CHURCH AND SOCIETY
IN ENGLAND
1770–1970

CHURCH AND SOCIETY IN ENGLAND

1770-1970

A Historical Study

BY

E. R. NORMAN

CLARENDON PRESS · OXFORD

1976

Oxford University Press, Ely House, London W.1

GLASGOW NEW YORK TORONTO MELBOURNE WELLINGTON
CAPE TOWN IBADAN NAIROBI DAR ES SALAAM LUSAKA ADDIS ABABA
DELHI BOMBAY CALCUTTA MADRAS KARACHI LAHORE DACCA
KUALA LUMPUR SINGAPORE HONG KONG TOKYO

ISBN 0 19 826435 6

© Oxford University Press 1976

Printed in Great Britain by
Butler & Tanner Ltd, Frome and London

Preface

I am very grateful to the Master of Selwyn College, Cambridge, and to the Dean of Christ Church, Oxford, for reading the manuscript of this book and assisting publication; and to Professor Edward Shils for his encouragement. I am also indebted to Hazel Dunn for organizing the typing of the book; and to Canon T. G. King and the Central Board of Lay Readers of the Church of England, who first invited me to offer opinions on this subject.

Peterhouse, 30 January 1975   E. R. NORMAN

Contents

Introduction

This attempt to describe the social teachings and attitudes of the English Church in modern times is an amplification of some lectures delivered at the annual course for Lay Readers, held in Selwyn College, Cambridge, during the summer of 1972. About ten years earlier, the paper in Christian Ethics had been dropped from the general examination which candidates for ordination in the Church of England are normally required to take; and one of the reasons for the change was the lack of books able to bring the subject up to date. Time has done little so far to alter the situation, despite the contemporary Christian emphasis on the importance of social issues, and on the application of social ethics. It has always been a weakness of the Church of England that its clergy have received insufficient instruction in social and political morality. The failing has not been unpopular, however. It corresponds to what Neville Figgis described as 'the disinclination of average opinion to admit that the Church has any real social entity or any standard either of doctrine or discipline, except that of the nation at large'.[1] The popular erastianism of the Englishman's approach to his religion demands that the parson keeps out of political matters. The education of the clergy has not really encouraged them to dissent greatly from this. Related by class and culture to the ruling and professional sections of society, they were, for most of the nineteenth century, simply qualified by residence at the Universities—institutions which, though under clerical control, at least until 1871, were not specifically given to vocational training. Thus the clergy were educated alongside the laity. They also married, and slid easily enough into a style of family life often indistinguishable from that of the lay members of the Church. When, after the mid-century, the Theological Colleges began to be founded, and it might have been supposed that a more characteristically ecclesiastical approach to temporal questions would be fostered, the atmosphere of clerical training remained surprisingly little altered. In tone and social outlook, the new colleges were usually similar in manners and social composition to the public schools and the University colleges. They were quite unlike the seminaries of the Roman Catholic Church, with their much more enclosed and sacerdotal qualities. 'The normal training of the English clergy, at school and university, is entirely non-professional,' wrote Hensley Henson in 1900; 'hence they are the most theologically ignorant and the best educated ministry in existence, and the worst informed on all matters

[1] J. N. Figgis, *Churches in the Modern State*, 2nd edn. (London, 1914), p. 43.

of ecclesiastical technique; but hence also they are the most vigorous and healthy in moral tone, and the sanest in political action.'[1]

It is interesting and instructive that although numerous texts have been written by Roman Catholic scholars seeking to convey Christian teaching in moral theology, only a handful have emerged from the Church of England during the last hundred years. The author of one of these attributes the contrast to the less authoritarian nature of the English Church—'so much is left to the judgment of the individual conscience'.[2] So much, in fact, that one of the first problems in trying to describe the Church's attitude to social questions is to decide what actually does constitute official teaching. 'It is surprising, and a little alarming', wrote Maurice Reckitt, the lay 'Christian Socialist' writer whose works influenced the clerical generations of the 1930s and 1940s, 'to observe how easily the Christian social enthusiast will come to claim ecclesiastical authority for his individual convictions, and even to be found to declare "the Church teaches", when all he ought to say is "I think".'[3]   For most of the nineteenth century there lacked the means of defining Church teaching—at just the moment in English history, with its huge social and economic changes, when adjustments were necessary. Such means as did exist altered during the century. For the first half, Christian instruction in social questions came from the pulpit directly, at the discretion, and according to the preferences, of the local parson. At the top, it derived its lead from the legislative attitude of the bishops in the House of Lords. Episcopal *Charges*, delivered with general regularity to the clergy, contained the most coherent body of instruction and advice in social questions. The Convocations of Canterbury and York were the appropriate canonical bodies for the definition of ecclesiastical teaching, but their revival in the mid-nineteenth century did little to clarify social policy: such questions were not often discussed in them. The bishops preferred to arrive at a common mind, where this was possible, in occasional gatherings at Lambeth Palace. Diocesan Conferences were a development of the second half of the nineteenth century, but they reflected opinion in the Church, rather than created it. The annual Church Congresses, held after 1861, were valuable and highly articulate in the discussion of social issues—particularly useful as sources since issues were debated alongside theological and moral questions in a manner which revealed common points of reference. But the Congresses, though fairly representative of opinion in the Church, were unofficial. They helped to publicize attitudes and ideals, but not to establish teachings. They did, however, more or less take over from episcopal or archdeaconal

---

[1] *Church Problems. A View of Modern Anglicanism*, ed. H. Hensley Henson (London, 1900), p. 21.

[2] Lindsay Dewar, *An Outline of Anglican Moral Theology* (London, 1968), p. vii.

[3] Maurice B. Reckitt, *The Christian in Politics* (London, 1946), p. 65.

Charges as the means of disseminating the attitudes of the leaders of the Church. 'The time is past', Mandell Creighton wrote in 1894, at the start of an immensely long *Charge*, 'when it is profitable to attempt, in an Episcopal Charge, a massive survey of important questions, or to influence opinion by learned investigations which are more fitted for reading at leisure than for apprehending at the moment.'[1] The creation of the Church Assembly, under the terms of the Enabling Act of 1919, gave the Church its first official means of autonomous expression, but its debates of social issues, right up until its supersession in 1970 by the General Synod, were neither extensive nor comprehensive. Its time was mostly absorbed by ecclesiastical finance, canon-law revision, and issues relating to the technicalities of property and jurisdiction. 'On general subjects the House is inclined to pass rather easily and quickly far-reaching resolutions which should demand much more thought and consideration,' as Archbishop Garbett noticed in 1947.[2] The General Synod has reflected contemporary interests in the extent of its discussion of social issues. Some may believe that Garbett's observation still applies. Lambeth Conferences have provided the nearest the Anglican Church can offer in the way of authoritative teaching on social and economic questions. These gatherings of the Anglican bishops of the world, which began in 1867, take place every ten years. Yet the resolutions passed are only advisory, even though they have an authority which few in the Church would seek to ignore. It is clear, then, that for most of its recent history, the English Church has lacked a sure source of social teaching, a truly authoritative definition of its mind on the temporal questions with which it has been confronted.

To some, indeed, it has appeared as if the Church had almost no social teachings at all; as if it merely offered a spiritual sanction for existing arrangements, as an arm of the ruling interests in the State. 'It adhered to its practice—indulge the rich and keep down the poor.'[3] This sort of judgement has attracted a lot of belief. To the extent that it contains truth, however, it is such an abridgement of the complicated realities of Christian experience that it constitutes a distortion valuable only for the polemical purposes it is used to serve. Only the 'vulgar' Marxists have supposed that the Church ignored social evils and the sufferings of the working classes. Philosophical Marxists know better. They see that churchmen were full of concern for the poor; but they see also that they were victims of their own class moralism, presenting solutions which comprehended neither the subtleties of working-class social custom nor the possibility of social reconstruction. It was a clergyman of the Church of England—Charles

[1] *A Charge Delivered to the Clergy and Churchwardens of the Diocese by Mandell Creighton, D.D., Lord Bishop of Peterborough* (Peterborough, 1894), p. 5.
[2] Cyril Garbett, *The Claims of the Church of England* (London, 1947), p. 193.
[3] G. D. H. Cole and Raymond Postgate, *The Common People, 1746–1946*, revd. edn. (London, 1946), p. 270.

Kingsley—who struck an image which acquired international currency, 'we have used the Bible as if it were a mere special constable's handbook, an opium dose for keeping beasts of burden patient while they are being overloaded'.[1] Churchmen, paradoxically, have themselves been the most addicted to 'vulgar' Marxist interpretations of the Church's record in social questions. They seem almost to enjoy dwelling on what they take to be the past inadequacies of vision; they are often full of censorious criticism of their predecessors. It is not a particularly recent habit. The Lambeth Conference of 1897, for example, reported that social and economic morality were subjects 'to which numberless Christians have as yet never thought of applying Christian principles'.[2] This was an extraordinary observation—following, as it did, a century of intense social activity by churchmen. Each generation of churchmen has appeared to imagine that it is the first to espouse social policies, the first to be concerned with the conditions of the working classes. The reason is partly to be found in the vicarious nature of so much social concern; the tendency to declare principles, to offer brotherhood to the workers, and yet unconsciously to retain the essentials of class interests. It is also to be found in the assumption that past social policies, which were later rejected as unsatisfactory, were not really policies at all. Thus there has been a tendency among twentieth-century critics of Political Economy and *laissez-faire* practices to suppose that the Victorian churchmen who endorsed those doctrines did so in a resignation from involvement in the social and economic concerns of men.[3] In fact, those ideas were found attractive because they were presented by the informed economic opinion of the day as being most likely to conduce to the physical prosperity and well-being of the whole of society. It is also evident that the Nonconformists' campaign against the legal Establishment of religion in the nineteenth century has obscured much of the Church's social work. So much attention was directed to depicting the Church of England as an arm of landed society, soaked in privilege and wealth, unconcerned with the fate of the poor (and so forth), that the screen of polemicism has often been too thick for subsequent observers to penetrate. And churchmen, with all their characteristic *penchant* for self-criticism, have now inherited the Nonconformists' case at its own valuation.

There has been a tendency for some contemporary writers to judge the Churches *solely* in terms of their social concern. But for most of the period covered by this study, churchmen had another priority. They regarded the

---

[1] *The Common People, 1736–1946*, p. 322.

[2] *Conference of Bishops of the Anglican Communion holden at Lambeth Palace in July, 1897* (London, 1897), p. 140.

[3] This view was especially propagated by Tawney and Temple. But for a contemporary version of it, see David Sheppard, *Built as a City. God and the Urban World Today* (London, 1974), p. 335.

alleviation of social ills, and care for the temporal welfare of mankind, as important aspects of the Divine Will for ordered and just life, but not as the essential purpose of the Church's mission. The pursuit of eternity remained the first and absorbing preoccupation of organized religion. The subject dealt with in this book was, therefore, a secondary consideration. The stability of English political institutions allowed this an uninterrupted course: there were no threats on a scale which placed the Church in the position where it would have to take sides over a real clash of political ideologies—as occurred in Europe. When English Christianity really did begin to become aware of a world reference for political and social divisions (which did not happen until the 1930s, with the European confrontation of Communism and Fascism), it increased reserve and reinforced the existing tradition of defining the general principles, and not the particular applications, of political and social morality.

The adoption of social teachings in the Church was also complicated by the unprecedented acceleration in social change. The Church never caught up with the demographic and economic transformation of the nineteenth-century world—though it was far from being unaware of the problems themselves, as some have liked to suppose. The difficulty lay in translating awareness into activity; it was the difficulty of an elaborate, hierarchical, and largely rural institution, which required the sanction of Parliament for its own adjustment and reform. And the Church was also often internally divided about the nature of the adjustments to modern society which ought to be sought, and about the solutions appropriate in the novel social conditions. For the problems really did seem, as Troeltsch remarked, 'entirely new'. They were problems 'with which Christian social work has never been confronted until now', which 'includes the problem of the capitalist economic period and of the industrial proletariat created by it; and of the growth of militaristic and bureaucratic giant states; of the enormous increase in population, which affects colonial and world policy; of the mechanical technique, which produces enormous masses of material and links up and mobilizes the whole world for the purposes of trade, but which also treats men and labour like machines'.[1] Nor could the Church, in contemplating these realities, turn to the State or to public life in general for a systematic response to the new conditions. Characteristically, the response by politicians and journalists was pragmatic; it looked to the reform of institutions, to the broadening of the bases of public life, to the adjustment—not the reconstruction—of the political Constitution. Parliament adapted by expediency. It declined to define real principles of change; it worked to preserve the national polity without a coherent political theory. Questions were considered on their own merits, piecemeal.

[1] Ernst Troeltsch, *The Social Teaching of the Christian Churches* (London, 1931), ii, 1011.

The Church found itself in the position of being one dimension of this practical adjustment. Hence its survival as an Establishment: because public men did not allow the clamour of the Dissenters to be pushed beyond practical reforms—there was no acceptance of any theoretical case against the maintenance of established religion as such. But there were practical alterations. The Church was reformed; the Constitution was adjusted. Exclusive privileges were removed from the Establishment. But in these operations a distinct political doctrine of change was not allowed to become the directing genius. There was, in consequence, no clear theory about social and political change to which the Church—even had it the will to do so—could bring a distinct critique, or around which it could assemble a Christian social policy for the new age. In this, the Church of England differed from the Roman Catholic Church, whose social and political teachings reflected Papal contact with European, and especially Italian, Liberalism and Nationalism, and later with totalitarianism of the Left and the Right. The Catholic Church had a world context throughout the nineteenth century. Its social and political teachings have been, both because of this experience, and because of its own inherent authoritarianism, theoretical and systematic.

In view of these difficulties it may seem surprising that the English Church had any social teachings at all. But they are there, interwoven with the fabric of public life like the Church itself. In order to isolate and to identify them a good deal of pruning has to be done, to make a survey of the whole period from the end of the eighteenth century to the present, manageable and useful. A great deal has to be left out, and the field of inquiry narrowed to the point where specialists in some contiguous areas of study will complain, perhaps with justice, that dimensions of the subject have been inadequately served. This book is about the attitudes of the Church of England to English society and its problems over a period of nearly two centuries; it is about the Church's social and economic teaching; and, because the control and welfare of society and calculations for social change or social stability require collective action, it is about the Christian attitude to politics, the relationship of Church and State, of law and public morality. These themes are treated broadly, and an attempt is made to sketch the contexts in which these attitudes and teachings were formuated. But it is only indirectly concerned with applications: it is not a description of two centuries of Christian social work. What is sought is the mind of the Church—of that part of the Church which was influential in the adoption of social attitudes. The book is not really concerned with what the people thought about religion or the Church, except to the extent that they looked to the Church for certain social functions. This is not, therefore, another commentary on the decline of religion: some acquaintance with all that sort of thing is assumed in the reader. It seeks, instead, to depict the mind of the Church as an institution; it is not really concerned with 'high politics', with how Lambeth Palace influenced Downing Street, but with the ideas and attitudes which formed the context of the influence Lambeth brought to bear. The analysis, furthermore, is largely restricted to England. Conditions in Scotland, Wales, and Ireland are considered to the extent that they introduced variants into the English debate. The distinct religious traditions of those other countries do not readily combine to make a coherent single analysis, and they would certainly make a thematic study like the present one quite unmanageable. There are still further austerities. The Church considered here is ordinarily the Church of England, and not the Protestant Nonconformist bodies or the Roman Catholics. There are several reasons for this. It is, first, the Established religion, the Church of the Nation, with a relationship to public life which has placed it far above the other Churches in its engagement with temporal questions. On most issues—the most notable exception being the constitutional position of religion itself—the social teachings of the Church of England can be taken as reasonably typical. This is also due to its comprehensive quality; its parties incorporate Protestant and Catholic, pietist and activist: religious psychologies in uneven but permanent distribution. In practice, too, the Church of England has exercised a leadership of the other Protestant Churches in social questions—which the great public dispute between Church and Dissent over political issues of 'religious equality' has rather obscured. The Church's output of records also makes it the most balanced to study: they are fairly good at both local and national levels. It is true that the social composition of the Church of England is rather different from that of the Nonconformist bodies, but this can be exaggerated. If the weight of the Establishment is in the upper-middle and upper classes, then the weight of Protestant Dissent is certainly not working class, as is often supposed. It is middle and lower-middle class, touched with additions from the 'aristocracy of labour', the skilled artisans, pushing upwards through status aspiration to lower-middle-class gentility. This has always been the case, with a few local exceptions where there have been real working-class Churches, like the Durham mining villages or the South Wales valley Chapels, where, anyway, urban living is still mixed with strong surviving rural qualities. The Roman Catholic Church has had a strong working-class element. But the Irish immigrants who formed it tended either to defect from the faith in the second generation or to move up the social scale.

Despite the Establishment's comprehensive nature, there were occasional differences in social teaching from the other Churches—especially from the Roman Catholic Church in the twentieth century. Sideways references to these variations have been written into this account, but space and balance has not allowed extensive explanation of them. A number of specific issues have been omitted too. The question of pacificism, the morality of war, international relations, have been left out since they raised ancillary areas which would obscure the main themes. Some other issues, such as education, have been treated only as they affect the main developments described in the book, and this account of them is not, therefore, a complete one. Care has also been taken about the concept of 'leadership' in the Church, but it remains rather unsatisfactory. There is, in the tradition of the English Church, less of a distinction between clerical and lay elements than in some other Churches. But even after their formal admission to organs of Church government—as in the Church Assembly after 1919—the laity do not easily fall within the conventional concept of 'leadership'. Politicians were usually Christians, and a majority were churchmen. But they have not acted politically like a conscious Church laity—except for occasional great men of single purpose, like Wilberforce or Shaftesbury, or perhaps Gladstone. Normally the expression 'Church leadership' is here taken to refer to the officers of the institutional Church. The thoughts of influential lay writers on the Church's social role are also discussed. One of the results is that a study of this nature tends to become an analysis of episcopal opinion, or of specific groups like the 'Clapham Sect' or the 'Christian Socialists'. Attempts have been made to balance this tendency where it has been noticed—but not to eliminate it, for in an episcopal Church the bishops naturally have a superior voice in the discernment of religious policy. And lastly it must be declared that this is not a sociological but a historical work: it is concerned with the historical development of an institution in its most important temporal function.

Several general conclusions emerge from this survey. The most obvious is the class basis of the social ethics the Church has adopted. It has, of course, long been assumed in the 'vulgar' Marxist attitude to social history, that the clergy propagated the morality and politics of the ruling class, of which, indeed, they were a part. In such a version of things, a few men of conscience and 'prophetic' discernment were believed to have emancipated themselves sufficiently to promote social radicalism—the 'Christian Socialist' school of the nineteenth century is usually the favoured example. Its leading members were supposed to have transcended the ordinary assumptions of their class. It is the contention of the present study that most of the social attitudes and ideas adopted by churchmen were a reflection of class-consciousness—including the radical and critical ideas. Receptivity to new influences was strictly limited to ideals promoted by sections within the intelligentsia, of which the clergy were themselves a part. Radical attitudes adopted by churchmen derived from an area of debate largely restricted to the educated classes; theirs was a partisan gesture, a taking of sides in a division of opinion over ideas currently appealing to groups within their own class. Social radicalism within the Church was as much the result of class moralism as was the more prevalent conservatism. The social composition of the clergy helps to explain the mechanics of this. Towards the end of the eighteenth century the proportion of the clergy drawn from the upper classes and the nobility increased.[1] In the first half of the nineteenth century about two-thirds of the bishops came from aristocratic or landed families: this indicated a considerable increase in the status of the Church as a profession.[2] During the century the strictly aristocratic element declined, but the landed and professional middle-class element filled in the gap. Many clergymen were themselves the sons of clergymen. By the 1960s the pattern had altered surprisingly little. The general social tone of the ministry was by then still middle to upper class. The bishops tended to approximate more to the upper than to the middle class. The over-all background, especially of those who have risen to senior and influential position in the Church, is public school and ancient University.[3] Apart from a relative reduction in personal wealth compared with lower social groups, the contemporary clergyman of the English Church is still as described by Masterman at the start of the century: 'the amiable young man of pleasing manners and limited intelligence who has taken an ordinary degree at the University, lived a life of contented and blameless indulgence, been crammed with a few assorted pieces of chopped-up theology at a theological college'.[4] Public support for the Church—at least as far as attending its worship—has shown a similar class correspondence, as well as a certain economy. Diocesan returns at the end of the eighteenth century indicated that church attendance had declined. The available figures are patchy and localized, but it appears that in many places fewer than 15 per cent of the population regularly went to church or were communicants.[5] By the 1960s the figures were perhaps marginally less—perhaps 13 or 14 per cent.[6] But if increases in the membership of Catholic and Protestant Nonconformist Churches are taken into account, the figures probably level out. Yet most Englishmen continue to claim membership of one or other of the Churches. In fact, by the end of the 1960s an astonishing 95 per cent of the population claimed

[1] Norman Ravitch, *Sword and Mitre. Government and Episcopate in France and England in the Age of Aristocracy* (The Hague, 1966), p. 125.

[2] R. A. Soloway, *Prelates and People. Ecclesiastical Social Thought in England, 1783–1852* (London and Toronto, 1969), p. 8.

[3] *The Deployment and Payment of the Clergy. A Report by Leslie Paul* (London, 1964), pp. 111–14, 275.

[4] Charles F. G. Masterman, *The Heart of the Empire. Discussions of Problems of Modern City Life in England* (London, 1901), p. 44.

[5] Soloway, *Prelates and People*, pp. 50–1.

[6] See the tables in *Facts and Figures about the Church of England*, no. 3 (ed. R. F. Neuss), prepared by the Statistical Unit of the Central Board of Finance of the Church of England (London, 1965), p. 59.

religious affiliation: 60 per cent Anglican; 12 per cent Roman Catholic; 11 per cent Free Church; 1 per cent Jews; 5 per cent other faiths; and 5 per cent with no religion.[1] What has happened? Over a perspective of two centuries it can be seen that institutional Christianity in England underwent a modest boom in the first half of the nineteenth century—modest in numerical terms, but hugely important in terms of influence. It represented the adhesion of the middle classes, and most of the intelligentsia, to Christianity, as the vehicle of their moral seriousness. It was a middle-class boom, and it infused the English Churches with the class attitudes and the moralism which are still, in some measure, the style of Christianity familiar today. The enthusiasm of the middle classes was infectious: it drew in many from the old landed classes. It accelerated a religious machinery whose slow running down, after the mid-nineteenth century, has become particularly apparent in very recent times. But the working classes were only indirectly affected by all this. They still did not go to church, and it was the slow erosion of the middle-class membership, not the disappearance of the working classes from church, that has led to modern attendance figures. Thus the Church today, in terms of regular and committed support, is not dissimilar from what it was in the later years of the eighteenth century. It cannot now be said, as Gladstone said of society in his earlier years, 'that not only the noble and the wealthy, but the almost unbroken bulk of the well-educated classes are in the Communion of the Church; that her pale comprehends the great majority of the learned lay professions; that the literature of the country is generally in the hands of her members; that the warm young blood of the nation, at the universities and great schools, which from day to day recruits its life, is enthusiastic in her behalf'.[2]

It is also clear that the leadership of the Church has been internally divided on a number of issues in each successive generation. Some, often a majority, have readily adopted the progressive idealism common to liberal opinion within the intelligentsia, of which they were a part. The parochial clergy and the laity have often been less open to shifts of intellectual attitude—they were less immediately related to the sources of ideas in the Universities and in public life. They have been more reflective of conservative values, slower to adapt to the fashions of thought which take hold at the top of the Church. Divisions of opinion within the intelligentsia have always been faithfully reproduced within the Church's leading thinkers. This points to another general conclusion of the present study: that the social attitudes of the Church have derived from the surrounding intellectual and political culture and not, as churchmen themselves always seem to assume, from theological learning. The theologians have always

---

[1] John D. Gay, *The Geography of Religion in England* (London, 1971), p. 37.
[2] W. E. Gladstone, *Church Principles Considered in their Results* (London, 1840), p. 379.

managed to reinterpret their sources in ways which have somehow made
their version of Christianity correspond almost exactly to the values of
their class and generation. Thus theological scholarship justified the
structural social obligations of the eighteenth-century world; then it
provided a Christian basis for Political Economy; later collectivist principles were hailed as the most perfect embodiment of the compassion
prescribed in the New Testament; and even the contemporary doctrines
of 'liberation' and 'secularization' have been given powerful theological
support. Theologians, after all, are intellectuals, and they have a natural
interest in representing social changes in terms of ideas. It is not surprising
that they should believe that their own social preferences are derived from
straight intellectual calculation, rather than, as is the case, from the
complicated and mixed world of ideas and moral postures characteristic
of the intelligentsia as a whole. This is, no doubt, the way of all truth; it
takes on the form and the idealism of the intellectual preoccupations of
each generation. 'Christian theology, Christian ethics, Christian institutions,
have all been demonstrably shaped by contemporary non-Christian
influences,' as Hensley Henson observed; 'it is a condition of the Church's
terrestrial mission from which there is no escape.'[1] It is a condition
familiar enough to sociologists. 'As we may see from history,' Max Weber
wrote, 'almost all the platforms of religious organizations have been
religiously relative so far as sacred values, ethical rationality, and lawful
autonomy are concerned.'[2] And Archbishop William Temple noticed that
'it is not legal bonds that make the Church too closely to follow the State;
it is personal ties and economic interests'.[3] Temple, however, never quite
followed his analysis to the point where he could see the effects of class
moralism. Henson did. In 1939 he noticed that the debates in Convocation
'reflected the intellectual, social, economic, and even political fashions of the
day'. Churchmen were 'more interested in social ethics than in theology'. He
saw also that the public affairs which so absorbed the Church leaders were
'everywhere debated by the laity, and discussed in the newspapers, with no
less knowledge, often with larger practical experience, and sometimes with
superior intellectual equipment'.[4] Where contemporary theological liberals
have been conscious that their social idealism is derived from the culture
of the intelligentsia, and not from theological learning, they have spoken
of their affirmation of the value of 'the secular', of the Divine 'immanence'
in the world, of the 'adulthood' of humanity, which explores God in the
'process' of human development. It is certainly true that too sharp a
distinction ought not to be made between the values of the 'secular' ideas

[1] H. Hensley Henson, *Bishoprick Papers* (Oxford, 1946), p. 38.
[2] *From Max Weber: Essays in Sociology*, ed. H. H. Gerth and C. Wright Mills (London, 1948), p. 338.
[3] William Temple, *Citizen and Churchman* (London, 1941), p. 67.
[4] H. Hensley Henson, *The Church of England* (Cambridge, 1939), p. 215.

of the intelligentsia and religious thought—but for another reason. Lay culture has for so long been impregnated with diluted versions of theological concepts, and English education has so familiarized men with a Biblical frame of reference (however much it is a rejected one), that 'secular' values still convey traces of religion. During the nineteenth century this was even more important than it has since become. It is because Church social thought has reflected the preferences of the intelligentsia of each generation that the periods into which it can be divided for study are the conventional ones familiar to political historians.

Despite all this, another constant theme in this study is the avoidance by the Church of partisan politics. The great political bishops of the eighteenth-century gave place, early in the nineteenth century, to men who attempted to dissociate the Church from party allegiance. It began as an aspect of the movement for 'economical reform' at the end of the eighteenth century: the increasing distaste, in public life generally, for the association of public office with political reward. At around this time Church leaders began to emphasize that the proper role of the Church as a corporate body was to define general principles of political and social morality; that the detailed and particular applications of them must be left to those who were expert or experienced. 'It gives out general principles, which will work an amendment by degrees,' said Bishop Samuel Horsley, in 1799; 'and trusts, for the eradication of moral evil, to the slow and silent operation of those general principles.'[1] It has often been supposed that the nineteenth-century Church had a very partisan political character: 'the Tory Party at Prayer'. This study does not sustain that view. 'The Church, if she is true to her mission, has to declare truths which are far higher than any political realities', as the Revd. Dr. Barry, Principal of Cheltenham College, told a meeting of working men in 1867.[2] In spite of a few individual lapses, the Church as an institution has kept itself free of party allegiance. The impression that it was an adjunct of the Conservative Party derived less from the old sympathy of Tory squires and Tory parsons in the first half of the nineteenth century, than from the Nonconformists' attempt to depict the defence of the Establishment by Conservative politicians at the end of the century—particularly at the time of the agitation against the Welsh Church—as the fruit of a distinct political alliance with the Church. Public opinion always distrusted the idea of the clergy becoming involved in politics. Men frowned upon the part taken by the Irish Catholic priests in the political life of that part of the kingdom. The clergy of the Established Church in England were sometimes unpopular with the working classes because they were thought to be politically involved. But this was often a misunderstanding, based on the working man's inability to dis-

---

[1] *The Speeches in Parliament of Samuel Horsley* (Dundee, 1813), i. 250
[2] *Report of the Wolverhampton Church Congress, 1867* (London, 1867), p. 237.

tinguish the parson's upper-class speech and manners from his actual political conduct.

The Church has also, consistently, refused to endorse particular forms of government or social organization. This position, too, has been widely misunderstood. For the Church has, of course, stood for the maintenance of civil order, and for respect to civil authority according to the teaching of Scripture. But this has been carefully separated from consecrating any actual form of government as more Christian than another—aristocracy more than democracy, or whatever. 'History is littered with various orderings of society, and none of us is yet competent to say which of them was the most divine or nearest to the divine pattern,' Archbishop Fisher told the Church Assembly in 1957; 'I take it that to the end of time men will be experimenting with societies which will be nearer to, or further from, the divine mind.'[1] Here, again, a number of individuals have transgressed the convention, especially in more recent years. But most have not. 'To identify any particular form of government with Christianity is a dangerous error,' wrote T. S. Eliot—who was associated with Anglican social radicalism in the later 1930s—'for it confounds the permanent with the transitory, the absolute with the contingent.'[2] Most modern Church leaders have shared the empirical approach to political organization which has characterized so much English political experience. They have supposed, as Bishop Mortimer has written, that 'what is desirable must always be correlated with what is possible', and that 'changes and disturbances in the existing order of things must be so engineered that the old pillars of law and order be not removed until there are new and firm ones to take their place'.[3] It might have been expected that the relative separation of Church and State in recent times would have heightened political consciousness in the Church: that the Church, with a diminished national role, would find in a greater 'denominational', or even 'sectarian' self-identification, the springs of a more committed political outlook.[4] In a number of individual cases—where particular clergymen have sought to find a new social identity for themselves in the complicated dislocations of modern life—this has indeed happened. But there has been no discernible general change as yet. This is in part, no doubt, because the clergy of the Church of England continue to be so closely related, by class and education, to the intelligentsia. Many do not yet see themselves as outside the centres of national life. It is also because the clergy have often tended not to reject the secularized culture around them, despite its relativism, its

[1] *The Archbishop Speaks. Addresses and Speeches by the Archbishop of Canterbury*, selected by Edward Carpenter (London, 1958), p. 107.

[2] T. S. Eliot, *The Idea of a Christian Society* (London, 1939), p. 57.

[3] R. C. Mortimer, *The Elements of Moral Theology* (London, 1947), p. 208.

[4] See H. Richard Niebuhr, *The Social Sources of Denominationalism* (1929) (New York, 1959 edn.), p. 18.

agnosticism, and its materialism. Leaders of Church opinion in the 1960s and early in the 1970s have often, astonishingly, continued to reflect the values of their class, despite the increasing secularization of those values. This explains, on the one hand, the contemporary theological upheaval—necessary in order to accommodate the otherwise antipathetic version of human nature found in secular humanism; on the other hand, it accounts for the continuing absence of a distinctively ecclesiastical view of political questions.

Through all these developments, the English Church has in the last two centuries persistently responded to a central tension in the relationship of Christianity to the world: a dialectic between that attitude which would seek to regenerate men individually to render them fit to change society; and that which, on the contrary, would first change society by immediate political means in order to create the conditions necessary for educating men into regeneration. It is a central theme. Sometimes it is crudely translated into a difference of religious psychology, between the pietist and the radical, between 'other-worldliness' and social activism. More often a real dialectic is envisaged, each aspect of change, individual and social, informing the other as men extend the frontiers of experience. In 1895 Archbishop Frederick Temple wrote:

There is always a considerable difficulty in defining with any precision the relations between the things of this world and the things of the other, because on the one side there is a very serious danger that, if these two things are allowed to come into too close a contact, the things of the other may seem to be absorbed into the cares of this world, and on the other hand there is a very great danger, perhaps the more serious danger of the two, that, if the demarcation between them be made too strong, the result will be that the principles of religion will be altogether excluded from their proper influence on our conduct in this life.[1]

This judicious balance is characteristically Anglican. The conflict between the two attitudes remains unresolved, and the contemporary Church can furnish clear examples of both. It is a conflict which corresponds to the permanent tension in Christian truth between 'Hellenism' and 'Hebraism',[2] between spirit and matter. And the Church has ever been subject to that 'gravitational pull in human nature which draws the highest things downwards'.[3] Wise churchmen also know, as Archbishop Sumner pointed out early in the nineteenth century, that 'men, in every state, are less induced to a change of their present habits by reason, than by example'.[4] This has been silently witnessed, in the parishes of the land, during the last two centuries.

[1] Frederick Temple, *Lectures on Disendowment* (London, 1895), p. 7.

[2] Matthew Arnold, *Culture and Anarchy* (1869), ed. J. Dover Wilson (Cambridge, 1960), p. 130.

[3] Herbert Butterfield, *Christianity and History* (1949) (London, 1957 edn.), p. 56.

[4] John Bird Sumner, *A Treatise on the Records of The Creation* (London, 1816), ii. 40.

I

Christian Social Teaching at the End of the Eighteenth Century

It was the identity of sentiment between Church and State that most impressed contemporaries about the social and political attitudes of the Church in the last two decades of the eighteenth century. The harmony of interests which had given so practical an expression during the century to the theological orthodoxy of Natural Philosophy—and the fact that the Church was so fully integrated into political and social relationships—appeared to have produced a providential end to the sort of tensions which had, in what men regarded as less enlightened centuries, provoked discord between religious and secular institutions. The Church upheld the 'natural' hierarchy of mutual obligations which were thought to provide social cohesion; the State, for its part, protected the legal Establishment of Christianity as the appropriate agent for the diffusion of benevolence and public morality. Church and State seemed at last to have become the ideal to which medieval Christendom had aspired: two aspects of an agreed unity.[1] The laity exercised a large influence. Since the discontinuation of the meetings of the Convocations, in 1717, the Church had lacked a place at which ecclesiastical debate could occur. Professor Sykes wrote of the consequent 'Laicisation' of the Church in the eighteenth century: 'The clerical order generally was characterized by a markedly unprofessional temper, the laity not only deemed themselves a proper and necessary part of the organization of the Christian Church, but acted upon that persuasion with vigour and conviction.'[2] Whether the laity were unduly vigorous is a judgement dependent upon inclination—to the Oxford divines of the next century the practice of the eighteenth century seemed almost intolerable, and it is often their opinions which have tinctured subsequent interpretation. In reality, both laity and clergy drew upon a common body of social ideas, and by the end of the century it was evident that the Church was on the whole satisfied that this disclosed a nearly perfect version of what a religious Establishment should be.[3] By the close of the century, as a result, the teaching of 'the Church' really did tend to mean the opinions of the laity

[1] See G. F. A. Best, *Temporal Pillars, Queen Anne's Bounty, the Ecclesiastical Commissioners, and the Church of England* (Cambridge, 1964), p. 70.

[2] Norman Sykes, *Church and State in England in the XVIIIth Century* (Cambridge, 1934), p. 379.

[3] See Soloway, *Prelates and People*, p. 9.

like William Wilberforce and Hannah More as much as it meant those of influential bishops, like Samuel Horsley or Richard Watson.

Some of the most distinguished theological writing belonged decidedly to the first half of the century,[1] but some of the more seminal political and social speculations belonged to the end—when churchmen, aware of the corruptions of social manners, and fearful of the effects of events in France, became disillusioned with Natural Theology. The Evangelicals were not alone in this. A more general, if subtle, change may be discerned in many areas of Christian thought and attitude. No doubt there would be hazards in assuming that the tone set by individual divines or reformers became pervasive: many others must have remained attached to the certainties they had absorbed from the intellectual and social culture of the century. That is always the way with movements of thought: the observer can follow the reasonings of the articulate; it is much less easy to trace the practice of those who do not choose to follow changing opinion. Yet developments early in the nineteenth century make it clear that the heightened social awareness of the Church leadership at the end of the eighteenth century had enjoyed a successful propagation.

The Church stood for the maintenance of existing social order, and for a wide range of the social values. Eighteenth-century churchmen, that is to say, espoused a practice which many modern Christians would find theoretically agreeable: they identified with the secular aspirations of the society in which they lived. It is, however, important to notice that although this had the advantage, at times, of coinciding with the class interests of the clergy—interests which were, in eighteenth-century terms, legitimate elements of social cohesion—the defence of the existing social order was not just a matter of self-interest. Churchmen also held other notions, some humane, some very critical of aspects of society, upon which their social service ultimately depended.

The interdependence of Church and State, of religion and civil government, remained the first consideration which men proposed for a right social constitution. Bishop Warburton's *Alliance between Church and State*, published in 1736, had given an extensive and acceptable explanation of the propriety of this notion. It continued to serve as a major text, as the authority to which public men referred in supporting the view that religion was a necessary adjunct of a stable civil order.[2] The clergy, as Shute Barrington said when he was Bishop of Llandaff in 1781, were 'incorporated with the laity, connected in one common interest, citizens of the State holding their property by the same laws'.[3] The idea that society and religion stood or fell together found its most celebrated expression at the

[1] G. R. Cragg, *The Church and the Age of Reason* (London, 1960), p. 169.
[2] Sykes, *Church and State*, p. 319.
[3] Quoted in Best, *Temporal Pillars*, p. 61.

end of the century in Burke's assault upon the apologists of the French Revolution. Burke had developed the view in his earlier work, too.[1] In the *Reflections on the Revolution in France* (1790), he gave the most sacred significance to the mutual dependence of Church and State: 'We know, and what is better, we feel inwardly, that religion is the basis of civil society.'[2] The 'consecration' of the State by religion was made 'that all who administer the government of men, in which they stand in the person of God Himself, should have high and worthy notions of their function and destination'.[3] This coincided with the traditional teaching of the Western Church. For Burke, of course, the Revolution had sharpened the reality of this teaching by furnishing evidence of the consequences of its abandonment. 'When religion shall have lost its hold on men's consciences, government will lose its authority over their persons, and a state of barbarous anarchy will ensue.' So wrote Richard Watson, Barrington's successor in the see of Llandaff, in 1795.[4] Unlike most of the episcopal bench, Watson was a Whig. He had held the chairs both of Chemistry and of Divinity at Cambridge, and was, despite his advocacy of Church Reform, a noted pluralist. He was also one of the most influential churchmen of his day. 'There never yet hath existed, and there never can exist, a nation without religion,' he wrote; 'If Christianity be abolished, paganism, mahometanism, some religious imposture or other must be introduced in its stead, or civil society must be given up.'[5] And William Wilberforce, the doyen of the Evangelicals, followed the custom of the age in cementing the social fabric with religious sanction. 'To the decline of Religion and morality our national difficulties must both directly and indirectly be chiefly ascribed', he wrote in 1797.[6] The Evangelicals' application of the interdependence of religion and society in fact had few features which were peculiar to themselves. Attempts were made in most sections of the Church, at the end of the century, to re-establish social ethics upon 'Revealed' rather than 'Natural' religious truth. Wilberforce's *Practical View of the Prevailing Religious System* enjoyed an astonishing success, and sold over 7,000 copies in six months—hugely exceeding any expectation for religious publications at the time. Its appeal was evidently universal, and not just to those conventionally regarded as Evangelical. 'The better part of the religious world, and more especially the Church of

---

[1] Alfred Cobban, *Edmund Burke and the Revolt against the Eighteenth Century*, 2nd edn. (London, 1960), p. 238.

[2] Burke, *Reflections*, Nelson edn. (London, 1958), p. 299.

[3] Burke, *Reflections*, p. 301.

[4] Richard Watson, *A Defence of Revealed Religion in Two Sermons Preached in the Cathedral Church of Llandaff*, 3rd edn. (London, 1806), p. 400.

[5] Ibid., p. 401.

[6] William Wilberforce, *A Practical View of the Prevailing Religious System of Professed Christians in the Higher and Middle Classes in the Country Contrasted with real Christianity*, 2nd edn. (London, 1797), p. 489.

England, prize it most highly, and consider it as producing an era in the history of the Church', according to Henry Thornton, one of the Evangelical luminaries of the 'Clapham Sect'.[1] The book certainly established Wilberforce as the first churchman of his generation. Burke spent the last two days of his life reading it.[2]

Churchmen could also claim with some accuracy that the notion of the interdependence of religion and civil society was actually popular with the English people, however much Unitarian philosophers or disaffected men might criticize it. 'The majority of the people of England, far from thinking a religious national establishment unlawful, hardly think it lawful to be without one,' wrote Burke. 'They consider it as the foundation of their whole constitution.'[3] And in 1790 Bishop Samuel Horsley noted that 'the inseparable union of religion and Civil Government is the grand Desideratum with respect to human happiness'.[4] In 1796 he told the clergy of Rochester that 'Popular opinion, in this instance, is, fortunately for us, on the side of truth'.[5] Horsley shared with Watson the effective leadership of clerical opinion in his generation. Bishop successively of St. David's (1788), Rochester (1793), and St. Asaph (1802), he was a High Churchman, a scientist, and a Tory. In his 1796 *Charge* he went on to warn the clergy that they could not rely upon this public support remaining unconditional. He urged them to reside in their parishes and generally to reform standards.[6] It was a theme to which he returned in 1800, referring then to the 'strategem' of subversive persons 'to alienate the minds of the people from the Established Clergy, by representing them as sordid worldlings, without any concern about the souls of men, indifferent to the religion, which they ought to teach, and to which the laity are attached'.[7] They should avoid easy living, conduct public worship with greater care, see to the welfare of young people in their parishes, and so forth.[8] This linking of the survival of the religious Establishment with Church reform was to become immensely important in the next century. So was the polemical assumption, described by Horsley, that the clergy were all given over to unworthy living. The new century also inherited intact the idea of the mutual interdependence of religion and society. 'The Church of England has partaken of the stability and security of the State,' Southey ended his

[1] Quoted in Samuel Wilberforce, *The Life of William Wilberforce*, revd. edn. (London, 1872), p. 170.

[2] Ibid., p. 173.

[3] Burke, *Reflections*, p. 309.

[4] Fulham Papers, Lambeth Palace Library (Horsley Collection), MS. 1767, f. 201.

[5] *The Charge of Samuel, Lord Bishop of Rochester to the Clergy of his Diocese, 1796* (London, 1796), p. 22.

[6] Ibid., p. 27.

[7] *Charge to the Clergy of Rochester, 1800*; printed in *The Charges of Samuel Horsley* (London, 1830), p. 103.

[8] Ibid., pp. 105 ff.

Book of the Church in 1824. 'Whatever should weaken it, would in the same degree injure the common weal; whatever should overthrow it, would in sure and immediate consequence bring down the godly fabric of that Constitution, whereof, it is a constituent and necessary part.'[1]

It is important to notice that it was the interdependence of Church and State, and not the dependence of the Church upon the State, that formed the basis of the eighteenth-century view. Almost no one advocated 'entire subservience to the purposes of government'[2] on the part of the Church, and this did not actually happen in practice. The belief that it did was again derived from a later uncritical acceptance of the polemical views put out by Dissenters in their early nineteenth-century attacks upon the Church. The closeness of the connection of religious and civil sanctions in men's minds meant that they were in practice inseparable. In 1790 Pitt 'considered the Church of England, as by law established, to be so essential a part of the Constitution, that whatever endangered it, would necessarily affect the security of the whole'.[3] Civil upheavals overseas seemed to confirm these suppositions. Although the revolt of the thirteen American colonies did not in all cases lead immediately to the formal separation of Church and State in the various Colonial assemblies, a clear connection was established between radical politics and the termination of state favour for particular Churches. The process was very far from being complete. The new federal constitution of 1787 sought to end the exclusive protection of one Church at the expense of others—there was no general intention, however, to separate religion as such from the foundation of civil government.[4] Yet the formal disestablishment of the Church of England in Virginia became an object-lesson for those who feared that political revolution had the severance of Church and State as a necessary corollary.[5] The 1798 Rebellion in Ireland was also led by men who advocated disestablishment: by Protestant radicals of the Society of United Irishmen, attached to the 'natural rights' theories of their American and French predecessors.[6] But it was the Revolution in France that provided English churchmen of this generation with—to them—the most appalling indictment of the unhappy consequences for civil order of the removal of the State from religious sanction. The cataclysmic events hung upon their political analysis for more than half a century. So near to their shores, the

---

[1] Robert Southey, *The Book of the Church* (London, 1824), ii. 528.

[2] Alan Smith, *The Established Church and Popular Religion, 1750–1850* (London, 1970), p. 3.

[3] Quoted in Edward Royle, *Radical Politics, 1790–1900, Religion and Unbelief* (London, 1971), p. 7.

[4] E. R. Norman, *The Conscience of the State in North America* (Cambridge, 1968), pp. 45–8.

[5] Ibid., p. 38.

[6] E. R. Norman, *A History of Modern Ireland*, Penguin edn. (London, 1973), p. 31.

worst had happened in France—'Her Government Demolished! Her Altars overthrown!', as Bishop Horsley exclaimed.[1]

There was never much doubt in their minds that it was the rejection of religion that had brought disaster and tyranny to France: religion was seen as the guarantee of political freedom, and the establishment of religion by law secured that freedom for all citizens in the State. To later generations, who came to regard state religion as illiberal, on grounds of civil justice, this eighteenth-century conviction has been unapparent. But it was of the greatest significance. The example of France was at once applied to conditions at home. 'I pray God', wrote Bishop Watson in a lengthy refutation of the principles of Tom Paine in 1796, 'that the rising generation of this land may be preserved from that evil heart of unbelief, which has brought ruin to a neighbouring nation; that neither a neglected education, nor domestic irreligion, nor evil communication, nor the fashion of a licentious world, may ever induce them to forget, that religion alone ought to be their rule of life.'[2] And in another place Watson wrote,

This impious fever of the mind, this paralysis of human intellect, originated in a neighbouring nation; its contagion has been industriously introduced, and is rapidly spreading in our own; it becomes us all in our several stations to endeavour to stop its progress; for of this we may all be well assured, that when religion shall have lost its hold on men's consciences, government will lose its authority over their persons, and a state of barbarous anarchy will ensue.[3]

This opinion was very widely shared. It is echoed throughout Wilberforce's *Practical View of the Prevailing Religious System*.[4] Hannah More's popular works conveyed the lesson to the humble men for whom she wrote—her rustic defender of the existing social order in her most famous tract is made to declare that he would 'sooner go to the Negers to get learning, or to the Turks to get religion, than to the French for freedom and happiness'.[5] So terrible, indeed, did the prospect appear that Horsley actually demanded, in 1798, that the clergy be mobilized into an armed militia for the defence of the country against the spread of the Revolution from France.[6] Wesley had also offered to muster a force of volunteers to defend the country.[7] Such practical aid was not, happily, called upon; but the prominence of the clergy in preaching and writing against 'French'

---

[1] Samuel Horsley, *A Sermon Preached Before the Lords Spiritual and Temporal* (London, 1793), p. 22.

[2] Richard Watson, *An Apology for the Bible in A Series of Letters Addressed to Thomas Paine*, 9th edn. (London, 1806), p. 393.

[3] Richard Watson, *A Defence of Revealed Religion*, p. 400.

[4] See op. cit., p. 10.

[5] *Village Politics, Addressed to all the Mechanics, Journeymen, and Day Labourers in Great Britain by Will Chip*, 3rd edn. (London, 1793), p. 5.

[6] Soloway, *Prelates and People*, p. 33.

[7] R. F. Wearmouth, *Methodism and the Working-Class Movements of England, 1800–1850*, 2nd edn. (London, 1946), p. 38.

principles later led many, including themselves, to suppose that they had been the country's most effective defence against revolution.[1]

Church and State combined to make provision for the exiled French clergy: a clear indication not only of public dismay at the fate of religion in France, but also an application of the need to give public support to religion, even if it was Catholic and foreign.[2] John Wilmot's 'Committee for the Relief of the Suffering Clergy and Laity of France exiled in England', set up in 1792, came under close government patronage—and was not disbanded until the 1820s. The clergy of the Church of England supported the relief work liberally, and within the first year most of the bishops had subscribed.[3] In April 1793 they received authorization from the Crown to make collections for the French clergy in the parish churches, and £41,314 was donated in this way.[4] In some places, however, the people put up resistance. 'I sincerely wish we had been able to collect a larger sum,' wrote the Revd. John Phillips from East Ham, 'but the parish is very small, consisting chiefly of farmers, who are not in general liberally disposed to the clergy, even of their own persuasion.'[5] The Government lodged a large number of priests at Winchester Castle; Oxford University Press published a Vulgate Testament for their use. The French, for their part, were left with an impression that the English Protestant clergy were 'learned, hospitable, and generous'.[6] The English had seen the worst that could happen when religion was severed from the State. The presence of the exiled French priests seemed a vivid proof of their general political contentions.

Many churchmen had anyway—quite independently of the example of the Revolution in France—begun to bring a new critical spirit to bear upon the moral condition of English society. They linked the moral corruptions of the age to the dissemination of wrong political values. Deism, Unitarianism, French atheism: all appeared to symptomize a deep malaise. In 1793 Horsley thought he saw the centre of all loosening of Christian social attitudes in that 'freedom of dispute, in which, for several years past, it hath been the folly of this country to indulge, upon matters of such high importance as the origin of government, and the authority of sovereigns.'[7] There was scarcely a bishop on the bench who did not call upon the Government to prosecute the publishers of radical literature. Most seemed unaware of the real differences between the 'philosophical' radicalism of

[1] Soloway, *Prelates and People*, pp. 45–6.

[2] I am indebted to Mr. Dominic Bellenger, of Jesus College, for information about the émigré clergy. His research into this subject is producing interesting new evidence about religious attitudes in these years.

[3] Public Record Office, T. 93, vol. 8.   [4] Ibid., col. 24, item VII.

[5] Fulham Papers, Lambeth Palace Library, MS. 150.

[6] *The Memoirs of Chateaubriand*, selected and translated by Robert Baldick (London, 1961), p. 198.

[7] Horsley, *A Sermon Preached Before the Lords Spiritual and Temporal*, p. 1.

the *salons* and the diluted and confused stirrings amongst groups of urban and rural labourers whose ideas were very much less attracted to atheism. Some churchmen, however, did isolate, and render respectable, reforming proposals which came from within existing political society. Thus Wilberforce argued that the existence of philosophical radicalism ought not to impede the passage of a measure of franchise reform. In 1792 he wrote, 'Unless some reforms be made, though we shall get well through our present difficulties, they will recur hereafter with aggravated force'.[1] A great deal of confusion surrounded attempts by churchmen to locate the exact source of the political evils to be eradicated. They were impressed by the progressive nature of decline, as it seemed to them: they believed that all radicalism which contained the seeds of French or Deistical ideas would inevitably result in the eventual adoption of atheism, and therefore furnish the dissolution of the religious sanction at the basis of civil society. 'There never was an age since the death of Christ, never one since the commencement of the history of the world, in which atheism and infidelity have been more generally professed,' said Watson in 1795. 'Nature and reason have been proclaimed as gods, festivals have been instituted in honour of abstract ideas, and all revealed religion has been scoffingly rejected as a system of statecraft and priestcraft, as a gross imposition on the understanding of mankind.'[2] It was a common exaggeration. Churchmen were too sensitive to the fashionable atheism of London literary society, and mistook the almost universal refusal of the working populations to go to church as evidence of unbelief—and not, as it in fact was, evidence of the working men's association of the Church with higher social classes.

So appalling did the tendencies of the age appear that apocalyptic expectations flourished in all sections of English society in the 1790s. Horsley reflected upon the possibility that the time of persecution for the Church, predicted in the New Testament, was almost upon them.[3] By 1800 he was able to be precise: the spread of political infection from France was inaugurating the sufferings spoken of by Christ Himself.[4] With these sorts of speculation went the theory of a grand conspiracy, originating with French philosophers, Bavarian *Illuminati*, and Freemasons, to overthrow society everywhere. Belief in some sort of actual plot became very widespread. Its details were revealed by the Abbé Barruel, an émigré Jesuit, and 'proved' by John Robison, a Scottish professor of mathematics. The clergy divided in attitude, some regarded the conspiracy with great scepticism—like John Randolph, Bishop of Oxford[5]—some appear to have

---

[1] Samuel Wilberforce, *The Life of William Wilberforce*, p. 115.
[2] Watson, *A Defence of Revealed Religion*, p. 399.
[3] Horsley, *Charge* (1796), p. 21.
[4] *The Charges of Samuel Horsley*, p. 83.
[5] See Soloway, *Prelates and People*, p. 43.

extended full credence. Horsley warned his clergy in extravagant language; against 'a machine of stupendous size and endless complications',[1] a 'vast enterprise of impiety'[2] by those who, knowing atheism to be unpopular with the common people of England, 'must pretend that their object is not to demolish but to reform'.[3] It is hardly surprising, with such opinions issuing from Church leaders, that reform programmes of the most ordinary and constitutional kind were unable to make much progress during the Jacobin scare. Amongst humbler social groups, millenarian speculations were widespread in these years.[4] These, too, contributed to the almost universal feeling of impending social crisis.

Churchmen, like public men generally, inclined to suppose the first priority was to dam up the source of error. Even William Paley, with all his adhesion to Whig principles of toleration, had declared it 'no infringement of religious liberty to restrain the circulation of ridicule, invective, and mockery, upon religious subjects'.[5] The *British Critic*, which Joshua Watson and Henry Norris acquired in 1812, and made an expression of the views of the 'Hackney Phalanx',[6] had already established itself as a Tory journal wherein clerical writers demanded the censure of Jacobin opinions. The very large sales of Tom Paine's works, especially in the 1790s, heightened the demands for some sort of action against radical literature. The prosecutions of Daniel Eaton (the publisher of Paine's *Age of Reason*) in 1793 and 1796, and of Thomas Williams in 1799 (who had published Paine on behalf of the London Corresponding Society), were largely brought about through the efforts of churchmen acting as members of the Proclamation Society. Their action was popular, and reflected the inclinations of a large majority in society. One of the most active in procuring the censorship of immoral literature—for so the works which attacked the position of religion in society were described—was the devout and respected Beilby Porteus, Bishop of Chester from 1776, and of London after 1787. In 1794 he instructed his clergy to preserve the principles of the people 'uncorrupted and unshaken by those pernicious and dangerous publications' which were being sent 'with dreadful industry and activity' throughout the country.[7] His objection to Paine's *Age of Reason* lay especially in its potential appeal to ordinary people—'It compressed the whole poison of infidelity into the narrow compass of an

[1] *The Charges of Samuel Horsley*, p. 90.

[2] Ibid., p. 91.   [3] Ibid., p. 101.

[4] See Alan Smith, *The Established Church and Popular Religion*, pp. 41–50; and E. P. Thompson, *The Making of the English Working Class*, Pelican edn. (London, 1968), p. 54.

[5] William Paley, *The Principles of Moral and Political Philosophy* (1785), printed in *Works* (Edinburgh, 1822), iv, Book VI, p. 466.

[6] A. B. Webster, *Joshua Watson* (London, 1954), p. 29.

[7] Robert Hodgson, *The Life of the Right Reverend Beilby Porteus, D.D.* (London, 1811), p. 119.

essence or extract, and rendered irreligion easy to the meanest capacity'.[1] He correctly believed that it furnished the first popularized account of Deism.[2]

Leaders of religious opinion were also considerably exercised by the social consequences of personal corruption; with vice, which they saw among the great as well as among the humble. In the last two decades of the century opinion generally was becoming conscious of what seemed to be a huge increase in crime and violence.[3] And amidst the contemporary exaggerations of the prevalent immorality there were many who were prepared to listen when clergy urged the need for social controls to stop the rot. The new consciousness of the state of public morals affected much wider sections of opinion than the Evangelicals alone. The Evangelicals, it is true, came to promote the most energetic agencies of publicity and correction; they prescribed solutions with a clarity which some others were unable to achieve. It was the moral *earnestness* of the Evangelicals that marked them off from their contemporaries; it was the linear quality of their social vision, rather than their diagnosis of the social ills around them, that gave the Evangelicals their distinctive qualities. Others complained of the things they complained of, and demanded action, too. There has been a tendency among historians to suppose that anyone who suggested higher standards of personal and social morality at this time must have been either an Evangelical or open to their influence. But this was not so; Lord Liverpool used to refer to any clergymen who was known to be attentive to his duties as 'Evangelical', whether he actually belonged to that school or not.[4] The definition was often as loosely applied. It is probably correct to see the last two decades of the eighteenth century as a time when an increasing volume of concern about the social consequences of personal immorality was becoming apparent to, and becoming acceptable to, prevailing opinion in Church and State.

The new movement for the 'reformation of manners' preceded the Revolution in France. Churchmen had already begun to point to the gulf between religious sanction and social practices even before the revolutionary political ideas rained upon the country. The Revolution served to reinforce the diagnosis of contemporary social ills which already had a considerable acceptance amongst the religious sections of educated and ruling opinion. A very large number of philanthropic agencies, under distinctly Christian inspiration and direction, came into existence in the 1770s. It is not true, as is sometimes supposed, that Christian concern with social evils originated in a wish to patch things up quickly to prevent

---

[1] *The Life of the Right Reverend Beilby Porteus, D.D.* p. 126.
[2] Royle, *Radical Politics*, p. 20.
[3] Best, *Temporal Pillars*, p. 138.
[4] W. R. Brock, *Lord Liverpool and Liberal Toryism*, 2nd edn. (London, 1967), p. 200.

the Revolution from spreading. The new agencies were devoted to many issues: to improvements of the conditions in which people lived, to the establishment of hospitals and dispensaries for the poor, to the creation of refuges for the destitute, to the prevention of cruelty to animals, and so forth.[1] The 'Society for Bettering the Conditions of the Poor', founded as a result of the collaboration of Bishop Barrington, William Wilberforce, and Sir Thomas Bernard, in 1796, gave publicity to the ideas for social improvement which the humanitarian enterprises were generating. It sent out questionnaires and published results; it provided essential statistical evidence of social conditions. Some societies were explicitly concerned with attracting the attention of the Government to the condition of society. In this, the State was seen to have a legitimate interest, as the supreme agency for the maintenance of a Christian society. The most celebrated of these bodies was the 'Society for Enforcing the King's Proclamation Against Immorality and Profaneness', set up in 1787 to promote the Royal Proclamation which Wilberforce and others had helped to elicit. The Society got the support of seventeen bishops. It promoted the prosecutions of publishers of immoral literature—a definition which included political immorality. It was also concerned with the evils of gambling, prostitution, drunkenness, and so on. In 1801 another body, the 'Society for the Suppression of Vice', took over some of this work. A lot of their efforts, like those of most of the agencies of the period, went into the question of Sunday observance—in 1794 legislation was secured which reinforced the existing Sabbatarian code.

The appeal to state support for the enforcement of moral conviction did not go uncontested. The objections, however, did not usually arise from any general belief that the State ought not properly to be concerned with these sorts of functions, but came from those who just did not like the moral earnestness of the high-minded, and who sometimes managed to represent their revulsion as a defence of the rights of the poor. Bishop Porteus noticed that hostile writers in the newspapers argued that Sunday laws were really intended 'to take away from the common people all the usual comforts of the Sunday'.[2] Defenders of the code, for their part, contended that Sabbatarian legislation protected the people from Sunday labour. A special appeal was made to social superiors to respect the Lord's Day. 'If, therefore, the rich and great will not, from a liberal spirit of doing right, abstain from these offences, for which the poor are to suffer fines and imprisonment, effectual good cannot be done,' Hannah More wrote in her *Thoughts on the Importance of the Manners of the Great to*

---

[1] For details of these works, see E. M. Howse, *Saints in Politics. The 'Clapham Sect' and the Growth of Freedom* (London, 1953), pp. 124 ff., and Ford K. Brown, *Fathers of the Victorians, The Age of Wilberforce* (Cambridge, 1961), pp. 83 ff.

[2] Hodgson, *Life of Porteus*, p. 141.

General Society (1788).[1] Wilberforce, too, went to considerable lengths to make it quite clear that action against the social evils of the age should not involve class discrimination. In 1797 he attacked those who thought otherwise—

Vices are held to be grossly criminal in the lower ranks, because manifestly ruinous to their temporal interests: but in the higher, they are represented as . . . flowing naturally from great prosperity, from the excess of gaiety and good humour; and they are accordingly regarded with but a small degree of disapprobation, and censured very slightly or not at all.[2]

The belief that social reformation disguised discrimination against the poor was given a famous expression—and so projected from contemporary polemicism to posterity—by Sydney Smith, Canon of St. Paul's, in an attack upon the 'Society for the Suppression of Vice' which he wrote for the *Edinburgh Review* in 1809. 'A man of ten thousand a year may worry a fox as much as he pleases—may encourage the breed of a mischievious animal on purpose to worry it; and a poor labourer is carried before a magistrate for paying sixpence to see an exhibition of courage between a dog and a bear!'[3] Smith was among those who opposed some of the moral agencies of these years out of distaste for men who appointed themselves accusers of others.[4] Fashionable gambling duly escaped legal penalties, and the games of chance of the poor did not; just as fox-hunting survived bear-baiting. But this was not for want of effort by the reformers. They did not consciously avoid attacking the rich and influential, though the assumption that they did has survived.[5]

The most well-known philanthropic undertaking of the period, of course, was the movement for the abolition of the slave-trade. Here, again, there was an Evangelical spearhead. Yet initial interest arose from agitation by Quakers, led by Granville Sharp, for the release of Negro slaves imported into England itself. This had been achieved as a result of Mansfield's judgement in 1772. The relationship between that legal decision and the general campaign against the slave-trade, and the priority of philanthropic over economic motives in the new campaign, have recently been questioned.[6] Whatever the motivations, however, it remains certain that agitation by the teachers of religion emphasized the moral aspects of the issue. Slavery was condemned by Paley as an obligation to labour which did not involve contract or consent; it was, as a result, 'merciless and

[1] Hannah More, *Thoughts on the Importance of the Manners of the Great* (London, 1788), p. 97.
[2] Wilberforce, *A Practical View*, p. 286.
[3] Reprinted in Sydney Smith's *Works*, 3rd edn. (London, 1845), ii. 335.
[4] Ibid., ii. 328.
[5] See Ford K. Brown, *Fathers of the Victorians*, p. 84.
[6] See F. O. Shyllon, *Black Slaves in Britain* (London, 1973).

tyrannical'.[1] By the end of the century all the bishops had come out against the slave-trade.[2] It is important to notice that this involved them in a violation of property rights, because the owners of slaves had a legal property in the persons of their slaves. It was the attack on this aspect of slavery that was at the centre of the debate: it affected the institution of property as such, and not just the conditions of slave-owning or transport. Many churchmen saw a need to postpone the emancipation of the slaves until they had been adequately prepared for the life of a free subject, but eventual abolition of slavery itself was, from the start, the real object of most reformers. In 1783, for example, Bishop Porteus conceived a plan for 'the Civilization and Conversion of the Negroes' in the West Indies.[3] Conversion to Christianity was regarded as an essential element of citizenship, since religion and social order were inseparable and interdependent. In 1787 Porteus instructed the clergy in the West Indies (who were within his episcopal jurisdiction) to inquire into the living conditions of the slaves and to begin Christian instruction on a systematic basis.[4] Not everyone agreed about so radical a step: the Society for the Propagation of the Gospel had, in 1784, declined to act on the Bishop's suggestion that they undertake the education of the slave population.[5] Since the slave-owners and their agents and dependents were all Christians, too, the reforming beliefs of the bishops involved them in something resembling a confrontation with a section of the laity of their own church.

The clerical abolitionists went to great lengths to declare that slavery was the only issue over which they believed it proper to violate the rights of property. Wesley, in his *Thoughts on Slavery* (1774) had so respected those rights that he had argued for emancipation through individual action rather than legal compulsion. The campaigners in the 1790s had to claim that their doctrines about the essential humanity of the Negroes, and the exceptional violability of property, were not hedged with what appeared to some opponents to be Jacobin presuppositions. Bishop Horsley, speaking in July 1799, in support of a bill to regulate the slave-trade, was sensitive to the change:

I know well, my Lords, that the advocates of the slave-trade have long endeavoured to represent the project of abolition as a branch of Jacobinism . . . My Lords, we who contend for the abolition proceed upon no visionary notions of equality and imprescriptible rights of man; we strenuously uphold the gradations of civil society: But we do indeed, my Lords, affirm that those gradations both ways, both ascending and descending, are limited. There is an exorbitance

---

[1] Paley, *Principles of Moral and Political Philosophy*, in *Works*, iv, Book III, p. 154.
[2] *The Speeches in Parliament of Samuel Horsley*, i. 247.
[3] Hodgsen, *Life of Porteous*, p. 85.
[4] Ibid., p. 104.
[5] Howse, *Saints in Politics*, p. 31.

of power to which no good king will aspire; and there is an extreme condition of subjection to which man cannot without injustice be degraded; and this, we say, is the condition of the African carried away into slavery.[1]

It is true that radicals sympathetic to French ideas were also active in the movement against the slave-trade. But quite apart from the spectre of Jacobinism—easily raised against any reform—the fears for property were a serious difficulty, and survived the Jacobin scare as a major ground of opposition to the abolition of slavery in the debates in Parliament and in public opinion in the first three decades of the nineteenth century. Thus the Earl of Westmoreland, denouncing the abolitionists in 1807, the year in which the trade (but not slavery itself) was in the end abolished, referred to the threat to 'titles and estates' from all who, in the campaign, had 'combined against property'. He identified them as 'the Presbyterian and the Prelate, the Methodist and the field preacher, the Jacobin and the murderer'.[2] Many at the time regarded the reforming enthusiasm of the abolitionist bishops with the same sort of distaste which, a century and a half later, for example, men of business felt for bishops who sought to change the policy of the South African Government by the withdrawal or manipulation of investments.

The literature produced by the campaign against the slave-trade, and the reasonings of the reformers, had thus begun to describe some moral attributes of humanity which the State ought to protect, against the normal considerations of property. The question of Christian missionaries in India raised a comparable problem. Here, it was the corporate rights of the East India Company that got in the way of the Christian humanitarians. Evangelicals led the campaign. In 1793 they failed, and in 1813 they succeeded, in amending the charter of the Company, whilst it was being renewed, allowing the entry of missions to India. Wilberforce was careful to point out that his hope was not 'to force our faith upon the natives of India; but gravely, silently, and systematically to prepare the way for the gradual diffusion of religious truth'.[3] It was because humanity appeared to be so degraded by such Hindu practices as the suttee rites that a Christian attitude to human life was thought to be essential. In this, as in the case of the Negro slaves, therefore, Christian philanthropists were appealing to a view of humanity which they believed required legislative protection. 'Christianity, independently of its effects on a future state of existence, has been acknowledged even by avowed sceptics, to be, beyond all other institutions that ever existed, favourable to the temporal interests and happiness of man,' Wilberforce remarked of the prospects for India.[4]

[1] *The Speeches in Parliament of Samuel Horsley*, i. 196–7.
[2] Howse, *Saints in Politics*, p. 62.
[3] S. Wilberforce, *Life of Wilberforce*, p. 119.
[4] Quoted in Howse, *Saints in Politics*, p. 89.

Many of those who did not agree were concerned lest the introduction of Christianity should result in conflicts with the native religions, civil strife, and the eventual loss of the country.[1] Some others simply did not regard Indians as capable of a suitable reception of Christianity.

These inroads on corporate and property rights in the interests of humanity were, and were regarded as being, exceptional: required by conditions outside the British Isles and by peculiar conditions of personal degradation. The Church, in most other areas, envisaged the State as the guarantor of property and contract. The dissemination of radical ideas at the end of the eighteenth century in fact obliged churchmen to formulate with a new precision exactly what duties men owed to the State, and what protection they received in return. The resulting restatement of Christian teaching combined the precepts of Natural Theology, Utilitarian political philosophy, and the traditional sanctions of Scripture.

The most systematic explanation of political obedience was furnished by Archdeacon William Paley, the Cambridge Whig divine whose works established a moral and political reference to which the clergy resorted for a length of time—over a century—out of all proportion to their originality or theoretical durability. To some extent Paley's significance 'lay in the exactitude with which he represented the *Zeitgeist*',[2] but in reality his premises belonged to the eighteenth-century world which had already begun to slip away. Yet his writings acquired great authority, and his defence of the notion of Established religion, even on Whiggish grounds, enjoyed a renewed vogue in the 1830s when the Church was actually under attack as an Establishment. It was this that gave Paley's thought an extended life beyond normal expectation. His *Principles of Moral and Political Philosophy* was written in 1785. It rejected the idea that the duty to obey civil government rested on contract: 'Wherefore, rejecting the intervention of a compact, as unfounded in its principle, and dangerous in the application, we assign for the only ground of the subject's obligation, the will of God as collected from Expediency.'[3] It was God's Will that human happiness be promoted—civil society conduced to that end—civil society could not be upheld unless the interest of the whole society was binding upon every member of it—conclusion: 'that so long as the interest of the whole society requires it, that is, so long as the established government cannot be resisted or changed without public inconveniency, it is the will of God (which *will* universally determines our duty) that the established government be obeyed'.[4] The application of the principles of utility and the observations of natural evidence coincided with the precepts of Holy

---

[1] Sydney Smith argued this case in 1808; see *Works*, i. 142.
[2] Sykes, *Church and State*, p. 326.
[3] *The Principles of Moral and Political Philosophy*, in *Works*, iv, Book VI, p. 333.
[4] Ibid., p. 334.

Scripture, with Revelation; and for Paley Scripture was therefore the great source of Christian obedience to the State.[1]

The command of Christ that obedience was due to Caesar in the things belonging to Caesar, and the teaching of St. Paul in the thirteenth chapter of the Epistle to the Romans, had supplied Christendom with the obligation of civil obedience since the beginning; they were still, at the end of the eighteenth century, the basis of the Church's attitude to government. When Bishop Horsley preached before the House of Lords in January 1793 on the anniversary of the martyrdom of King Charles I, his text was from Romans, 'Let every soul be subject to the Higher Powers'. He attacked the notion that political power could be based upon any natural rights of man;[2] that there was ever a 'state of nature'—since God made men for civil society[3]—and that the idea of a 'contract of government' could be Christian.[4] It was God himself who had instituted civil order; 'be the form of any particular government what it may, the submission of the individual is a principal branch of that religious duty which each man owes to God'.[5] This traditional teaching was the staple matter of the popular religious propaganda of the age. Hannah More's 'Cheap Repository Tracts' (1797–8) were full of this sort of view. They were intended to counteract the effects of Jacobin literature among the poor,[6] and copies were distributed by the Government.[7] Hannah More said that *Village Politics* (1793), her most successful composition, was intended 'for the most vulgar class of readers'.[8] As a former school-teacher, and as one who came herself from a fairly humble family, she was well acquainted with people for whom she wrote. *Village Politics* was an imagined dialogue between two rustics: Jack, who upheld obedience and quoted scriptural texts to justify himself,[9] and Tom, corrupted by French ideas about the rights of man, but who was, of course, in the end persuaded by his colleague. The *Anti-Jacobin Review*, started in 1798, and intended for a slightly higher social level of readership, contained numerous articles by the clergy enjoining obedience to civil authority as a religious duty. In such arguments, churchmen were usually careful to emphasize that obedience was owing to political, rather than social superiors. Yet it was in practice clear that social status and political power were inextricable.[10] Churchmen also declared another aspect of the traditional teaching of the Church: that no explicit *form* of civil government was prescribed by God. Horsley said that 'the Christian religion is an institution not adapted to any

---

[1] *The Principles of Moral and Political Philosophy, in Works,* iv, Book VI, p. 340.

[2] Samuel Horsley, *A Sermon Preached before the Lords Spiritual and Temporal,* p. 2.

[3] Ibid., p. 6.   [4] Ibid., p. 7.   [5] Ibid., p. 8.

[6] For an analysis of their content, see Ford K. Brown, *Fathers of the Victorians,* pp. 135–50.

[7] Ibid., p. 124.   [8] Ibid., p. 123.

[9] *Village Politics,* p. 13.   [10] Best, *Temporal Pillars,* p. 153.

particular nation, to any age, or to any particular form of government, without exception'.[1] He also maintained, on a previous occasion, that Christian principles 'ascribe no greater sanctity to Monarchy than to any other form of established government'.[2] This sort of distinction must be borne in mind when considering the clergy's defence of the existing British Monarchy and Constitution against its revolutionary enemies. It was not a blind defence of a particular form of government, but a support of order in a particular historical circumstance. The clergy went to some lengths to try to make this clear.

Some of the enemies of the existing order seemed traditional ones, too. 'The descendants of the puritans are still found among us in great numbers,' observed the *Anti-Jacobin Review* in 1799; 'they have, with few exceptions, admired, extolled, nay, even encouraged and promoted, to the utmost of their power, the French Revolution, because it was founded upon their principles.'[3] Unitarian leaders, like Priestley and Price, were seen as the embodiment of a continuing opposition to throne and altar, as the representatives, at the end of the eighteenth century, of those who, a century and a half before, had overthrown Crown and Church. This identification was made often. Thus in 1793 the Dean of Middleham, the Revd. R. B. Nickolls, said,

All that is urged now by the enemies of our Church and State was urged, and what is more, was tried in the last century; and after Republicans and Levellers had overturned both the Church and the Monarchy, together with the morals and happiness of the nation, affairs came at last, as they generally do in such cases, into the hands of a Dictator.[4]

France certainly seemed set fair to fit this canon. It has been noticed that memories of the seventeenth-century upheaval reverberated in the popular millenarianism of the 1790s.[5] To clerical defenders of the existing order, therefore, the period seemed to present some familiar as well as some novel dangers.

It was a matter of inquiry whether the Methodists did not also belong, by adoption, to this English republican legacy. They were certainly held in considerable suspicion.[6] But most of the more informed observers were able to distinguish between the followers of Wesley—who were still, at this time, inseparable from the Established Church, using its Prayer Book and sometimes still attending its public worship as well as their own services—and extreme groups which had lodged within the Methodist

[1] *The Speeches in Parliament of Samuel Horsley*, i. 249.

[2] Horsley, *A Sermon Preached Before the Lords Spiritual and Temporal*, p. 7.

[3] *Anti-Jacobin Review*, iii (1799), 319.

[4] R. B. Nickolls, *The Duty of Supporting and Defending our Country and Constitution* (York, 1793), p. 23.

[5] E. P. Thompson, *The English Working Class*, p. 54.

[6] Wearmouth, *Methodism and Working-class Movements*, pp. 36–7.

fold. Horsley believed, in 1800, that Jacobins were 'making a tool of Methodism'; yet he saw that 'the real Methodist' was 'kept in utter ignorance of the wicked enterprize the counterfeit has in hand'.[1] Many of those most noted for their democratic politics and primitive egalitarianism in fact seceded from Wesleyanism with Alexander Kilham in 1797—a number of these men really were influenced by Jacobin ideas.[2] After 1790 the Methodist Conferences made regular declarations of their attachment to the Constitution and urged the duty of civil obedience upon their members.[3] When considering E. P. Thompson's diverting and influential belief that Methodism provided the 'work discipline' enabling an efficient and profitable factory economy, it is as well to remember that the Methodists were still often indistinguishable from the members of the State Church. Thompson gives little attention to the Church of England. It was, he remarks, so far removed from the people anyway, because of its class identity, that its influence was negligible—'its homilies had ceased to have much effect'.[4] It is certainly true that the Church was seen as a class institution, but the ineffectiveness of its social influence can be exaggerated. Some clergy had shown themselves rather adept at inciting 'Church and King' mobs in provincial cities in 1791 and 1792.[5] And not all of Hannah More's tracts were 'left to litter the servants' quarters of the great houses' as Thompson suggests.[6] In 1802 William Cobbett—no friend of the Established Church—noticed that the clergy 'are, from necessity, *everywhere*; and their aggregate influence is astonishingly great'.[7]

There is sometimes a tendency amongst observers of religious phenomena to suppose that uneducated people inevitably absorb religious ideas because of ignorance or superstition, or because they are indoctrinated by the agents of 'social control'. These suppositions were around in the 1790s too. Bishop Horsley remarked that it had become 'fashionable' to regard the common people as incapable of true religion because unable to perform the necessary intellectual calculations. But religious truth depended upon Revelation, he insisted, and the most humble of men were perfectly capable of spiritual wisdom.[8] This has always been the orthodox view of the Church. Intellectuals are often the last to perceive the wisdom of the unsophisticated. Thompson hints that Methodism was deliberately

[1] *The Charges of Samuel Horsley*, p. 105.

[2] See W. R. Ward, *Religion and Society in England, 1790–1850* (London, 1972), p. 34; E. P. Thompson, *The English Working Class*, p. 48.

[3] Wearmouth, *Methodism and Working-Class Movements*, pp. 38–48.

[4] Thompson, *The English Working Class*, p. 386.

[5] See E. J. Hobsbawn, *Primitive Rebels. Studies in Archaic Forms of Social Movement in the 19th and 20th Centuries* (Manchester, 1959), p. 7.

[6] Thompson, *The English Working Class*, p. 386.

[7] Quoted Brown, *Fathers of the Victorians*, p. 47.

[8] Samuel Horsley, *The Charge of the Bishop of St. David's* (1790) (Gloucester, 1791), p. 11.

exploited by factory owners in order to contrive a passive work force,[1] but in fact he is less concerned with establishing agency than with tracing the ideological suitability of the Methodist outlook for inducing the ethic of hard work among those who could expect little earthly reward for their efforts.[2] His only solid documentary evidence comes from Andrew Ure's *Philosophy of Manufactures*—a book which influenced Engels and Marx, and not published until 1835. There, it is true, the sober qualities that belief in eternal verities demands are seen to be conducive to factory discipline. That is hardly surprising. It would be novel to expect religious men to imagine the practice of their beliefs to issue in sloth. In 1804 the *Evangelical Magazine* offered typical advice to its readers: 'Religion promotes industry, industry gains respect, respect gains recommendation, recommendation gains business, business gains wealth; and thus religion itself naturally leads to prosperity.'[3] This sort of liturgy was quite popular, and has fallen upon the satisfied ears of later sociologists as proof enough of the real nature of the Protestant ethic. But just as many contemporary cautions against too much involvement with the business of making money, or with worldly preoccupations, can be found. In 1796, for example, a Canon of Christ Church exhorted men not to be 'overpowered by the restless agitations of business'.[4] Wilberforce stressed the 'danger to true Christians from mixing too much in worldly business'.[5] And in fact the writings of *secular* moralists of the time covered by Thompson's analysis were just as emphatic in commending the ethical qualities of hard work and personal discipline to working men as religious writers were. The most systematic prescription for factory discipline did not come from a Methodist preacher but from a Freethinker, Robert Owen.[6]

Thompson is also anxious to explain how 'Methodism obtained its greatest success in serving *simultaneously* as the religion of the industrial bourgeoisie . . . and of wide sections of the proletariat'.[7] The masters, he believes, prospered according to the virtues discussed by Weber and Tawney: for them Methodism 'served as ideological self-justification'— their endeavours were rewarded, religion was conducive to the rise of capitalism. The operatives, on the other hand, had to be persuaded to work

---

[1] Thompson, *The English Working Class*, p. 390.

[2] Ibid., p. 398. See also the 'Postscript' (in the Pelican edn.), pp. 917–23, where the author answers his critics.

[3] 'The Folly of Vice', *Evangelical Magazine*, May 1804, p. 201.

[4] Robert Holmes, *A Sermon Preached Before the Honourable House of Commons* (London, 1796), p. 10.

[5] William Wilberforce, *A Practical View of the Prevailing Religious System*, p. 274.

[6] See Owen's *A New View of Society, or Essays on the Formation of the Human Character Preparatory to the Development of a Plan for gradually Ameliorating the Condition of Mankind* (1813); printed in *Robert Owen on Education*, selections, ed. Harold Silver (Cambridge, 1969), especially pp. 79–99.

[7] Thompson, *The English Working Class*, p. 391.

diligently even though their efforts were 'unlikely to bring any temporal gain'.[1] For them, Methodist theology and worship provided emotional sustenance through the sublimation of their desires. (Thompson does not actually say it was their opiate.) Since he dwells upon the 'perverted eroticism of Methodist imagery'[2] it comes as rather a surprise to read some of Thompson's own verbal images to describe the appeal of Methodism. It was 'a ritualized form of psychic masturbation'[3]; there were 'Sabbath orgasms of feeling'.[4] But this inquiry is scarcely necessary at all. The number of working men who became Methodists was not as large as Thompson seems to think; nothing like a majority even of the factory owners were Methodists. There was, anyway, nothing unique about the simultaneous appeal of a religious outlook to both masters and men. The same was true of the Church of England, whose greater comprehensiveness, and whose reduced numerical strength over-all, disguised the fact that it retained a far larger following from all classes than Methodism did. All the churches used their influence to encourage disciplined labour; it is a lesson much administered to the ill-disciplined by modern Marxists. There were also those, at the end of the eighteenth century, who were extremely anxious to make sure that Christianity did not become what Wilberforce called 'a cold compilation of restraints and prohibitions', or 'simply a set of penal statutes',[5] that it should not 'dwindle away into a mere matter of police'.[6] Christianity, according to Wilberforce, was intended to elevate human life beyond anything that could be achieved by the mere 'moral teacher'—by one who was concerned with religion as a matter of social control, the 'Methodist' minister described by Thompson in fact.

Let the Socinian and the moral teacher of Christianity come forth, and tell us what effects they have produced on the lower orders [Wilberforce wrote]. But, blessed be God, the Religion which we recommend, has proved its correspondence with the character originally given of Christianity, that it was calculated for the poor; by changing the whole condition of the mass of society in many of the most populous districts in this and other countries.[7]

Those who have been interested in the Church's teaching on civil obedience and the virtues of labour as evidences of the part played by religion in 'social control' usually emphasize the effect of clerical magistrates. During the reign of George III the number of Justices in holy orders noticeably increased; a reflection of the improved social status of the clergy.[8] It was a practical sign of the close proximity of Church and

[1] Thompson, The English Working Class, p. 398.   [2] Ibid., p. 407.
[3] Ibid., p. 405.   [4] Ibid., p. 406.
[5] Wilberforce, A Practical View, p. 180.
[6] Ibid., p. 285.   [7] Ibid., p. 410.
[8] G. Kitson Clark, Churchmen and the Condition of England, 1832–1885 (London, 1973), p. 34.

State. But it also appeared, to some contemporary radicals and their later sympathizers, as if the Church was merely a part of the coercive machinery of the State. This impression derived not only from the more dramatic occasions when clerical magistrates took action against political subversion, but from the regular and familiar enforcement of tithe, and of other local duties and levies, which associated the magistracy with the protection of the interests of landed society. It was the Church's educational work, however, that has most involved it in the later odium apparently attaching to 'social control'. Robert Raikes began his Sunday Schools in 1780. The Sunday School Society was founded in 1785. Hannah More's schools were started at Cheddar in 1789; and by the end of the century both Church and Dissent had established an impressive number of Sunday Schools. Some bishops, like Porteus, when he was Bishop of Chester (a diocese which contained extensive new industrial areas), experimented with schools in the cities first, and then encouraged their establishment in the country areas.[1] They were intended to teach children to read—in order, principally, that they might be able to read the Bible—and sometimes to write. Quite a lot of them also prepared children in the personal and moral attitudes considered appropriate for life and work in adult society. Some modern writers have seen the schools as an attempt by established order to instil loyalty into the children of the poor; institutions of 'discipline and repression'.[2] Men of the time were indeed worried lest the enthusiasm of the Church for education accidentally encouraged sedition, a fear which sometimes conveyed itself to Church leaders. Bishop Horsley, who had strenuously encouraged popular education in 1792—including vocational training in trades[3]—was by 1800 persuaded that some Dissenting Sunday Schools were under Jacobin control, that 'sedition and atheism are the real objects of these institutions'.[4] The *Anti-Jacobin Review* opposed the schools in the belief that literacy was contrary to the diffusion of virtue among the lower orders.[5] In Hannah More's schools, as doubtless in most others, it was clearly understood that the children were not to be educated out of their social station.[6] The schools, that is to say, operated within the conventions and expectations of the society which created them. They reflected the prevailing sense of social order. It is always so; there can be few societies which actually try to educate their children into the will to destroy their own social values—though it is arguable that modern exponents of 'open' moral teaching in the schools

[1] Hodgson, *The Life of the Right Reverend Beilby Porteus, D.D.*, p. 92.

[2] Thompson, *The English Working Class*, p. 441.

[3] Samuel Horsley, *The Abounding of Iniquity. A Sermon Preached in Quebec Chapel, Mary-le-Bone* (London, 1792), p. 17.

[4] *The Charges of Samuel Horsley*, p. 104.

[5] *Anti-Jacobin Review*, iii (1799), 180.

[6] Howse, *Saints in Politics*, p. 97.

came close to it. And those who did not fear the consequences of literacy were clearly the most effective, for the Sunday Schools thrived. As William Otter, who became Bishop of Chichester, wrote in 1820: it was mistaken 'to take refuge in ignorance from the lessons of sedition'.[1]

Most Church leaders certainly regarded social inequality as an essential part of the Divine Will. Differences of station, inherent personal qualities, and social function, were seen as the bases of social authority, the incentive, and the actual mechanism of national prosperity. The Church also taught the *obligation* of responsibilities, as well as the enjoyment of privileges. It was a social view which, once again, shows the proximity of Christian thinking to the conventional lay thought of the ruling classes of the age. 'A natural equality amongst mankind is contradictory to the actual condition of human nature,' as George Horne, Bishop of Norwich, wrote to his clergy in 1791, in a *Charge* which he was too unwell to deliver verbally. 'Equal liberty', he added, 'is another idea which cannot take place in society, because men are not equal in virtue.'[2] Social inequality was thought to be founded, therefore, in natural inequality. Bishop Watson explained the connection and its consequences:

Sincerely as I am attached to the liberties of mankind, I cannot but profess myself an utter enemy to that spurious philosophy, that democratic insanity, which would equalise all property, and level all distinctions in civil society. Personal distinctions, arising from superior probity, learning, eloquence, skill, courage, and from every other excellency of talents, are the very blood and nerves of the body politic; they animate the whole and invigorate every part; without them, its bones would become reeds, and its marrow water; it would presently sink into a fetid, senseless mass of corruption—Power may be used for private ends, and in opposition to the public good; rank may be improperly conferred, and insolently sustained; riches may be wickedly acquired, and viciously applied: but this is neither necessarily, nor generally the case. I cannot agree with those who, in asserting the natural equality of men, spurn the institutional distinctions attending power, rank and riches.[3]

Paley had also argued for the practical and moral basis of the social hierarchy. Like most of his contemporaries, he believed that distinctions of class provided the incentives necessary for social amelioration. In a work published in 1792, *Reasons for Contentment, Addressed to the Labouring Part of the British Public*, Paley declared that 'The change, and the only change to be desired, is that gradual and progressive improvement in our circumstances which is the natural fruit of successful industry'.[4] It was also usual

---

[1] Quoted in Best, *Temporal Pillars*, p. 159; from Otter's *Reasons for Continuing the Education of the Poor.*

[2] George Horne, *Charge, Intended to have been Delivered to the Clergy of Norwich at the Primary Visitation* (Norwich, 1791), p. 28.

[3] Richard Watson, *An Apology for the Bible*, p. 378.

[4] Printed in *Works*, iii. 442.

for clerical apologists of prevailing social arrangements to cite scriptural authority. William Jones, the Vicar of Nayland and a member of the High Church 'Hackney Phalanx', wrote an anonymous critique of Priestley's work in 1792, in which he observed, 'that man must be an atheist or an infidel, who forgets that there is a foundation of law, by which all men are bound, in their relation to God and to one another; and that the ten commandments are made for men in a state of inequality'.[1] Although Professor Soloway is generally correct in remarking that eighteenth-century bishops did not ordinarily seek to console the sufferings of the poor by pointing to the compensation of heavenly rewards,[2] a few examples can be found. 'Religion smooths all inequalities because it unfolds a prospect which makes all earthly distinctions nothing,' Paley told the labourers.[3] And Hannah More's village sage declared that 'instead of indulging discontent, because another is richer than I in this world (for envy is at the bottom of your equality works) I read my bible, go to church, and think of a treasure in heaven'.[4]

With the necessity of social inequality went a justification of property. Here, too, the arguments used by churchmen were eighteenth-century commonplaces. Paley taught that inequality of property 'abstractly considered' was an evil, but one which incited men to industry—'if there be any great inequality unconnected with this origin, it ought to be corrected'.[5] The institution of property was itself of Divine ordering; 'It is the intention of God, that the produce of the earth be applied to the use of man: that intention cannot be fulfilled without establishing property: it is consistent therefore with his will that property be established.'[6] The same laws that created wealth also provided work for the poor. 'Fixed rules of property are established for one as well as another,' Paley wrote; 'to abolish riches would not be to abolish poverty, but, on the contrary, to leave it without protection or resource.'[7] In an important amplification of this rule, Paley made it clear that the first responsibility of wealth was the relief of poverty: 'When the partition of property is rigidly maintained against the claims of indigence and distress, it is maintained in opposition to the intention of those who made it, and to his, who is the Supreme Proprietor of every thing.'[8] This was the teaching which generations of clergy learned from their resort to Paley's writings as standard texts. The

---

[1] William Jones, *A Small Whole-Length of Dr. Priestley, from his Printed Works* (London, 1792), p. 10.

[2] Soloway, *Prelates and People*, p. 75.

[3] Paley, *Reasons for Contentment*, in *Works*, iii. 443.

[4] More, *Village Politics*, p. 18.

[5] Paley, *Principles of Moral and Political Philosophy*, in *Works*, iv. 73.

[6] Ibid., p. 79.

[7] Paley, *Reasons for Contentment*, in *Works*, iii. 433.

[8] Paley, *Principles*, in *Works*, iv. 160.

responsibilities of the rich, in fact, were a prominent theme in the clerical writings of the period. That Tory cleric, William Jones, preaching to a London congregation in 1796, said 'wealth is given to *some* for the sake of *all* . . . no man has a right to consider himself as an absolute proprietor, with power to dispose of everything he has, according to his own will'.[1] Criticisms of the unnecessary luxury of upper-class life were frequent. In 1798 Bishop Porteus devoted a course of Lenten lectures to flaying the 'upper ranks' of society for the misuse of their wealth—as well as warning the lower about the dangers of atheism. The lectures, when published, went through several editions.[2] Both Wilberforce and Hannah More, in addressing themselves to the rich as the natural leaders of society, pointed out that they needed to reform their manner of living. 'Reformation must begin with the GREAT, or it will never be effectual,' wrote Hannah More. 'Their example is the fountain from whence the vulgar draw their habits, actions and characters.'[3] Wilberforce taught that the obligations of the rich to the poor ought to involve some element of actual sacrifice. There was no real Christianity 'in the case of one who by his liberality in this respect is curtailed in no necessary, is abridged of no luxury, is put to no trouble'.[4] Paley, too, had told the owners of estates to help the less fortunate through a productive use of their wealth, 'by building cottages, splitting farms, erecting manufactories, cultivating wastes, embanking the sea, draining marshes', and so on—even if 'the profits of these undertakings do not repay the expense'.[5] Those who influenced Church opinion in the formulation of Christian teaching in these years were therefore careful to regard wealth as only properly held by Christians when used according to certain conditions. It had to be conducive to the common good.

During the last two decades of the eighteenth century Christian opinion divided within itself. Some continued to adhere to characteristically utilitarian social attitudes. A section became activist: it sought to provide a more 'vital' basis for the creation of a Christian society. Many Church leaders tended to support this feeling, and most active among them, of course, were the Evangelicals. These activists were anxious to place morality upon distinctly Christian foundations: they accused the other members of their class of too ready an acceptance of worldly conventions. They denounced the tendency to allow Christianity to become merely a series of moralistic propositions scarcely distinguishable from secular natural philosophy. The man described by the Age of Reason—auton-

---

[1] William Jones, *The Use and Abuse of this World. A Sermon* (London, 1796), p. 9.

[2] Hodgson, *Life of Porteous*, p. 131.

[3] Hannah More, *Thoughts on the Importance of the Manners of the Great to General Society*, p. 95. This theme is also developed in her *Estimate of the Religion of the Fashionable World* (London, 1790).

[4] William Wilberforce, *A Practical View*, p. 312.

[5] Paley, *Principles*, in *Works*, iv. 165.

omous, benevolent, suited to 'Natural Religion'—was becoming discredited even before the world, reeling under the impact of the French Revolution, appeared to be sliding into social chaos. 'Mistakes about the nature of man are almost as dangerous as about the nature of God,' wrote Bishop Horne in 1791;[1] 'Natural Religion, *as a system*, is a phenomenon risen up in these latter times; infidelity seems to have been increasing upon us ever since.'[2] Churchmen, in fact, were rediscovering the doctrine of Original Sin. They were realizing that human motive and social virtue were more ambiguous and less susceptible to calculation than they had supposed. Horsley attacked not only the Deists, but the intellectual fashion of almost a whole age, when he condemned the proposition 'That Moral Duties constitute the whole, or by far the better part of practical Christianity'.[3] Hannah More blamed the upper classes for supposing themselves exempted from the personal obligations essential to the profession of Christianity. 'Charity must not supplant faith,' she warned them.[4] It was wrong to confuse benevolence with Christianity—'A man may correct many improper practices, and refrain from many immoral actions, from merely human motives'.[5] Wilberforce applied the distinction between Christianity and 'mere morality'[6] with systematic stringency. It was the corner-stone of his religious structure, of his social vision. Erroneous opinions about human nature were very widespread among the most influential in society, he believed. Everywhere people 'speak of man as a being who, naturally pure and inclined to all virtue, is sometimes, almost involuntarily, drawn out of the right course, or is overpowered by the violence of temptation'. This fallacy in fact bred the worst instincts: 'vice with them is rather an accidental and temporary, than a constitutional and habitual distemper; a noxious plant, which, though found to live and even to thrive in the human mind, is not the natural growth and product of the soil'.[7] Another consequence of this wrong view led some to exaggerate 'the merit of certain aimiable and useful qualities, and of considering them as of themselves sufficient to compensate for the want of the supreme love and fear of God'.[8] Men's actions were, as a result, estimated 'not by the proportion in which, according to scripture, they are offensive to God, but by that in which they are injurious to society'.[9] And so 'a fatal distinction is admitted between Morality and Religion: a great and desperate error'.[10] The nineteenth century therefore began with many of the most influential Christian leaders determined to relate social teaching to vital religion; to prepare for the redemption of human society by the redemption of the individual

---

[1] Horne, *Charge* (1791), p. 10.   [2] Ibid., p. 18.
[3] Horsley, *Charge* (1791), p. 7.
[4] More, *Thoughts on the Importance of the Manners of the Great*, p. 18.
[5] Ibid., p. 15.   [6] Wilberforce, *A Practical View*, p. 7.
[7] Ibid., p. 26.   [8] Ibid., p. 246.
[9] Ibid., p. 286.   [10] Ibid., p. 248.

soul. It was an attitude well suited to the reception of another body of ideas about to appear within educated opinion. Political Economy, too, was espoused by those churchmen closest to the progressive intelligence of the new century.

2

Social Attitudes, 1800–1830

The response of Church leaders to Political Economy, as its influence spread within political society and the intelligentsia early in the nineteenth century, was like that of other leaders of society: some accepted the new attitudes and arguments, some did not. The Church, once again truly reflecting the dispositions of the class and the society in which it was set, divided. But Political Economy effected men as individuals; it did not significantly redefine party political attitudes. Converts were found among both the Whig and the Tory leadership. London radicalism was considerably attracted by the new ideas; provincial radicalism hardly at all. Men who espoused the principles of Political Economy saw themselves as disciples of progressive thinking, of a new 'scientific' attitude to society. The vogue for Political Economy within the intelligentsia was associated with the contemporary fascination for statistics, for quantifying social information. Lord Liverpool's Tory administration, especially after the reconstruction of the Government early in the 1820s, contained a strong representation of converts, including Peel, Canning, and Liverpool himself. The progressive abandonment of tariff protection, and the application of non-interventionist economic policies, indicated the practical influence of the new ideas. Social thinking on such issues as the relief of poverty, the monetary system, population increase, and the general approach to crime, police, and education, were all transformed by the impact of Political Economy in the first half of the nineteenth century. Yet it was not a popular science, and always attracted only a minority in Church and State. Whig magnates and Tory paternalist squires, popular radicals and country parsons, found the cold calculations of Political Economy offensive to their sense of human relationships and social responsibilities. 'Scientific administration'—the consequence of applied Political Economy—also generally had the additional disadvantage, from the point of view of traditional interests, of disrupting or altogether abolishing parts of their local influence. But Political Economy did not define party politics: party loyalties were still not derived from systematic acceptance of policy in the sense which later defined English party government. Exponents of Political Economy were found within the traditional fabric of political society, often applying their new learning very selectively and sometimes in considerable ignorance of its real implications. Despite a widespread feeling that Political Economy was 'progressive', its general political tendency was probably conservative. In providing an intellectual and 'scientific' basis for free contractualism in social and economic relationships, and in emphasizing the virtues of individual exertion and the freedom of economic laws from state interference, Political Economy, in the hands of the traditional politicians and churchmen who were its converts, usually underpinned existing concepts of social authority. It was its individualism that attracted the London radicals: the skilled artisans and craftsmen who were the backbone of radical politics in the capital hoped to raise themselves, once free from the interference of an aristocratic state machinery, to independent prosperity—to become, themselves, owners of capital. But elsewhere radical groups resisted the new ideas as alien to their traditions of social responsibility.

It was those Church leaders most in touch with the academic and political world who formulated or adopted Political Economy; men like John Bird Sumner, later Archbishop of Canterbury; Richard Whately, Archbishop of Dublin; Edward Copleston, Bishop of Llandaff; Charles James Blomfield, Bishop of London; and the Revd. Thomas Malthus, Fellow of Jesus College, Cambridge. Their adoption of the most progressive ideas of their age, the ideas of a minority of 'informed' opinion, had the unhappy effect of cutting them off from the sympathy of the poor they were trying to assist. This became especially obvious in 1834, when leading churchmen were prominently associated with the reform of the Poor Laws according to some of the favourite doctrines of Political Economy. Their conduct in this and other areas of social policy illustrates a constant theme in the social attitudes of the Church of England—the adoption, in almost every generation, of diluted versions of the most progressive ideas available, by that section of the leadership most in touch with academic idealism. Inevitably they have been hurt to find that they have further separated themselves from the common people, in whose interests they had tried to act, in the process. It is a strange paradox. Church leadership has often been ineffective not because it has lagged behind the progressive intelligence of each age, as churchmen so often seem to think; but because it has been too much in advance, too academic, too removed from the practical assumptions of ordinary men.

Resistance to the adoption of the precepts of Political Economy was very extensive within the Church, as it was generally in society. The leading episcopal opponents were Phillpotts of Exeter and Van Mildert of Durham. The lower clergy were probably mostly hostile; but here the evidence is hidden away in the parishes of the land, and it is only in occasional glimpses that it is seen. Thomas Arnold, in 1825, called the Political Economists 'those one-eyed men', who fostered 'too much of the oligarchical spirit in

England, both in Church and State'[1]—as a result of the growing cult of expert opinion. John Keble, who in 1830 was actually persuaded that Malthus had 'hit the right nail on the head', at least over the Poor Laws, remarked that he had nevertheless been taught by his father, and by Southey, to dislike Political Economy. Malthus, he continued to believe, was 'hard and vulgar'.[2] This sort of individual resistance gradually disappeared as fashions of thought and general attitudes adjusted, in the mid-century, to accommodate popularized versions of Political Economy—laissez-faire. But from the start of the century, the Church leaders who adopted the new ideas exercised an influence quite out of proportion to their numbers. In 1815 the Revd. Richard Yates, the exponent of Church extension, noted that Political Economy had already 'become so fashionable' that men tended to 'blend and mix' it 'with every discussion relating to the Ecclesiastical part of our Constitutional Government'.[3] Yates, however, also typified those who, despite their dislike for the new science, recognized the advantages of statistical inquiry in its preparation of opinion for reforms. Yates placed 'the general and increasing diffusion of liberal and scientific knowledge' first in his list of things 'promoting the advance of the Kingdom of Christ' in his day.[4] His own propaganda for Church extension was heavily dependent on the statistical and comparative methods of inquiry which the Political Economists encouraged.

Quite a lot of churchmen began to use some of the chief texts of the Political Economists as sources of social information. From Adam Smith and Ricardo, and from clerical writers like Malthus and Sumner, they found a harmony between Christianity and the new science. Malthus's *Essay on Population*, of course, was initially unpopular with almost everyone, seeming not only to present an impersonal analysis of the operations of immutable social laws but also an apparent denial of God's foresight and Providence. It was Sumner who salvaged his reputation and made Malthus acceptable reading within the Church. John Bird Sumner was an Evangelical; Bishop of Chester from 1828 to 1848, and thereafter Archbishop of Canterbury until his death in 1862. He had, before his episcopal career, been a master at Eton and a rural incumbent. It was in 1816 that he published *A Treatise on the Records of the Creation*, a work of large and enduring influence, which made Political Economy, and Malthus, acceptable to the Christian frame of reference by drawing attention to their compatibility with Scripture. Malthus had himself pointed to the effects of Provi-

---

[1] A. P. Stanley, *The Life and Correspondence of Thomas Arnold, D.D.*, 15th edn. (London, 1892), i. 68.

[2] J. T. Coleridge, *A Memoir of the Revd. John Keble*, 2nd edn. (Oxford and London, 1869), i. 191.

[3] Richard Yates, *The Church in Danger* (London, 1815), p. 6.

[4] Richard Yates, *The Gospel Kingdom . . . A Sermon Preached in the Parish Church of Halstead in Essex* (London, 1818), p. 20.

dence in the first edition of his *Essay* (1789), but this had been left out of the more celebrated (or notorious) and widely read second edition (1802) because he intended to develop this theme in a separate work.[1] Sumner recognized that Malthus had unfolded an 'important branch of human history', and described his *Essay* as already 'too well-known to justify any abridgment of its leading doctrines'.[2] Another who helped to render Malthus, the 'everlasting value of his work',[3] and the general attitude to Political Economy, acceptable to Christian opinion was Edward Copleston, Provost of Oriel College, Oxford, friend and teacher of Peel, and Bishop of Llandaff from 1828 to 1849. But the popular odium attaching to Malthus's name did not disappear quickly. In 1834 Lord Chancellor Brougham attempted to boost Malthus's reputation at the time of the Poor Law Amendment Act—a measure correctly associated by its opponents in the country and in Parliament with Malthusian principles. Brougham declared that 'the character of this estimable man has been foully slandered'.[4] Yet despite the continuing unpopularity, the ideas and social attitudes of Political Economy had captured the centre of 'enlightened opinion' and was beginning to seep downwards. It was, as Malthus himself noticed, in 1820, still at a point of critical growth.[5]

In one area of Christian concern, however, the application of Political Economy was seen to be limited by its advocates. Yates, who defined the new principle simply as 'leave things to themselves and supply follows demand', remarked that it 'may be generally true, and yet not applicable to the peculiar circumstances of religion'.[6] To most churchmen—though not to an increasing number of Dissenters—the notion of a 'free trade in religion' seemed extremely inappropriate. Peel, arguing against the objection of some Dissenters to the parliamentary grant for church building, in 1824, said that 'even if the people were indifferent on the subject, that was no reason why they should not be supplied with the means of obtaining religious instruction'.[7] Those most in need of religious instruction were precisely those least likely to realize it: the defence of Established religion on these grounds was most systematically expounded in Thomas Chalmers's famous lectures on religious Establishments in 1838.[8]

---

[1] Soloway, *Prelates and People*, p. 102.

[2] J. B. Sumner, *A Treatise on the Records of the Creation*, ii. 103.

[3] Edward Copleston, *A Second Letter to the Right Hon. Robert Peel, M.P. for the University of Oxford, on the Causes of the Increases of Pauperism and on the Poor Laws*, 2nd edn. (Oxford, 1819), p. 22.

[4] Hansard, *Third Series*, xxv. 224, (21 July 1834).

[5] T. R. Malthus, *Principles of Political Economy, Considered with a View to their Practical Application* (1820) (Oxford, 1951 edn.), p. 12.

[6] Richard Yates, *Patronage of the Church of England: Concisely Considered in Reference to National Reformation and Improvement; to the Permanence of our Ecclesiastical Establishments* (London, 1823), p. 22.

[7] Hansard, *New Series*, xi. 342 (9 Apr. 1824).

[8] See Ch. 3, p. 98.

For churchmen at the end of the Napoleonic Wars the maintenance of special state protection for religion was beyond question. The teaching of the eighteenth century passed to them virtually unaltered, and they saw little need for adjustment. The old interdependence of Church and State, guaranteed in the Coronation Oath of the Sovereign, secured not only the moral sanction of law but also the basis of personal liberty. The Establishment continued to be hallowed as the historic bulwark against the foreign sovereignty of the Papacy; it still meant 'the preservation and permanence of those constitutional rights, privileges, and duties, which are the parents and guardians of our personal security, our domestic comforts, and our national prosperity'.[1] Opposition to state religion increased during the 1820s, amongst radicals and Dissenters, but few churchmen, outside a very rarefied High Church group of clerical dons who were worried about the 'liberalism' of Parliament, were prepared to envisage a dissolution of the historic ties. Sumner wrote a Hulsean Prize Essay at Cambridge in 1802 which contained the classic argument that the sanction of religion was essential to the stability of civil government, for 'the highest moral sanctions are insufficient to confine the bulk of mankind within the bounds of duty: what can be expected from a nation by which all moral sanctions are at once disowned?'.[2] The traditional supposition that a dissolution of the ties of religion and government must result in moral anarchy was a position from which Sumner, for all his contributions to Political Economy and for all his general subscription to the clamour against state intervention in social and economic relationships, never retreated. George Law, Bishop first of Chester, and then of Bath and Wells after 1824, told the clergy that 'a free Government cannot subsist without Religion'.[3] Law belonged to the older generation of Tory prelates, untouched by Political Economy. But differences of generation made no discernible impact on attitudes to the relations of Church and State. Sumner, in fact, emphasized the social utility of religious Establishments. He pointed to the 'general improvement of habits' derived from 'the new views of the nature and destination of man, unfolded by the Gospel' as ones which the State must find it in its interests to encourage. Cruelty had been diminished, the savagery of warfare curtailed, women had been raised to a 'just level in society', the duty of benevolence had been recognized, domestic slavery had ceased.[4] As a country clergyman informed Ricardo, 'the State cherishes and protects religion', because religion was 'the main source of the State's

[1] Yates, *Patronage of the Church of England*, p. 35.

[2] J. B. Sumner, *An Essay Tending to Show that the Prophecies, now Accomplishing, are an Evidence of the Truth of the Christian Religion* (Cambridge, 1802), p. 22.

[3] George Henry Law, *A Charge Delivered to the Clergy of the Diocese of Bath and Wells* (London, 1825), p. 29.

[4] J. B. Sumner, *The Evidence of Christianity, Derived from its Nature and Reception* (London, 1824), p. 388.

welfare, the great stay and security of all its use as a wisely-devised engine of social happiness'.[1] Yates addressed Lord Liverpool in similar vein. Established religion was to be esteemed 'not only as an integral part of the Constitution, but also as the most stable and solid Basis of a liberal and enlightened Government; the best guardian of our Civil as well as Ecclesiastical Liberties'.[2] So the eighteenth century lived on, largely unquestioned within the Church—held in suspension alongside new ideas. But outside the Church the questioning had very definitely begun.

To churchmen, indeed, the Establishment and society itself appeared beset by many threats in post-war England. 'Now all is changed,' William Howley told his clergy in 1818, when he was Bishop of London; 'it is our lot to have fallen on days of innovation and trouble: the political character of the age has produced an alteration in the circumstances of the country, and an agitation in the public mind, affecting the Church as well as the State.'[3] The Church of England certainly came under fire from the radical press in the disturbed years after the war, when rapid deflation of the economy and cyclical depressions produced considerable and widespread hardship in both rural and manufacturing districts. The Church was easily made to look like an institution unwilling to attend to the people's welfare, loaded with abuses, associated with illiberal political interests: these aspects of the Church were sometimes the only ones which men saw. For the multitudes who did not attend the worship of the Church it was as a supporter of the squire or the local bench of magistrates that the authority of the parson and his parish institutions appeared so often. Yet the Church was very aware of the destitution of the masses, and tremendously anxious to adapt the antiquated ecclesiastical machinery in order to elevate their lives with Christian truth. 'Exposed to all the disadvantages of temptation attendant on populous neighbourhoods,' Bishop Charles Sumner noticed of the people in his Diocese of Llandaff—which contained the industrial and mining areas of South Wales—'they are restrained by few of those checks, which impose elsewhere a salutary restraint on human passions.'[4] Nearly all churchmen looked to the State to help the Church with the work of bringing the masses within the fold of Christianity. In 1817, the year of the Spa Fields rioting and the suspension of Habeas Corpus, Richard Yates published the following warning:

It is not only from the absence of Religious Instruction that the Danger to our existing institutions is to be estimated; we must also take into consideration the

---

[1] William B. Whitehead, *Prosecutions of Infidel Blasphemers briefly Vindicated in a Letter to David Ricardo, Esqr., M.A.* (Bristol, 1823), p. 13.

[2] Yates, *The Church in Danger*, p. 5.

[3] William Howley, *A Charge Delivered to the Clergy of the Diocese of London* (1818), 2nd edn. (London, 1818), p. 7.

[4] Charles Richard Sumner, *A Charge Delivered to the Clergy of the Diocese of Llandaff* (London, 1827), p. 8.

positive introduction of licentious, irreligious, and blasphemous principles; which are promulgated, and, as there are no Religious Impressions to counteract them, are received, to a much greater degree than seems at all to be supposed by many who are living in elegance and plenty, on an apparently peaceful surface; unheeding the gathering elements of commotion, which might be discovered, and perhaps dissipated, by a timely examination of the Basis on which their enjoyments rest; and the danger which must be augmented by confining their attention in fancied security to the amusements of science and literature, or to the somewhat more serious avocations of doctrinal discussions, and palliative legislation;—while the Social Foundation is undermined, and the materials of volcanic violence are accumulating beneath them. An accurate idea of the full extent of these dangers can only be ascertained by a personal intercourse with the lower classes.[1]

Yates's suggestion that the clergy give up discussing theological niceties and get out among the working classes falls agreeably upon the modern ear. His call was actually listened to in 1817, as well. As a propagandist for state support for the extension of church building in the new industrial areas he was astonishingly successful. Many other clergy, too, spoke of the responsibilities of the rich to the poor in these years of economic dislocation. In 1820 Thomas Calvert, who was Norrisian Professor of Divinity at Cambridge, said, 'We live in times when the evils of life press heavily on the lower orders of the community, and when more than ordinary exertions and sacrifices are required on the part of the rich, to enable them to bear up under the weight of their privations and sufferings'.[2] Even John Bird Sumner, despite his Political Economist's reluctance to allow any charitable hand-out which might inhibit industry among the poor, wrote in 1816 that 'the superfluity of the rich' imposed on them 'the peculiar duty of judicious expenditure'.[3] The rich, in fact, were to use their resources not merely to alleviate suffering, but to correct the social ills which produced it—'the charity which is often employed to wipe away the tear of distress might, by a more prudent application, stop the source from which it flows'. The rich, accordingly, were exhorted to use their wealth 'to invigorate drooping industry'.[4] Or, in the language used by later churchmen, 'ambulance work' was insufficient; the basis of the economy had itself to receive attention.

It is possible that the extent of the Church's unpopularity in the post-war years has been exaggerated—first by contemporaries, and later by

[1] Richard Yates, *The Basis of National Welfare: Considered in Reference chiefly to the Prosperity of Britain, and the Safety of the Church of England . . . In a Second Letter to the Right Honourable the Earl of Liverpool* (London, 1817), p. 62.

[2] Thomas Calvert, *The Rich and the Poor Shewn to be of God's Appointment and Equally the Objects of His Regard, in Two Sermons Preached in His Majesty's Chapel, Whitehall* (Cambridge, 1820), p. 27.

[3] Sumner, *A Treatise on the Records of the Creation*, ii. 86.

[4] Ibid., ii. 87.

historians who believed the reasons they gave for their attacks upon the
Church, or who heard the cries of dismay raised by its defenders. It is
certainly true that the clergy sided with order: 'their constitutional principles', as a Norfolk parson wrote in the gloomy year of 1819, 'have been
marked at all periods by a strict adherence to that limited form of monarchy
which providentially obtains in this empire, and by a decided opposition
to every movement that has for its object the exaltation of the democratic,
and the degradation of the aristocratical branches of government'.[1] But it
was precisely for their support of order that they were valued. It was only
the radicals who loathed the clergy for supporting existing society; and
those whose estimate of these years was largely derived from the voluminous radical literature have accordingly seen a deeply unpopular clergy.
Most later nineteenth-century Liberals and many modern historians have
depended heavily on the polemicism of these contemporary radicals. But
although the clergy were certainly not popular, nor were they especially
unpopular; or at least, if some were, it did not particularly derive from their
support of existing social order. The measures which Lord Liverpool's
Government took to preserve order between 1816 and 1820 were only really
offensive to those radical minorities against whom they were directed. Nor
were the measures especially savage: in the absence of a civil police force
the Government was itself obliged to undertake the direction of the maintenance of order, and this centralization was easily made to look oppressive.
Modern governments regularly use most of the legal powers which Lord
Liverpool acquired in these disturbed years. Professor Gash has remarked
that most provisions of the infamous 'Six Acts' of 1819 are indispensable
to modern governments,[2] but they are today used, when necessary, by
regionalized police forces and few really notice them. Liverpool's actions
were popular with many humble men, who, in a deferential society, looked
to traditional rulers to preserve them from social disruption. The matter
is one of degree and emphasis. The Church was no more unpopular for
siding with order than other institutions, and even that degree of unpopularity may well have been confined to minority groups. It is not particularly helpful, for example, to regard the Peterloo episode in 1819 as a
decisive moment in the loss of popular support for the Church, as some
have done.[3] It is true that two of the precipitate magistrates at the Peterloo
affray were clergymen, and that the incident marked the least popular
period of the Government. But it is also true that Peterloo was deliberately
inflated by radical propagandists in order to inspire those who regarded

---

[1] George Burges, *Reflections on the Nature and Tendency of the Present Spirit of the Times in a Letter to the Freeholders of Norfolk* (Norwich, 1819), p. 301. (Burges was Vicar of Halvesgate.)

[2] Norman Gash, *Mr. Secretary Peel, the Life of Sir Robert Peel to 1830* (London, 1961), p. 248.

[3] W. R. Ward believes this; see *Religion and Society in England, 1790-1850*, p. 104.

themselves as guardians of liberty with hostility to the Government. It was used in an attempt to discredit an administration by associating it in the popular mind with excesses for which it was scarcely responsible. The voices of those who opposed the force used at Peterloo without branding the Government with infamy, have not been listened to by posterity with the attention given to the less balanced radical polemicism. But they were often heard at the time; before Peterloo had become incorporated by repetitive condemnation into the radicals' catalogue of the evils of landed society, and passed to later uncritical acceptance. Henry Phillpotts, a Tory who was at the time a Prebend of Durham (and later Bishop of Exeter) believed the action of the magistrates to have been mistaken, but he also found the protest meetings contrived and out of proportion to what had occurred, and easily and deliberately turned into demonstrations against the Government by small groups of radical agitators.[1]

Whatever loss of public esteem the Church had suffered in these years was quite rapidly recovered. In the healthier economic climate of the 1820s Church leaders themselves felt a happier atmosphere around them, despite the increasing restiveness of middle-class Dissenters and the continued attacks from 'philosophical radicals' like Hume and Bentham. 'The immediate danger is now passed,' the Bishop of London told his clergy in 1822, in a general review of institutions and society.[2] Two years later Hobhouse, then radical Member for Westminster, expressed to Parliament his conviction 'that the religious feelings of the people of England had very much increased' since the start of the century.[3] In the same year Sumner wrote that there was 'just cause for believing that real religion never flourished more in any age or country than at the present time in Britain', despite the 'vast number' who rejected it 'either avowedly or virtually'.[4] What in fact these men were observing were the first evidences of the mid-nineteenth-century boom in religion among the middle classes. They were aware that radical attempts to excite the unchurched masses against the Church had not succeeded, but they also saw that the revival of religious practice was in another class—a class, however, to which men were looking for energy and enterprise. Churchmen were also becoming conscious that the relationship between economic distress and political discontent was a more powerful threat to social disruption than the dissemination of atheist literature among the poor. In 1825 Thomas Arnold said he did not think there would be a revolution. His reason was an economic and social one. 'I do not see what the labouring classes would gain by it,' he explained.

---

[1] Henry Phillpotts, *A Letter to the Freeholders of the County of Durham* (Durham, 1819), p. 10.

[2] William Howley, *A Charge Delivered to the Clergy of the Diocese of London* (London, 1822), p. 10.

[3] Hansard, *New Series*, xi. 334 (9 Apr. 1824).

[4] J. B. Sumner, *The Evidence of Christianity*, p. v.

'For them the work has been done already, in the destruction of the feudal tyranny of the nobility and great men.'[1] The social confidence of the Victorian bourgeoisie was just beginning to sustain a religious confidence.

Confidence was needed if churchmen were to begin to tackle the problems of 'Spiritual Destitution' among the masses. A great deal of information about this was accumulating, from the various philanthropic agencies,[2] and from the clergy in the parishes most affected by the growth of population and industry. The writings of Sir Frederick Eden and of Patrick Colequhoun had a wide public—especially the former's *State of the Poor*, published in 1797. There was also a series of inquiries by parliamentary select committees early in the new century, into the education of the poor, the operation of the criminal code, vice and crime in the metropolis, the police, the relief of poverty. These, too, helped to create a public opinion disposed to do something about the condition of society. The clergy were leaders in encouraging a feeling that extraordinary measures were needed to deal with the unprecedented scale of social suffering. They saw a defection from formal religious affiliation in the body of the nation, and associated, in classic eighteenth-century style, the return of social cohesion and general prosperity with the diffusion of Christian truth and morality. Churchmen had already noticed that the small attendance at the churches of the Establishment was not due in any really significant degree to the rise of Methodism or the expansion of Dissent in general. Nor was it the result of the industrial revolution in any simple sense—though the clergy were less clear about this. Despite many authoritative opinions to the contrary, it is difficult to see a straightforward correlation between urban dwelling and defection from formal religious practice in modern society. It was not until the 1960s, for example—a century after their first growth— that 'church-relation' in North American cities began to decline. Industrial cities in some of the eastern European countries, like Poland, have not seen a dramatic lapse from Catholicism, despite attendant political difficulties. And in Ireland, industrial Belfast is notorious for its religious belief. The Irish who settled in English and Scottish cities in the nineteenth century, on the other hand, certainly demonstrated a considerable 'leakage' from church attendance. In this instance, the 'cultural shocks' involved in moving to England, often from something like a peasant society, have to be balanced against the exiles' tendency to retain his religious affiliation as a badge of identity. This is always less necessary to the second generation, who assimilate to general British society so well, in fact, that they pick up the habit of not going to church along with other social attitudes. It is also clear that the urban working class of the English cities at the start of the nineteenth century had not lapsed from church attendance *as*

[1] Stanley, *Life of Arnold*, i. 68.
[2] For a list of their activities, see Ford K. Brown, *Fathers of the Victorians*, p. 328.

a result of their movement into the towns. It rather looks, from the admittedly thin evidence available, as if they did not attend the churches in the rural areas from which they originally came. The new social relationships of the urban environment merely served to reinforce an existing disinclination to go to church, and the breakdown of the ancient parochial system in the new cities therefore did nothing but confirm an existing collapse of organized religion. To the extent that this is a balanced picture, it must modify the view, popular among historians, of ideal rural relationships in which the vicar and his poor parishioners sustained a reasonable social intercourse, even if one of unequals, before the industrial revolution broke it all up. The failure of the rural labourers to go to church had received some documentation at the end of the eighteenth century. Bishop Butler of Hereford compared returns of church attendance in his diocese for 1792 with those of 1747: there had been a very large decline, which the Bishop attributed to clerical neglect, and to the evils and luxuries of the age.[1] In 1800 a group of Evangelical parsons in the diocese of Lincoln, the largest in England, sampled seventy-nine parishes and discovered that fewer than 5,000 of the 15,000 who lived in them had any connection with the Church, and that only 1,800 were communicants. The inquirers balanced the loss due to the growth of Dissent, but still found a huge lapse from religious attendance. They, too, attributed it to the failings of the age and of the clergy—though they noticed, also, that the abuses of the Church had been greatly exaggerated by opponents.[2] In 1799 Bishop Cleaver of Chester, the diocese which contained the industrial cities of south Lancashire, found one parish of 40,000 souls in which no one went to church, Established or Dissenting, at all.[3] It was against this sort of background, and with a belief that there was no real reason why industrial society should not go to church if provision and encouragement were forthcoming, that churchmen at the start of the nineteenth century regarded the new cities. They were to be objects of missionary assault. Church and State could stand together in a great social experiment: the alleviation of unprecedented urban social problems through the agency of religion; the morals of society to be improved; the rate of crime to be reduced; loyalty to the Constitution to be fostered; personal industry encouraged. Apart from the field of national education, it was the last occasion on which the British State employed the Established Church, at the public expense, as the machinery of social control.

Very few new churches had been built during the eighteenth century, despite appeals by Shute Barrington and Richard Watson at the end of the century. This was, in part, due to the legal difficulties surrounding the creation of new ecclesiastical districts. It was not until 1843 that

---

[1] Soloway, *Prelates and People*, p. 50.
[2] Ibid., p. 51.   [3] Ibid., p. 306.

parishes could be divided without the promotion of legislation. Dissenters did not suffer these legal disadvantages, and as Lord Liverpool was able to point out in 1818, 'by building additional churches, the Establishment and the Dissenters would be placed on a fair and equal footing'.[1] In 1809 the Government, seeking some means of providing religious instruction for the urban districts, made the first of eleven annual grants of £100,000 to Queen Anne's Bounty to augment poor livings.[2] An 1811 plan of Spencer Perceval's—the Evangelical Prime Minister—to build new churches in the areas of greatest population growth, at the public expense, was postponed by his assassination. Lord Sidmouth had, in the previous year, drawn attention to the problem by moving for returns of the numbers and seating capacities of existing churches.[3] It was in the context of these stirrings of opinion that the Revd. Richard Yates, Chaplain to the Chelsea Hospital, produced his decisive works in support of Church extension. He was by far the most influential clerical propagandist of his generation. In 1815 he published *The Church in Danger*, and in 1817 he followed it up with *The Basis of National Welfare*. Both were addressed to the Prime Minister.

Yates was quite clear, in 1815, that the State had a responsibility to foster religion amongst the working class: a matter 'of very high importance to the stability and prosperity of our Constitutional Government'.[4] In 1817 he reaffirmed the view that Church and State were interdependent, that sound religion was 'necessary to the well-being of Civil Society', and he cited Hooker, Warburton, and others as authorities.[5] In both his works there was a battery of statistical evidence, drawn from parliamentary returns, about the condition of society. But he argued that the appalling conditions were consequences and not causes. A due provision of Christian instruction would elicit the virtues which would eliminate misery.[6] Without it, he saw 'the source of that unexampled and early depravity, which fills our prisons with desperate offenders, and our streets with juvenile ignorance, wretchedness, and plundering rapacity'.[7] There were, in London, 800 children 'in regular training as thieves'.[8] Only Christian enlightenment could lift them out of thrall of vice, and could instil the sobriety and social responsibility needed to establish a good moral basis to labour and a stable family life. But the problem looked almost overwhelming; it 'appals the imagination'; 'the mind shrinks from the contemplation of such a concentrated mass of exclusion . . . such a mine of Heathenism, and con-

---

[1] Hansard, xxxviii, 712 (15 May 1818).
[2] Best, *Temporal Pillars*, pp. 203 ff., and Soloway, *Prelates and People*, p. 289.
[3] Hansard, xvii. (19 June 1810).
[4] Yates, *The Church in Danger*, p. 3.
[5] Yates, *The Basis of National Welfare*, p. 34.
[6] Ibid., p. 152.
[7] Yates, *The Church in Danger*, p. 84.
[8] Ibid., p. 85.

sequent profligacy and danger, under the very meridian (as is supposed) of Christian illumination'.[1] Yates took the rich to task for failing in their obligations to the poor. They had built chapels for themselves and had not bothered with the working population and its spiritual needs: 'The first object of the proprietors is to obtain the highest possible rent for the pews.'[2] He was severe with those who had grown rich through the profits of the new industrial towns—'the tendency of the Commercial and Manu-facturing System to the rapid increase of gain, by denying a proper atten-tion to moral improvement, has degraded the Artificers and Workmen into a condition that almost extinguishes the rational faculties, and debases and curtails the animal powers and enjoyments'.[3] Nor were the landed mag-nates any better: 'Modern arrangements in Agriculture have almost anni-hilated the former independent peasantry, and lowered the character of those that still exist as labourers and servants.'[4] Engels himself, more than twenty years later, was not more decisive in his strictures on the classes with economic power. But for Yates the solution to these ills lay in an Act of Parliament to furnish public money for the building of new churches in the populous districts, providing also for the easy subdivision of parishes, and for the stipends and accommodation of the clergy to serve them.[5] This plan, so widely approved, made the traditional assumption that religion was the essential basis for social well-being and class harmony.

Yates's works achieved almost immediate success. They were com-mended by both Whig and Tory political leaders, recommended to the clergy in the *Charges* of the bishops; they became a frequent source of reference by the Prime Minister himself.[6] Church building became a popular panacea for social evils. The idea acquired a vogue which carried it, virtually without opposition, into legislation in 1818. In February of that year a group of laymen associated with the 'Hackney Phalanx', led by George Bramwell and Joseph Cotton, had secured the blessing of Archbishop Manners-Sutton for the establishment of the Church building Society.[7] In the next few years their example was copied in numerous Diocesan Societies. In March 1818 the Government introduced its 'New Churches Bill', allocating £1 million for new building and giving legal protection to subscriptions raised in aid from private sources. A body of permanent commissioners was appointed to carry out the provisions of the Act and to make annual reports to Parliament.[8] It was a substantial first measure of ecclesiastical collectivism, anticipating—at least in the creation of a government body of expert opinion concerned with Church

---

[1] Yates, *The Church in Danger*, p. 51.   [2] Ibid., p. 34.
[3] Yates, *The Basis of National Welfare*, p. 179.
[4] Ibid.   [5] Ibid., p. 184.
[6] Lord Liverpool; see Hansard, xxxviii. 712-14 (15 May 1818).
[7] A. B. Webster, *Joshua Watson*, p. 62.
[8] For their work, see M. H. Port, *Six Hundred New Churches* (London, 1961).

resources—the later Ecclesiastical Commission. By 1830, 134 new churches
had already been built, and fifty more were in construction; and the Church
had by then raised an additional subscription of £1½ million. The Act[1]
embodied the confessional obligations of the State in a very clear form. It
was a direct recognition by Parliament of the duty to provide for the public
worship of the Church of England. And there was, in 1818, no opposition
to the principle of the measure in either of the Houses of Parliament, as
Archbishop Manners-Sutton was delighted to note in his speech supporting the Bill.[2] Lord Holland suggested that the money needed could have
come from a reform of ecclesiastical revenues rather than from the Consolidated Fund, but he also agreed 'that the situation of the country did
call for a bill of this nature'.[3] But there was Commons opposition in 1824,
when Parliament voted a further £500,000. It registered the growing confidence of radicals and Dissenters, and prompted the Chancellor of the
Exchequer (Robinson) to remark that 'in the legislature of a country which
possessed a Church establishment, and which establishment it was bound
to maintain, he did feel considerable astonishment in observing an opposition to a plan, having for its object to afford facilities to professors of the
established religion to attend divine service'.[4] There was no opposition in
the House of Lords.[5]

The idea of a mission to the masses in the industrial towns caught the
imagination, and engaged the labours, of several generations of churchmen.
It sent the clergy into the slums to see conditions for themselves; they
became appalled at what they saw, and added to the reform dialectic by
demanding still further action. It inspired Newman, serving his title in
the parish of St. Clement's, Oxford, in 1824, to visit every family, 'going from house to house, asking the names, numbers, trades' of the
parishioners;[6] and to help raise the £6,000 required to build a new church
in the parish.[7] It led the young Walter Hook, future apostle of Leeds—
who in 1824 was acting as a curate to his father at Whippingham in the
Isle of Wight—to use a sail loft as a church for the local fishermen when
he found them without a place of worship.[8] Men felt they were doing
something which met the challenge of the new age: there was a buoyant
atmosphere. 'The Church of England has apparently never contemplated
a case analogous to the present,' said Bishop Charles Sumner in 1827. 'It

[1] 58 Geo. III, cap. 45; An Act for Building and Promoting the Building of Additional
Churches in Populous Parishes.
[2] Hansard, xxxviii. 712 (15 May 1818).   [3] Ibid. 717.
[4] Hansard, New Series, xi. 328 (9 Apr. 1824).   [5] Ibid. 1430 (16 June 1824).
[6] Letters and Correspondence of John Henry Newman During his Life in the English
Church, ed. Anne Mozley, new edn. (London, 1898), i. 75.
[7] Ibid., i. 82–3.
[8] W. R. W. Stephens, The Life and Letters of Walter Farquhar Hook, 3rd edn. (London,
1879), i. 59.

has made no provision for the religious instruction of a population which ebbs and flows.'[1] The Church was soon to discover that the population increase was not a temporary phenomenon. It struggled to keep up with the pace of change. It never quite succeeded even in meeting the needs of the existing multitudes, but the problem was clearly seen and clearly tackled.

There was resistance in some places. Richard Potter, a Manchester Unitarian and a radical, compiled his own religious statistics in order to suggest that there was no need for the Church Building Commissioners to expend public money in the city. He claimed to have found the existing churches less than a third full. As a result of this and other local agitation, the vestry petitioned against the parliamentary grant in 1824.[2] In 1818 the Sheffield vestry had protested at paying Church Rate because, it was alleged, the number of privately appropriated pews was the cause of the insufficient church accommodation.[3] The opposition to private pews caused a considerable amount of embarrassment to Church leaders, and complicated the case for Church extension. Most bishops condemned excessive pew-renting; 'the inequitable allotment of pews by which an undue proportion of sittings is invidiously reserved for the thin and uncertain attendance of the higher classes'.[4] An episcopal campaign against excessive pew-renting accompanied the movement for building new churches, in order that 'so considerable a portion of the nation' might no longer be deprived of the benefits of religion.[5] The purpose of the extension movement, as a Durham incumbent wrote in 1818, was to encourage social harmony: 'to know God from the highest to the lowest, to participate in one common salvation, to eat the same spiritual meat, and to drink the same spiritual drink'.[6] This scheme of social cohesion became a central purpose of the clergy. Later, they were to discover that their new churches were often poorly attended, and that inadequate endowment strained local resources. But for a couple of decades the vision remained untarnished.

Similar in the enthusiasm it evoked among churchmen, and similar also in social intention, was the contemporaneous movement for the education of children of the working classes. It was an extension of the Sunday-school successes of the 1790s, a more ambitious hope to provide full-time schools for young children. In the field of education, as in Church extension, the

[1] C. R. Sumner, *A Charge Delivered to the Clergy of the Diocese of Llandaff*, p. 9.

[2] Ward, *Religion and Society in England*, p. 111.

[3] E. R. Wickham, *Church and People in an Industrial City* (London, 1957) (1969 edn.), p. 71.

[4] Howley, *Charge* (1818), p. 19.

[5] Walter King, *A Pastoral Letter to the Clergy and Other Inhabitants of his Diocese* (Rochester) (London, 1819), p. 8.

[6] John Brewster, *A Sketch of the History of Churches in England: Applied to the purposes of the Society for Promoting the Enlargement and Building of Churches and Chapels* (London, 1818), p. 84.

Church looked to the State for support in the expectation that public men would regard it as the proper right, as well as the duty, of the religious Establishment to educate the nation's children. There was less initial success here than there had been with church building. In public debate, three different views were emerging: the Church claimed that children should be instructed not only in 'useful knowledge' but in the Catechism and worship of the Establishment; some liberal churchmen and nearly all Protestant Dissenters believed that unadorned Biblical study was all that was required since it avoided sectarian advantages; a small minority of radical opinion, mostly within the intelligentsia, contended that education should be wholly secular. Most men agreed that the task of educating the nation's children was too great to be financed wholly by private agencies and the Church. Some Dissenters and many radicals were coming to think that education should be controlled by the State. But Parliament, in the first half of the nineteenth century, had a limited view of its own responsibilities—limitations which the impact of Political Economy reinforced—and the education of children was something which public men were willing to assist financially but not undertake directly. Few outside the circle of the 'philosophical' radicals could envisage an educational scheme not associated with religious instruction. The system to which Dissenters tended to subscribe was the 'British and Foreign School Society', created in 1814 out of the Royal Lancastrian Institution of 1810, itself the consolidation of Joseph Lancaster's Borough Road schools. Since the later years of the eighteenth century the clergy had been founding schools for poor children in many parishes on their own initiative, and getting them endowed by appeals to local rich families. These supplemented older charitable foundations and the 2,000 schools provided by the Society for Propagating Christian Knowledge earlier in the eighteenth century.[1] In 1811 a group of influential laymen and bishops set up the 'National Society for the Education of the Poor in the Principles of the Established Church' —a body which still exists—in a deliberate attempt to claim the education of the English people for the Church. Both the National and the British and Foreign schools used the 'Madras' monitorial system of teaching; both taught the Bible; the National schools, like the older Church schools (many of which were soon affiliated to the National Society) also gave Catechistical instruction. The radicals became increasingly estranged from the religious education of the Lancastrian schools, which they had originally tended to support, and began to agitate for some sort of parliamentary initiative. But radicals in Parliament were obliged to recognize that the temper of opinion required that any state provision for education would have to be based on the parochial system and would have, in some way, to recognize the claims of the National Church. Thus Samuel Whitbread's Bill of 1807, which

[1] F. Warre Cornish, *The English Church in the Nineteenth Century* (London, 1910), i. 86.

looked to parish schools paid for out of a local rate, was defeated in the House of Lords because Archbishop Manners-Sutton would not contemplate a school system under the control of the local magistrates. Lord Brougham, another radical who sought a state system, declared with realism in 1816 that 'nothing will be admitted offensive to any religious opinions, while care must by all means to be taken that nothing be allowed to interfere with the just privileges of our national Establishment'.[1] Brougham was responsible for the collection of educational statistics in his 1816 Select Committee on the education of the poor of London, whose terms of reference were in 1818 widened to include the whole country. In 1820 his attempt to get a national system of parochial schools on the local rate was dropped when attacked from two sides. The Church rejected the Bill for excluding the Catechism; the Dissenters rejected it because the clergy of the Church were to have a right of veto over the appointment of teachers, and other privileges of supervision. This was a predictable conclusion. The Revd. Tindal Walmsley, in his evidence to the 1818 Select Committee, had already declared the fixed opposition of the National Society to any plan which might weaken the confessional character of education.[2]

The Church therefore looked to the State to sustain its educational work. 'The education of the Young in the doctrines of pure Christianity is admitted on all hands to be a public duty,' said Bishop Howley in 1818, 'and, without any direct interposition of Government, the principal persons in Church and State have expressed their unequivocal approbation of the principles adopted by the National Society.'[3] It was only a mild exaggeration. The same appeal to public approval was made by Mrs. Sarah Trimmer, editor of the *Guardian of Education*, a magazine which began a systematic attack upon the latitudinarianism of the Lancastrian schools. In 1803 Mrs. Trimmer wrote:

That the interference of the Legislature, in respect to the education of the common people, is highly necessary in these times, we are ready to allow; but whilst we have a *Church Establishment*, the doctrines and ordinances of which are perfectly consonant with the Revealed Word of God, it is to be hoped, that nothing will ever be done by the Legislature to throw it down.[4]

And when in 1811 Dr. Herbert Marsh, Lady Margaret Professor of Divinity at Cambridge, and subsequently Bishop of Llandaff (and later of Peterborough), made a famous assault upon the Lancastrian system, he was even more specific about the obligations of the Government. 'In every

---

[1] *Opinions of Lord Brougham* (Paris, 1841), p. 51.

[2] Parliamentary Papers, 1818, iv. 12, *Second Report of the Select Committee On the Education of the Lower Orders* (Evidence on 14 Apr. 1818).

[3] Howley, *Charge* (1818), p. 22.

[4] *Guardian of Education*, ii (1803), 174.

country the national education must be conducted on the principles of the National religion,' he said. 'For a violation of this rule would involve, not only an absurdity, but a principle of self-destruction: it would counteract by authority what it enjoins by authority.'[1] But such was the pragmatism of the English political tradition that the 'absurdity' was precisely what did come to pass in the nineteenth century: the Constitution which continued to profess an exclusive Church also subsidized education given by its rivals. In 1811 the *Edinburgh Review*, representing liberal support for the non-sectarian schools, denounced both Marsh and churchmen who thought like him, as 'enemies of the Poor', who would 'bring ruin upon the Establishment, by opposing the most enlightened and disinterested attempt that ever yet was made, in any country, for scattering the blessings of knowledge and moral improvement among the more helpless classes'.[2] It was a very polemical attack, intended to brand the Church with obscurantism. For liberal opinion within the Church tended to defend exclusive Church education on grounds of realism. Bishop Blomfield—a characteristic example of what men were beginning to call 'the steam-age intellect', a man soaked in utilitarian social thought—poured scepticism on the chances for effective co-operation in education, 'without a compromise of principle on one side or the other', between Church and Dissent. The two religious groups simply had different conceptions of the nature of religious education. Blomfield added: 'I hold it to be morally impossible to give religious instruction which shall not have a tendency either to promote or to weaken the interests of the Church'.[3] Indeed, the truth of this appeared evident in the case of the Sunday schools. Early co-operation between the local churchmen and Dissenters in these ventures had ended long before the 1820s almost everywhere. Howley declared that the content of religious education must relate defined truths, 'if Religion is anything beyond a contrivance of State, or a creature of philosophical Speculation'.[4]

The Church was concerned about the education of the working classes for a number of reasons. First of these was the traditional ministry of teaching. In England this was embodied in the 77th and 79th Canons of the Church, which required all schoolmasters in the land to hold a bishop's licence. The strict observance of this requirement had been relaxed in the eighteenth century, and in 1812 Lord Liverpool's administration had exempted Dissenting schoolmasters from having even to apply for a magis-

---

[1] Herbert Marsh, *The National Religion the foundation of National Education, a Sermon preached in the Cathedral Church of St. Paul, London on Thursday, June 13th, being the time of the Yearly Meeting of the Children educated in the Charity Schools* (London, 1811), pp. 4-5.

[2] *Edinburgh Review*, 37 (Nov. 1811), 41.

[3] Alfred Bloomfield, *A Memoir of Charles James Bloomfield, D.D.* (London, 1863), i. 153.

[4] Howley, *Charge* (1818), p. 24.

trate's licence. But the theory remained, and many apologists of the Church's priority in national education cited the canons as evidence of their claim. A lot of the Church's interest in popular education also reflected a realization—sharpened by the new awareness of the spiritual destitution of the masses—of the need to preserve the Church as an institution by implanting its teachings in the hearts of those who might so easily otherwise become the enemies of social order.[1] Early in the nineteenth century there was a great change in general attitudes towards popular education. Old fears about the risk of creating social disruption by educating the poor were largely abandoned: Van Mildert was almost alone among the bishops in retaining reservations.[2] The Political Economists within the Church's leadership added their arguments to the calculation. The poor, according to Sumner, would perform their labours with less reluctance if they were in a position to comprehend the essentials of the economic and social laws which had determined their place in society. Popular education, he believed, far from disturbing the social fabric, would actually reinforce social cohesion:

Few will any longer venture to assert that ignorance makes a necessary ingredient in industry, or that stupidity is essential to subordination. Which will be the best servant or the best subject? He who returns unwillingly, or at best mechanically, like the patient animal he drives, to his daily routine of employment; or he who has learnt in his youth, that the object of his life is the performance of appointed duties?[3]

The emptiness of the fears which some had entertained of the Sunday schools added to the growing impression that popular education would assist, and not hinder, social stability. In 1819, the year of Peterloo, the Chaplain to Lord Kenyon—the ultra-Tory peer—observed that 'all who were open to conviction soon perceived the folly of these fears, and the sophistry of that argument, which had been adopted and urged without hesitation against the safety, or the expediency, or the utility of affording means of knowledge in the education of the children of the labouring poor'.[4] Popular education was proclaimed in almost every episcopal *Charge* in the first half of the nineteenth century. Modern writers have laid great stress on the element of social control in the motives of churchmen in the promotion of education.[5] And this was, indeed, one of the benefits both State and Church hoped would result. But it by no means followed that a blind class deference, or adhesion to the most reactionary political

---

[1] William Davis Bayly, *The State of the Poor and Working Classes Considered* (London, 1820), p. 96.

[2] Soloway, *Prelates and People*, p. 783.

[3] J. B. Sumner, *A Treatise on the Records of the Creation*, ii. 295.

[4] Harvey Marriott, *Essay on the Madras System of Education* (London, 1819), p. 11.

[5] Gillian Sutherland, *Policy-Making in Elementary Education 1870–1895* (Oxford, 1973), p. 5.

principles, was in the minds of the bishops and clergy who founded modern popular education. It clouds the matter to see their labours merely as an attempt 'to induce complacency at the present situation and disgust at those who would try to change it radically'.[1] That is too gross an abridgement of what the bishops were trying to do for the moral characters of the poor. Nor were the schools 'a factory put into an educational setting'.[2] The preservation of the conventions and attitudes of a deferential and graded society was certainly a prominent motive of those who promoted popular education; it could scarcely have been otherwise in a society in which those ideas were popular with almost everyone outside the minority radical groups. It is also clear that the Church undertook education in order to make men better in themselves, in the perspective of their eternal expectations. This obligation, as much as its social utility, lay behind the hope that education would diminish vice and crime and lead to a more stable family life. The Church was concerned with transforming the lives of humble men whose social and moral degradation, they now realized, was on a greater scale than they had imagined possible. They believed that the work was urgent, and they responded generously. By 1824 the National Society supervised over 3,000 schools, mostly in the manufacturing districts.[3] The funds for most of this effort were collected privately by the clergy.

The Church schools not only aimed at correct religious belief, morality, and literacy; many were also places of elementary vocational training. 'Without religion man is little better than the beast that perisheth,' said Bishop Law in 1827. 'Without the ability of pursuing some trade or occupation, he may be turned out into the world a bane and a burthen to all around him.'[4] The values of the society in which the schools operated naturally required vocational training to fit children for the characteristic employments of the classes from which they were drawn. But as well as teaching the propriety of social inequality and the legitimacy of wealth, Church schools also informed the children about the duties of the rich. 'We are taught that prosperity is, in general, a state of danger, and that an humble station is more secure,' declared a text used in Church schools, in what looks like almost a caricature of social indoctrination. But the con-

---

[1] Valerie E. Chancellor, *History for their Masters. Opinion in the English History Textbook; 1800–1914* (London, 1970), p. 38.

[2] David Wardle, *English Popular Education, 1780–1970* (Cambridge, 1970), p. 22. See also Anthony Armstrong, *The Church of England, the Methodists and Society, 1700–1850* (London, 1973), p. 181, and John Hurt, *Education in Evolution, Church, State, Society and Popular Education, 1800–1870* (London, 1972), p. 14, for other versions of this view of the motives of the educators.

[3] For the location of schools in the industrial areas, see Parliamentary Papers, 1818, iv. 11–12.

[4] George Henry Law, *On Education, A Sermon Preached in the Cathedral Church of Wells* (London, 1827), p. 16.

ditional nature of wealth was also taught: 'for those who have received much, will have much to answer for; and the rich and the great will therefore have a dreadful account to make up at the last day, if they neglect to apply in a proper manner, the talents which their Maker has given them'.[1] This sort of instruction was very much a preparation for the world as it was. The schools also had a ministerial utility in 'the opportunity which they give to the clergy in populous places, of becoming known to the rising generation in the character of Pastors'.[2] Those who imagine the educational effort of the Church at this time solely inspired by an attempt 'to combat dangerous egalitarian doctrines'[3] can have given little attention to the Church—as the Church saw itself—as an agency for the salvation of souls.

That other great social issue, the relief of poverty, also absorbed a great deal of clerical attention. In this matter the Church, reflecting political society in general, spoke with several voices. It was the rising expense of poor relief that provided the background to the debate on the Poor Laws. A peak of £8 millions was reached in 1817, at the worst point of the post-war deflation; by 1824 it had fallen back to £5½ millions, which had been the normal figure for the war years—a reduction which Edward Copleston managed to predict.[4] The simultaneous growth of population, seen by some in Malthusian terms, and of fluctuations in the economy, producing unrest, raised the most serious questions of social order. At one level of the resulting public debate, the Political Economists stressed the relationship between unemployment relief and the reduction of incentive to labour among the poor; at another, and more popular level, the debate turned on ways of adjusting the Poor Laws so that they could work more effectively and yet preserve the old obligations of parochial charity to the poor. The actual conditions under which the Poor Law operated have themselves been rather obscured by the doctrinaire arguments used by the Poor Law Commission of 1832–4, dominated as it was by Edwin Chadwick and the Political Economists. Their Report ignored the fact that the 'allowances system', possible because of legal adjustments made to the code in 1776 and 1782, in reality contained two elements: relief in the form of family allowances, with supplements related to the number of children, and relief in the form of ordinary wage subsidies. Not only were these lumped together by the Commission of 1832, but they were never really separated in the popular debate either. Yet it was clearly the family-allowances element that most obviously offended Malthusian orthodoxy.[5] There is little

---

[1] *The Cottager's Religious Meditations* (London, 1803); the scriptural reference is to Luke 6:20.

[2] Howley, *A Charge Delivered to the Clergy of the Diocese of London* (1822), p. 18.

[3] Wardle, *English Popular Education*, p. 26.

[4] Copleston, *A Second Letter to the Right Hon. Robert Peel*, p. 91.

[5] See Mark Blaug, 'The Poor Law Report Re-examined', in *Journal of Economic History*, 24 (1964), 229.

evidence that the allowances system actually had much relationship to the causes of distress, despite its tendency to depress rural wages, or that it was spreading, as contemporaries believed, in the 1820s. But the popular attack on all forms of taxation after the war included the poor rate,[1] and suffused the old Poor Laws in an odium which extended far beyond the advocates of Political Economy. Fear of population mobility, as much as of the increase in population, added to the unease about the prevailing methods of poor relief. William Cobbett was perhaps the only man in England who actually supposed that the population had declined.[2] His romantic illusions about the social and charitable work for the poor performed by the medieval monasteries, however, reflected a popular notion[3] which was not without effect in the thought of those who opposed the Political Economists' view of the poverty question on the grounds of its supposed inhumanity. Copleston, for the Political Economists in the Church, dismissed the 'old notion that monasteries were the main support of the poor' as 'pretty well exploded'.[4]

The Church divided over the Poor Law question. A group of bishops followed the diagnosis of Political Economy—those, generally, who were most closely related to the values of contemporary 'informed' opinion. It was these bishops who were consulted by Government and actually took part in the reform of the law. They shared views to be found in a fairly small section of public opinion, but, again, a section which regarded itself as in the vanguard of 'progressive' social thought, and which managed to acquire an influence with parliamentary opinion quite out of proportion to its size. Probably most men in society were deeply suspicious of the theoreticians, some out of popular hatred of any sort of centralized 'scientific administration'; some others, the local possessors of influence and patronage, because the new devices of social control and amelioration favoured by the Political Economists tended to weaken their local authority. In a very large number of places, squires and parsons came together to protect the existing parish administration of poor relief against the centralizing tendencies of the London thinkers. A majority of the clergy, in fact, sided with local interests rather than with the parliamentary prelates who supported Political Economy. They spoke of the traditional obligation of personal charity.

The Political Economist bishops were influenced by the notion that laws in social and economic questions should be as free of moral compulsion as

---

[1] J. D. Marshall, *The Old Poor Law, 1795–1834* (London, 1968), p. 24.

[2] William Cobbett, *A History of the Protestant 'Reformation' in England and Ireland, Showing how that Event has impoverished and degraded the main body of the People in these Countries* (Dublin, 1826), p. 269. Cobbett was impressed by the size of medieval churches, and imagined they indicated a larger population than the 1820s.

[3] See Robert Pashley, *Pauperism and Poor Laws* (London, 1852), p. 179.

[4] Copleston, *A Second Letter to the Right Hon. Robert Peel*, p. 40.

possible: it was no proper duty of the State to impose morality in matters which were best left to the individual, and where, anyway, economic laws would themselves inevitably produce a predictable consequence. In terms of the Poor Law debate, this translated into a conviction that public relief had a corrupting effect on its recipients. In his *Treatise on the Records of the Creation* (1816) Sumner argued that popular complaints about the high cost of poor relief were misplaced because, if the poor were in normal employment, the consumer 'would pay much more in the enhanced price of every article from the augmented wages of labour'. This was a conclusion derived from his understanding the 'fixed wages fund' doctrine supplied by Ricardo and MacCulloch. For Sumner, 'the principal mischief is due to the moral character of the receiver, who is extravagant, in confidence of sure support; or, if he is not positively taught improvidence, at least does not learn prudence'.[1] By this time a number of Church leaders had come to imagine that for some men poverty indicated a personal failing, a fault in the moral character. Copleston argued that the Poor Laws had anyway been formulated long before the laws of Political Economy were known. They were bound to have a mischievous effect.[2]

The fundamental mistake which I allude is the confusion of moral duty with the task of legislation. That what all individuals *ought to do*, it is the business of the laws to *make* them do, is a plausible position, and has actually been adopted by some of the ablest and most virtuous men. But nothing in reality is more fallacious—nothing less congruous with the nature of men, and with the state of discipline and trial which his present existence is clearly designed to be. In the first place it destroys the very essence not only of benevolence, but of all virtue, to make it compulsory: or to speak more properly it is a contradiction in terms. An action to be virtuous must be voluntary. It requires a living and a free agent to give it birth.[3]

Here was the very heart of the moral attitude of Political Economy. Later churchmen, like Westcott and Temple, who argued that *laissez-faire* had removed morality from economic life, may have noticed a technical effect of the doctrine: they were wrong, however, to suppose that men advocated it because they somehow failed to associate morality with economic conduct. It was because the Political Economists started with so clear a moral purpose, with such a view of the relationship between morality and law, that their system was proposed for the highest moral ends. Copleston wrote that the attempt 'to invest the laws with the office of humanity' resulted in men becoming 'charitable *by proxy*': for 'to throw off the care of want, and disease, and misery upon the magistrate, is to convert humanity into a police, and religion into a statute book'.[4] This sort of view separated the

---

[1] J. B. Sumner, *A Treatise*, ii. 300.   [2] Copleston, *Second Letter*, p. 17.
[3] Ibid., p. 18.   [4] Ibid., p. 19.

Political Economist bishops only marginally from the Constitutional ideas of the mid-century Dissenters—with their insistence on the corrupting effect of state compulsion of religious duty. But the Dissenters were not consistent in their 'Voluntaryism'; they freely called upon the State to legislate in the moral sphere: in sexual, Sabbatarian, liquor-licensing, and a vast number of similar issues. Nor were the bishops consistent: they held to the idea of state religion, of the necessity of the law to provide religious instruction. It is also to be noticed that, in the longest perspective, the argument that morality loses its value through compulsion cuts the ground from beneath the modern Welfare State. For men like Copleston, however, a more limited application was in view. The independence of morality from law was of Divine institution: Copleston praised Malthus for having shown 'that all endeavours to embody benevolence into law, and thus impiously as it were to effect by human laws what the Author of the system of nature has not effected by his laws, must be abortive'.[1] The Irish national politician, Daniel O'Connell, an advocate of 'Benthamite' utilitarian reforms, also believed that concern for the poor was a moral duty which ought not properly to be compelled by legislation. In this he spoke for a section of Liberal Catholic opinion; a section in opposition to some of the Liberal Catholic bishops, who favoured a Poor Law for Ireland.[2] The Catholic Church, that is to say, was divided, like the Church of England, according to its general attitude to Political Economy.

English churchmen who were influenced by Political Economy increasingly distinguished between poverty and indigence.

Poverty is often both honourable and comfortable; but indigence can only be pitiable, and is usually contemptible [wrote Sumner]. Poverty is not only the natural lot of many, in a well constituted society, but is necessary, that a society may be well constituted. Indigence on the contrary, is seldom the natural lot of any, but is commonly the state into which intemperance and want of prudent foresight push poverty: the punishment which the moral government of God inflicts in this world upon thoughtlessness and guilty extravagance.[3]

It is important to realize that this view, so easily parodied in subsequent anti-Church polemicism, was the conclusion also arrived at by most of the 'philosophical radicals' of the 1820s and 1830s; men also under the sway of Political Economy. Without the reference to Divine intention, it is to be found in the thought of Place, Hume, Bentham, James Mill, and Ricardo. Some would have liked to see the Poor Laws entirely repealed. But the implication for most of those persuaded by the new economic

---

[1] Second Letter., p. 22.
[2] W. J. FitzPatrick, The Life, Times and Correspondence of the Rt. Revd. Dr. Doyle (Dublin, 1861), ii. 369. See also, A. MacIntyre, The Liberator, Daniel O'Connell and the Irish Party, 1830–1847 (London, 1965), p. 209.
[3] Sumner, A Treatise, ii. 92.

science was that some relief had to be retained, but that it should contain a deterrent quality, an incitement to labour. This became Chadwick's notorious 'less eligibility' principle, built into the Poor Law Amendment of 1834. The Political Economists were aware of fluctuations in the economy, and of the difficulty of defining the types of poverty and the variations of their incidence. Sumner accepted that *some* legal device was required: 'It may be justly doubted whether irremediable poverty, and the helplessness of sickness, infancy, and old age, can ever be safely left, in a large and fully peopled community, to the care of that spontaneous charity on which they must devolve in the absence of all legislative provision.'[1] Even Bishop Phillpotts, an old-fashioned advocate of ordinary charity, who went to great lengths in his distrust of the Political Economists, denounced 'the misjudging tenderness' of the Poor Law, which 'has proved in its effects the very reverse of true mercy'—because it assisted the indigent in their idleness—and imagined that 'the truest humanity to the poor would be to put the laws for their relief on such a footing as should least tend to make them dependent on the aid of parishes rather than on their own industry, morality, and prudence'.[2] Phillpotts looked to strictly indoor relief, the workhouse system, but under existing parochial jurisdiction.

Despite the relative smallness of their numbers, the Political Economists in the Church leadership exercised a large influence. They dominated the Royal Commission on the Poor Laws in 1832, and, as a result, associated the bishops with the most unpopular legislation of the nineteenth century. Bishop Blomfield of London became chairman, and brought to the Commission, as Nassau Senior remarked, 'great knowledge both of principles and of details'.[3] As recently as 1826, Blomfield had chaired a committee which had urged the Government to make special provision for distressed weavers; by 1832 he was convinced that public relief only encouraged indigence, that the real solution to social distress lay in the provision of popular education and Christian worship.[4] Speaking in the House of Lords in 1834, in support of the Poor Law Amendment Act, Blomfield said 'he hoped that the people would soon be induced to exercise a foresight which would render relief unnecessary; and that the time would come when it would be thought, as once it was, disgraceful to receive relief, except in case of extreme urgency'.[5] The education of the people would help in this. Sumner was also a member of the 1832 Commission. So was Richard

---

[1] Ibid., p. 299.

[2] Henry Phillpotts, *A Letter to the Right Honourable William Sturges Bourne, M.P., on a Bill introduced by him into Parliament 'to amend the laws respecting the settlement of the poor'*, 2nd edn. (London, 1819), p. 25. For the circumstances surrounding its publication, see G. C. B. Davies, *Henry Phillpotts, Bishop of Exeter, 1778–1869* (London, 1954), p. 21.

[3] Blomfield, *Memoir* i. 203.

[4] Soloway, *Prelates and People*, p. 150.

[5] Hansard, *Third Series*, xxv. 583 (24 July 1834).

Whately, Archbishop of Dublin. Whately had taught both Newman and Senior at Oxford—though with rather different consequences—where he had been Professor of Political Economy until 1831. This episcopal weight on the Commission very clearly showed the co-operation of Church and State in the reform of the law. The Act itself, in 1834, rationalized the administration of poor relief within 600 new Poor Law Unions—it ignored the old parish basis of administration altogether. The Unions came under the centralized direction of a Board in London; the system was administered by paid officials, the Poor Law guardians. Indoor relief, in the workhouses, was obligatory. Opposition to these provisions came both from the poor, who disliked the workhouse test, and from traditional figures of local authority, who resented their loss of influence. Popular radicals in the province—but not the London 'philosophical' radicals—denounced what they took to be the inhumanity of the 'scientific administrators' and described the workhouses as 'bastilles'. In the House of Lords, the bishops voted for the Act. Only Phillpotts raised difficulties, and these were on technical matters related to the bastardy clauses.[1] As popular opposition developed in the country, during the next decade, however, Phillpotts was to become a vehement enemy of the Act. The Archbishop of Canterbury secured an amendment providing for chaplains in the workhouses, and with that he appears to have satisfied himself that the measure was sound in principle.[2]

The currency question was another issue in which the voice of the Church which was heard was often the voice of Political Economy. It is likely that in this sensitive area, too, the local clergy were frequently at variance with the leadership in London and the Universities. During the war, the Bank of England had suspended cash payments, and this had at the time received a lot of influential support—among others from Henry Thornton, one of Wilberforce's lay associates in the 'Clapham Sect'. Thornton had argued that paper credit did not stimulate a rise in prices, as many supposed.[3] In 1810 a Select Committee (the 'Bullion Committee') had attempted to secure a resumption of cash payments—the weight of Ricardo's opinion and the authority of Political Economy was behind the movement for resumption. In 1817 a partial return to cash was made. By then leading 'inflationists' such as Peel had been converted to the bullionist position. Postponements of a full resumption were caused by the extreme unpopularity of the policy amongst agriculturalists, suffering, as they were, from the sharp deflation. Popular radicals were also opposed; they attributed the fall in wages and industrial unemployment to the manipulation

---

[1] Hansard, *Third Series*, xxv. 586. See Blomfield's reply, 594.

[2] Ibid. 455.

[3] Henry Thornton, *An Enquiry into the Nature and Effects of the Paper Credit of Great Britain* (London, 1802), p. 312. This work, praised by John Stuart Mill, went into many editions, the last in 1939.

of currency by the Bank of England.[1] In fact some radicals, and especially Thomas Attwood and the Birmingham Political Union, gave currency reform a priority even greater than the reform of Parliament in their agitations. The currency question was a hidden but important issue in the general elections of 1830 and 1831: many looked to a reformed Parliament to adopt Attwood's, or some other, soft-currency programme.

It was in 1819 that Lord Liverpool's Government finally fixed the date for the resumption of cash payments. Edward Copleston (who was at that time the Provost of Oriel) took a leading part in the public discussion of the currency issue and published two pamphlets in the form of open letters to Robert Peel. He was a convinced bullionist; he maintained that the paper currency had been founded 'upon the denial of all the soundest maxims of political economy'.[2] He believed the fluctuations in the value of the currency affected people's attitude to the Church as an institution. The clergy were constantly having to readjust tithe payments—'at each successive operation of the same kind, fresh irritation is produced, and a general ferment and exasperation pervades a community which ought to be the residence of harmony and good-will'.[3] Copleston's concern was really with the moral and social effect of the currency question. He showed a very considerable sensitivity to the living conditions of ordinary men; he understood the hardships of the labourers and the working population:

The things which they have to buy are the necessaries of life, and the only commodity they have to sell, their labour, it is impossible they should keep back. They came into the market therefore with a double disadvantage, and the effect is invariably found to correspond with this disadvantage. A depreciation of the currency always depresses the lower classes. They must buy, and they must sell, and that immediately. The parties with whom they deal are intent upon gain. To drive a bargain is the business of their life, and they will not fail to employ the advantage thus thrown into their hands. Besides which, it is easy to persuade themselves, and even the workmen they employ, that the high price of provisions is a temporary evil—that it must be borne accordingly—that they ought patiently to wait for better times. In the mean time the labourer is by degrees inured to a harder condition of life; to inferior food, lodgings, and clothing. With his habits of living, his habits of thinking also undergo a change; and many of those comforts which formerly belonged to his station, being found to be no longer strictly necessary, are by degrees forgotten. In this manner, unless an extraordinary demand for labour comes to his aid, his condition is permanently and irrecoverably degraded.[4]

---

[1] Gash, *Mr. Secretary Peel*, p. 239.

[2] Edward Copleston, *A Letter to the Right Hon. Robert Peel M.P. for the University of Oxford, on the Pernicious Effects of a variable Standard of Value, especially as it regards the Condition of the Lower Orders and the Poor Laws* (Oxford, 1819), p. 6.

[3] Ibid., p. 28.

[4] Ibid., pp. 30–1.

It is interesting to find so perceptive a description of the creation of the proletariat from the pen of an Oxford divine in 1819. Copleston was a Tory, as well, and his attitude illustrates the close sympathies which were not uncommon between Toryism and the people at this time. Yet advocacy of cash payments was not a popular cause, and Copleston actually rejected Attwood's currency plans explicitly,[1] so throwing up a practical barrier to any hope—at least on this issue—of implanting the Church in the sympathies of the popular radicalism of the provinces. Copleston did urge the employers to increase wages.[2] Those bishops who on other issues were influenced by Political Economy agreed with Copleston's view on the currency question. The most prominent national leaders of the Church were therefore ranged on the side of intellect and against a lot of popular sentiment in the country.

On matters like the factory legislation of 1802 and 1819, or the general issue of agricultural protection, the bishops had no particularly distinctive voice. When questions became too clearly a matter of party politics—as, at times, with the question of agricultural protection—it was thought improper for the leading clergy to be active. But questions more straightforwardly concerned with morality were considered within their province. One of these was penal and criminal law reform. The clergy tended to divide here; some adopting the Whig-radical belief in the need for an amelioration of the law, and some supporting the more characteristically Tory resort to the enforcement of order, of police, and agencies of morality like the new churches. Bishop Blomfield, a Tory, espoused the Whig view in this question, and in 1828 he argued for a range of penal reforms tending to promote 'the restoration of an offender to society'.[3] He believed that young criminals needed special treatment; that those convicted of minor offences ought not to be confined with real and habitual criminals; that no one in prison should go without instruction to help him return to society.[4] Church concern with the welfare of criminals was extensive. There were chaplains in prisons, and a large number of Christian philanthropic agencies for helping criminals both in gaol and on release. A number of prison chaplains, like the Revd. John Clay at Preston, were influential exponents of prison reform.[5] But in many questions the Church had to walk carefully to avoid the charge of involvement with party politics. In 1811 the *Edinburgh Review*, in a declaration that the pulpit ought only to preach religion, voiced a familiar and popular prejudice:

---

[1] Copleston, p. 47.   [2] Copleston, *Second Letter*, p. 107.

[3] Charles James Blomfield, *The Christian's Duty Towards Criminals, A Sermon Preached in St. Philip's Chapel, Regent Street, For the Benefit of the Society for the Improvement of Prison Discipline* (London, 1828), p. 16.

[4] Ibid., p. 15.

[5] J. J. Tobias, *Nineteenth-century Crime, Prevention and Punishment* (Newton Abbot, 1972), p. 153.

When it is perverted to common secular purposes (a prostitution became almost habitual since the French Revolution);—when we find it a mere rostrum from whence the vulgar effusions of political faction may be distributed, under the guise of Christian homilies, and the multitude cajoled with the jobs of a party, by its emissaries in the pious garb of spiritual pastors—then we view the ground as no longer holy.[1]

Men have been saying the same thing ever since.

The social interests of the Church in these years did greatly strengthen the desire for utilitarian reform within the Church itself. Reform was advocated by bishops anxious to make the Church more effective to face the challenge of the unchurched masses. It was an inclination which preceded the attacks on the Church, as an unreformed institution, by radicals and Dissenters in the mid-1820s. There was scarcely a bishop on the bench who did not, after the 1790s, allocate some space in almost every *Charge* to the need for reforms in the discharge of their duties by the clergy. Their complaints were not against infamous living—cases of this were rare, despite the publicity they received at the hands of radical propagandists. The bishops were concerned with non-residence above all other problems of the clergy. In 1823 Richard Yates compiled tables to show that over 5,300 of the estimated 12,000 beneficed clergymen in England and Wales did not ordinarily reside in their parishes.[2] There were sometimes good reasons for this—an inadequate income attached to a single cure, for example—but in a large number of cases it amounted to an abuse. 'It seems to be admitted on all sides that reformation and improvement are necessary', Yates wrote.[3] Bishop Howley instructed the clergy of London 'not to provide a hireling' but to perform their parochial duties in person.[4] 'The ties which bind the Pastor to his people are of a sacred and hallowed nature', Bishop Law reminded the West Country clergy.[5] 'If there be a failure in activity and zeal on the part of the clergy, the *establishment* must sink beneath them,' Bishop Blomfield told the clergy of Chester; 'but it will never cease to be respected and maintained while it is useful.'[6] The clergy were also enjoined to hold services with greater solemnity and to see that 'all things be done decently and in order'.[7] In its internal efficiency, therefore, it can be seen that the Church at the beginning of the nineteenth century was preparing to fit itself for an effective place in society. Nor was it only in the English Church that internal reforms were thought necessary. The Irish Catholic priests, too, were often given to the manners of the society in which they lived. In 1819 Dr. James Doyle, the Roman Catholic Bishop of Kildare

---

[1] *Edinburgh Review*, 37 (Nov. 1811), 26.
[2] Yates, *Patronage of the Church of England*, pp. 60–1.
[3] Ibid., p. 4.
[4] Howley, *Charge* (1822), p. 7.
[5] Law, *Charge* (1825), p. 28.
[6] Blomfield, *Charge* (1825), p. 11.
[7] C. R. Sumner, *Charge* (1827), p. 2.

and Leighlin, began a systematic campaign to raise his clergy to a due sense of their calling. They were forbidden to speculate in land, to attend public amusements, and they were told to dress soberly. They were also forbidden to hunt, for 'they ejaculated "Tally Ho!" as often as *Dominus Vobiscum*'.[18] The Church of England was evidently not unique in at least one particular.

[1] FitzPatrick, *The Life, Times and Correspondence of the Rt. Revd. Dr. Doyle*, i. 97.

3

Constitutional Adjustments of
Church and State, 1828–1846

During the first two decades of the nineteenth century churchmen had looked upon the condition of England and established their priorities: the extension of education to the poorer classes, and the building of churches in the populous districts in order to bring the masses within Christian truth and morality. These priorities, however, did not prepare the Church for the sort of dangers it encountered in the later 1820s and in the 1830s, when political expediency altered the relationship of the State to the Church in ways which churchmen had not adequately envisaged. The constitutional implications of the repeal of the Test and Corporation Acts in 1828, of Catholic Emancipation in 1829, and of the struggle over the Reform of Parliament in 1831 and 1832, were quite clearly seen but less clearly accommodated. The Church of England had recovered a considerable optimism after the gloomy years of the French Revolution. Its expansionist policies at the start of the new century had assumed a settled constitutional relationship with the State, which the State itself had encouraged. When churchmen found themselves on the political defensive in the later 1820s, therefore, they found themselves in a situation which was completely unexpected. Nor were they victims of a peculiar ecclesiastical lack of discernment. Few public men had predicted the pressures for constitutional reforms, or the preparedness of those in power to conciliate them, which now fell upon the country. The new strength of extra-parliamentary opinion, the growth of Dissenting militancy, the prestige of radicalism with some influential intellectual circles, were not developments which had been widely predicted. The Church was not spiritually ill-adapted to meet the challenges of a new age—as High Churchmen of the Tractarian School were at some pains to suggest. Touched by the late eighteenth-century ferment of spiritual and organizational renewal, the Church scarcely, as the Oxford apostles claimed, reflected the 'loose unreality of ordinary religious morality'.[1] The style of public worship was certainly not, in general, such as to suit the sensibilities of a later age, but the spiritual life of the Church in the early years of the nineteenth century had an impressive integrity, and the aspiration to extend Christianity to

---

[1] R. W. Church, *The Oxford Movement* (London, 1892), p. 22.

the masses was an external indication of a considerable religious vitality. Despite all the assertions to the contrary, there was a sense in which the Oxford Movement was not so much a protest against a totally arid religious terrain as itself a manifestation of an existing religious renaissance.

Although it was an institution closely related to the State and to the machinery of government, the Church of England was surprisingly weak politically. Since the suppression of the deliberative functions of the Convocations in 1717, the only effective means of ordering ecclesiastical affairs resided in Parliament, and although the bishops sat in the Upper House, in practice it was the laity in Parliament who directed the policies of the Church. This situation was tolerable because of the relatively small scale of eighteenth-century politics, with its closely knit connections, and when erastian principles were common to both clergy and laity. In the first two decades of the nineteenth century the machinery continued to operate without too much difficulty—symbolized in the votes of public money for church building. The clergy were intimately associated with the political order. The relationship of parsons and squires, the extent of lay patronage in the Church, the use of parochial administration for secular purposes, the clerical magistrates, the support of the unreformed municipal corporations for Church education, the dispensation of charities: the fabric of the social and political order incorporated the clergy at many levels. Yet despite all this, the clergy were not 'political'. They did not, in general, associate the Church with political causes or act as political agents. To some extent this was because the genius of English Protestantism looked with disdain upon ecclesiastical power—in a long tradition of lay religion which looked back to the Reformation and beyond. It was in some measure, also, the neutralizing consequence of incorporating the clergy into the constitutional structure. Unlike their Dissenting brethren, they were familiar with the way political society operated, they were at home in it, and without either the need or the inclination to organize themselves around political parties. This simple point is often lost for those who list the involvements of the clergy in the fabric of the political order and assume that this propelled them automatically into political organization, or who assume the truth of Dissenting propagandist attempts to depict the Church as a mere political contrivance. In fact the political opinions of men considered for preferment in the Church were ceasing, at the start of the century, to bear much weight with statesmen. Lord Liverpool was more concerned, in the nomination of bishops, with the professional competence of his candidates than with their political sympathies.[1] Lord Melbourne was reverting to a practice no longer generally approved when, in the 1830s, he elicited the political opinions of men he was considering for the episcopacy. Sir Robert Peel, in

---

[1] Best, *Temporal Pillars*, p. 264.

the 1840s, resumed Liverpool's practice. It was easier for a Tory Prime Minister to show this detachment since he could calculate that most of the candidates were likely to be Tories anyway.[1] Thereafter the appointment of bishops and deans was ordinarily without decisive reference to political opinion: a practice assisted by Queen Victoria's increasing reliance on the views of churchmen themselves—and especially on the views of the Deans of Windsor and the Archbishops of Canterbury—when making appointments in the Church.[2] Her liking for men of broad theological opinion was more powerful in the matter of promotion than any political consideration. It is also true that the general movement for 'economical reform' at the start of the nineteenth century had encouraged the tendency to separate public office from the system of political rewards and management. It was a movement from which the Church, though not directly involved (since it was reformed separately) was, in the sense that office-holding in general came to be freed from political obligation, a beneficiary.

The clergy also themselves attempted to apply a sort of ban on party politics. The bishops in Parliament normally only took part in debates which they considered affected the interests of religion. In 1811, for example, Bishop Porteus's biographer pointed out that his subject 'never spoke except on points strictly ecclesiastical'.[3] Bishop Blomfield, the most involved of the bishops of his generation in legislative activity and social administration, was noted for his 'principle of eschewing the character of a politician'.[4] Edward Maltby, a Whig prelate—Lord Grey's first nomination to the bench—described himself as devoid of 'the spirit of a Polemic, still more of a politician'.[5] These were not just conventional pieties either. To some extent, it is true, churchmen meant by 'politics' a peculiar addiction to faction—rather than politics in the more usual modern sense. It is also true that the clergy were popularly thought of as being Tory,[6] however much they might seek to avoid 'party' activity. In their instructions to the clergy the bishops gave clear advice on the avoidance of political involvement, unless the interests of religion were clearly at issue. 'In referring thus to the political state of the country', Bishop Copleston told the clergy of South Wales in a comment on the recent Reform Bill excitement, in his *Charge* of 1833, 'you will not suspect me of alluding in the remotest degree to the measures or views of this or that party in the State, or indeed to any of those national interests which are unconnected with religion.'

[1] Owen Chadwick, *The Victorian Church*, Part I (London, 1966), p. 226.

[2] Ibid., Part II (London, 1970), p. 332.

[3] Hodgson, *The Life of the Right Reverend Beilby Porteus, D.D.*, p. 276.

[4] G. E. Biber, *Bishop Blomfield and His Times* (London, 1857), p. 50.

[5] Edward Maltby, *A Charge Delivered to the Clergy of the Archdeaconry of Lewes by Edward, Bishop of Chichester* (London, 1834), p. 8.

[6] For evidence of the Tory voting habits of the clergy, see J. R. Vincent, *Pollbooks. How Victorians voted* (Cambridge, 1967), p. 52.

He went on:

We must all indeed feel, in common with our fellow-countrymen, an interest in the *temporal* prosperity and happiness of our country. We do not put off the citizen when we assume the garb of a minister of religion; neither are we called upon to abandon those opinions and affections which attach men to individuals or to parties most consonent with their own inclinations . . . but I must be permitted to remind you, that those attachments are inferior in worth, and ought to be kept strictly subordinate to the one great purpose of our calling—the nourishment of the Church of Christ, and the increase of His Kingdom.[1]

This was an opinion widely approved and frequently expressed. Copleston was careful to note the perils which even the union of Church and State placed in the way of the disinterested minister.

This union may lead clergymen to forget the sacred character of their peculiar office;—to mix in worldly affairs, and party politics, so far as to discredit their calling, and to weaken its influence in society. These are the *corruptions* to which it is exposed—not the necessary or natural consequence of its existence. It has been well said that the object of the alliance is, not to make the Church political, but to make the State religious.[2]

This, then, was the formula: concern for the needs of men in their temporal condition but without involvement in party politics. It was a view particularly well suited to the limited politics of the early nineteenth century, when parties did not have programmes for social reform in the modern sense, and when the limited sphere of legitimate governmental competence defined 'political' issues reasonably clearly. Yet the course advocated by the bishops was not entirely an obvious one. Considering the circumstances of the 1830s, when it might have been expected that the Church, with its Tory bishops, under sharp attack from Whig reformers and radical agitators, would turn to an alliance with Tory politics, it was a remarkable piece of restraint. 'Let our teaching be that of Christian ministers, not of partisans and adherents of exclusive systems,' Bishop Monk of Gloucester, a very Tory prelate, told his Tory clergy in 1835: 'Political agitation cannot, under any circumstances, befit the Minister of the Gospel.'[3] Archbishop Howley of Canterbury, reviewing the attitudes of the parliamentary parties to the question of Church reform in 1831, advised the Irish Primate, Beresford, of his wish to remain unconnected with politics.

I am anxious to avoid communication of these subjects as much as possible, with the leaders of parties, however well disposed to us, lest we should in appear-

---

[1] Edward Copleston, *A Charge Delivered to the Clergy of the Diocese of Llandaff by Edward, Lord Bishop of Llandaff* (London, 1833), p. 7–8.

[2] Ibid., p. 10.

[3] James Henry Monk, *A Charge Delivered to the Clergy of the Diocese of Gloucester* (London, 1835), pp. 29–30.

ance at least, be made subservient to political tactics [he wrote]. My hope is to be able to take a straightforward part with no other object in view than the real interests of the Church.[1]

It has, of course, been the opposition of the bishops to the Reform Bill in 1831 that has most frequently been taken to represent the political character of the bishops at this time. It will be necessary to examine the Reform crisis shortly, but it is appropriate to notice at this point that defenders of the Church's role over the Reform issue argued that the distinction between party politics and larger questions, in which the interests of religion were involved, was preserved intact. A wide definition was accorded the latter, since the nature of the Constitution itself was involved— a Constitution which incorporated the Church.

It was lawful for the clergy, under proper restriction, to join with their fellow-citizens, either in resisting or in promoting those changes, while they were in progress, if they deemed them likely to affect the future happiness and prosperity of their Country;—for the Constitution of the Country is not a subject of mere vulgar politics, but a matter in which every man ought to feel an interest.

So wrote the Archdeacon of Colchester. He also advised the clergy to reapply the code of practice in normal conditions: 'now that those charges have received the sanction of the Legislature, and have become a part of the actual frame-work of the Constitution, our opinions as to the probable working of those changes must not be allowed to exercise any influence upon our conduct, as teachers of religion'.[2] Charles Sumner, Bishop of Winchester, whilst warning his clergy, in 1833, to 'take no share, indeed, in the rivalries and struggles of party faction', and to exercise 'reserve on subjects connected with the conduct of affairs of state', was another Church leader who pointed, nevertheless, to the wider interests which the clergy must have in 'what affects the moral well-being and eternal condition, as well as the temporal happiness of the community'. It was under this head that he noted 'there can be no public measures, of any importance, which do not exercise an influence directly or indirectly, upon the course of religion'.[3] But no Church leaders, at this time, believed that any of their number applied the wider definition of 'religious interests' rashly. An examination of subjects touched upon in the episcopal *Charges* of the period shows that political issues not immediately affecting the welfare of the Church were very rarely made the subject of instruction or comment.

The Methodists, following the practice of the Establishment, also sought

[1] Lord George Beresford Papers, Library of the Representative Church Body, Dublin. Howley to Beresford, 15 Dec. 1831.

[2] William Rowe Lyall, *Sentiments of the Clergy on the Question of Church Reform, Briefly Stated in a Charge delivered to the Clergy* (London, 1833), p. 8.

[3] Charles Sumner, *A Charge Delivered to the Clergy of the Diocese of Winchester* (1833) (London, 1834), p. 9.

to avoid party political involvement,[1] although the Wesleyan Conference, like the Church of England, was largely Tory in sympathy during these years.[2] Dean Walter Hook, a Tory High Churchman, noticed that among Dissenters overt party politics were acquiring a wide acceptability in the 1830s, however. 'If the clergy are too much inclined to Toryism,' he wrote from Coventry in 1834, 'the Dissenting ministers are to radicalism, and some of the Dissenting meeting-houses in this city are, every Sunday evening, converted after service into political debating societies.'[3] This, of course, was one of the main developments of popular radicalism in the 1830s and 1840s: the alliance with religious Dissent. Not all Dissenters were attracted to radicalism. Jabez Bunting and the Wesleyans retained their Toryism. Not all the clergy of the State Church were Tories. For Thomas Arnold, 'Liberal principles were not merely the expression of his adherence to a Whig ministry, but of his belief in the constant necessity of applying those principles of advance and reform which, in their most perfect development, he conceived to be identical with Christianity itself'.[4] Sydney Smith, Canon of St. Paul's, was an influential Whig publicist. Henry Bathurst, Bishop of Norwich until his death in 1837, and his successor, Edward Stanley, were both articulate Whig Liberals; so were Archbishop Whately of Dublin, Bishop Maltby of Chichester, Bishop Denison of Salisbury, Bishop Thirlwall of St. David's, and Bishop Grey of Hereford (the brother of the Whig Prime Minister). But there had only been two Whig prelates on the bench before Grey and Melbourne began their scrutiny.

The Church of England was able to apply a working distinction between party politics and public issues affecting the Church because the limited nature of the politics of the period actually allowed the distinction to operate without too great a measure of inconsistency. In the first decades of the nineteenth century men had a very circumscribed view of the proper competence of the State. Its duty was to preserve order, to secure the conditions in which contractual relationships could be fulfilled, and to protect religious truth and morality. Since men did not look to the State—not even radicals—as a social regulator, the conventional area of politics was in practice quite small. It was much easier for churchmen to decide what was a party or political matter, and what was a constitutional issue affecting the interests of the Church, or a moral question affecting religion, when legislation was little concerned with social and economic relationships. The growing orthodoxy of Political Economy reinforced the limited function of government—indeed, its practical tendency was to reduce still further

---

[1] D. M. Thompson, *Nonconformity in the Nineteenth Century* (London, 1972), p. 65.
[2] Wearmouth, *Methodism and Working-Class Movements*, p. 151.
[3] Stephens, *The Life and Letters of Walter Farquhar Hook*, i. 261.
[4] Stanley, *The Life and Correspondence of Thomas Arnold, D.D.*, i. 173.

the laws concerned with social and economic regulation—and perpetuated, for a time, an ease of definition. When later churchmen like Westcott or Temple opted for a more collectivist view of government, they ran at once into the problem of redefining the political and the religious spheres.

The constitutional adjustment which so disturbed the relationship of the State to the Church—and which clearly fell within the sphere which Church leaders regarded as their proper concern—began with little realization that anything momentous was occurring. In fact the repeal of the Test and Corporation Acts, in 1828, attracted a lot of distinguished clerical support. It seemed a fitting compliment to the proved loyalty and public responsibility of the Dissenters. Within a couple of years, however, churchmen could already see the dangers. 'I refer our calamities to the Repeal of the Test Act, for then the State *virtually* renounced every connexion with religion,' Hook observed in 1831, amidst the Dissenters' new assault upon the Church Establishment: 'It pronounced religion to be, so far as the State is concerned, a thing indifferent.'[1] But when the Repeal Bill had been proposed, many churchmen had regarded the concession as a maturation of the principles of toleration. When, in 1811, Lord Sidmouth had unsuccessfully attempted legislation to control the conditions according to which Dissenting teachers were licensed—some were thought to be procuring licences in order to avoid militia service[2]—Archbishop Manners-Sutton had spoken against the proposal in the House of Lords. Far from seeking the containment of Dissent by legal restrictions, in fact, the age looked to greater freedom for Dissenters. In 1812, Lord Liverpool's administration repealed the Conventicle and Five Mile Acts; and in the next year Unitarians were accorded equal legal standing with Trinitarian Dissenters.[3]

For eighty-five years orthodox Protestants outside the Established Church had been able to sit in Parliament, and to hold municipal and other public office, by the passage of annual Acts of Indemnity exempting them from the statutory penalties formally imposed upon those taking office without receiving the sacrament of Holy Communion at the hands of the Church of England. The bishops themselves believed this situation ought to end. In March 1828 the two Archbishops, and the Bishops of London, Durham, Chester, and Llandaff, met with Peel, the Home Secretary, and agreed the terms of a Bill to repeal the Test and Corporation Acts. A full meeting of the bishops later approved this.[4] A new declaration, required of office-holders, replaced the sacramental test. The change in constitutional theory was very considerable: the Legislature now be-

---

[1] Stephens, *Life and Letters of Walter Farquhar Hook*, i. 221.

[2] B. L. Manning, *The Protestant Dissenting Deputies* (Cambridge, 1952), p. 130.

[3] W. G. Addison, *Religious Equality in Modern England, 1714–1914* (London, 1944), p. 39.

[4] William James Copleston, *Memoir of Edward Copleston, D.D.* (London, 1851), p. 123.

came, in theory as well as in practice, a body of mixed religious membership—it no longer consisted solely of the laity of the Establishment. Church
leaders were perfectly willing to acquiesce in this at the time, for the Dissenters were Protestants, and had shown themselves well adapted to public
office. There was also no intention, by any of the parties to the legislation,
to weaken the position of the Church as an Establishment. Churchmen saw
the reform as a removal of a premium on the sacrament which Pusey, an
enthusiastic Whig Liberal, called 'disgraceful'.[1] But in wishing to dissociate
the rites of the Church from the qualification of fitness for public office,
churchmen were in fact tacitly recognizing that great changes were rendering aspects of the Establishment of religion anomalous. 'Religious tests,
imposed for political purposes, must, in themselves, be always liable, more
or less, to endanger religious sincerity', said Vernon-Harcourt, the Archbishop of York, in supporting the Repeal Bill in 1828. 'Nothing, therefore,
but paramount necessity—I mean some obvious and urgent danger apprehended to the State—can, in my opinion, justify their being so imposed.'[2]
It was an advanced opinion at the time that it was uttered. John Kaye,
Bishop of Lincoln, pointed to the absence of real protection to the Church
in existing provisions, or, indeed, in the preamble to the Repeal Bill, with
its declaration that the Church was 'inseparably united with the State'. For
'when the hour of danger arrives', he said, 'the feeling of the legislature
and the country will either be favourable to the Established Church or
adverse to it'.[3] No paper safeguards could do much about that. Bishop
Van Mildert of Durham objected to the claims based on Natural Rights
doctrines advanced in some of the Dissenters' petitions supporting Repeal:
'It has been assumed that it is a natural, inherent, and inalienable right,
belonging to every member of the community, to be deemed eligible to
offices of trust and power in the State, without regard to his religious
opinions, and even if his opinions be diametrically opposite to those which
the State has adopted as its own.'[4] Van Mildert thought he discerned a
whiff of the Jacobin radicalism of the 1790s, but even so he supported
concession to the Dissenters, with a generous tribute to the 'obligations
we owe to them in literature, in arts and sciences, in religion, in biblical
criticism, and even in government itself'.[5] Charles James Blomfield, Bishop
of Chester (it was just before his translation to London) spoke strongly in
the House of Lords against the 'profanation and abuse of the most holy
ordinance of our religion' by the sacramental test. It was inappropriate 'in
the present state of the Christian world'.[6] Like Kaye, he discounted legal
safeguards as a real protection of 'the Christian character of the country'.

---

[1] H. P. Liddon, *Life of Edward Bouverie Pusey*, 4th edn. (London, 1894), i. 133.
[2] Hansard, *New Series*, xviii. 1483 (17 Apr. 1828).
[3] Ibid. 1490.   [4] Ibid. 1492.
[5] Ibid. 1496.   [6] Ibid. 1512.

The real danger, he believed, came from attempts to exclude religion from popular education.[1] In justifying this general agreement of the bishops over Repeal—and a justification was evidently necessary, because the lower clergy were much less accommodating than the leaders of the Church— Bishop Bethell told the clergy of Gloucester that the bench had 'not been led away by what are called liberal opinions, nor by vague and impracticable notions of religious liberty'. They were motivated by the growth within the Church itself of a conviction that sacramental tests were improper.[2] This sort of appeal to the spiritual integrity of the Church contained the seeds of conflict with the practical erastianism upon which the ecclesiastical polity of the country rested. But there were more immediate implications.

Catholic Emancipation in 1829 made the bishops realize that they were no longer living in the sort of friendly political climate where they could afford to compromise principles and tolerate the creation of constitutional anomalies, as those can who occupy positions of unassailable strength. The Emancipation question involved an alteration in the parliamentary oath, so that Roman Catholics entering Parliament could take their seats without having to denounce their religion. It also involved the admission of Catholics to most offices of State and to municipal government. Since the maintenance of a legislature theoretically composed of members of the State Church had already been abandoned in the recent concession to the Dissenters, men of broad opinion could see no reason why the anomaly should not be extended to include Roman Catholics. Sydney Smith wrote with truth, indeed, that 'in their tenets, in their Church government, in the nature of their endowments, the Dissenters are infinitely more distant from the Church of England than the Catholics are'.[3] But the issue could not be simply detached from either the emotional repulsion which Englishmen had for some centuries felt towards Roman Catholicism, or from the fact that most of the proposed beneficiaries of Emancipation were believed to be Irish agitators under the control of O'Connell and the Catholic priests. These considerations, as much as concern for the place of the Church Establishment in the British Constitution,[4] explain why Lord Liverpool had declared the matter an 'open' question as a way of preserving the unity of his ministry. In constitutional principle, the only real difference between the Catholic and the Protestant Dissenters was that the former were held to owe allegiance—some said temporal as well as spiritual

[1] Ibid. 1516.

[2] Christopher Bethell, *A Charge Delivered at the Triennial Visitation of the Diocese of Gloucester* (Gloucester, 1828), p. 11.

[3] *Peter Plymley's Letters on the Subject of the Catholics*, in Sydney Smith, *Works*, 3rd edn. (London, 1845), *Letter V*, p. 366.

[4] See Geoffrey Best, 'The Protestant Constitution and its Supporters, 1800–29', in *Transactions of the Royal Historical Society*, 5th Series, 8 (1958), 105.

allegiance—to the external sovereignty of the Pope. Nor were they trusted who pointed out that only spiritual obedience was owed to Rome. 'Spiritual and temporal domain run imperceptibly into each other, and are separated by almost evanescent boundaries', wrote Bishop Law in opposition to the Catholic claims.[1]

As parliamentary and public opinion in England shaped itself during the 1820s, in the discussions of Plunket's Bill in 1821, and Burdett's Bill in 1825, it became clear that those in favour and those against Emancipation differed very little in their attitude to the Catholic religion itself. That system continued to be loathed and distrusted. Political division arose over the differing attitudes to the means most likely to preserve the Constitution and the Established Church. Whigs tended to believe that the Constitution was most likely to survive by broadening its basis by the admission of Catholics; most Tories continued to regard a compromise of the principles of the Constitution as calculated to undermine its foundations. Both positions were, in the terms available, perfectly tenable. But the emotions released by the Catholic question, and the belief (not well founded) that a civil war might start in Ireland if the question was not attended to, converted the Emancipation issue into a full-dress constitutional crisis.

Attitudes among the clergy followed those of the public. The bishops, in correspondence to parliamentary opinion, divided over the Emancipation question; the parochial clergy, like the people of the country generally, were more solidly against concession. In the Lords' vote in 1829, eight bishops supported Emancipation, and sixteen were against. In the country, the clergy helped the formation of the Brunswick Clubs in 1828—as did the Methodist ministers[2]—and encouraged the circulation of petitions against relief.[3] The academic clergy divided very publicly, over the Oxford election of February 1829, caused by Peel's determination to seek the confidence of his University constituents following his own conversion to Emancipation. He was opposed by Sir Robert Inglis, a stout defender of the Protestant Constitution. Keble organized the opposition to Peel, with the assistance of Newman, Froude, and Robert Wilberforce. Peel was supported by Bishop Lloyd, and Whately, with Pusey canvassing on his behalf. Blanco White, the former Spanish priest and Protestant convert, was Pusey's most notable convert to the Emancipation cause.[4] The Oxford controversy exposed the divisions within the Church in their most doctrinaire light. But it should be noticed that some of the bishops who

---

[1] George Henry Law, *A Charge Delivered to the Clergy of the Diocese of Bath and Wells*, p. 25.

[2] G. I. T. Machin, *The Catholic Question in English Politics, 1820 to 1830* (Oxford, 1964), p. 141.

[3] Ibid., p. 148.   [4] Liddon, *Life of Pusey*, i. 199.

eventually voted in favour of concession had no real enthusiasm for it: it was a regrettable necessity, a concession to the evil temper of the times. Only the old Whig Bishop of Norwich, Henry Bathurst, was a warm advocate of Emancipation for its own sake. 'For more than half a century I have been uniformly of opinion that civil disabilities, on account of religious tenets, are inconsistent with all true ideas of justice, of policy, and of Christian charity', he said in 1829 as he put his name to a petition in favour of Emancipation.[1] More typical of the bishops who in the end supported relief was Lloyd of Oxford. 'I should have preferred', he told the Lords in 1829, 'to see the educated persons of the country declaring themselves in favour of the old and existing institutions of the kingdom—but such, my Lords, is not the case.' Concession, he supposed, was realistic, in accord with 'the progress and continuing course of public opinion'.[2] The Bishop of St. David's, John Banks Jenkinson, offered a model version of the Whig view. Emancipation, he said, was not only compatible 'with the maintenance of the Constitution and the Protestant establishments of the country, but would tend to strengthen those establishments, by uniting all parties in attachment to the Constitution'.[3] In view of Wellington's Bill, this was a point to which many parliamentary Tories were obliged to turn.

The bishops opposed to concessions in 1829 used 'constitutional' rather than 'religious' arguments: a distinction familiar to the vocabulary of the Emancipation debate. Archbishop Howley declared simply that 'the Constitution would be changed by the measure'.[4] He repeated the words of the Coronation Oath, which obliged the Sovereign to 'preserve unto the bishops and clergy of this realm, and to the churches committed to their charge, all such rights and privileges as by law do or shall appertain to them'. As the fulfilment of the terms of the Oath depended on the fidelity of the King's ministers, there must be a guarantee that they should be of the same Protestant faith.[5] The Coronation Oath was frequently cited by opponents of Emancipation, for it was a sanction outside Parliament. George IV, like his father, believed that Emancipation was really incompatible with his Oath, and had to be persuaded by his ministers to acquiesce in the measure of 1829.

In his consideration of the Emancipation Bill, Howley did at any rate acknowledge one good feature. There were no provisions for the creation of a state interest in Roman Catholic ecclesiastical appointments.[6] The idea of reducing the risk of Catholic disloyalty by allowing a Crown veto of Catholic episcopal nominations had been canvassed many times since the Act of Union with Ireland. A royal veto had been approved in principle

---

[1] Henry Bathurst, *Memoirs of the late Dr. Henry Bathurst* (London, 1837), i. 319.
[2] Hansard, *New Series*, xxi. 77 (2 Apr. 1829).
[3] Ibid., p. 41.
[4] Ibid., p. 66.
[5] Ibid., p. 63.
[6] Ibid., p. 66.

by the Papacy in 1808 and in 1814. O'Connell and his Irish supporters were vehemently opposed to the idea, but not to another device with a similar intention—the state payment of the Catholic clergy. This plan was actually included in Burdett's Bill in 1825, and in the first draft of Wellington's measure in 1829. State payment of the priests was considered an effective way of separating them from dependence on their flocks, who, in Ireland, were thought to be, and usually were actually, in O'Connell's political control. Yet there was a great deal of exaggeration of the real influence of the priests in Irish political life. Archbishop Beresford of Armagh believed that, after Emancipation, Catholic members returned to Parliament would 'in effect be the agents and commissioners of the Roman priesthood, sent hither to give utterance to the sentiments, and to manage the interests of that body; a body, it should be recollected, which has objects to gain and views to promote, irreconcileable with the general good of the empire'.[1] This sort of opinion was commonly heard.[2] But in fact it misunderstood the true nature of O'Connell's achievement in Ireland. The priests tended to derive their politics from their flocks, not the other way round: O'Connell had incorporated the Catholic Church within his general scheme of locally based national organizations. The priests were his agents. The devices of a Crown veto on episcopal appointments, and a stipendiary priesthood, were just as liable to free the Catholic Church from O'Connell's control as they were to reduce the shared political sympathies of priests and people. In the end, neither of these expedients appeared in the Emancipation Act: it was considered too dangerous, from the point of view of constitutional principle, to create any sort of link between the Catholic Church and the State. As Howley said, 'interference with the Catholic priesthood would have recognized something like a Roman Catholic establishment, and acknowledged, to a certain degree, the power of the pope'.[3]

The Act of 1829 contained, in the new parliamentary oath, the chief safeguard to the constitutional position of the Protestant Establishment. Catholics had to swear not to attempt to subvert the position of the Church, to abjure the power of the Pope, and to owe full allegiance to the Protestant House of Brunswick. The state offices of Regent, Lord Chancellor, Viceroy of Ireland, and High Commissioner of the Church of Scotland, were reserved to Protestants. There were a number of minor securities. Catholic clergy were forbidden to wear ecclesiastical dress in public; religious orders were regulated and no new members were to be admitted to them; Catholic bequests were still liable to scrutiny as donations to 'superstitious use';

[1] Hansard, New Series, xxi, 72.
[2] See e.g. the Letters addressed to Canning by Phillpotts in 1825, in Davies, Henry Phillpotts, Bishop of Exeter, 1778–1869, p. 63.
[3] Hansard, New Series, xxi. 66.

bishops were prohibited from assuming existing territorial titles; the symbols of municipal authority were not to be paraded in Catholic places of worship. In two separate Acts, O'Connell's Catholic Association was outlawed, and the Irish franchise was increased to £10. Opponents of Emancipation, whilst recognizing that these securities did something to recognize the constitutional position of the Church Establishment, remained sceptical of their practical effect. 'I have no opinion of oaths, declarations, etc. etc., as real securities', Howley wrote to Beresford in September of that year.[1]

The debate of the Emancipation question had occasioned an exhaustive examination of the basis of political society in Britain. Issues had emerged with great clarity. Blomfield pointed to this in his speech to the House of Lords in April 1829—the real question, he said, was about 'the duty of a Protestant government to distinguish between truth and error', and 'the only duty of a Protestant state to make a distinction between fundamental truth and dangerous error, so far as not to make them co-ordinate powers in the State'.[2] Emancipation had in fact logically moved the State further from its confessional character, and the implications were fully recognized by opponents of the concession. They did not see themselves—as their opponents did—as defenders of selfish religious privilege, but as defenders of a Christian political order. Emancipationists argued that there was no reason to extend the logic of the reform, and that the flexible genius of the British Constitution, which was able to absorb seemingly any number of internal inconsistencies without undue harm to its operation and effectiveness, was on their side. Opponents claimed that a precedent was now on the statute book which opened the way for further changes in the very foundations of political society, that no paper guarantees could protect the Church. And the Church, with no government of its own, was controlled by Parliament. 'Laws upon parchment', as Bishop Copleston remarked in 1831, 'will never save the establishment, if the public mind is quite alienated.'[3] Unhappily for the Church, an issue was about to break upon the country which had exactly that effect.

The opposition of the bishops to parliamentary reform has borne a great deal of service as evidence of the reactionary political instincts of the nineteenth-century Church of England. To some it has seemed a symbol of the Church's adhesion to the least enlightened political ideas of the century. In reality, however, it indicated the proximity of the leaders of the Church to prevailing parliamentary practice. Public men divided over the Reform question, and the Church found itself on one side of the division. Like most of those with Tory sympathies, who could see large

---

[1] Beresford Papers, Howley to Beresford, 6 Sept. 1829.
[2] Hansard, *New Series*, xxi. 122.
[3] W. J. Copleston, *Memoir of Edward Copleston*, p. 139.

dangers inherent in any attempt to alter the system of representation, the bishops and clergy would doubtless have preferred no changes at all. In 1830, therefore, their opposition to Reform was characteristically Tory: at this stage it did not look as if their preference could possibly isolate them from the general texture of political debate. Tory opposition to Reform in 1830 was not especially out of step with opinion in the country—which was divided, as parliamentary opinion was. There were a lot of popular disturbances in the country in 1830, but they were not obviously stamped, as they were in 1831, with the burning issue of parliamentary reform. The new Whig ministry, in December 1830, did not display any particular sympathy for popular radicalism: their first action in office was to introduce coercive measures to put down popular disturbances. Special commissions were set up; nine labourers were executed and 457 were transported to penal servitude overseas. At the start of the new year, the Whig Cabinet turned to the Reform question—one they had always tended to regard as properly within the Whig tradition—and a committee was set up to frame legislation. Grey had no particular plan prepared on taking office, and there was no reason why he should have had. Despite the Whigs' commitment to some sort of reform, the issue did not achieve paramountcy until Grey had himself taken it up as government policy and adopted advanced positions from which it was tactically difficult to withdraw. The view of Reform as a continuous pressure leading up to 1832 has been so popular that it is difficult to realize, at this distance, that the really rapid development of the question took place after 1830. Supporters of Reform during the ensuing crisis, and later radicals and historians, have gone carefully through all the various movements for franchise and borough reform, from Wilkes's proposals of 1776, and have telescoped them together to give the impression of a steadily accumulating popular pressure—arrested temporarily by the Jacobin scare in the 1790s—which by 1830 had become so irresistible that the flood waters engulfed any who stood in the way. But the Reform impulses were in fact very disconnected and often incoherent, and it was only when the Whig Cabinet had actually made Reform a parliamentary policy, with actual proposals, that the country caught the enthusiasm. The Government itself elicited a lot of the Reform clamour, merely by its action in lifting Reform to a political possibility. The Church, like the Tory Party, could not at first see that the Reform question would excite such a public response: they envisaged an internal parliamentary battle of the conventional sort. Wellington's declaration against Reform, in November 1830, did not look quite so opposed to the spirit of the times as it has since come to be seen.

Yet by October 1831, when the House of Lords rejected the revised Reform Bill, the position had greatly changed. The scale of the popular enthusiasm for the Bill, and Grey's determination to use every constitutional expedient to get it through Parliament, had led many of the leading Tories to adjust their position. By then, they recognized that *some* measure of Reform was necessary, and their continued opposition derived from detailed objections to the actual provisions of the Whig Bill. The bishops who had voted against the Bill in October 1831—all, that is, except the two Whig bishops, Bathurst and Maltby—were also by then clear that they were not opposed to Reform in principle but hoped for better legislation than that proposed by Lord Grey. They aimed at prompting suitable amendments to make the Bill less partisan. By May 1832, when the King accepted the resignation of the Whig ministers following the Lords' insistence on their own amendments, Wellington was quite ready to form a Tory administration and pass a Tory Reform Bill. Had Peel co-operated, the Duke might well have succeeded: a minority Tory Government passed a Reform Bill in 1867. When Grey resumed office at the end of May, the passage of his Bill was assured, for by then there were few grounds for opposition in principle to reform which the Tory leaders had not conceded. The bishops, reflecting these adjustments, were no more and no less detached from the internal shifts of parliamentary opinion than everyone else—certainly most of them did not turn to absolute opposition to all change as some of the ultra-Tory peers did. It was quite by chance that the Lords' division in October 1831, when half of those voting against the Bill were prelates, represented the Church to popular opinion as the reactionary guardians of the old order. In fact they were caught up in a perfectly conventional attempt to get the Bill, which many believed contained partisan Whig clauses, modified in Committee. Nor did the bishops act in collusion. As Bishop Monk later explained, 'each was ignorant of the manner in which the others proposed to act' when it came to the actual voting on that occasion.[1] It was also fortuitous that the movement was the right one for Dissenting and radical opponents of the Establishment to seize upon the bishops' vote and stage a set-piece propaganda assault. Bishops were burned in effigy by local mobs, some were abused in the streets, the Bishop of Bristol had his palace set on fire, and leaflets were distributed by radicals to inform the public about the extent of episcopal wealth.[2] Grey had warned the bishops that they should put their house in order. But the bishops feared that unless they voted to get a moderated Reform Bill, the new House of Commons might well ransack the Church. It was a fear which 'had a very solid basis in the observable temper of the times'.[3]

The position in which the bishops found themselves was quite clear.

[1] Hansard, *Third Series*, xii. 405 (13 Apr. 1832).
[2] Chadwick, *Victorian Church*, Part I, p. 27.
[3] Olive J. Brose, *Church and Parliament. The Reshaping of the Church of England, 1828–1860* (Oxford, 1959), p. 22.

'To a Reform synonymous with the extermination of abuses, and the restoration of the excellencies of the Constitution, he professed himself a sincere friend,' Archbishop Howley told the House of Lords in Otcober 1831, just before the storm broke over the Church. 'Amongst the right reverend Prelates who sat on the bench', he added, 'he did not believe there was a single individual who did not concur with him in that sentiment.' He hoped for a 'union of men of all parties' to prepare a new Bill more representative of opinion.[1] The bishops took almost no part in the debate on the Bill, in fact, despite the later assumption of the mobs that they were its leading enemies.[2] In the earlier debate of April 1831, when Grey's first and most radical Bill was before Parliament, that same Bishop of Bristol whose palace was later burned down, Robert Gray, had declared himself 'not unfriendly to rational reform', but believed the measure before them went too far. Bishop Gray favoured legislation to end bribery and corruption at elections, and limiting election expenses. But he did object to the removal of representation from the scheduled boroughs on the ground that it was an attack on property. 'If Parliament once commenced a course of spoliation of one species of property, there was no telling what species of property would long continue safe.'[3] This argument, looking ahead as it did to the need to protect ecclesiastical property from an antipathetic Parliament, reflected older notions of property rights invested in a borough patron. Pitt's Reform proposals in 1785 had envisaged cash compensation for the borough-owners who lost their representation; and when, in 1800, the Act of Union was passed, the Irish boroughs which were not transferred to Westminster, on the extinction of the old Irish Parliament, were compensated in cash. The principle was not included in the Whig Bill.

After their public discomfiture in 1831, the bishops took care to explain their position more clearly in the Reform debate of 1832. They had all been taken by surprise at the public reaction, and admitted they had misjudged the extent of public feeling.[4] Old Bishop Bathurst predicted that many of the bishops would consent to modifications and then pass the Bill.[5] Nearly all were willing for this, in fact. 'I had been desirous of voting that the bill might go into committee with a view to amendment,' Copleston wrote of his behaviour in October 1831, 'but the declaration of Lord Grey that no material amendments would be agreed to, determined me and several others to vote against the second reading.'[6] In 1832 many of the bishops were determined not to be manœuvred into this position again. A few

---

[1] Hansard, *Third Series*, viii. 303 (7 Oct. 1831).
[2] Soloway, *Prelates and People*, p. 247.
[3] Hansard, *Third Series*, iii. 1333 (14 Apr. 1831).
[4] Soloway, *Prelates and People*, p. 251.
[5] Henry Bathurst, *Memoirs*, ii. 3 (January 1832).
[6] W. J. Copleston, *Memoir*, p. 143.

retained their earlier opposition. Van Mildert, who said he 'viewed the measure proposed with respect to the effect it would have on the religious and moral interests of the country',[1] was attempting to operate the distinction between 'political' issues and larger questions affecting the interests of the Church. He still did not believe that the 'religious and moral interests of the country' would be served by the Bill. Indeed, he had observed the signs of the times, he said; he 'had attended to what was called the march of intellect, and he found abroad a restless disposition—a love of innovation—a wish to destroy institutions because they were ancient—a desire to set the subject over the ruler, and to trample the ruler under the subject'.[2] These, clearly, were very traditional Tory fears. Van Mildert also sought to defend the Church from class bias. He embodied Tory paternalism, a desire to protect the ordinary people from the new middle classes. 'It had been said that they thought only of their own interests, and that they cared not for the welfare of the lower classes,' he said of the bishops. 'These were gross and unjustifiable aspersions', for it was the Bill that would do nothing to help the lower classes.[3] In that conclusion, as the popular radicals were shortly to discover, he was quite right.

Bishop Blomfield had been prevented, by his father's death, from voting on the Bill in the crucial division of October 1831. He had no objection to the principle of Reform, though reservations enough about 'the extremely democratic character of the Bill introduced by the Government'. But 'holding himself bound in principle to eschew the role of a politician', he said, 'he naturally viewed the whole question in reference to its effect upon the Church'.[4] These were reasonable grounds. For it was Parliament that governed the Church; and its composition, and how it was controlled, were clearly of great importance to churchmen. In November 1831 Blomfield seems to have agreed to promote a modified Bill after a meeting with Lord Grey. He did, in fact, persuade a number of bishops to change their votes in 1832. In April of that year he declined to say 'whether or not a more cautious and sparing application of the pruning-knife to the ancient Constitution of the country would not have been sufficient to pare off its excrescences, to remove its encumbrances, to renovate its vigour, and to restore its virtue'.[5] This sort of language was very much at the centre of what parliamentary reform was intended to promote. Archbishop Howley, too, had spoken of Reform as a work of 'restoration'. So did Grey and the Whig ministers. Palmerston, indeed, declared that the Bill was

---

[1] Hansard, *Third Series*, xii. 48 (9 Apr. 1832).
[2] Ibid., 50.
[3] Ibid. 51.
[4] Biber, *Bishop Blomfield*, pp. 110–11.
[5] Hansard, *Third Series*, xii. 269 (11 Apr. 1832).

meant to restore the landed interest to an influence he believed indispensable;
he 'considered the soil to be the country itself'.[1] Reformers like these saw
the Constitution as unbalanced in their day by the shifts in population
and the growth of the industrial and commercial interests. Their legislation
was an attempt to 'restore' the balance by redefining constituencies so
that each should represent a coherent interest; to discriminate between
proper and improper political influence; and to adhere the middle classes
to the representational system by enfranchising them.[2] Once a measure of
Reform had become politically acceptable, there was little difference of
view between Whigs and Tories on these priorities; but differences
continued over the means to achieve those ends. The bishops, too, in
general, came to agree that a restoration of the balance of the Constitution
was necessary. Even Phillpotts of Exeter, who opposed the Bill to the end
as a device 'to effect a complete and entire change in the whole representative system',[3] was in private prepared to allow the need for a moderate
reform.[4] Lord George Murray, the Bishop of Rochester, was out of step
when he announced bluntly that he 'did not think their Lordships ought to
legislate on expediency upon a question involving the total subversion and
annihilation of law and justice'.[5] But in his belief that 'the lower classes
should not be called into council; they should not be suffered to interfere
with matters connected with legislation',[6] he said no more than Lord
Althorp had said, nor disagreed with the intention of the Whigs to avoid
the enfranchisement of the dependent men below the middle classes.

At the end of the debate in the House of Lords on the second reading
of the amended Bill in April 1832, twelve bishops voted in favour of its
passing and sixteen against. The Archbishop of York supported the Bill,
the Archbishop of Canterbury was still opposed. Throughout the country
the parochial clergy were less conciliatory in their general opposition.
There were a few Whig activists. Sydney Smith, speaking on a Reform
platform at Taunton in 1831 warned the Tories of the consequences of the
spread of literacy: 'you have a different sort of man to deal with—you must
change because the beings whom you govern are changed'.[7] Keble was an
unrepentant Tory; hissed by the crowd as he drove out of Fairford with
his father to vote for the anti-Reform candidate.[8] Keble told Pusey he
expected the reformed Parliament to do 'something really illegal' to the
Church; perhaps alterations to the Liturgy, perhaps the transference of

[1] Quoted in Norman Gash, *Politics in the Age of Peel* (London, 1953), p. 14.
[2] See D. C. Moore, 'Concession or Cure: The Sociological Premises of the First Reform
Act', in *Historical Journal*, 9, 1 (1966), 44.
[3] Hansard, *Third Series*, xii. 273 (11 Apr. 1832).
[4] Soloway, *Prelates and People*, p. 248.
[5] Hansard, *Third Series*, xii. 400 (13 Apr. 1832).
[6] Ibid. 401.   [7] Smith, *Works*, iii. 77.
[8] Georgina Battiscombe, *John Keble. A Study in Limitations* (London, 1963), p. 137.

its corporate property to others.[1] Blomfield was rather more optimistic. 'It had been said that the first consequence of this Bill would be an attack on ecclesiastical property,' he said during the parliamentary debate; 'but he hoped that, when the leaven of agitation had worked off, and when the country was restored to calmness and tranquillity, the people . . . would look with reverence to their ancient institutions.'[2] By 1834, however, this optimism had become tempered by a realization that a considerable change had occurred—that the radicals and Dissenters, in selecting the Reform Bill crisis as a good issue on which to attack the Church 'had recourse to the grossest calumnies, and the most unfounded accusations' and that there was no sign of this diminishing.[3] A bleak interlude of extreme unpopularity had opened for the Church. Church leaders considered it out of all proportion to their conduct over the Reform question. Their behaviour had been within the conventional parliamentary dealings; they could not understand why Dissenting and radical propagandists should wish to single them out for such treatment.

'I can find nothing to account for the existence of this hostile spirit', Bishop Kaye declared to the Lincoln clergy in 1834.[4] There were, the new Bishop of Bristol, Joseph Allen, wrote in the following year, 'undisguised attacks' upon the Church which, he correctly observed, were likely to acquire a permanent habitation in the national memory. 'When sentence of condemnation is once passed upon supposed delinquents, it is never reversed; nor are the calumnies we are assailed with, however often and satisfactorily refuted, ever forgotten.'[5] Churchmen had supposed that the Repeal of the Test and Corporation Acts, and possibly even the concession of the Catholic claims, would make for greater mutual esteem between the churches. The Reform Bill crisis had destroyed any hope of that. Instead, it confirmed the Dissenters in a new sense of their grievances, of their inferior legal standing compared with the Establishment; it allied them with radical politics in opposition to the 'aristocratic' state. The spearhead of the attack was provided by Baptists and Independents (Congregationalists). But not all Dissenters assailed the Church; the Wesleyans in particular remained generally friendly. Nor did all radicals attack the Church. The London intellectual radicals were more anxious to see the places of worship converted into secular libraries of 'useful knowledge' than were the various brands of provincial radicalism, many of which

---

[1] Liddon, *Life of Pusey*, i. 266.

[2] Hansard, *Third Series*, xii. 270 (11 Apr. 1832).

[3] C. J. Blomfield, *A Charge Delivered to the Clergy of the Diocese of London by Charles James, Lord Bishop of London* (London, 1834), p. 3.

[4] John Kaye, *A Charge Delivered at the Triennial Visitation of John, Lord Bishop of Lincoln* (London, 1834), p. 2.

[5] *A Charge Delivered to the Clergy of the Diocese of Bristol by the Right Reverend Joseph Allen, D.D.* (London, 1835), p. 6.

C S E—D

sought to remove the wealth of the Church, but not its existence. 'Philosophical radicals' had long made use of the wealth of the Church in their propaganda against religion. Bentham, for example, had fallen upon the renunciation of 'the pomps and vanities of this wicked world' in the Church of England catechism with especial delight. What he beheld, he wrote, was 'the Lords Spiritual, with fine linen on their shoulders, the purple on their liveries, the purple and the mitre on their equipages'. He asked: 'If not of these things, of what things is "pomp" made?'[1] The same query was articulated with much less elegance by other propagandists. There was no obvious correlation between intelligence and accuracy in the radicals' polemicism. Bentham wildly exaggerated the wealth and abuses of the Church, regarding as typical evils which were very occasional, or which were sustained by Parliament rather than by the will of Church leaders. John Wade, a Unitarian propagandist and a leader-writer for the *Spectator*, issued periodical attacks upon various institutions anonymously in the 1820s. In 1831 these were collected into a bumper edition and published as *The Extraordinary Black Book*. It was full of the grossest inaccuracies. The section on the abuses in the Church, which was the most exaggerated of all, had a huge vogue in its day, and is, characteristically, still cited by historians as a reliable source for evidence about the state of the Church. When the Royal Commission on Ecclesiastical Duties and Revenues began to produce the first reasonably accurate account of the wealth of the Church and its management, after 1836, the radicals' assertions were seriously undermined. But by then the damage to the Church's standing had been done; attitudes had been adopted; a damning case supported by intellectual opinion had acquired acceptance.

There was, of course, a great deal which really was wrong with the financial structure of the Church, and there were many abuses which needed reform. The Church was anxious for Parliament—a Parliament they could trust—to attend to these reforms. Archbishop Howley had been discussing possible methods of initiating these with Wellington's administration at the time of its collapse in 1830. In the following year he went ahead with three modest measures to tackle the problem of pluralism. Only one of them, on augmentations, got through Parliament. It was in this situation that the Reform Bill crisis intervened: it is little wonder that the bishops were anxious about the composition of a more radical Parliament, and what it would do to the Church. For everyone knew that the necessary reforms of the Church would have to be a joint Church and State enterprise.[2] The constitutional position of the Church left no alternative. Churchmen looked to legislation to end the abuses of non-

[1] Jeremy Bentham, *The Church of England Catechism Examined*, new edn. (London, 1824), p. 15.
[2] Brose, *Church and Parliament*, p. 20.

residence and pluralities, and for a limited internal redistribution of ecclesiastical financial resources.[1] Episcopal *Charges* had urged these reforms since the 1780s. Howley, whose vision of the future of the Church did not include 'rash innovation', was especially anxious for some sort of reforming initiative.[2] Some Church leaders included better arrangements for the education of candidates for Holy Orders among their reforming priorities—one of the things which a more reasonable distribution of financial resources could allow.[3] In December 1832, following the shock of the Reform crisis, the leading bishops gathered at Lambeth Palace to discuss the principles upon which Church Reform should proceed, and, as Van Mildert said, 'to enable the Archbishop to communicate to the Government our general feelings and persuasions'.[4] Thus Phillpotts was able to tell his clergy that 'the question of change, or no change, is in fact decided' both by Church and State. 'A change there will be, and it is the part of every faithful and prudent friend of the Church, especially of its Ministers, to exert all the best faculties which God has given to them, in the endeavour to make that change productive of as much good . . . as human prudence . . . can effect.'[5] Copleston later declared, 'We have nothing to conceal—nothing to gloss over: we desire that what is amiss may be corrected: and our chief regret is, that the measures prepared in Parliament for this object have not proceeded with that expedition which the governors of the Church themselves desired'.[6] It must not be forgotten, on the other hand, that clergy outside the episcopal bench, with its immediate contacts with the shifting ideas and tactics of the world of political possibilities, were often very unenthusiastic about reform. Nor should the radicals' exaggerations of abuses obscure the fact that some very disgraceful conditions were present in the Church. At the start of the 1830s, nearly half the clergy were non-resident—although this abuse was not quite as appalling as might at first appear because some parsons resided close to, but not technically inside, the ecclesiastical boundaries of their parishes (which did not always coincide with the civil boundaries). Non-residence did not typically leave the flock unattended: curates were usually provided by the non-resident incumbent to perform religious duties. Pluralism was commonplace. In 1832 it was estimated that of the

[1] Blomfield, *A Charge Delivered to the Clergy of the Diocese of London*, p. 17.

[2] William Howley, *A Charge Delivered at his Primary Visitation by William, Lord Archbishop of Canterbury* (London, 1832), p. 38.

[3] Thomas Burgess, *A Charge Delivered to the Clergy of the Diocese of Salisbury by Thomas, Lord Bishop of Salisbury* (Salisbury, 1832), p. 24.

[4] E. Hughes, 'The Bishops and Reform, 1831-2: Some Fresh Correspondence', in *English Historical Review*, 56 (1941), 477.

[5] Henry Phillpotts, *Charge Delivered to the Clergy of the Diocese of Exeter by the Right Reverend Henry, Lord Bishop of Exeter*, London, 1833, p. 9.

[6] Edward Copleston, *A Charge Delivered to the Clergy of the Diocese of Llandaff by Edward, Lord Bishop of Llandaff* (London, 1836), p. 7.

12,000 preferments in the Church, 3,853 clergy held only one title, whilst 3,304 held two, 370 held three, 73 held four, and 59 held five or more.[1] The internal inequalities of financial distribution meant that nearly 5,000 clergy got stipends of less than £150 a year; whilst the Bishop of London got over £12,000 and the Bishop of Durham got £19,000. The Church certainly needed reform, as its leaders saw.

The history and internal consequences of the ecclesiastical reforms which took place in the 1830s are not immediately relevant to the theme of the present analysis. Yet they did reveal the Church operating within the general assumption that the normal relationship of Church and State would continue despite the clamours from Dissenters and radicals, and despite the Oxford critics of erastianism within the Establishment. But those normal relationships were strained by the pressures to which the Whig ministry was itself subjected from its radical wing. In 1833, following the Reform crisis, the Protestant Dissenting Deputies in London drew up a list of six 'practical grievances'.[2] Early in 1834 these were rearranged as five points and managed to appeal to many Dissenting groups which had not previously been particularly attracted to political agitation.[3] They demanded an end to the exclusive registration of Baptism by the state Church; an end to the obligation of all except Quakers and Jews to be married in the parish church; the right to hold denominational burial services in parish churchyards; the abolition of compulsory Church rates; and the removal of religious tests at the Universities of Oxford and Cambridge.[4] 'They pave the way for the success of the attack which they meditate in due season on the Establishment,' observed Bishop Kaye; 'since under the plea of seeking the redress of practical grievances, they demand concessions in which the very principle of a Church Establishment is involved.'[5] Not only in constitutional principle, but in scale, the leaders of the Church realized that they faced a formidable assault. 'It is the accession of the great body of Protestant Dissenters to the number of those who seek the ruin of the Church, which constitutes the most surprising as well as the most alarming event of the present times', Bishop Monk sadly remarked, with pardonable exaggeration of the extent the shift of opinion had reached by 1835.[6] It seemed a thin reward for the legislative gestures made towards the Dissenters in the preceding decade.

Churchmen tried to distinguish between 'religious' and 'political' Dissenters in the new climate of opinion. 'The *religious* dissenter is not

---

[1] Desmond Bowen, *The Idea of the Victorian Church* (Montreal, 1968), p. 11.

[2] Manning, *Protestant Dissenting Deputies*, p. 274.

[3] See Robert Winter, *Brief Statement of the Case of Protestant Dissenters, Signed on behalf of the Committee of Dissenters of the Three Denominations*, London, 1834.

[4] Chadwick, *Victorian Church*, Part I, p. 80.

[5] John Kaye, *A Charge Delivered at the Triennial Visitation*, p. 7.

[6] James Henry Monk, *A Charge Delivered to the Clergy of the Diocese of Gloucester*, p. 23.

to be confounded with the *political* dissenter,' said the Chancellor of the Diocese of Winchester in 1834; 'among the religious dissenters, as we most cheerfully admit, are doubtless many good and valuable men: and I have reason to believe that there is a large body who view the proceedings of their political associates with strong disapprobation.'[1] An examination of the Dissenting literature of the time shows differences of view between the various branches of Dissent over all the 'practical grievances'.[2] Yet the more advanced wing, those most involved in the alliance with radical politics, were already beginning to coalesce around demands for total disestablishment of the Church, and for the general adoption of the Voluntary System of religious endowments. In May 1834, Edward Baines, the M.P. for Leeds, presided at a conference of 400 Dissenters which called for an end to the union of Church and State.[3] It was a policy that thrived. Early in the 1840s the 'Religious Freedom Society', founded in 1839 to promote 'the Civil Equality of all Religious Denominations'— and in fact to attack the church rates—committed itself to disestablishment.[4] In 1844 the first Anti-State-Church Conference assembled in London 'to commence efforts for the disenthralment of religion from the secularizing influence of State control', and to bring about 'the extinction of the union between Church and State'.[5] Support for this frank avowal of disestablishment was still fairly sectional. The Baptist union was the only body formally represented at the Conference. But the dynamic was being generated which led the 'British Anti-State-Church Association', founded at the Conference, to transform itself, in 1853, into the astonishingly influential 'Society for the Liberation of the Church from State Patronage and Control'. Leaders of the Church of England saw the writing on the wall early in the 1830s. They also realized that an attack upon ecclesiastical property was likely to be the first occasion Dissenters would choose to try out their new militancy—since it was a popular policy, fed by radical propaganda, and least likely to divide them internally. Joseph Hume's pressure in Parliament for a radical inquiry into the nature of ecclesiastical property had preceded Grey's appointment of a Commission in 1832.

Hence the gloom of the bishops and clergy. 'Perhaps one of the most alarming characteristics of the present time', wrote Bishop Bagot of Oxford in 1834, 'is the rapidity with which questions of the deepest importance are brought before the public, and hurried in in such quick

---

[1] W. Dealtry, *A Charge Delivered in the Autumn of 1834 at the Visitation in Hampshire* (London, 1835), p. 2.

[2] See F. R. Salter, 'Political Nonconformity in the 1830's', in *Transactions of the Royal Historical Society*, 5th Series, 3 (1953).

[3] W. H. Mackintosh, *Disestablishment and Liberation. The Movement for the Separation of the Anglican Church from State Control* (London, 1972), p. 4.

[4] Manning, *Protestant Dissenting Deputies*, p. 50.

[5] Mackintosh, *Disestablishment and Liberation*, p. 27.

succession, as to give no respite to the constant irritation of popular excitement.'[1] The amount of legislation was indeed new: the reform of Parliament, of municipal corporations, of the Irish Church, of the factory regulations, of the old Poor Law. Some churchmen doubted if the Church could survive a reform passed by a Parliament they believed to be in the grip of a reforming mania. To a few in Oxford it seemed as if the liberal temper of the age, coming on top of the repeal of the Test and Corporation Acts and Catholic Emancipation, had torn the last shred of propriety from erastianism. When the Whigs reformed the Irish Church in 1833, Keble preached his famous Assize Sermon on 'National Apostasy'. In his account of the birth of the Oxford Movement, William Palmer wrote of the prevailing sense of upheaval: 'The press was wholly in favour of revolutionary liberalism in religion; so were the leaders of opinion—the fashionable prophets of the age.'[2] Samuel Wilberforce, meditating in 1831 upon the fate of the martyred King Charles, lamented 'the true march-of-mind spirit' which described the opinions of those about to reform the Church.[3] It was Newman whose sensitivity to liberal errors was the most finely attuned. In 1841 he assailed the unfortunate Robert Peel for a speech he had delivered at the opening of a Reading Room in his constituency at Tamworth. Peel, of course, was a devoted lay member of the Church, a distinguished Church reformer, a Tory. But he was also touched by the 'steam-age mentality', a man who believed in the cultivation of 'useful knowledge', a practitioner of empiricism in politics. At Tamworth in 1841 he appeared to suggest that virtue and morality could be acquired by all men of goodwill, whatever their religious party, through education. Newman was astonished. 'Christianity is faith, faith implies a doctrine, a doctrine propositions, propositions yes or no, yes or no differences,' he pointed out. 'Differences, then, are the natural attendants on Christianity, and you cannot have Christianity and not have differences.' There was a conclusion: 'when, then, Sir Robert Peel calls such differences points of "party feeling", what is this but to insult Christianity?'[4] His logic was a little austere, yet Newman had caught the atmosphere of liberalism correctly. Its prevalence amongst educated opinion appeared a grave threat to the spiritual integrity of a Church governed by the State. Newman was perhaps unusual in the clarity with which he isolated alien ideas, but in some degree or other fears comparable to his furnished the context in which

---

[1] Richard Bagot, *A Charge Delivered to the Clergy of the Diocese by Richard, Lord Bishop of Oxford* (Oxford, 1834), p. 2.

[2] William Palmer, *A Narrative of Events Connected with the Publication of the Tracts for the Times* (1843) (London, 1883 edn.), p. 49.

[3] A. R. Ashwell, *Life of the Right Reverend Samuel Wilberforce, D.D.* (London, 1880), i. 59.

[4] J. H. Newman, 'The Tamworth Reading Room' [1841], printed in *Discussions and Arguments* (London, 1872), p. 284.

many churchmen viewed the prospects for the Church in the period after the great Reform Bill. It is important to realize this; it helps to explain the opposition of so many of the clergy to political liberalism—it was the creed of an antipathetic erastianism, as well as of Dissent. Theirs was not a wilfully ignorant adhesion to a comfortable old order from which they derived social privilege. It was a fear for the very survival of exclusive Christian truth. That, at any rate, is the way they saw the situation of the 1830s and 1840s. They pointed out that state protection of the Church's teaching was the sole justification for the Church's subjection to Parliament. Before 1829, when the State appeared confident of the Church, Church leaders were happy to countenance liberal reforms, like the repeal of the Test Act. After that time, when public men seemed impressed with a need to conciliate the hostile pressures for Church reform, from radicals and Dissenters, Church leaders fought concessions. Accepting the terms of reference available to them, it is difficult to see how the Church could have acted differently. But it did make the Establishment capable of being represented as the foe of liberal reform. The Dissenters, too, were caught in a dilemma. They sought a number of civil concessions and were obliged to appeal to far-reaching theories of liberal government in order to seal the necessary alliance with political radicalism, and in order to put pressure on a State which, while not unwilling to assist them, operated according to a legislative framework which continued to insist upon the maintenance of a single religious Establishment. In this situation, the most advanced Dissenters soon exaggerated their real civil disadvantages until they had inflated their device of a free Church in a free State to the proportions of a dogma. Many aspects of the popular radical politics of mid-nineteenth-century Britain accumulated around the various agencies the Dissenters created to achieve 'religious equality'.

For these reasons the 1830s were the most significant years for the relations of the Church of England with the State and with society in the nineteenth century. In reply to the alien liberalism which affected so much of the parliamentary view of ecclesiastical polity, Church leaders restated the traditional teachings on the obligation of the State to the National Church. Whigs and Tories agreed with the general principles of those teachings, of course, but they differed, as usual, over the degree of concession required to buy off the opponents of Established religion. In their new defence of old arguments, churchmen still placed the utility of religion to the State as the first advantage of a national Establishment. Bishop Bethell told the Gloucester clergy that the State had an interest in providing for the religious welfare of its subjects 'because religious motives are the only effectual security for their orderly and virtuous behaviour, and for the peace and prosperity of the commonwealth'.[1] The Archbishop of

[1] Christopher Bethell, *A Charge Delivered at the Triennial Visitation*, p. 27.

Armagh commended the Church to the Whig Chief Secretary for Ireland in 1832, on the grounds that churchmen always supported 'the side of established order and security'.[1] In 1834 Bishop Blomfield argued that 'the true peace and real prosperity of the country depend, not upon the multiplicity of minute legislative provisions, nor upon any economic regulations, however ingeniously devised, and however useful, as subsidiary aids; but upon its Christianity'.[2] Political Economy and a National Church, in short. In a sermon preached at St. James's in Westminster four years later, Blomfield explained the Christian obligation of civil obedience in language completely untouched by any accommodation with the world of the Reform Bill. The thirteenth chapter of the Epistle to the Romans, he said, provided the foundation for 'the tendency of Christianity to strengthen and uphold the institution of civil government, and to make it effectual to the purposes for which God has given it to mankind'.[3] All the other traditional justifications of state religion were reiterated in the 1830s as well. Churchmen clearly still continued to regard Church and State as mutually dependent. 'The interests of the Church', as Bishop Monk said in the House of Lords during the Reform Bill debate, 'were inseparable from those of the country, and whatever tended to the happiness, prosperity, and liberty of the people of England was so far conducive to the interests of the Church.'[4] Those who today find the notion of religious support for civil authority distasteful will be surprised at the extent to which, in the 1830s, lay politicians of all but the most radical persuasion assumed its importance as one of the first conditions for a sound social order. Gladstone and Coleridge, two of the theorists of the Constitution most esteemed by succeeding generations, both defended the Establishment of religion for, among other benefits, providing the foundations of civil obedience.[5]

The Establishment was also defended for religious reasons, just as it had always been in the past. It was a public provision for teachers 'exempted from the necessity of pursuing any secular calling, or resorting to any unworthy expedient for a livelihood', as Howley put it in 1832.[6] The Church defended national religious endowments, not as a basis of privilege, but as the means of bringing religion to the poor—to those who could not pay for the maintenance of a pastor. 'The endowments of the Church', Phillpotts argued, are 'mainly to be valued as a means to an end, the

---

[1] Beresford Papers. Beresford to Stanley, 4 Oct. 1832.

[2] C. J. Blomfield, *A Charge Delivered to the Clergy of the Diocese of London* (1834), p. 2.

[3] C. J. Blomfield, *The Duty of Prayer and Intercession for our Rulers. A Sermon preached in the Parish Church of St. James's, Westminster* (London, 1838), p. 8.

[4] Hansard, *Third Series*, xii. 403 (13 Apr. 1832).

[5] See W. E. Gladstone, *The State in its Relations with the Church*, 2nd edn. (London, 1839), p. 4; and S. T. Coleridge, *On the Constitution of the Church and State According to the Idea of Each* (1830), ed. John Barrell (London, 1972), p. 43.

[6] William Howley, *A Charge Delivered at his Primary Visitation*, p. 45.

greatest of all ends, the full instruction of the *people* in the knowledge of those truths which can "make them wise unto salvation".'[1] It is interesting that the popular presentation of the case for the Establishment often stressed the purely religious benefits of the Church. In May 1835 the *Churchman*, a monthly begun in January of that year to provide a cheap and popular organ for the defence of the Church, listed six 'reasons for supporting the Established Church at all times'. Only one of those reasons —that the Church had been 'instrumental in securing many and great blessings to the nation'—was not directly concerned with spiritual cultivation. The Establishment was defended on the grounds of the truth of its doctrine, the purity of its Liturgy, the pastoral office of the clergy, its devotional life, and the benefits of diffusing spiritual care throughout the land.[2] On another occasion the same journal presented arguments to prove the mutual dependence of Church and State: 'the destruction of the one cannot happen without the subversion of the other'.[3] This too was untouched by anything that had happened since the end of the eighteenth century.

The Church, furthermore, continued to urge the State to give more instalments of direct financial support for the building of new churches— the last grant had been made in 1824—and for popular education conducted by the Church. Blomfield had taken the opportunity afforded by his speech on the Emancipation Act in 1829 to remind the House of Lords that the Church 'was entitled to look to their lordships for an increase of the means of doing good, for the security of her property, and for the augmentation of the number of places of worship'.[4] Bishops frequently remarked on the duty of the Government to give financial subsidies. Blomfield was unmoved in this by the impact of the Dissenters' attack upon the confessional nature of the State; in 1838 he still insisted that it was 'incumbent upon the government of a Christian country to make an adequate provision for the religious instruction of the people'. He even hoped 'that the time may not be far distant when this duty will be again distinctly recognized by the legislature of this country'.[5] As late as 1842 Julius Hare maintained that the State had a clear obligation to help the Church financially, and 'should not excommunicate itself from the duties of Christian love'.[6] In 1839 the University of Oxford petitioned Parliament in favour of more financial aid to the Church. But despite these appeals, the temper of public life really had changed. By the end of the 1830s the reports of the Ecclesi-

---

[1] Henry Phillpotts, *Charge Delivered to the Clergy of the Diocese of Exeter* (1833), p. 7.
[2] *Churchman*, i, No. V (May 1835), 98.   [3] Ibid. i, No. X (Sept. 1835), 198.
[4] Hansard, *New Series*, xxi. 123 (2 Apr. 1829).
[5] C. J. Blomfield, *A Charge Delivered to the Clergy of the Diocese of London, by Charles James, Lord Bishop of London* (London, 1838), pp. 44–5.
[6] Julius Hare, *A Charge Delivered to the Clergy of the Archdeaconry of Lewes* (London, 1842), p. 39.

astical Commission had begun to reveal that the existing wealth of the Church, however redistributed, was not the bottomless purse which the radicals and Dissenters had represented it as being. Yet Parliament did nothing to help the Church with the problems of expansion. Peel, on forming his Conservative administration in 1841, contemplated a further measure of state aid but abandoned the idea when he also considered the uproar it would cause amongst Dissenters.[1] Instead, he passed the District Churches Act of 1843, which enabled the Ecclesiastical Commissioners to augment the stipends of clergy serving newly founded churches through loans from Queen Anne's Bounty. Parliament never again made any grants of public money to help the Church. Another point had been reached in the modification of the confessional nature of the State.

Churchmen did reply to the Dissenters' attack on ecclesiastical endowments by themselves pointing to the difficulties in the central principle of the Dissenters' Church polity—the 'Voluntary System' of religious endowments. The most influential critique of that system came, not from the Church of England, but from the Scottish Presbyterian divine, Thomas Chalmers. In 1838 he was invited to London to give a series of public lectures in defence of national Establishments of religion. These were hugely successful, attended by fashionable audiences, and extensively reported. At the heart of his analysis was an attack on 'Voluntaryism', or a 'Free Trade' in religion. Those most in need of receiving the Gospel were also those least likely to pay for ministers to teach them, he argued.[2] The Establishment principle *was* compatible with what Chalmers called external, or 'ab extra' Voluntaryism: voluntary offerings in support of additional religious enterprises undertaken by existing churches, or to set up new missions. Such, he maintained, were parliamentary votes in aid of Church schools. But internal Voluntaryism, 'ab intra', when a congregation paid their own minister directly, and where the sustenance of religion was entirely dependent upon the will of the people and the market forces, made no adequate provision for the diffusion of truth amongst those without the ability to pay for it. In the end he went on to show that the State could not be 'denationalized'. Legislators could not dissociate their actions from their religious beliefs, and as Parliament was collectively the sum of the individual opinions of which it was composed, religious measures would be promoted by religious men.[3] This atomistic view of the State, and the derivation of its religious obligations, contrast strongly with Coleridge's essay of 1830 on Church and State, with its organic concepts and almost mystical doctrine of group personality. Chalmers's lectures were

---

[1] Chadwick, *Victorian Church*, Part I, p. 223.

[2] Thomas Chalmers, *Lectures on the Establishment and Extension of National Churches; delivered in London from April 25th. to May 12th., 1838* (Glasgow, 1838), Lecture II.

[3] Thomas Chalmers, Lecture III.

much more influential with public men; they corresponded to the empiricism of British Constitutionalism.

Yet Chalmers's analysis did not apply universally. English Dissenters and Irish Roman Catholics had shown that a very extensive system of religion could be sustained on the Voluntary System. But he was correct in pointing to the premium which Voluntaryism imposed on the freedom of ministers. It was something which most worried English churchmen about the effect of the Voluntary System. They saw the risk that a minister would teach 'not so much in accordance with the vital spirit of the Gospel, as to meet the taste of his hearers'.[1] Both Irish priests and English and Scottish Dissenting ministers were believed to reflect the political passions of their flocks as a result. Opponents of Voluntaryism ignored the fact that such ministers and flocks were usually drawn, anyway, from the same social class, and had a natural political sympathy. They pointed to the example of America, where, it was supposed, 'the evil spirit of sectarianism has wrought its perfect work,' as Arnold wrote,[2] and where, as a result of Voluntaryism, the Government would eventually, as Gladstone believed, 'own no Christian name or ordinance whatever'.[3] In this Gladstone was, at least in the perspective of time he had set himself, incorrect. Despite the formal separation of Church and State in the federal and state instruments of government, and despite the universal Voluntaryism and the luxuriance of religious sectarianism, civil government in the United States retained a Christian character.[4] Blomfield, too, used the example of America to exhibit the disadvantages of the Voluntary System: 'great numbers are without any teachers at all, or at least without any who deserve the name ... vast districts are, to all appearances, rapidly sinking into heathenism'.[5] But in the first half of the nineteenth century it was the masses in England who were, as churchmen kept declaring, sinking into heathenism. America displayed an impressive and widespread religiosity.

The Voluntary System of religious endowments was in fact fairly neutral. Its consequences depended upon the enthusiasm for religion available in a society at any given time. State provision for religion did not, of itself, generate further support unless other social forces were calculated to regard religious practice as necessary for eternal deserts or social well-being. In mid-nineteenth-century England, as it happened, the middle-class enthusiasm for religion provided just such an available social force: the financial support given to religion by that class laid the groundwork for the Victorian religious boom. The defence of Established religion was best

---

[1] James Henry Monk, *A Charge Delivered to the Clergy of Gloucester*, p. 27.

[2] Thomas Arnold, *Principles of Church Reform*, 3rd edn. (London, 1833), p. 14.

[3] Gladstone, *The State in its Relations with the Church*, p. 287.

[4] See Norman, *The Conscience of the State in North America*, p. 75.

[5] C. J. Blomfield, *The Uses of a Standing Ministry and an Established Church. Two Sermons* (London, 1834), p. 39.

set upon another basis. The arguments about endowment were not theoretically central to the Establishment principle, however much they were forced on by the Dissenters' selection of ecclesiastical property as the spearhead of their attack. Established churches could exist without state endowment. Their best defence lay in a recognition of their service in offering religious sanction, Christian morality, as the basis of law and political order. Churchmen saw this, although they found themselves diverted into a defence of endowments by the Dissenters' assault. This defence was on weaker ground, but it was, again, characteristic of the nature of English political experience that questions of money and fairness took up the centre of attention, while the theoretical basis of civil society was relegated to the fringe of the debate. Discussions generally came down to property. And the Church maintained that a lot of the ecclesiastical endowments, which radicals and Dissenters claimed were public property, originally derived from private donation, by pious gift and testation. How would Dissenters like it, Blomfield asked in 1834, at the height of the political row over the 'surplus' revenues of the Irish Church, if 'an attempt were made to interfere, by legislative enactment, with all the wills, and trust-deeds, which secure a certain amount of property to the various places of dissenting worship throughout the country; and to appropriate the whole, or a part of that property to secular purposes'?[1] His answer came in 1844, when orthodox Dissenters turned their wrath against the Dissenters' Chapels Bill. This was an attempt by Parliament, arising out of a number of controversies caused by Presbyterian congregations converting their chapels to Unitarianism, to regulate the legal application of Dissenting trusts. The measure was intended to help Dissenters. Yet Church and Dissent actually united in opposition. Blomfield presented a petition drawn up by the London Deputies against the Bill; both Archbishops spoke against it in the House of Lords.[2] The question of endowments formed the pivot upon which the entire debate about the Establishment of religion rested. As the rare accord of Church and Dissent over the 1844 Bill showed, property considerations were seen to be central to the propagation of religion.

This was one of the themes in Coleridge's essay *On the Constitution of Church and State According to the Idea of Each*, which was published in 1830. It consisted of arguments originally formulated in opposition to Catholic Emancipation, to Burdett's Bill in 1825. Coleridge held that state endowment was the crucial test of a national religious Establishment. A 'nationalty' or reserve of land[3] was originally set aside by society for the

[1] C. J. Blomfield, *A Charge Delivered to the Clergy of the Diocese of London* (1834), p. 10.
[2] Manning, *Protestant Dissenting Deputies*, p. 89.
[3] S. T. Coleridge, *On the Constitution of the Church and State* (1830), ed. by John Barrell (London, 1972 edn.), p. 34.

support of a class of learned men, the 'clerisy'.[1] The 'National Church', which Coleridge often uses as a sort of synonym for whatever constitutes the moral guardianship of public virtue, through historical circumstances, became confined to the Church of Christ—'a blessed accident, a providential boon, a grace of God'.[2] The nation, however, could not now alienate the clergy from the national reserve without obliterating the moral entity of the State. Coleridge elaborated this outline and introduced a number of modifications. The work was rather less influential than many modern writers have supposed. The pragmatic nature of British political and constitutional debate meant that most theoretical works were of limited appeal to men in public life. Politicians grounded themselves 'in expediency': it was an expression frequently used and conventionally agreed to mean that the blessings of the Constitution were such that no theoretical defence was required; and that reforms were much better seen as adjustments of existing practices, not attempts to make political life correspond to theoretical propositions. Coleridge's own debt to German Idealist philosophers, to the influence of Herder, was not such as to coincide with the genius of the English political tradition. His book exercised a certain influence with a few intellectuals in the Church: with Gladstone, F. D. Maurice, Julius Hare, F. W. Robertson, and Thomas Arnold. But as a practical contribution to the debate on the relations of Church and State, Coleridge's thought was nowhere near as influential as some modern commentators have supposed. The idea of a national reserve of Church property, it is true, was often raised in parliamentary discussions—but the idea did not come from Coleridge so much as from the popular historical myth, propagated by (among others) Major Cartwright, the organizer of the radical Hampden Clubs, and widely imagined to be historical fact, that the 'free' Saxon institutions of England, before the 'Norman yoke', had provided for the communal endowment of the Church with land. The frequent parliamentary discussions of the Canadian 'clergy reserves' in the later 1830s and 1840s—themselves important occasions for defining the obligations of the State in regard to ecclesiastical endowments, and judged as such by contemporaries—also popularized the notion and the vocabulary of national ecclesiastical land reserves quite independently of Coleridge's influence. Coleridge wrote that his 'nationalty' was a concept, not a historical description—'my object has been to present the idea of a National Church, not the history of *the* Church established in this nation'.[3] But the parliamentary debate turned on the actual historical origin and development of the Church: wealth and property—it was essentially practical, not theoretical. Occasionally parliamentary speakers mentioned

---

[1] Ibid., p. 36.
[2] Ibid., p. 44.
[3] Ibid., p. 45.

Coleridge's essay, usually in a context that suggests that they supposed he was writing an actual historical explanation of English ecclesiastical revenues. It is difficult to escape the conclusion that these references are to be taken as attempts to back up arguments already very familiar. Quotations from Hooker, Warburton, Paley, were much more frequent than those from Coleridge. As an essay in political theory, furthermore, the *Constitution of Church and State* is not particularly respected by political theorists. Later churchmen did not, in general, rate Coleridge's influence highly. Hensley Henson, at the end of the century, wrote, 'To chain his generous conception of the national clerisy to so relatively insignificant a factor in the national life as the established clergy is to stamp his arguments as merely polemical, designed with a view to immediate political exigencies'.[1] Henson's judgement reflected English Church opinion much more accurately than Maurice—whose admiration of Coleridge's essay has only recently begun to appeal to scholars. To one recent writer the essay has seemed 'a remarkable contribution to the theory of political obligation';[2] to another, 'his frequent anticipations of the modern standpoint seem of an almost uncanny appositeness'.[3] The contemporary respect for Coleridge's contribution to the discussion of the relations of Church and State is no doubt explained by this observation.

Gladstone certainly admired Coleridge's essay. There are several references to it in his own work, *The State in its Relations with the Church*.[4] But those philosophical explanations of the relations of Church and State that Gladstone acquired from Coleridge were precisely those that he immediately abandoned—even as his own book was rolling off the press in 1838.[5] Gladstone's own contribution had enduring political importance; not because of its theoretical arguments, which were largely ignored, but because of the author's frequent retractions of the position he had sought to establish in it. The book became a sort of textual guide to the old Tory view of the confessional office of the State. As the architect of the Disestablishment of the Irish Church in 1869, and as the favourite of the Nonconformists, Gladstone became the most important British advocate of the doctrine of 'a free church in a free state'—a doctrine he none the less applied selectively. *The State in its Relations with the Church* was the work of a Tory High Churchman. It claimed that the State, which was conceived organically, in the Coleridge manner, had a 'personality' which could identify the sacred truths of religion and which had the obligation to

[1] H. Hensley Henson, ed., *Church Problems*, p. 57.

[2] John Barrell, in his Introduction to the 1972 edition of Coleridge's essay, p. xix.

[3] Bernard M. G. Reardon, *From Coleridge to Gore. A Century of Religious Thought in Britain* (London, 1971), p. 89.

[4] Gladstone, *The State in its Relations with the Church*, pp. 6 and 12.

[5] For Gladstone's explanation, see D. C. Lathbury, *Correspondence on Church and Religion of William Ewart Gladstone* (London, 1910), i. 18.

protect the Church as the institution which transmitted them. Gladstone believed

That in national societies of men generally the governing body should, in its capacity as such, profess and maintain a religion according to its conscience, both as being composed of individuals who have individual responsibilities to discharge and individual purpose to fulfil, and as being itself, collectively, the seat of a national personality, with national responsibilities to discharge, and national purposes to fulfil: that it must have the extrinsic, and, in proportion as it is good government, will have the intrinsic, qualifications for professing and maintaining such religion.[1]

Part of this doctrine of the State Gladstone tried to keep going for a few years, but most of it began to fall away at once. In 1840 he was still able to write that if the rulers of the State had given support to the Church 'merely because she propounds opinions which are theirs, and not because she is the actual holder of Divine truth and authority, then, whatever be her merits, they are acting in the spirit of error'.[2] The trouble with so philosophical a notion of the British State was that it clearly did not square with the reality. Men had only to look at its actual conscience—at Lord John Russell, Lord Melbourne, Lord Palmerston—and find it all rather unconvincing. Gladstone himself, indeed, noticed enough to modify his grand design. Five years later he wrote to Newman

The State cannot be said now to have a conscience, at least not by me, inasmuch as I think it acts, and acts wilfully, and intends to go on acting, in such a way as no conscience . . . can endure. But the State still continues to act in many ways *as if* it had a conscience. The Christian figure of our institutions still remains, though marred by the most incongruous associations. There are, therefore, actual relations of the State to Religion—I mean to determinate religion—which still subsist and retain much vitality, and offer opportunities of good in proportion to it, however they may be surrounded with violent moral contradictions . . . I have clung to the notion of a conscience, and a Catholic conscience, in the State, until the idea has become in the general mind so feeble as to be absolutely inappreciable in the movement of public affairs.[3]

Even in this awakening Gladstone was self-deceived. There had certainly been dramatic changes in the degree of support Parliament was prepared to give to aspects of the Church Establishment in the 1830s, but almost nobody before that had believed that the State had a conscience. The articulation of the theory of the British Constitution in this fashion was quite alien; it was an intellectual's figment. Gladstone's book, Macaulay remarked, 'is a measure of what a man can do to be left behind by the

[1] Gladstone, *The State in its Relations with the Church*, p. 26.
[2] Gladstone, *Church Principles Considered in their Results*, p. 296.
[3] Lathbury, *Correspondence of Gladstone*, i. 71 (19 Apr. 1845).

world'.[1] Gladstone himself rapidly saw the need to scramble back to constitutional realities.

His work, however, did have considerable merit in identifying some significant changes in parliamentary attitudes. He catalogued a large number of instances in which the State was already giving recognition and support to religious bodies other than the Establishment. He pointed to the 'gross anomaly of principle' implied by state financial support for most denominations in the Colonies.[2] Like Newman's meditations upon the Tamworth Reading Room, Gladstone's logic isolated the real division between parliamentary practice and the maintenance of an exclusive State Church. 'This divorce of religion from government will proceed upon the principle that men of all religions, or none, are alike to be considered competent for the duties of citizenship[3]—a state of affairs, of course, which exactly corresponded with the effects of Catholic Emancipation. Gladstone was not ready to surrender the lower grounds of Establishment.

I still think, as firmly as ever, that the connection between Church and State is worth maintaining [he wrote in 1847], but I cannot pledge myself to uphold, under all circumstances, all the civil and proprietary claims of the Church, and this for two reasons, both weighty: the one, that I think some of them may require to be qualified in deference to the spirit and recognized principles of our modern legislation; the other, that I have too plainly seen them, with my own eyes, hampering and obtruding the fair demands of the Church upon the State for her own more essential purposes.[4]

Gladstone had gone through a great deal to arrive at this position, including resignation from Peel's administration in 1845 because he believed that his support for the Maynooth Grant policy was a violation of his own published arguments in defence of the exclusive protection of the Established Church.[5]

Another work written in these years to defend the idea of a national religious establishment incorporated a certain amount of theoretical argument. Thomas Arnold's *Principles of Church Reform*, published in 1833, was less theoretical than Coleridge's or Gladstone's books, and was, accordingly, more widely read. But it attracted very little actual support, and a good deal of scorn. Van Mildert thought it 'exquisitely absurd'.[6] Arnold was oppressed by the 'evil of Dissent'—the weakening consequence for a national profession of religion of the existence of so large a body of Dissent. He therefore proposed 'to constitute a Church thoroughly

[1] Quoted in Alec R. Vidler, *The Orb and the Cross. A Normative Study in the Relations of Church and State with Reference to Gladstone's Early Writings* (London, 1945), p. 52.

[2] *The State in its Relation with the Church*, p. 277.

[3] Ibid., p. 304.

[4] Lathbury, *Correspondence of Gladstone*, ii. 7 (15 Feb. 1847).

[5] E. R. Norman, *Anti-Catholicism in Victorian England* (London, 1968), p. 29.

[6] E. Hughes, 'The Bishops and Reform', p. 478.

national, thoroughly united, thoroughly Christian, which would allow great varieties of opinion'. The Church Establishment, in fact, was to be broadened and expanded in order to incorporate most brands of Dissent: only Roman Catholics, Quakers, and Unitarians were to be omitted. 'As all classes of society require the services of the ministers of religion, the ministry should contain persons taken from all; and in a national church, all the great divisions of the nation should have a share in the government.' Laity as well as clergy were to be incorporated into ecclesiastical government. This new contrivance, Arnold supposed, would prevent 'the dissolution of the Establishment altogether—that is, in other words, the public renouncing of our allegiance to God; for, without an establishment, though it may happen that the majority of Englishmen may still be Christians, yet England will not be a Christian nation—its government will be no Christian government—we shall be wholly a kingdom of the world, and ruled to none but worldly principles'.[1] This was exactly the result which the Dissenters, then at the height of their assault upon the Church, denied would be the result of a withdrawal of state patronage from religion. Few Dissenters had as yet advanced to the frank espousal of secularism in government; few, when they did so, really grasped the implications of what they were demanding. Most certainly envisaged a Christian State—though one not giving legal preference to one church over another. Arnold's position was more logical. Churchmen who denounced his essay usually did so because of its latitudinarianism, and its clear bias to political liberalism. Arnold's belief in the absolute unity of Church and State—they were to be literally the same body—and his abhorrence of the 'superstitious' doctrines of the Church confessed by those opposed to his sort of total erastianism, were enough to dispatch the work from the realm of possibilities. It awaited the latitudinarianism associated with modern ecumenical endeavour, to discover a prophetic quality in Arnold's historical insensitivity.

The legislative measures which, in these years, actually adjusted the relationship of Church and State were the work of both Whig and Tory administrations. Precedents steadily accumulated as the Dissenters' 'practical grievances' were disposed of practically, on grounds of expediency. The ultimate constitutional issues were seen with great clarity by opponents of each measure, but politicians were usually unprepared, either out of conviction, or out of a desire to avoid widening the area of controversy, to halt the gradual diminution of the State's confessional obligations once the process had begun. Both the main political parties were largely composed of churchmen; it was the radicals, and O'Connell's Irish Catholic liberals, who, in parliamentary terms, represented advanced opinion on the religious question. The major political parties were content

[1] Arnold, *Principles of Church Reform*, pp. 28, 31, 41, 45, 75.

to make piecemeal concessions, declining to consider the theoretical implications of their actions. Thus the materials of the liberal State were being assembled with no clear intention of making structural alterations. This general refusal to see individual issues through a screen of ideology allowed the Church of England to survive as an Establishment. But it began to apear more and more anomalous.

The Irish Church Act of 1833 admitted the principle, as Bishop Bathurst gleefully told the Archbishop of Canterbury, 'that the State has a right to re-model the Church as to its internal arrangements'.[1] Precedents were made for the parliamentary deployment of ecclesiastical property, although, after considerable discomfiture to the Whig ministry, the principle of applying 'surplus' Church revenues to secular purposes was avoided. The radicals were disappointed. But for many churchmen the Act appeared extremely drastic: church cess (rates) were abolished in Ireland; a graduated tax on benefices replaced the old First Fruits, incomes and revenues were placed under the management of a permanent Royal Commission; eight bishoprics were amalgamated or suppressed. There was opposition to the suppression of the ancient sees; still more to the permanent Commission. Archbishop Howley was more upset by the centralizing tendency of the Commission than by the powers over ecclesiastical property given to it.[2] He was also alarmed about 'the possible extention of the principle on which the measure is framed'.[3] It was as an indication of the sort of drastic reform the Whigs were likely to apply to the English branch of the Establishment that the Irish Act prompted most fears. The Oxford divines who gathered at Hadleigh rectory hoped to arrive at a clear defence of Church principles to counter the coming storm. Newman hurried back from Italy, Keble preached his sermon on 'National Apostasy'. Archbishop Beresford, the Irish Primate, saw the Irish Act as 'a prelude to the downfall of the national Church'.[4] It looked like the first-fruits of the reform of Parliament.

By the time the Whigs managed to deal with the English Church, however, radical enthusiasm was already seeping away. Peel's brief Tory administration in 1834–5 had succeeded in giving friendly churchmen a large share in the Commission of inquiry which preceded legislation. The Church Act of 1836, and subsequent measures of 1838 and 1840 helped to establish the changed temper of opinion in which churchmen defined their political options. The controversy over the English Ecclesiastical Commission was important. This permanent body, composed of laymen and clerics, incorporated in 1836, elicited a number of attitudes to the new

[1] Henry Bathurst, ii. 30.

[2] Olive J. Brose, 'The Irish Precedent for English Church Reform: the Church Temporalities Act of 1833', in *Journal of Ecclesiastical History*, 7, no. 2 (1956), 215.

[3] Beresford Papers. Howley to Beresford, 14 Feb. 1833.

[4] Beresford Papers. Beresford to Stanley, 23 Feb. 1833.

relationship of Church and State. Most of those involved in the machinery of the Commission were, not surprisingly, prepared to use it as a helpful instrument for the sound distribution of ecclesiastical resources, and, in that sense, as a proper co-operation of Church and State. Of the original thirteen members, it was provided that the two Archbishops and three other bishops should sit *ex officio*, but two of the bishops were removable at the pleasure of the Crown. This caused a lot of offence, and in 1840 all the bishops, and three deans, were added to the Commission.[1] Blomfield, its leading and most energetic member, was its most consistent apologist. He pointed out to 'those persons who have raised such an outcry against the powers of the Ecclesiastical Commission' that in many respects its powers were 'trifling and inconsiderable compared with those which have been exercised for many years past by the Church Building Commissioners, a body partly lay and partly clerical'.[2] Phillpotts was predictably a leading opponent. The Commission, he insisted, embodied 'the vice of modern legislation—all is "centralization", as it is called; a word not more strange to our language than the practice, which it indicates, is foreign to our ancient habits and feelings'.[3] Christopher Wordsworth also expressed this familiar objection: 'the dangers which our liberties, both civil and ecclesiastical, may be likely to undergo by these transfers of the deliberative and legislative duties and rights of both Houses of Parliament, our Constitutional protectors, into the hands of Commissioners and Central Boards', were not ones to dismiss lightly.[4] This sort of opposition to centralization echoed fears found everywhere in English society at the time, as the first collectivist reforms began to set up administrative machinery. This was the age which, in reaction, produced Toulmin Smith's 'Anti-Centralization League', and the popular antipathy to Edwin Chadwick. State administrative machinery seemed a sinister and un-English encumbrance to individual liberty. Opposition to centralization, in fact, was so much part of the current vocabulary of politics, that there is almost no clearer evidence of the extent to which the attitudes of the Church mirrored prevailing assumptions. Some men were prepared to make an exception in their general hostility to state interference and centralized administrative machinery in the interests of reforming particular social evils. So in the Church, too, there were some like Blomfield, who recognized the need for exceptional measures to deal with the antiquated structure of ecclesiastical finance. Regarded in this perspective, as an instance of state collectivism,

---

[1] Chadwick, *Victorian Church*, i. 139.

[2] C. J. Blomfield, *A Charge Delivered to the Clergy of the Diocese of London, by Charles James, Lord Bishop of London* (1838), p. 22.

[3] Henry Phillpotts, *Charge Delivered to the Clergy of the Diocese of Exeter by the Right Reverend Henry, Lord Bishop of Exeter* (London, 1836), p. 33.

[4] Christopher Wordsworth, *The Ecclesiastical Commission and the Universities* (London, 1837), p. 6.

the creation of the Ecclesiastical Commission has another significance. Whereas the tendency of the century was towards a partial disengagement of Church and State, the Commission moved the State in the opposite direction. It inaugurated an increased intimacy of Church and State, concerned with property, the very centre of social values. This sort of ecclesiastical collectivism, much as it was loathed by some churchmen, gave a renewed lease of life to the practice of Established religion.

The State acquired some of its new administrative machinery as a result of reforms which transferred to the secular responsibility of government tasks previously entrusted to the Church. Here the Dissenters' agitations unwittingly helped the growth of government. The Marriage Act of 1836, which allowed the licensing of Dissenting chapels for weddings, ended the exclusive rights of the Church over matrimony. Purely civil marriages were also provided for. Under the centralized control of the Registrar-General, civil registrars in each locality were required to send in returns under the conditions prescribed in the Registration Act of 1836. Registration of births, deaths, and marriages was, as a result, transferred from the parochial administration of the Church to the State—to the new Poor Law machinery. After ten years, however, fewer than 8,000 weddings had been performed in Dissenting chapels,[1] an indication, no doubt, of the extent to which the Dissenting agitators had exaggerated the prevailing sense of grievance—as well as the dislike of associating registration with the Poor Law administration. Most of the clergy of the Church of England rather welcomed the new arrangements, which released them from the obligation—which some had performed with a noted inefficiency—of making returns of marriages. But there were reservations about the constitutional implications, and a feeling that the religious nature of the marriage contract had somehow been undermined by the State, as Phillpotts said in Parliament.[2] 'It would certainly have been more consonant with the principle of a Government professing Christianity to have recognized Marriage as a sacred institution, and to have required the sanction of religion in all cases, as essential to the contract', Copleston argued—but he added that he did not really expect 'much actual evil' to follow. He regarded the new arrangements for registration as 'the supply of a defect in our civil institutions which one only wonders should have so long existed'.[3] Bagot was perhaps more typical of the episcopal attitude to the Acts. He wrote of 'the degradation of the holy rite of Matrimony, from a religious to a mere civil contract; and the tendency which the other Act has to lower the value of the sacrament of Baptism in general estima-

[1] Addison, *Religious Equality in Modern England*, p. 63.

[2] Hansard, *Third Series*, xxxv, 604 (28 July 1836).

[3] Edward Copleston, *A Charge Delivered to the Clergy of the Diocese of Llandaff by Edward, Lord Bishop of Llandaff* (1836), p. 15.

tion and respect'.[1] The legislation certainly extended the practical separation, in a particular field, of religion and national life. It also added directly to the accumulating machinery of the State—and provided the State with some accurate statistical information. It was perhaps this last result that was in the end the most significant for the development of modern government.

Lord John Russell's Tithe Commutation Act of 1836 also created a new department of government: a permanent Board of Tithe Commissioners. The Act was not, in general, opposed by the Church. According to Copleston, writing in 1833, at the time of Althorp's Tithe Bill, the advantages of a tithe settlement 'would consist in the removal of that popular declamation, which is always at hand, whenever either national or local discontent affords occasion to the disturbers of the public peace'.[2] This was certainly true. The Church had an immense amount to gain by the removal of the popular discontent tithe caused—an ill will frozen for posterity in the Staffordshire 'Tithe Pig Groups', made for cottage decoration in the early nineteenth century.[3] It was an ill will the more unwelcome to the clergy because a large portion of the tithes were anyway owned not by themselves, but by ordinary landowners.[4] Phillpotts had defended tithes as a species of property: 'to legislate about tithe on any principle not applicable to property of other descriptions, would be to violate the right, and shake the title, of all property whatever'.[5] But when it came to Russell's Act in 1836—'that great change in the temporal relation between the clergy and the people'—even Phillpotts saw the advantages of a settlement which 'for ever extinguished those heartburnings and jealousies, which a collision of the temporal rights of the clergy with the pecuniary interests of their people, are at all times likely to enkindle'.[6] Not a single clerical or episcopal petition against the Bill was presented. As the Act went into effect, another link of Church and national life began to disappear. It disappeared very slowly. It was not until 1936, after many legislative adjustments to the scales of tithe rentcharge, and after a final flourish of anti-tithe agitation in rural East Anglia early in the 1930s, that the end of commuted tithe finally came within sight.

The payment of compulsory Church rates, that other unpopular tax for the maintenance of the State Church, was not abolished until 1868. The

---

[1] Richard Bagot, *A Charge Delivered to the Clergy of the Diocese of Oxford* (Oxford, 1838), p. 16.

[2] Copleston, *A Charge Delivered to the Clergy of the Diocese of Llandaff by Edward, Lord Bishop of Llandaff* (1833), p. 21.

[3] See H. A. B. Turner, *A Collector's Guide to Staffordshire Pottery Figures* (London, 1971), p. 115.

[4] Warre Cornish, *The English Church in the Nineteenth Century*, i. 119.

[5] Phillpotts, *Charge* (1833), p. 20.   [6] Phillpotts, *Charge* (1836), p. 8.

conflict with Dissent was very bitter. In the definition of liberal political principles, and as a catalyst in the alliance of Dissenters with political radicalism, the Church-rate controversy had a major importance. The Church continued to insist on the continuation of the legal rights of Establishment. In a lot of parishes, it is true, rather than face local disruption, the Church either suspended the levy of rate or arranged local compromises with the Dissenters. But compromises were not possible with the more militant, who were out to make a point—who were stirring up the campaign against the rate in order to contrive a general debate on the legal position of the Establishment. Full of the confidence inspired by the reforming atmosphere of the early 1830s, and additionally anxious to free themselves from the obligation to pay for the maintenance of the parish church at a time when they were building hundreds of chapels of their own,[1] militant Dissenters recognized in Church rates a perfect target for attack.

Church rates were levied on all occupiers of property, for the upkeep of churchyards and the naves of parish churches. They were voted each year by the Easter vestry meeting, to which all parishioners, regardless of their religious affiliation, were entitled to go, on the principle that the National Church included everyone. Early in the 1830s, Dissenters began to pack vestry meetings in some parishes and refuse to levy the rate. The legal obligation to maintain the fabric of the parish church was clear, but the means of enforcement were impractical. The offence was punishable by ecclesiastical courts, which, of course, by the mid-nineteenth century, were highly inappropriate tribunals for hearing cases about local taxation. The enforcement of their rulings would also depend upon the ordinary secular processes of law. This enabled the Dissenters to raise a secondary uproar about the evils of ecclesiastical jurisdiction. Before long, as was inevitable, a few Dissenters were imprisoned for refusing to pay the rate, and then test cases were seized upon by agitators to give extravagant publicity to the case against Established religion. So were the protracted legal cases arising over refusal to levy rates by packed vestries. The notorious Braintree case, begun in 1837, did not reach a final decision, in the House of Lords, until 1853. Legislative clarification was the obvious solution, but the Dissenters' agitation had exposed the central principles of Establishment too much for politicians to be able to agree on an accommodation. The Church itself hoped for what Connop Thirlwall, the Bishop of St. David's, described as 'a measure which, without a sacrifice of existing rights, would remove the occasions of discord afforded by the present state of the law'.[2] The Dissenters hoped for a simple abolition. In 1834

[1] Manning, *Protestant Dissenting Deputies*, p. 176.
[2] Connop Thirlwall, *A Charge Delivered to the Clergy of the Diocese of St. David's by Connop, Lord Bishop of St. David's* (London, 1842), p. 12.

Althorp attempted legislation to make the repair of church fabrics a charge on the Treasury: a principle equally offensive to Dissenters, for it continued to recognize the national obligation to maintain the Church. In 1837 Spring Rice abandoned a scheme to replace the rate with funds drawn from the Ecclesiastical Commission, after strong representations from Church leaders.[1]

The Church's contention that Church rates involved 'the very principle of a National Establishment of religion'[2] was not without some measure of popular support. In 1836 Parliament received more petitions seeking the retention of the rates than praying for their abolition,[3] and this was in a year of great excitement over the question. Local disputes polarized around political division—Tories standing for the union of Church and State, radicals and liberals seeking a change. The rate question was assuming a very large importance. In 1840 the Tories actually managed to get a rate voted in Rochdale, after the most intense conflict with local Dissenters, led by John Bright, in which the ultimate issue of the survival of an Established Church was directly placed before the public.[4] Popular appeals did not always go the way the Dissenters claimed they would. To the Dissenters' argument that they ought not to be taxed for the maintenance of another man's religion, churchmen could cross-reference their several 'practical grievances' to show up an inconsistency: 'they demanded that their dead should be interred in the Church-yards, their own ministers officiating', Bishop Monk argued, 'at the very moment that they required a special exemption from those rates by which the church-yards are fenced and maintained'.[5] Others noticed that the Dissenters' principle 'virtually asserts that no man is to be taxed, for any thing which is not beneficial to himself *individually*'. And out of that, as Dr. Dealtry, the Chancellor of the Diocese of Winchester, suggested in 1834, a considerable principle of welfare arose—'he is not to allow a public grant to be made for eminent services to the State, nor a starving dependency to be relieved, nor a slave colony to be emancipated, if these measures involve expense, unless it can be proved that he gains some direct personal advantage'.[6] But the Dissenters, of course, would allow all these things. Their battle was a propaganda exercise. Basic constitutional principles were laid bare; exaggerated rhetoric wrapped the issues in advanced extensions of logic which almost no one really intended. Churchmen answered in kind. As Lord Shaftesbury said of Spring Rice's Bill in 1837, 'This measure cuts up by the roots all our national homage to God, which is the meaning of a Church Establish-

---

[1] Chadwick, *Victorian Church*, i. 147.
[2] John Kaye, *Charge* (1834), p. 5.
[3] Gladstone, *Church Principles*, p. 378.
[4] Ward, *Religion and Society*, p. 188.
[5] James Henry Monk, *Charge* (1835), p. 25.
[6] Dealtry, *Charge* (1835), p. 6.

ment'.[1] Most parliamentarians, whilst recognizing the gravity of the constitutional issues, were, as usual, unprepared to allow a fundamental scrutiny of the basis of the national political order over an issue like Church rates if they could avoid it.

The question of education was another one which churchmen and Dissenters saw in terms of religious Establishment. And in this field, too, the Church adhered strongly to the belief that the State had an obligation to preserve the national profession of Christianity. In 1831 the Whigs set up a system of state primary schools in Ireland, which provided for religious instruction on non-denominational lines—according to a formula known as 'Common Christianity'. It consisted of basic Trinitarian tenets, with what were thought of as sectarian luxuries creamed off.[2] As a social enterprise the scheme had merit: it was an attempt to educate the children of Catholic and Protestant populations in the same classrooms, so forging, it was hoped, a future social cohesion. But it was religiously premature, intruded upon a society in which people really did believe in their differences. All the Churches had initial reservations, yet all gave the scheme a trial. By 1850 the Catholics had had enough, and at the Synod of Thurles the principles of the system were condemned as theological 'Indifferentism'. This was the view taken of the scheme all along by the Church of England, which resolutely refused to allow anything like it to be mooted for her own schools. Churchmen insisted on the State's duty to assist catechistical instruction. Manning, when Rector of Lavington in 1838, said that the education question 'wears only by accident a political, or civil aspect; its real character is moral and spiritual: and its importance not temporal alone, but eternal; involving the everlasting welfare of souls for whom Christ died'.[3] This was the view most commonly heard within the Church. It was a view attacked by liberal intellectuals—especially by the 'Central Society for Education', a radical agency for propagating the ideals of national, secular, compulsory education, on the Prussian model. But the appeal of that was very slight. When, in 1833, the radical Roebuck introduced a motion for national secular education to Parliament, he was opposed by both Whigs and Tories. The Dissenters, too, were independently complaining about the Church's practical monopoly of education. They were divided about what to do. Some sought the creation of a state system on the Irish model, with 'common Christianity'—which was anyway very similar to the religious teaching in the British and Foreign Society's schools—as the form of instruction. Some of the more advanced argued for a secular system, as favoured by the radicals, seeing this as the

---

[1] Lathbury, *Correspondence of Gladstone*, ii. 344.

[2] D. M. Akenson, *The Irish Education Experiment* (London, 1970), p. 159.

[3] *National Education. A Sermon Preached in the Cathedral Church of Chichester by Henry Edward Manning, M.A.* (London, 1838), p. 10.

only device which could effectively guarantee that no religious body would enjoy an ascendancy over any other. As a corrective to the Church's educational seniority—which Dissenters usually failed to appreciate was largely due to the Establishment's greater enterprise, for the Church, and not the State, had planned and built their schools—this was a drastic solution. Its full implications were not appreciated by its Dissenting exponents. But churchmen feared that the Whigs would make some concessions. They did not fear concessions to secularism, for the Whigs were as opposed to this as almost everyone else. But they did think a measure of 'common Christianity' might be required in schools receiving state financial maintenance grants (and that included most of the Church's National Schools). As a possible alternative, reformers might seek to separate religious from other instruction in the school curricula. Blomfield, a lifelong advocate of confessional education, denounced 'all attempts to divorce religious from secular instruction in the process of education; a separation which must of necessity be made if the Government of the country were to take the education of the people into its own hands'.[1] Gladstone was just as adept at sniffing out the tendencies to religious indifferentism in education. 'Not contented with excluding religion from the province of government, the spirit of the age struggles with no less zeal to introduce, as its substitute, education', he wrote in 1838.[2] It was a perceptive long-term forecast.

The Church's insistence on state financial support for Church education was brought to something of a test in 1839. In that year Lord John Russell prepared to establish a state training (normal) school for teachers in which both denominational and undenominational instruction was to be given. The rights of the Established Church did not appear to be recognized, and after strong episcopal representations the plan was dropped.[3] It was immediately after this that the Whigs set up the Committee of the Privy Council on Education, charged with the distribution of the parliamentary grants to the schools of the National Society, and the British and Foreign Society. In 1833 a sum of £20,000 a year had been voted. In 1839 this grant was increased by £10,000 and allocated to all schools which passed inspection by the new Committee, regardless of their religious affiliation. The bishops of the Church of England were not especially happy about the whole arrangement, but their conflict with the Government came over the inspectorate question. The Committee of Council intended to divide religious instruction into 'General' and 'Special' categories, and this looked

---

[1] C. J. Blomfield, *A Charge Delivered to the Clergy of the Diocese of London by Charles James, Lord Bishop of London*, 2nd edn. (London, 1846), p. 45.

[2] Gladstone, *The State in its Relations with the Church*, p. 315.

[3] James Murphy, *Church, State and Schools in Britain, 1800–1970* (London, 1971), pp. 19–21.

like a device to separate secular and religious education. Following the guidance of Kay-Shuttleworth, the Committee did not contain any clerical members and that, too, offended the Church. After a short period of mutual non-co-operation, Archbishop Howley and the Government came to an arrangement in 1840, whereby the two Archbishops were empowered to veto the appointment of inspectors of Church schools, or dismiss them if necessary.[1] It looked like an impressive victory for Church principles. The bishops had not restrained themselves in seeking to defeat what they saw as a scheme 'of indifference to all considerations, if not of Religion, yet of truth or falsehood in religion'.[2] For the Church, 1839 was a key year in its determination to be the educational agency of the nation. 'Though we do not assert an empire over the consciences of those who are not within the pale of her communion, nor presume to interfere with them in the education of their own children,' Blomfield declared, at one of the public meetings called to oppose the government plans, 'we say that the Church is the authorized and recognized organ and instrument of National Education in the largest sense in this country.'[3] Copleston chose the occasion of the crisis to point out the evils of state interference in education on *laissez-faire* grounds: 'I entertain serious doubts, whether it is for the public good that such matters should be under the control of Government —and whether they ought not to be left wholly to private competition, and to that desire of secular advantage, which is sufficiently strong to raise up the means of instruction wherever they are wanted.'[4] Edward Stanley, the Whig Bishop of Norwich, advanced the claims of the Church on grounds of social utility—'Christian education alone deserves the name of education; it is through Christian knowledge only that we can hope to see the social and political condition of our countrymen purified and perfected'.[5] There were some who disagreed. Thirlwall favoured education based on undenominational principles; and Hook, in 1846, proposed a state system of education as the only way to provide an adequate number of schools at a time of rapid population growth.[6]

The success of the Church against the Whigs in 1840 was not repeated with the Tory Government in 1843—when the educational clauses of

---

[1] James Murphy, *Church, State and Schools in Britain, 1800–1970*, p. 29.

[2] Henry Phillpotts, *Charge Delivered to the Clergy of the Diocese of Exeter by the Right Reverend Henry, Lord Bishop of Exeter* (London, 1839), p. 21.

[3] *Speech of the Lord Bishop of London on National Education at the Public Meeting held in Willis's Rooms on Tuesday, May 28th, 1839; His Grace the Archbishop of Canterbury in the Chair* (London, 1839), p. 10.

[4] Edward Copleston, *A Charge Delivered to the Clergy of the Diocese of Llandaff by Edward, Lord Bishop of Llandaff* (London, 1839), p. 31.

[5] *A Charge Delivered to the Clergy of the Diocese of Norwich by the Right Reverend Edward Stanley, D.D.* (Norwich, 1838), p. 19.

[6] C. K. Francis Brown, *The Church's Part in Education, 1833–1941* (London, 1942), p. 27.

Graham's Factory Act had to be abandoned in the face of Dissenters' claims that they favoured the Church of England. According to the London Dissenting Deputies, the clauses were 'a severer blow at religious liberty than has been aimed at since the rejection of Lord Sidmouth's bill in 1811'.[1] Even the Wesleyans, usually noted for their friendliness to the State Church, joined the attack on the educational clauses. Graham's proposal was that schools should be established for children in workhouses and in textile factories, paid for with government loans, and maintained by the poor rate. The schoolmaster was to be a member of the Church of England, and the school managers were to be placed under the local incumbent. Religious instruction was to be according to the forms of the Church, with a right of exemption for Dissenters. The Church had not in fact asked for this plan, was not a party to it, and was rather taken aback by the storm of abuse which now fell about it. Peel's Government was only attempting a very limited extension of the State's interest in education, and believed it was continuing existing practice in recognizing the position of the National Church. But the Dissenters' outburst, which was successful, left the Church's claims in a much weaker position than before. In 1845 Bishop Denison told his clergy that the chances for state support for Church education for the poor had diminished—'I presume that the result of the attempt which was made two years ago to effect this object, as regards the manufacturing districts, has convinced most persons that no such endeavour is likely to be successful'.[2] It had become inevitable that eventually the State would have to promote its own schools if pressures from Dissent would not allow it to use the Church. This collectivist solution was postponed until 1870, largely because opinion was still reluctant to concede that the State was the appropriate body to educate the nation's children. Behind the pamphlets and the petitions inspired by the Dissenters' opposition to the educational claims of the Church, in this area of national life too Dissenters were forcing the State towards the accumulation of still more powers. This was not their real intention. With all their belief in self-help, and private enterprise 'Voluntaryism', their view of the proper role of the State was the reverse of collectivist. The great Dissenting politicians of the second half of the century, like John Bright, envisaged a liberal State whose virtue would be judged on a scale calculated according to its inactivity in large areas of private contract and individual initiative. But in agitations against the Church's position in education, as elsewhere, the Dissenters in practice obliged the adoption of new responsibilities by the State.

Some of the Dissenters' agitations failed. In 1834 a radical motion to

---

[1] Manning, *Protestant Dissenting Deputies*, p. 343.

[2] *A Charge Delivered to the Clergy of the Diocese of Salisbury, by Edward Denison, D.D., Bishop of Salisbury* (London, 1845), p. 21.

exclude the bishops from the House of Lords, which got some Dissenting support in the country, secured sixty-seven votes. But the many subsequent attempts to raise the question never reached anything like success, and the bishops are still in Parliament. Their entitlement was defended for some very erastian reasons—Bishop Maltby declared that the bishops' presence in the Upper House was 'a very important and effectual check upon their exercise of spiritual, as well as temporal, power'.[1] For most practical men, resistance to a reform of this sort derived as much from a desire to avoid tinkering with the Constitution, with attendant risks of creating dangerous precedents, as it did to respect for the religious Establishment. 'If, therefore, it be possible to remove the Bishops from the House of Lords by any *legal* act of Parliament,' remarked Samuel Butler in 1834, 'it is possible by the same process to abolish the Bill of Rights, the Habeas Corpus, and every constitutional provision.'[2] That was, in fact, precisely what Parliament had the power to do if it chose; but as usual in British experience politicians were unwilling to go into such ultimate matters.

Parliament was not ready, either, for the admission of Jews. In 1830 a Bill based on similar principles to the Catholic Emancipation Act was introduced to the Commons and defeated by 228 to 165 votes. Most of those who objected to the measure believed the admission of Jews to Parliament was incompatible with the Christian character of the Constitution. Some had additional reservations about having Jews in the House: 'a few of the leading men among them would soon obtain as much influence there as they already possess over Three Per Cent Consols'.[3] After the rejection of several further Bills, Jews were admitted to Parliament by Tory legislation in 1858, subject to the same sort of securities which protected Church patronage and certain offices of State in the Catholic Act of 1829. The clergy of the Establishment were generally hostile to attempts to abandon Christian tests for membership of the body which governed the Church; but many prominent laymen, and notably Gladstone, were converted to the cause of Jewish relief by appeals to civil liberty.

The Dissenters' campaign for the opening of the ancient Universities was protracted as a result of the opposition it encountered. Yet it was helped by internal liberalism. In 1834, sixty-three resident members of the University of Cambridge petitioned Parliament for the admission of Dissenters to degrees. Dissenters could already matriculate at Cambridge; at Oxford, subscription to the Articles of the Church had to be made on admission. London University was founded as a secular corporation in 1836, and this to some extent lessened the pressures on the ancient

---

[1] Maltby, *Charge* (1834), p. 30.

[2] Samuel Butler, *A Charge Delivered to the Archdeaconry of Derby* (London, 1834), p. 16.

[3] A. M. Hyamson, *A History of the Jews in England*, 2nd edn. (London, 1928), p. 266.

foundations. But the matter was not a purely practical grievance. Within the ancient Universities themselves, liberal dons urged the admission of Dissenters as a lever in their own internal strife; to represent their conservative colleagues as the reactionary guardians of unreformed abuses. And the Dissenters, for their part, were out to subvert the Establishment as much as they were concerned with securing higher education. 'So intimate is the connexion of the Church and the Universities, so closely are their interests blended and entwined', said Bishop Monk in preaching to the University of Cambridge in 1835, that those seeking to destroy the Church began by 'putting restraint and force upon the Universities'.[1] In 1854 the statutes of Oxford were reformed following a Royal Commission of inquiry, and scholarships and the degree of Bachelor of Arts were opened to Dissenters. In 1856 the reforms for Cambridge included the admission of Dissenters to the Master's degree. But it was not until 1871 that the Test Act removed most of the offices and the administration of the Universities from the control of the clergy of the National Church.

In opposing reform in order to preserve the Christian basis of the Constitution—which was the way the Church saw its office as an Establishment—the bishops and clergy were easily made to appear extremely illiberal. Some, of course, actually were. But most churchmen tried to isolate conciliation of genuine 'practical grievances' from propagandist attempts by radical Dissenters to discredit the principle of Established religion by making its actual operation appear oppressive. 'While, however, I renounce as vain and illusory the hope of softening by concession the hostility of the enemies of the Established Church,' Bishop Kaye declared in 1834, 'I am prepared to cooperate cordially in the removal of any real grievance to which the Dissenters of this kingdom may be subject, for this I conceive to be not a concession, but an act of justice.'[2] In practice, as they discovered, churchmen were rarely able to apply this distinction, because the Dissenters themselves did not.

With each concession the Establishment was further compromised in constitutional theory. It looked, by the 1840s, as if the State was moving not to some future secularity, however, but to a broader practice of religious Establishment—to 'concurrent endowment', to an admission of all Christian opinion to the benefits of official patronage. Some Dissenters feared this potential development, believing that any connection between Churches and Government was corrupting to the integrity of both. The Church of England saw in concurrent endowment, or some allied device, not merely its own reduction of status, but an advance of religious 'indifferentism' by the State. In 1845 the question of concurrent endowment

---

[1] James Henry Monk, *A Sermon Preached before the University of Cambridge* (London, 1835), p. 22.
[2] Kaye, *Charge* (1834), p. 4.

was brought to a head by Peel's proposal to convert the annual grant to the Roman Catholic seminary at Maynooth, in Co. Kildare, into a permanent charge upon the Treasury. Parliament passed the necessary legislation, but only after a national outburst of popular Protestantism, mixed with considered objection to concurrent endowment as an acceptable constitutional expedient. Dissenting 'Voluntaryists' used the Maynooth furore to stage a great public assault upon the Establishment principle in general. The Anti-Maynooth Conference at Exeter Hall in April 1845 was disrupted by the secession of the militant Voluntaryists from the Anti-State Church Association.[1] Some churchmen, like Peel and Gladstone, came to see the Maynooth grant as a tolerable sort of concession to Dissent—even to Irish Catholic Dissent. Bishop Pepys explained to the clergy of Worcester that, in opposition to their declared views, he had voted in favour of the grant because he did not believe Catholicism was 'so full of errors, so corrupted from its original purity, as to make it a sin in a Protestant State to contribute towards the education of its ministers'.[2] Those who opposed the grant had to admit, as the Archdeacon of London put it, that 'the proposal does not differ in principle from the policy which this country has for many years pursued'. The grant was, all the same, 'a formal recognition of the Roman Catholic religion as a religion fostered and protected by the State'.[3] Gladstone, in agreeing to the justice of the grant, noticed that it was, none the less, 'a proposal reopening so much of the great question of Church and State—in principle almost reconstructing their relation for Ireland, and, depend upon it, seriously modifying the aspect of the case for England also'.[4] Nor was Ireland the only area of obvious inconsistency. It was Gladstone who had in 1838 drawn attention to the 'gross anomaly of principle' involved in the state support of all the Christian churches in the Colonies.[5] Phillpotts was concerned about the same discrepancy.[6] In England too the *Regium Donum* was a state grant to Protestant Dissenters; and it was not until 1851 that militant Voluntaryists had persuaded the Government to withdraw it. Despite this, and despite the failure of the House of Lords to get a general concurrent endowment in Ireland, at the time of disestablishment in 1869, practical concurrent endowment has continued in several forms in Britain—in educational grants to the different denominations' schools, in stipends to chaplains in the armed forces of the Crown, and in prisons, hospitals, and other public

---

[1] Norman, *Anti-Catholicism in Victorian England*, p. 46.

[2] *A Charge Delivered to the Clergy of the Diocese of Worcester by Henry Pepys, D.D., Bishop of Worcester* (London, 1845), p. 23.

[3] William Hale Hale, *The Approaching Contest with Romanism Considered in a Charge addressed to the Clergy of the Archdeaconry of London* (London, 1845), pp. 7, 15.

[4] Lathbury, *Correspondence of Gladstone*, i. 68 (Jan. 1845).

[5] Gladstone, *The State in its Relation with the Church*, p. 277.

[6] Phillpotts, *Charge* (1839), p. 2.

institutions. The 1840s and the Maynooth question saw the issues raised with greater clarity than was usual. In this moment of transition in 1843 the Disruption of the Scottish Presbyterian Church Establishment and secession of a large number to form a new Dissenting denomination weakened the Establishment principle still further. For the Scottish controversy was over patronage; it involved a rejection of erastianism; it was a very serious crisis in the relations of Church and State. The Church of England, nurturing within itself those with 'Puseyite' distaste for state control of religion, looked on with unease.

By the 1840s there were therefore impulses directing the Church to reconsider the exact nature of its association with the State. Many who believed that the changed relationship of the State to the Church had heavily compromised the competence of Parliament to govern the Church began to contemplate the possibility of an independent vehicle for the expression of ecclesiastical opinion. More extreme advocates of Oxford anti-erastianism began to scrutinize the propriety of any sort of National Church in the novel conditions of a mixed legislature. Some, despairing of a neat arrangement of complicated realities, departed to Rome. The most extreme of the Oxford purists was Richard Hurrell Froude, whose early death in 1836 saved him from the logic of his ideas. It was Froude who divided the Church into 'Z's' (Establishmentarians) and 'X's' (those more concerned with spiritual autonomy than national religion). Froude's linear vision had discerned that the Repeal of the Test Act and Catholic Emancipation commenced 'a new system of Ecclesiastical Polity', in which Parliament had forfeited its legitimate claim to govern the Church by compromising its own religious composition.[1] Newman, much under Froude's influence, had in 1833 come near to endorsing disestablishment —'not that I would advocate a separation of Church and State unless the nation does more tyrannical things against us; but I do feel I should be glad if it were done and over, much as the nation would lose by it, for I fear the Church is being corrupted by the union'.[2] Keble too believed that the Church might be corrupted by the State, in the new terms of their association, and criticized Parliament in 1839 for having too low (too liberal) a doctrine of the Church.[3] The Tractarians were not alone in believing that the time had come for the independent spiritual authority of the Church to receive a structural expression. As early as 1826 Whately had anonymously suggested something of the sort,[4] though he later modified his opinions. Most of those who, by the 1840s, were interested

[1] See R. H. Froude, *Remains* (London, 1838), Part Second, i. 184; 'Remarks on State Interference in Matters Spiritual' (1833).
[2] Mozley, *Letters of John Henry Newman*, i. 395.
[3] *British Critic*, Oct. 1839.
[4] See his *Letters on the Church: By an Episcopalian* (1826).

in the idea were not opponents of Establishment; they saw an instrument of Church autonomy as simply a necessary development in view of the practical disengagement of the State from its exclusive religious professions. A number of bishops began to suggest the restoration of the deliberative functions of the Convocations, or the creation of synods, in their *Charges* during the 1840s. The reluctance of Parliament to take up needed ecclesiastical reforms—both because of the opportunity it gave Dissenters to ransack the Church, and because of the difficulty of conciliating divergent parties within the Church—was beginning to impose intolerable strains. Bishop Denison noticed in 1842 that this situation 'really preserves us from change', for 'alterations which the Church cannot make for herself are not made without her, either by the civil power, or in any other mode'.[1] There had been earlier straws in the wind. Lord Henley's *Plan of Church Reform*, written in 1832, and influential with parliamentary reformers o the Church at that time, had envisaged a revival of Convocations; Arnold had maintained in 1833 that it was the absence of proper ecclesiastical government that had led directly to the multiplication of Dissent.[2] In 1843 and 1844 numerously signed petitions, got up by the clergy, favoured some sort of autonomy. In 1844 Whately remarked on the 'increased and still increasing interest taken in the question'.[3] The first stirrings of new life had begun. In 1847 the last of the old formal Convocations presided over by Archbishop Howley included a petition for the restoration of synodical powers in its address to the Crown; and in 1851 a 'Society for the Revival of Convocation' was established. Some bishops and many of the laity were extremely dubious, suspecting that ecclesiastical party interests were seeking influence.[4] By a series of stages, the Convocation of Canterbury began to debate ecclesiastical business, and by 1855 it had more or less recovered a proper existence as a deliberative assembly. In 1861 a similar revival of the York Convocation occurred—after the death of Archbishop Musgrave, who disapproved of the whole enterprise. Convocation was unreformed, antique, unused to the practices of debate; but a significant step had been made towards the 'denominalization' of the Church of England. The partial disengagement of Church and State, that is to say, was on both sides: the Church was beginning to create a practical independence—as yet only a germ, a tendency—which was eventually to replace the old interdependence of religious truth and civil order. As the evolution of ecclesiastical self-government proceeded during the following hundred years, Church and State matched each other, step for step, in the

[1] Edward Denison, *A Charge Delivered to the Diocese of Salisbury* (London, 1842), p. 34.

[2] Arnold, *Principles of Church Reform*, p. 46.

[3] Richard Whately, *Thoughts on Church Government* (London, 1844), p. 25.

[4] See P. J. Welch, 'Revival of the Convocation of Canterbury, 1852-5', in *Journal of Ecclesiastical History*, 10 (1959).

withdrawal from Hooker's model of a single Christian polity.[1] Churchmen had very little alternative. In 1843 the Archdeacon of Bristol noted that the Church had witnessed 'repeated interference of legislation in affairs strictly ecclesiastical, without any opportunity of exercising her own judgment upon them'.[2] But very few at this time supposed the creation of ecclesiastical deliberative bodies incompatible with the Establishment of religion, otherwise they would not have been created.

The condition of ecclesiastical law also pointed to the need for some drastic clarification of the civil and religious spheres. In 1832 Bishop Blomfield, in advising one of his clergy about the rights of the civil courts in ecclesiastical matters, wrote that the decay of Church discipline and the prevailing chaos of jurisdictions were evils for which the Church was itself 'not altogether answerable'.[3] This was true. It was another aspect of the nineteenth-century dilemma: an erastian Establishment subject to a Parliament unwilling to discharge its ecclesiastical responsibilities. The reform of ecclesiastical law, when it came, further separated the spheres. In 1857, for example, wills and testamentary cases were removed from the jurisdiction of the Church, and in the same year matrimonial cases were handed over to the civil courts. There were some unforeseen consequences of ecclesiastical law reform. Following the Report of a Royal Commission, in 1832, the old Court of Delegates was abolished and its jurisdiction transferred to the Privy Council. In 1833 appellate jurisdiction passed to the Judicial Committee of the Privy Council. Under the provisions of the Church Discipline Act of 1840 appeals against episcopal judgements in clerical cases also went to the Judicial Committee. In these arrangements the State was actually practising a very thorough erastian control of the Church. And the body involved, the Judicial Committee, was not even one that provided that its membership was restricted to members of the Church. The possible consequences were not appreciated until 1850, when the Judicial Committee, in giving judgement about the Church's exact teaching on the nature of Baptismal Regeneration, in the Gorham case, appeared to be determining the doctrines of the Establishment. The resulting crisis in the relations of Church and State threw into a disagreeable clarity the problems a liberalized machinery of government placed before churchmen. Manning left the Church of England. The Church survived that: but the Gorham case appeared to symbolize all the theoretical anomalies which the reforms of the preceding twenty years had stacked up. Yet in spite of everything, the Church adhered to its traditional

---

[1] A concept which never had the historical clarity churchmen tended to suppose anyway: see E. T. Davies, *The Political Ideas of Richard Hooker* (London, 1946), p. 94.

[2] Thomas Thorp, *A Charge Delivered to the Archdeaconry of Bristol* (Bristol, 1843), p. 22.

[3] Fulham Papers, Lambeth Palace Library. Blomfield Letter-Books, 336, Blomfield to the Revd. G. Woodroffe, 13 Aug. 1832.

insistence on the union of Church and State. And there were a few compensations to be derived from public interest in the various religious controversies. 'Even the discussions with which the press teems upon Ecclesiastical questions', noticed Copleston in 1848, 'are evidence of the interest now felt in such things—deeper interest than was ever felt within the remembrance of the past generation.'[1] In 1844 old Archbishop Howley deposed 'that at no other period in our history has more affectionate reverence been felt towards the Church'.[2] Yet the Victorian religious revival was full of anxieties and disputation. Today men look back to the golden days of Victorian Christianity as to a time of wonderful stability. To Victorian churchmen it seemed as if the Church was lurching from one crisis to another, in a painful adaptation to the hostile realities of a liberalizing political Constitution. And to these torments were about to be added the intellectual difficulties over Biblical authority. To contemporaries it seemed a bleak period.

[1] Edward, Copleston, *A Charge Delivered to the Clergy of the Diocese of Llandaff by Edward, Lord Bishop of Llandaff* (London 1848), p. 4.

[2] William Howey, *A Charge Delivered at his Ordinary Visitation by William, Lord Archbishop of Canterbury* (London, 1844), p. 16.

4

The Victorian Church and the Condition of Society

Just as in the first half of the nineteenth century a section of the leadership of the Church assimilated the body of social and economic ideas that contemporaries believed represented the progressive intelligence of the age—Political Economy—so in the second half of the century a section adopted the new attitudes of collectivism. This shift of opinion again demonstrated the extent to which Church leadership was responsive to the development of social and political attitudes within the intelligentsia. Unhappily for the prospects of a single Church approach to social questions, however, the adoption of collectivist solutions by Church leaders took place at a time when the ideals of *laissez-faire* had just acquired an orthodoxy among the parochial clergy—among those less in contact with the centres of political and intellectual thought. This seepage downwards in society of the advanced thought of one generation, to become the commonplace reference of the majority in another, was again the reflection of developments in the secular world. After the mid-century, simplified versions of Political Economy became popular with all classes.

The self-help ethic and the competitive principle, public economy, and the belief that those forms of government were best which least interfered in social or economic relationships: these became the staple matter of the 'Gladstonian' popular politics of the second half of the nineteenth century. In adopting criticisms of *laissez-faire* practice and the competitive principle at the same time, Church leaders managed, once again, to cut themselves off from the main current of working-class social thought. Both in adopting Political Economy, and in rejecting it, therefore, the leadership of the Church fostered intellectual assumptions which contributed to making the rapport with the working classes they so earnestly sought little more than a pious hope. There were, of course, many exceptions to the general trends. Not all Church leaders adopted collectivist social attitudes, but clearly those who did were the more influential, or at least the most vocal. Not all the parochial clergy assimilated *laissez-faire* values; many continued to reflect older, paternalistic attitudes. The Church, that is to say, was a fair reflection of the diversities and aspirations of the society in which it existed. Where it failed to join its authority to the reform of social or economic evils, its failure can usually be explained not by its adhesion to reactionary politics or class selfishness, but by the considered application of what were supposed the most enlightened social theories. Sometimes the failures resulted from class attitudes of which the clergy were often wholly unconscious: their remorseless goodwill was often ineffective, despite their social idealism and their hard work for the removal of social evils, simply because it was ignorant of working-class cultural values.

Church leaders of the mid-century continued to build more churches in the populous districts, and the masses continued to decline to attend them. Most thought a break-through would eventually come, and pressed ahead with preparations for further church extension. 'It is true that during the last twenty-five years much has been done,' wrote Blomfield, on launching a new appeal to end the 'Spiritual Destitution' of London in 1836.[1] Yet there were only 140,000 seats in church for a population of 1,380,000 in London.[2] The problem still seemed formidable. It also seemed a clear priority: provision of worship was, for those of convinced Christian belief, the first and essential condition for the creation of a better society. That is why so many churchmen saw church building as more urgent than social reform. The precepts of Political Economy, which placed a limit on the amount of direct interference which would anyway be conducive to social improvement, underlined this priority. Blomfield therefore looked to the State to help in the Church-extension programme. This form of help to the poor, he wrote, 'appears to me to be implied in the very principle of a religious establishment'.[3] By 1851, the year of the religious census, the Church of England had actually built 2,529 new churches, at a cost of £9 millions, since the start of the century. Two-thirds of the money had been constituted through voluntary offerings, and the rest had been met by the parliamentary funds made available to the Church Building Commissioners.[4] Yet the new churches were usually more than half empty; and those who did attend them were more likely to be drawn from the lower-middle class then from the working classes. Church leaders began to realize that the anticipated break-through had not occurred: that as a way of preparing for social amelioration the attempt to create a wor-shipping Christian society was less and less likely to be successful. When Bishop Tait started a new building fund in 1862 he declared, 'Let it not be supposed that I am speaking as if the sole way to remedy the social evils of an overwhelming population, and to propagate true religion, was to multiply Churches'.[5] The religious census of 1851 had itself assisted this

---

[1] C. J. Blomfield, *Proposals for the Creation of a Fund to be applied to the Building and Endowment of Additional Churches in the Metropolis* (London, 1836), p. 6.

[2] Ibid., p. 7.   [3] Ibid., p. 13.

[4] Soloway, *Prelates and People*, p. 314.

[5] R. T. Davidson and W. Benham, *Life of Archibald Campbell Tait* (London, 1891), i. 445.

realism. It had shown that 66 per cent of available seats in churches of the Establishment were unoccupied on Sundays. It has also shown that 3,773,474 people attended the worship of the Church of England on the sample day chosen, and that 3,487,558 attended Catholic or Protestant Dissenting churches. The Church barely enjoyed an over-all majority: it was a finding that added to Dissenting buoyancy. But most significantly of all, it was the absence of the working classes from any place of worship at all that appeared to stand out from the survey. This was clearly stated by Horace Mann in the Report which he published with the census in 1854— a Report otherwise notable for its historical inaccuracies and its propagandist tone.[1] Church building, in the second half of the century, did not keep pace with the increases in the population, and at the end of the century, in fact, the Church actually began to decrease absolutely in size.

Working-class men and women were not irreligious, though middle-class churchmen did not usually appreciate this, not having adequate tests by which to identify the nature of working-class religiosity. The propaganda of reformers had depicted the poor as so sunk in appalling conditions that the practice of morality and religion was scarcely possible. 'My first surprise about East London was its extreme respectability,' wrote Winnington-Ingram, later Bishop of London, on his arrival as head of Oxford House in 1888; 'in morality and a sense of decency they are far ahead of dwellers in some other parts of London.'[2] To most working-class men in Victorian England this sense of 'decency' was how they recognized Christianity. Amongst the unchurched masses—those working men whose manner of living so terrified the middle-class reformers—there resided a sturdy and inarticulate culture of religious belief. Most churchmen failed to recognize its existence. At the turn of the century, for example, Charles Masterman supposed that only between 1 and 4 per cent of the population of south London were practising Christians. He was astonished to learn, from Mudie Smith's *Daily News* census of 1902-3, that in his own area one in every six of the population went to church.[3] His miscalculation was characteristic of the prevalent tendency to overemphasize the extent of the national refusal to go to church or chapel. Church leaders had long imagined that working men were easily opened to irreligious ideas. 'An Uneducated Multitude', Bishop J. B. Sumner observed in 1832, were 'the prey of any designing writer who, from whatever motive, finds it his interest to persuade them that the Gospel is a "cunningly devised fable".'[4] As it

---

[1] C. J. Blomfield, *A Charge Delivered to the Clergy of the Diocese of London by Charles James, Lord Bishop of London* (London, 1854), pp. 6-7.

[2] A. F. Winnington-Ingram, *Fifty Years' Work in London (1889-1939)* (London, 1940), p. 2.

[3] Chadwick, *Victorian Church*, Part II, p. 237.

[4] *A Charge Delivered to the Clergy of the Diocese of Chester by the Rt. Revd. John Bird Sumner, Lord Bishop of Chester* (London, 1832), p. 9.

turned out, however, it was the intelligentsia who turned away from Christianity because they came to see it as a 'cunningly devised fable', and the working classes who continued a stable adhesion to a diluted version of the faith. The religious sense of working men penetrated the early Labour movement. It combined with self-help doctrines to give English popular thought its most characteristic moralistic qualities. But it found no real home in the Churches. To some extent the Catholic Church, with its Irish labouring congregations, captured some working-class enthusiasm: but this was Irish and not English in style. The Dissenting Chapels attracted the lower-middle classes rather than the labourers. The Church of England seemed, to most working-class men, an institution for the well-to-do. 'Look at them rich wagerbonds as the parsons hunt and dine and drink with,' remarked a country woman whose words Engels recorded in 1844.[1] This was, by the mid-nineteenth century, largely a social myth too: the country clergymen depicted in this fashion was already part of folk memory. Most mid-century parsons were becoming more earnest, less happy with the crude country pursuits of the generation that had preceded them. But their reputation with the labouring classes did not change.

The Church continued to see its most important social function as the recovery of social harmony. It hoped to act itself, through the parish network, as the cohesive force which would knit the classes together in a return to what was imagined as the more stable relationships of the past—before the industrial towns and the disruption of rural society had intruded the existing evils. The parish system was thought to be ideal for this because it was territorial. 'It leaves no corner of the country, however dim the spot, without a pastor bound to look to it', according to Blunt's manual on the duties of the parish priest, published in 1856.[2] Contemporaries did not regard the parish system, despite the obvious difficulties of adapting it to conditions of social mobility, as 'the bane of Victorian Anglican planning' that some modern writers have considered it.[3] The parish clergyman was charged with responsibility for everyone within his appointed area, regardless of their particular religious profession, or absence of one. Social leadership within such small units was, in theory, easily attained; the clergy also continued to be responsible for a considerable amount of secular administration attached by law to the parish as an area of civil government. In reality, of course, these conditions often tended merely to identify the parson with the State, or with local landed wealth or other

---

[1] Frederick Engels. *The Condition of the Working Class in England* (1844) (Blackwell edn., Oxford, 1958), p. 304.

[2] J. J. Blunt, *The Acquirements and Principal Obligations and Duties of the Parish Priest*, 5th edn. (London, 1856), p. 215.

[3] J. H. S. Kent, 'The Role of Religion in the Cultural Structure of the Later Victorian City', in *Transactions of the Royal Historical Society*, 5th Series, 23 (1973), 156.

predominant class interest. Clashes with Dissenters over church rates or other issues destroyed the practical chances for social harmony in the parishes. But churchmen continued to hope that the parish system would still prove the best machinery for fostering social unity. The Church-extension programme assumed this, too. Yet in these expectations the Church was disappointed. It never managed to adjust to the life of the new industrial cities.[1] Its vision of social harmony was more crudely translated by its opponents who depicted the clergy, often with some truth, as the interested upholders of fixed social inequality. The clergy were upper and middle class. Their class assumptions and their manner of living were ineradicable. Even those who sought emancipation—who adopted 'radical' or even 'socialistic' political ideas, in the belief that this freed them from class reference—were unable to convince the working classes that the Church was on their side. It is interesting that the Church of England, which contained a much larger number of clergymen attracted to 'Christian Socialist' ideas than any other denomination, was also the Church that most noticeably failed to attract a working-class membership. A few slum priests who were socialists achieved working-class congregations for a time because they were sympathetic pastors—not because of their politics. Working-class men, like all Englishmen, did not expect their clergy to preach political opinions, and did not like it when they did so. The Baptist Church, the denomination least concerned with a 'Social Gospel', actually grew in size at the end of the century.[2] The clergy seemed unable to grasp that it was their social behaviour rather than their social ideas that kept the working people out of church. The more radical their ideas, in fact, the less sympathetic were they often likely to appear: many forms of socialism and collectivism were unpopular because they were bourgeois in origin.

It was at the parish level that most of the social work of the Victorian Church was actually carried out. The obligation was a traditional one—the clergy were charged by the Church with the duty of visiting the sick, caring for orphans, for the widowed, for the destitute. With the expansion of popular education, most parsons also had a school to supervise. Local charities and charitible institutions represented other aspects of this traditional role. The growth of state activity in social questions during the century still left the clergy as the most energetic and effective agents of welfare in each locality. Sometimes, indeed, as in the case of parsons who got themselves elected as Poor Law Guardians, new state machinery partially integrated with existing clerical duties. Because it was assumed that the clergy would ordinarily perform these sorts of services their work usually failed to excite remark. Cases of notorious neglect or dereliction of duty attracted attention—and have passed, through the publicity given by

[1] See S. Meacham, 'The Church in the Victorian City', in *Victorian Studies*, 11 (1968).
[2] P. d'A. Jones, *The Christian Socialist Revival, 1877–1914* (Princeton, 1968), p. 64.

Dissenting propaganda, into the conventional conclusion that Victorian Christianity was little concerned with social suffering. The ordinary welfare work of the clergy was also without centralized control; there was no central body to give it publicity, no output of records which historians can use to trace its extent.[1] It was work hidden away in the parishes of the land, undertaken according to local conditions, by men who did not apply a single set of social rules but who recognized the need to adjust the palliation of social evils in sympathy with variations in local conditions. In an age of individual exertion, the clergy exerted themselves individually. Men worked on their own: there were no periodic clerical gatherings, or diocesan circulars, of the sort that were familiar in the later experience of the Church. They were faced with puzzling new problems, often terrifying in their scale. If they failed to seek political solutions, that was because the general assumptions of the political culture in which they were set was in general opposed to the idea of state intervention in such questions. There were, of course, some who neglected their duties, or who failed to increase the volume of their welfare work in correspondence with the increasing awareness of the extent of social evils; there were some others who applied the least appropriate or the most tactless solutions. But probably, in the undramatic circumstances of their parishes, most were responsible for the alleviation of a great deal of suffering, and their work has passed, as Christian work ought to pass, without personal memorial.

The clergy were frequently exhorted to care for the physical welfare of the people. 'No man can know the Gospel, of which it is the characteristic that to the poor it is preached,' Bishop Denison told the Salisbury clergy in 1845, 'without feeling for the poor a melting pity.' This, he added, was a practical obligation: 'the duty of the Christian teacher is not to proclaim mere abstract truth, but to give to each one of those committed to his charge his portion of meat in due season'.[2] The Hon. and Revd. S. Best, author of *Parochial Ministrations* (1839), considered the care of the poor in each parish 'a chief object of our ministry'; for 'temporal as well as spiritual interests are committed to our care'.[3] Gladstone wrote in 1840 that the Church was 'responsible as an institution, before the bar of impartial judgment, for the social condition at large'.[4] Thomas Arnold believed that 'the social improvement of man is one of the direct objects of

---

[1] This was not only true for England: "The comparative lack of evidence for the attitude of the Church in the Social pressures of the time is a very odd gap in the story of the Church in Victorian Scotland'—A. L. Drummond and J. Bulloch, *The Church in Victorian Scotland, 1843–1874*, (Edinburgh, 1975), p. 137.

[2] Denison, *Charge* (1845), pp. 42, 44.

[3] S. Best, *Parochial Ministrations* (London, 1839), pp. 24, 40.

[4] Gladstone, *Church Principles*, p. 373.

a Church establishment'.[1] Such opinions were commonplace. Sometimes they referred to the general, national sense in which the Church sustained a 'higher' view of mankind, and so contributed to social advancement; often they related directly to the welfare duties of the parish priest. Despite the later supposition that the Victorian Church taught the poor the blessings of a heavenly reward, but left their earthly condition unattended, the emphasis of Church writers was usually on the practical service of the ministry.

The considerable numbers of clerical witnesses who appeared before parliamentary Select Committees, or Royal Commissions of inquiry, into social conditions in nineteenth-century England, was an indication not only of the extent to which the clergy were actually involved in social work, but also of the preparedness of public men to accept them as expert opinion in the various fields of inquiry. The parson was usually the local agent for one of the many philanthropic societies produced by what some contemporaries called the 'humanity mania' of the times. The organization of parish activity was sometimes such as to inspire wonder in observers: in 1884 the Bishop of Liverpool actually had to warn the clergy not to exhaust themselves in the effort. Committees and agencies had 'all multiplied enormously within the last twenty years', he wrote. 'It sometimes almost takes my breath away to hear the programme of weekly work which some excellent clergymen announce upon a Sunday, from the reading-desks, as the parochial bill of fare for the next six days.'[2] Some of them were concerned with missionary or other purely spiritual activity, but many others involved the organization of social-relief works. At St. Alban's Church in Holborn in the 1870s, for example, the well-known Ritualist priest Alexander Mackonochie ran a choir school, an orphanage, an infant nursery, a Youth Club, a Sunday breakfast for destitute boys, and a soup kitchen.[3] In many parishes there had been Clothing Clubs and Mutual Benefit societies for the poor since the 1820s. A lot had dispensaries for the sick too: these were the most important means of giving medical care to the poor. In some places—as Hook found at Coventry[4]—they ran into hostility from local doctors. The clergy were well represented on the governing bodies of hospitals, many of which were anyway under the control of Church trusts. In 1838 Christopher Wordsworth (later Bishop of Lincoln) preached a sermon in which he used the existence of the London hospitals as evidence of the social concern of the Church: 'in them we behold Him among us, as He was once in the streets of Capernaum:

---

[1] Arnold, *Principles of Church Reform*, p. 2.
[2] *A Charge Delivered to the Clergy of the Diocese of Liverpool by John Charles Ryle, D.D. Lord Bishop of Liverpool* (1884), p. 70.
[3] E. R. Russell, ed., *Alexander Heriot Mackonochie* (London, 1890), p. 213.
[4] Stephens, *Life and Letters of Walter Farquhar Hook*, i. 216.

in them we still see Him healing the sick'.[1] Gladstone cited the sermon as a testimony to the social utility of religion.[2]

Friendly Societies and Savings Banks, intended to foster the habits of thrift and family responsibility among the working classes, were also founded by the clergy in many parishes. These were not always successful, as Keble discovered, when the Savings Bank he had inspired at Hursley failed because the labourers lost interest in it.[3] One parish priest who was enthusiastic in the promotion of Friendly Societies—W. Lewery Blackley, Vicar of King's Samborne in Hampshire—moved on to advocate a state scheme of compulsory National Insurance for sickness benefit and old age. In 1880 he got the support of Edward Browne, Bishop of Winchester, for his plan.[4] In 1897 the Lambeth Conference Report on Industrial problems recommended old-age pensions;[5] by then the idea had been canvassed in parliamentary circles for some time, and had a wide measure of support among political groups. The Church's approval indicated, as was usually the case, how close the leadership was to prevailing opinion. In addition to Friendly Societies and Savings Banks, the clergy often tried to help the independence of working men by the provision of 'allotments'. Land was purchased, or donated by local landowners, or a part of the church glebe was set aside, for subdivision into plots for individual men to cultivate their own vegetables. This was not only a rural enterprise. Allotments on the edges of town and city parishes were common. To some extent, it is possible to see in this a shadow of the romanticized belief in the ideal nature of rural pursuits which so attracted nineteenth-century reformers. The Chartist Land Plan of the 1840s made the same appeal to the ideal of rural self-sufficiency, but on a much more ambitious scale. In the 1830s the Bishop of London sponsored allotment schemes on the edge of the metropolis. Later in the century they were often supported by speakers at Church Congresses.[6] A few churchmen went rather further, and became concerned in the promotion of ideal communities. Bishop Stanley of Norwich was interested in them. The Utopian Community attempted in Wales by the Revd. J. M. Morgan, with the help of a group of clergy, was not successful.[7] More realistic was the planned migration of poor families

---

[1] Christopher Wordsworth, *Heathen and Christian Philanthropy, Their Practical Results Compared* (London, 1838), p. 21.

[2] Gladstone, *The State in its Relations with the Church*, p. 310.

[3] Battiscombe, *John Keble*, p. 162.

[4] See Blackey's speech at the Leicester Church Congress in 1880, in the *Official Report of the Church Congress held at Leicester* (London, 1881), pp. 60 ff.; and Browne's speech, ibid., p. 78. See also Blackey's further appeal at the Reading Congress in 1883, in the *Official Report* (London, 1883), p. 241.

[5] *Conference of Bishops of the Anglican Communion holden at Lambeth Palace in July, 1897* (London, 1897), p. 142.

[6] e.g. see *The Official Report of the Church Congress held at Leicester* (1880) (London, 1881), p. 76.

[7] Kitson Clark, *Churchmen and the Condition of England*, p. 172.

to counties or districts where there was employment. A number of clergy financed and organized schemes for this. Edward Girdlestone, a parson who became famous for his advocacy of the right of rural labourers to form unions, found that his migration scheme in north Devon forced up rural wages as a result of the creation of labour shortages in the areas from which the migration had taken place.[1] Another device often used by the clergy to help the labouring classes, and the lower-middle classes, was the co-operative combination. 'The Co-operative principle', said Bishop Mackarness of Oxford in 1873, 'has some analogies with the principles of Christian fellowship.'[2] He was a warm supporter. In 1897 the Lambeth Conference Committee on Industrial Problems gave the Co-operative principle very high praise—'it has helped to spread and strengthen the feeling of mutual membership or brotherhood, and to conciliate the interests of the capitalist, the workman, and the purchaser'.[3] In enterprises of this sort the clergy joined with leaders of the working classes themselves in the belief that self-help, individual exertion, and thrift were the qualities most likely to foster the improvement of the working man's lot. It is difficult to assess the scale of this sort of social work by the clergy: nearly all of these local schemes were transient, they passed away when the general level of working-class standards of living no longer required them. But it is clear that in very many places they were regarded by the clergy as of the utmost value in lifting working men from a wretched dependence.

Parish priests often acted as the local organizers of the large national philanthropic bodies, centralized in London. These were usually conducted by laymen—like George Williams, founder of the Y.M.C.A., and the circle of Anglican philanthropists who worshipped at the Portman Chapel in the mid-century.[4] The increase in the numbers of charitable and philanthropic bodies continued during the second half of the century; between 1850 and 1860 alone, 144 new societies for social or moral improvement were founded.[5] A lot of the work overlapped, especially as Evangelical charities usually embodied an individualistic outlook and an emphasis on their leading personalities which rendered co-operation with similar enterprises conducted by other bodies difficult.[6] Many of the organizations were interdenominational; most had some religious connection. A measure of order between the competing agencies came in 1869, when the Charity

---

[1] Bowden, *Idea of the Victorian Church*, p. 246.

[2] *Authorized Report of the Church Congress held at Bath* (London, 1873), p. 27.

[3] *Conference of the Bishops of the Anglican Communion holden at Lambeth Palace in July, 1897*, p. 144.

[4] Clyde Binfield, *George Williams and the Y.M.C.A. A Study in Victorian Social Attitudes* (London, 1973), p. 209.

[5] Kathleen Woodroofe, *From Charity to Social Work in England and the United States* (London, 1962), p. 23.

[6] Kathleen Heasman, *Evangelicals in Action. An Appraisal of their Social Work in the Victorian Era* (London, 1962), p. 20.

Organization Society was set up at a meeting which, with its attendance of bishops and the nobility, itself indicated the degree to which social good works had became fashionable. The consolidation of charitable agencies helped to prepare for the later entry of the State into the social areas they had, by their work and their propaganda, revealed as in need of greater attention.

The relief work of the clergy both in these philanthropic bodies and in their ordinary parish duties gave them a first-hand knowledge of social conditions. Each generation of priests, however, had to start from scratch: they became acquainted with realities for which their social background and training had made no preparation. But once in their posts, many went to great lengths to become experts in the social evils which encompassed the lives of their flocks. 'You possess, from the nature of your duties, a larger experience than almost any other persons of the actual state of the dwellings of the poor,' Blomfield told the London clergy in 1847.[1] The cholera epidemics of these years saw the clergy visiting the infected homes to comfort the sick and dying. Bishop Denison actually called at every house in Salisbury where a case of cholera was notified in the epidemic of 1849. A knowledge of the dwelling conditions of the working population was the inevitable consequence of such experience. Some parsons, it is true, lacked the ability or acumen to evaluate the conditions they witnessed. They did not always make the sort of correlation between environment and moral behaviour which to later generations became an obvious part of social work. One of Hook's curates, for example, was surprised to discover, in the 1840s, that there were thirteen brothels within a hundred yards of his own house—he eventually learned the information from police reports.[2] To later generations it seems astonishing that a man actually living among the poor, and in daily attendance to their needs—as this curate was—should have been so unperceptive. It is characteristic of the upper- or middle-class clergy of the Church that they sometimes attempted to acquire their knowledge of social conditions, not from the evidence of their experiences, but from newspapers, and official reports. But there were just as many parsons who did learn to evaluate the social evidence which their pastoral experience threw in their way. Church leaders were especially ready to recognize that palliatives were of little effect if the basic conditions of social life were too wretched to allow men to have a decent opportunity of living healthy and moral lives. The cholera epidemics were again important here. Blomfield urged the clergy to teach the working classes about sanitation and personal cleanliness during the epidemic of 1847, though he confessed that 'under their actual

[1] C. J. Blomfield, *A Pastoral Letter to the Clergy of the Diocese of London* (London, 1847), p. 8.
[2] C. J. Stranks, *Dean Hook* (London, 1954), p. 93.

circumstances' it was 'nothing less than an impossibility' for the poor to practise cleanliness. He also noticed that drunkenness, like filthiness, was 'too frequently the result of want', and reminded the rich of their obligations to the poor.[1] Archbishop Howley had connected environment with health and morals when supporting factory reform in 1832: 'it was a disgrace to a Christian and civilized community to allow such a system to continue merely for putting money in the pockets of master manufacturers.'[2] Bishop Samuel Wilberforce made the same sort of point when speaking of the Corn Laws in 1846. 'I know that the clergy of this country believe that the state of the great mass of the labouring population and the peasantry of England is such that they cannot desire it long to continue as it is,' he said; 'they do not wish to see them living in cottages from which the decencies of domestic life are necessarily banished.'[3] In the language of later critics, that is to say, those clergy most perceptive in their social experience were already becoming conscious that 'ambulance work' alone was inadequate: that the lives of men could only be elevated morally and spiritually if the physical circumstances in which they lived and worked were tolerable. Since the theory of the Establishment pointed to the utility of religion in the cultivation of social harmony and national well-being, a powerful reforming impulse lay within the reach of the Church. As they saw this, Victorian churchmen increasingly developed an environmental approach to social improvement—a commonplace notion to later generations, it was novel to them. The emphasis on environmental circumstance in the contemporary movement of expert opinion for sanitary reform was related to the adoption of these attitudes. The clergy were among the most enthusiastic readers of parliamentary reports, inspired by such as Chadwick and Simon, on the sanitary conditions of the poor. The allied question of urban burials—tackled as a health problem in the mid-century—directly concerned the interests of the clergy. In 1861 the first Church Congress met, and for the rest of the century these unofficial but influential annual gatherings were often taken up with issues which indicate the ready acceptance of environmentalist attitudes in the Church. In 1874, for example, at the Brighton Congress, the debate on 'The Influence of Social and Sanitary Conditions on Religion' disclosed a great willingness by almost everyone to sponsor the reform of social conditions as the essential first step in moral and spiritual cultivation. 'Any one who has attempted any schemes of improvement in any large parish', said Archdeacon Henry Fearon of Leicester, 'will find his efforts often foiled by the miserable places in which the poor live.'[4] The Revd. R. J. Simpson, Rector of St.

[1] Blomfield, *A Pastoral Letter*, pp. 8–9.
[2] Hansard, *Third Series*, x. 985 (1 Mar. 1832).
[3] Ibid. lxxxvii. 330 (12 June 1846).
[4] *Authorised Report of the Church Congress held at Brighton* (London, 1874), p. 495.

Clement Danes in London, appealed to the clergy to ask themselves 'whether the sorrows and sins of our poor people are not aggravated, if not produced, by the small, crowded, and foul dwellings in which they herd, and the unhealthy conditions by which they are surrounded'.[1]

By the last decades of the century these attitudes had acquired an orthodoxy within Church leadership. In 1897 the Lambeth Conference's Report on Industrial Problems reflected it: 'Character is influenced at every point by social conditions,' the Report declared, 'and active conscience, in an industrial society, will look for moral guidance on industrial matters.'[2] Publicists had been active in the formulation of opinion. One of the most effective—William Booth, of the Salvation Army—had himself been converted to the need for social reform because he saw that the conditions of poverty inhibited the profession of religion.[3] This is far from the crude assumption of much modern commentary that Victorian Christianity was almost solely concerned with eternal deserts and ignored the social conditions of men. Booth's conversion to social reform took place at about the same time as that of many bishops. His was a not untypical experience. 'I have keenly felt the remedial measures usually enunciated in Christian programmes and ordinarily employed by Christian philanthropy to be lamentably inadequate for any effectual dealing with the despairing miseries of those outcast classes.'[4] Many bishops of the Church of England were saying precisely this at Church Congresses in the 1880s and 1890s. Several influential works published towards the end of the century publicized the conditions of working-class life. William Booth's own *In Darkest England* (1890) had been preceded by an anonymous Congregationalist pamphlet, *The Bitter Cry of Outcast London* (1883), which similarly dwelt on the miseries of the poor. Charles Booth's great surveys of *Pauperism* (1892) and *Life and Labour of the People of London* (1899–1903) also enjoyed a considerable vogue with the upper- and middle-readers. Charles Booth actually wrote at the urging of Samuel Barnett, the Marylebone curate and social reformer who later guided the first years of Toynbee Hall. Barnett belonged to that well-known band of slum priests whose work among the poor was one of the most noble achievements of the Victorian Church. To this group belonged Brooke Lambert of Whitechapel, Watts-Ditchfield of Bethnal Green, Charles Lowder of Pimlico, Bryan King of Wapping, A. B. Goulden of the Elephant and Castle, Arthur Stanton of Holborn, Robert Dolling of Stepney and Poplar. The influence of men like these in acquainting and inspiring young clergy in the idealism

[1] *Authorised Report of the Church Congress held at Brighton*, p. 493.

[2] *Conference of Bishops* (London, 1897), p. 137.

[3] K. S. Inglis, *Churches and the Working Classes in Victorian England* (London, 1963), p. 195.

[4] William Booth, *In Darkest England and the Way Out* (London, 1890), Preface.

—even the romanticism—of social work among the working classes, was very great.

Despite their high level of interest in social conditions Victorian bishops and clergy have acquired a poor reputation in social issues. To some extent this reflects the criticism made by later social radicals, or those with more advanced collectivist solutions to social problems, that the Victorian Church on the whole declined to attempt political means of redressing social evils. Later churchmen were themselves often the first to accuse their predecessors on these grounds. To some extent, also, it reflects deliberate attempts by militant Nonconformists to discredit the public image of the Established Church by representing its officers as so involved in the preservation of their privileges as to show scant concern for the social conditions around them. As a part of the old aristocratic State, the bishops and clergy could be lumped together with landed wealth in the Dissenters' propaganda depicture of an illiberal and selfish opposition to the progressive forces in society. With their own adhesion to *laissez-faire* practices, of course, the Nonconformists had no more systematic plans for social reform than the Church; and their actual record for social relief, through their own ministers and philanthropic agencies, was perhaps less impressive than that of the Church. But the Dissenters were quick to criticize the social record of the Establishment. In 1894 the Liberation Society published an attack on the State Church which conrained a section on 'The Bishops as Legislators'. It included a table showing 'the record of the principal votes given by the Bishops in recent times' in the House of Lords, and meant to convey the impression that the bench had consistently supported every illiberal cause in the nineteenth century.[1] The same device was used by Joseph Clayton, a High Church layman whose *Bishops as Legislators*, published in 1906, began with an essay by Stewart Headlam, founder of the Socialist Guild of St. Matthew. Clayton actually conceded that the episcopal record had improved a little during the century, but contended that on social issues there was a large debit balance which had begun in the 1820s, when the bishops had voted against the abolition of capital punishment for minor crimes.[2]

It was certainly true that the bishops generally refused to assume a legislative role in social questions. But they are not to be isolated from prevailing attitudes among public men in this: most parliamentary leaders were slow to approve the planned entry of the State into the social field. For most of the century they supported individual acts of state intervention in particular fields because of necessity—it seemed the only way to deal with particular social evils. But these were always regarded as exceptional violations of a generally agreed principle that it was no proper function of

[1] *The Case for Disestablishment*, revised edn. (London, 1894), pp. 88–9.
[2] Joseph Clayton, *Bishops as Legislators* (London, 1906), p. 47.

the State to act as a social regulator. Church leaders had an additional reason for following this practice: they were anxious to avoid 'political' conduct. For many acts of state intervention included upsetting vested interests, and the opposition this elicited usually took on a political colour. Yet whenever social reforms were promoted—factory legislation, slum-dwelling clearance measures, sanitation and public-health reform, and so on—the bishops were inevitably in favour. Despite the reputation they later acquired, the Victorian bishops were earnestly interested in social reform. 'The Bishops of today', as Archbishop Benson told the Queen in 1884, 'were not like the Bishops of fifty years ago.' Their attendance to various causes put them frequently before the public; 'now meetings, lectures, temperance gatherings, constant openings of mission rooms and churches, and above all schools, familiarize them with the people as the people with them'.[1] And a sure sign of the involvement of the clergy in social questions was the growth of criticism of them for interferring too much in secular matters. In 1894 Randall Davidson, who was at the time Bishop of Rochester, addressed the clergy on industrial problems, and directly referred to these criticisms. 'We have heard', he said, 'that "the clergy are mischievously interfering in matters with which they have no concern," or that "the Church is now, as always, casting its weight on the side of capital and landlordism," or that "the growing socialism of the younger clergy is becoming seriously harmful." ' Davidson added: 'the variety of criticism serves at least to rebuff the accusation that the clergy are swayed by an ignorant unanimity of prejudice on one side or the other'.[2] It was a fair point.

By then the layered filtration of ideas within the Church was particularly pronounced. *Laissez-faire* attitudes had become the most characteristic ones among the ordinary parochial clergy, just as they had come to penetrate social thought among the nation at large. By then, the leaders of opinion had already begun to follow a section of the intelligentsia in espousing collectivist notions of the duties of the State: the most influential of the bishops reflected this in their own adoption of opinions critical of *laissez-faire* orthodoxies. This development came only after a period during which Political Economy had ousted older Tory paternalism as the most prominent feature of episcopal social thought. The vanguard of Sumner, Blomfield, Copleston, and Whately, was followed by a rising generation of bishops who readily absorbed Political Economy: Thirlwall, Wilberforce, Kaye, Stanley, and many others. By the end of the 1830s indeed, the most influential of the Church leaders were all soaked in the

---

[1] Benson Papers, Trinity College Cambridge, Diaries, 1884, p. 193 (11 July). See also A. C. Benson, *The Life of Edward White Benson*, new edn. (London, 1901), p. 277.

[2] *A Charge Delivered to the Clergy of the Diocese of Rochester by Randall T. Davidson, Bishop* (London, 1894), p. 47.

attitudes of Political Economy. 'Society will work out its own good of a temporal nature, through the medium of private interest, much better than Government can do it for us,' wrote Copleston in 1839, in a sort of summary of the prevailing ideas; 'while the general error into which all plans of centralization naturally fall—that of treating in the same manner districts wholly different in circumstances and habits—is thus avoided.'[1] Some resisted the new social doctrines, and continued to adhere to the old Tory paternalism, with its attachment to fixed rural relationships and obligations, its loathing of the new towns and the new social principles. Phillpotts stood out as the greatest of the old-style bishops until his death in 1869. Divisions of opinion between the old and the new were frequently revealed in episcopal attitudes to legislation. Thus in 1833 Blomfield had opposed the Duke of Richmond's Bill to provide public relief for distressed agricultural labourers—a model of the old view of social responsibilities —on the grounds that the measure would 'affect the free circulation of labour', and would 'relieve one class of the Community at the expense of another'.[2] This was the voice of Political Economy. Bishop Law of Bath and Wells, on the other hand, supported the Bill because it 'would have the effect of preventing much misery',[3] regardless of the economic principles involved. He spoke for the paternalists. Whately, who was Archbishop of Dublin, criticized aspects of Lord John Russell's Irish famine-relief policy in 1847 because it ignored the laws of laissez-faire— 'from what he knew of human nature he did feel that it was a perilous experiment to hold out the prospect of relief provided by law for all parties in want'.[4] The ascendancy of Political Economy in the Church's leadership had been shown in the debates on the Corn Laws in 1846— bishops who stood by the agriculturalists were fewer in numbers than before. Sixteen bishops voted for repeal of the Corn Laws, nine against. But it is not absolutely clear that a vote against Repeal was a gesture against Political Economy: the issue was a complicated one involving attitudes to the relationship between landholding and political power. Copleston voted against Repeal because he did not wish to see landed influence weakened. Some of the bishops who supported Repeal had succumbed to the propaganda of the Anti-Corn Law League: they believed that free trade would help the poor by reducing the price of provisions. But many who supported Repeal were directly under the influence of laissez-faire doctrine. Samuel Wilberforce, Bishop of Oxford, declared in the parliamentary debate that 'of this whole matter the very alphabet is to be found in the science of political economy'. It was, he

---

[1] Edward Copleston, A Charge Delivered to the Clergy of the Diocese of Llandaff (1839), p. 32.
[2] Hansard, Third Series, xviii. 673–4 (13 June 1833).
[3] Ibid. 678.   [4] Ibid. xcii. 112 (29 Apr. 1847).

went on to say, 'on the surest principles of political economy' that he himself approved the repeal. The Corn Laws were 'unnatural', since 'legislation, for the most part, is an interference with nature; good legislation is a necessary interference with nature; but where it is shown to be a needless interference, it is bad'.[1] The agricultural labourers would profit from the laws of free trade.[2] It was because of what he took to be its effect on the poor that Phillpotts attacked Repeal. What they needed, he argued, was better wages, not cheaper provisions: a clear assault upon the middle-class manufacturers, who had sponsored the Anti-Corn Law League. The manufacturers had gone to some length to show that their object in seeking Repeal was not the reduction of wages—it was Richard Cobden's achievement to have lifted the Corn Law agitation onto a moralistic level where such considerations were obscured. Phillpotts was not deceived. 'He was not capable of dealing with it as a political economist, for of political economy he was altogether ignorant,' he told the Lords with some irony. But as 'a man of plain understanding and ordinary observations', he contended that Repeal would depress wages.[3]

Bishops who supported factory reform, and yet were in general adherents of the new learning, had to explain their inconsistency. Factory regulation clearly involved state interference with contractual relationships. In 1847 Wilberforce supported the Ten Hours Day Bill by establishing humanitarian grounds for defining it as an exceptional area. This was typical of the mid-nineteenth-century difficulty over the strict application of Political Economy, and Wilberforce's solution was in fact a conventional one for Political Economists to apply.

This measure formed no exception to the rules of political economy [he said of the Ten Hours measure]. If, indeed, they attempted by legislation to regulate the wages of labour, it would be an infraction of the principles of political economy; but by this measure they did not make any such proposition—they merely said it was wrong to create wealth by the sacrifice of the health and morals of a portion of the people—that wealth so obtained was unlawfully obtained.[4]

Connop Thirlwall, Bishop of St. David's, supported factory reform, despite his belief that 'the principles of political economy were the principles of common sense', because it was 'a wholesome restraint against the abuse of power—it was substituting a system of restraint for a pernicious system of coercion'.[5] For the free operation of contractual relationships, that is to say, reasonable freedom must first be allowed to both sides of the contract, not just to the employees of labour. 'The Political Economist may declare

---

[1] Hansard, *Third Series*, lxxxvii. 322 (12 June 1846).

[2] R. G. Wilberforce, *Life of the Right Reverend Samuel Wilberforce, D.D.* (London, 1882), i. 367.

[3] Hansard, *Third Series*, lxxxvii. 316–17 (12 June 1846).

[4] Ibid. xcii. 941 (17 May 1847).   [5] Ibid. 945.

against interference with the price of labour,' declared Best in 1839; 'but every law that is made necessarily does this more or less; and non-interference in this case has the effect of delivering one party into the hands of another.'[1] The Dissenters did not have all these difficulties with the application of *laissez-faire*: following Bright, many simply opposed factory reform as undue interference by the State.

The recognition of exceptions to the general rule against state intervention cumulatively prepared for the displacement of Political Economy by collectivist ideas as the most advanced social teachings of the end of the century. It was a practical change in opinion and attitude, characteristic of English political experience. It was also an uneven change, rarely accepted systematically. The advocates of *laissez-faire* themselves acquiesced in the reforms which pulled down its edifice. Particular social evils were seen to be so urgent, so huge in scale, so protected by vested interests, that only the State had the authority and the resources to intervene in the interests of humanity. At times this was seen with great clarity. 'The whole series of laws affecting mines and factories, approved by the nation at large, directly contravenes *Laissez-faire* doctrines', V. H. Stanton, a Fellow of Trinity College, Cambridge, told the Church Congress meeting in 1880.[2] Usually the effects of reforms upon the general orthodoxy of Political Economy were less easily recognized. Men convinced of the essential virtue of *laissez-faire* attitudes nevertheless overcame their general abhorrence of state regulation in order to attend to individual social evils. Expert opinion, in the name of particular acts of social improvement—sanitation, industrial employment, food adulteration, and so forth—appealed increasingly to the central authority of the State as the only effective agency for change. Public interest, and the insistence of individual experts, eventually elicited parliamentary inquiries in the various fields of social concern. These inquiries, in turn, created a larger opinion in favour of some sort of action. Church leaders like Blomfield took a prominent part in this reform dialectic. It was intended that each issue should be tackled separately by the State; and it was precisely because social evils became the subjects of state intervention in isolation, one from another, that legislation was possible at all—that it passed with the approval of men who in general stood by *laissez-faire* orthodoxy. Thus the machinery of modern collectivism accumulated haphazardly, without a *theory* of government planning, without systematic direction, and certainly without the intention of undermining the principles of Political Economy. The influence of the parochial clergy was an important element in the hidden pressures making for state intervention. As the local organizers of

[1] Best, *Parochial Ministrations*, p. 35.
[2] *The Official Report of the Church Congress held at Leicester* (1880) (London, 1881), p. 108.

the various philanthropic agencies which called upon the State to intervene
in social conditions, on humanitarian grounds, they looked to a very
limited legislative role. 'All legislation is but a series of experiments,'
Samuel Wilberforce explained in 1846: 'You meet a certain evil by the
tentative remedy which promises to embrace the greatest possible amount
of good.'[1] On a later occasion he said 'The folly of legislation was needless
interference—the wisdom of legislation was necessary interference where
it was demanded by the moral and physical condition of the people . . . to
protect those who could not safely protect themselves'.[2] This described
the impulse which led to the accumulation of state machinery with a
simplicity which nevertheless summarized a whole dimension of nineteenth-century social reform. In England the modern State, with its
collectivist machinery of social regulation, was created by the pressures of
expert opinion, operating against the orthodoxies of social thought; it was
not popular. Towards the end of the century those who adopted frankly
collectivist views of the function of the State—intellectual critics of
laissez-faire, and the sort of radicals inspired by Chamberlain and the
'Unauthorized Programme' of 1885—found that they had a great amount
of popular opinion against them. By then most working-class political
consciousness assumed the validity of the 'Gladstonian' doctrine of the
State, which was anti-collectivist—absorbed in the preservation of individual liberty, and, through the dogma of retrenchment and state economy,
quite unable to contemplate the intervention of the State in the ordinary
operations of society and the economy. This limited, anti-collectivist view
of the State was adopted by the early Labour movement. It was only, in
general, the intellectual, bourgeois socialists who were attracted to a
dynamic view of the State. Because of this, the general espousal of *laissez-
faire* attitudes by the main body of the parochial clergy was in fact in
sympathy with working-class social beliefs in the second half of the
century: they shared the same body of references when it came to the
limited nature of the State over social reform. It was the simultaneous
conversion of many of the leading bishops, towards the end of the century,
to collectivist criticisms of *laissez-faire* practices and ideas that separated
the Church from popular politics. This was the same paradox that had
occurred at the beginning of the century, before Political Economy had
started to filter downwards in public esteem—when the adoption of that
system by Church leaders cut them off from the sympathy of the masses.
Few modern writers on the nineteenth-century Church seem to have
appreciated that social reform was generated by enthusiasts for Political
Economy who allowed exceptional incursions of the State because of the
supervening considerations of humanity. They do not seem to realize that

1 Hansard, *Third Series*, lxxxvii, 323 (12 June 1846).
2 Ibid. xcii. 942 (17 May 1847).

the modern State was not created in response to the adoption of a theory or recognition of collectivist principles. Had social reform actually been proposed on such grounds, had it been only a part of a socialist political programme, it would unquestionably have been held back. Surely, therefore, Bishop Wickham was wrong to believe that 'the major defect of the nineteenth century Church' was 'a failure of prophecy, a failure to understand and interpret the phase of history into which the age had come'.[1] It is not true that they were most conscious of the need for social reform 'who saw the prophetic calling of the Labour movement'.[2] In fact the bishops attracted to collectivism, who often called their new criticism of *laissez-faire* 'socialism', whose advanced ideals placed them far from popular political thinking, were much less 'prophetic' than those who adhered to the widespread subscription to *laissez-faire* social attitudes. Those closest to the pragmatism of the impulse to social reform, that is to say, were usually the advocates of limited doctrines of the State. In this sense the nineteenth-century Church was extremely 'prophetic'. It was full of men who tempered *laissez-faire* orthodoxy by appeals to humanitarian exceptions. It was at the very centre of the forces working for the modern State. Mandell Creighton, when he was Bishop of Peterborough in 1894, recognized the role of the Church in helping to create the conditions of social reform.

Legislation can only follow slowly upon the development of the national conscience. Christian zeal on the other hand is always in the van, and striving to occupy new regions. Before society can turn its attention to subjects, religious minds are slowly bringing them into prominence. When questions have once entered within the sphere of politics, religion may leave them to the conscience which she has educated. The Christian claims no reward, not even that of recognition of her labours.[3]

Creighton was interested in 'socialist' ideas, and was himself an advocate of some collectivist solutions of social issues. He believed it necessary that 'the rights of the individual will be less and less regarded when they evidently clash with the welfare of the people as a whole'.[4] But this did not differ from the humanitarian grounds of exception to *laissez-faire* practice which were generally agreeable to advocates of Political Economy in the second half of the century.

The surviving remnants of the old Tory paternalism within the Church operated alongside the humanitarian critique to modify the application of Political Economy. Some of this had a sharp political edge. Thus clerical enthusiasm for factory reform was often as much a reflection of their class

---

[1] Wickham, *Church and People*, p. 191.   [2] Ibid., p. 216.
[3] Creighton, *Charge* (1894), p. 28.
[4] W. G. Fallows, *Mandell Creighton and the English Church* (London, 1964), p. 25.

hatred of the new capitalist entrepreneurs as it was of disinterested humanitarianism. The middle-class manufacturers, whose industrial cities had broken up what many regarded as the old social harmony of rural England, were also often Dissenters in religion—leaders in the assault upon the position of the Established Church. Many of the Church of England clergy in the manufacturing districts, and especially in Yorkshire, were local leaders of the factory-reform agitation. One of the most celebrated of these was the Revd. George Bull, a Tory, an Evangelical, a lifelong opponent of Political Economy on the one hand and of state intervention on the other. He was fairly typical of the tenacity of old Tory paternalism: he looked to the restoration of old social responsibilities. He was attacked by Dissenters.[1] Churchmen who adopted Political Economy were just as liable to criticize the manufacturers as a class because of their social irresponsibility. Thus Blomfield, in 1842, denounced the conditions of employment in factories and mines as 'a system which was eating into the very vitals of the country'.[2] Since a great deal of the finance for the various Dissenting attacks upon the Church came from the manufacturers, churchmen sometimes replied by contrasting the Dissenters' demand for state education with their actual behaviour towards the young in the industrial plants. In a *Charge* of 1856, for example, the Archdeacon of Lindisfarne (an area which included industrial Tyneside) observed,

The very men who are most prominent in contending for a comprehensive system of instruction, or education, as they term it, are the foremost also in promoting and glorying in an industrial system which entails the necessity of labour, so continuous and so exhausting, even from those of tender age, as to render instruction almost hopeless—education altogether impracticable. And this system both the legislature and the country at large, commend and encourage. But surely, while this industrial furor has proceeded so far as to render some legal intervention necessary to protect the young . . . it is a mere mockery . . . to be parading schemes of intellectual cultivation.[3]

Old-fashioned paternalists within the Church were, for their part, anxious to preserve the principle of the confessional obligation of the State to compel moral duty. In a clash with the Earl of Radnor directly on this issue, in the parliamentary debate on the Mines Bill of 1842, Bishop Monk of Gloucester said emphatically that 'as Christian legislators it was the most important of their duties to enforce morality by legislation'.[4] The application of Political Economy was thus under pressure at the very

---

[1] J. C. Gill, *Parson Bull of Byerley* (London, 1963), pp. 66, 79–81, 106.
[2] Hansard, *Third Series*, lxiii. 199 (6 May 1842).
[3] R. C. Coxe, *A Charge Delivered to the Clergy of the Archdeaconry of Lindisfarne* (London, 1856), p. 19.
[4] Hansard, *Third Series*, lxv. 122 (14 July 1842).

height of its orthodoxy with influential opinion, and from more than one direction.

The intellectual attack on Political Economy, which in the last two decades of the century was becoming fashionable with the more moralistic sections of the intelligentsia (and those under their immediate influence) had Church leaders among its most eager converts. This transition once again illustrated how reflective Church leadership was of trends in the class of which they were a part. Converts to more critical attitudes to *laissez-faire* practice sought to restore the old ideal of social harmony by removing the competitive social ethic which, they believed, had helped create class feeling. 'I think the tendency of the present day', said Samuel Wilberforce in 1867, 'in all its strong rivalry in trade, in all its strong competition for the advantages of the earth, and the like, has a marvellous tendency to set class secretly against class.'[1] Some clergy came to support the idea of trade combination as a way of protecting the working men against the advantages of employers and the competitive system. The Reverend G. W. Gent, a tutor of Keble College, Oxford, was persuaded of this. 'In opposition to the pure trading spirit which would grind him into the dust beneath the wheels of competition,' he wrote in a paper on the duty of Christianity to the working man, published in 1890, 'it insists that he shall be defended from his own weakness, and not betrayed into unjust contracts or plundered by unscrupulous middle-men.'[2] In 1894 Winnington-Ingram described the working class as 'the prey of ceaseless competition'.[3] Once the notion that the competitive principle, in addition to creating wealth, also had the effect of dividing the classes, had lodged in the minds of Church leaders, it was adopted rapidly. For such men a sort of guilty class moralism thrived on the criticism of *laissez-faire* orthodoxies. During the last two decades of the century, the most vocal, the most intellectual, the most influential bishops were those who rushed to denounce Political Economy and to espouse collectivist solutions to social evils. The change was a quick one. Characteristically, these men exaggerated the practical application of *laissez-faire*, failing to account for the extent to which its exponents had tempered its rigours by humanitarian adjustments. The growing profession of collectivism was noticeable at the annual Church Congresses; few went against the strongly flowing current —despite the fact that most of the parish clergy were at first untouched by the conversions at the top. It took some years before the new attitudes began to filter down. By the bishops who took up collectivism, Political Economy was represented as a body of practice and ideas which separated

[1] *Report of the Wolverhampton Church Congress* (London, 1867), p. 248.

[2] *Oxford House Papers*, 1st Series (London, 1890), p. 186.

[3] A. F. Winnington-Ingram, 'The Classes and the Masses', in *The Church of the People*, ed. Randall Davidson (London, 1894), p. 174.

Christianity from concern with social change: they were creating a myth which was to become extremely powerful. 'Modern theories of the isolation of our Christianity from the living, breathing, acting life which environs us every day in a Christian State are a delusion,' wrote Archbishop Tait of the effects of Political Economt, in 1880.[1] Tait was a Liberal: yet the impact of the new political moralism did not follow party divisions, just as the attraction of Political Economy itself had not. In 1880 also V. H. Stanton described the evil character of Political Economy at the Leicester Church Congress.

We are met by a theory which leaves no place for any motive in the production or exchange of wealth except the desire of individual gain. It is said that the interests of all are best secured by every man pursuing his aim. The hold which this theory has obtained upon the minds of Englishmen in the middle and upper classes is probably in part to be traced to the great benefit which resulted, in the early days of the influence of economic science, from removing all kinds of unwise restrictions upon trade. Hence arose a suspicion, not unwarranted, but too unreasoning and excessive, of all interference by the State with the course of trade or the conditions under which it is carried on. In its dogmatic shape this became the doctrine of *Laissez-faire*. Closely allied to, and no doubt fostered by, this doctrine, there sprang up a disposition to think that every interference with perfect liberty of individual action was bad. Hence notably all combinations of workmen were condemned, on the ground of the restraint put by them upon the actions both of capitalists and of their own members. And political economy seemed to support this view, with its theory that the whole capital available for wages must distribute itself among the working classes in fair proportions, according to the nature of different employments.[2]

This description was allied to an attack upon the competitive principle which won a good deal of approval at the Church Congress of 1880. The spread of collectivist attitudes within the leadership of the Church had become so effective by 1897 that the Lambeth Conference of that year appeared to represent almost no other view. The Conference's Committee on 'Industrial Problems', chaired by Bishop J. Percival of Hereford, took up a very clear collectivist position, despite its formal declaration that it declined 'to interfere with the legitimate evolution of economic and social thought and life by taking a side separately in the debate between rival social theories or systems.'[3] It in fact rejected what it thought were the principles of Political Economy in almost every recommendation. The Committee, instead, supported what it called 'The Principle of Public Responsibility'. By their manner of defining this, the Committee followed the new fashion for supposing that Political Economists had deliberately

---

[1] A. C. Tait, *The Church of the Future* (London, 1880), p. 141.

[2] *The Official Report of the Church Congress held at Leicester* (1880), pp. 107–8.

[3] *Conference of the Bishops of the Anglican Communion holden at Lambeth Palace in July, 1897*, p. 138.

separated social and economic order from moral considerations: 'A Christian Community, as a whole, is morally responsible for the character of its own economic and social order, and for deciding to what extent matters affecting that order are to be left to individual initiative, and to the unregulated play of economic forces.' There were instances of this—factory and sanitary legislation, the institution of Government labour departments and the influence of Government, or of public opinion and the press, or of eminent citizens, in helping to avoid or reconcile industrial conflicts'. But there should be a wider application of collectivist principles:

Christian opinion should be awake to repudiate and condemn either open breaches of social justice and duty, or maxims and principles of an unChristian character. It ought to condemn the belief that economic conditions are to be left to the action of material causes and mechanical laws, uncontrolled by any moral responsibility. It can pronounce certain conditions of labour to be intolerable . . . It can speak plainly of evils which attach to the economic system under which we live, such as certain forms of luxurious extravagance, the widespread pursuit of money by financial gambling, the dishonesties of trade into which men are drawn by feverish competition, and the violence and reprisals of industrial warfare.[1]

The Committee went on to recommend the creation of such state collectivist agencies as 'Labour bureaux, Boards of Conciliation and Arbitration, and some judicious use of public works in times of distress'.[2] The acceptability of these ideas to the Lambeth Conference of 1897 shows just how far opinion had shifted within Church leadership by the end of the century.

The bishops of this new generation seemed ignorant of the inconsistencies in the practical application of Political Economy by their predecessors. In one of the most important fields of social welfare for example—the care of the poor—churchmen had often tried to temper the operation of the law of 1834. In many places, the clergy themselves adhered to popular anti-Poor Law feeling in great numbers;[3] but this, no doubt, represented surviving notions of traditional paternalism by parsons who were as yet unconvinced by the principles of Political Economy. Bishop Denison of Salisbury spoke for a very large body of feeling in the Church when he declared that the new Poor Law was typical of 'the current of modern legislation' in that it 'interrupted the connexion between the parish priest and the most destitute members of his flock'.[4] Yet the clergy in general co-operated with the new law; many were elected

[1] Ibid., pp. 139–40.   [2] Ibid., p. 143.
[3] N. C. Edsall, *The Anti-Poor Law Movement, 1834–44* (Manchester, 1971), p. 63.
[4] Denison, *Charge* (1845), p. 44.

as Poor Law Guardians and directly administered it. As the orthodoxy of Political Economy filtered down to the parochial clergy in the mid-century, however, there was little sign that criticism of the law was diminishing. For most parsons the relief of the poor clearly formed one of those areas in which, on grounds of humanity, they were prepared to disregard the logic of accepted academic science. In many places the clergy, with lay assistants, supplemented the provisions of the Poor Law with quite sophisticated poor-relief machinery of their own. In the 1870s Octavia Hill's social work began when W. A. Freemantle, the Vicar of St. Marylebone, put her in charge of the poor-relief scheme operating in his own parish. It was also common for the clergy to demand that Parliament consider a reform in the law—especially as the public image of the workhouse system had not changed with the diffusion of popularized *laissez-faire* ideas. For many, as Dr. Hannah, the Vicar of Brighton, said in 1873, the Poor Law had come 'to be regarded as little more than a machinery to promote its harsh and undiscriminating repression'.[1] Most Church Congresses had the Poor Law question on their agenda to the end of the century. As the ideals of Political Economy spread, so the clergy spoke more often of the need for self-help and individual exertion by the poor: but they still, in general, called for legislative adjustments to render the law more humane. The whole question is a good illustration of the truncated form in which *laissez-faire* ideas were in reality put into effect. Thus W. L. Blackley, the Vicar of King's Samborne, attacked the Poor Law for not being stringent enough: he claimed it operated as an incentive to laziness—the very last thing the 'less eligibility' principle had intended. The law, Blackley said in 1880, 'corrupts the social conscience at the beginning, and makes men improvident through all this time by telling them that their bread is sure, and that they will never want'.[2] Yet he was also the campaigner for a collectivist solution to the question of poverty: it was Blackley who, from the 1870s, advocated a system of state national insurance. The Poor Law question elicited some very confusing responses. Taken out of context, the emphasis by churchmen on what Edward Sturges (Vicar of Wokingham) called 'the moral degradation of dependence'[3], and the exhortations to thrift and self-help, look like undiluted Political Economy. In fact they were simply imposed upon existing attitudes to the Poor Law, and were the form and the vocabulary in which popularized *laissez-faire* reached the parish clergy. Those who used such exhortations were also those who demanded parliamentary reforms to make the Poor Law more humane. The same Lambeth Conference (1897) which proposed a fairly frank collectivist view of the social obligations of the

---

[1] *Authorized Report of the Church Congress held at Bath* (London, 1873), p. 78.
[2] *The Official Report of the Church Congress held at Leicester* (1880), p. 63.
[3] *The Official Report of the Church Congress held at Reading* (London, 1883), p. 247.

State was the one that observed of the poor that 'the perpetual temptation of their lives is to throw off their burdens and expect to obtain aid without any exertion on their part'.[1] The responses of churchmen to ideas and to actual social conditions were much more inconsistent and difficult to categorize than later observers allowed.

The other major areas of social concern showed the same preparedness of churchmen, following the general practice of public men, to temper the application of *laissez-faire* doctrines with humanitarian considerations. In 1847 Bishop Wilberforce pointed out that in factory reform it had been necessary for the State to intervene 'against the greatest of all human passions—the love of gain'.[2] By the 1840s even Blomfield's addiction to Political Economy had been sufficiently modified on this issue to enable him to support state intervention along with the rest of the bishops.[3] Public health and sanitary reform was another field where the Church joined the pressures of expert opinion, in support of state intervention. Here the opponents often represented the sort of local vested interests with which the Church was normally associated in the parishes. Public-health reform was very heavily—and often successfully—resisted: it involved a high degree of centralization. Yet the leading advocates, men like Chadwick and Simon, were themselves convinced Political Economists who had become persuaded that it was necessary to make some exceptions to economic science in the interests of humanity. Church leaders followed them. Blomfield was an early convert to sanitary reform. At first, like Chadwick himself, he sought to effect reform by voluntary means. In 1839 he attempted to start a fund to help the sanitary conditions of the poor; but on finding the task too gigantic for private exertion, he appealed for state intervention. The size of the cholera epidemics in the 1840s confirmed him in this violation of Political Economy.[4] Even John Bird Sumner, the doyen of the episcopal economists, was convinced of the need for state intervention in the field of public health by the cholera. In 1848 Blomfield supported the Public Health Bill—he called it 'the Poor Man's Bill'— as a measure to protect those who could not protect themselves: the classic reason for infringing *laissez-faire* orthodoxy. 'He had always held that in any legislation for the improvement of the sanitary condition of the country the welfare of the labouring part of the population ought to receive especial attention, for in these matters the rich could take care of themselves.'[5] Over the allied question of urban interments, too, Blomfield advocated state intervention. The overflowing city cemeteries were an

[1] *Conference of Bishops* (Encyclical Letter) (London, 1897), p. 16.
[2] Hansard, *Third Series*, xcii. 941 (17 May 1847).
[3] Soloway, *Prelates and People*, p. 202.
[4] Blomfield, *A Pastoral Letter* (1847), p. 2.
[5] Hansard, *Third Series*, c. 895 (27 July 1848).

obvious hazard to public health.[1] In 1854 it was Blomfield who defended the Board of Health, an early collectivist experiment, in the face of successful attacks by the anti-centralization lobby.[2] The public Health Act of 1872 showed that Parliament was once again responsive to a collectivist solution, and the clergy reflected the awakening interest in sanitary reform which the Act symptomized. In 1874 the Church Congress, meeting in Brighton, discussed 'The Influence of Social and Sanitary Conditions on Religion'. Speakers vied with one another in supporting state initiatives. 'I do not say the clergy have been so active as they might have been,' declared Archdeacon Henry Fearon, 'but it should be remembered that it is only of late that sanitary questions have taken hold of the public mind; and no one can deny that the clergy have kept pace with the movement in knowledge and in endeavouring to promote it"[3] This was the period in which *laissez-faire* ideas enjoyed their greatest vogue among the clergy. Clearly their application was extremely selective.

The related question of working-class housing was also one in which Blomfield early established an ecclesiastical view. Again, his normal advocacy of Political Economy was adjusted in the face of the conditions he saw. In 1847 he condemned 'excessive' rents charged by landlords, together with polluted water supply, lack of ventilation, poor washing facilities, and inadequate sewerage, in 'the miserable tenements or apartments occupied by the poorest classes'.[4] A number of clergy in the worst areas took up the question and began small-scale measures of relief—men like Quekitt and Denton in East London. But it was in the 1860s and 1870s, when the slum-clearance legislation initiated by Torrens and Cross elicited a growing body of support within Parliament and educated opinion for the acceptance of state intervention, in the housing question, that the clergy responded along with other humanitarian interests. Richard Cross, a loyal churchman himself, had been influenced in preparing his legislation by being taken on a tour of the slums of Whitechapel by Samuel Barnett, then one of Freemantle's curates in Marylebone, who himself urged legislative action.[5] In 1866 Robert Bickersteth, Bishop of Ripon, reflecting the interest in the Torrens slum-clearance Act of that year, addressed the Church Congress at York on 'the importance of attending as a primary question to the condition of the dwellings of the poor'. He spoke from experience. For many years he had been the incumbent of a large London parish where, in his own words, people lived in conditions which 'made it almost impossible

[1] Hansard, *Third Series*, cxxi. 1341 (27 Mar. 1854).
[2] Ibid. cxxxv. 240 (14 July 1854).
[3] *Authorized Report of the Church Congress held at Brighton* (1874), p. 495.
[4] Blomfield, *A Pastoral Letter* (1847), p. 9.
[5] D. O. Wagner, *The Church of England and Social Reform since 1854* (New York, 1930), p. 103.

for them to be moral, much less religious'.[1] Bishop Walsham How, who also had a considerable personal acquaintance with the slums, remarked in 1884 on the large amount of work then being done by the clergy to improve working-class housing in their parishes. He also noticed that, despite all this, 'a supposition was got abroad that the Church has been exceptionally supine and apathetic in the presence of a gigantic evil'.[2] With such contemporary impressions, it is hardly surprising that later observers should have failed to notice the extent of the Church's work. There were, no doubt, cases where priests were reluctant to attack the influence of landlords, but there were also plenty of examples of their doing so. In 1874 the Bishop of Chichester (Richard Durnford) spoke of the opposition his own attempts to get proper sanitation in working-class dwellings in Lancashire had encountered from the owners of the property.[3] J. W. Horsley, Rector of St. Peter's, Walworth, referred to 'Lord's side' as 'frequently not that of the land-lords'. He urged the Church to effect such a transformation of the housing conditions of the working classes as would amount to 'a revolution in every place where there are slums'.[4] In 1884 Walsham How urged the clergy to create 'the impetus of an awakened and enlightened public opinion', which would get the Torrens and the Cross slum-clearance legislation—which was permissive, not obligatory— put into effect by local authorities. He praised the work of Octavia Hill. He called on the Church 'to stir up the owners of property to a higher conception of their responsibilities'.[5] In the following year, the 'Houses of the Working Classes Act' marked a collectivist advance: the measure was compulsory. It got a lot of clerical support.[6] In 1897 the acceptance of state responsibility for slum improvement was confirmed at the Lambeth Conference. What was needed, the Conference reported, was 'stronger control by public opinion and authority over the housing of the poor, both in town and country, and methods by which the existing laws may be more effectively carried out so as to secure the conditions necessary for a decent moral life'.[7] No doubt these exhortations represented the enthusiasm of particular reformers within the Church, and no doubt the response, in the actual results achieved, may seem slight in the face of the proportions of the problem. But it can hardly be said that Church leadership was lacking in energy or opinion on the question.

Subsequent generations have not forgotten the part taken by the clergy

[1] *Authorized Report of the Proceedings of the Church Congress held at York* (1866) (York, 1867), p. 61.

[2] *The Official Report of the Church Congress held at Carlisle* (London, 1884), p. 48.

[3] *Authorized Report of the Church Congress held at Brighton* (1874), p. 499.

[4] Randall Davidson, *The Church of the People*, pp. 35–6.

[5] *Official Report of the Church Congress held at Carlisle* (1884), p. 49.

[6] See the Speech of the Vicar of Wakefield (N. D. J. Straton) at the 1886 Church Congress, held in Wakefield; *Official Report* (London, 1886), p. 269.

[7] *Conference of Bishops* (London, 1897), p. 143.

in the attempt to reduce drunkenness in the nineteenth century, however. This was an area of social concern which stressed environmental conditions very markedly. The effect of intemperance on the domestic budgets of the working classes, as well as on the general stability of family life, were persistent themes in sermons and pamphlet literature. So was the relationship between drink and crime—an aspect of the question given publicity by William Caine and John Clay, both prison chaplains.[1] In this area, too, Christian opinion did not rest content with personal attempts to persuade men to virtue: here also demands were made for the State to intervene and control the accessibility of liquor. It was a movement of opinion which, unlike most of those so far discussed, attracted more Nonconformist than Church involvement. Blomfield was an early enthusiast from the Church. At the formation of the London Temperance Society in 1831, he became its president. But the Establishment lagged behind the Dissenting Churches in the organization of opinion. It was not until 1862 that the Church of England Temperance Society was set up, and not until 1875, when Queen Victoria consented to become its patron, that the Temperance movement within the Church acquired a prestigious place within the increasing number of agencies for social reform. In 1869 a report of the Convocation of Canterbury indicated not only a correlation between intemperance and crime, but a large increase in drunkenness among the working classes.[2] This Report, too, became one of the pressures, preparing the question for legislative attention. In 1871 H. A. Bruce unsuccessfully made a first attempt at conciliating the various interests in the question— brewers as well as moralists. In 1872 a modified version of his legislation was passed: it restricted the issuance of licences by magistrates, so reducing the number of public houses. The Act completely failed to satisfy the United Kingdom Alliance—the great Liberal and largely Nonconformist Society—which had campaigned for something like prohibition. For the Church of England, William Magee, Bishop of Peterborough, regretted the modifications made to the measure made during the parliamentary debate. 'Nothing', he said of the working classes, 'would do more to win their hearts to the cause of law and order than that they should see your Lordships earnestly and deeply considering how far you can not merely repress intemperance and check the evils arising out of it, but doing this in a manner to satisfy them that the highest interests of the working classes of the country will be clearly and fairly considered.'[3] Magee, who was an Irishman, had made himself something of an expert on the drink question. Archbishop William Thomson of York agreed that greater res-

---

[1] Brian Harrison, *Drink and the Victorians, The Temperance Question in England, 1815–1872* (London, 1971), p. 163.

[2] Warre Cornish, *The English Church in the Nineteenth Century*, ii. 103.

[3] Hansard, *Third Series*, ccxi. 87 (2 May 1872).

trictions were required on the traffic in liquor.[1] The Lambeth Conference of 1888 was cautious, however. The bishops condemned 'the evil effects of this sin' of intemperance, but they also sought 'to discountenance the language which condemns the use of wine as wrong in itself, independently of its effects on ourselves or on others'.[2] The cellars of Lambeth and Bishopthorpe were saved. The Church, in this field of social reform, was second to the Nonconformists in appealing for state intervention, to assist the moral and physical condition of the people.

A considerable measure of modern interest has surrounded attempts by Victorian churchmen to use the authority of the State to secure Christian standards in sexual conduct. In fact the calls for the use of law—again more characteristic of Nonconformists—were much less typical than the conviction that 'Purity' was something that could best be achieved by direct evangelism, and that the care of those who were victims of their own sexual irresponsibility could be adequately undertaken by religious agencies alone. But as the dimensions of the various problems were revealed by social work among the poor, and by parliamentary inquiries, the need for public action became increasingly evident in particular questions. Those who have found Victorian concern over vice distasteful or suggestive forget that it worked to promote the eventual creation of state social welfare. The 'Purity' movement was a continuation of the sort of work promoted by the philanthropic bodies which had so greatly expanded since the end of the eighteenth century. New features derived from social experience. Environmental considerations were increasingly recognized. The Churches were largely responsible for drawing attention to miseries which men had before often regarded as merely to be borne as part of the ordinary burdens of life. In creating a public attitude to sexual questions, that is to say, the Churches were seeking to define a new dignity in human relationships—that is the way contemporaries viewed the question. Most of this work was restorative and reconciliatory. The Church Penitentiary Association, founded in 1851, aimed at returning prostitutes to normal social life. By 1880 it was running twenty-five penitentiaries and thirteen refuges. Some of the inspiration came from Bishop Wilberforce's 'Protection of Females Bill'—an attempt, in 1848, to prevent 'the practice of entrapping, by unfair arts, young and unsuspecting females for prostitution'.[3] Religious opposition to the Contagious Diseases Acts, of 1864, 1866, and 1867, was generally because they were seen as an 'embodiment of materialism'[4] rather than for the sort of reasons that prompted Josephine

[1] Ibid. 568.
[2] *Conference of Bishops of the Anglican Communion holden at Lambeth Palace in July 1888* (London, 1888), p. 8.
[3] Hansard, *Third Edition*, xcix. 333 (5 June 1848).
[4] See the speech of the Principal of Liverpool College (the Revd. G. Butler) at the Nottingham Church Congress; *Authorized Report* (London, 1871), p. 410.

Butler's campaign. The Acts, which were passed after representations from military authorities worried about the incidence of venereal disease in seaports and garrison towns, empowered magistrates to order medical examinations of suspected prostitutes; powers which were regarded by some as gross violations of individual liberty.[1] Religious opposition derived additionally from the belief that the laws were too clinical—that they had created a link between the State and sexual morality which inadequately protected moral considerations. In 1880 the Chaplain to the House of Mercy in Fulham, reporting on the Church's rescue work, noticed that 'new interest seems to be awakening, on many sides, in a work long left to this silent operation'.[2] One of the signs of this was the establishment, in 1883, of the Church of England Purity Society and the White Cross Army. Gladstone took an active interest in this work; so did the new Anglican sisterhoods—the religious communities of women. Nor was this work always undertaken with the insensitivity or sublimated enjoyment so often supposed in modern commentary. 'I do not desire to inculcate or to see any morbid spirit of narrow asceticism,' said Bishop James Fraser of Manchester of purity work among young men, in 1876. 'There are often sad reactions from that', he added.[3] It was a realism sustained by later knowledge of psychology.

Similarly, not all parsons supported the Sunday-observance code in a spirit of gloomy piety. Many clergy in the Church of England were prepared to see Sunday games, to make it a proper day of recreation for the working classes. 'I honestly think this is a question which should not be treated with Puritanical moroseness', said E. J. Randolph, one such clergyman, in 1866. He was speaking at one of the usual Church Congress discussions of the 'Social Conditions and Recreations of the Poorer Classes'.[4] But clergy who maintained this sort of view came into conflict with enthusiasts of the great Sabbatarian movement within both Church and Dissent. Yet even those who contended for a complete observance of Sunday often did so for reasons, among others, of social utility. 'Without those laws', declared Canon Tristram in 1872, 'the lust of gain, and the love of pleasure, would rapidly divide the land into two classes, the money-making classes and the slaving classes.' Sunday observance protected the poor from excessive labour.[5]

The question of class division worried Church leaders increasingly. The growth of working-class political consciousness, the working-class suffrage

---

[1] G. S. R. Kitson Clark, *An Expanding Society, Britain 1830–1900* (Cambridge, 1967), p. 166.

[2] *The Official Report of the Church Congress held at Leicester* (1880), p. 189.

[3] James Fraser, *Charge Delivered at his Second Visitation by James, Lord Bishop of Manchester* (1876), p. 13.

[4] *Authorized Report of the Church Congress held at York* (1866), p. 43.

[5] *Authorized Report of the Church Congress held at Leeds* (Leeds, 1872), p. 348.

following the parliamentary extensions of the franchise in 1867 and 1884, the development of consolidated trade unionism, had stimulated a public awareness of the division of labour and capital which occupied the attention of public men in the last three decades of the century. The leaders of the Church were fascinated and appalled by class antagonisms. Without in general translating their feelings into political terms, they were extremely anxious to foster better class relationships by an open recognition of the claims of labour to a greater esteem, and sometimes, even, to a more generous share in the wealth of industry. They exuded goodwill. They rushed to abandon the sort of attitudes to social class which the preceding generation of bishops had learned from the Political Economists. Such views continued to be professed among the parochial clergy long after the Church leadership, with its correspondence to the world of the intelligentsia, had adopted its new class moralizing. The old view was summarized in the thought of John Bird Sumner, Archbishop of Canterbury from 1848 to 1862. In 1845, when Bishop of Chester, this distinguished Political Economist had written,

The first aspect of a society like ours has a very anomalous appearance. We see wealth and poverty in close contact and violent contrast: both in extremes. It would be unreasonable to complain of this, which in long settled and prosperous countries is the inevitable course of things. Money is accumulated in large masses: population verges hard upon the means of subsistence; or, in other words, the demand for employment is greater than the demand for labour, legislation cannot reach the case: can neither produce nor prevent it. But like every other providential arrangement, the evils which belong to it have a corresponding remedy. In a community thus circumstanced, many possess both the leisure and the means to attend to wants which ought to be relieved, and to correct the irregularities and vicissitudes of temporal condition. And the Gospel, the faith that is in Christ Jesus, imposes upon those who enjoy such opportunities the duty of employing them in compliance with the will of God, according to each man's 'several ability' . . . If wealth is used merely for the purpose of increasing wealth, of amassing more, the intent is frustrated for which it was awarded: but if it is employed to feed those who would otherwise be naked, to educate those who would otherwise be ignorant, to raise up those who would otherwise have fallen irrecoverably, then the design of God's providence is answered, and his wisdom justified by his children. How different a scene we should contemplate, if this were made the general principle of action![1]

In contrast to this description of social relationships and personal obligations, regulated by self-correcting mechanisms, is the frank recognition of the extent of class conflict evident in clerical pronouncements in the second half of the century. 'If we are to do any real good we must have some true insight into the nature and causes of the antagonism between the different

[1] *A Charge Delivered to the Clergy of the Diocese of Chester by John Bird Sumner, D.D., Lord Bishop of Chester* (London, 1845), pp. 22–3.

classes,' said the Revd. V. H. Stanton, Fellow of Trinity College, Cambridge, at the Leicester Church Congress of 1880—during a debate on 'The Church in relation to the Organization of Labour'. 'We must candidly and gladly admit anything that is just in the claims of the workmen,' he added, 'we must not suffer ourselves to be blinded by any narrow prejudice of the classes of society to which we ourselves belong.'[1] The annual Church Congresses discussed the issue time and time again. At the 1885 gathering in Portsmouth, during a consideration of 'The Bearing of Christianity upon the Mutual Relations of the Rich and the Poor—Employees and Employers', the Revd. M. S. A. Walrond (Vicar of the London church of St. Lawrence Jewry), gave typical expression to the new enthusiasm of churchmen for making gestures towards the claims of working men—whom he called, following a usage still widespread, 'the poor':

As to the poor, what shall we say? 'Be content with your wages', and that is all? No. Let us listen to their side of the story, though we may not always agree with it. Let us show at least that we understand them; let us acknowledge that there are evils in their social condition which are sad, grievances to be borne, and which need speedy remedying. Let us instruct them as to the causes of these, and the possibilities of cure. Let us frankly admit that in much society has wronged them.[2]

This sort of attitude was not confined to a handful of advanced clerical thinkers. With astonishing rapidity it became a fashionable view in the leadership of the Church. It became the new orthodoxy, the new social piety to which reference was made at every point. The trouble with the Victorian Church, was not that it demonstrated an unthinking disregard of social change, but that it took the matter up with such unthinking enthusiasm; using the existence of class feeling and social misery as the basis for the release of moralizing sympathy, rather than as the criterion for hard social and economic analysis. At the Lambeth Conference of 1897 the bishops announced their openness to the claims of working men in characteristically large language. 'The industrial problems of the present day present themselves under the double aspect of justice between man and man, and sympathy with human needs,' they declared. 'It is widely thought in some classes that the present working of our industries is unjust to the employed and unduly favourable to the employer.'[3] The Church had every wish to be associated with the justice of that feeling, but declined to give an actual judgement. At its highest, in the thought of such as Mandell Creighton, episcopal understanding of the nature of class antagonism attained some reality. 'The social problems of the present day are in their nature economic,' he said in 1894; 'they are concerned with the more equal

---

[1] *The Official Report of the Church Congress held at Leicester* (1880), p. 107.
[2] *The Official Report of the Church Congress held at Portsmouth* (London, 1885), p. 586.
[3] *Conference of the Bishops* (London, 1897), p. 15.

distribution of material advantages.' He believed that 'among right-minded men' there was an agreement that as wide a distribution as possible was to be desired. But the difficulty, of course, was 'how far it is possible to distribute them, and how experiments can best be made to determine this point'.[1] Bishops less enthusiastic than Creighton for 'socialist' attitudes to the distribution of wealth nevertheless shared the agonizing about class conflict, and about what Christopher Wordsworth, in the later 1870s, called 'the din of discord' and the 'war' which had broken out 'between Labour and Capital'.[2] Modern views of the Victorian clergy assume a distaste for the claims of working men, a rejection of the class conflict from the partisan heights of the comfortable classes. They are quite wrong. The bishops almost fell over themselves in their sympathy—though they did little that was practical to adjust the balance of labour and capital.

The attitude of the Victorian Church to trade unions was similar. Orthodox Political Economy had regarded unions as improper combinations in restraint of trade: during the period when Political Economy was ascendant within the leadership of the Church there was little sympathy for the idea of working-class combination. By the 1870s, when the rural clergy were confronted with renewed attempts at agricultural combination, and by the 1880s and 1890s, with 'new Unionism'—amalgamations of skilled and unskilled workers in single trades—the more influential levels of the Church were already critical of *laissez-faire* ideas and willing to be sympathetically inclined to the case for organized labour. Clerical opposition to unionism usually came, when it came at all, from the lower clergy, still soaked in diluted Political Economy. The 1870s was the testing period. The judgment in Queen's Bench of *Hornby* v. *Close* in 1867, and the Report of the Royal Commission on Trades Unionism in 1869, made the organization of labour a matter of current debate and controversy. In 1871 the Criminal Law Amendment Act reflected Gladstonian ideals of free contract: trade unions were subjected to the law of conspiracy, so rendering industrial action of questionable legality. This was replaced in 1875 by the Conservatives' Conspiracy And Protection Of Property Act, which gave legal sanction to collective bargaining. The Employers And Workmen Act, in the same year, removed breach of contract by an employed person from the criminal law. The Church had no clear opinion on these reforms. The bishops took no part in the debates in the House of Lords, regarding them as concerned with issues outside the conventional legislative concern of the Church.

In 1872, however, the clergy found themselves involved in the union question in their own rural strongholds. This was the year of the strike by agricultural labourers, a disruption on their doorsteps which obliged

---

[1] Creighton, *Charge* (1894), p. 25.
[2] Christopher Wordsworth, *Miscellanies* (London, 1879), iii. 402.

many clergy to face up to the issue of trade combination. The leader of the strike was Joseph Arch, organizer of the Agricultural Labourers' Union. It was in Arch's interest to show up the parsons as the natural enemies of the labourers: he saw this as a powerful way of eroding rural social deference, one of the impediments to agricultural unionism. He was also a Primitive Methodist preacher, a convinced opponent of the Church of England as an Establishment. Examples of clerical opposition to his Union were given swift and exaggerated publicity. But it was the Bishop of Gloucester who presented him with the materials for a propaganda triumph. At a dinner for Gloucestershire landowners in August 1872, Bishop Ellicott spoke astringently about union agitators—advising his hearers to resist the temptation to throw them into horse ponds. Ellicott later claimed these words were spoken in 'a jocular mood'.[1] He was actually opposed to labour combinations, but had misread the temper of the times. It was necessary to make amends very hurriedly. At a conference which met in his palace, consisting of employers, labourers, and union officials, he suggested a programme to improve the conditions of agricultural employment.[2] But the damage had been done. Arch used the Bishop's indiscretion with considerable skill to suggest to many contemporaries—and to posterity—that the entire bench of bishops were enemies of the agricultural labourers. In May 1873 another incident was used to similar effect. Two clerical magistrates gaoled sixteen women from Ascott, in Oxfordshire, for assaulting blackleg labourers with sticks during the agricultural strike. The magistrates had in fact attempted to persuade the employer concerned from pressing the case. In this they were not successful, and as the women were guilty, and as the bench was obliged by the terms of the Criminal Law Amendment Act to give sentence, the women went to prison for one week each. The affair was given huge publicity, and was raised in Parliament. The clerical magistrates were depicted as insensitive reactionaries; the clergy everywhere as the mere agents of landowners. These incidents did a great deal to foster the view of the Victorian clergy which many later came to assume. In reality the clergy were divided in their attitudes to the agricultural unions.[3] A minority were either overtly hostile, like Archdeacon C. W. Holbeche, Rector of Banbury, who supported the counter-organization of landowners, or completely sympathetic, like Edward Girdlestone, the Devonshire agrarian reformer. A majority of the clergy, probably a large majority, were reluctant to take sides, but were full of goodwill towards the labourers and certainly prepared to listen to the labourers' case for organization.[4] Most of the bishops favoured a sym-

---

[1] *Authorized Report of the Church Congress held at Leeds* (1872), p. 363.
[2] Kitson Clark, *Churchmen and the Condition of England*, p. 248.
[3] Wagner, *The Church of England and Social Reform*, p. 160.
[4] Kitson Clark, *An Expanding Society*, p. 256.

pathetic neutrality. Bishop Frazer of Manchester articulated more good-will than accuracy, however, when he claimed that 'there is not a clergy-man of the Church of England who does not feel in the bottom of his heart that the agricultural labourer has suffered . . . great hardships'. Fraser was among those who believed, and said he thought the clergy also believed, that the labourer had 'a legitimate right to combine for the pur-poses of improving his earthly condition'.[1]

In the following year, in 1873, the Church Congress at Bath considered the entire issue of 'The Church's Duty in Regard to Strikes and Labour'. The Bishop of Oxford, J. F. Mackarness, opened the debate by referring to the odious reputation being acquired by the clergy at the hands of Arch's propaganda: 'meetings have been held in hundreds of parishes at which the abuse of the clergy has been the prominent topic of discourse'.[2] He then put the case for neutrality by the clergy on the question of wages and contracts. He also criticized the Church for not adequately instructing employers in the duties 'of charity, kindly treatment, friendly considera-tion, and respect' towards their workers; 'her training of the youth of the whole upper class has been deficient in that very important part of it which makes the rich humble'.[3] Following speakers repeated the ideal of neutrality by the clergy, and generally expressed sympathy with the working men's claims to better treatment in society. Those who complained about the inconvenience of strike action were themselves criticized by the Revd. J. Llewelyn Davies, of Marylebone—such complaints, he said, were 'apt to be expressed most forcibly by those who must be conscious of a class sympathy with employers'.[4] The general desire to sympathize with work-ing men, which characterized this particular debate, was typical of attitudes prevalent in the more influential sections of the Church. It was demon-strated at every meeting of the Congress. Yet very little actually resulted. Church leaders simply went on declaring their goodwill. Twenty years later Scott Holland warned the Church that it was becoming 'so very late in the day for her to be still employed in striking an attitude' on such issues.[5] The chief difficulty lay in clerical opposition to some of the *practices* of the trade unions: it often obscured the recognition which most were prepared to give to the *principle* of combination. Creighton, a friend to organized labour, remarked in 1894 that a lot of industrial bar-gaining was 'carried on in terms of struggle and conflict, by weapons which the Church cannot use, and in language which the Church cannot speak'.[6] A great deal has been made by some writers of the sympathy between

[1] *Authorized Report of the Church Congress held in Leeds* (1872), p. 363.
[2] *Authorized Report of the Church Congress held at Bath* (1873), p. 23.
[3] Ibid., p. 27.　　　　　　　　　　　　[4] Ibid., p. 31.
[5] *The Official Report of the Church Congress held at Folkestone* (London, 1892), p. 71.
[6] Creighton, *Charge* (1894), p. 23.

the Church and the working classes inspired by those bishops who tried their hand at industrial conciliation in the later decades of the nineteenth century. But this practice was very exceptional and usually unsuccessful. Westcott's mediation in the Durham miners' strike of 1892, in which the bishop took no part in arbitration but invited both sides to mediate under his own roof, was probably the only really successful, as well as the only well-known, Anglican adventure of this sort.[1] The close links between the Catholic Church and the Irish immigrant labourers allowed Cardinal Manning his extremely successful intervention in the Dock Strike of 1889. The opportunity had been passed up by the Church of England: Frederick Temple, the Bishop of London (and later Archbishop of Canterbury), managed to offend Ben Tillett, the dockers' leader, and then go off on a holiday in Wales at just that moment when the chance for mediation was offered to him.[2] Manning stepped in instead. In 1878 Bishop Fraser failed in an attempt to mediate during a strike of mill hands in Lancashire. In 1895 Creighton achieved no success in a direct attempt to settle a strike in the boot and shoe trade. 'I own that on a matter of principle I deprecate episcopal interference with economic questions,' Creighton wrote at the time.[3] The feeling that the clergy ought not to be involved in such issues as wage negotiations or labour relations was also pretty general in the Church—a good thing too, because the English popular dislike of parsons interfering in secular issues would have rewarded the Church with a considerable measure of public disapproval had it been tried. Christian 'Socialist' priests who dreamed of an England where the Church acted as the natural regulator of industrial conditions always seem to have ignored this prejudice. But it was one which, in practical terms, set a very clear limit to Church involvement in temporal conditions. Even those bishops most notable for their social concern were sufficiently realistic to see that the Church must keep out of involvement with the terms of employment. 'The position of the clergy in these social questions', said Fraser in 1872, '—questions affecting the relation of employer and employed, questions touching the hours of labour or the amount of wages—are extremely delicate and difficult questions for a Minister of Christ's Gospel to deal with.'[4] Mackarness of Oxford said in the following year that it was 'not the duty of the Church, or of the clergy, to fix the rate of wages; in the first place, because they have not the requisite knowledge; secondly, because neither the payers nor the receivers of wages have consented to abide by their decision; thirdly, because the attempt would be contrary to the very nature

[1] See G. F. A. Best, *Bishop Westcott and the Miners* (London, 1967).
[2] *Memoirs of Archbishop (Frederick) Temple by Seven Friends*, ed. E. G. Sandford (London, 1906), ii. 142.
[3] *Life and Letters of Mandell Creighton*, by his Wife (London, 1904). ii. 120.
[4] *Authorized Report of the Church Congress held at Leeds* (1872), p. 363.

of the Church of Christ'.[1] Creighton believed the clergy had 'the most ardent desire to promote the welfare of their people', but this did 'not enable them always to judge decisively that any particular scheme for that purpose is immediately practicable'.[2] In 1897 the Lambeth Conference Report on Industrial Problems summarized these sorts of feelings. 'In this work the clergy, whose special duty is to ponder the bearings of Christian principles, have their part; but the Christian laity, who deal directly with the social and economic facts, can do even more.' The Report recommended that committees be set up 'as a part of local Church organization', consisting chiefly of laymen, to examine 'social and industrial problems' like unemployment; they should 'fearlessly draw attention to the various causes in our economic, industrial, and social system, which call for remedial measures on Christian principles'.[3] This reflected the suggestion made in 1892 by Charles Gore, that 'small consultative bodies of men who know exactly what life means in workshops, in different business circles, among employers of labour, among workmen' should be set up by the Church to determine policies in industrial questions.[4]

With all this social concern, how was it that the Church failed to draw any closer to the working classes? By the end of the Victorian era the masses still did not go to church or look to the Church as an institution incorporating their interests. Bishop Walsham How offered an explanation of the type modern observers have seized upon. In 1884 he said 'A Church which talks about another world, but does not seem to take much interest in this, is one which will embrace within its fold a limited number of the working class'.[5] It was certainly true that a lot of bishops, in their enthusiasm for collectivism, said this sort of thing at the end of the century in an attempt to persuade others to adopt their new ideas. But as an explanation of the alienation of the working classes from organized religion it is unsatisfactory. It represents a self-critical moralism, fashionable within the Church itself; but the working classes themselves, progressively soaked in practical *laissez-faire* ideas, did not look to the Church for interference in earthly conditions and would have resented the clergy if they had attempted it. English popular spirituality actually expected the Church to cultivate an 'other-worldly' concern, to elevate men and direct them to another realm of values altogether. Furthermore, working-class men were largely unaware of the new fashion for collectivism in the Church's leadership—the discussions and the declarations of sympathy were all given off in episcopal palaces and at Church gatherings. And whatever churchmen

[1] *Authorized Report of the Church Congress held at Bath* (1873), p. 24.

[2] Creighton, *Charge* (1894), p. 27.

[3] *Conference of the Bishops* (1897), pp. 138, 141.

[4] Charles Gore, *The Mission of the Church* (London, 1899), p. 135 (Lectures at St. Asaph, 1892).

[5] *The Official Report of the Church Congress held at Carlisle* (1884), p. 46.

might say, the fact remained—and it was the side of the Church that was most apparent to working men—that the Church was a class institution. Its social moralizing was characteristic of the class moralizing of that section of the intelligentsia to which Church leadership was related.

The Church sought a work of reconciliation. In reply to the class antagonisms of the later Victorian period, of which churchmen were fully conscious, they offered to restore the old balance of social interests, to proclaim an ethic which would act as the cohesive element in a new harmony, like the one they supposed pre-industrial England to have been. This social ethic churchmen came to declare under the title of 'Brotherhood'—it was the scriptural word used at every Church gathering after the mid-sixties. Subsequently a commonplace expression, it is difficult now to recapture the social goodwill (and the shock to genuine reactionaries) which the normative adoption of the word indicated. 'I think it is the special office of Christianity to keep alive that brotherhood of man and man, especially in those teeming multitudes which are gathered together in the centre of human industry,' said Wilberforce in 1867.[1] The 'brotherhood' ideal was thought to be reached when men recognized that their class differences were dissolved by mutual respect and 'higher' common ends. Mackarness said that the Church 'teaches that all her members are workers together for the common good, bound to consider one another's welfare in the progress of their united toil'.[2] Bishops began to describe themselves as 'workers' at public meetings. But this practice can scarcely have appealed to those who really were trapped on the wrong side of the prevailing distribution of wealth. Class or economic adjustment was not seriously on the agenda of the Church, despite the vague declarations of the bishops. 'Brotherhood' was a courtesy ideal; it was not intended to change economic relationships very radically. ' "Brotherhood" is the fundamental relation in which human beings stand to one another,' the *Oxford House Papers*, written for working men, declared in 1890; 'the ordinary "classes" of society are, by the side of it, conventional and transitory.'[3] As a solution to social disharmony, the ideal of 'Brotherhood' was acclaimed at the Lambeth Conference of 1897. 'We think it our duty to press the great principle of the Brotherhood of Man, and to urge the importance of bringing that principle to bear on all the relations, between those who are connected by the tie of a common employment,' the Bishops said in their *Encyclical Letter*. 'Obedience to this law of brotherhood would ultimately in all probability, prevent many of the mischiefs which attend our present system'.[4] Class and economic arrangements were not to be changed very

---

[1] *Report of the Church Congress held at Wolverhampton* (1867), p. 248.
[2] *Authorized Report of the Church Congress held at Bath* (1873), p. 27.
[3] *Oxford House Papers*, 1st Series (London, 1890), p. 178.
[4] *Conference of Bishops* (1897), p. 16.

drastically, that is to say: they were to be reanimated by a spirit which would dissolve their divisive effects. It was a message that satisfied the social idealism of the clergy, but it can have done little to attract the toiling masses to the Church.

Yet the eagerness of the Church to win the sympathy of the working classes was very real. And so was the continued assumption that society was naturally divided into classes. 'The great idea which the Church has to teach men is the idea of duty,' Bishop Magee said to the special meeting for working men at the Southampton Church Congress in 1870; 'and she has to teach it to all classes, so that every man may feel—"It is for me to do my duty whether I rise high or sink low in the social scale." '[1] Exhortations like this have often been lifted in isolation from the general body of social ideas current in the Victorian Church, and, taken on their own, have been used to represent the Church as concerned solely with 'social control'.[2] In fact the Church saw its primary social duty in working to influence the creation of conditions in which men were capable of moral and spiritual development. There was a consistent realization that social conditions affected the nature of moral consciousness. This had depended in the steady revelation of the extent of social misery through the work of philanthropic bodies and the reports of parliamentary commissions. The clergy had encouraged the development of a considerable auxiliary lay ministry, composed of Lay District Visitors and Licensed Scripture Readers, and these men and women had added their experience of the urban and rural working classes to the growing deposit of social knowledge available to the Church. There were even those who saw the possibility of employing this ministry to impart a greater sense of social mobility to the ordained ministry. A speaker at the first Church Congress, which met at Cambridge in 1861, suggested that Scripture Readers should be admitted to the priesthood, to 'disabuse the public mind of the notion that Greek and Latin made a clergyman, and that the gifts of the Spirit were recognized only in the highly-educated gentry'.[3] The Evangelicals' 'Pastoral Aid Society' of 1836 and the 'Society for Promoting the Employment of Additional Curates', set up in 1837 by central churchmen, were attempts to reach the poor. So was the Church Army, inspired by Wilson Carlile in 1882, as a result of parish work in the slums of Walworth. In 1876 the 'Church of England Working Men's Society' had been founded, with the intention of training laymen for special work among the poor. Within a

---

[1] *Authorized Report of the Church Congress held at Southampton* (Southampton, 1870), p. 396.

[2] See e.g. E. Royston Pike, *Human Documents of the Victorian Golden Age* (London, 1967), p. 37.

[3] *Report of the Proceedings of the Church Congress held in the Hall of King's College, Cambridge* (1861) (Cambridge, 1862), p. 107 (Speech of the Revd. Henry Mackenzie).

decade it had 10,000 members.[1] The Convocations were also attentive to the problem. In 1889 the Convocation of Canterbury received a report of its Committee on 'Organizations to Reach Classes Now Outside Religious Ministrations'. From 1866 the Church Congresses held special meetings for working men. These, however, illustrated the ineradicable class nature of the clergy: the meetings were always held in the afternoons, when the working men were at work. It was at such gatherings that bishops claimed that they, too, were 'workers', in clumsy but well-intentioned attempts at creating the atmosphere of social harmony.[2] Authentic workers then beheld them departing to their palaces.

The class references of the Church of England were revealed in many ways. They point to the real cause of the alienation of the working population: the clergy appeared as emissaries of another class. All the goodwill of the bishops and clergy was frustrated by this. They could never comprehend how misunderstood they were; but their beliefs were all drawn from intellectual attitudes; they were too vicarious; too unacquainted with working-class cultural assumptions, and in consequence they much too readily appeared patronizing. Creighton had the wisdom to see some of this. 'It is easy in the retirement of the study, to make the small assumption that a change in the outward conditions of human life will at once produce an increase of human capacity,' he remarked.[3] Too many of the enthusiasms of the clergy ended up as paper solutions; they were too academic.

Some contemporaries blamed the absence of the working classes from Church on the system of pew-renting. There can be no doubt that the appropriation of seats, resulting as it did in a visible class segregation in Church, kept many working people away. In 1863 the Revd. W. R. Wroth represented their view as 'We don't like to go where we don't appear to be wanted—where we have to sit in seats marked "free seats" or "for the poor", and where rich folk seem to think we ain't fit to come near 'em'.[4] Yet the Church of England was not alone in having rented pews. Indeed, the system lasted rather longer among the Nonconformists, owing to the later commencement of the campaign against them in those churches. Class-consciousness was scarcely less evident in Nonconformist places of worship than in the Establishment. In some, separate weekday services were held for tradesmen, and rolls of Church membership sometimes listed working-class members by surnames only, omitting the courtesy

[1] See the report on the work in the *Official Report of the Church Congress held at Wakefield* (London, 1886), p. 177.

[2] See e.g. the address by Bishop Lonsdale of Lichfield at the Wolverhampton working men's meeting, in 1867, in the *Report*, p. 234.

[3] Creighton, *Charge* (1894), p.21.

[4] *Report of the Proceedings of the Church Congress held in the Free Trade Hall, Manchester* (1863) (Manchester, 1864), p. 134.

titles given to others.[1] The Roman Catholic Church had very few rented pews, and this was not without its disagreeable consequences: Fr. Dalgairns complained to Newman in 1849 that some upper-class Catholics were giving up Church attendance because of the smell arising from the Irish worshippers.[2] There were those in the Church of England who defended pew rents. In 1842 Samuel Wilberforce supported 'the convenient separation of worshippers of different stations' for reasons derived from a fixed view of social class. 'Diversity of rank and station do exist among us: they are evidently part of God's appointment for maintaining quick and real mutual charity,' he explained.[3] But most Church leaders were opposed to pew rents, and episcopal *Charges* had inveighed against them since quite early in the century. By the 1890s, most seats were free. Pew rents do not in themselves account for the absence of the working classes from Church; but they symptomized, for working people, an institution which was not for them. In Ireland the Catholic Churches were sometimes segregated on class lines even more rigorously, with a separate communion rail for the poor[4]—and this did not have the effect of keeping them away from church, because the Church did not represent an alien social order.

The academic quality and the social insensitivities which so often frustrated the desire of Church leaders to reach the working classes was nowhere better illustrated than in the Settlement movement. This was an attempt at social service which was noble, and which often involved considerable personal sacrifice. But class barriers were never breached. The work often did more for the social consciences of the upper and middle-class envoys to the slums than it did for the poor—as Hensley Henson noticed during his brief time as head of Oxford House, Bethnal Green, in 1888.

The notion that undergraduates might usefully supplement their normal academic experience by some personal contact with the lives of the poor was not sufficiently correlated with the condition under which alone any permanent influence can be gained [Henson later wrote]; a few weeks spent in Bethnal Green during the vacation might benefit the undergraduate, but can hardly have much effect on the East End.[5]

In the settlements some achievements were attained—more often in the work of public relations than in social experiment. It left the established classes with the impression that important steps were being made to bring

[1] Kenneth Young, *Chapel* (London, 1972), p. 221.

[2] Chadwick, *Victorian Church*, Part I, p. 330.

[3] David Newsome, *The Parting of Friends, A Study of the Wilberforces and Henry Manning* (London, 1966), p. 272.

[4] Inglis, *Churches and the Working Classes*, p. 130.

[5] H. Hensley Henson, *Retrospect of an Unimportant Life* (Oxford, 1942), i. 28.

religion and comfort to the poor. But apart from the relatively small numbers who received direct help from the settlements, the working classes were largely untouched by their existence. Their value lay in preparing young men from the upper and middle classes to assist in the creation of a reforming opinion. Toynbee Hall and Oxford House led the way in 1884; by the start of the Great War in 1914 over forty settlements had been established in working-class districts of the cities. Some followed the practice of Toynbee Hall in subordinating evangelistic to social-relief work. Probably most were like Oxford House in trying to fulfil both together. Radical politics often went with those who directed these enterprises, but this was not invariable. The Hon. and Revd. 'Jimmy' Adderley, the first head of Oxford House, was a 'Christian Socialist'. He was the author of *Stephen Remarx*, a nearly autobiographical novel about an Etonian who discovered a social conscience through work in the slums. But Adderley's successors were not so radical. The impetus to go among the poor expressed a moral fervour which did not necessarily translate into political terms—as it did for some later generations. It was also found in all the Churches, in some degree or other, by the last two decades of the century, the years which produced the settlements. 'Mix freely with the people,' Hugh Price Hughes, the great Nonconformist leader, told the comfortable classes; 'it will help to purify you of your innate selfishness, and you will come out of the crowd glowing with the enthusiasm of humanity.'[1] Bishop Fraser urged churchmen in the same sort of language: 'do try and go out among these poor, these outcasts, you men and women on whom Providence has showered so undeservedly, so far as we are concerned, the choicest gifts'.[2] And they did. It was probably W. W. Champneys, the Vicar of Whitechapel between 1837 and 1860, who first began to take the children of the upper classes to visit the slums and see for themselves. In 1869 Uppingham School, under the headmastership of Edward Thring, began the first School Mission among the working classes. This stimulated one of the most powerful social influences of the next hundred years: the public-school social conscience. An earnest desire to help the poor was encouraged by a line of distinguished headmasters—who included all the Archbishops of Canterbury in the second half of the century. Tait, Benson, and Temple had all been public-school heads. Young men at the Universities continued the ideals of social service, and in the Settlement movement they achieved a permanent form.

It is astonishing that the young men who went into the slums knew so little about them. For a century the Church had been giving vast publicity to the 'Spiritual Destitution' of the masses; the philanthropic agencies had collected huge sums of money within the upper classes for social work.

[1] Hugh Price Hughes, *Social Christianity*, 2nd edn. (London, 1889), p. 8.
[2] *Authorized Report of the Church Congress held at Nottingham* (1871), p. 421.

Yet of his arrival at Bethnal Green in 1889, Winnington-Ingram wrote, 'I plunged into the unknown'.[1] His biographer added that he was 'entirely ignorant of East End life' and had 'known only the public school, the University, and the Cathedral City'.[2] The conditions in Bethnal Green, however, had been exposed to an incredible amount of publicity during the nineteenth century. Bishop Blomfield had built twelve new churches there.[3] In 1877 Stewart Headlam had founded the Guild of St. Matthew there. It was perhaps the most well-publicized slum area in the whole of England, yet still it was possible for it to appear completely unknown. How could such ignorance have existed? The explanation, of course, lies in the class background of the clergy. Each generation was reared in middle and upper-class isolation from the social conditions they later found so repellent. Each generation had to rediscover the miseries of the working classes for themselves. 'Now the sting of truth seems to be this,' wrote Winnington-Ingram in 1894, after he had discovered the social conditions of the working classes for himself: 'We, that is to say the well-to-do, the educated, the cultivated, are sinning against the poor and the non-cultured classes by allowing a million and a half of them to live herded together at one end of the town, whilst we keep all the leisure, all the culture, all the higher education at the other.'[4] This observation suggests a further quality typical of those who undertook social work in the slums: insensitivity to the cultural values of the working classes. The middle and upper-class reformers were horrified by everything they saw in the 'non-cultured'. Their dislike of every aspect of working-class life was all-embracing—they tried to change everything; they were unable to separate working-class values from the evil consequences of an appalling environment and economic hardship. Their simple instinct was to educate the working classes into acceptance of their own cultural values. A chasm existed between styles of life which the Settlements did not bridge. They became little oases of upper-class life. Thus in their spare time, the residents at Oxford House relaxed in a Fives Court. 'I don't think I ever heard of anybody who defeated the Head at Fives', was the recollection of the happy days spent at Bethnal Green by one of the graduate residents.[5] A trivial illustration: but it was an outward sign of the more or less complete inability of churchmen to recognize that it was their class identification, not their religious beliefs, that alienated the working population. Some adopted radical political ideas, and evidently supposed that this

[1] Winnington-Ingram, *Fifty Years' Work*, p. 1.

[2] Percy Colson, *Life of the Bishop of London* (London, 1935), p. 29.

[3] See Hugh McLeod, *Class and Religion in the Late Victorian City* (London, 1974), p. 104.

[4] A. F. Winnington-Ingram, 'The Classes and the Masses', in *The Church of the People*, ed. Davidson, p. 173.

[5] S. C. Carpenter, *Winnington-Ingram* (London, 1949), p. 38.

would attract the working classes. But the advanced ideas they adopted were in themselves indications of class reference, removed from the common assumptions of contemporary working-class politics. Victorian Christianity had become integrated with the class values of the established classes: separating religious truth from the mixture was a problem each generation of Christian men has had to face since the beginning. Even the most enthusiastic Victorian churchmen failed to realize just how difficult that problem always is.

5

Political Attitudes of the Victorian Church

It was conventional for Victorian ecclesiastics to regard it as one of their duties to keep the Church free of political involvement. Christian laymen, those who actually conducted the terms of political debate, also agreed that it was right to separate religion as far as possible from the area of party politics; and it was only in unfortunate and occasional parliamentary lapses, like Disraeli's Public Worship Regulation Act, or the Bradlaugh affair—issues which themselves cut across normal party loyalties, so unused were public men to the practice of party division on such matters—that religion formally entered the arena of controversial political discussion. The areas of conflict between Church and Dissent formed a large exception to this. In maintaining the position of the Establishment, churchmen were often drawn unwillingly into political division, since their opponents had political objectives. But this was never regarded as a particularly suitable state of affairs; it was always considered an exceptional, and, it was hoped, a transient lapse from normality. Nonconformists themselves argued that after the attainment of 'religious equality' a return could be made to the proper separation of religion and politics, and they blamed the Establishment of the Church as having, in fact, obliged them to mix religion with political questions at all.

The collection of attitudes known as 'Christian Socialism' forms, at least at first sight, an interesting exception to the conventional separation of religion and politics. These ideas and attitudes deserve prior and extensive consideration, not merely because of the sympathetic attention they have received from the modern Church, but because they established a way of regarding the relationship of the Church to the world of secular activity which has sustained a nearly continuous existence since the mid-nineteenth century. The first appearance of 'Christian Socialist' ideas in England came between 1848 and 1855, when Maurice, Ludlow, Kingsley, and others, came together to promote their own solution to the 'spiritual destitution' of the masses. The times were opportune. The 'Hungry 'Forties' inspired several versions of folk romanticism within the intelligentsia; and in 1844 W. G. Ward, the Oxford High Church extremist, had outlined the ideal of a Church of the working class, whose 'ordinary condition will be one of opposition to those high in worldly station'.[1] The first impetus of Christian Socialism did not last, and it was not until the later 1870s, with the ideas of Headlam, and then of Westcott, Gore, and their associates, that an enduring tradition of Christian social radicalism took root. But the Christian 'Socialist' school was not really socialist. Maurice and his circle were classical bourgeois 'utopians'; they regarded existing social structures as satisfactory and necessary, and sought only to iron out the unfortunate conditions of industrial society by voluntary co-operative enterprise.[2] Westcott's vision was similar. In his thought the rejection of Political Economy—for this is, at basis, what Christian 'Socialism' was all about—was perhaps rather more explicit. It reflected in a particularly well-publicized form the growing tendency of some intellectuals to criticize *laissez-faire* practices. Christian Socialism, in fact, was deeply academic. The Christian Socialists' rejection of Political Economy was much more agonized than that of others in public life, because of their own insistence on giving the most moralistic and theoretical tone to their observations on the state of society. To the extent that they managed to give a theological backing to the critique of *laissez-faire* social and economic practice it served only to separate them from the characteristically pragmatic, and non-theoretical basis of almost everyone else's view of the social state. Maurice and Westcott, in particular, have had a tremendous impact on modern theological learning, and there are soundly based reasons why this has been so. They adjusted the relationship of the sacred and secular in order to see the world as a single unity in the providential design of God. As social and economic theorists, however, their ideas were not distinguished.

Christian Socialism first emerged, in fact, in opposition to the extension of the suffrage to the working class. It arose in opposition to Chartism. Nothing so clearly shows its academic nature. For Chartism was a genuine working-class movement for parliamentary reform. The six points of the Charter were all derived from the old radical reform programme—all had appeared as long before as Cartwright's proposals in 1776. Chartism was not a socialist movement, though socialists like Harney and Jones emerged within it, and were the most important influences to survive the Chartist collapse after 1848. The movement in effect represented the simultaneous outburst, in years of economic depression, of a number of different and highly localized agitations, each reflecting regional variations in economic conditions and traditional social interests. The policy of parliamentary reform was its sole unifying element: without it, Chartism would have been simply a widespread collection of agitations generated by local feelings over

---

[1] W. G. Ward, *The Ideal of a Christian Church considered in comparison with Existing Practice* (London, 1844), p. 50.

[2] For a critical survey, see Torben Christensen, *Origins and History of Christian Socialism, 1848–54* (Aarhus, 1962).

the Poor Law, factory reform, the currency question, 'religious equality', local labour relations, demands for a cheap press, and so forth. When the Christian Socialists opposed the policy of universal suffrage, in explicit opposition to the main point of Chartism, they were, therefore, placing themselves well outside the references of popular political consciousness. 'For all widespread popular troubles and general discontents do indeed point at some great social want or evil', as Samuel Wilberforce said when speaking of Chartism in 1842. He was himself sensitive to the Chartists' cry for attention but unsympathetic to Christian Socialism. 'It is therefore a short-sighted policy which would merely stifle the voice of complaint; rather should its accents, broken and inarticulate as they must needs be, guide us to the redressing of the evil which they indicate.'[1] Socialism, he saw with considerable penetration, was 'but the outgrown religious dissent of the preceding generation'.[2] Most churchmen were opposed to Chartism. Phillpotts was well supported by other bishops when in 1840 he moved for a parliamentary inquiry into what he took to be the 'crimes' of Chartists and socialists[3]—whom, like many of his contemporaries, he appears to have bracketed together. Chartism seemed to stand for the overthrow of institutions; public men in the 1840s rather exaggerated its potential revolutionary threat. A lot of sermons attacked the Chartists, some of them reprinted by the Religious Tract Society. Relations had been made bad by the Chartists' own attacks on the Church and on the relationship of Church and State, for much the same sorts of reasons as led to the Dissenters' attacks: because the Church appeared to be an inseparable part of the aristocratic, landed basis of the State. But the Chartists went on to attack the Church for further reasons—reasons which applied equally against the middle-class Dissenters. They regarded nearly all organized religion in their day as too corrupted by worldly respectability, too involved in the unequal distribution of wealth and social influence. Chartists were not irreligious. Their opposition to the formal Churches in fact expressed their belief that the Churches were unworthy; that they had departed from the primitive purity and equality of early Christian society. 'Study the New Testament,' advised a Chartist newspaper; 'it contains the elements of Chartism.'[4] In Chartist literature, Christ was represented as a teacher of democratic politics. The religious wing of Chartism sought to overthrow the religious conventions of the age and re-establish a practical, egalitarian dimension to Christianity —it was the British counterpart of the 'frontier' religious experience of America. A very few men inside the formal Churches sympathized: the

[1] *A Charge Delivered at the Ordinary Visitation of the Archdeaconry of Surrey*, by *Samuel Wilberforce*, M.A. (London, 1842), p. 28.
[2] Ibid., p. 30.
[3] Soloway, *Prelates and People*, p. 227.
[4] H. U. Faulkner, *Chartism and the Churches* (New York, 1916), p. 22.

Revd. Dr. A. S. Wade and the Revd. Thomas Spencer in the Church of England; the Revd. Henry Solly, the Unitarian; the Revd. J. R. Stephens, the celebrated Methodist Chartist. But most were hostile. And some Chartists instead turned to religious organization of their own. The 'Christian Chartist Churches' began to spread south from Scotland, where they had started, after 1840. These were congregations of working men, and from their pulpits contrasts were made between the true practice of Christianity and the 'exactions' of the Church.[1] Chartist leaders were also anxious to avoid too great a sympathy for the crusade of the middle-class Dissenters against the Church. 'Give us religious liberty, as well as every other—but do not give us religious liberty alone,' Ernest Jones told a Chartist meeting at St. Pancras in 1846. 'Will religious liberty give you a leg of mutton on your spits, or a coat on your backs?'[2] The opposition of the Chartists to the Church was not merely rhetorical, it was practical. The practice of invading church services began at Stockport in 1839: demonstrators occupied church buildings at service times and demanded that the minister preach a sermon in support of the claims of labour. Such was the style and quality of preaching in the 1840s that the Church could usually be cleared by agreeing to do so.

That the Christian Socialists found Chartism antipathetic was not because they had, themselves, some more subtle diagnosis of the ills of industrial society, or because they recognized that in parliamentary reform the Chartists had backed a political solution to grievances which were social and economic. It was because F. D. Maurice supported the union of Church and State, which the Chartists did not, and opposed the extension of the franchise, which was the centre of the Chartist programme. In 1838 Maurice wrote that 'confused, disorderly notions' were stirring up the Chartists and Socialists.[3] In 1848 he volunteered as a special constable to help put down the expected Chartist rioting. (He was rejected: clergymen were not enrolled.) It was the Chartist alarm in April 1848 that first brought Maurice, Ludlow, and Kingsley together in political sympathy—they published a placard addressed to the 'Workmen of England', in which Chartists were told that they were not yet ready for the vote. 'Workers of England, be wise, and then you *must* be free, for you will be fit to be free', they declared. Only educated men could properly exercise a vote. It was a message they explained in *Politics for the People*, a paper which lasted for some months and which was not untypical of the moralistic literature in favour of popular education which was quite common at the time. Charles Kings-

---

[1] R. B. Pugh, 'Chartism in Somerset and Wiltshire', in *Chartist Studies*, ed. Asa Briggs (London, 1959), p. 201.

[2] *An Anthology of Chartist Literature*, I. O. B. Kobaneba (Moscow, 1953), p. 356.

[3] F. D. Maurice, *The Kingdom of Christ* (1838), new edn. (London, 1958), ii (Part III), 336.

ley's 'socialism' was as idiosyncratic as Maurice's. He believed, according to Thomas Hughes, 'that a landed aristocracy was a blessing to the country, and that no country would gain the highest liberty without such a class'. Kingsley was excited by the 1848 revolutions in Europe. Indeed, he believed that a cataclysmic 'Day of the Lord' was imminent.[1] Some other intellectuals were similarly excited by it all. Arthur Stanley, future Dean of Westminster, and a sympathizer of mid-century Christian Socialism, said he 'could hardly get through' his lectures when the news of the Paris revolution reached Oxford.[2]

It is sometimes difficult to see how the label 'socialist' can be applied to Maurice and his circle at all. Their concern for the conditions of the working men was like that of most old-fashioned paternalist clergy who hated the middle-class manufacturers and the industrial England they had created. But the description 'socialist' was applied by Maurice to himself in 1850, evidently because he supposed that the espousal of the co-operative ideal—which became the most characteristic feature of his economic thought—was 'socialist'. But Maurice's thought was not really economic at all; it was moral, and the co-operative idea, in his mind, described a social attitude rather than an economic device. It was like the small co-operative enterprises[3] encouraged by parish priests, in the hope of securing a degree of independence for working men, in all parts of the country. Maurice was indirectly influenced by the utopian socialism of Buchez, Blanc, and de Lamennais, and through his association with John Ludlow, who had himself absorbed French co-operative ideas while being brought up in France. Ludlow was a barrister. At Lincoln's Inn he met Maurice, who was Chaplain there. He did have a positive attitude to the State, regarding it as competent to act for social regulation. He was a critic of the non-interventionist teachings of the *laissez-faire* formula. Maurice, however, did not follow Ludlow's endorsement of state action. He had already opted for a quasi-mystical, organic view of the State, professing its own sacred character as part of the Divine dispensation, but institutional at basis, made up of corporate entities. Maurice's *Kingdom of Christ* was published in 1838, the same year as Gladstone's *State in its Relations with the Church*. Both works owed something to Coleridge's view of the State. Maurice's book was not even remotely a treatise on practical socialism. The moral personality of the State which he described had no collectivist function. It was, indeed, the old confessional State, dressed up in the style of German Idealism. Maurice was, in plain language, a Tory pater-

[1] *Charles Kingsley, His Letters and Memories of his Life*, ed. by his Wife (London, 1899), pp. 61, 63, 110.

[2] R. E. Prothero and G. G. Bradley, *The Life and Correspondence of Arthur Penrhyn Stanley, D.D.* (London, 1893), i. 390.

[3] On the incoherence of co-operative enterprise at this time, see P. N. Backstrom, *Christian Socialism and Co-operation in Victoria England* (London, 1974). p. 41.

nalist with the unusual desire to theorize his acceptance of the traditional obligation to help the poor. Gladstone moved on from the hopeless and un-English attempt to express traditional relationships in philosophical language: he abandoned his Coleridgian inheritance. But Maurice never did; he always remained in intellectual detachment from the realities of practical political experience. His espousal of the co-operative ideal was a perfect vehicle of his idealism. It was voluntary; it did not call upon the State; it would come about through the education of the working men by their social superiors. The union of the Church and State, which Maurice believed to be sacred and inviolable, was not to be compromised by unbalancing the mechanism—no collectivist powers needed to be added for the work of social reconciliation to proceed through the body of society. The contrast with Ludlow's ideas was very considerable. Ludlow *was* an economist theorist. He believed that society really did have to be reconstructed in the interests of economic justice. The co-operatives he envisaged were to be introduced by the State—not the mystical entity envisaged by Maurice, but the actual English State. And because that State was loaded with aristocratic associations and landed influence, it needed actual—parliamentary—reform. Maurice did not agree with that sort of thing at all. He believed that his Kingdom of Christ was already in physical existence. It was the English State in his own day. If men would reconcile their differences by recognizing the purposes of God in the State as it was, they would would find the State truly ethical. To Ludlow, as to some more distinguished thinkers, the purpose of philosophy might be to explain the world, but the point was to change it.

Maurice as a gentle person; shy and academic. His concern for the working class was not a sort of optional extra which he added to his Christian ministry—as it sometimes was for others. It was central to his view of life. His own life was passed among intellectuals—as a Professor at King's College, London, until 1853, in the planning of the Working Men's Colleges, as a Cambridge Professor after 1866. He was deeply impressed with the need for popular education, a quality widespread in the Church of England in his day. The working classes were to be raised by education until they were capable of assenting to the sort of values he himself believed. Like an advance guard of the 'Adullamite' Liberals, Maurice was appalled at the prospect of the rule of ignorance. He loathed popular opinion. In 1867 he opposed the Reform Bill. The only progressive political scheme he did subscribe to was female suffrage, an idea hardly likely to attract working-class support. 'Acquiescence in a popular opinion is the obvious, easy course for every man,' Maurice explained in 1865.[1] In attacking the reasons given by reformers for extending the vote to the

---

[1] F. D. Maurice, *The Conflict of Good and Evil in Our Day* (London, 1865), p. 47.

working classes, at the time of the parliamentary discussions in 1866, he declared that he would always ignore the will of the majority. 'If it could be put to the vote of the greatest number what they would have for happiness, I have no security that they would not decide for something profoundly low and swinish.'[1] It was an opinion typical of the liberal intelligentsia of the second half of the nineteenth century. Yet he also rejected the 'fancy franchises' and similar devices promoted by those anxious to exclude working men insufficiently intelligent to exercise an independent vote, and thought that reformers of Parliament should 'seek for the organic portion of the working classes, in these they will find the best and most effectual guarantees against any mere mob dictation'.[2] It was a revealing conclusion: the 'organic portion' were those educated to the point at which they had become reconciled to the existing operation of the State and the Constitution as the present embodiments of the Divine order. Maurice underlined this definition by deploying arguments for the sort of popular education required before the vote could be conferred. It was to be a programme directed at concentrating all existing social and economic diversities and disparities in a single unifying doctrine of the State: 'the education of the workmen should be directed not to extinguish any one of the convictions which are striving among us now, but to find some centre for them all'.[3] As in some diluted Hegelian explanation, the poor were to be raised from *Verstand* to *Moralität* by self-realization, by recognizing their function in the providential arrangement of things. It was not exactly a vision which made them rush to the barricades. When Maurice's doctrine of nationality is added to these ideas, his 'centre' of social consciousness becomes even more removed from the common assumptions of English working-class radicalism. He admired the rise of German nationalism, and believed that national identity in its purest form was established through warfare. In fact the morality of war derived from its ability to create and preserve national identity.[4] These developments in Maurice's organic view of the nation-state took place in the 1860s and 1870s, as Bismarck, whose career he admired, was consolidating the German State. He delivered his views on the morality of this sort of thing to his students in Cambridge. He taught them to venerate national institutions, as the embodiments of the national will, 'the form of Government under which we have been nurtured, which has moulded the thoughts of us and our fathers'.[5] But it is probably best not to apply the logic of these ideas too rigorously. Maurice's sensitivity to human suffering and his universal view

[1] F. D. Maurice, *The Workmen and the Franchise* (London, 1866), p. 203.
[2] Ibid., p. 233.
[3] Ibid., p. 239.
[4] F. M. McClain, *Maurice: Man and Moralist* (London, 1972), pp. 119, 130, 132.
[5] F. D. Maurice, *Social Morality. Twenty-one lectures Delivered in the University of Cambridge* (London, 1869), p. 198.

of the Divine mercy, should be allowed to soften his political philosophy. He was a theologian; it is as well that he is remembered as one.

Maurice's social and economic ideas were a little more conventional than his ideas about the nation-state. They were, that is to say, an early and partial rejection of Political Economy. He objected to the competitive spirit in economic relationships for being, simply, 'the selfish principle'.[1] Yet with characteristic individuality, he favoured *laissez-faire* as a trading practice; he approved of classical economic liberalism and only regretted, apparently, that it had not had a more beneficial effect in promoting manliness and energy of character.[2] His solution to the unpleasing social effects of *laissez-faire* economic practice was not to change the system as such, but 'to make men fellow-workers instead of rivals', through the cultivation of 'the old feeling that trades are brotherhoods'.[3] This reference to the idealized world of the medieval guilds struck familiar enough nineteenth-century chords: it belonged to the intellectual culture of the medieval revivalists, of Carlyle, Ruskin, and Morris, and it faintly anticipated the 'arts and crafts' bourgeois socialism of the end of the century. In opposition to the views of Edward Neale and Thomas Hughes, two other prominent members of the Christian Socialist circle of the early 1850s, Maurice was opposed to trade unionism.[4] In 1849, his antagonism to the idea of state intervention to promote social reform was such that his colleagues had to abandon plans for an agitation on public-health reforms.[5] All that is left, to define the sense in which Maurice called himself a 'socialist', is the co-operative ideal and his work for popular education—both of which were, anyway, encouraged by clergymen of all political tinctures in the middle years of the nineteenth century. These, however, were the areas in which Maurice was practical rather than purely theoretical. The 'Society for Promoting Working Men's Associations' was, it is true, largely organized by Neale; but Maurice was personally concerned with the work of establishing workshops in London and the provinces, especially at the beginning. These enterprises themselves were undercapitalized and, as a result, were unsuccessful. Yet many other co-operative ventures were started in emulation. In 1853 Maurice was dismissed from the Chair of Divinity at King's College, London, for his liberal attitudes to the Doctrine of Eternal Punishment—by a Council which included Gladstone. It has been suggested that his political beliefs were the real reason behind his dismissal,[6] but this is hardly likely. If all the clergymen who sponsored co-operatives had lost their appointments a very large gap would have

---

[1] F. D. Maurice, *On the Reformation of Society, and How all Classes may Contribute to it* (Southampton, 1851), p. 15.

[2] Ibid., p. 17.   [3] Ibid., pp. 32, 36.

[4] P. d'A. Jones, *The Christian Socialist Revival*, p. 23.

[5] McClain, *Maurice*, p. 65.   [6] Ibid., p. 40.

appeared in the Church. It was a time when theological opinion was important. A recent study of the controversy surrounding the doctrine of Eternal Punishment suggests the strong possibility that it was this alone that was quite adequate to get Maurice removed from his Chair.[1] At any rate Maurice was freed to devote himself to the pursuit of his educational ideals, and in 1854 he founded the Working Men's College in Red Lion Square—a fairly successful venture which attracted some distinguished lecturers and inspired similar establishments throughout the country.

The Working Men's College absorbed most of Maurice's energies and his 'socialism' declined. The Christian Socialist circle dissolved: it had anyway more or less completely lacked any common political bond. In 1851 Ludlow and Neale had quarrelled, and then Maurice and Ludlow had differed over the policy—and even the title—of their journal, the *Christian Socialist*. Ludlow also believed that Maurice's second wife, Georgina, was persuading her husband to abandon Christian Socialism.[2] In 1855 Maurice closed down the Society for Promoting Working Men's Associations, and with the collapse of this practical vehicle of the co-operative ideal, the first phase of Christian Socialism in England passed out of existence. Its importance is to be gauged by the impression it created that some churchmen were really experimenting with socialist ideas— rather than with the reality—and by the respect it has earned from modern scholars, searching around for early exponents of political preferences of their own. It did not even manage to outrage contemporary conservative opinion. Kaye of Lincoln appears to have been the only bishop[3] who criticized what to most, no doubt, seemed a rather eccentric but reasonably acceptable attempt to assist popular education. The only significant economic thinking had come from Ludlow—yet it was not his ideas, but Maurice's, that impressed Westcott, Temple, and the later tradition of Christian Socialism within the Church.[4] The most effective result of the Christian Socialism of these years came from Slaney's parliamentary Select Committee of 1850 on Limited Liability. Six of the seventeen witnesses before the Committee were Christian Socialists, and they managed to influence the adoption of the legislation of 1855 and 1856 for the protection of working-class savings through limited liability.[5]

The Christian Socialism which re-emerged in the 1870s and 1880s was quite different from Maurice's. It remained an upper-class affair of aesthetes like Stewart Headlam and intellectuals like Brooke Foss Westcott, Henry Scott Holland, and Charles Gore. But it was more diversified.

[1] Geoffrey Rowell, *Hell and the Victorians. A study of the nineteenth-century theological controversies concerning eternal punishment and the future life* (Oxford, 1974), pp. 62 and 84.
[2] McClain, *Maurice*, p. 26.   [3] Soloway, *Prelates and People*, p. 265.
[4] P. d'A. Jones, *The Christian Socialist Revival*, p. 10.
[5] J. Saville, 'Sleeping Partnerships and Limited Liability, 1850–56', in *Economic History Review* (Apr. 1956), p. 418.

Headlam and the Guild of St. Matthew (1877) did have, despite some marked eccentricities, a grasp of socialism. Westcott's Christian Social Union (1889), on the other hand, was really a large and respectable body of academic churchmen who sought to replace what they supposed *laissez-faire* economic practice to be with 'brotherhood'. It was this second group that attracted attention—that became the most influential exponent of social principles in the Church of England at the end of the nineteenth century. It is not clear that the members of the C.S.U. were acquainted with the technicalities of socialist political thought, but when they did refer to them they were generally dismissive. Christianity, said William Alexander, the Bishop of Derry and Raphoe, at the Church Congress discussion of 'Socialism and Christianity' in 1887, 'is not Karl Marx's *Capital* in a religious form'.[1] Members of the C.S.U. were unlikely to suppose it was. They agreed with Alexander's denunciation of Bakunin's anarchist ideas for involving the 'universal destruction of the present social system', and for making land and capital 'the collective property of the inhabitants'.[2] When in 1890 Westcott himself told the Church Congress that 'the term socialism has been discredited by the connection with many extravagant and revolutionary schemes',[3] he does not seem to have been conscious that it was *his* definition of 'socialism' that was extravagant, not the political creed itself. The Christian 'Socialists' of the C.S.U. school were, like Maurice in the 1850s, not really socialists at all. They represented the synthesis of Victorian intellectual liberalism with Chamberlain's 'constructionism' or collectivism. They differed only in the scale of their moralizing from those of their class and profession whose criticisms of Political Economy, and partial acceptance of collectivist functions for the State, were marked features of the last three decades of the century. So far were they from being the daring social theorists of their own imagining, and so respectable did their attitudes become, that between 1889 and 1913, sixteen of the fifty-three episcopal appointments went to members of the Christian Social Union.[4]

Definitions of 'socialism' used by sympathetic churchmen in the later years of the nineteenth century make it quite clear that they used the term in various and unorthodox senses. Most did not regard the socialism of Marx, or Bakunin, or the S.D.F., as remotely acceptable, and appeared to regard 'socialism' as—in the words of Bishop Alexander—'an inspiration' aimed at 'ameliorating the moral, intellectual, and social condition of the greatest number'. Alexander rejected the idea 'that social equality

---

[1] *The Official Report of the Church Congress held at Wolverhampton* (London, 1887), p. 159.
[2] Ibid., p. 158.
[3] *The Official Report of the Church Congress held at Hull* (London, 1890), p. 320.
[4] P. d'A. Jones, *The Christian Socialist Revival*, p. 164.

must be established in the most rigorous form, and social inequality abso-lutely levelled', because this involved 'complete redistribution of property and re-casting of human society'.[1] In 1888 the Lambeth Conference had before it a Report from its Committee 'Appointed to consider the subject of the Church's practical work in relation to Socialism', whose chairman was James Moorhouse, Bishop of Manchester. The Committee began by confessing that 'Socialism' was a word 'used at present in very different senses'.[2] Furthermore: 'any scheme of social reconstruction may be called Socialism which aims at uniting labour and the instruments of labour (land and capital), whether by means of the State; or the help of the rich, or of the voluntary co-operation of the poor'. Defined this way, 'Socialism' could be Christian, the Committee reported. But they went on to denounce atheists and anarchists, and those opposed to private property—with whom the Church could have no alliance. In the end, indeed, this definition of acceptable 'socialism' was so diluted as to be virtually meaningless: 'every wise endeavour which has for its object the material and moral welfare of the poor'.[3] That would have made every clergyman in the nineteenth cen-tury a 'socialist'. The Committee recommended the adoption of the co-operative principle, and offered three reasons for rejecting 'state socialism'. First: 'if full compensation were given to the present holders of property the scheme could hardly be realised, while if full compensation were with-held it would become one of undisguised spoliation'. Secondly: 'it is diffi-cult to see how the affairs of any great commercial undertaking could be conducted by the State or the Commune with the energy, economy, and sagacious foresight which are necessary to secure success'. And thirdly: 'if all men had to work under State or Communal inspection and com-pulsion, it would be difficult for them to retain freedom, the sense of parental responsibility, and those numerous traits of individuality which give richness to the human character'.[4] These reasons confirmed the Com-mittee's very insubstantial comprehension of socialism.

It is clear, in fact, that most of what passed for 'Christian Socialism' in the later nineteenth century was Liberalism, with all its moralistic qualities, but with Gladstonian economic ideas hacked out. Most who called themselves 'Christian Socialists' in the C.S.U. sense favoured col-lectivist reforms of individual social evils, but opposed the notion of sys-tematic state power or state compulsion. 'Socialism' was to be adopted voluntarily—the co-operative ideal most easily fitted this scheme, hence its ready acceptance. Christianity, Bishop Moorhouse declared, 'seeks to make men prosperous and wise and good, not by the force of laws or

---

[1] *The Official Report of the Church Congress held at Wolverhampton* (1887), p. 156.
[2] *Conference of Bishops of the Anglican Communion Holden at Lambeth Palace in July 1888* (London, 1888), p. 50.
[3] Ibid., p. 52.   [4] Ibid., pp. 53–4.

bayonets, but by the change of individual hearts, and the introduction of a new brotherhood in Christ'.[1] Like so many of the leaders of the Church towards the end of the century, Westcott had come to support state intervention to eliminate social evils—and seems to have believed this to be the essence of 'socialism'—yet he relegated state power to a secondary capacity. 'Legislation is the last and not the first thing in social reform,' he said in his address to the Christian Social Union in 1894. 'Its proper function is to register each successive advance in the popular conception of the just conditions of life.' He added, 'We need, in fact, far more to reform the unwritten laws of social intercourse than to alter the statute book'.[2] Churchmen who criticized socialism, however, generally meant the real thing: their criticisms usually centred on the issue of state compulsion. Bishop Magee of Peterborough denounced 'Christian Socialism' as 'only one of many attempts to make the laws of the State and the Laws of the Church one and the same; and, as such, is foredoomed, like all its predecessors—the Papacy, and the Fifth Monarchy men, and the Puritan laws of New England—to certain and speedy failure'.[3] In October 1889 he told the Peterborough Diocesan Conference that 'if the State took the law of the Church and tried to enforce it by the penalties of the State, it would set up an absolutely intolerable tyranny'.[4] Yet he saw that Christian Socialists were trying just that: to insist that their social teachings were essentially Christian, and that, as such, they should have the force of law. Archdeacon William Cunningham, the Cambridge critic of *laissez-faire*, who was prepared to allow the State to regulate the conditions upon which property was held,[5] objected to joining the C.S.U. precisely because he objected to state compulsion of Christian morality.[6]

The only group that had a convincing acquaintance with systematic socialist theory was the one that Stewart Headlam gathered to himself in East London. Headlam was one of the curates at St. Matthew's, Bethnal Green. He was aesthetic and eclectic; but he did have a real knowledge of practical politics as a result of his membership, as a Fabian Socialist, of the London County Council from 1888.[7] He had been educated at Eton and Cambridge, and enjoyed the sort of private income which enabled him to pursue his propagandist work and to indulge his artistic tastes. His failure

[1] *Conference of Bishops of the Anglican Comunion Holden at Lambeth Palace in July 1888* (London, 1888), p. 52.

[2] Brooke Foss Westcott, *Christian Social Union Addresses* (London, 1903), p. 12.

[3] J. C. MacDonnell, *The Life and Correspondence of William Connor Magee* (London, 1896), ii. 261.

[4] Ibid., p. 277.

[5] W. Cunningham, 'The Church's Duty in Relation to the Sacredness of Property', in *The Church of the People*, ed. Randall Davidson, p. 29.

[6] Kitson Clark, *Churchmen and the Condition of England*, p. 337.

[7] A. M. McBriar, *Fabien Socialism and English Politics 1884–1918* (Cambridge, 1962), p. 198.

ever to secure a parish of his own almost certainly reflects his eccentricity rather than his politics. His interests were varied: he advocated secular education, though a High Churchman; he campaigned for freedom of thought, for the abolition of liquor licensing, for disestablishment, and for the adoption of Henry George's scheme for a single tax on land.[1] He was a devotee of the theatre and of ballet; his rooms were done up by fashionable interior decorators, and there he entertained the artistic society of London. All this culture did not leave him without a genuine compassion for the working classes, however, and Headlam's socialism, despite its uneven quality, was real enough. His political views were similar to those of two other left-wing Christian publicists, H. H. Champion and J. L. Joynes, both of whom were members of the S.D.F. Joynes, who edited the *Christian Socialist* in 1883, was the son of Headlam's housemaster at Eton. And like Percy Dearmer and Conrad Noel, two of the leading 'medievalists' in the socialist movement within the Church, Headlam spoke at 'Labour Churches'—the secular societies for working men which John Trevor inspired in 1891, and which were closely associated with emerging labour politics.[2]

'For men and women to put up with circumstances which hinder their mental, moral, or physical growth, is not only a sin against themselves,' Headlam wrote in 1875, 'it is a sin against the Brotherhood and against God the Father.'[3] This was not merely descriptive: Headlam believed that society had to be recast, to provide for the redistribution of wealth by the power of the State. At the 1887 Church Congress, he called for legislation to 'put a stop to the robbery of the poor that has been going on for so long'.[4] His *Fabian Tract* (No. 42) on *Christian Socialism*, published in 1892, envisaged the Church as 'mainly and chiefly for doing on a large scale throughout the world those secular, socialistic works which Christ did on a small scale in Palestine'.[5] His view of socialism was a total one: 'If you want to be a good Christian, you must be something very much like a good Socialist.'[6] There was nothing voluntary about it either. There was to be a political—but not a revolutionary—struggle for the control of state power, in order to use it for the recreation of social priorities. 'The State is a sacred organisation as well as the Church', and churchmen 'can unite with Socialists of every sort in their endeavour to seize the state and use it for the well-being of the masses instead of the classes'.[7] It scarcely needs to be said that this is not what the Christian Social Union understood

---

[1] P. d'A. Jones, *The Christian Socialist Revival*, p. 103.

[2] Inglis, *Churches and the Working Classes*, p. 231.

[3] Stewart D. Headlam, *The Church Catechism and the Emancipation of Labour* (London, 1875), p. 3.

[4] *The Official Report of the Church Congress held at Wolverhampton* (1887), p. 175.

[5] Stewart D. Headlam, *Christian Socialism* (London, 1892), p. 6.

[6] Ibid., p. 4.   [7] Ibid., p. 9.

by 'Socialism'. Headlam really did intend to change the basis of society.
As it happened, his own peculiarities of character, as well as the unpopular
nature of his ideas, made his practical influence slight within the Church.
He went too far for the fashionable radicals in the C.S.U.

Headlam's propagandist skills, however, did manage to give his ideas a
currency out of all proportion to the size of his immediate following. The
Guild of St. Matthew, which he founded at Bethnal Green in 1877, never
had a membership of more than 400, about a quarter of whom were priests,
and none of them working class. The Guild was beset with disintegrating
tendencies: personal conflicts and ideological dissensions. Yet it was, in
certain ways, influential. Its attempts to get the Lambeth Conference of
1888 to consider socialism as a serious matter were successful. The Guild
sent a memorial to the assembled bishops. And the bishops, in their Encyclical Letter, declared that 'No more important problems can well occupy
the attention—whether of clergy or Laity—than such as are connected with
what is popularly called Socialism'.[1] But the Guild's influence had been
only secondary: it was the respectable 'socialism' within the Church hierarchy that was really receiving attention. Scott Holland had addressed the
Lambeth Conference on Socialism; his words, together with Bishop
Moorehouse's Conference Committee, were the more effective reasons
for the bishops' willingness to look favourably on the question. It is also
important to notice that the Anglican Communion did not stand alone in
its openness to new social influences. Its attitude compared with contemporaneous adjustments in the Roman Catholic Church, especially with
Leo XIII's Encyclical of 1891, *Rerum Novarum*.[2] The Guild of St.
Matthew was at its strongest in the mid-1890s. Thereafter it declined—
a decline assisted to some extent by the adverse publicity arising from
Headlam's aid to Oscar Wilde during the latter's trial in 1895.[3] Headlam
himself dissolved the Guild in 1909. It had earned the respect of most of
the leading Fabians in England, and, whatever its eccentricities, it had at
least familiarized some with the notion that systematic socialism and formal
Christianity were not irreconcilable.

The Christian Social Union was quite different. Unlike the socialist
groups which flowered unpredictably on the fringe of the intelligentsia,
the C.S.U. was central, respectable, and vague. A number of clergymen
with advanced opinions managed to sustain memberships both of the
C.S.U. and of the Guild. Percy Dearmer was one such; he became secretary of the London branch of the C.S.U.—he was typical of the 'arts and
crafts' wing who seemed capable of finding a niche almost anywhere. The

---

[1] *Conference of Bishops* (London, 1888), p. 10.

[2] For the text, see Anne Freemantle, ed., *The Papal Encyclicals* (New York, 1956), pp.
166–95.

[3] P. d'A. Jones, *The Christian Socialist Revival*, pp. 128 and 147.

C.S.U. was not a socialist body. Although many of its members called themselves socialists, or allowed themselves to be called socialists, the Union was not even formally committed to socialist doctrines. It had been started in 1889 by Scott Holland, Gore, and Westcott. Like the Guild of St. Matthew, it was exclusively Anglican. Almost at once, the C.S.U. achieved a considerable measure of approval in the Church; perfectly expressing the social-service idealism of the upper-class clergy who organized and sustained it. The Union never had any working-class members. Its membership did become quite large, however, and at one point reached 6,000. Whereas the Guild had some influence upon Fabian Socialists, the Union had no influence with any political group—but it was immensely influential inside the leadership of the Church. The Church of England led the field in the espousal of social radicalism. When other denominations started comparable organizations—the Quaker Social Union (1904), the Methodist Social Union (1905), the Catholic Social Guild (1909)—it was to the C.S.U., and not to the Guild of St. Matthew, that they looked for inspiration. In origin the Union expressed some of the common assumptions of an Oxford group called by Scott Holland 'the Holy Party'. From 1875 this small company began to meet for occasional discussions of liberal theology.[1] Then, as later, there was usually a correlation between liberalism in theology and radical political idealism, and 'the Holy Party' began to cross the line. The convenor of the group was a tutor of Keble College, J. R. Illingworth, Rector of Longworth from 1883. It was a very academic, very upper-class gathering. Henry Scott Holland, who in 1884 became a Canon of St. Paul's, was the grandson of Lord Gifford, and went to Eton. Charles Gore, vice-principal of Cuddesdon Theological College in 1880, and in 1884 the first Principal of Pusey House, was descended from the Irish peerage; he went to Harrow. All three men were influenced by T. H. Green at Oxford. All came to believe that the Church was neglecting social and economic teaching. The greatest of 'the Holy Party', however, was Brooke Foss Westcott, once pupil of Prince Lee at King Edward's School in Birmingham. Westcott had been Headmaster of Harrow, Canon of Westminster, and in 1890 became Bishop of Durham. He was the first President of the C.S.U., and it was Westcott who made it the clearing-house for the radical conscience of the Church of England.

In Westcott's economic and political thinking there was no real socialism. There was actually no socialism at all: he was a Chamberlain-style Liberal, whose strong sense of compassion for the working men released itself in the assemblage of an intellectual apparatus to criticize the unpleasing consequences of what he took to be Political Economy. In his thought is to be found all the frustrated outrage that intellectuals experience when the

---

[1] *The Life and Work of John Richardson Illingworth*, ed. by his Wife (London, 1917), p. 33.

world does not appear to respect theoretical explanations of the ills of society. In 1890 he addressed the Church Congress on 'Socialism', and offered a lucid and characteristic definition of his political and social vision—it was a standard criticism of *laissez-faire* practice of the sort that had been spreading among sections of the intelligentsia for some years.

Socialism is the opposite of Individualism, and it is by contrast with Individualism that the true character of Socialism can be discerned. . . . Individualism regards humanity as made up of disconnected or warring atoms. Socialism regards it as an organic whole, a vital unity formed by the confirmation of contributing members, mutually interdependent. . . . The method of socialism is co-operation; the method of Individualism is competition. The one regards man as working with man for a common end; the other regards man as working against man for private gain. . . . Socialism, as I have depicted it, is not, I repeat, committed to any one line of action, but everyone who accepts its central thought will recognise certain objects for immediate effort. He will seek to secure that labour shall be acknowledged in its proper dignity as the test of manhood, and that its reward shall be measured not by the necessities of the indigent, but by its actual value as contributing to the wealth of the community.[1]

Christianity, he explained 'which has dealt hitherto with the individual, deals also with the State, with classes and not only with men, with social conditions and not only with personal character'. Men were waiting, he believed, 'for the next stage in the growth of the State, when in free and generous co-operation each citizen shall offer the fullness of his own life that he may rejoice in the fullness of the life of the body'.[2]

Westcott's description of Political Economy, of the system of 'Individualism', is rather a model of his own devising; it is far too unsubtle, an intellectual foil with little real existence. No doubt men could be found who acted in the way he described. But the actual operations of society and the State, in the period when *laissez-faire* ideals were in their ascendency, bore little relationship to Westcott's model. For him, evidently, 'socialism' turned on the voluntary principle, the co-operative ideal, as the means of changing society from selfishness to brotherhood. 'Socialist' Christians were to have a mission to the State and to the employers of labour. Then society, under their influence, would be permeated by the ideals of brotherhood and service until society was transformed. There was, in Westcott's thought, no suggestion that state coercive authority would be used to reorganize society, even though he clearly retained an organic concept of the State derived from F. D. Maurice and T. H. Green. His collectivism was to come about through the agitations of enlightened reformers—according to existing practice, in fact, among Political Economists themselves. This accumulation of state collectivist machinery as

[1] *The Official Report of the Church Congress Held at Hull* (London, 1890), p. 320.
[2] Ibid., p. 322.

a result of piecemeal social reform was what Westcott meant when he spoke of 'the growth of the State'. It is hard to believe that Westcott's speech in 1890 really 'fluttered the ecclesiastical dovecotes' as it was said to have done.[1] There was no vision of the overthrow of class society, no redistribution of wealth through state power, no attempt to define the false consciousness which held the working people in involuntary subjection to prevailing social custom. It was not that Westcott had ruminated on these ideas and arrived at sophisticated theoretical objections to them. He just did not seem to have regarded them as essential to 'socialism'. In 1895 he went so far as to declare that 'in considering the problems of industry, we have to take account of the distribution of wealth no less than that of the production of wealth'.[2] But he offered no concrete proposals to do anything about it. Westcott's personal spirituality, and his extraordinary ability to move others by his enthusiasm, explains how he was able to lead a movement of opinion whose real objects were so imprecisely defined. Scott Holland significantly recalled that no one could remember a word of Westcott's address at the founding of the C.S.U. in 1889—'only we know that we were lifted, kindled, transformed,' he wrote; 'we pledged ourselves; we committed ourselves; we were ready to die for the cause; but if you asked us why, and for what, we could not tell you'.[3]

Westcott and his followers overemphasized their own originality: they did not see that others before them had burned with a desire to bring the Church to the social and economic conditions of men. They simply assumed —with all the ignorance of practical politics characteristic of academic thought—that their predecessors had failed to see the problem. Hence Westcott's crude antithesis between 'socialism' and 'individualism'. And hence his claim, picked up later by Temple and his school, that no one had before sought to apply Christian teaching to modern economic life. 'What ought I to do as a Christian?' was a question Westcott said, which was not asked in 'commercial and political life'.[4] He was assisting the creation of a quasi-mythical interpretation of the social attitudes of the nineteenth-century Church which later became generally accepted as true. In opposition to the *laissez-faire* model he had devised he in fact offered a not dissimilar one—at least in the sense that it was voluntary. Classical Political Economy had supposed that individual exertion would create the wealth from which all would benefit. Westcott's alternative was the more nebulous creation of a sense of corporate mutual responsibility, not through state power, but by individual assent to the Christian ideals of brotherhood. Capitalism was not to be interfered with, except by the continuation

---

[1] Arthur Westcott, *Life and Letters of Brooke Foss Westcott* (London, 1903), ii. 111.
[2] Brooke Foss Westcott, *The Christian Social Union* (London, 1895), p. 8.
[3] Arthut Westcott, *Brooke Foss Westcott*, ii. 16.
[4] B. F. Westcott, *Christian Social Union Addresses*, p. 2 (Address at Cambridge, 1894).

of the existing piecemeal reforms to regulate particular excesses. The social structure of society was to remain the same. 'As citizens we are all bound to be workers,' he told the C.S.U. meeting at Macclesfield in 1898; 'and it has been one of my chief joys to watch the gradual acceptance of the master-thoughts of corporate obligation and corporate interdependence, till now it is (may I not say?) universally acknowledged among Englishmen that we all belong to one body, in which the least member has his proper function.'[1] How anyone could have used these words to describe the state of English society in the 1890s—a decade of particularly sharp class antagonism—it is almost impossible to imagine.

The Christian Social Union itself avoided exacting definitions of its purpose. Its first principle was 'to claim for the Christian Law the ultimate authority to rule social practice'.[2] This, of course, was precisely what the churchmen who had adopted Political Economy had been trying to do. The C.S.U. could not see it; they supposed their own methods were the first serious attempt to arrive at a Christian social polity. The methods themselves were inexplicit. In 1898 Westcott wrote that 'the members of the Union are by no means pledged to what is called Christian Socialism— a most vague phrase'.[3] In 1895 he had declared that the Union 'has no programme of immediate reforms'. The members 'reserve their freedom of opinion, and use it; but it would be disastrous if the Church itself were to be identified with a party or with a class'.[4] Since the C.S.U. was pretty exclusively upper class anyway, the second consideration was rather vacuous. But the aim of not having a programme was fulfilled. The Union became a place for its academic members to talk about goodwill and social harmony between the classes. Social action was very restricted. In 1893 the Oxford branch were moved in characteristically academic fashion: they began to compile 'white lists' of trading firms whose wages were thought an adequate reward of labour.[5] It is surprising how low they considered an adequate wage to be; and the practical result was a boycott of sweated industry by handfuls of intellectuals, a gesture which did in the end manage to draw some public attention to the evil working conditions in some small trades. The device was copied elsewhere in the country. Westcott also advocated frugal living by the rich as a means of diminishing social friction —'we must seek to live on as little as will support the full vigour of our life and work'.[6] Gore proposed that they should apply moral criteria when investing their money: 'to put one's money, or allow it to be put, into any "concern" without enquiring into the moral or social tendency of the

---

[1] Brooke Foss Westcott, Lessons from Work (London, 1901), p. 30.
[2] Westcott, The Christian Social Union, p. 15.
[3] Arthur Westcott, Brooke Foss Westcott, ii. 261.
[4] Christian Social Union Addresses, p. 25.
[5] P. d'A. Jones, The Christian Socialist Revival, p. 183.
[6] Christian Social Union Addresses, p. 60 (Liverpool, 1899).

concern, is to serve mammon at the expense of Christ'.[1] Like Westcott. Gore did not regard the 'socialism' he professed as involving systematic state action. He saw it as a 'moral ideal'; it was 'the great Christian principle of the brotherhood of man as based upon the fatherhood of God', a scheme which 'sums up all that is best in the social and moral aspiration of our time, whether it does or does not call itself Christian'.[2] Gore frequently insisted on the Church's guilt in having failed in its responsibilities to the poor; it was a constant theme in his entire public life and considerably influenced twentieth-century attitudes to the Church's past record.

The political detachment of the C.S.U. was demonstrated in 1893 when the Independent Labour Party was founded. Only a very few C.S.U. members, like the Hon. and Revd. James Adderley, supported the new political venture—whose constitutional respectability and muted objectives were anyway hardly likely to compromise the Union. (It is interesting that Stewart Headlam, who disliked the idea of a distinct working-class political party, also refused to support the I.L.P.) The C.S.U. membership were divided on conventional lines over questions of imperialism but this, too, failed to translate into overt political sympathy. Thus Scott Holland and Gore opposed the Boer War, along with a lot of Liberal opinion; Westcott supported it. At a prayer meeting for those involved in the war, he declared:

It is not only our paramount authority in South Africa which is at stake, but, as involved in that, our dominion in India, and our fitness to inspire and guide the life of Greater Britain. We have to show that we are still worthy to hold, both by might and counsel, the Empire which has been entrusted to us, to protect those who rightly look to us for help, and to bear patiently the thankless burden of the white man and train uncivilized races to a nobler life.[3]

He saw imperialism as a global extension of his domestic ideal of social service and goodwill between the classes. 'Imperialism is the practical advocacy of a fellowship of peoples with a view to the completeness of their separate development,' he said at Tufnell Park in 1900. 'An Empire, in other words, is the embodiment on a large scale of two ideas characteristic of our generation—association and service.'[4]

It is clear that Christian Socialists of the C.S.U. tradition did not regard their ideas as requiring political expression. They saw 'socialism' as a moral dimension to be added to existing political parties. So it was possible for Canon Henry Parry Liddon to regard himself both as a Christian Socialist

---

[1] Gore, *The Mission of the Church*, p. 119.

[2] Ibid., p. 142.

[3] Brooke Foss Westcott, *The Obligations of Empire* (London, 1900), p. 6.

[4] Westcott, *Lessons from Work*, p. 320. For another sympathetic appraisal of imperialism by a 'socialist' churchman, see 'The Church and the Empire', by B. R. Wilson in *Church Problems. A View of Modern Anglicanism*, ed. H. Hensley Henson, p. 379.

and as a supporter of Gladstone's Liberal Party[1]—a Party whose economic ideas and whose doctrine of economic individualism made it the enemy of collectivism. In the 1880 election Liddon voted Liberal with enthusiasm, and in 1885 he switched his vote to the Conservatives because he believed that the Liberals were menacing the Church Schools.[2] Mandell Creighton, another who leaned to Christian Socialism, campaigned on behalf of Liberal candidates in the 1880 election, when he was an incumbent in Northumberland. As a bishop, he was opposed to the involvement of the clergy with politics of any sort.[3] In this practical discouragement of party-political behaviour, the Christian Socialists of the C.S.U. school were very centrally in the tradition of the nineteenth-century Church.

It was a tradition that continued to be preserved, as far as possible, by nearly all Victorian churchmen. Of Edward King, Bishop of Lincoln, it was written: 'In politics and social questions the bishop was satisfied to enunciate great principles rather than to undertake any active work for their immediate application. He was a bishop first, not a politician or a social reformer'.[4] Yet King was noted for his social conscience and his desire to help working men. Frederick Temple, when Bishop of London in 1895 insisted on the duty of the clergyman 'to make religion penetrate into politics as far as he possibly can', yet insisted at the same time that 'politics shall never absorb religion'.[5] He was opposed to party loyalties. During the 1885 election, the vicar of a church in Upper Clapton, in London, preaching on the duty of churchmen in the election, said he 'should think it most wrong to pervert the pulpit into a platform, whence to denounce one political party and uphold another'.[6] This was very typical: a continuation of an earlier nineteenth-century tradition of behaviour. So was the belief that churchmen should be politically responsible as good citizens, deciding for themselves how to vote. Even the Revd. W. Tuckwell, Rector of Waltham, Lincolnshire, a supporter of Chamberlain and the National Liberal Federation, who campaigned for the Caucus radicals in the 1885 election at Rugby—for which he was cautioned by Henry Philpott, Bishop of Worcester—believed as a matter of general principle that the clergy ought not to get involved with party politics.[7] And the anonymous lay author of an 1865 tract urging voters to consider whether the Liberals or Conservatives were the better supporters of the Estab-

---

[1] G. W. E. Russell, *Dr. Liddon* (Leaders of the Church) (London, 1905), p. 168.

[2] Ibid., pp. 161 and 165.

[3] Fallows, *Mandell Creighton and the English Church*, p. 24.

[4] B. W. Randolf and J. W. Townroe, *The Mind and Work of Bishop King* (London, 1918), p. 251.

[5] *Lectures on Disendowment*, by the Bishops of London, Bangor, Stepney, and others (London, 1895), p. 12.

[6] Leonard E. Shelford, *Twenty Years at St Matthew's, Upper Clapton, 1866–1886* (London, 1886), p. 102.

[7] W. Tuckwell, *Reminiscences of a Radical Parson* (London, 1895), p. 17.

lished Church, admitted that 'it is not the Church as a collective body' that was the appropriate body to decide such a question, but 'Churchmen as individuals'. The author added, 'it is not proposed to bring the Church to the level of party, or to mix her up with politics'.[1] The tract itself, of course, identified the Conservatives as the better friend of the Church.[2]

One of the consequences of the non-partisan political preference of the Church was that the clergy did not advise the laity about their political conduct—as the European clergy usually did. Very deliberate attempts were made to persuade the newly enfranchised working-class voters that the Church, whilst exhorting them to a responsible use of political experience, did not wish to prejudice their actual party preferences. 'Now my advice to you is this: Think for yourselves,' said Basil Jones, Bishop of St. David's, to the Working Men's Meeting at the Swansea Church Congress in 1879; 'and mind when you vote that it is according to your conscience.'[3] It was typical advice. 'I know that all of you working men at the present day are politicians, and I am not in the least sorry for it,' Samuel Wilberforce said in 1870, when he was Bishop of Winchester; I want you to be politicians and philosophers, and everything else which the intellect God has given you enables you to be.'[4] This was, of course, a declaration for social mobility, not for the removal of social hierarchy. As the Nonconformists' assault upon the Church Establishment became increasingly associated with the Liberal Party—in the 1860s and 1870s, when the sectional alliances which constituted the Gladstonian party began to coalesce—churchmen began to be worried lest the Church became associated, by implication and necessity, with the Conservatives. This in practice happened: the Conservatives did stand out as the party of loyalty to the Church,[5] especially over the education question. It is from this period, rather than from the early nineteenth century, with its bench of Tory bishops, that the Church of England came to be popularly identified with Conservative Party politics. Gladstone himself gave one of the earliest indications of what was happening. Meditating at length in 1868 upon his own political conversion to the Nonconformists' case, Gladstone criticized the use of the term 'Political Dissenters' by defenders of the Establishment. 'If they, because they object to the union of the Church and the State, are Political Dissenters,' he said, 'it follows that all who upheld it

---

[1] *Church and Party: being some Remarks on the Duty of Churchmen in and out of Parliament with particular reference to the Coming General Election*, by a Lay Churchman (London, 1865), p. 21.

[2] Ibid., p. 20.

[3] *Nineteenth Annual Meeting of the Church Congress, Held at Swansea* (1879) (London, 1880), p. 459.

[4] *Authorized Report of the Church Congress held at Southampton* (1870), p. 389.

[5] Anglican clergy were especially identified with the Conservatives in local politics; see Hugh McLeod, *Class and Religion in the Late Victorian City* (London, 1974), p. 173.

are political Churchmen.'[1] The point was being picked up by others. Even those Church leaders most Conservative in politics were anxious to avoid a party political link as the price of preserving the Establishment. 'It is rather of bad augury that Lord Salisbury has made political Church Defence a watchword (for the present) with his party,' wrote Archbishop Benson in his Diary in November 1885; 'the effect will be that the Liberals will be afraid of meddling with the support of the Church lest it should cause any to doubt of their Liberalism.'[2] In 1882 Stanley Leighton, himself a Member of Parliament, had advised the Church Congress to organize a distinct political group in the House of Commons to protect their interests.[3] But this was exactly the sort of political involvement most anathema to churchmen. In 1887 the Earl of Selborne, a Liberal, was able to defend the Church against the charges made by the Liberation Society that the Establishment was merely an adjunct of the Conservative political interest, by pointing to the refusal of the clergy to take part in party politics.[4] The attempts to disestablish the Welsh Church, made by the Liberals in 1894 and 1895, gave a new substance to the cry that the Church and the Conservatives were in alliance. Indeed, Sir Michael Hicks-Beach told Archbishop Benson that it was no longer possible to avoid 'the defenders of the Church being Conservative, since "Welsh Disestablishment" has become a party cry'.[5] At a public meeting in Winchester, called in January 1895 to oppose Welsh disestablishment, George Sumner, Bishop of Guildford, said 'it was not the wish of the Church simply to vote Tory; they wished to be free as regarded their politics as Churchmen'.[6] But declarations like this were largely in vain. The Liberals' and Nonconformists' propaganda was successful: the Church went down in the record as an adjunct of the Conservative Party.

The political role of the bishops in the House of Lords continued to diminish in the second half of the nineteenth century, as the new clarity of party division, and the bipartisan nature of most sorts of social reform, perpetuated a distinction between 'political' and 'moral' questions. It became usual for the bishops to attend Parliament only for debates more or less directly concerned with the interests of the Church—measures on patronage, ecclesiastical discipline, public worship, education, the defence of the usual rights and privileges of the Establishment, and ethical questions such as marriage and divorce. The change was noticed

---

[1] W. E. Gladstone, *A Chapter of Autobiography* (London, 1868), p. 56.

[2] Benson Papers, Trinity College, Cambridge—Diaries, 1865, p. 331 (27 Nov.); see also A. C. Benson, *The Life of Edward White Benson*, p. 292.

[3] *The Official Report of the Church Congress held at Derby* (1882), p. 209.

[4] Roundell Palmer, Earl of Selborne, *A Defence of the Church of England against Disestablishment*, new edn. (London, 1887), p. 304.

[5] Benson Papers, Letter Books (1893–6), Benson to Randall Davidson, 8 Mar. 1894.

[6] *Memoir of George Henry Sumner*, compiled by Mary E. Sumner (Winchester, 1910), p. 128.

at the time. 'The attendance of Bishops in the House of Lords, except upon Church and semi-Church questions, has immensely fallen off,' Gladstone wrote to Lord Hartington in 1884; 'and the political function is, properly on the whole, sacrificed to diocesan duty.'[1] This last consideration was important. The sheer increase of ordinary ecclesiastical duties, as the Church expanded its ministration in the century, set a definite limit to other public duties the bishops had the time to perform; a situation only slightly eased by the appointment of suffragans. As Bishop of Manchester between 1848 and 1869, James Prince Lee did not attend the Lords once,[2] although he was entitled to do so, despite the newness of his see. Benson was a frequent attender when Archbishop of Canterbury,[3] but this reflected as much his personal sense of historical grandeur as it did the pressure of affairs of state or a defined political role. One sign of the new confinement of the bishops' interests was their attitude to parliamentary reform. In 1832 they had burned their fingers by regarding franchise reform within their proper sphere. In 1866 and 1867 they took no part in the parliamentary debates on the Second Reform Bill. In 1884 some bishops did concern themselves with the Third Reform Bill—at the invitation of Gladstone, the Liberal Prime Minister. Archbishop Benson had kept his own unfavourable view of the Bill, which he believed advanced 'fast into revolution',[4] to himself. Early in July 1884 Gladstone wrote to all the bishops seeking their support over the Bill. With the impending crisis in the Lords over the Redistribution clauses every vote for the Government was crucial. Without explicitly saying so, Gladstone's letters to the bishops in effect held out the possibility of their appearing to be 'on the side of the people'.[5] It was an appeal the bishops could not bring themselves to ignore: the Bishops of Ely (Woodford), Manchester (Fraser), and Truro (Wilkinson) all dispatched favourable replies. The Bishop of Durham (Lightfoot) agreed to record his 'first political vote'. In the actual division on the Bill in the Lords only the Bishop of Gloucester (Ellicott) voted with the Conservatives.[6] Gladstone had understood the bishops well. Queen Victoria, on the other hand, was 'puzzled to find so many whom she considers good' on the wrong side.[7] By the 1880s an appeal to the political high-mindedness of the bench was only likely to succeed if made on behalf of the popular parties. There had been a considerable change.

[1] *Correspondence on Church and Religion of William Ewart Gladstone*, ed. Lathbury, i. 181 (21 Mar. 1884).

[2] David Newsome, *Godliness and Good Learning. Four Studies on a Victorian Ideal* (London, 1961), p. 127.

[3] A. C. Benson, *Edward White Benson*, p. 294.

[4] Benson Papers, Diaries, 1884, p. 165 (13 June 1884).

[5] Andrew Jones, *The Politics of Reform, 1884* (Cambridge, 1972), p. 150.

[6] Ibid., pp. 150–1.

[7] Benson Papers, Diaries, 1884, p. 193 (11 July).

The defence of the Establishment of the Church against the Nonconformists may have had the unfortunate consequence of associating the
Church with a particular political party, but in defending the idea and the
practice of Establishment churchmen still tried to avoid party association.
It was the disestablishment of the Irish Church in 1869 that for the first
time really made the issue of state religion correspond to national party
divisions. Before then, the demands of the Nonconformists for 'religious
equality' were absorbed within political society through piecemeal reforms
by both major parties. It was the chance adoption of the policy of Irish
disestablishment by Gladstone in 1867 that suddenly adhered one of the
parties to a practical opposition to the continuation of the Establishment
in a section of the kingdom. The Church had by then already come to see
the need for organized resistance to the Nonconformists. It had in fact
been 'the restless attacks, the systematic organization, and the avowed
purposes of the opponents of the Church of England' that had prompted
the committee of the Cambridge Church Defence Association to call the
first Church Congress in 1861.[1] Since 1859 the 'Church Institution' in
London had sought to counter the arguments of the Nonconformists. In
1871 it was converted into the 'Church Defence Institution' by the leading
Tory prelate, Bishop Ellicott of Gloucester: Archibald Tait, Archbishop
of Canterbury (a Liberal), became its honorary president, and all but five
of the bishops—Liberal appointments made by Gladstone—became vice-
presidents. By 1874, the year of the collapse of the Liberal Government,
there were 450 local associations.[2] The Institution certainly had Conservative political sympathies—and in view of the growing association between
the Liberal Party and the Nonconformists this was scarcely surprising—
but it preserved a formal political neutrality. An additional body, the
'Central Church Committee', formed in 1894 at a meeting in Lambeth
Palace to plan the defence of the Welsh Church, was even more linked
with the Conservatives. The initial meeting was attended by Salisbury,
Cross, Cranbrook, and other Conservative leaders, as well as by a number
of senior bishops.[3] In 1896 this Committee amalgamated with the Church
Defence Institution. This sort of protective activity, which went so much
against the taste and instinct of churchmen, did have the undesired effect
of adding to the Church's appearance as an ally of the Conservative Party
politics, a feature which the Liberals were quick to exploit.

The Nonconformists, by the same token, are not to be regarded as
merely a limb of Liberalism. They certainly formed the most vocal of the
sectional alliances which constituted the Liberal Party over which Glad-

---

[1] *Report of the Proceedings of the Church Congress* (Cambridge, 1862), p. iii.

[2] P. T. Marsh, *The Victorian Church in Decline. Archbishop Tait and the Church of
England, 1868–1882* (London, 1969), p. 145.

[3] Benson Papers, Diaries, 1894, p. 125 (5 May).

stone presided. Their political influence was largely expressed through three great agencies—the Liberation Society, the United Kingdom Alliance (the Temperance movement), and the Education League. But a party sustained upon alliances tends to fall apart when the objectives of the groups involved turn out to be mutually incompatible. During his first ministry, from 1868 to 1874, Gladstone found that his other supporters, who were anyway unable to agree among themselves—whigs, radicals, Irish Catholics, English manufacturers, and intellectuals—were unable to agree with the Nonconformist wing on a number of issues. The Irish Catholics' demand for state-supported denominational education was the most obvious incompatibility and it was on this issue that the Government was defeated in 1873. By then most vocal Nonconformist leaders believed in secular education. Early in the 1870s Gladstone had upset the Nonconformists over Forster's Education Act and Bruce's Licensing Act. Realizing that it was useless to look to the Liberal Party in such circumstances to carry the policy of disestablishment further than Ireland, Edward Miall and the Liberation Society began an independent campaign for English disestablishment.[1] In May 1871 his motion for the disestablishment of the Church of England was defeated by 376 to 91 votes. The Irish Catholic members of Parliament, who had agreed to support the Liberation Society over disestablishment, in return for the Nonconformists' help in overthrowing the Irish Church, did not support the motion.[2] Another weakness had appeared in the Liberal alliance. Gladstone, for his part, stood by the English Church Establishment. In his election address of 1885, he declared that the question was not ripe in England; a sentiment which did not calm the fears of the Church —Lord Salisbury pointed out that two years before actually disestablishing the Irish Church, Gladstone had said that that prospect was in the dim and distant future.[3] Others in Gladstone's own party did not even share his intent. Chamberlain's 'Unauthorized Programme' envisaged a general disestablishment, in England, Wales, and Scotland. Gladstone's dislike of the Radical programme largely arose from its abandonment of economic retrenchment, but its religious policy cannot have commended it either. Yet in 1891 sufficient ground had slipped away for Gladstone's Newcastle Programme to endorse the policy of Welsh disestablishment. When the party had divided over Home Rule in 1886, the Liberal Unionists led by Hartington had stood by the Establishment principle; and despite its Whiggish associations, even Chamberlain was prepared to put up with this in order to preserve political opposition to Gladstone.

With these developments within the Liberal Party, it is not surprising

---

[1] For details of this see W. H. Mackintosh, *Disestablishment and Liberation*, pp. 238 ff.

[2] E. R. Norman, *The Catholic Church and Ireland in the Age of Rebellion, 1859–1873* (London, 1965), p. 364.

[3] A. C. Benson, *Edward White Benson*, p. 292.

that churchmen once more needed to defend the Establishment of religion. Inside the Church the principle of Establishment, in fact, was more widely accepted than it had been since before the 1830s. Even the High Church-men who had looked upon parliamentary control of the Church with such loathing, were prepared to tolerate the idea of Establishment by the end of the century—by then organs of ecclesiastical autonomy were already beginning to develop anyway. In 1871 Canon Gregory of St. Paul's had delivered what Bishop Fraser called an 'intemperate paper'[1] to the Church Congress, which denounced as 'miserable and pernicious' the consequences of the union of Church and State, and referred to 'the tyrannical action of the State towards the Church'.[2] Such sentiments were quite common for High Churchmen in the years following the Gorham judgment in 1850, the Ritual Commission of 1867, the Public Worship Regulation Act of 1874, and the prosecutions of Ritualist priests in the latter 1870s. But by the 1890s the exercise of erastianism seemed less evident, and the militant Protestantism of the Nonconformists was poised to strike down the Church in Wales. Most High Churchmen supported the Establishment principle rather than see the victory of the Welsh Chapels.[3] Another development which helped to lessen the Establishment question as a burning contro-versy at the centre of national life—and so allowed High Churchmen not to have to stumble over sharp definitions of it given by other churchmen—was the decline, at the very end of the century, of the Liberation Society. This was due to 'the failure of the voluntary principle in meeting the Society's financial needs'.[4]

The Nonconformists' objections to religious Establishments were little different from those put forward in the 1830s. The middle years of the century had seen those arguments and attitudes acquire a very large measure of support from most sections of Dissenting opinion, however. The militants had won over the majority. They spoke, still, of the cor-rupting effects for both parties of the union of Church and State. In prac-tice, their assault upon the Church of England remained a dimension of the middle-class radicals' attempt to discredit 'aristocratic' government. They were concerned with status, with 'religious equality'. They attacked the Church because of its 'privileges'. Their earlier successes had added to the logic of their cause by rendering the connection of Church and State still more anomalous. 'It is the absurdity and impolicy of attempt-ing to manage the affairs of a body like the Anglican Church by means of an assembly constituted as the House of Commons now is',[5] that the

---

[1] *Authorized Report of the Church Congress held at Nottingham* (1871), p. 139.

[2] Ibid., p. 117. The paper was actually read to the Congress in Gregory's absence.

[3] P. M. H. Bell, *Disestablishment in Ireland and Wales* (London, 1967), p. 262.

[4] Mackintosh, *Disestablishment and Liberation*, p. 293.

[5] *The Case for Disestablishment: A Handbook of Facts and Agreements in Support of the*

Liberation society sought to convey to the public. The Nonconformists also made effective use of the growth of Ritualism in the Church—the Church could no longer claim to be the 'bulwark of Protestantism'. 'The greatest danger to Protestantism now lies in what is being said and done, with the connivance or open encouragement of the archbishops and bishops, in the Church of England itself.'[1] A great deal of use was still made of the old arguments about Church property being national property. It was also becoming clear that beneath all these claims to justice on individual questions, the Nonconformists were in fact appealing to a new sort of State altogether. By the 1880s the matter was no longer disguised: a neutral state, a State 'free' of preference for a particular version of religious truth, was now increasingly advocated in unambiguous language. 'The question of disestablishment', declared the Liberation Society in 1884, 'is no petty dispute between Churchmen and Dissenters, but a great question of national policy.'[2] The new liberal State was not to be wholly secular, however. The Liberation Society pointed to the examples of the United States, the Colonies, and, indeed, to Ireland, to show that the disconnection of Church and State did not necessarily result in a godless system of government. A society and its government could profess a general adhesion to religion without having to protect one Church at the expense of another, they contended. 'The dominant force in favour of disestablishment is a religious force,' they pointed out; 'it may safely be assumed, therefore, that in putting an end to the political ascendancy of a particular Church, care will be taken, possibly at the expense of some logical consistency, to do nothing that will be prejudicial to the religious interests of the nation.'[3] In effect they sought the replacement of one anomaly, the National Church, by another: state recognition of a broadly based society resting on Christian morality, with the protection of law, but without public endowment. No serious attempt was made to define the philosophical basis of such a State, or to explain how sovereignty would operate towards those who really did dissent from the Christian basis of legislation. In removing the confessional principle from the existing relationships of the State to religious opinion, the Nonconformists were setting up a greater logical inconsistency than they realized. In the United States and in Ireland they saw Christian laws without a State Church, operating in countries with active and large Churches, supported by a majority of their citizens. But to contrive such an arrangement in England could only be done if no one raised against their new logical inconsistency precisely the sort of objections they had raised against the 'anomaly' of the State Church.

Claim for Religious Equality, published by the Society for the Liberation of Religion from State Patronage and Control (London, 1884), revd. edn. (1894), p. 47.
[1] Ibid., p. 29.   [2] Ibid., p. 12.   [3] Ibid., p. 220.

Occasionally defenders of the Establishment saw this, but in general their defence against the Nonconformists' claims was pragmatic and constitutional, rather than theoretical. The first principle of national policy, said Dean Stanley at Sion College in February 1868, 'is that the state should recognise and support some religious expression of the community; the second, that this religious expression should be controlled and guided by the state'.[1] The logical effects of a real disconnection of Church and State (rather than an anomalous one as in America) were evident to many churchmen. 'My whole soul revolts at the thought of such a nation treating its subjects as if they were no better than civilized gorillas without souls, in order to avoid the charge of sectarianism,' said J. C. Ryle (Bishop of Liverpool after 1880) at the Church Congress discussion of the relationships of Church and State in 1871[2]—a topic which was regularly debated at the Congresses. The legal Establishment of religion still seemed to most churchmen the only way of preserving a higher end for human social life. 'A national Church is a national protest for God and for Christ, for goodness and for truth,' said Archbishop Tait in 1876.[3] It was not that other bases of national morality were inconceivable: they were conceived and rejected. Francis Paget, when a Canon of Christ Church, Oxford, in 1887 preached a sermon in which he declared that 'other plans of work, other systems, may seem to us at times more likely to conciliate, or more compact and prompt in action, or more convenient and opportune; but we believe that in this plan we see God's Will for England'.[4] This general mind of the Church was well expressed by William Inglis, President of the Church of England Working Men's Society, in 1886: 'An Establishment or National Church is "an outward and visible sign" of the recognition of God by the nation, and provides that all public acts of the state shall be hallowed by religion.'[5] It was, that is to say, sacramental.

Those who defended the Establishment sometimes ignored the difficulties which the existence of a real denominational pluralism interposed. The Church still saw itself as what Disraeli called the 'remedial agency',[6] the bond of social cohesion. 'This Established Church', maintained Tait, 'is an instrument devised by Providence for welding this great people into one compact Christian body.'[7] Frederick Temple, when he was Bishop of London in 1892, said, 'we desire to defend the Established Church of this country quite as much on behalf of the Country itself as on behalf of the

[1] A. P. Stanley, *An Address on the Connection of Church and State* (London, 1868), p. 4.
[2] *Authorised Report of the Church Congress held at Nottingham* (1871), p. 126.
[3] Archibald Campbell Tait, *Some Thoughts on the Duties of the Established Church of England as a National Church* (London, 1876), p. 3.
[4] Francis Paget, *This Church and Realm* (London, 1887), p. 7.
[5] *The Official Report of the Church Congress held at Wakefield* (1886), p. 174.
[6] Robert Blake, *Disraeli* (London, 1966), p. 193.
[7] Tait, *Some thoughts on the Duties of the Established Church*, p. 96.

Church'.[1] And Mandell Creighton, another prelate notably influential in the defence of the Church, said in 1899 that 'the Church is a great witness to the continuity of national life, and the method of divine training of our race'.[2] There had been, as these illustrations show, very little change in this manner of explaining the utility of a Church Establishment since the end of the eighteenth century. Emphasis was still placed on the parochial system, the territorial basis of the 'mission to the whole people'.[3] 'Everyone has a priest upon whom he has a claim,' said Harvey Goodwin, Bishop of Carlisle, when listing the gains and losses of a State Church in 1881.[4] As the century developed, however, the Church was less frequently defended as a force for social control, the body that taught the duty of civil obedience. But examples were still not uncommon, for the Biblical teaching on the Divine basis of all civil authority was seen as an important aspect of the Church's social function. Thus Dr. Alfred Barry informed the working men of Wolverhampton in 1867—the year of the Reform Bill, which he told them he fully supported—that the Church 'recognises authority as sacred, from the fatherly authority which God has sanctified to every other authority of which that is the type'.[5] Preaching in 1877 before the University of Cambridge, Christopher Wordsworth, Bishop of Lincoln, declared that 'The Church of England, of all Churches in Christendom, is one of the best teachers of loyalty, and one of the most faithful guardians of Order, Liberty and Law'. He added: 'to disestablish such a Church as this, would be to inflict the heaviest blow that could fall on the English Nation'.[6]

Erastianism continued to have exponents—not only in the common attitude of much parliamentary opinion but within the Church's ministry as well. Archbishop Tait not only rejected the view that Convocation should take over the legislative functions of Parliament, in ecclesiastical issues, but he defended the Judicial Committee of the Privy Council as a suitable court to deal in ecclesiastical cases.[7] It was also Tait who induced Disraeli to promote the Public Worship Regulation Act in 1874—an emphatic exercise of erastianism by Parliament, deeply offensive to the High Church opinion which was still growing in the Church. But, on the other hand, Tait denied that the Church was 'bound hand and foot with our

[1] *A Speech by the Right Honorable and Right Reverend the Lord Bishop of London, at the Annual Meeting of the Church Defence Institution May 17, 1892* (London, 1892), p. 3.

[2] Mandell Creighton, *The Church and the Nation, Charges and Addresses* (London, 1901), p. 264.

[3] Archibald Campbell Tait, *The Present position of the Church of England*, 3rd edn. (London, 1873), p. 162.

[4] *The Official Report of the Church Congress held at Newcastle-on-Tyne* (1881) (London, 1882), p. 162.

[5] *Report of the Wolverhampton Church Congress* (1867), p. 238.

[6] Wordsworth, *Miscellanies*, iii. 428.

[7] Archibald Campbell Tait, *The Church and the Law*, 4th edn. (London, 1877), p. 11.

connexion with the State, so that we are quite unable to accommodate ourselves to the changed circumstances of the changing ages through which the Church of England has to minister'.[1] He listed examples to show that necessary adjustments were possible under parliamentary control—the simplification of oaths and subscriptions, the amendment to the Act of Uniformity in 1872.[2] Although, therefore, the defence of the Church's subordination to Parliament was characteristically a layman's contention, it still attracted distinguished clerical support. Dean Stanley always contended for the subordination of the clergy to the law as a major virtue of Establishment.[3] The presence of the bishops in the House of Lords, he believed, brought them 'under the direct control of public opinion and public questioning'.[4] James Prince Lee had an almost passionate belief that the clergy should be subject to lay control.[5] Benson, who delighted in sacerdotalism, in contrast, found that the House of Lords had 'a thorough conviction of the infallibility of laymen (if not too religious) on all sacred subjects'.[6] It was common to support erastian controls on the ground that they kept the clergy out of party politics. Lord Selborne supposed that disestablishment would render the clergy a political force in their own right, and defended the Establishment because, under legal restraint, it had not been 'the general habit' of the clergy 'to endeavour to overbear, or intimidate, or control by spiritual influence, the independence of laymen'.[7] In his Bampton Lectures of 1871, George Curteis, who was the Principal of Lichfield Theological College, had urged the continuation of existing arrangements for the government of the Church on 'the principle of *government by fixed laws* and not by the mere will and pleasure of any man or set of men—government by known and established rules, and not by the swaying impulses of a congregationalist majority, not yet by the *ipse dixit* of an Infallible Pope'.[8] The defence of the Establishment as an erastian institution, therefore, was still very much alive, in opposition to a sectarian characterization of the Church.

Yet in 1869 all the arguments for the defence of Established religion were deployed in vain. The Irish Church was not a good test case. Nor were the opponents of the Irish Establishment always prepared for a general battle of ideologies: Gladstone promoted Irish disestablishment because of the *exceptional* nature of the case—grounds which the Whigs within the Liberal Party would accept, and which anyway corresponded

[1] Tait, *The present position of the Church of England*, p. 55.

[2] Ibid., pp. 57–60.

[3] Prothero and Bradley, *The Life and Correspondence of Arthur Penrhyn Stanley*, ii. 183.

[4] Stanley, *An Address on the Connection of Church and State*, p. 25.

[5] Newsome, *Godliness and Good Learning*, p. 143.

[6] Benson Papers, Letter Books (1883–8), Benson to Westcott, 22 Mar. 1884.

[7] Selborne, *A Defence of the Church of England*, p. 305.

[8] George Herbert Curteis, *Dissent in its Relation to the Church of England*, 2nd edn. (London, 1892), p. 413.

to his own continued adhesion to the Establishment principle in places where the Church concerned enjoyed something like a majority support. But over the Irish issue, Gladstone finally abandoned the belief that the State had the capacity to determine religious truth. It was a formal withdrawal from a position he had long since given up. His attitude to the Irish Church in 1868, he wrote, 'connects itself with silent changes which are advancing in the very bed and basis of modern society'.[1] The first result of this prophetic discernment was the claim that when 'the State has come to be the organ of the deliberate and ascertained will of the community, expressed through legal channels—then the inculcation of religion can no longer rest, in full or permanent force, upon its authority'.[2] Thus religious Establishments should be tested 'by a practical rather than a theoretical test'.

An Establishment that does its work in much, and has the hope and likelihood of doing it in more: an Establishment that has a broad and living way open to it, into the hearts of the people: an Establishment that can commend the services of the present by the recollections and traditions of a far-reaching past: an Establishment able to appeal to the active zeal of the greater portion of the people, and to the respect or scruples of almost the whole, whose children dwell chiefly on her actual living work and service, and whose adversaries, if she has them, are in the main content to believe that there would be a future for them and their opinions: such an Establishment should surely be maintained.[3]

This was to adopt the old notions of Warburton and Paley, the old Whig view: that an Establishment of religion must be justified on a majority principle. Gladstone's clarification was, however, assembled in order to eliminate the Irish Church. Its chief difficulty, as he later discovered in his opposition to the clamour of his Nonconformist supporters for English disestablishment, was that it made the survival of a national Church dependent on current opinion. In opposition to such a position, defenders of the Establishment released their traditional arguments all over again. And, as in the 1830s, it was the issue of Church property and ecclesiastical endowments that came first into prominence. This was not because a selfish hold on this property was the immediate reflex of churchmen: it was because the Irish Roman Catholics and the English Nonconformists chose to attack on that ground.

These two bodies were in working alliance. In 1867 the Liberation Society and the National Association of Ireland—the Irish Liberal agitation, supported by the Catholic hierarchy—had agreed to a policy of mutual assistance.[4] One of the results was a general assent by the two parties to the policy of disendowment. The Irish Catholic Church was anyway a

[1] Gladstone, *A Chapter of Autobiography*, p. 7.
[2] Ibid., p. 60. [3] Ibid., p. 63.
[4] Norman, *The Catholic Church and Ireland*, p. 326.

monument to the practical virtues of the Voluntary System of religious endowments. But it had not come to any theoretical adhesion to Voluntaryism as such—indeed it was contrary to the normal practice of Catholicism in Europe. It was the alliance with English Dissent that converted the Irish Catholic leadership to hardened Voluntaryism. When, in July 1867, Gladstone consulted Sir John Gray, of the National Association, he was assured that disendowment, as well as disestablishment, was the object of the Catholic agitations against the Protestant Establishment.[1] Therefore, in March 1868, Gladstone's three Resolutions on the Irish Church in the House of Commons proposed disestablishment, disendowment, and the secularization of excess ecclesiastical revenues—the old 'appropriation clause' policy. 'That which I renounce for the future', he said, 'is the attempt to maintain, in association with the State, under the authority of the State, or supported by the income of the State, or by public or national property in any form, a salaried or stipendiary clergy.'[2] Gladstone's adoption of the leading point in Irish popular agitation left the minority Conservative Government with an unsupported Irish policy. Gladstone's success in the consequential general election, in November 1868, made Irish disestablishment certain.

Characteristically, the parliamentary debate turned on the question of endowments. Church defenders continued to argue that ecclesiastical property was not national property in the ordinary sense. It was also rightly held that establishments were anyway not to be defined by their possession of national endowments (the Coleridge view), but by the existence of legal connections between the State and religious opinion. But endowments were advantageous, and since they derived from private and royal donations it was 'spoliation' to strip them from sacred use. Tait, in the Lords' debate on the second reading of the Church Bill said that 'the curse of Ireland is the repeated political and religious agitation on which voluntaryism necessarily rests'.[3] To many defenders of the Church, time seemed to confirm this. In 1880, ten years later, Bishop Wilberforce blamed the existence of the Home Rule Party and the agrarian agitation on the Disestablishment of the Church.[4] The Irish Protestant bishops, of course, were solidly against Gladstone's Bill, and refused to co-operate with the Government in adjusting its clauses. Their attempt to convene a Synod or Convocation to discuss it was blocked by Gladstone.[5] In the House of Lords the Archbishop of Dublin, Richard Chenevix Trench, spelled out the national implications of the Government's policy, and the grave evils involved 'in the dissociation of the State from all connection with the Church, in the

---

[1] Norman, *The Catholic Church in Ireland*, p. 332.
[2] Hansard, *Third Series*, cxci. 472 (30 Mar. 1868).
[3] Ibid. cxcvi. 1708 (14 June 1869).
[4] Ibid., cclii. 1019 (3 June 1880).   [5] Bell, *Disestablishment*, p. 124.

renunciation by the State of all that authority which a wielding of the sword and sceptre in the name of God has hitherto lent it, in the unconsecrating of all those mysterious agencies which bind a human society'. It was an 'experiment of tremendous magnitude'.[1] Bishop William Plunket, himself a Liberal—and Trench's successor as Archbishop—asked the congregation of St. Patrick's Cathedral, 'Is the disestablishment of the English Church so remote a contingency that it is folly to assume its possibility?'[2] The English bishops were fully aware of the precedent being created. They were, nevertheless, more adaptable than their Irish brothers. Once it was clear that the success of the Government's legislation was inevitable, they turned their attention to salvaging what they could. The first move was to support a 'concurrent endowment' solution for Ireland, rather than see a secularization of ecclesiastical revenues. It was not an impossible solution to try—Whig politicians had been attracted to something of the sort. In 1866 Lord Lifford had outlined a scheme for state financial support of the Roman Catholic Church in Ireland.[3] In 1867 Earl Russell's motion for an inquiry into the reform of the Irish Church had been coupled with an appeal for concurrent endowment of the other Irish denominations out of any surplus revenues.[4] Earl Grey outlined a similar proposal in 1868.[5] Faced with Gladstone's Bill in June 1869, Tait announced in the Lords that he neither accepted nor rejected it as it stood, but that he would look for suitable amendments.[6] Tait had long supported concurrent endowment for Ireland,[7] and had only just, in the previous year, succeeded Longley as Primate: as a Liberal, he found his position extremely difficult. He abstained in the vote on the second reading of the Bill—as did the Archbishop of York, and the Bishops of Oxford, St. David's, and Chester. Bishop Magee of Peterborough, an Irishman himself, made the most effective speech against the Bill,[8] and he, together with fifteen other prelates, voted against it. Very few ecclesiastics in the Church generally supported Gladstone, and those who did—like Frederick Temple, Headmaster of Rugby, and later Archbishop of Canterbury—were inevitably Liberals. F. D. Maurice, in an astonishing essay in the *Contemporary Review*,[9] declared that the Church of Ireland had been 'set up for the furtherance of Protestantism'—an opinion which denied the claim of most churchmen

---

[1] Hansard, *Third Series*, cxcvi. 1812 (15 June 1869).

[2] F. D. How, *William Conyngham Plunket. A Memoir* (London, 1900), p. 79.

[3] Hansard, *Third Series*, clxxxi. 1063 (26 Feb. 1866).

[4] Ibid. clxxxvii. 116, 354, 362. See also J. T. Ball, *The Reformed Church of Ireland* (London, 1886), p. 266.

[5] Hansard, cxcii. 2060; see also Grey's *Letter to John Bright respecting the Irish Church* (London, 1868).

[6] Hansard, cxcvi. 1707-8 (14 June 1869).

[7] Marsh, *The Victorian Church in Decline*, p. 25.

[8] Macdonnell, *The Life and Correspondence of William Connor Magee*, i. 229.

[9] Jan. 1868.

that the Irish Church was as much the national and legal successor of the Church founded by St. Patrick, as the English Church claimed to be that founded by St. Augustine. Maurice's 'astounding blunder' was at once denounced by Bishop Magee: 'It would be much nearer the truth to say that it became Protestant because it was established than to say it was established as a condition of teaching Protestantism.'[1]

Tait had his opportunity to see the Bill satisfactorily amended when the Lords went into Committee at the end of June 1869. The result was an attempt to alter the preamble, which declared the secularization principle for ecclesiastical property. An amendment of Lord Cairns's was carried, which postponed the application of any surplus revenues. Lord Stanhope's amendment, providing free glebes for the disestablished Church, the Roman Catholics, and the Presbyterians, was also carried.[2] There was, of course, little real possibility that the Irish Catholics, who had so recently adhered themselves to strict Voluntaryism, would accept concurrent endowment. David Moriarty, Bishop of Kerry, was the only one known to be sympathetic. The President of Maynooth, Dr. Russell, had also approached Gladstone in the hope that the parliamentary grant to the College might survive in some form.[3] The Presbyterians in Ireland would also, no doubt, have been willing to continue to receive the Irish *Regium Donum*. By the terms of Gladstone's Bill, both the Maynooth Grant and the *Regium Donum* were wound up. The Lords' amendments were supported by Tait and by Thomson, Archbishop of York. Tait pointed out that even if the surplus revenues of the Church were appropriated to secular utilities they would probably end up in denominational hands anyway, since many of the agencies of social welfare in Ireland were conducted by the Churches.[4] Bishop Wilberforce, also supporting concurrent endowment, took the opportunity to define the 'fundamental difference between an established religion and that which is merely endowed'. He said 'that establishment consists in its essence, not in the payment of the clergy, higher or lower, but in the recognized form of teaching which the State has assumed to be its representative in the religious instructions of the people'.[5] This was a correct definition. From it, he deduced that concurrent endowment did not violate the proposed disestablishment in Ireland.

The Government was unprepared for concurrent endowment, because of Irish Catholic and English Nonconformist opinion, and the Lords' amendments were rejected. The resulting conflict between the two Houses was settled by an agreement, to which Tait was a party, between the Government and the Conservative leaders.[6] As finally passed, the Irish

---

[1] Macdonnell, *William Connor Magee*, i. 167.
[2] Norman, *The Catholic Church and Ireland*, p. 379.   [3] Ibid., p. 303.
[4] Hansard, *Third Series*, cxcvii. 729 (29 June 1869).   [5] Ibid. 714.
[6] John Morley, *The Life of William Ewart Gladstone* (London, 1905 edn.), i. 909.

Church Act did not explicitly sanction the secularization principle: any surplus revenues and property of the Church, after disestablishment and attendance to vested interests, were to be applied, 'in such manner as Parliament shall hereinafter direct'.[1] But it was clear that Gladstone had in effect carried the day. Concurrent endowment had disappeared from the settlement. The Irish disestablishment was at once seen by Nonconformists as a precedent for England. For all the weight of its constitutional authority, the Church had been unable to prevent the legislation. Even the promotion of concurrent endowment, as a practical way of recognizing religious pluralism without severing the links of religion and public life, had been in vain. John Percival, who became Bishop of Hereford in 1895, was almost alone in suggesting a concurrent endowment solution when the Nonconformists pressed the Welsh Church question.

It was the 'Unauthorized Programme' in 1885 that lifted the issue of Welsh disestablishment to the level of practical politics. After that, the Welsh Liberals, under the leadership of Stuart Rendel—an Englishman and an Anglican—placed Disestablishment first in their list of political priorities.[2] In 1886 their motion for Welsh disestablishment was defeated by only twelve votes in the Commons. A campaign against tithe in rural Wales between 1888 and 1890 provided a further incentive for vilification of the Established Church;[3] and then in 1891 Gladstone's adhesion to the cause was signalled in the Newcastle Programme. The agitation in Wales was much more bitter than the campaign against the Establishment in Ireland had been: the Welsh Nonconformists were extremely vindictive.[4] 'Nowhere', declared the Liberation Society, 'are Church establishments more strongly condemned in principle, and as contrary to the teaching of Scripture, than in Wales.'[5]

The Welsh Establishment was eventually swept away by Liberal legislation of 1914; but for a time after 1893, when a Bill was before Parliament to suspend appointments in the Welsh Church, as a prelude to further consideration of the Church's constitutional position, it looked as if the fate of the Welsh Church was already sealed. And in 1894 and 1895 two Bills to secure disestablishment were introduced to Parliament. Both measures also provided for disendowment. The 1895 Bill actually passed a second reading and went into Committee—it lapsed when Rosebery's administration resigned. The Church of England, which regarded the four Welsh dioceses as an integral part of itself, responded with all the usual arguments in defence of established religion. Two bishops were favourable to Welsh disestablishment: Gore, who felt guilty about the record of the

[1] 32 & 33 Vict., cap. 42.   [2] Bell, *Disestablishment*, p. 229.
[3] K. O. Morgan, *Wales in British Politics, 1868–1922* (Cardiff, 1963), p. 84.
[4] Bell, *Disestablishment*, p. 293.
[5] *The Case for Disestablishment*, p. 183.

Welsh Church, and Percival, a Liberal who wanted concurrent endowment. The otheɪ prelates appeared on many platforms in a national campaign to defend the Church. Although a lot of the debate, as in Ireland, was about the endowment question, Archbishop Benson was more concerned with the effects on the nature of the State. 'The Christian State is the Christian Church in another character,' he said at Rhyl in 1891.[1] When the Suspensory Bill was introduced to Parliament in 1893, both Convocations were summoned especially to declare their opposition. Creighton, in his presidential address to the Peterborough diocesan conference in 1893, denied that the Welsh Church was not a Welsh institution, as was so often claimed in Wales.[2] Benson actually believed that the Bill had 'done the Church a good turn' by showing up the nature of its enemies.[3] That would have been pretty cold consolation had not the Conservatives returned to office in 1895 and laid the question on one side. The most instructive feature of these events had been the revelation of the strength of feeling for Establishment principles inside the Church of England. Those who had wavered, out of dislike of erastianism, were returning to the fold.

The separation of Church and State which had taken place in the Colonies were precedents which Nonconformist agitations often utilized. 'The British Colonies in all parts of the world supply evidence in favour of the Free Church System', the Liberation Society declared in 1884.[4] One by one, the various statutory measures affecting the separation of Church and State in each place had passed through Parliament during the century, familiarizing public men with the notion that Established religion was incomparable with the religious diversities of British societies overseas. In 1854 the Canadian clergy reserves question was finally settled by secularizing them. State financial aid to religion was abolished in New South Wales in 1863, in Queensland and Tasmania in 1866, in the West Indies in 1868, in Jamaica and in Victoria in 1870, in Honduras and St. Lucia in 1871, in St. Kitts and Grenada in 1873, in Cape Province in 1875, and in Ceylon in 1881. It was a formidable list. In most cases these were not formal disestablishments in the English sense—since the Establishment of religion had rarely been closely defined in the Colonies anyway. They were terminations of public endowment, but this was, effectively, and was taken by the inhabitants to be, disestablishment. Each was greeted in turn by English Nonconformists as a further precedent. As early as 1838 Gladstone had noticed that 'in some British Colonies there does not actually exist a state of things, in which religious communities are so equally

---

[1] Edward Benson, *The Church in Wales: Shall We Foresake Her?* (London, 1891), p. 4.
[2] Creighton, *The Church and the Nation*, p. 13.
[3] Benson Papers, Letter Books (1893–6), Benson to Randall Davidson, 6 Apr. 1893.
[4] *Case for Disestablishment*, p. 237.

divided, or so variously subdivided, that the Government is itself similarly chequered in its religious complexion, and thus internally incapacitated by disunion from acting in matters of religion'.[1] The imperial Parliament did nothing to prevent the colonial legislators giving a logical expression to this diversity.

The question of national education in England, however, raised principles of religious Establishment in a form which, due to Nonconformist pressures, made the issue one of the most intractable the Victorian Church had to face. In this area, as in the formal disestablishment debates, the Church was deeply involved in political action, largely, again, against its wish. Churchmen felt wounded at the scant credit they got for their efforts to secure education for the working classes. They resented the Nonconformists for making education a political issue. 'Let the Nonconformist advocates of the voluntary system tell us why they have not provided schools for the young during the last fifty years,' said Ryle in 1871.[2] It was a reasonable question. 'It may be possible for some persons, great philanthropists, here and there to take up the movement for education, and endeavour to support it out of pure philanthropy, apart from religion,' said Tait in 1865, when Bishop of London; 'but we find no widely extended scheme for spreading education, no persons who have sacrificed money and time, and their best energies to the service of education, except those who have been stirred by a desire to spread education, because they believed it a great religious duty to do so.'[3] This too was a good point. The Church really had made a huge effort, and the persistent attacks upon it by the Nonconformists seemed quite gratuitous to most churchmen. The actual reasons why Nonconformists did so little for popular education in the nineteenth century remain unclear.[4] It cannot have been simply that their available financial resources were used up in the construction of places of worship, since the Establishment spent huge sums on Church building too; sums vastly in excess of the public grants of 1818 and 1824. And the landed wealth available to those who donated to the Church must easily have been equal to the commercial and industrial wealth available to Dissent. The ministers of Dissenting congregations simply do not seem to have regarded education as one of their prime duties. By the time of the Newcastle Commission's Report on popular education in 1861, the State had contributed £4½ millions for education since 1833—half the figure raised by the Church of England from voluntary donations. By the mid-century, 81 per cent of the schools receiving state financial aid had been

[1] Gladstone, *The State in its Relation with the Church*, p. 73.

[2] *Authorized Report of the Church Congress held at Nottingham* (1871), p. 127.

[3] A. C. Tait, *Middle Class Education: A Speech Delivered at the Devon County School, West Buckland* (London, 1865), p. 9.

[4] See Kitson Clark, *Churchmen and the Condition of England*, pp. 124-5; and Gillian Sutherland, *Policy-making in Elementary Education*, p. 90.

built, and were run, by the Church.[1] These were elementary schools. The Church had also begun to increase its concern for secondary education, not only in an attempt to protect the ancient endowed schools from Nonconformist attacks, but to attend to the needs of the middle classes. Quite a number of clergy were especially involved in this second area of responsibility—they saw it as an attempt to win back the middle classes to the Church.[2] 'By middle class', said the Revd. W. C. Sharpe, in the discussion of the question at the first Church Congress in 1861, 'I mean that portion of our population which declines to send its boys to our old county grammar schools, as teaching things too high for their wants, and yet refuses to use our village National Schools, as being too low in the social scale for their position in life.' He identified these as farmers, tradesmen, and 'higher artisans'.[3] It was not a definition that all would have accepted, but it indicated firmly enough the class references which the movement for middle-class education reflected. For some of those so defined, the commercial schools which the Church encouraged were probably adequate. The Bishops of London and Winchester had established a society to start commercial schools in 1838, and many were in operation by the mid-century.[4] Some Church leaders, like Thirlwall, encouraged evening classes for children sent out to work at an early age because of the 'selfish calculations of petty immediate advantage' made by parents who hoped to get their wages.[5] Some supposed that adult evening classes helped to draw the classes into greater mutual understanding and harmony.[6] Certainly the definition of 'middle classes' given by churchmen anxious to promote their education fell lower in the social scale than was later conventional. Nathaniel Woodard, whose *Plea for the Middle Classes* (1848) inspired the foundation of Lancing College and other successful schools, appears to have envisaged tradesmen as the typical social model of middle-class society.[7] The movement was slow and expensive, and by 1865 it was still possible for Tait to remark that 'there has been somewhat of a standstill in the education of that most important class, which forms the very bone and sinew of the kingdom'.[8] For the upper-middle class, and for the landed and aristocratic families, the development of public-school education in the nineteenth century was closely linked with ideals of Christian moral earnestness, through the inspiration of the great clerical headmasters—Arnold, Prince Lee, Tait, Benson, Temple. 'No blessings of God on England have been

---

[1] Soloway, *Prelates and People*, p. 426.

[2] Brian Heeney, *Mission to the Middle Classes. The Woodard Schools, 1848–1891* (London, 1969), p. 13.

[3] *Report of the Proceedings of the Church Congress held in the Hall of King's College, Cambridge, 1861* (1862), p. 89.

[4] Ibid., p. 99.   [5] Connop Thirlwall, *Charge* (1842), p. 32.

[6] *Report of the Proceedings of the Church Congress* (1861), p. 98.

[7] K. E. Kirk, *The Story of the Woodard Schools* (London, 1937), p. 29.

[8] Tait, *Middle Class Education*, p. 4.

more full and free and dear than the spirit of her public schools,' said Benson in 1887.[1] Some would have pointed out that spirit was about the only thing which was 'free' in the public schools, but whatever view may be held of the educational nature of those institutions, there can be little doubt of their importance in adhering the upper classes to Christianity in Victorian England.

The defence of religious education, in schools conducted by the State Church with public financial assistance, was the core of the great conflict between Church and Dissent which overshadowed the educational debate in the second half of the nineteenth century. In 1869 Jessie Collings, Dixon, and Chamberlain organized the National Education League from their radical base in Birmingham, to campaign for rate-supported, compulsory, secular education, under local-government control, in schools which were to be entirely free.[2] This great pressure group united radicals and Nonconformists: both objected to paying through taxation for the maintenance of Church schools. The Church was no less insistent on its educational rights as the Establishment. It replied to the foundation of the League by setting up, in the same year, a propagandist body of its own known as the Education Union. The National Society, which actually had the oversight of most Church schools, became increasingly intransigent in its insistence on the Church's position; a stand encouraged by the truculent opinions of Archdeacon Denison of Taunton. In 1861 the Newcastle Commission —on which the Dissenters' leading publicist, Edward Miall, had sat— recommended a national system of schools. But this did not reflect a bias to the Nonconformists' case. It was a recognition that a collectivist solution was required to a social need too great for the Church to meet. Despite all its efforts, the Church just did not have the resources to cover the cost of national popular education.[3] The National Society did not agree, as its annual report for that year made plain.[4] The scene was prepared for a considerable conflict, and with Gladstone's new administration under pressure from its Nonconformist backers, it was certain to come on soon.

Forster's Act in 1870 was the first statutory recognition of the principle that the State has a direct responsibility for education. This recognition, as Canon John Pilkington Norris, of Bristol, observed two years later, could have taken two forms: 'either to ignore all that was being done by the religious bodies, and establish a wholly new system of state schools, or to adopt what was being done, so far as it went, and supplement it where necessary'. Both schemes had supporters in 1870; the secularist radicals

---

[1] *Church Education. A Sermon Preached at the Dedication of the Chapel of St. Chad's College, Denstone, 27 July, 1887, by Edward, Archbishop of Canterbury* (London, 1887 p. 10.

[2] Sutherland, *Policy-making in Elementary Education*, p. 165.

[3] Warre Cornish, *The English Church in the Nineteenth Century*, ii. 271.

[4] Francis Brown, *The Church's Part in Education*, p. 69.

and the Nonconformists favoured the first, those in the Church who conceded that some state initiative was required, favoured the second. 'In a
happy hour', wrote Norris, who approved of the 1870 Act, 'Mr. Forster
suggested that "the religious difficulty" might be simply *ignored* by the
State, and left for solution to the *local* authorities; and thus the secularists
were defeated, and the schools, both new and old, were left free to incorporate religion with their teaching.'[1] Certainly most public opinion assumed
that religion ought to be taught in the schools. Only a small group of intellectual Liberals and militant Nonconformists promoted real secularism—
the latter simply believing it the only way to guarantee 'religious equality'
in the educational sphere. Forster's Act set up a 'dual system' of Church
and state schools, but very few of the schools founded by the local Boards,
elected under the terms of the Act, opted to have no religious teaching at
all.[2] In Board schools, according to the compromise arrived at in the
Cowper-Temple clause, no denominational instruction was permitted, but
a 'common Christianity', like that used in the Irish National System since
the 1830s, was to be adopted. The Act also required all schools in receipt
of public funds, both Church and Board schools, to implement the 'conscience clause'—exempting children from religious instruction and observance at the request of individual parents. Church schools in receipt of
state financial grants were to be subject to inspection, as in the past, only
in secular subjects.

It was the 'conscience clause' that Church advocates of religious education found most difficult to accept in their schools. Archdeacon Denison
had said in 1865 that he would never allow such an arrangement in Church
schools.[3] 'For a Christian Country it sounds like a paradox, but so it is,
that henceforth no school of ours can receive pecuniary help from public
taxes—towards which members of the Church are by far the largest contributors—unless on the condition that no religious teaching should be
given in it except at fixed periods,' said the Revd. A. R. Ashwell, Principal
of Durham Training College in 1870; 'I say that the new state of things
in our Church Schools is not one of impartial neutrality, but of practical
discouragement to religious teaching.'[4] This view was widely echoed in
the Church. The 'conscience clause' ran counter to the whole teaching of
the Church during the century: that it was not possible, or proper, to
separate religious and secular instruction in the classrooms. Adherence to

[1] J. P. Norris, 'The Present and Future Relations of the Church to National Education',
in *The Church and the Age*, ed. Archibald Weir and William Maclagan (London, 1872), p.
136.

[2] Chadwick, *Victorian Church*, Part II, p. 301.

[3] *Authorized Report of the Proceedings of the Church Congress held at Norwich* (1865), p. 26ʻ

[4] *Authorized Report of the Church Congress held at Southampton* (1870), p. 94. Ashwell's
paper introduced the debate on the 'Duty of the Church in the present phase of the
Education Question as affected by the Bill in Elementary Education'.

this position accounts for the initial caution, or hostility, of many of the clergy to the 1870 proposals. Yet a realistic recognition of the advantages the Church would in fact derive from the Act began a softening of attitudes. 'The Church's duty in regard to the new Education Act is to make the best of it,' said Walsham How (later Bishop of Bedford and then of Wakefield). 'An Education Act was necessary,' he added, 'and I doubt much if in any other hands we should have got one less detrimental to the cause of religion and of the Church.' There was a lesson in it, too—'the Church is not the nation; and this is a national measure'[1]—a frank enough recognition of religious pluralism. Cowper-Temple himself told the clergy to make the new system work, 'to offer themselves as the leaders in this as in every other good and righteous popular movement'.[2] Tait, recovering from a stroke, was too ill to take any part in the debate on Forster's Act.[3] Although he believed strongly that 'a system of mere secular instruction is not education',[4] he was realistic enough to see the benefits the Church could get. Frederick Temple, who became Bishop of Exeter while the legislation was actually going through Parliament, was very friendly to it. He was a Liberal. He was also an informed judge, having worked at the Education Office from 1848 to 1857. Forster was a close personal friend, and Temple was consulted about the framing of the Bill, and possibly about amendments too.[5]

Church leaders opposed to the Act used their local influence to reduce the number of School Boards elected under its provisions by rapidly multiplying the number of Church schools in their dioceses.[6] Wordsworth was particularly successful in this at Lincoln.[7] Resistance to the creation of School Boards continued through the 1880s and, by 1890, the Voluntary Schools (Church schools) had grown to 14,479—a peak from which there was later a decline,[8] as some schools opted to come under the control of sympathetic local Boards. The main cause of suspicion of Forster's Act, however—the 'conscience clause'—was not a stumbling-block for long. Very few Nonconformist children in practice applied for exemption from religious instruction in the Voluntary schools conducted by the Church of England. By the end of the 1880s fewer than 3,000 of the 2,000,000 children in these schools had sought exemption.[9] The Church came to accept the 'dual system' of public education. But the anger of the Nonconformists with Gladstone and Forster over the 1870 Act did not rapidly

[1] Ibid., p. 111.　　　　　　　　　　　　　[2] Ibid., p. 115.
[3] Marsh, The Victorian Church in Decline, p. 77.
[4] Davidson and Benham, Life of Archibald Campbell Tait, i. 532.
[5] Memoirs of Archbishop Temple by Seven Friends, ed. Sandford, pp. 341–3.
[6] The Case for Disestablishment, p. 40.
[7] J. H. Overton and E. Wordsworth, Christopher Wordsworth, Bishop of Lincoln (London 1888), p. 281.
[8] Chadwick, Victorian Church, Part II, p. 305.　　　[9] Ibid., p. 189.

abate. To them, it seemed a statutory recognition of the claims of the Church Establishment in national education. Feeling was very bitter, and opposition on this question helped to bring about the defeat of the Liberals in the 1874 election. Church leaders urged the clergy to see that even the non-denominational religious teaching (based on the Bible, the Lord's Prayer, the Ten Commandments, and the Apostles' Creed) was as well conducted as it could be by the teachers in Board schools.[1] Churchmen everywhere watched the development of the new system carefully, in the belief that there was 'a strong tendency to secularization in education to be resisted'—as a clerical member of the Manchester School Board said in 1884.[2] The continued pressure of Nonconformist agitation for the removal of Church influence from all state-aided education kept churchmen in a condition of wary defensiveness. Sandon's Education Act, in 1876, was very strenuously opposed by Nonconformists because it increased financial assistance to Voluntary schools, and seemed a Conservative gesture of friendliness to the Church.[3]

The direct entry of the State into the field of education marked an important stage in the diminution of the national role of the Established Church. In two other areas of public controversy, the question of the marriage laws, and of burials, the Establishment principle was compromised still further. On both, the Church took a broadly defensive position. Nonconformists had urged a settlement of the burials question right through the middle years of the century. They had a common-law right to burial in parish churchyards, but not to any religious service other than that prescribed in the Book of Common Prayer. The issue was a simple one. The Church opposed the Nonconformists' claim that it was an injustice for them not to be allowed their own services in the parish churchyards; the Church stood by its rights as an Establishment to have control of the parish church. Feeling ran very high, especially because of a few unfortunate cases, given huge publicity, where parsons refused burial to Dissenters who had not been baptized.[4] Many attempts were made in Parliament to change the law. The Liberation Society, the Protestant Dissenting Deputies in London, the Nonconformist press, hammered away at the grievance. Defenders of the Church stuck to principle. The issue, according to the Bishop Wordsworth, 'concerns the destinies, and may imperil the existence of the Church of England, not indeed, as a spiritual society, but as a national institution; and, therefore, it affects the welfare of the Realm of England as intimately connected with the Church'.[5] Even

[1] A. C. Tait, *Some Thoughts on the Duties of the Established Church of England*, p. 94.
[2] *The Official Report of the Church Congress held at Carlisle* (1884), p. 396 (Revd. J. Nunn).
[3] Mackintosh, *Disestablishment and Liberation*, p. 259.
[4] See Manning, *The Protestant Dissenting Deputies*, p. 299; and Ronald Fletcher, *The Akenham Burial Case* (London, 1974).
[5] Hansard, *Third Series*, cclii. 1013 (3 June 1880).

Tait, who favoured concessions on the question, said in 1876 that he was 'quite aware that the greatest difficulty which presents itself in this matter comes from the distinct conviction, which it is impossible to banish from one's mind, that the claims of the Nonconformists in this matter are but a step to something further'.[1] Many, too, supposed it was rather a paper grievance, got up to embarrass the Establishment, part of the general and undisguised attempt to bring about her demise. In 1878, when Bishop Selwyn presented the petition of 15,000 clergymen—three-quarters of the whole number in the Church—against any alteration in the law, he said he had never come across a single instance in which the existing burial laws were a real grievance.[2] A very few churchmen, like Dean Stanley, 'fought to preserve the good will between the Church and the Nonconformists',[3] by supporting attempts at legislation.

Bills to open the parish churchyards to Nonconformist burial rites were introduced frequently during the 1880s by Sir Morton Peto, and during the 1870s by Osborne Morgan. In 1877 a batch of bills was presented. It was clear that if the Liberals should come into office the burials question would prove to be an ideal one to help consolidate Nonconformist opinion behind an administration. Hence the measure of 1880, introduced by Gladstone's new Government. It provided that any Christian and 'orderly' form of burial service might be used in parochial churchyards, or that burials might be conducted in silence. No anti-Christian services or words might be used. The Act, therefore, recognized that Church property, in the form of churchyards, was national property, not for the exclusive use of the Establishment. The Act also recognized the continued national profession of the Christian faith, yet freed from exclusive protection of one denomination. Most Church leaders regarded the legislation as wrong in principle. But they divided over its expediency. Temple had been the first to see the advantage in safeguarding the Church, once again, by removing a leading ground of opposition to it. 'No greater mischief could be done to her than to alienate the sympathies and affections of the great body of the people,'[4] he had said of the burials question in 1876. Tait accepted the 1880 Act: 'it is my belief that in conceding what is felt to be right by men who are steadfast members of the Church of England you strengthen the position of the Church'.[5] A majority in the Church were clearly unconvinced. The Lower House of the Convocation of Canterbury described the Act as 'a dishonour to Almighty God'—to the intense annoyance of both Tait[6] and

---

[1] Tait, *Some Thoughts on the Duties of the Established Church*, p. 108.

[2] H. W. Tucker, *Memoir of the Life and Episcopate of George Augustus Selwyn* (London, 1879), ii. 367.

[3] *A Victorian Dean. A Memoir of Arthur Stanley*, ed. Hector Bolitho (London, 1930), p. 295.

[4] *Memoir of Archbishop Temple*, i. 579.

[5] Hansard, *Third Series*, cclii. 1024 (3 June 1880). [6] Ibid. 1025.

Gladstone.[1] Tait believed they lived 'in dangerous times' with 'systems abroad, both here and on the continent, which threaten both social and family life', and that in such circumstances men of insight should lay aside their differences.[2] In May a meeting of the bishops convened by Tait had not been able to arrive at a common mind on the expediency of accepting the legislation. Indeed, Magee of Peterborough and Lightfoot of Durham had quarrelled at the meeting.[3] In the parliamentary debate it was Wordsworth of Lincoln who led those bishops opposed to concession: 'If no civil distinctions are henceforth to attach to any body of men by reason of their religious profession, then we must be prepared for other more sweeping changes in Church and State.'[4] But this position was in defiance of the great adjustments which had been made to the Constitution in the nineteenth century, which were precisely aimed at removing religious profession as a qualification for civil responsibility. Similar ground, however, was occupied by other opponents of the Bill. In the vote on the Lords' second reading, the two Archbishops and eight bishops supported the Bill, and six voted against it. Opinion among the parochial clergy did not follow their expediency. Feeling in the Church remained very hostile. But once on the statute book the matter was virtually closed. A number of remaining grievances were cleared up by the Burials Act of 1900. The Nonconformists had won another round in the fight against the surviving remnants of the confessional State.

The question of marriage and divorce was much more serious for the Church, for here there was always a risk that the law of the Church and the law of the State would come into collision. A Royal Commission of 1850 on the marriage law had recommended changes which were embodied in Lord Cranworth's Divorce Act of 1857. Up to that time dissolution of marriage was only possible by private Act of Parliament. The 1857 measure allowed divorce on the ground of a wife's adultery—adultery by a husband did not constitute ground for divorce until 1923. In moving the second reading of the 1857 Bill in the House of Lords, Lyndhurst pointed out that no great novelty of principle was involved: divorce bills had been going through Parliament for the preceding 150 years, during which time there were 'only one or two instances in which any opposition had been made by the right rev. prelates'.[5] There was within the Church some disagreement about the propriety of divorce, and the debate over the 1857 Act during the next couple of decades sharpened it. Some bishops held to the absolute indissolubility of marriage. Others allowed divorce for adultery,

---

[1] *Correspondence on Church and Religion of William Ewart Gladstone*, ed. Lathbury, i. 173.
[2] Hansard, cclii. 1025.
[3] Macdonnell, *Life and Correspondence of William Connor Magee*, ii. 130.
[4] Hansard, cclii. 1018.
[5] Hansard, *Third Series*, cxliv. 1692 (3 Mar. 1857).

the single exception endorsed by Christ Himself (St. Matthew's Gospel, ch. 5, v. 2). Theologians referred to this as 'the Matthaean exception'.[1] Archbishop Sumner subscribed to this view, and accepted the 1857 Act despite disapproval of the clause which allowed the remarriage of the guilty party.[2] Bishop Phillpotts of Exeter believed that in some cases divorce could be permitted, but considered the question as an exceptionally difficult one to determine, and thought that all legislation on it 'ought to have regard to the principle of Divine Law'.[3] As the clergy were the interpreters of Divine Law in a country with a National Church, they should have been consulted by the 1850 Commission, and had not been.[4] Phillpotts opposed the 1857 Act because it established one law for the rich and another for the poor; for only the rich, he contended, could afford to travel to the Divorce Court in London and to pay the legal expenses involved in a matrimonial action. 'Their Lordships must remember that they were legislating, not for the benefit of the opulent, but on a question which was essentially the people's question.'[5] So, on this issue too, Phillpotts remained the guardian of old Tory paternalism. Wilberforce led the attack on the Bill by those bishops who did not accept even adultery as a ground for the dissolution of marriage. In his judgement, the measure simply afforded 'every facility to those who wished to violate the marriage tie'. The law ought not to be used to protect unchristian views of marriage.

At present persons separated were in an anomalous and not creditable position because the law did not sanction their separation [he argued]; but if the law stepped in and recognised the position of the separated parties, the law must be held to some extent to invite that separation, by giving them a *status* in society which they did not at present possess.[6]

Any statutory acknowledgement of the concept of a matrimonial offence as a proper ground for divorce, Wilberforce believed, must rest on nobler foundations than these adduced—Parliament must remember that 'it was dealing with a great institution of God, upon which the purity and happiness of this Christian land, more than upon any other matter, did depend'.[7]

These were clear positions. Those who believed in the indissolubility of Christian marriage found the 1857 Act a threat to the union of Church and State, because it opened up a division between the law of the Church and the law of the State; others did not see any immediate difficulty. The division of opinion continued through the second half of the century. But there were practical aspects of the matter which were often urgent: whether

---

[1] *Marriage, Divorce, and the Church. The Report of a Commission appointed by the Archbishop of Canterbury* (London, 1971), p. 5.
[2] Warre Cornish, *The English Church*, ii. 92.
[3] Hansard, cxliv. 1699 (3 Mar. 1857).
[4] Ibid. 1701.
[5] Ibid. 1699.
[6] Ibid. 1705.
[7] Ibid. 1707.

the divorced should be admitted to the sacraments of the Church, and whether remarriage was permissible. The 1857 Act allowed remarriage of the divorced; the law of the Church seemed clear that the guilty party could not be remarried, although the position of the innocent party was unclear. In the Church Congress Debate on Marriage and Divorce in 1880, Canon Henry Temple, Vicar of St. John's, Leeds, pinpointed the central problem. 'I am one of those who deeply value Establishment; who think it unwise in the extreme to strain the relations which exist between Church and State,' he said, but if the State 'proceeds to enforce by civil penalties the admission to Church Communion of those who break the Church's law, the Church must reconsider her whole situation'.[1] It was a situation that the State did not force to an issue. But the threat haunted Victorian churchmen. In 1888 the Lambeth Conference had before it a Report from its Committee on Marriage Law, chaired by the historian, William Stubbs, Bishop of Chester. The Committee emphasized the problems of disputed teaching on the nature of marriage. They agreed

to declare that, inasmuch as Our Lord's words expressly forbid Divorce, except in the case of fornication or adultery, the Christian Church cannot recognise Divorce in any other than the excepted case, or give any sanction to the marriage of any person who has been divorced contrary to this law, during the life of the other party.[2]

In no cases, they declared, ought the guilty party to be remarried by the Church. They recognized the fact 'that there has always been a difference of opinion in the Church on the question whether Our Lord meant to forbid marriage to the innocent party in a Divorce for adultery'; and they recommended that the clergy should not be instructed 'to refuse the sacraments or other privileges of the Church to those, who, under civil sanction, are thus married'. They were unable to make any recommendation on the disputed question of remarriage of the innocent, believing that such decisions were, in view of the differences of opinion, best left to the discretion of diocesan bishops.[3]

Attempts to secure legislation on the law of affinity and consanguinity—the question of marriage with a deceased wife's sister—were frequently made in the later nineteenth century, and here, in general, churchmen were able to offer a united opposition. It seemed to involve a much more obvious separation of civil and ecclesiastical law.[4] In 1847 a Royal Commission chaired by Bishop Lonsdale of Lichfield had actually recommended a relaxation of the legal prohibition of such marriages—though the Commis-

---

[1] *The Official Report of the Church Congress held at Leicester* (1880), p. 405.
[2] *Conference of Bishops of the Anglican Commission Holden at Lambeth Palace in July 1888*, p. 43.
[3] Ibid., p. 44.
[4] T. A. Lacey, *Marriage in Church and State*, revd. edn. (London, 1947), p. 182.

sion admitted a great difference of opinion on the issue. It was not an obscure matter, either. Public discussion was voluminous and frequent—opinion, if anything, hardened against change after the Report of Lonsdale's Commission. In 1883 a Committee of Bishops, and the Lower House of Convocation, both declared against change at a time when further attempts were being made to get private legislation through Parliament.[1] The issue had been brought to a head. Archbishop Benson regarded the threat to the union of Church and State as a grave one. In June 1883 he wrote in his diary: 'Arnold said, when the steam of the first locomotive passed Rugby, "This is the death-blow of the Feudal system." This [Bill] is the first real disseverance of the law of England and the Law of the Church.'[2] In this portentous manner most churchmen viewed the question. The 1883 Bill was defeated, as were similar attempts, and it was not until 1907 that the law was finally amended to allow marriage with a deceased wife's sister. As parliamentary opinion gradually began to shift on the issue, the Church had felt the ground trembling beneath the Establishment. 'The system of Marriage Laws, which the Church erected on the basis of principle, and maintained on that basis so long as it was committed to her charge, is now under the guardianship of the state, and is consequently exposed to criticism and amendment on the ground of social expediency,' Bishop Creighton said in 1895.[3] Referring explicitly to his own opposition to legalizing marriage with a deceased wife's sister, he said 'we must expect to find that the relations between the sexes will always be the great battleground of social principles', for 'it is indeed a fundamental test of the power of self-restraint and subordination to a higher law than individual feeling'.[4] It is interesting that some bishops were additionally opposed to changing the law of affinity because it was an agitation promoted solely by the wealthy; a 'desire for freedom among the upper classes'.[5]

Further adjustments in the relationship of Church and State in the second half of the nineteenth century marked the continued advance of the political system towards the practical recognition of religious diversity. Churchmen broadly contented themselves with rearguard actions in each case, reserving the position of the Establishment, but often offering no systematic opposition to changes which were promoted in order to secure civil equality. Thus in 1858, when Jews were admitted to Parliament, the bishops stood aside. The Relief Act, like the Catholic measure of 1829, contained securities for the Establishment in the exclusion of Jews from

---

[1] Warre Cornish, *The English Church*, ii. 95.

[2] Benson Papers, Diaries, 1883, p. 162 (11 June).

[3] Creighton, *The Church and the Nation*, p. 143.

[4] Ibid., p. 148.

[5] *The Present State of the Church. A Charge Delivered to the Clergy and Churchwardens of the Diocese of Hereford by John Percival, D.D., Bishop of Hereford* (London, 1898), p. 51.

the offices of Lord Chancellor, Lord Lieutenant of Ireland, and High Commissioner of the General Assembly of the Church of Scotland. Only the aged Bishop of Cashel, Dr. Robert Daly, brother of Lord Dunsandle, opposed the Bill in Parliament. 'I have no doubt that the mere money-changing, money-brokering Jew would come in,' he observed (rather than the 'good Jews' whom he would not mind having in the House), and to admit such, he was 'unwilling to be a party to withdrawing the profession of the Christian faith'.[1] This opinion was not shared by his colleagues. A few laymen, like Lord Cranworth, professed respect for Jews but opposed the Relief Bill in order to protect the Christian character of the Constitution.[2] There was, on the other hand, no doubt that much 'general church opposition'[3] existed to the idea of admitting Jews: it was just that realism decreed that no success, and only the earning of a lot of odium, would attend any attempt to oppose the reform. In 1886 the Qualification for Offices Act was passed, in response to agitation by Irish Roman Catholics,[4] although English Nonconformists were equal beneficiaries. The Bill was three times rejected by the House of Lords, where fears were still expressed for the safety of the Established Church. As passed, the Act removed the declaration required of municipal and other public office-holders that they would not, by virtue of their position, 'interfere with or weaken the Protestant Church as by Law Established'. The Marquess of Westmeath entered a formal protest against the passing of the Act,[5] but the bishops thought it politic to avoid public opposition. Similarly, in 1867 all but one of the bishops abstained from opposing the abolition of the Declaration Against Transubstantiation (the Offices and Oaths Bill). Only the Bishop of Carlisle objected in the Lords, because the repeal of the Act was 'inconsistent with the principle of an Establishment'.[6] The bishops certainly took part in the public controversy over the right of freethinkers to affirm— rather than take the parliamentary oath with its references to God—but then this was a question that divided political society pretty evenly, and the Church did not stand out in the character of sole opponent of liberal reform. The issue was constantly before Parliament in the clumsy and disagreeable debates between 1880 and 1886 instituted by Charles Bradlaugh's insistence on raising the matter as one of principle. Most of the parochial clergy were quite strongly opposed to Bradlaugh's claims to take his seat in Parliament[7]—it was an opposition as much to his militant and

---

[1] Hansard, *Third Series*, cxlix. 1794 (25 Apr. 1858).
[2] Ibid. 1768.
[3] R. G. Wilberforce, *Life of the Right Reverend Samuel Wilberforce*, iii. 85.
[4] Norman, *The Catholic Church in Ireland*, pp. 291 ff.
[5] Hansard, *Third Series*, clxxxii. 1354 (16 Apr. 1866).
[6] Ibid. clxxxviii. 1377 (11 July 1867).
[7] Walter L. Arnstein, *The Bradlaugh Case: a Study in Late Victorian Opinion and Politics* (Oxford, 1965), pp. 55 and 161.

propagandist atheism as to the constitutional case for the admission of those with no religious beliefs to the legislature. The Convocation of Canterbury resolved against the Affirmation Bill of 1883, and Archbishop Benson was himself opposed to Bradlaugh's claims. Yet he took no part in the public agitation on the question.[1] In 1888 the Affirmation Act was finally passed, Benson voting for it; and in 1891 the Religious Disabilities Removals Act at last deleted religious subscription from the qualifications required of those who sat in parliament. Yet Parliament was still the government of the Church: it was an extraordinary situation, which churchmen suffered because there was really no practical alternative. Not many would have agreed with Stewart Headlam's later conclusion that 'the Church, looking back, must acknowledge that it owes a deep debt of gratitude to Charles Bradlaugh'.[2] By the end of the century, as a result of these changes, the Establishment had been rendered even more anomalous within the texture of the Constitution.

Other reforms, passed to conciliate Nonconformist agitation, had removed some practical benefits the Church had enjoyed. In 1860 the grammar schools were opened to the children of Dissenters by the Endowed Schools Act. There were nearly 700 schools which came within the terms of the legislation, most founded and endowed to provide education according to the principles of the Church of England. Many had a long tradition of admitting Dissenting and Jewish children anyway—as Tait pointed out in 1860, giving as an illustration the case of King Edward VI's School at Birmingham.[3] But the endowed schools were mostly conducted by governors and trustees who had to be members of the Church, and practically speaking, this meant that most of the available secondary education of the country was in the hands of the Church of England. The immediate background to the reform of 1860 was furnished by the Ilminster Grammar School case. In 1857 the local vicar had successfully procured the removal of Dissenters from the Board of Trustees of the Ilminster School. The case was given national publicity by the Nonconformist press, and turned into part of the general propaganda against the Establishment. The Church was conciliatory in response. In 1860 the bishops offered no opposition to the admission of Nonconformist children, but they were anxious to preserve the Christian education given in the schools, and to maintain the relationships between sacred and secular learning. Archbishop Sumner objected to the 'conscience clause' in the Bill which, before amendment, appeared to allow the trustees of each foundation to vary the terms of religious instruction.[4] Tait wanted a clear declaration that the 5,000

---

[1] Ibid., pp. 171–2.
[2] *Champion of Liberty: Charles Bradlaugh*, issued by the Centenary Committee (London, 1933, p. 54.
[3] Hansard, *Third Series*, clvi. 1214 (17 Feb. 1860).
[4] Ibid. 1210 (17 Feb. 1860).

National schools which had their own endowments, founded during the nineteenth century itself, would not be included in the legislation.[1] In 1869, when the governing bodies of the endowed schools were opened to persons of all denominations, the threat to religious education in the sense understood by the Church was even greater. The Act set up a royal commission empowered to frame new statutes for each trust. Churchmen resisted attempts to remove the requirement that religious instruction should be according to the principles of the Church. Cases were fought individually once the Act had passed. In 1873 Tait and the Conservatives in Parliament had managed to defeat an attempt to remove King Edward's School from the control of the Bishop of Worcester, and hand it over to the Birmingham municipality[2]—then dominated by Chamberlain and the members of the Education League.

The abolition of compulsory Church rates in 1868, the first reward for their support which Gladstone gave the Nonconformists when he formed his Liberal Administration in that year, was another of the issues which the Church leaders were anxious to let by rather than raise a whirlwind. The rates had been ably defended at the first Church Congress in 1861, by the Revd. A. Hume, an officer of the Church Defence Institution.[3] But fewer and fewer men were prepared to stand by them as a test of Establishment, as they had done in the 1830s and 1840s. It was in the interests of the Nonconformists to portray the Church as still grasping the rates as essential to survival, however. 'Considering that many men fail to appreciate abstract principle, except it be reduced to a concrete form, we could hardly desire a better battle-ground than the Church-rate question,' noticed the *Christian Spectator*, a journal unsympathetic to the Establishment, in 1866; 'but it is surely impolitic for our opponents to represent that the very existence of the State Church is bound up with the maintenance of an odious tax.'[4] But the Church avoided doing so. Both Archbishops supported the Abolition Bill in 1868. Archbishop Thomson pointed out that in thousands of parishes the rate was already voluntary anyway. If Dissenters would now respond by keeping away from Church vestry meetings, and stop their disruption of normal parochial administration— features of the long campaign against the rates—a considerable gain would have been made.[5] The Bishop of Carlisle said he would have liked to have voted against the Bill, but 'he felt it his duty to make the best of it'.[6] The remark was like a summary of the Church leaders' general attitude to the dismembering of the confessional State. With the 1868 Act there ended, after a short debate in Parliament, one of the longest and most bitter and

[1] Hansard, *Third Series*, clvi. 707 (9 Feb. 1860).
[2] Marsh, *The Victorian Church in Decline*, p. 70.
[3] *Report of the Proceedings of the Church Congress* (1861), pp. 42 ff.
[4] *The Christian Spectator*, N.S. vii (Apr. 1866), 245.
[5] Hansard, *Third Series*, cxciii. 602 (3 July 1868).   [6] Ibid. 606.

most successful of the Nonconformists' campaigns against the Establishment of the Church.

The opening of the ancient Universities was another issue which, in the end, the leaders of the Church were unwilling to fight over to the last ditch. The Oxford University Act of 1854 and the Cambridge Act of 1856 were, as the Liberation Society noticed,

due in great part to the fact that, from the first, an earnest band of University reformers have co-operated with the friends of religious equality, prompted by the conviction that the narrow and sectarian basis on which the Universities were administered, was as injurious to the cause of learning as it was unjust to all who could not subscribe to the formularies of the Established Church.[1]

These reforms, which opened degrees to Nonconformists, were, that is to say, greatly assisted by academic liberal reformers within the Church of England. Similarly in 1871, when the University Test Act was passed, liberal opinion among academics welcomed it. The churchmen who opposed the reform were again reluctant to expose themselves by open opposition. Both Archbishops were in favour of the Act,[2] which threw open all University offices, except the Regius chairs of Divinity, to persons of all denominations. 'As regards the Church of England there will, of course, be many who will regret the loss of the exclusive privileges which it has hitherto enjoyed,' said Lord Kimberley, in moving the second reading of the Bill in the Lords, but 'the Church lives in the affections of the people as a reformed church; and the admission into the Universities of a number of Nonconformists is by no means likely to impair its character in that respect'.[3] It was cold comfort. The Bill was another of Gladstone's essays in conciliation of his Nonconformist followers. Yet liberal ecclesiastics rushed to say how much they valued the liberty of opinion the Bill symbolized—Westcott, who was then Regius Professor of Divinity at Cambridge, expressed this view.[4] The bishops took no part in the parliamentary debate. Ten years later, however, Tait regretted the effect of the Act in diminishing the utility of the Universities as places for the preparation of candidates for Holy Orders. The numbers of these were falling off. 'You are aware', he told the clergy in 1880, 'that over our Universities, in the course of the reforms which have recently been introduced into them, a wave of free-thought has rolled, exalting the secular above the ecclesiastical.'[5] In 1882 headships and fellowships at Oxford and Cambridge were freed from clerical restrictions.

[1] The Case for Disestablishment, p. 253.
[2] Chadwick, Victorian Church, Part II, p. 444.
[3] Hansard, Third Series, ccv. 42 (16 Mar. 1871).
[4] Owen Chadwick, Westcott and the University, Bishop Westcott Memorial Lecture: 1962 (Cambridge, 1962), p. 19.
[5] A. C. Tait, The Church of the Future, p. 145.

Like the accumulation of the collectivist machinery of the State, there-fore, the practical steps to the attainment of religious neutrality were piece-meal, each taken up singly and considered in isolation from others, and in isolation from the theoretical implications of the ultimate consequences. In touch with the pragmatism of parliamentary opinion, and with all their upper-class liberalism, the leaders of the Church adapted themselves to the new circumstances and swam, only sometimes reluctantly, with the current. The parish clergy were much less accommodating, and a good deal more confused by what was going on. Their hostility was often sharp, but it was never effective. 'Government has thrown its weight altogether into the Nonconformist scale,' said Archdeacon Denison in 1865, of the various adjustments in the relationship of Church and State. 'It makes much of the Nonconformist conscience. It makes nothing of the Church conscience.'[1] It was an understandable complaint in the unfamiliar world which was coming into existence. The contrast of old and new attitudes to State confessionalism was interestingly illustrated in 1858, when the proposal to abolish the 'political services of the Church of England'—the State Prayers for 5 November, for King Charles the Martyr, and for the Restoration of the Monarchy—came before Parliament. Archbishop Sum-ner readily agreed to their deletion from the Prayer Book: they 'savoured of politics as much as religion', he said.[2] But old Christopher Bethell, Bishop of Bangor, argued for the retention of the services in order to 'acknowledge and adore the superintending power of the Almighty in the blessings which we enjoyed as a nation'.[3] The services were deleted.

Despite the emphasis placed by both churchmen and Nonconformists on the practical separations of Church and State which took place, the extent to which the State continued to support religious belief was still, by the end of the century, enormous. The Establishment in England re-mained possessed of its ecclesiastical, if not of all its educational, endow-ments and property. Its clergy continued to receive precedence in numer-ous areas of public life, and especially a seniority in the appointment of service and institutional chaplaincies. The bishops still sat as Spiritual Peers in the House of Lords—despite many attempts to get them removed. One such effort, in 1884, was lost by only eleven votes. Their increasingly infrequent attendance in Parliament may have saved their seats. 'Nothing is more likely to lead to the immediate expulsion of the Bishops from the House of Lords than by making a practice of residing two months a year in London,' remarked Lightfoot in 1884.[4] The parliamentary commission which administered the property and revenues of the Church was a very

---

[1] *Authorized Report of the Proceedings of the Church Congress held at Norwich* (1865), p. 28.
[2] Hansard, *Third Series*, cli. 487 (28 June 1858).
[3] Ibid. 494.
[4] Benson Papers, Letter-Books (1883–8), Lightfoot to Benson, 19 Apr. 1884.

intimate link of Church and State. So was the Crown nomination of bishops and deans. So also was the continued integration of Church Schools with the national system. The parochial clergy, too, retained a lot of their civil functions. It was not until the Parish Councils Act of 1894 that the incumbent was relieved of the chairmanship—and even of membership—of parish councils. The Act in theory secularized the parish as a unit of local government: in practice the association with the Church lingered on in many places, especially as the Church had usually built the village halls where they met.

The country continued to regard itself as possessing a Christian government. Only small groups of intellectuals looked to a rigorous secular State. Nonconformists who said they did really retained a greater belief in the Establishment of religion than they knew. For Nonconformists were among the first to demand that there be a connection between the law and Christian morality, especially when it came to sexual conduct, temperance, Sunday observance, and similar matters. Nonconformists, like churchmen, expected Christianity to provide the ultimate sanction of the morality of government: the principle of Establishment in its purest form. For all their appeals to a secular state, the Nonconformists were really only out to end the legal ascendancy of one denomination over another. Sunday observance was a clear example of the united appeal to a Christian State. The Revd. James Hessey, Headmaster of Merchant Taylor's School, and an Anglican, delivered his Bampton Lectures at Oxford on Sunday observance in 1860. He had no doubt that the State had an obligation to enforce Christian observance. When he considered John Stuart Mill's objection to Sunday laws, that they were an illegitimate interference with the liberty of the subject, he had no difficulty in defining an answer. 'Such statements', he said, 'ignore, first, the Christianity of Government; secondly, the duty of Government to promote, so far as it can, the welfare of its subjects in accordance with Christian principles.'[1] Similarly, popular attitudes to Roman Catholicism assumed the duty of the State to protect society against Roman errors. This belief, which was as strong in the United States and in Canada as it was in Britain, lay behind popular 'No-Popery' movements.[2] It was, however, in decline. The Ecclesiastical Titles Act of 1851, a symbol of the willingness of militant Protestantism in the mid-century to use the authority of the State against Catholic claims, was repealed in 1871. By then, the sort of Nonconformity represented by the Liberation Society, and the sort of Liberalism represented by Gladstone, found the use of the law to penalize religious organization unsupportable. But with arge sections of public opionion, the belief that the State ought to

---

[1] J. A. Hessey, *Sunday. Its Origin, History, and Present Obligation*, 3rd edn. (London, 1866), p. 245.

[2] Norman, *The Conscience of the State in North America*, pp. 89–103.

discourage Catholicism lingered on to the end of the century and beyond. It was again a version of state confessionalism. With the publication of the Syllabus of Errors in 1864, and with the Vatican Council in 1870, some learned men too found themselves wondering if the law really should decline to control Catholic error. In 1874 Gladstone himself was on the brink, as he surveyed the Vatican Decrees. 'A religious society which delivers volleys of spiritual censures in order to impede the performance of civil duties', he wrote of the Roman Catholic Church, 'brings into question, in the face of the State, its title to civil protection.'[1] It was, however, for Gladstone at any rate, a temporary uncertainty. By the close of the century the belief that the State ought properly to control religious opinion was rarely heard amongst educated opinion. A great change had taken place.

[1] W. E. Gladstone, *The Vatican Decrees in their Bearing on Civil Allegiance: A Political Expostulation* (London, 1874), p. 36.

6

Christian Social Ideals, 1900–1920

During the first two decades of the twentieth century the permeation of the leadership of the Church of England by the ideals and attitudes previously largely confined to the enthusiasts of the Christian Social Union was truly remarkable. Much of the language used to describe this movement of social opinion was very loose: the terms used by both the upholders and the detractors of the new social orthodoxies confused 'socialism' and 'social concern' pretty freely. But a general awareness of the extent of the movement of opinion was evident by 1908—the year of the Pan-Anglican Congress, at which Lord William Cecil said he felt 'almost out of place in speaking as a person with no belief in socialism';[1] the year, also, of a Lambeth Conference which could be described as a 'socialist field-day'.[2] It was the Christian Social Union that served as the primary catalyst. Serious and high-minded men joined it at the Universities and carried its ideals into their later ministries. In 1907 Bishop Stubbs of Truro in a speech to the Upper House of the Convocation of Canterbury, credited his own conversion to social principles to the influence of F. D. Maurice when he was at Cambridge.[3] In 1909 at Swansea he went on to attribute the spread of social ideals in the new generation to 'the teaching, in the Cambridge class-rooms thirty years ago, of Maurice and Seeley and Lightfoot and Westcott and Hort' and to 'its assimilation by that school of younger theologians, both at Oxford and Cambridge, who are mainly responsible for the organization of the Christian Social Union'.[4] Handley Moule, Bishop of Durham, joined the C.S.U. in 1900, while Norrisian Professor of Divinity at Cambridge.[5] Even Archbishop Randall Davidson's wife was a member. And in 1913 Scott Holland, too ill to attend the Church Congress at Birmingham—it was the year before his death—sent a letter in which he observed that 'the whole world has become Christian Social Union now'.[6] The change was astonishing; a

[1] Quoted in Roger Lloyd, *The Church of England, 1900–1965*, revd. edn. (London, 1966), p. 193.
[2] P. d'A. Jones, *The Christian Socialist Revival*, p. 216.
[3] *The Chronicle of Convocation, 1907*, p. 104 (1 May).
[4] *The Official Report of the Church Congress held at Swansea* (1909), p. 121.
[5] J. B. Harford and F. C. MacDonald, *Handley Carr Glyn Moule, Bishop of Durham*, 3rd edn. (London, 1922), p. 156.
[6] *Guardian*, 29 Nov. 1917: 'The Christian Social Union—Annual Conference at Birmingham'.

generation of upper-class and upper-middle-class clergy was adopting social ideals far more radical than the general currency of the political world. Archdeacon William Cunningham of Ely suggested a wide and perceptive explanation. 'The attraction of socialism lies not in the reasoning which supports it, but in the hope it holds out and the sense of duty it inspires,' he said in 1909. 'It is the form which the enthusiasm for humanity takes in the present day.'[1]

The influence of social radicalism quite rapidly spread through the Church. There were very few Church leaders who did not adopt attitudes critical of existing industrial organization and social order—attitudes expressed in language, and according to a frame of reference, which was clearly furnished by the sort of atmosphere nurtured by the C.S.U. The respectability of social criticism within the Church's leadership not only diluted the dynamic element but created a new othodoxy of opinion which more or less completely failed to translate itself into political terms. Nor did the adoption of social criticism on this scale appear to have much discernible effect upon the class attitudes of churchmen. Indeed, their new radicalism was still a product of class moral consciousness. In the 1880s and 1890s they had offered the working men the ideal of 'brotherhood' as the consequence of their awareness of the injustices of society; in the first two decades of the twentieth century the catch-phrase changed. The working class were now offered 'fellowship'. 'We find that one idea runs through all our work in this Conference,' declared the bishops after the Lambeth Conference of 1920; 'it is the idea of fellowship.'[2] The Church insists, they said, that 'industry is not a conflict, but a fellowship'.[3] They formulated social problems in a manner, and with a rhetoric, which suggested political solutions to the ills of society, yet very few ever actually contemplated political action. But with all the enthusiasm of the converted, Church leaders advanced the most radical social criticism. Their first assumption was that their predecessors had wholly neglected the social implications of the Gospel. 'Christian people everywhere are awakening to the claim which Christianity makes upon our whole social life', wrote Randall Davidson in 1914.[4] The later nineteenth-century criticism of Political Economy was important in this. After 1900 the views of those who had attacked 'individualism' as an economic ethic were now supreme. In 1918 Bishop Gore was

---

[1] W. Cunningham, *Christianity and Socialism* (London, 1909), p. 11.

[2] *The Six Lambeth Conferences, 1867–1920*, compiled by Randall Davidson (London, 1929), p. 9 (Encyclical Letter of the Bishops).

[3] Ibid., p. 18. Goerge Orwell characterized this disposition vividly—'Stop calling me "Sir", you chaps! Surely we're all men? Lets pal up and get our shoulders to the wheel and remember that we're all equal . . . ,'—*The Road to Wigan Pier*, Penguin Books edn. (London, 1968), p. 141

[4] Davidson Papers, Lambeth Palace Library, 1914, S.9, Davidson to Miss Lucy Gardner (Secretary of the Congress of Social Christianity), 17 Feb. 1914.

able to write that the ideals of Political Economy 'have been largely discredited';[1] that 'to-day you get unquestioning acceptance in the most
conservative circles for ideas which would have been listened to with
horror a short time ago'.[2] In fact the movement of opinion had been far
greater among Church leaders than among some other sections of the
intelligentsia, and churchmen like Gore often failed to realize how out of
touch with prevailing political assumptions the Church was becoming. In
1909, for example, while the Liberal administration was putting forward
housing legislation, Bishop Percival of Hereford prepared an amendment to
force the owners of rented property to display their names on the buildings
they let, in the belief that this would inflame public opinion against slum
landlords.[3] This was far too radical for the Government, and the amendment was refused. Archbishop Randall Davidson attacked them for trying
'to shield from public knowledge' and 'wholesome discipline' those who
owned slum property.[4] But very few in Parliament were prepared to see so
far-reaching a violation of the rights of property as Percival was sponsoring.[5]
In 1906 the Convocation of Canterbury had held an inquiry into housing
conditions because, in the words of the Archdeacon of Worcester (William
Walters), it was an issue which involved 'fair dealing between man and man,
class and class'.[6] It was certainly a question to which Convocation gave a
lot of attention.[7] The public became accustomed to hearing quite radical
assaults upon existing property rights from leading churchmen. 'If it
appears', wrote Gore in 1913, 'that the conditions of property-holding at
any particular period sacrifice the many to the few, and tend to starve the
vitality or destroy the hope or depress the efforts of masses of men and
women, there is no legitimate claim that property can make against the
alteration of conditions by gradual and peaceful means.'[8]

There is almost an impression of benevolent unreality hanging over
these years of social criticism; as churchmen failed to see the implications
of their enthusiastic espousal of views so antagonistic to the existing
practice of industry and commerce. Diocesan conferences dwelt upon the
theme of the Church's relation to industrial organization.[9] The Lambeth
Report on Industrial and Social Problems in 1920 wrote of the Church as
becoming 'a reservoir of social service', undertaking 'welfare work of all

---

[1] Charles Gore, *Dominant Ideas and Corrective Principles* (London, 1918), p. 5.
[2] Ibid., p. 7.
[3] Hansard, *Fifth Series*, 1909, vol. 3, Lords' Debate on the Housing, Town Planning
Bill (21 Sept. 1909), 94.
[4] Ibid. 210 (22 Sept.).
[5] G. Stephens Spinks, ed., *Religion in Britain since 1900* (London, 1952), p. 92.
[6] *The Chronicle of Convocation* (1906), p. 109 (22 Feb. 1906).
[7] See Garbett's speech in 1918, *The Chronicle of Convocation* (1918), p. 348.
[8] *Property, Its Duties and Rights*, Introduction by the Bishop of Oxford (London, 1913),
p. xvii.
[9] Stephen Mayor, *The Churches and the Labour Movement* (London, 1967), p. 146.

kinds'.[1] Social change was recommended to almost every clerical gathering; it was given intellectual authority in numerous lectures and books. Dr. Bussell, Vice-Principal of Brasenose College, Oxford, ended his very successful 1905 Bampton Lectures by urging the Church to see that 'Christian belief and the welfare of society are one'.[2] It was exactly what the new generation of churchmen wanted to hear. Religion and the role performed by Protestantism in the growth of the competitive ethic of capitalism was another favourite theme of the learned clergy. Archdeacon Cunningham had in 1913 given a lecture at the London School of Economics on 'Calvinism and capital' in which he attacked Political Economy, claimed that all 'the human activities with which Economics deals lie within the sphere of Christianity',[3] and pointed out that it was the Reformation that had 'rejected the authority by which Christian morals had been enforced at active centres of economic life'.[4] In 1917 *Competition*, the compendium published by William Temple's group of social critics (the 'Collegium'), attributed 'the spirit of capitalism to Protestant ethics';[5] and the moral was: 'Nothing but a new Reformation can deliver us from the evils of capitalism'.[6]

Church leaders were faced with a problem which political society in general faced. Social policy in the 1900s was becoming influenced by the results of social investigation: the official inquiries of 1904 and 1908 into the operation of the poor-relief system finally dispatched the philosophy of the 1834 Poor Law by showing that the lowest-paid labourers lived in conditions which were harmful to physical and industrial efficiency—a death-blow to the 'less eligibility' principle. The continuing revelation of social conditions, an activity in which the Church was prominent, prepared the ground to receive Alfred Marshall's teaching that payments to the poor by the State did not necessarily depress wages nor discourage thrift.[7] Marshall's ideas were popularized by social reformers. 'Every clergyman will be the better for reading the pages in which Professor Marshall has shown that the omission of what is needed for efficiency in food, clothing, dwelling place, education, and recreation is really waste,' said the Principal of Pusey House, Oxford, in a course of pastoral lectures at Cambridge in 1905.[8] Bishop Gore recommended Marshall's doctrine, too, though he

[1] *The Six Lambeth Conferences* (1920), Report No. II, p. 76.
[2] F. W. Bussell, *Christian Theology and Social Progress* (London, 1907), p. 331.
[3] W. Cunningham, *Christianity and Economic Science* (London, 1914), p. 1.
[4] Ibid., p. 58.
[5] *Competition. A Study in Human Motive*, written for 'The Collegium' by John Harvey, Malcom Spencer, J. St. G. C. Heath, William Temple, H. G. Wood (London, 1917), p. 41.
[6] Ibid., p. 45.
[7] José Harris, *Unemployment and Politics. A Study in English Social Policy, 1886–1914* (Oxford, 1972), p. 212.
[8] V. S. S. Coles, *Pastoral Work in Country Districts* (London, 1906), p. 79.

added the reservation that Marshall still laid too great an emphasis on the possibilities of individual exertion as opposed to state action.[1] Churchmen were not alone in reacting positively to the new outlook on social problems. Among Liberal politicians, too, there was, in 1906, and in the policies of 'Reconstruction' mooted in 1917, an acceptance of the notion that society had itself to change in order to foster social justice in economic relationships.[2] While the Liberals were moving moderately to this accommodation with the new ideas, the Church rushed into full acceptance. In 1918 Canon Cyril Garbett, future Archbishop of York, led a debate in the Convocation of Canterbury on 'Reconstruction' policies and moved a successful resolution.

That this House, convinced that the demands of labour for a national minimum wage, for state provision against unemployment, and for the recognition of the status of the workers in the industries in which they are engaged, are in accordance with the principles of Christianity, calls upon the Church both to support these demands, and at the same time to further all efforts now being made to promote closer fellowship and co-operation between employers and employed in the service they are both rendering to the whole community.[3]

Churchmen frequently supported the policy of a 'living wage'. The Lambeth Conference 'Report on Industrial and Social Problems', in 1920, called upon employers to give a wage sufficient 'to live a decent and complete, a clean and noble life'. This was 'the fundamental Christian principle of the remuneration of labour'; but the Report left it rather imprecise.[4] Similarly, on the question of unemployment, the Church was full of sympathy and calls for action during these years; but when it came to hard details, the Lambeth Report in 1920 was only able to say that it was 'beyond our compass to discuss methods of solving this troublesome problem'.[5]

It was unusual, after 1900, to find a bishop who did not regard the declaration of social principles a primary duty. Winnington-Ingram, who at the end of his period as Bishop of Stepney, in 1901, had urged the return of men in the L.C.C. elections who would clear up the slums,[6] marked his elevation to the see of London by ordering a denunciation of slum properties to be read in all his churches.[7] Henry Paget, Bishop of Stepney in 1909—after Lang's departure for the Archbishopric of York— became Chairman of the Stepney Council for Social Welfare.[8] Cosmo Gordon Lang was not hesitant in adopting fairly adventurous social ideas.

[1] The Chronicle of Convocation (1907), p. 100 (1 May).
[2] Bentley B. Gilbert, British Social Policy, 1914–1939 (London, 1970), p. 9.
[3] The Chronicle of Convocation (1918), p. 344 (1 May).
[4] The Six Lambeth Conferences 1867–1920 (1920), Report No. II, p. 71.
[5] Ibid., p. 70.   [6] Carpenter, Winnington-Ingram, p. 109.
[7] Colson, Life of the Bishop of London, p. 106.
[8] E. K. Paget, Henry Luke Paget (London, 1939), p. 175.

His years at Stepney had given him a real regard for the poor; 'there are qualities of character in our working folk which are beautiful in themselves and full of promise', he wrote in 1904.[1] In order to prepare the clergy to formulate correct social attitudes, he advocated a training which would produce a 'knowledge of Economic History, of the Poor Law, of the Economics of Industry, of the Laws of Health and Housing, of the problem of the unemployed'.[2] In 1911 he remarked that as the nineteenth century had been concerned with the creation of wealth, the twentieth should be concerned with its distribution: 'We cannot but be appalled by the contrast of increasing prosperity and great wealth and of great poverty, of increasing luxury and of great squalor.'[3] By 1917 Lang had advanced to a degree of social criticism which allowed him, in a House of Lords debate on industrial unrest, to attribute the disturbances 'to profiteering at the expense of the community' by capitalists.[4] He spoke of the 'just and reasonable demands' of labour; denounced the 'unequal distribution of the rewards of industry'; pointed to the 'dehumanization of industry' by the prevalence of the competitive spirit.[5] He then asked that 'our workers may have a very much larger share in the actual control of their industry'.[6]

Randall Davidson, Archbishop of Canterbury from 1903, was scarcely a radical figure. He had, nevertheless, come under the influence of Westcott's ideas—and constantly quoted him[7]—insisting as early as his 1894 *Charge* (when Bishop of Rochester) on the need to penetrate economic practice with Christianity. He was also unwilling to involve himself and his office in sectional interests. In 1906 when the C.S.U. got Scott Holland to approach him over the electoral success of the Liberals—'to try and show that the Church is not in alarm and despair at the new government' and that the Church 'looks keenly forward to good work that may be done to improve the condition of labour'—Davidson was cautious and imprecise, but not dismissive.

It is in my judgement most important that the Church should give visible evidence that its thoughts are not concentrated simply upon matters ordinarily known as ecclesiastical, but that we are always keen, and never more keen than now, to set forward the things which make for righteousness, sobriety, and true progress in the nation's life and well-being.[8]

In 1911, still reluctant to sponsor actual schemes for social change, he looked forward to the end of poverty, in 'a couple of generations'. 'I can see

[1] C. G. Lang, *The Opportunity of the Church of England* (London, 1906), p. 41.
[2] Ibid., p. 75.
[3] J. G. Lockhart, *Cosmo Gordon Lang* (London, 1949), p. 239.
[4] Hansard, *Fifth Series*, xxvi. 915 (7 Nov. 1917).
[5] Ibid. 917–18. [6] Ibid. 924.
[7] G. K. A. Bell, *Randall Davidson* (Oxford, 1935), i. 227.
[8] Davidson Papers, 1906, S. 17. Scott Holland to Davidson, 31 Jan. 1906; Davidson to Scott Holland, 1 Feb. 1906.

no obvious or simple road,' he added, 'but that there is a road, and a Christian road, I am sure.'[1] Churchmen even more naturally conservative in these matters than Davidson were nevertheless anxious to join the chorus of social criticism. Ralph Inge, Dean of St. Paul's, disagreed with all the social panaceas of his contemporaries, but he shared a lot of their social diagnosis. In 1906 he spoke of the 'vulgarity of industrial competition',[2] and in 1912 he said 'the present distribution of wealth is absurd'.[3] And Hensley Henson, preaching to working men in 1891, had agreed 'that Labour does not receive its due reward in England to-day'.[4]

The new respectability of criticizing the social order became more articulate, of course, among the block of C.S.U. bishops, whose thought received its clearest expression in the young William Temple. Temple's rise to prominence in the social movement was rapid: he was inspired first by the Workers' Educational Association, then by the Student Christian Movement, and finally, in 1916, he became the leader of 'Life and Liberty', which, though an agitation for Church legislative autonomy, was always closely associated with social radicalism. In 1922 he accepted the bishopric of Manchester. Temple was in many things rather more radical than the C.S.U. membership in general—though to some extent this is an impression created solely by his ability to clarify, and thereby to show the truly radical implications of, positions and attitudes general among his C.S.U. contemporaries. His position was a simple one. 'Our lives are moulded very largely by the secular environment of our nation; but that secular environment is not yet Christian, and until it is, there is not the remotest chance of any individual person being completely Christian,' he said in a Cambridge lecture of 1912. 'Consequently, we are bound to secure that the society in which we live shall itself become as Christian in all its institutions as it can be made.'[5] First priority in this task was social justice. 'I find no room whatever for doubting that the root of the labour unrest in England is a sense that the whole organization of our life constitutes a standing insult to the personality of the poor man,' he declared in 1915, during a visit to America.[6] Therefore he became the leading exponent of the view that previous Christian society—at least since the Reformation—had neglected to apply religious principles to economic and social relationships: that the great object of the Church in his

---

[1] *The Character and Call of the Church of England. A Charge Delivered at his Second Visitation by Randall Thomas Davidson, Archbishop of Canterbury* (London, 1912), p. 119.

[2] W. R. Inge, *All Saints' Sermons* (London, 1907), p. 51.

[3] W. R. Inge, *The Church and the Age* (London, 1912), p. 71.

[4] H. Hensley Henson, *Light and Leaven. Historical and Social Sermons* (London, 1897), p. 266.

[5] William Temple, *The Kingdom of God* (London, 1912), pp. 72–3.

[6] William Temple, *Church and Nation* (London, 1916), p. 81.

generation was 'to be delivered from the poisonous heresy that business is business'.[1]

It was this belief, held in various degrees of association with other social ideas, that cemented the convictions of most Church leaders. During the last three decades of the nineteenth century it had become usual within the Church to attack both the social order and the conduct of industry for embodying the evils of the competitive principle. It followed the assaults by churchmen upon Political Economy: now the implications were extended. 'Competition is not a thing limited to business,' said Temple in 1912. 'It is a thing that pervades the whole of our life. It is simply organized selfishness . . . a great deal has been said in praise of competition, and most of it is rubbish.'[2] The solution he first advanced was the old co-operative ideal; later he took to more systematic collectivist politics. In 1908, at the Pan-Anglican Congress, Temple had not yet crossed this line: 'If Christianity is to be applied to the economic system, an organization which rests primarily on the principle of competition must give way to one which rests primarily on co-operation.'[3] Temple became deeply influenced by R. H. Tawney, whom he had known at school (Rugby). When Tawney's *Acquisitive Society* was published in 1920 the indictment of capitalism for its competitive ethic, and the contrast with what was imagined to be the economic teaching of the medieval Church, were at once absorbed by Temple and his colleagues. The evil effects of competition became an ever more familiar theme in the social commentary of most Church leaders. In 1913 Scott Holland wrote that 'the law of competition, working under our present capitalism, while offering scope and fulfillment to the very few, wrecks and undermines the individuality of the many'.[4] It was an opinion repeated time and time again by other Church writers. In 1918 the Archbishops' Second Committee of Inquiry— one of the five official committees on the work of the Church set up as part of the National Mission in 1916—attributed the relative failure of the population to be attracted to public worship to the effects of competition: 'the idea of fellowship which is an essential conception in that worship has been largely lost through the individualism and the antagonism of classes resulting from the competitive system'.[5] The message got down to the popular preachers, too. G. A. Studdart Kennedy had first been drawn to a compassionate desire to improve the condition of life among the poor when he was Vicar of St. Paul's, Worcester—a working-class parish—

---

[1] *Guardian*, 29 Nov. 1917; 'The Christian Social Union'.

[2] Temple, *The Kingdom of God*, pp. 96–7.

[3] F. A. Iremonger, *William Temple, His Life and Letters* (Oxford, 1948), p. 94.

[4] 'Property and Personality', Essay VII, by Henry Scott Holland, in *Property, Its Duties and Rights*, p. 184.

[5] *The Worship of the Church, Being the Report of the Archbishops' Second Committee of Inquiry* (London, 1918), p. 13.

just before the Great War.[1] After his remarkable period as an Army Chaplain he became one of the great preachers of the post-war years, and a missioner with the Industrial Christian Fellowship. He, too, absorbed the familiar arguments. 'History', he wrote in 1919, 'is the tale of how the truth of Co-operation has fought the falsehood of strife and competition all down the ages.'[2]

Another feature of the social attitudes of Church leaders in these years was the insistence, in the face of all the evidence to the contrary, that the Church had, until then, failed to bother with social and economic questions. It is quite astonishing that they could have been as ignorant as they clearly were of all the developments of the preceding century. This may, in part, be explained by their disapproval of any social teaching suggestive of individualism—which they did not regard as social thought at all, since it resulted from premises different from their own. But it is one thing to castigate a preceding generation for adopting social ideas which are considered improper; quite another to assert that preceding generations did not have any social ideas at all. Already the habit was growing of isolating a few committed thinkers, like Maurice and Westcott, and assuming that they—the forerunners of ideas similar to those later found acceptable—had been unique in their social concern. Like the young men who went into the slum settlements at the end of the nineteenth century, and discovered for themselves what their predecessors had come to know, but what their own class upbringing had shielded them from: the generation who grew up in the first two decades of the twentieth century fell upon the conditions of working-class life as if they were the first churchmen to have realized how appalling they were. In 1901 it was possible for Tissington Tatlow, General Secretary of the S.C.M., to say he 'knew nothing about social questions'.[3] With such ignorance apparently quite common, it is perhaps not surprising that when their own eyes were opened to social realities outside their own class churchmen scrambled to criticize the previous record of the Church in social questions. It also became a convenient explanation of the rise of socialism—'precisely because the Church of to-day has so largely failed us', as Conrad Noel explained.[4] Temple told the Pan-Anglican Congress in 1908 that they were all 'guilty of a whole system of oppression' of the workers.[5] The confession of guilt was again a familiar theme. 'It is undeniable that the Church's own record in the past stands in its way to-day,' declared the Archbishops' Third Committee of Inquiry in 1918; 'old abuses—child labour, sweated labour,

---

[1] William Purcell, *Woodbine Willie* (London, 1962), p. 83.

[2] G. A. Studdert Kennedy, *Lies!* (London, 1919), p. 21.

[3] Tissington Tatlow, *The Story of the Student Christian Movement of Great Britain and Ireland* (London, 1933), p. 340.

[4] Conrad Noel, *Socialism in Church History* (London, 1910), p. 9.

[5] Iremonger, *William Temple*, p. 95.

the intolerable conditions of housing and the monstrous evils of the slums
—long continued to exist with scarcely a protest from the Church at large'.[1]
This statement, coming from an official source too, is simply unhistorical;
its authors' ignorance of the positive passion of the nineteenth-century
Church for social improvement is remarkable. Yet in 1920 the Lambeth
Conference Committee on Industrial and Social Problems, under the
chairmanship of Bishop Kempthorne of Lichfield, also came out with an
apologetic statement on the bad record of the Church: 'since the beginning
of the industrial revolution only a minority of the members of our Church
have insisted on the social application of the Gospel'.[2] The evils of the
Industrial Revolution frequently appear in Church writing at this time—
stimulated by the innocent absorption of Fabian history through reading
the Hammonds. Garbett, who was greatly impressed, was appalled to
think (what he need not have thought, had he known more about it) that
'during that time the Church raised no protest'.[3] This generation was
reinterpreting the past: their opinions have come down to later generations
as virtually unquestioned truths. But their opinions were formulated in
ignorance, in an earnest appraisal of their own social vision. To the less
socially obsessed the insistence on the Church's guilt was usually very
irritating. In July 1917, following the inauguration of the 'Life and Liberty'
movement, Davidson criticized Temple's speech for the sharp nature of his
criticisms of the Church's failure to adopt social questions. Since later
twentieth-century churchmen have come to rely upon Temple for a good
deal of their own knowledge about the conduct of the Church in the last
century, Davidson's criticism is important. 'I try to picture, if it were
conceivable, someone reading that speech fifty years hence', wrote
Davidson fifty years ago.[4] Historians and moralists are apt to overlook the
English addiction to guilty self-criticism when assessing the value of
evidence from the past. In 1918 the Archbishops' First Committee of
Inquiry warned the younger clergy, especially, not to get things out of
proportion. 'Though much criticism at the present time' the Committee
remarked, came from a genuine desire 'to see a better age', yet 'it has
become a habit to say hard things of the Church'.[5]

Those who attacked the record of the Church in social questions were
also given to discrediting her past charitable efforts as mere 'ambulance
work'. The Church, as Charles Masterman, a future Liberal Cabinet
Minister, wrote in 1901, 'is far too much inclined to the doctrine of doles

---

[1] *The Evangelical Work of the Church, Being the Report of the Archbishops' Third Committee of Inquiry* (London, 1918), p. 2.

[2] *The Six Lambeth Conferences* (1920), Report No. II, p. 62.

[3] *The Chronicle of Convocation* (1918), p. 345.

[4] Bell, *Randall Davidson*, ii. 962.

[5] *The Teaching Office of the Church, Being the Report of the Archbishops' First Committee of Inquiry* (London, 1918), p. 5.

and devotion, to the benevolences of the rich and the grateful humility of the poor'.[1] It was certainly true that acceptance of state interventionism, the growth of collectivist attitudes, had overtaken much nineteenth-century charitable enterprise. 'All observers are agreed as to the ineffectiveness on a large scale of our "ambulance work" ', wrote Gore in 1908.[2] Temple, in 1916, went so far as to envisage the possibility that the State should take over medical services because of the ineffectiveness of charitable institutions to cope with the scale of the work.[3] But it was easy for a realistic appreciation of collectivist solutions to slide into a vilification of the Church for its past record of charity work, and some of the more radical clergy did this quite often. 'Not individual charity, but the administration of social righteousness is the test by which the Lord of Glory will condemn or will commend the nations of the earth', said F. Lewis Donaldson, of the Christian Socialist League, in a sermon of 1917, after denouncing social inequalities and the unjust distribution of wealth.[4] J. E. Watts-Ditchfield, priest of Bethnal Green, and later Bishop of Chelmsford, condemned philanthropy as an insult to the poor. Its source was tainted by social injustices. In 1913 he lectured Cambridge undergraduates on the evils of the rich and on the impurities of life in the West End of London. 'Here reign Luxury and Pleasure on the Throne of Materialism', he said: 'Yet some, while living the life of modern Sodom, will pose as philanthropists, and their gifts will swell the exchequer of the Hospital or even of the University.'[5] But not all philanthropy was sprung from the 'modern Sodom', and however much charitable works may have inhibited a realization that in some readjustment of personal wealth alone lay effective provision for social welfare, it would be absurd to suppose that the rich gave to charity in a deliberate attempt to preserve the existing distribution of wealth. That may have been a consequence of their practice: it was not the motive.

It is, however, impossible to avoid the impression that, as in the nineteenth century, the development of social attitudes within the Church after 1900 closely corresponded to class moralism in the clergy. Their moral earnestness, their sense of social guilt, their academics' distaste for business practice, their willingness to criticize the organization of industry in which they had no stake, their detachment from the self-help ethic of the lower-middle class and the working classes, and even their attraction to the fashionable social criticism of the intelligentsia of the period—all these are class indicators. The Church remained an upper-class,

---

[1] C. F. G. Masterman (ed.), *The Heart of the Empire*, p. 45.

[2] *Christianity and Socialism*, by the Bishop of Birmingham; *Pan-Anglican Papers, Being Problems for Consideration at the Pan-Anglican Congress, 1908* (London, 1908), p. 5.

[3] *Church and Nation*, p. 82.

[4] *Guardian*, 11 Oct. 1917: 'The Harvest and Social Justice'.

[5] J. E. Watts-Ditchfield, *The Church in Action* (London, 1913), p. 110.

and an upper-middle-class, institution; its leaders reflected the social preferences of Edwardian England. Archbishop Davidson had gone to Harrow and Oxford, and had married Archbishop Tait's daughter. His knowledge of working-class conditions was acquired by reading up about the condition of the poor in Charles Booth's volumes.[1] Lang went to a Scottish private school, Glasgow University, and Oxford, where he became a Fellow of All Souls. He picked up his knowledge of the working population by residence at Oxford House in Bethnal Green, and a curacy at Leeds. His knowledge in fact became quite impressive. Gore, who was descended from the Earls of Arran, was educated at Harrow and Oxford. Temple was the son of the Archbishop of Canterbury: he went to Rugby and Oxford, and seems at first to have imagined that the working classes were all like the intelligent artisans he encountered in the W.E.A.—whose president he became.[2] 'Except for the butler at Fulham and Lambeth and his scouts [servants] at Balliol and Queen's he had hardly spoken to an adult hand-worker till he joined the W.E.A.', according to his biographer.[3] Temple was the first to admit that his knowledge of the working class was rather academic, and he came to see that the W.E.A. was untypical.[4] The most radical Church leaders were also the most upper-class. This cannot be said of the leading critic of their social views: Hensley Henson, who became Dean of Durham in 1913, Bishop of Hereford in 1918, and Bishop of Durham in 1920. He came from a Nonconformist middle-class background, attended a small private school in Broadstairs, and was too poor whilst at Oxford to belong to a college.[5] Henson lacked the patrician detachment from world of wage-earning and social aspiration which characterized his episcopal colleagues: it is the key to his conservatism. He saw values and sympathies invested in the social attitudes of ordinary people which the upper-class leadership of the Church, for all its goodwill and determination to improve the lot of the less fortunate, always managed to misunderstand or not to notice.

Although churchmen usually failed to see that their social idealism was often at variance with their own class and cultural behaviour, many did notice the class basis of the Church's appeal and lament it. Dr. Fry, the Headmaster of Berkhamsted School, had spelled the matter out clearly in Gore's widely read volume on Church Reform, published in 1898.

The Church is mostly administered and officered by the classes; her influential laity belong almost wholly to the classes [he wrote]; she is doing a great and growing work amongst the masses; but the deep sympathies of her clergy with

---

[1] Bell, *Randall Davidson*, i. 208.   [2] Temple, *Church and Nation*, p. 81.
[3] Iremonger, *William Temple*, p. 87.
[4] *The Chronicle of Convocation* (1918), p. 350.
[5] C. A. Alington, *A Dean's Apology. A Semi-Religious Autobiography* (London, 1952), p. 42; see also p. 51.

the poor as such are largely obscured to the eyes of the masses by the fact that social rank and social position secured by wealth and tradition still count for so much in her service, both amongst clergy and laity.[1]

The Kelham experiment was one attempt to broaden the social basis of the Church's ministry, by training boys from the lower-middle class and the working classes—boys from elementary schools—for ordination. The Revd. Herbert Kelly began his work by training priests for the Korean mission. In 1903 he moved to Kelham to start his new experiment. He pointed out that upper-class boys left school at eighteen or so and went straight on to the universities, but that in 'the wage-earning classes' boys left school at fourteen, and had no means of financing further education. Kelham was an attempt to deal with the 'unbridged gap'[2] for poor boys, so removing the practical financial bar to the ministry of the Church. The bishops were not altogether happy, and in 1908 they declared that candidates for ordination must have a university degree.[3] Kelham continued to provide a sound preparation for the ministry, but some of its initial social intentions were, as a consequence of the bishops' attitude, frustrated. When he was Rector of Northolt, Middlesex, in 1918, Dr. Bussell wrote a perceptive and rather elliptical book about the Church, in which he criticized its social basis. 'We are a "gentleman's" Church, with a married clergy and a ministry entered as a profession, not merely as a vocation', he wrote.[4] It was also criticized for 'snobbery', and for 'its distaste for all genuine business'. Bussell gave some examples: the 'bishop who delights to pose as an advocate of Labour, a true friend of democracy, and indeed half a socialist' who nevertheless insisted that his clergy live in dwellings fit for gentlemen; and another prelate 'known for his noble lineage, high principles and advanced views' who refused to consider anyone for ordination who had not been to a university. 'It seems to my humble judgment', he concluded, 'another (quite involuntary) instance of the "snobbism" which honeycombs our social life, that the Church should thus be bound up with a particular university degree in her ministries, with a certain and stipulated number of bedrooms and reception-rooms in its manses.'[5] It was this sort of class reference that many churchmen managed to avoid recognizing. Frank Weston, the Bishop of Zanzibar—and the leader of the Anglo-Catholic wing of the Church—compared the earnest good intentions of the missionaries in Africa with the Church

[1] *Essays in Aid of the Reform of the Church*, ed. Charles Gore (London, 1898), p. 303. This is the Dr. Fry, later Dean of Lincoln, whose personality is described so candidly in Graham Greene's autobiography: see *A Sort of Life*, (Penguin edn., London, 1974), p. 50.
[2] Herbert Kelly, *England and the Church* (London, 1902), p. 184.
[3] Lloyd, *The Church of England*, p. 187.
[4] F. W. Bussell, *The National Church and the Social Crisis, or, The Churchman's Attitude to Political Panaceas* (London, 1918), p. 8.
[5] Ibid., pp. 11–12.

social workers in the English slums: both unconsciously patronized those whom they sought to serve.[1] Weston was himself a passionate advocate of social reform. 'You cannot claim to worship Jesus in the Tabernacle if you do not pity Jesus in the slum', he told the Anglo-Catholic Congress, in appropriate language, in 1923.

If you are prepared to say that the Anglo-Catholic is at perfect liberty to take all the money he can get no matter what the wages that are paid, no matter what the conditions are under which people work; if you say that the Anglo-Catholic has a right to hold his peace while his fellow citizens are living in hovels below the levels of the streets, this I say to you, that you do not yet know the Lord Jesus.[2]

It was a famous declaration. Lang did actually describe the slums as 'a mission field',[3] and Weston's criticism could be substantiated from numerous examples.[4] Another form of class reference was the supposition that the workers were by nature sympathetic to their social superiors. 'Anyone who has lived among workmen knows that until they are stirred up by some demagogue they have no bitter feeling against the upper classes,' Winnington-Ingram, the Bishop of London, told the Church Congress at Swansea in 1909; 'I have seen members of the aristocracy night after night taking coppers in boys' clubs.'[5] But the class conflict was real enough, however much the Bishop might have hoped it was not. The practical works prompted by the social conscience of the clergy did not usually interfere with their normal class style of living. Sometimes, indeed, they were actually combined—as in the Cavendish Club, inspired by H. R. L. Sheppard, before he became Vicar of St. Martin-in-the-Fields in 1914. This was an ordinary social club, with all the usual amenities of a London club, for 'young men of wealth and leisure', but membership was for those who also undertook social welfare work.[6] The social position of the parson was not easy. He was beset by the conventions of the class to which he belonged, in a period when class conventions were particularly rigid. 'The contrast is sometimes brought home sharply to the clergyman, who may have to divide his morning between preparing a sermon on Dives and Lazarus', noted Inge, 'and writing letters about life insurance or investments.'[7] But the extent to which even the most radical in the Church failed to comprehend their own class assumptions is remarkable. *Competition*, the book written by Temple's 'Collegium' in 1917, illustrated one of

---

[1] H. Maynard Smith, *Frank, Bishop of Zanzibar* (London, 1926), p. 262.
[2] *Report of the Anglo-Catholic Congress, 1923* (London, 1923), p. 185.
[3] Lang, *The Opportunity of the Church of England*, p. 39.
[4] Mayor, *The Churches and the Labour Movement*, p. 334.
[5] *The Official Report of the Church Congress held at Swansea* (1909), p. 140.
[6] R. Ellis Roberts, *H. R. L. Sheppard, Life and Letters* (London, 1942), p. 67.
[7] Inge, *All Saints Sermons*, p. 70.

its points with the case of a bricklayer who had jumped the unemployment queue ahead of a workmate: in the book he is credited with saying 'I feel a real cad'.[1] Temple himself, when visiting the fun-fair on Blackpool sands as Bishop of Manchester in 1923, had to ask someone to explain what a big dipper was.[2] Radical churchmen acquired too many of their social attitudes from books and mutual discussions. They often knew very little about the social classes whose lives they sought to change.

The class moralism of the Church of England was an extremely effective conductor of the social idealism generated within the intelligentsia by revelations of social ills. But there were other Churches that vibrated with the same currents—though to a lesser degree. Nonconformists continued to fall behind the Church of England in the rush to espouse social radicalism, but there were plenty of men within their ranks who responded. John Clifford, for example, the leading opponent of the Establishment's educational claims, wrote two essays endorsing Christian Socialism which became Fabian Tracts.[3] And in 1914 the National Free Church Council appointed a 'Commission of Enquiry into Christianity and the Social Order', which raked a lot of ground already disturbed by social critics in the Church of England. The most interesting parallel movement of thought, however, was the one that occurred contemporaneously in America. The 'Social Gospel' idea grew in respectability in the 1890s within the Protestant Churches, and was characterized, like its English counterpart, by criticism of industrial conditions.[4] As in England, the movement was academic. F. G. Peabody was Professor of Christian Morals at Harvard. His *Jesus Christ and the Social Question*, published in 1902, became a classic indictment of social conditions—and was read and commented upon in England, too. 'The industrial conflict of the present day', he believed, 'is simply the form assumed by that profound sense of moral distrust which is stirring in the hearts of the hand-working classes, and expressing itself in a passionate demand for industrial justice.'[5] Walter Rauschenbusch, Professor of Church History at Rochester Theological Seminary, went into greater detail to attack 'the hostile ethics of commercialism'[6] in his *Christianity and the Social Crisis* (1907). His conclusion that 'competitive industry and commerce are based on selfishness as the dominant instinct'[7] echoed the social thinking of Westcott and

---

[1] *Competition, A Study in Human Motive* (London, 1917), p. 181.
[2] See the letter to his wife, 6 Aug. 1923, printed in Iremonger, *William Temple*, p. 315.
[3] *Socialism and the Teaching of Christ* (1897), and *Socialism and the Churches* (1908).
[4] Richard Hofstadter, *Social Darwinism in American Thought*, revd. edn. (Boston, 1955), p. 105.
[5] F. G. Peabody, *Jesus Christ and the Social Question* (New York, 1902), p. 272.
[6] Walter Rauschenbusch, *Christianity and the Social Crisis* (New York, 1912 edn.), p. 308.
[7] Ibid., p. 310.

Gore. Developments were not in isolation: American writers were conscious of English social criticism and cited it frequently.

The progressive infiltration of social radicalism can be traced quite clearly within the Church of England—as it continued in an unbroken line from the influence of Westcott. The Christian Social Union remained its most influential and successful agent. The influence of the C.S.U. was reinforced early in the new century by the conversion of the Student Christian Movement, which had begun in 1892, to social principles. By 1913, the year in which the S.C.M. summer conference at Matlock held its first discussion on social problems, there were branches of the movement in every university in Britain and in most others throughout the world. The growth of social criticism within the S.C.M. was then rapid, and in 1909 it acquired a particular importance when Temple turned the Matlock Conference into a Christian Socialist platform. 'Till then, for most of us', noted the S.C.M.'s paper on the conference, ' "social problems" had always raised the thought of a slum, with its penury and degradation; but then it was revealed to us that the spiritual problem is found in germ wherever men cast off the yoke of Christ.' Tissington Tatlow, General Secretary of S.C.M., wrote of the Matlock Conference of 1909: 'Here was something quite new. We had never before thought of the re-ordering of society'. They had only thought of 'providing palliatives for the benefit of those who suffered.'[1] Temple's impact was retained; he joined the social study committee of the S.C.M.

The official deliberations of the Church were also moving to the expression of ever more radical opinion. In 1907 the Convocation of Canterbury received, and approved, the Report of a committee it had set up on 'The Moral Witness of the Church on Economic Subjects'. The Report was in fact a manifesto of the C.S.U. viewpoint—all five episcopal members of the committee, including Gore, were members of the Union. In the Upper House, the bishops fell over each other in welcoming the Report and it was passed unanimously; in the Lower House some were sceptical, and Henson declared that the Report 'with all its Christian fervour, was full of contentious statements on a subject of infinite complexity'.[2] The Report in fact argued the familiar objections to the competitive basis of industrial organization, urged the acceptance of a Christian criterion for economic law, dwelt upon the responsibilities of property and the conduct of business, and declared the value of 'fellowship' between workers and employers. Gore said in the debate that it marked the acceptance of the views of Ruskin on economic questions and that previously men had tended 'to regard commercial economic dealings as outside the influences of morality and religion', but that attitudes had now changed.

[1] Tissington Tatlow, *The Story of the Student Christian Movement*, p. 349.
[2] *The Chronicle of Convocation* (1907), p. 91.

He made a reference to Marshall's thesis: 'the cheapest labour was constantly found to be the dearest, because physiologists and biologists had constantly brought into evidence the fact that the value of man's labour depended upon the adequacy of his nourishment and the conditions of life in which he lived'.[1] This realization, Gore contended, must lead them to 'a re-statement of the Christian principles of society'.[2] There was 'a stirring of the public conscience', in which the Church must take a directing role.[3] The enthusiasm for social doctrines and the unanimity of the bishops in the acceptance of advanced social criticism, which the reception of the 1907 Report revealed, were again displayed in the following year, at the Pan-Anglican Congress. This was concerned primarily with missionary organization, but social radicalism and Christian Socialism captured a lot of attention. The discussions of the Congress Report on 'The Church and Human Society' saw speaker after speaker declare that the Church should aim at social change—many went on to argue for 'socialism', and for an alliance with the Labour Party. John Ludlow, visibly disintegrating after fifty years of adhesion to the Christian Socialist cause—he was now eighty-seven—addressed the Congress. Temple, moved to extend still further the advance of his opinions, advocated nationalization of industry, and pronounced the inherent Christianity of collectivism.[4] 'If Christianity is to be applied to the economic system,' he said, 'an organization which rests primarily on the principle of competition must give way to one which rests primarily on co-operation.'[5] The Congress Report, *Christianity and Socialism*, compiled by Gore, was an uneven document. In it the 'levelling' socialist was criticized for ignoring 'the vast inequality of faculty and considerable inequalities of need among men'. The managerial class and 'the thinker', the Report maintained, 'have needs in the way of leisure, house room etc., which the ordinary worker has not'.[6] Of 'the socialistic idea', on the other hand, the Report claimed it as 'closely allied to the Christian idea'. State socialism was condemned: it failed to account for 'the average level of human character as it exists at present'. After all, the Report urged 'we have no socialistic State in existence, or near to coming into existence'.[7] In what, then, did the Report regard 'socialism' as residing? 'The indictment of our present social organization is indeed overwhelming', it continued, with reference to the contrasts of wealth and poverty; 'we must identify ourselves, because we are Christians, with the positive ethical ideal of socialistic thought.'[8] This was all rather insubstantial. It was the sort of 'socialism' suggested by Westcott—a socialism, apparently compatible with a leisured class. The

[1] Ibid., p. 95.　　　　　　　　[2] Ibid., p. 96.　　　　　　　　[3] Ibid., p. 101.
[4] Lloyd, *The Church of England*, p. 193.
[5] Iremonger, *William Temple*, p. 94.
[6] *Christianity and Socialism*, by the Bishop of Birmingham. *Pan-Anglican Papers*, p. 2.
[7] Ibid., p. 3.　　　　　　　　[8] Ibid., p. 5.

Report, indeed, identified this affinity: 'In their claiming that the Christian should, because he is a Christian, co-operate with the ideal which men like Dr. Westcott have called Socialist, it is not of course intended that Christians or Churchmen should tie themselves to any one political party, or should behave as partisans of any one class.'[1] Despite all the euphoric acclamations made at the Congress, therefore, it is quite clear that its understanding of socialist ideas was extremely imperfect. It is only surprising that assailants of the Congress's conclusions failed to notice its essential weakness. Thus the paper on 'Socialism, Abstract and Actual' contributed to the Congress Report by the Revd. C. F. Rogers, author of several influential works on the pastoral ministry, chose instead to attack socialism by defending self-help individualism. Socialism, he argued, does 'moral harm in the discouragement of individual effort'.[2] It ignored the labour of managers in the creation of wealth, regarding manual labour alone as real labour. Socialism encouraged materialism—not philosophical materialism, to which Rogers does not refer—but 'stress on material things, on comfort, food, wages, houses'.[3]

In the same year, 1908, the Lambeth Conference Report on the 'Moral Witness of the Church' was another manifesto of social radicalism. The Committee which produced the Report was chaired by Bishop Kempthorne of Lichfield, a member of the C.S.U. The Report began by considering the advance of democratic government. 'It is the privilege of the Church to welcome this movement as one of the great developments of human history, which have behind them the authority of God.' It was, in addition, the duty of the Church to apply 'the fundamental truths of the Fatherhood of God, and the Brotherhood of Man, to the solution of social and economic difficulties, to awaken and educate the social conscience, to further its expression in legislation (while preserving its own independence of political party)'.[4] The Report did go on to criticize 'the new democracy' for its limited vision, for appealing 'too often to individual selfishness or to class interests', and furthermore, 'it can hardly be denied that the movement is characterized by a quite inadequate perception of the need for the redemption of the individual man from the power of sin as a condition essential to social regeneration'.[5] The Report encouraged the laity to join with the clergy in forming local committees to agitate for social reform.

It is of the greatest importance that in the religious teaching of the Church a prominent place should be given to those practical principles of morality which are already recognized by the people as true—e.g., brotherhood, justice, including

[1] *Christianity and Socialism*, by the Bishop of Birmingham, *Pan-Anglical Papers*, p. 7.
[2] 'Socialism, Abstract and Actual', p. 6 (printed in *Pan-Anglican Papers*).
[3] Ibid., p. 4.
[4] *Conference of Bishops of the Anglican Communion Holden at Lambeth Palace* (1908), Report No. IX, p. 156.
[5] Ibid., p. 157.

justice to other races than our own, honesty, purity, peaceableness, self-education, cleanliness, and care of health; and that there should be put plainly before the rich and leisured classes the sin of idleness, the responsibility of property, the paramount duty of public service, the incompatibility of selfish luxury with professing Christianity, and the duty of substituting justice and sympathy and brotherly effort for a condescending and thoughtless benevolence.[1]

The Report ended by endorsing the principles of the Report of Convocation on the 'Moral Witness of the Church' (1907), and by reprinting extracts from it. The Resolutions adopted by the bishops at Lambeth followed the recommendations of the Committee, and also reminded Christians of 'the moral responsibility involved in their investments', and the need to have regard to the 'character and general social effect' and 'the treatment of the persons employed' in any business in which investment was made.[2] In their Encyclical Letter the bishops commended the 'ideals of brotherhood, liberty, and mutual justice and help'.[3] The Lambeth Conference was, altogether, an impressive official recognition of the influence of C.S.U. propaganda. A whole generation of Church leadership had given its blessing to the principle of social change.

The Great War, after 1914, pushed the preparedness of Church leaders to contemplate social changes still further. The 3,000 Anglican chaplains who served with the forces during the war were often appalled by the lack of Christian knowledge displayed by ordinary Englishmen, appearing to confirm once again the failure of the Church to penetrate the masses. Their own efforts at bringing a Christian influence to bear upon the troops were, to say the least, uneven.[4] Yet they were also impressed by the survival of a low-level spirituality, an 'inarticulate religion',[5] the sort of 'religion of fellowship' described by Coningsby Dawson in *The Glory of the Trenches*.[6] Many of the chaplains no doubt found themselves in the same position as others of their social class—able 'to rub shoulders with the poorer classes in a way which they have never done before'.[7] The result was usually a conviction that social reform, and a more equitable distribution of the wealth of industry, must be high on the agenda for post-war reconstruction. This was the impression of 'Tubby' Clayton, founder of the Toc H movement, based on his experiences in Flanders. 'The War',

---

[1] Ibid. pp. 158–9.

[2] Ibid., p. 57, Resolution 49.

[3] Ibid., p. 39.

[4] Albert Marrin, *The Last Crusade. The Church of England in the First World War* (Duke University Press, 1974), p. 207.

[5] 'When the Priests Came Home', by Kenneth Kirk, in *The Church in the Furnace. Essays by Seventeen Temporary Church of England Chaplains on Active Service in France and Flanders*, ed. F. B. Macnutt (London, 1917), p. 410.

[6] Coningsby Dawson, *The Glory of the Trenches* (London, 1918), pp. 154–5; see also his *Khaki Courage*.

[7] Bernard Keymer, in *The Church in the Furnace*, p. 135.

he wrote, 'erased, or at least softened, the horizontal divisions of class; and the time was ripe for a great forward movement on the part of the Church itself towards the ideas already seen in the working at Kelham and Mirfield.'[1] There was a general agreement that this was the case, although a good deal of ephemeral romanticism surround the chaplains' social observations on the one hand, associated with a sort of appalled fascination at the lives of the lower-class creatures they now beheld so closely on the other. 'The wage-earners are filled with a vague but profound sentiment that the industrial system, as it is now, denies to them the liberties, opportunities, and responsibilities of free men,' wrote one chaplain.[2] Canon MacNutt of Southwark, wrote from the front, 'we can never again be content with much that we accepted as quite natural in those far-away days before we came out here'.[3] The volume on *Competition* produced by Temple's group in 1913 also remarked upon those stirrings: 'during the present war the country has realized that men who would willingly work their hardest for the sake of their country in the production of munitions are reluctant to put forth their best efforts to enrich their employers'.[4] For Winnington-Ingram, the Bishop of London, the need to introduce 'a fair chance for everyone' in the new world created by the war was very immediate—if not, he said in a Lenten Sermon, 'unrest will become revolution, and the good-natured apathy about religion which we remember in the masses of the people will become acute hostility, as it has in Russia, where eighteen bishops and three hundred priests have been cut to pieces'.[5] The war effort also brought Church and State into a very public working alliance: 'clergy and laity alike took it for granted that, as a servant of the state, the Church would contribute directly to the allied cause by explaining to the people the causes and meaning of the war'.[6] The bishops and clergy assisted the recruiting campaign by urging men to do their duty.

It was during the war that Temple's 'Collegium' produced its most important contribution to the development of social radicalism in the Church: the publication in 1917 of the volume on *Competition*, to whose importance reference has already been made. The 'Collegium' itself had begun to meet after the Matlock Conference in 1909; it was a group of a dozen or so, under Temple's informal leadership, 'called into existence to take part in satisfying the widespread desire for further light on the relation of Christianity to social life, through a fuller understanding of the social teaching of the Gospel in its application to the facts of modern

[1] Melville Harcourt, *Tubby Clayton. A Personal Saga* (London, 1953), p. 93.
[2] Keymer, in *The Church in the Furnace*, p. 130.   [3] Ibid., p. x.
[4] *Competition. A Study in Human Motive*, p. 133.
[5] A. F. Winnington-Ingram, *Victory and After* (London, 1919), p. 116.
[6] Marvin, *The Last Crusade*, p. 179.

life'.[1] The secretary was Miss Lucy Gardner, who later became secretary to Temple's C.O.P.E.C. movement. *Competition* summarized the criticism of the competitive basis of economic life, and the rejection of Political Economy, which had been going on throughout the second half of the nineteenth century. Its collectivist leanings were more advanced than many previous publications by churchmen had allowed.

Many forms of competition should be suppressed as immoral. Private enterprise requires supplementing in various directions, and will always require it. The provision of certain services which individuals cannot supply at a profit; the control of monopolies; the caring for those who are beaten and broken in the industrial process—these and similar duties will always call for collective action. The policy of equalizing opportunity by improving education, and perhaps by limiting the right of bequest, must be carried out, that competition may be fair and effective.[2]

The work also argued for a system of graduated personal taxation and an increase in death duty, so that 'all undue profits would be transferred to the community as a whole'. National income thereby gathered in could be used for social services—for 'experiments in education, sanitation, housing and the like'.[3] This ideal of state interventionism coincided with the growing post-war assumption by the working classes that the State did have an obligation to safeguard the economic welfare of its citizens.[4]

Another consequence of the stimulus provided by the war was the appointment of five committees set up by the Archbishops of Canterbury and York as part of the National Mission in 1916. The Mission itself was a rather unsuccessful evangelistic campaign. The Reports, published in 1918, and covering five main aspects of the Church's work and concern, were soaked in the vocabulary and the idealism of the social radicalism current in the Church during the pre-war years. The most directly concerned with social policy was the Fifth Report, on *Christianity and Industrial Problems*. Like the study of *Competition* by the 'Collegium' this was something of a summary of preceding radical thought. The Report, indeed, opened with the now familiar reference to the 'lamentable failure' of the Church to concern itself adequately with social issues.[5] Then followed the claim that the Church must be as concerned with the economic morality of society as it is with individual moral conduct. There was, in the Report, no actual attack upon the existing structure of industrial organization, but a conviction that the spirit which pervaded it required changing. Business ethics must be free of the competitive principle which

---

[1] *Competition. A Study in Human Motive*, p. v.
[2] Ibid., p. 63.   [3] Ibid., p. 127.
[4] Gilbert, *British Social Policy, 1914–1939*, p. 31.
[5] *Christianity and Industrial Problems, Being the Report of the Archbishops' Fifth Committee of Inquiry* (London, 1918), p. 2.

allowed the value of men to reside solely in their labour as producers of wealth for others. Profits should be restricted; taxation should be calculated to redistribute wealth; workers should be guaranteed a 'living wage', and unemployment studied and prevented. Though the Report was cautious about the detail of industrial management, it was emphatic that the social system in general was antipathetic to the fulfilment of a Christian social order.[1] Nevertheless the solution offered related primarily to the conditions and rewards of industrial employment: there was to be co-operation between employers and workers in the management of industry. At this point, however, the Report disclosed a divergence of opinion— the more radical members of the Committee hoped for direct participation by the workers in the management of industry; others plumped for a vaguer formula about 'co-operation', retaining a degree of managerial executive control.[2] This difference of opinion no doubt corresponded to the balance on the Committee between the C.S.U. bishops and the Christian Socialist League members.[3] The C.S.L. had only two of their men on the Committee, but it is likely that on the question of worker participation the more radical of the C.S.U. members, like Gore and Tawney, must have sided with Lansbury and the C.S.L. view. The Chairman of the Committee was Bishop Talbot of Winchester (C.S.U.). The two Tory M.P.s who sat on it must have felt very much out of place. The 'dominating spirit' of the Committee, according to Hensley Henson, 'was evidently supplied by Messrs. Lansbury and Tawney, and their episcopal shadows, Gore, Talbot, Kempthorne, and Woods'.[4] The Report also argued for an increase of clergy from less privileged sections of society, for courses in economic and social teaching in the preparation of ordination candidates, for clerical participation in agitations for social change, and for national education animated by the concept of an educational 'highway' rather than a 'ladder' —an idea clearly picked up from Temple, who had been saying this sort of thing for some years.[5]

The Fifth Report did not encounter much opposition in the Church. The Lambeth Conference Committee on Industrial and Social Problems in 1920 found itself 'substantially in agreement' with both the 'opinions and suggestions' of the Report[6]—but then that was hardly surprising, because of the considerable overlap in the personnel of the two committees.

---

[1] *Christianity and Industrial Problems, Being the Report of the Archbishops' Fifth Committee of Inquiry*, (London 1918), pp. 79–81.

[2] Ibid., pp. 135–8.

[3] Maurice B. Reckitt, *Maurice to Temple. A Century of the Social Movement in the Church of England* (London, 1947), p. 162.

[4] Henson Papers, Durham Chapter Library, Journals, vol. 25 (1 June–22 Oct. 1919), p. 205; see also *Retrospect*, i. 318.

[5] See Temple's *Church and Nation* (1916), p. 187, where he criticized modern education: 'Its ideal is the educational ladder.'

[6] *The Six Lambeth Conferences*, Report No. II, p. 67.

The Report did draw out a small group of distinguished opponents—
Hensley Henson, whose dismissive attitude has just been noticed; and
A. C. Headlam, Regius Professor of Divinity at Oxford, and later Bishop of
Gloucester, who warned the Church 'to meddle as little as possible, as a
Church, with definite political or economic issues'—his opposition was
regarded as serious enough to receive attention in the Lambeth Report.[1]
But the most detailed critique came in a short book by Archdeacon William
Cunningham. It was his last service to the Church before his death.
Remarking at the outset of his demolition of the Report's main premises
that they would, none the less, be 'welcomed in a very wide circle'[2]—a
prediction which certainly proved true—Cunningham isolated two chief
'misunderstandings'. The first was economic: 'The economic misunderstanding consists in separating and contrasting the material progress of the
country with moral progress—the welfare of the population—as if they
were quite distinct, and in some sense even opposed.'[3] He affirmed the
advantages of the materialism necessary to the creation of wealth—it was
essential for the improvement of the condition of the whole population.
Theological objection to the Report resided in the belief that 'the attempt
to formulate maxims on economic affairs which are true for all time has
led to the claim that these laws have a divine sanction, and to a reverential
treatment of economic science as if it was engaged in expounding the
Divine Will'.[4] On the contrary, Cunningham argued, 'our Lord Himself
did not regard it as part of His mission to try and set the industrial and
social injustices of His own day aright'.[5] This last was the argument from
Scripture often employed against attempts to identify Christianity with
exact social systems and social panaceas. Cunningham's discussion of the
Fifth Report summed up his distinguished record as a critic of those who
would too readily assume the immediate compatibility of Christianity and
Socialism—although he was himself a noted critic of *laissez-faire* practice.
In 1909 he had pointed to the differences of socialism and Christianity—
'both aim at an improvement in society, but socialists try to attain it by
compelling other people to do their duty, Christianity by inducing every
man to do his own'. Christianity 'appeals to each individual personally, by
holding out an ideal, and stirring up his will; it does not hope to accomplish
its object by pressure from without, but by inspiration from within'.[6]
Cunningham had also dared to attack Westcott's co-operative ideal—'It
does not foster a sense of duty to the community, but aims instead at
securing objects which men have in common, and at satisfying wishes of

[1] Ibid., p. 72.
[2] W. Cunningham, *Personal Ideals and Social Principles. Some Comments on the Repor*
of the Archbishops' Committee on Christianity and Industrial Problems (London, 1919), p.;
[3] Ibid., p. 6.   [4] Ibid., p. 13.   [5] Ibid., p. 24.
[6] W. Cunningham, *Christianity and Socialism*, p. 13.

which they are conscious,' he said in 1914.[1] He also defended the utility of social inequality: 'In a society where the economic life is determined by the hope of reward' there was 'a range of ambitions which afford a stimulus that would not otherwise exist for a man to work energetically at his calling'. To assist this, a high degree of social mobility was also desirable.[2] Cunningham's opinions were just passing out of the range of those closer to the influential centres of the Church: he left little mark on Church thought.

The other four Reports of the Archbishops' Committees concerned issues less obviously related to the social system, yet each of them in some way reflected the pervasive social criticism which the Fifth embodied. The Report on *The Worship of the Church* concluded that 'only by the removal of the worst features of our social and industrial system, or even by a radical change in the system itself, will the way be made clear for the return of the people to the public worship of the Church'.[3] The Report on *The Evangelistic Work of the Church* insisted that concern with social and industrial problems was 'vitally related to the evangelistic work of the Church',[4] and added that 'a presentation of the Gospel which ignores the social obligation of Christianity will not receive serious attention from increasing numbers of the people to-day'.[5] The Reports were, altogether, a remarkable testimony to the growing orthodoxy of social-radical ideas within the leadership of the Church.

In 1920 yet another Committee appointed by the Archbishop of Canterbury reported on *The Church and Social Service*. Its terms of reference themselves indicate the acceptance of collectivist principles within the Church: the Committee was charged to consider 'the ways in which the clergy, churchworkers, and churchpeople generally can best co-operate with the State in all matters concerning the social life of the community'. The Report noted that 'a vast web of new social machinery has been created in the form of salaried and other agents to give effect to the long series of legal enactments to secure better conditions of life for those who have not always been able to help themselves'. The Report was an acceptance of the scale of social welfare: it was now seen to be too great for private or religious agencies to handle alone. It therefore recommended the co-operation of the Church with the State, rather than any attempt by the Church to duplicate public effort with its own welfare agencies.

---

[1] W. Cunningham, *Christianity and Politics*, the Lowell Lectures, 1914 (London, 1916), p. 207.

[2] W. Cunningham, *Christianity and Social Questions* (London, 1910), p. 111.

[3] *The Worship of the Church, Being the Report of the Archbishops' Second Committee of Inquiry* (1918), p. 14.

[4] *The Evangelistic Work of the Church, Being the Report of the Archbishops' Third Committee of Inquiry* (1918), p. 16.

[5] *Ibid.*, p. 17.

'Systematised teaching on social subjects' was recommended for theological colleges; the clergy were urged, once again, 'to bear witness to Christian principles in their social application'.[1]

It is, in view of the tone and content of these official Church documents, not at all surprising that the Lambeth Conference of 1920 should have echoed the criticism of existing social relationships. In their Encyclical Letter, the bishops declared that everyone must 'share equitably in the results of labour', and that 'fellowship' was 'imperilled by any form of industrial slavery'. This followed a condemnation of the 'internecine conflict between capital and labour'.[2] Resolution No. 74 of the Conference, which was often referred to later as being the main guide to the Church's teaching on these questions, was rather less radical than the over-all tone of the Fifth Report of 1918, but still, by most of the standards applied in 1920, an advanced pronouncement.

An outstanding and pressing duty of the Church is to convince its members of the necessity of nothing less than a fundamental change in the spirit and working of our economic life. This change can only be effected by accepting as the basis of industrial relations the principle of co-operation in service for the common good in place of unrestricted competition for private or sectional advantage. All Christian people ought to take an active part in bringing about this change, by which alone we can hope to remove class dissensions and resolve industrial discords.[3]

To complement that, Resolution 78 declared that the Church was 'bound to use its influence to remove inhuman or oppressive conditions of labour in all parts of the world'.[4] To later twentieth-century readers, accustomed to hearing the rhetoric of oppression banded around by interested priests, the radical impact of this sort of declaration seems rather muted. But to contemporaries in 1920 the Church really did appear to be in the vanguard of social change—so much so, indeed, that the Lambeth Report on 'Industrial and Social Problems' went out of its way to say that 'violent revolution' was not considered a proper means of achieving the ends they recommended. Bertrand Russell was quoted as an authority on the evils of revolution.[5] The Report also cited Westcott as the great exponent of the social conscience. God, the Report urged again in all the familiar language, 'cannot be excluded from politics, or industry, or from any of our social relationships'. The Gospel 'includes a social message'.[6]

The Lambeth principles were popularized in the Church by the work of the Industrial Christian Fellowship, founded in 1919 by amalgamating the C.S.U. with the Navvy Mission (founded in 1877). Bishop Kempthorne

---

[1] *Guardian*, 6 Feb. 1920: text of the Report.
[2] *The Six Lambeth Conferences 1867–1920*, Conference of 1920, p. 18.
[3] Ibid., p. 46.   [4] Ibid., p. 46.
[5] Ibid., p. 72.   [6] Ibid., p. 61.

became the Chairman of the Executive Committee and Prebendary P. T. R. Kirk presided over the actual organization. The country was divided into missionary districts under clerical directorship, working with lay agents.[1] Studdert Kennedy became the most celebrated of the district missioners of the I.C.F. The new Church Assambly, set up according to the terms of the 1919 Enabling Act, also took steps to provide for the dissemination of the Lambeth social ideals. In 1923 it appointed a Standing Committee on Social and Industrial Questions, so institutionalizing the social interest of the preceding years of discussion and propaganda. The Committee was chaired by Winnington-Ingram, on whose motion it had been constituted.[2] In describing the reasons for a permanent Church body on social issues, Bishop Talbot repeated the old C.S.U. contention that Christians tended 'to confine themselves, and to represent the Church as confined to a certain limited range of subjects connected with discipline, instruction, and the salvation of the individual soul'—a 'fundamental mistake'.[3] Gore also took steps to spread his interpretation of the social implications of the Gospel. Having retired from the see of Oxford in 1919, largely because of his opposition to the compromises made in the franchise provisions of the Enabling Act, Gore had gone off, 'full of beans, as the boys say'[4], to London, where he worked as a lecturer and author. In 1920 he presided over the Christian Social Crusade, the successor of the Council for Christian Witness on Social Questions, founded in 1913. This body, too, sought to propagate and to implement the Lambeth resolutions of 1920.

While the leadership of the Church was thus adapting and absorbing quite radical social attitudes, the development of the more distinct Christian Socialist outlook had also been marked. It was now even more clearly separated from the fashionable social postures of the C.S.U. than it had been in the 1880s and 1890s. Most Christian Socialists in the first years of the new century were collectivists, with a positive belief in the use of the machinery of the State to bring about social and economic transformation. 'Many members of the Church of England are Socialists', wrote Conrad Noel in 1910, 'and would establish a commonwealth whose people should own the land and the industrial capital and administer them co-operatively for the good of all.' Public ownership, in fact, was 'a necessary deduction from the teachings of the Church'.[5] In 1906, at a conference in Morecambe, the Church Socialist League was founded. The movement marked a further decline in the old Guild of St. Matthew under Stewart Headlam. It also reflected the possibilities which radical priests saw opened up by the

---

[1] Lloyd, *The Church of England*, p. 303.

[2] Winnington-Ingram, *Fifty Years' Work in London*, p. 212.

[3] *National Assembly of the Church of England. Spring Session, 1923, Report of Proceedings*, vol. iv, No. 1, p. 117.

[4] Bell, *Randall Davidson*, ii. 973.

[5] Conrad Noel, *Socialism in Church History*, p. 7.

return of fifty-three Labour and Lib-Lab members to Parliament in the 1906 General Election. 'The mood was one of almost unbounded confidence', Maurice Reckitt has written of the atmosphere surrounding the creation of the C.S.L.[1] The League was inspired by priests from the north of England, with Mirfield—where Gore's influence had gathered together Fr. Paul Bull, Fr. Samuel Healy, and Fr. J. Neville Figgis—as a particularly important centre of Church Socialist ideas.[2] This also indicated another feature of the League: its Anglo-Catholicism. It was a clerical movement. But despite the internal divisions over political doctrine, and despite the eccentricity of some of the leaders—publicized in caricatures of socialist priests then often found in plays and novels[3]—the League did promote serious political analysis. The Revd. Algernon West, first President of the C.S.L., was a systematic thinker whose ideas were similar to those of the Marxists in the S.D.F. He did not have the usual upper-class background, and had come from a lower-middle-class home, educated in a Church school in Islington. The Revd. Frederic Lewis Donaldson, inventor of the slogan 'Christianity is the religion of which Socialism is the practice', and well known as the leader of the Leicester Unemployed March to London in 1905, joined the League's committee in 1906 and was its champion from 1913 to 1916. Like Noel and West, he was formerly a member of the G.S.M. In Leicester, where he was an incumbent (until he became a Canon of Westminster), Donaldson established the League in local Church circles, with the assistance of the young Hewlett Johnson, later Dean of Canterbury. The most durable of the League's leaders, however, was Conrad le Despenser Roden Noel, grandson of the Earl of Gainsborough, and son of a gentleman-in-waiting to Queen Victoria. After being sent down from his Cambridge college for frequent intoxication, Noel proceeded to Chichester Theological College, where he discovered that the early Fathers of the Church had all been putative revolutionaries. At Chichester, he said, he 'compared socialism with the Gospels, and contrasted them both with the contemporary commercial individualism'.[4] On ordination, in 1894, he went to serve under Fr. Dolling in Portsmouth, then for a time in Plymouth, and after that, living in a south London doss-house, he met Percy Dearmer.[5] After a couple more curacies, Noel became the organizer of the Morecambe Conference in 1906. In 1910 he entered his most famous work, when he was presented to the living of Thaxted by Lady Warwick, the patron, who was herself a member of the League. For the next thirty years Thaxted became the centre of Christian Socialism in England. For

---

[1] Reckitt, *Maurice to Temple*, p. 151.

[2] P. d'A. Jones, *The Christian Socialist Revival*, p. 228.

[3] See e.g. H. A. Bulley, *Father Clement, Socialist* (London, 1907); Morrell, in Shaw's *Candida*, is another, probably a G.S.M. priest.

[4] Reg Groves, *Conrad Noel and the Thaxted Movement* (London, 1967), p. 27.

[5] P. d'A. Jones, *The Christian Socialist Revival*, p. 245.

although Noel can easily be written off as an upper-class 'folk' romantic, addicted to Morris dancing and flying the red flag from the tower of his church, this would do his intelligence a considerable injustice. He was a critical thinker whose socialism, though its peculiarities will not allow exact categorization, had impressive qualities. He was an enemy of the sort of liberal social reformism which the C.S.U. bishops called 'socialism'. In 1917, in attacking the policies of Reconstruction, he declared 'Reconstitution without revolution is evil'.[1] In the same year he welcomed the Russian Revolution—though he entertained reservations about the Bolsheviks, whom he seems to have identified with the S.D.F.[2]

The Church Socialist League had an unequivocably socialist platform: 'The political, economic and social emancipation of the whole people, men and women, by the establishment of a democratic commonwealth in which the community shall run the land and capital collectively and use them for the good of all.'[3] By 1910 there were 1,200 members; it was therefore a small body (especially when compared with the C.S.U.), but with a skilled propagandist organization. It was most active in 1912, the year of greatest industrial unrest, the year also in which the League's committee petitioned the Convocation of Canterbury that 'private ownership of land and capital should forthwith be made to cease'.[4] By 1912 too, the membership included R. H. Tawney, Maurice Reckitt, and A. J. Penty. At the Bristol Conference of that year George Lansbury, later leader of the parliamentary Labour Party, was elected President of the League, and Hewlett Johnson joined the Executive. But 1912 also marked the opening of the first doctrinal fissures which later split the C.S.L. Noel and Widdrington, especially, were unable to agree about the religious (rather than the political) basis of association—as first became really clear at the Thaxted gathering of the leaders in 1912.[5] In 1916 Noel eventually seceded, and in 1918 formed the Catholic Crusade with a definitely Catholic theological constitution. A lot of members followed him.

The League itself was increasingly attracted to Guild Socialism. It was another indication of division within Christian Socialism, for Noel, in spite of a brief interest in syndicalism in 1912,[6] remained a convinced collectivist, an ardent believer in the use of centralized state power for social regeneration. The attractiveness of Guild Socialism to most of the other League leaders was a pointer to their 'medievalism'. Widdrington, Bull, Reckitt, Penty, and Tawney—all the intelligence of the League,

---

[1] Groves, *Conrad Noel*, p. 187.   [2] Ibid., p. 239.

[3] Maurice B. Reckitt, *P. E. T. Widdrington. A Study in Vocation and Versatility* (London, 1961), has incorrectly transcribed 'collectively' as 'co-operatively', by conflating the declaration with the 4th principle of the League, which was that land and capital should be used 'co-operatively for the good of all'.

[4] Groves, *Conrad Noel*, p. 111.

[5] Reckitt, *P. E. T. Widdrington*, p. 55.   [6] Groves, *Conrad Noel*, p. 124.

except for Noel—were in some degree absorbed by Guild Socialism after 1914. It represented a renewal of what seemed to them the ideal order of medieval Catholic christendom: diversity of vocation within a universal society. It was also an attempt to recreate the ethical conditions in which Tawney's account of pre-Reformation economic morality could again receive recognition. This was, indeed, one of the features that seemed less than realistic to those who stuck to moderate collectivism. Hence Temple's 'Collegium', and their condemnation of both full state socialism and syndicalism: 'No artificial changing of the framework of society would succeed if the members of that society remained unchanged.'[1] Neville Figgis, a Mirfield monk after his departure from a distinguished career as a teacher of history at Cambridge, was the most systematic and most philosophical exponent of the new acceptance of social pluralism. His *Churches in the Modern State*, a series of lectures to the clergy of Gloucester, given in 1911, became the most influential Christian Socialist attack upon the notion of state collectivism. For Figgis, the State was properly envisaged as a 'community of communities', and the Church as an independent and distinct spiritual society which, like other social entities, derived from a life quite independent of the State. Recognition of the legitimacy of the various aspirations of the components of this pluralism involved the most extensive alterations to conventional understanding of political organization. 'Since, as a fact,' Figgis wrote, 'religious bodies are only one class of a number of other societies, all laying claim to this inherent life, it is clear that the question concerns not merely ecclesiastical privilege, but the whole complex structure of civil society and the nature of political union.'[2] Figgis depended quite heavily on Otto Gierke's theory of the group personality of corporations in society. The difficulty of all such notions resides in the operation of sovereignty: how to construct a State that actually does work—through the exercise of necessary authority and directive capacity—without destroying the 'personality' of its components; how also to derive a mechanism which prevents the components devouring one another. The weakness of Figgis's lectures lay precisely there. His isolation of the problem was itself imperfect: his solution too vague. 'The business of Christians is with the moral standard of their own society and with themselves as its members,' he wrote. 'The raising of that will gradually bring about the elevation of the great mass of those who do not belong to it.'[3] This belief in permeation was apposite enough when applied in a context fashioned by those who were anxious not to involve the Church, collectively, in divisive political activity within a dynamic State; but for a theorist who has eliminated some of the basic exercises

---

[1] *Competition* (1917), p. 146.
[2] Figgis, *Churches in the Modern State*, second edn., (London, 1914), p. 40.
[3] Ibid., p. 130.

CSE—I

of sovereignty by the State, it involved some difficulties of survival which Figgis did not discuss.

Maurice Reckitt's version of Guild Socialism (he preferred to speak of 'National Guilds') was also a total one: 'a challenge both to the capitalist and the collectivist . . . the abolition of the wage-system, the attainment of self-government in industry, and the modification of state sovereignty'.[1] Reckitt became one of the most distinguished lay social thinkers of the Church in the years between the wars. Whereas Tawney, whose ideas were to some extent popularized by Reckitt, was a more distinguished thinker, whose influence was over intellectuals, Reckitt was read by thousands of parish clergymen and laymen. His books were frequent and popular. He came from a rich family, whose wealth derived from manufacturing, and, while at Oxford, had joined the Church Socialist League. During the vacations he set up a branch at St. Leonards-on-Sea.[2] He never regarded himself 'as a whole-hearted guild socialist',[3] and his socialism, indeed, mellowed. 'My objection to our leisured classes', he wrote in 1941, 'is that they make so poor a study—and therefore a use—of that in which they presume to specialize': leisure.[4] But in 1918 he contended for a balanced relationship between vocational groups and state supervision of resources. 'In every main industry', he wrote, 'the workers, organized in a self-governing National Guild, would have the monopoly and control of its working in partnership with the State, which would be the owner of the means of production.'[5] Collectivism and state socialism were rejected as devices which failed to secure popular control: 'To every problem the State Socialists applied their flyblown formula—"the nationalization of the means of production, distribution, and exchange"—as if putting industry into the hands of politicians were synonymous with putting it into the hands of the people.'[6] The trade unions were to be 'reconstructed' to fit into the National Guild social framework.[7] Fr. Widdrington had also come to distrust state socialism. 'What I see coming, unless the working class rouse themselves, is state capitalism', he said in 1912.[8] The Christian Socialists in fact quarrelled about the exact nature of the Guild Socialism to be adopted. Penty, with his insistence on the medieval craft ideal, disagreed with Reckitt. After the war, as it turned out, Guild Socialism largely passed out of the hands of Church thinkers, anyway, and became almost identified with the secular vision of G. D. H. Cole and William

---

[1] Maurice B. Reckitt and C. E. Bechhofer, *The Meaning of National Guilds* (London, 1918), p. xii.

[2] Maurice B. Reckitt, *As it Happened. An Autobiography* (London, 1941), pp. 104 and 247.

[3] Ibid., p. 141.   [4] Ibid., p. 73.

[5] *The Meaning of National Guilds*, p. 4.   [6] Ibid., p. 21.

[7] Ibid., p. 122.

[8] Reckitt, *P. E. T. Widdrington*, p. 55.

Mellor—almost, but not entirely: for Tawney continued to represent a Christian presence in post-war Guild Socialism.

With the exception of some of the Christian Socialists, the general acceptance of social radicalism among Church leaders in the first decades of the twentieth century did not suggest to them a need to alter their attitude to political involvement. The widespread assumption that party politics were to be avoided remained. The few Church leaders who were opposed to the new principles of social criticism always supposed that it would plunge the Church into radical politics; but their fears were unfulfilled. 'I can recall no instance of a Church which has gone into politics and not come out of it badly smirched', observed Dean Inge in 1912.[1] But this sort of fear was not based upon present realities: it did not appreciate the vicarious quality released in so much of the Church's social moralism. Despite the new ideals, and the repetitive exhortations to economic change, most churchmen had no intention of actually altering the social structure or of using systematic agitation to change society. 'Such agitation must almost necessarily involve the clergy in active participation in party politics, by signifying approval of the measures of one party, and denouncing the neglect of the other', said William Cunningham in 1914.[2] But the Church, on the whole, declaimed and postured rather than agitated. In 1905 Randall Davidson, replying to a complaint from Hensley Henson that the clergy were preaching politics from their pulpits, could find little evidence of it. 'Can anyone fairly say that anything occurs ordinarily in our churches which corresponds with the use made of Nonconformist chapels in this respect?', he asked; yet added that it was not desirable 'to dissociate our Christian teaching from our social life in such a manner as to make a preacher shun the application of Christian principles to the larger social issues which the community has to deal with'.[3] The general difficulty of avoiding the political implications of social and economic teaching was generally overcome by separating principles from application. Both opponents and defenders of social radicalism tended to do this—which was, indeed, the traditional practice of the universal Church. Thus Henson, preaching in 1891 to the Becton Gasworkers at Barking, where he was then Vicar, articulated the Church's position in concise language:

Why do not the clergy preach a crusade against the present organization of industry, and propound a better scheme of society for the acceptance of men? My brothers, these questions are commonly asked, and the view of the Church which suggests them is very widely spread. Nevertheless, I submit to you to-day

[1] Inge, *The Church and the Age*, p. 71.
[2] Cunningham, *Christianity and Politics*, p. 193.
[3] Davidson Papers, Lambeth Palace, 1905, O.2, Davidson to Henson, 3 Aug.; see also Bell, *Randall Davidson*, i. 491.

that it is a mistaken view. The Church never received from Christ any commission to deal directly with the social and political arrangements of men. . . . The clergy as such have nothing to do directly with political constitutions or schemes of social change, or projects of economic organization. Are they, then, strangers to the intensest interests of working men? Is their gospel so spiritual that it does not affect the course of terrestrial life? Is Christianity so much a matter of the next world as to be without value in this? No, my brothers; I beg you to believe that this is not so. The faith of Jesus Christ goes to the very roots of human conduct, and just because it does so it can afford to leave the details of conduct alone. Thus the Church affects the world not directly, but indirectly; not by prescribing a scheme of society, but by providing true principles of action.[1]

Archbishop Lang gave the same explanation of the Church's social action when preaching before the Sheffield Church Congress in 1922.

What, then, is the social mission of the Church? It is to assert the truth of these spiritual motives, and to inspire men loyally to them, so that the first question to be asked and answered, not, as so often now, the first question to be dismissed, shall be 'How can we apply these motives in our homes, our business, our industry, our national and international politics?' The primary duty of the Church as such is to insist upon the obligation of the question, rather than itself formulate the answer. It will give guidance through its moral teaching, sometimes its leaders will be justified in declaring a course of policy—e.g., the support of the League of Nations—to be a necessary application of Christian principles. But it must keep its independence. Christianity can never be a mere preface or appendix to any particular plan of economics or politics.[2]

Nor should it be supposed that this was a scheme put out by moderates, anxious to hold the Church back from radical solutions to social issues. The same case was argued by Gore,[3] and by Temple. 'The Church and the official representatives of the Church must keep themselves free from the entanglements of party politics,' said Temple in 1912: 'Their business is something far more fundamental and important; it is the formation of that mind and temper in the whole community which will lead to wholesome legislation by any party and all parties.'[4] Temple never really changed this early position, either. For the most famous statement of the division between principles and applications, according to the same formula offered by Henson and by Lang, was to come in Temple's *Christianity and Social Order*, published in 1942. 'It is of crucial importance that the Church acting corporately should not commit itself to any particular policy', he wrote then: 'The Church is committed to the everlasting

[1] H. Hensley Henson, *Light and Leaven*, p. 274.
[2] *The Official Report of the Church Congress, Sheffield, 1922* (London, 1922), p. 7; also printed in the *Church Times*, 13 Oct. 1922.
[3] *Christianity and Socialism*, in *Pan-Anglican Papers*, p. 7.
[4] Temple, *The Kingdom of God*, p. 90.

Gospel and to the Creeds which formulate it; it must never commit itself to an ephemeral programme of detailed action.'[1] In 1920 the Lambeth Conference resolved that 'The Church cannot in its corporate capacity be an advocate or partisan, "a judge or a divider", in political or class disputes where moral issues are not at stake'.[2]

Despite the existence of this principle, and its general acceptance and observance in these years, the Church's association, in the popular mind, with the Conservative Party continued. It was an impression fostered by the continued support of the Conservatives for Church education and for the Establishment of the Church in Wales. Nonconformists, as well as Liberals, were anxious to brand the Church as inherently Tory; the preceding decades of propaganda had stuck. Charles Masterman, a churchman and a Liberal politician, was correct when he remarked in 1901 that the Church was 'still regarded as having blindly thrown itself into the arms of one political party in order to prevent its own spoliation'.[3] Church leaders were naturally anxious to discount the impression. In the 1910 election campaign, for example, Randall Davidson refused to condemn the Liberals' Welsh Church and educational policies on the grounds that they were not major issues in the election—which was, indeed, being fought on constitutional questions raised by the Lords' rejection of the Finance Bill. For this he was even accused by some Tories of siding with the Liberals.[4] To Lord Salisbury he wrote, 'I honestly believe that we best serve the interests both of Church and Nation by abstaining from identifying ourselves vociferously with one side or other in an acute political conflict wherein Church questions occupy really a subordinate place'.[5] Davidson, in fact, inspired considerable respect among political leaders for his judicious approach to the moralistic claims of political pressure-groups.[6] He had nevertheless a consistent belief in the duty of the bishops to discharge their legislative function in the House of Lords; they were entrusted with this 'not only for what are technically called Ecclesiastical questions', he wrote in 1899, 'but for whatever things directly concern the moral life and social well-being of the English people'.[7] This was exactly the view taken by the early-nineteenth-century bishops, and the difficulty in it was still that of defining which issues really did concern general welfare and which were merely 'party' politics. The distinctions Davidson drew between issues were certainly applied often

---

[1] William Temple, *Christianity and Social Order* (Penguin Books, London, 1942), pp. 18–19.

[2] *The Six Lambeth Conferences*, Resolution 75, p. 46.

[3] *The Heart of the Empire*, ed. C. F. G. Masterman, p. 45.

[4] Bell, *Randall Davidson*, i. 603.   [5] Ibid. p. 604.

[6] David L. Edwards, *Leaders of the Church of England, 1828–1944* (London, 1971), p. 240.

[7] Bell, *Randall Davidson*, i. 318.

enough. In 1908, for example, he supported the Old Age Pensions Bill, but in 1909 he led most of the bishops in abstaining in the vote on the People's Budget. He explained his position to the House. In the past fifteen years, he said, the bishops had taken part in the parliamentary discussions of 'practically all those questions—moral, religious, educational, social— with which this House has constantly to deal.' Yet 'in recent years at least' the bishops have 'held themselves free from the ties of what is ordinarily known as Party allegiance'. As citizens, he maintained, the bishops were entitled to any view they liked on 'questions of a distinctly political character'; but they would not wish to represent the Church in such matters.[1] As the division on the Finance Bill was to be of 'a strictly Party character', he wished to take no part.[2] Archbishop Lang, making his maiden speech, following his translation to York, differed over the question of definition—not only from Davidson, but from Lord Newton's belief that the Budget was 'of interest only to professors and dons and persons who write letters to the *Spectator*'.[3] He went on to speak of the need to reform social conditions and increase the remunerations of labour; he cast doubts upon the alleged threat of socialism in the Bill. Of the socialists, he said, accurately, 'I know many of them to be as devoted to the property they have . . . as any of your Lordships'.[4] Socialism would anyway have no appeal if economic conditions were changed. 'Give a man a better chance, give him a feeling that the social system is not against him but with him' and, according to Lang, the country would be untroubled.[5] He did actually think the Finance Bill a bad measure, but not so bad as to justify the unprecedented step of rejecting it. Apart from Lang, Gore and Kempthorne voted for the Bill. Bishop Browne of Bristol voted against. The others followed Davidson's advice and abstained. Over the Parliament Act in 1911 Davidson and Lang worked together in supporting the Bill. Davidson urged conciliation and begged the peers not to make the constitutional crisis a question of 'party triumph or defeat'.[6] Eleven other bishops voted with the Liberals, so providing thirteen of the government's majority of seventeen; only two voted with the Conservative opposition. The bishops' behaviour was an indication of their belief that a defeat for the Government on so crucial an issue would wreck, if not the Constitution, at least the Upper House.[7] It was the nearest they came, in this period, to directly political behaviour. The Conservative Party was very shocked.

Some men, however, continued to charge the bishops with not being concerned enough with legislation. In 1907 Augustine Birrell (President of

---

[1] Hansard, *Fifth Series*, 1909, Lords, vol. 4, 940 (24 Nov. 1909).
[2] Ibid. 941.   [3] Ibid. 1236 (30 Nov. 1909).
[4] Ibid. 1240.   [5] Ibid. 1241.
[6] Hansard, *Fifth Series*, ix. 591 (20 July 1911).
[7] Lockhart, *Cosmo Gordon Lang*, p. 238.

the Board of Education when the Liberal administration had attempted educational reform in the preceding year) launched into the bench. 'I cannot remember a single great cause they ever advocated,' he said, 'I cannot recall a single victory they ever won, hardly a word they ever said in the cause of humanity.'[1] His words distilled the bitterness of the loss of his Bill in the face of episcopal opposition; the record he alleged of the bishops was quite untrue. Davidson was able to compile an impressive list of recent social questions in which the bishops had taken a direct legislative part: the Workmen's Compensation Act (1897), the Prisons Act (1898), factory and temperance reforms, the motions introduced to Parliament by bishops on the treatment of aborigines in Western Australia, the treatment of Jews in Russia, the issue of Chinese labour in South Africa, the conditions of labour in the Congo.[2] The list was an outline only. It was an interesting indication not only of the surviving strength of the bishops' legislative functions, but of the definition of social and moral, as opposed to political questions.

It was on the more radical wing of the Church of England that a temptation sometimes existed to break with this convention. Some did wish to commit the Church to Labour politics, and not just to social criticism; but they were a small number. Even the convinced Christian Socialists were not entirely happy about a complete association of the Church with a socialist political party. Conrad Noel wrote that Christianity should not 'be finally identified with any political or economic system',[3] though the Church must be prepared 'to make temporary alliances with political parties'.[4] The less socialistic (those given to the various shades of C.S.U. social radicalism) were certainly unprepared to identify the Church as such with the Labour Party—though individuals might, in their individual and not their corporate capacities; especially after the 1906 general election had given the new Labour Party a distinct parliamentary presence. Temple, who as early as 1912 had remarked that the Kingdom of Heaven would 'inevitably' be 'Socialistic',[5] had by 1918 decided that Labour was 'quite definitely a moral challenge thrown out to the whole order of society as it now exists'.[6] He announced in Convocation that he had just joined the Labour Party.[7] Although one writer has declared that those who criticized this action produced 'a display of the utmost nonsense'[8] the real disapproval of Temple's behaviour was simply because it appeared to break the convention of separating the Church from party politics. The timing of Temple's announcement, and the debating tactic he clearly intended it to

[1] Bell, *Randall Davidson*, i. 541.   [2] Ibid. 542.
[3] Conrad Noel, *Socialism in Church History*, p. 7.   [4] Ibid., p. 8.
[5] *The Kingdom of God*, p. 79.
[6] *The Chronicle of Convocation* (1918), p. 350 (Lower House, 1 May).
[7] Ibid., p. 351.
[8] John Oliver, *The Church and Social Order* (London, 1968), p. 47.

be, cannot have softened those fears. In a newspaper article published in the same month, Temple expressed his conviction that 'Churchmen ought to consider very carefully the formulated programme of the Labour Party, and whether they should individually subscribe it', because 'it is a scheme based on moral ideals'.[1] He had made his opinions extremely public. Randall Davidson, at the more conservative end of the Church was, for his part, careful to avoid saying anything which might appear unsympathetic to the Labour Party. In 1912 he privately disapproved of the activities of the Anti-Socialist Union of Great Britain, on the grounds, expressed to the Union's Secretary, that 'many Socialists are among our most devoted Christian teachers'.[2] Davidson gave his blessing to the annual 'labour weeks' at Browning Hall, at which Labour M.P.s and publicists gave lectures associating Christianity with socialism. His correspondence with the Warden of Browning Hall makes it clear that he was anxious to encourage this sort of work.[3]

In interesting itself in the Christian aspect of Labour politics, and in industrial relations, the Church went to some lengths to show that it was not just out for popularity—a criticism occasionally made by those who found the social radicalism of the Church leadership difficult to accommodate. 'Now that the conscience of the Christian community has been stirred,' declared the Lambeth Conference Report on Industrial and Social Problems, in 1920, 'we must be content to bear the accusation that we are only trying to make ourselves popular with labour, because labour is now a dominant power'. The Report added: 'We are honestly trying to see and to speak the truth'.[4] Henson certainly believed that this was not the case. 'The wheel has gone full circle, and the clerical toadies of the age do not flatter princes but mobs . . . They worship the possessors of power.'[5] (He was commenting in his Journal on a bishop who had supported the railway strikers in the press.[6]) Since the adoption of social reform was still not electorally popular, at least in the period up to 1914,[7] and since the overtures to social radicalism within the Church preceded their popular acceptance, there must be more inclination to agree with the Lambeth Report than with Henson.

The Church had also come, by 1900, to accept the legitimacy of collective bargaining and trade unions, and the later Victorian interest in the possi-

[1] *Daily News*, 14 May 1918: 'The Church and Labour'.

[2] Davidson Papers, Lambeth Palace, 1912, S. 25, Davidson to Mrs. Sumner, 22 July 1912.

[3] Davidson Papers, 1913, L. 1 (Labour and Religion).

[4] *The Six Lambeth Conferences*, Report No. II, p. 62.

[5] H. Hensley Henson, *Retrospect of an Unimportant Life*, i. 316.

[6] Identified as the Bishop of Peterborough: Henson Papers, Journals, Durham Chapter Library, vol. 25 (1 June–22 Oct. 1919), p. 201.

[7] See Henry Pelling, 'The Working Class and the Origins of the Welfare State', in *Popular Politics and Society in Late Victorian Britain* (London, 1968), pp. 1–18

bility of the Church fulfilling a mediatory role in industrial disputes continued to have an appeal for some. The religious press in these years gave a lot of support to trade unions; there was much goodwill combined with a certain amount of impractical commentary.[1] Scott Holland supported trade unions because, quite apart from their function of seeking justice for their members, they constituted a collective ownership of wealth and property—'every individual member of a strong union thus acquires something of the worth and dignity with which a man of property is endowed'.[2] The question of Church mediation in strikes became important during the two greatest periods of industrial unrest—between 1910 and 1914, and between 1919 and 1921. During these years, the Church newspapers tended to follow the currents of press opinion in general— sometimes supporting and sometimes opposing particular disputes.[3] Davidson's early record suggests great hesitancy. In June 1905, when Lewis Donaldson led the march of the 450 Leicester Unemployed to London, the Archbishop declined to see them at Lambeth Palace. It was certainly true that Donaldson had turned the march into a political event, calculated to win sympathy for socialist policies. Davidson explained his refusal to see the workers as due to 'the danger which is incurred by attempting rough and ready solutions of far-reaching and complicated economic problems'.[4] Donaldson replied that the Archbishop's presence 'would have done much to disabuse their minds of the idea, widely prevalent among them, that the tragedy and pathos of their condition is neither apprehended by the English Church, nor regarded by the Church as a matter with which she is most deeply concerned'.[5] In a private account of his decision, given to a local incumbent, Davidson wrote that he was 'quite aware that I have taken the less popular and sensational attitude, but I have from my earliest days in Holy Orders been so keen and eager a sympathiser with working men and their endeavours that my action ought not to be misunderstood'.[6] Again in 1913, when pressed by Lansbury, Davidson refused to support a workers' demonstration. 'It goes without saying', he then wrote, 'that anything relating to the well-being of those upon whom our industrial conditions press with harshness will always enlist my deep interest and sympathy' but he could not enter 'the merits of the case'.[7] When W. F. Watson, Secretary of the Amalgamated Society

[1] Mayor, *The Churches and the Labour Movement*, pp. 148–9.

[2] 'Property and Personality', by Scott Holland, in *Property. Its Duties and Rights*, ed. Gore, p. 189.

[3] Mayor, *The Churches and the Labour Movement*, p. 139.

[4] Bell, *Randall Davidson*, i. 488.

[5] Ibid. 490.

[6] For other correspondence relating to this episode, see Davidson Papers, 1905, O.2 ('Unemployment'). The letter here quoted is Davidson to the Revd. C. L. Robinson, 15 June 1905.

[7] Davidson Papers, 1913, L.2, Davidson to Lansbury, 8 July 1913.

of Engineers, read the text of this letter in the press he wrote furiously to the Archbishop. 'What hypocritical cant,' he exploded. 'Did the workers fully realize the insult contained in that phrase your life would not be worth a moment's purchase.'[1] It was not often that the benign verbiage of the current fashion for social radicalism in the Church was so effectively cut away. Yet although he was unwilling to support demonstrations, Davidson's self-acknowledged sympathy for working men's problems was not vacuous. In the railway strike of 1919 and the coal strike of 1921 he offered his services as a mediator. In 1919 his joint appeal with the Bishop of London, with Cardinal Bourne, and Nonconformist leaders, called for mutual conciliation.[2] In 1921 the Upper House of Convocation declared that Resolution 74 of the Lambeth Conference of 1920 was applicable in the dispute:[3] a very considerable gesture of sympathy with the coal-miners, in view of the terms of that Resolution. Davidson offered his services as a mediator in a press statement which reproduced the text of Resolution 74, with its call for workers to 'share equitably in the results of labour'.[4] Henson's attitude was in sharp contrast to Davidson's. The Yorkshire miners' strike of 1919 he attributed largely to the influence of Bolsheviks,[5] and in the same year he advised the Government to stand firm over the railway dispute and 'fight the strike to the end'.[6] Reflecting in fact upon the sermon he preached against the strikes in Hereford Cathedral, in October 1919, he observed: 'My difficulty is that the case of the men seems so thoroughly bad that there is nothing to mitigate the condemnation which one must needs express'.[7] This was the railway dispute in which Davidson offered mediation. Gore believed more in episcopal participation in industrial action than in mediation. In 1911 he intervened on behalf of strikers at Reading. In 1913 he intervened in a tram strike at Oxford—but this time he was against the men.[8] Bishop Handley Moule of Durham appealed to both sides in the shipbuilding strike of 1910, writing of his 'deep belief in the importance of collective bargaining for the artisan's protection'.[9] In the 1919 miners' strike, however, he blamed the militants, and accused them of exaggerating the evils of capitalism.[10] Lang refused, during this period, to arbitrate in industrial disputes, or to pronounce in the merits of the case on either side.[11] There was, therefore, a considerable diversity of attitudes among the leaders of

---

[1] Davidson Papers, 1913, Watson to Davidson, 11 July 1913.
[2] Bell, *Randall Davidson*, ii. 951.   [3] Ibid., p. 109.
[4] Davidson Papers, 1921, 5 ('Coal Dispute'—papers relating to the strike).
[5] Henson, *Retrospect*, i. 313.
[6] Ibid. i. 314.   [7] Ibid. i. 316.
[8] Mayor, *The Churches and the Labour Movement*, p. 219.
[9] Harford and MacDonald, *Handley Carr Glyn Moule*, p. 240.
[10] Ibid., p. 239.
[11] Lockhart, *Cosmo Gordon Lang*, p. 239.

the Church to the question of associating the Church with industrial arbitration.

In assessing the assimilation of social radicalism by the Church, it remains to determine the extent to which the leadership differed from the rest of the clergy. To what extent was the openness to social radicalism a fashion among the leaders only? It is a question which is difficult to answer. No doubt, on social issues, the inarticulate—or those whose words have passed unrecorded—followed the leadership in some of their opinions. Certainly Church leaders usually assumed that the clergy followed; and discussions at Church Congresses or in the Convocations do not indicate the existence of a groundswell of opposition to the liberal preparedness of the influential to espouse the social idealism characteristic of that section of the intelligentsia to which the bishops and divines belonged. Like the leadership, of course, the parochial clergy reflected the manners and class reference of the social station to which they belonged. There was usually a difference of generation—the lower clergy continued to adhere to the social attitudes they had absorbed at the universities and as young priests: they were often a generation or more behind the leaders, who were still in touch with the changing world of ideas and attitudes at the centres of learning and in London society. Amongst the upper- and middle-class laity there was usually a considerable resistance to social criticism. 'There does not appear to be any readiness in industrial circles to welcome the clergy as having a special capacity for the difficult task of solving industrial problems', wrote William Cunningham in 1919.[1] And he was right. The Lambeth Conference itself, in 1920, recognized that 'in the technical side of economics, which is a science for experts, the Church has no authority'.[2] But the enthusiasm of some clergy easily slid from general principles to particular applications, and the laity, unwilling to see clerical interference in economic relations, did not bother to balance out the distinction. To Lord Hugh Cecil, the new social conscience of the articulate clergy was simply 'the great evil of priestcraft' in its modern form: he deplored the use of 'the sanctions of religion' for 'secular purposes'.[3] Church leaders who sympathized with advanced social principles did, of course, often make it clear that in technical matters, as the bishops declared at Lambeth in 1920, they had no standing. 'Recommendations must emanate from those who are experts, not only in economic study but in administrative experience of national affairs', Davidson wrote about the question of Old Age Pensions in 1905—after he had already welcomed the general principle.[4] Inge was a little more pungent: 'It is a radical mistake

[1] Cunningham, *Personal Ideals and Social Principles*, p. 27.

[2] *The Six Lambeth Conferences*, Encyclical Letter of the Bishops, p. 18.

[3] *National Assembly of the Church of England, Spring Session, 1923, Report of Proceedings*, IV, No. 1, p. 115.

[4] Davidson Papers, 1905, O.2, Davidson to Frederick Rogers, 1 Aug. 1905.

to seek in the Gospel for legislation, instead of principles.'[1] Some years later he asked of Convocation: 'was it their business as Churchmen to commit the Church to one solution of an Economic question, one on which the wisest and best men were not agreed, and to stigmatize the other view as un-Christian?'[2] Even Figgis, on the left wing, denied that it was the duty of Christians 'to adopt some particular remedy and to identify the Gospel with some definite organization of society'.[3] His teaching about the prevalence of social pluralism also suggested to him one very important reason why not: no policy favoured by the Church ought to be 'imposed in its name in a State of which Churchmanship has no longer anything to do with the qualifications of a citizen'.[4] Those few within the leadership of the Church who were generally opposed to the tone of social criticism common in those years—principally Henson, Headlam, and Inge—were also the most popular with the laity. Once again the bishops had managed to miscalculate the public mood. To the extent that their adoption of social radicalism was a hopeful overture to the masses it fell flat; to the extent that it annoyed the laity, who objected to clerical interference, it was a nuisance. But they had no alternative, for there can be no doubt that their social moralism was not calculated, but really did arise from their own heightened sense of social concern. In martyred isolation, the bishops no doubt derived comfort from the supposition that those who make a stand for truth are always unpopular.

The Church's social capacity was not occupied solely with industrial and economic morality in these years: two other main issues—education and marriage—were important. On the education question, in fact, there are more letters and notes in Randall Davidson's papers than on any other topic, apart from Prayer Book revision.[5] The Church did not alter its teaching on the priority of doctrinal education, though there were, as in the nineteenth century, a few Church leaders who were willing to take a contrary view; and there was a marked gap between the preparedness of the bishops to compromise in the face of political realities and the more solid intransigence of the ordinary clergy,[6] who did not belong to the world of political bargaining and accommodation. Churchmen saw that any connection between the law and religious opinion is a form of Establishment. They were therefore anxious to vitiate the claim of the Nonconformists, and of many in the Liberal Party, that 'undenominational' or 'non-sectarian' Christianity in the schools was a satisfactory alternative to the confessional insistence of the Established Church. It was not unsatisfactory just because it was diluted Christianity—a separation of the

---

[1] Inge, *All Saints Sermons*, p. 71.
[2] *The Chronicle of Convocation* (1918), p. 356.
[3] Figgis, *Churches in the Modern State*, p. 126.
[4] Ibid., p. 128.   [5] Bell, *Randall Davidson*, i. 510.
[6] Lockhart, *Cosmo Gordon Lang*. p. 235

truth of religion from the teaching of 'secular' subjects—but because it was in itself the legal establishment of a religious formula, alongside the Establishment of the Church of England. 'At this moment,' Scott Holland sadly noticed in 1898, 'the spiritual expression of the State has to be made, not through the Church of the State; for to do this would be to offend religious equality; but through a curious form of Christianity which has been improvised for the occasion and is called "undenominationalism".'[1] Gore applied the anomaly in criticism of the Liberals' Education Bill in 1906—'the Bill "establishes" one particular kind of State religious teaching in the State schools at the expense of every other—the kind called "undenominational" '. For thus 'establishing' religious opinion, he pointed out, the Bill was 'contrary to the very idea of Liberalism'.[2] In the same year Canon Knox Little of Worcester confirmed the paradox of un-denominationalism: 'the intention of the present Bill is to endow it as a new religion'.[3] Christian Socialists like Scott Holland and Gore usually defended Church education very forcefully, especially as many belonged to the Catholic wing of the Church. Stewart Headlam's addiction to secular education was an eccentricity of his own. Churchmen had no reason to wish to surrender their place in the education of the nation. Church schools had certainly, by 1900, failed to keep pace with the increase in the population, but they were still an impressive and a growing system. Money was still given generously to build and maintain them: in the single parish of Heeley, in Sheffield, for example—and it is not an untypical case—£20,000 was donated for the local Church day-schools between 1888 and 1916.[4] Church schools were a standing testimony to the Church's continuing insistence on the intimacy of education and religion. This was nowhere better stated than in the Archbishops' Reports of 1918. 'Religion cannot be relegated to a separate department', declared the First Report; 'a general education which ignores God is in its effect atheistic or agnostic; and moreover the attempt to leave the fundamental questions untouched tends to undermine reverence for truth.'[5] The 'divorce of religious instruction from any denomination, which was clear to the theorists of the last century', according to the Second Report, had had 'evil results'—'the bond has been snapped between school attendance and Church attendance'.[6] The Third Report pointed to the general consequences for society: 'Among all classes material things have assumed

---

[1] Henry Scott Holland, 'Church and State', in *Essays in Aid of the Reform of the Church*, ed. Gore, p. 115.

[2] Charles Gore, *Objections to the Education Bill, 1906, in Principle and in Detail* (London, 1906), p. 4.

[3] *Hibbert Journal*, 4, No. 4 (July 1906), 739.

[4] W. Odom, *Fifty Years of Sheffield Church Life, 1866-1916* (London, 1917), p. 37.

[5] *The Teaching Office of the Church*, p. 35.

[6] *The Worship of the Church*, p. 9.

an exaggerated and false importance, which the spread of education, itself too often secular in its ideals, has done little to correct.'[1]

Balfour's Education Act, in 1902, was a friendly attempt by the Conservative administration to give public financial support to Church schools. It was devised by Robert Morant. All education was to come under a single local-government authority; the voluntary (Church) schools were therefore to be drawn into the national system. But the Local Authorities would maintain the schools and pay the salaries of the teachers, and denominational instruction was protected in the voluntary schools.[2] The Act, in effect, placed denominational religious instruction on the rates. There were all the usual 'conscience clauses' and carefully constructed provisions to protect Dissenting children. The Act, although it required some compromise from churchmen, was clearly a benefit to the Church— and as such was welcomed. Arthur Headlam urged a national acceptance of the Act as a safeguard to the Church.[3] Davidson welcomed it because it established a uniform national system, it organized secondary education, and it was clearly a great financial advantage. It helped 'to redress an injustice of which the Church has complained for some time—namely that the burden put upon her supporters is not fair'. Churchmen 'have to pay subscriptions for their own schools, which could not be maintained without subscriptions, and they have also to pay rates for Board Schools'. Further: 'the rates paid for the schools constitute a demand upon all alike, and whether a man approves of the school or not he has to pay'.[4] This line of argument, as it happened, unconsciously echoed the leading objections of nineteenth-century Dissenters to the Establishment of religion. Over Church rates and over education itself, they had contended that a man ought not to be taxed for a religious provision of which he was conscientiously unable to take advantage. The Nonconformists in 1902 were not slow to react to Balfour's Act. Their uproar tended once more to identify the Church with Conservative politics. The Free Church Council went so far as to set up a 'Passive Resistance Committee', with the intention of organizing a boycott of the education rate by Nonconformists. Even Hugh Price Hughes, the venerable Methodist leader, gave his support to this plan.[5]

Following their landslide success in the general election of 1906 the Liberals attempted to satisfy their Nonconformist element by redressing the balance. 'The electoral value of the educational grievance', as Hensley Henson put it, 'was too great to be lightly surrendered by political

[1] *The Evangelistic Work of the Church*, p. 2.

[2] Murphy, *Church, State and Schools in Britain*, pp. 92–4.

[3] Ronald Jasper, *Arthur Cayley Headlam, Life and Letters of a Bishop* (London, 1960), p. 68.

[4] Hansard, *Fourth Series*, cxv 1220–1.

[5] *The Life of Hugh Price Hughes*, by his Daughter (London, 1904), p. 503.

partisans.'[1] The new President of the Board of Education was himself the son of a Nonconformist Minister. Yet Augustine Birrell's proposed legislation was less moderate than he had hoped, because of Cabinet insistence on a clear gesture to the Nonconformists and to Liberal intellectuals. The 'dual system' was to be completely abandoned, and all schools in receipt of public financial aid were to come under public control. Local Authorities could opt to take over voluntary schools. Undenominational Christian education would usually be given in all schools, but, at the discretion of the authority, denominational teaching could be given twice a week, with the consent of parents, and by teachers brought in from outside. There were to be no religious tests of any sort for any of the school-teachers. Nonconformists attacked the Bill for still allowing a remnant of denominational education. Churchmen generally regarded the Bill as a straight assault on the Church schools, tempered with just a few grudgingly given vestiges of denominational teaching. 'The juncture at which we stand is a grave and critical one in our national life,' Davidson told Parliament in August,[2] by which time a constitutional conflict between the two Houses over the Bill had indeed projected the question of religious education into the very centre of political life. Davidson, in fact, hoped to amend the Bill, rather than see its complete dismissal[3]—a course which was out of sympathy with most of the clergy, who clamoured for outright rejection. Lang, Bishop of Stepney at this time, had no seat in Parliament but used his influence to support Davidson's position.[4] The bishops, meeting in April, declared their collective opposition to the Bill, and Bishop Knox of Manchester emerged as the leader of those who wanted to abandon Davidson's moderation and reject the Bill outright. In the country, three-quarters of a million people signed petitions in favour of rejection. The Convocation of Canterbury had prepared its opposition in advance. Meeting in February, two months before Birrell brought on his proposals, Convocation had accepted three resolutions in favour of denominational education moved by the Bishop of London.[5] Gore had declared, in the debate, that 'it would, indeed, be nothing short of a most grave national disaster if the elementary schools of the Church were secularized',[6] so anticipating his role as a leading opponent of the Bill.

Davidson went into negotiation with the Government: with Birrell, Lord Crewe, and Campbell-Bannerman.[7] During the autumn of 1906 the

---

[1] Henson, *Retrospect* i. 85.

[2] Hansard, *Fourth Series*, clxii. 941 (1 Aug. 1906).

[3] Bell, *Randall Davidson*, i. 520.

[4] Lockhart, *Cosmo Gordon Lang*, p. 233.

[5] *The Chronicle of Convocation* (1906), p. 60 (Upper House, 21 Feb.).

[6] Ibid., p. 70.

[7] Charles Herbert, *Twenty-Five Years as Archbishop of Canterbury* (London, 1928), p. 82.

Lords and the Commons conflicted over the amendments made in the
Upper House. At the end of November, the King intervened to urge the
Church and the Conservative Party, and the Government, to seek 'mutual
concessions', citing the 1869 arrangement between the two Houses over
the Irish Church Disestablishment.[1] Eventually the Bill was abandoned.
A dangerous internal crisis for the Church was, as a result, avoided. For
had Davidson been successful with his amendments, it would inevitably
have led to a clash with those clergy—probably a majority in the Church—
who were opposed to acceptance of the Bill in any form. Church parties
realigned around the issue, so did some political preferences—Gore's
opposition placed him in paradoxical alliance with the Conservative Party;
but he was quite clear that the Bill 'proceeds on lines which, by keeping the
religious controversy alive, not only in the political, but in the municipal
sphere, must serve to hinder social progress of all kinds'.[2] Yet it should be
noticed that Davidson, in his preparedness to make concessions, did not
go (at least in his judgement) outside the general principle that both
undenominational and denominational teaching should be supported by
the State. 'The instinct of the English people is sound and true that their
children should be Christianly brought up at school as well as at home',
he believed.[3] His amendments were, by his own description, 'pretty far-
reaching'; 'I say that definite religious teaching must be accessible to those
children whose parents desire them to have it, subject to such reasonable
limitations or restrictions as the authority may lay down.'[4] He had declared in Convocation that 'after all, it does not seem very much to ask or
to expect from a country which prides itself on being a Christian land with
a Christian Legislature'.[5]

Those who took a contrary view to the generally held insistence on
denominational instruction were a small minority in the Church. At one
end was Stewart Headlam and the Guild of St. Matthew—which campaigned in 1906 for a fully secular educational system.[6] At the other end
was Hensley Henson, who, in his own recollection, 'held a position of
central importance' between the views of churchmen and the Nonconformists on the education question.[7] He hoped for a compromise. He
urged the Church not to adopt 'an intractable attitude',[8] and looked to the
acceptance of undenominational teaching formulated according to 'those
fundamental doctrines of Evangelical Christianity upon which the main
body of the orthodox English Protestants of this country were agreed'.[9]

[1] Bell, *Randall Davidson*, i. 524.
[2] Gore, *Objections to the Education Bill*, p. 15.
[3] Hansard, *Fourth Series*, clxii. 924 (1 Aug. 1906).   [4] Ibid. 938.
[5] *The Chronicle of Convocation* (1906), p. 201 (3 May 1906).
[6] P. d'A. Jones, *The Christian Socialist Revival*, p. 211.
[7] Henson, *Retrospect*, i. 84.
[8] *The Chronicle of Convocation* (1906), p. 74 (21 Feb.).   [9] Ibid., p. 75.

Bishop Percival of Hereford, the Liberal prelate who was also out of step with his colleagues over the question of the Welsh Church Establishment, favoured the same course[1] and supported the 1906 Bill.[2] And the youthful William Temple made his first significant entry to Church affairs when he defended the Bill at the Oxford Union in April. He was at the time a Fellow of Queen's College. At the Church Congress in October, at Barrow-in-Furness, he lectured the delegates upon Plato's theories of child development, to support his views on the Bill. In 1910 his educational opinions were further expressed when he was a rather unsuccessful head-master of Repton.[3] 'I find myself obliged to separate myself from the express utterances of the leaders of the Church', he said at Oxford in 1906.[4] The Church leadership, he believed, was 'blinded to the true facts of the case by an exaggerated conception of the importance of dogma in the education of little children'.[5] Like Henson, he hoped for a 'common Christianity' formula which would unite churchmen and Nonconformists. It was one of the few occasions on which the opinions of these two men, who were to dominate Church opinion in the years between the wars, actually coincided.

There were several further attempts by the Liberals to do something to curtail the advantages the Church had acquired in the 1902 Act. In 1908 Walter Runciman attempted a compromise settlement—based on proposals originally framed by McKenna—which actually got Davidson's agreement. But Bishop Knox denounced the arrangement, and at a meeting of the Representative Church Council in December a considerable division within the Church was again revealed. Most of the bishops favoured Davidson's acceptance of the Bill; most of the clergy and laity rejected it outright.[6] The Church was once more saved from further internal dislocation when the Bill was withdrawn. At the Lambeth Conference in 1908 the bishops reaffirmed their adhesion to fully confessional education. 'We record our solemn protest and warning against any system of education which does not endeavour to fashion and upbuild the child's character in faith and fear of God,' declared the Encyclical Letter of the bishops; 'no teaching of the Bible can be regarded as adequate which does not steadily aim at inculcating personal holiness and a life of fellowship in the Church of Christ through the sanctifying grace of the Holy Ghost.'[7] H. A. L. Fisher's Education Act in 1918 was helped through the House of Lords by Davidson. It was really intended as a measure of educational expansion,

---

[1] William Temple, *Life of Bishop Percival* (London, 1921), p. 177.
[2] Ibid., p. 187.
[3] Edwards, *Leaders of the Church of England*, p. 301.
[4] W. Temple, *The Church and the Education Bill* (Oxford, 1906), p. 5.
[5] Ibid., p. 12.   [6] Bell, *Randall Davidson*, i. 538.
[7] *Conference of Bishops of the Anglican Communion Holden at Lambeth Palace, 1908* (London, 1908), pp. 32–3.

but it also prepared the way for an adjustment of the 'dual system'. In 1919 an attempt was again made to surmount the religious problems of national education. In that year Fisher invited Davidson to the Board of Education, together with Dr. Scott Lidgett, representing the Nonconformists. Bishop Knox, the leader of those opposed to extensive compromises, and Athelstan Riley were among others at the gathering. No Roman Catholics attended. Davidson defined three 'fundamentals' of the Church's position: the insistence on religious teaching; religious teaching conducted by 'competent men'; and religious teaching with 'some specific statement of doctrine'.[1] The emergent 'Fisher Proposals' were in fact within these principles, but as they involved a provision for religious instruction in *all* elementary schools—either undenominational or confessional teaching—the Nonconformists were unhappy, and Dr. John Clifford, the Baptist leader, actually withdrew from the Conference. The Roman Catholics, who had been consulted, also rejected the scheme. Churchmen in general welcomed the proposals, in the public discussion that followed their publication.[2] But, alarmed by Nonconformist restiveness, the Government did not adopt them.

The marriage question was the other area in which the Church found itself embroiled with legislative difficulties, and once again restated its teaching in the face of shifts of opinion in political society. The successful passage of the Deceased Wife's Sister Act in 1907 was in the face of sustained Church opposition. 'For the first time in the history of the Church of England', Davidson said, 'has the law of the State been brought on one specific point into direct, open, overt contrast with and contradiction of the specific and defined law laid down in the authoritative regulations of the National Church.'[3] He had tried, as he had with the Education Act in the preceding year, to get satisfactory amendments—to exclude the Church from the Act altogether. This had failed.[4] Only a very few clergy supported the legislation. Henson was among them.[5] 'The State must make its legislation accord with the actual condition of the citizens,' Henson wrote in 1907; 'and all that the Christian citizen can rightly or reasonably attempt to secure is that the action of the State shall tend towards the gradual but continuous raising of the national standard to the Christian ideal.'[6]

In 1908 the Lambeth Conference Committee on Marriage, under the chairmanship of Bishop G. F. Browne of Bristol, defined the future position of the Church on marriages contracted with a deceased wife's sister. Their Report noted that the Act of 1907 made canon 99 of the

---

[1] Bell, *Randall Davidson*, ii. 1127. [2] Ibid. 1129.
[3] Hansard, *Fourth Series*, clxxxii. 14 (26 Aug. 1907).
[4] Ibid. 15. [5] Henson, *Retrospect*, i. 292.
[6] H. Hensley Henson, *Christian Marriage* (London, 1907), p. 139.

Church 'no longer in correspondence with statute law'—a state of affairs which had already occurred in some of the colonies and in America.[1] Such marriages, though they were to be regarded as 'ecclesiastically irregular', were not to constitute the parties 'evil livers' and so exclude them from the sacraments of the Church.[2]

The question of divorce raised similar difficulties. Churchmen were not alone in lamenting 'the terrible increase in the facilities for divorce'.[3] There was a general awareness within all the denominations that public morality was at risk: this was reflected in the foundation of the National Social Purity Campaign in 1901. This movement, largely sponsored by the clergy, launched a 'forward movement' in 1908 to combat the moral evils of the age. Three bishops were active in it. In 1911 the movement re-formed itself into the National Council of Public Morals, and was supported by half a dozen bishops, some leading Nonconformists, by Ramsay Macdonald, and by Beatrice Webb.[4] Its object was to free society from prostitution and obscene publications, and to preserve the integrity of family life. When in 1909 a Royal Commission was appointed to look into the marriage laws, the question of divorce became political once more. Gore was among those who urged the Church to stand by its traditional teaching. 'It seems to me that the temptation which has beset the Church at various times to make compromise with current opinion, should not be found strong today,' he wrote in 1911; 'for it is evident that current opinion will not be satisfied with any compromise which it is possible for us to offer.'[5] Gore agreed that it was no longer reasonable to expect the modern State to embody Church law, but this increased the responsibility of churchmen to 'throw all our influence as citizens into resisting any proposal to relax the existing allowance of divorce by the State'.[6] In 1912 the Royal Commission reported. A majority recommended five new grounds of divorce; a minority report, signed by Archbishop Lang, Sir William Anson (Warden of All Souls), and Sir Lewis Dibdin (the Dean of Arches) objected to any new grounds of divorce at all.[7] The intervention of the war delayed immediate action, and it was not until 1917 that the Divorce Law Reform Union prepared a Bill, allowing divorce after three years of separation, which the *Church Times* declared 'reduces marriage to the level of concubinage'.[8] The English Church Union campaigned against the reformers. Lord Halifax described the proposals as 'an outrage on Christianity', and agreed that churchmen 'owed a duty not merely to

[1] *Conference of Bishops of the Anglican Communion Holden at Lambeth Palace, 1908,* p. 147.
[2] Ibid., p. 143.   [3] Ibid., p. 37 (Encyclical Letter).
[4] Samuel Hynes, *The Edwardian Turn of Mind* (Princeton, 1968), p. 287.
[5] Charles Gore, *The Question of Divorce* (London, 1911), p. 50.
[6] Ibid., p. 54.   [7] Lockhart, *Cosmo Gordon Lang,* p. 234.
[8] *Church Times,* 10 Aug. 1917: 'The Abolition of Marriage'.

the Church but to the State in this matter, and their duty to the State required that they should make it clear that, as those who desired to be guided by the teaching of Christ, they would refuse to countenance proposals which involved a definite turning away from Christianity'.[1] Athelstan Riley bluntly dismissed the proposals as 'the social economy of the rabbit hutch'. 'It was not possible', he contended, 'for the Christian to cut himself in two' and separate his religious duties from his citizenship: the law must, for a Christian, be made to reflect Christian belief. 'Today sexual questions are discussed both in the public press and in books and in general conversation with an absence of reserve which would have shocked a former generation', he remarked of England in 1917.[2] The discussions continued, however, and in 1920 Lord Buckmaster brought forward his Matrimonial Causes Bill. It was not the first, but it was certainly the most comprehensive attempt to give legislative sanction to the grounds of divorce recommended by the majority report of 1912. Five new grounds were to be added to the existing one of adultery: desertion, cruelty, insanity, habitual drunkenness, imprisonment under a commuted death sentence. The Bill passed its second reading in the Lords, and went into committee. Opposition was led by Davidson and Lang. Davidson allowed divorce for adultery according to the 'Matthean exception', but he attacked the new grounds for being a clear departure of the law of the land from Christian principle.[3] Lang, who spoke first in the Lords' debate, regarded marriage 'as dissoluble only by death'.[4] Yet he chose to place his opposition 'not upon the ground of religious authority, but upon the ground of public welfare'. It was the existing state of the political order that suggested this. 'Circumstances might arise in which it might not be possible for the State to impose Christian standards by law on all its subjects, many of whom would not accept the authority upon which those standards rest,' he said. 'After all, I admit that civil legislation cannot permanently sustain itself upon a level which the public opinion of the community is unable to reach.'[5] He therefore argued that the new grounds of divorce were to be resisted because they would lead to the dissolution of family life, and that this was a social evil.[6] Lang's position, like Gore's attitude to the relationship between the law and Christianity on marriage questions, appears to contain a realistic departure from the *theory* of the Christian Constitution —there were many nineteenth-century precedents for practical and expediential departures. Yet his realism was very muted. All Lang did, in

[1] *Church Times*, 30 Nov. 1917: 'The English Church Union and the new Divorce Proposals'.

[2] Ibid.   [3] Bell, *Randall Davidson*, ii. 992.

[4] Hansard, *Fifth Series*, xxxix. 368 (10 Mar. 1920).

[5] Ibid. 369.

[6] Ibid. 371. For extracts from the speech, see R. P. Flindall, *The Church of England 1815–1948. A Documentary History* (London, 1972), p. 355.

effect, was to shift the frontiers back a little: his speech was still a case for
the obligation of the law to protect Christian morality—only now he chose
to defend the integrity of family life for its positive benefit to social well-
being as the core of Christian moral order, rather than the superstructural
requirements of Christian marriage law as such. He did not attempt to
define a sort of natural-law morality, which might be prescribed by the
State because of its universal acceptability; he argued the essential
Christianity of a social order dependent upon stable family institutions.
It was a device commonly used by churchmen as the twentieth-century
State departed still further from daily acquaintance with religious considerations. Davidson adopted the same course as Lang on Buckmaster's Bill.
His opposition, he told Parliament, was 'upon the social grounds applicable to the well-being of the community as a whole'.[1] He lamented the
5,389 divorce applications in the preceding year;[2] he deplored the interference with the 'home life of England' which divorce threatened.[3] In
committee Davidson proposed an amendment allowing the clergy to
refuse marriage in church to those divorced on the new grounds. It was
defeated by a single vote. By then, however, the divisive nature of the
issue and a considerable public opinion against a change in the law led to
the abandonment of the Bill. The Lambeth Encyclical of 1920 reflected
the divorce controversy, and also the practical grounds of opposition
adopted by Davidson and Lang: 'The State's obvious interest in the
children should lead it to preserve the strictness of marriage law.'[4]
Resolution 67 of the Lambeth Conference also echoed the practical
debate of that year.

The Conference, while fully acknowledging the extreme difficulty of governments in framing marriage laws for its citizens many of whom do not accept the
Christian standard, express its firm belief that in every country the Church
should be free to bear witness to that standard through its powers of administration and discipline exercised in relation to its own members.[5]

Within the Church there were no shifts of ground at all. The Doctrine
Commission appointed by the two Archbishops in 1922 declared (when it
reported in 1938) that 'marriage is in its own principle a lifelong and
intimate union', as the New Testament teaches; and that 'grace is afforded
which, if reliance is fully placed upon it, will enable the persons concerned to fulfil the obligations involved and to rise to the opportunities
offered in their married life in spite of all difficulties however grave'.[6]
   The Church was also worried about the social as well as the moral

[1] Hansard, xxxix. 680 (24 Mar. 1920).
[2] Ibid. 688.   [3] Ibid. 690.
[4] The Six Lambeth Conferences, (1920), p. 17.   [5] Ibid., p. 44.
[6] Doctrine in the Church of England. The Report of the Commission on Christian Doctrine
Appointed by the Archbishops of Canterbury and York in 1922 (London, 1938), pp. 200-1,

consequences of artificial birth-control, and the Lambeth Conference of 1908, which considered the matter, condemned 'the practice of resorting to artificial means for the avoidance or prevention of childbearing'.[1] The Report of the Lambeth Committee on Marriage Problems was much more concerned with the declining birth-rate in western countries than it appeared to be with theological considerations; and they noticed, in evident alarm, that 'this decline has been most marked among English-speaking people once the most fertile of races'.[2] Nevertheless, the Report argued that 'the loss of the sense of responsibility to God for the fruits of marriage' was the primary cause of the widespread resort to contraceptives, and that 'the moral evil of this habit claims our first attention'. The tendency was to 'deprave the ideal of marriage'. But no systematic attempt was made in the Report to define an Anglican theological case on the issue, and practical considerations—of dubious authority—rather predominated: 'the verdict of Nature appears to endorse the moral instinct which condemns these practices, for there is good reason to believe that the use of artificial methods of prevention is associated with serious local ailments'. One result was 'nervous enfeeblement'.[3] Since the practice was more widespread among the rich than among the poor, the Report concluded, it could scarcely be excused on the ground that it alleviated the poverty imposed by large families. It was a matter of 'social ambition'; it arose 'from the wish to escape burdens which might lessen social prestige or limit the opportunities of pleasure'.[4] The Report called for the prosecution of those who publicized birth-control.[5] In 1920 the Lambeth Conference repeated those teachings, again with a mixture of moral, social, and practical considerations. 'We utter an emphatic warning', declared Resolution 68, 'against the use of unnatural means for the avoidance of conception, together with the grave dangers—physical, moral and religious—thereby incurred, and against the evils with which the extension of such use threatens the race.' The 'governing considerations' of Christian marriage are the procreation of children, and self-control.[6] Aldous Huxley, noticing in 1923 that clerical families were getting smaller, asked 'Is it too much to hope that these gentlemen may bring themselves in time to preach what they already practise?'[7]

It is interesting to see how greatly the Church in these years was concerned about the evils of racial discrimination—a question which it discussed with reference to the existence in overseas territories where the

[1] Conference of Bishops of the Anglican Communion Holden at Lambeth Palace, 1908, p. 38 (Encyclical); see Resolution 42.
[2] Ibid., p. 144.   [3] Ibid., p. 145.
[4] Ibid., p. 146.   [5] Ibid., p. 147.
[6] The Six Lambeth Conferences, p. 44. See also the Report on Marriage and Sexual Morality, p. 112.
[7] Aldous Huxley, Antic Hay (Penguin edn., London, 1948), p. 193.

Church had missions of the 'Colour Bar'. Churchmen were quick to attack writers who advocated doctrines of race superiority. Edmund McClure, Canon of Bristol, wrote at length in 1916, for example, criticizing Nietzsche for his racial opinions.[1] J. N. Figgis denounced as 'extremely superficial', and as morally indefensible, the 'race supremacy' ideals of Houston Stewart Chamberlain.[2] No doubt large numbers of clergy shared some of the common popular beliefs about the inherent inferiority of coloured races, but it is rare to find these ideas expressed in association with social or political policies: they were a matter for regret, and calling for special care. Archdeacon Cunningham, for example, was certainly conscious of 'the defects of the Lower Races', as he called them, in the vocabulary of the times, but these defects were for him the result of differences of culture rather than inherent biological determinism. He warned in 1910 that the 'constant danger that the temptation for the strong to oppress the weak may break out in some form or other'.[3] He condemned the 'sense of racial superiority';[4] he maintained 'the Christian belief that God has made of one blood all races of the earth' as 'the only foundation on which a wise and generous method of dealing with the native races can be established'.[5] And he insisted that 'a fair chance' must be given for the development of 'backward' peoples—it was 'a specifically Christian work'.[6] In 1904 the Convocation of Canterbury, responsive to the revelations made by Roger Casement, condemned the Belgian administration of the Congo for just such a failure to develop the population. Davidson contrasted the Congo with the 'beneficial' influence of the English in Africa.[7] In 1908 the bishops at Lambeth resolved that 'All races and peoples, whatever their language or conditions, must be welded into one Body, and the organization of different races living side by side into separate or independent Churches, on the basis of race or colour, is inconsistent with the vital and essential principle of the unity of Christ's Church'.[8] Thus in 1908 the practice of 'separate development' was condemned by the Church. Before the 1920 Lambeth gathering, there was a correspondence between Bishop Frank Weston of Zanzibar and Archbishop Davidson on the evils of the Colour Bar.[9] It was reflected in the strong language of the Conference Resolution: 'The Conference records its protest against the colour-prejudice among the different races of the

---

[1] Edmund McClure, *Modern Substitutes for Traditional Christianity* (London, 1916), p. 127 ff.

[2] J. N. Figgis, *Hopes for English Religions* (London, 1919), p. 7.

[3] Cunningham, *Christianity and Social Questions*, p. 40.

[4] Ibid., p. 42.

[5] Ibid., p. 43.

[6] Ibid., p. 44.

[7] Bell, *Randall Davidson*, i. 547.

[8] *Conference of Bishops* (1908), p. 50 (Resolution 20).

[9] Maynard Smith, *Frank, Bishop of Zanzibar*, p. 221.

world, which not only hinders intercourse, but gravely imperils the peace of the future.'[1] These were prophetic words.

One development of these years in the relations of Church and State suggested an adjustment to the realities of the Church's position in society which, in the long term, considerably affected the Church's social attitudes. This was the Enabling Act of 1919, and the tendency to reduce the national position of the Church of England by the creation of sectarian tests of membership. The Act was a result of a movement within the Church for greater legislative autonomy; a recognition of the increasing unsuitability of Parliament to govern the Church directly. To that extent, it was yet a further stage in the practical separation of Church and State which had been proceeding for a century, except that on this occasion, the initiative for a change came from within the Church. A few churchmen of the Catholic tradition looked to a formal disestablishment. Some radicals, like Watts-Ditchfield, regarded the maintenance of the Establishment as secondary in priority to social issues, to such questions as 'the housing of the poor or temperance reform', as he said in 1913.[2] Figgis thought the question of the Establishment was 'irrelevant', though, in arguing for pluralism and the spiritual independence of the Church, he added that 'it might be true as a matter of fact that disestablishment is the necessary condition in this country of the recognition in the Church of those principles I am trying to set down'.[3] Henson, at this time a firm supporter of Establishment, suspected Gore (who was not), of trying 'to employ the interval before the blow fell in making sure that the reconstruction of the disestablished Church should be carried out on Catholic principles';[4] which, once the animus is removed from remark, was probably true. But the defence of the Welsh Church in these years rallied most within the Church to the principle of Establishment. 'It is on grounds of intrinsic principle that the Church must be defended', said Lang of the Establishment question in 1904.[5] One of the clearest statements of the traditional position on the mutual dependence of Church and State came from Temple. It was a view he never abandoned. 'Both State and Church are instruments of God for establishing his Kingdom', Temple said in 1914. 'The State's action for the most part takes the form of restraint; the Church's mainly that of appeal.'[6] Before that, in 1906, he had even suggested an organic view of the State, full of Divine authority. 'The State is no mere secular machine, concerned only with the levying of taxes and administration of police', for 'in the innermost depths of its being the State is a religious body', whose 'highest obligation lies in the exercise of

---

[1] *The Six Lambeth Conferences*, p. 26 (Resolution 7).
[2] *Guardian*, 14 Nov. 1913: 'The Regeneration of England'.
[3] Figgis, *Churches in the Modern State*, p. 8.   [4] Henson, *Retrospect*, i. 209.
[5] Lang, *The Opportunity of the Church of England*, p. 63.
[6] Temple, *Church and Nation*, p. 53.

its religious functions'.[1] The prevailing Church opinion, again a traditional one, was summarized in 1910 by the Central Church Committee for Defence and Instruction: the Church defended Establishment not because it sought to cling to privilege, as the Nonconformists alleged, but because 'there would be great and grave spiritual losses to the nation through the removal of the organ by means of which it expresses itself spiritually'.[2] Very little emphasis was normally placed, compared with most of the preceding century, on the duty of the Church to enjoin obedience to the State, though examples can be found.[3]

The need for legislative autonomy was recognized in 1914 when the Representative Church Council (itself set up in 1903) secured the appointment of the Archbishops' Commission on the Relations of Church and State. Lord Selborne, vice-president of the Church Reform League, became the Commission's chairman. Balfour, who was 'strongly in favour of the principle of spiritual independence',[4] was a member. Gore, Temple, Walter Frere, Lord Hugh Cecil, Sir William Anson, and Sir Lewis Dibdin were also among the members of the Committee. Their Report, in 1916, unanimously recommended that the Representative Church Council should be enlarged and reformed, and should receive limited ecclesiastical legislative powers delegated by Parliament, but subject to parliamentary approval. Despite the advocacy of disestablishment by a few on the Committee, their Report ruled it out of consideration.[5] They took as a starting-point the supposition that 'the constitution of parliament prevents its being in any true sense representative of the Church, and the experience of recent years has shown that it possesses neither time nor inclination nor knowledge for dealing with ecclesiastical affairs'.[6] Quite apart from 'the congestion of secular business', the 'attitude of the House of Commons towards Church legislation is not so much one of hostility as of indifference, and of unwillingness to act, due in part to the realization of its unfitness to deal with religious affairs'. The Committee examined the fate of ecclesiastical legislation between 1880 and 1913. Of 217 Church Bills introduced in those years, 183 were dropped; and of the 74 Bills promoted for Nonconformity (mostly Chapel trusts and other property questions), 49 were dropped. 'It appears from this examination that the conditions that unfit the House of Commons for ecclesiastical legislation operate in the case both of established and of non-established bodies.'[7] This finding was important: it knocked a large hole in the Nonconformist case for disestablishment on the ground that 'free' Churches were untrammelled by

---

[1] Temple, *The Church and the Education Bill*, p. 12.
[2] H. J. Clayton, *Church Defence* (London, 1910), p. 135.
[3] See W. Cunningham, *Christianity and Politics*, (London, 1916,) p. 231.
[4] Bell, *Randall Davidson*, ii. 958.
[5] *The Archbishops' Committee on Church and State. Report* (London, 1918), p. 39.
[6] Ibid., p. 26.   [7] Ibid., p. 29.

parliamentary procedure. 'We submit that the time has come to arrange the relations of Church and State on a more elastic and rational basis', the Committee reported.[1] The key issue, however, and the one which caused the most controversy, concerned the nature of the franchise to be adopted for the new Church government. Selborne's Committee first reported in favour of all *Confirmed* persons being entitled to vote for the proposed reconstituted parochial councils, but this was later dropped in favour of a franchise based on *Baptism*.[2] The Catholic wing of the Church had insisted on a *Confirmation* test for enfranchisement, and when the existing Representative Church Council proceeded to endorse the Selborne Report a minority dissension signed by Athelstan Riley and four others objected to the baptismal-franchise recommendation for Catholic reasons.[3] The issue was indeed of the utmost importance. Central and Low Church opinion believed that a Confirmation franchise would reduce the Church to the level of a denomination[4]—it was a sectarian test, whereas the baptismal qualification still covered a large majority of Englishmen and was compatible with the concept and the reality of a territorial Church. The Catholic party believed, in contrast, that the Church of England had 'cheapened membership till it has come to mean nothing . . . the sacrament of continual fellowship has been ignored.'[5] The Enabling Act in 1919, which set up the Church Assembly, along the lines of Selborne's Report, prescribed a baptismal franchise for the parish electoral rolls, and a declaration that the qualified elector was not a member of another Church.[6] Even that was too much for Henson, who tried to organize opposition to the Bill in Parliament—he was at the time Bishop of Hereford. The Bill, he wrote, is 'the formal adoption by an unwitting legislature of a wholly novel conception of the National Church'.[7] His position was constitutionally perfectly sound, but it went against the general grain of the Church leadership. 'They have exchanged the status which was in principle Christian for one which is in principle sectarian,' Henson wrote; 'and they have banished from the realm of practical possibilities the ideal of a National Church.'[8] But the *change* was practical, it recognized the changed position of the Church; a sensible attempt to prevent Noncon-

---

[1] *The Archbishops' Committee on Church and State. Report* (London, 1918), p. 30.

[2] Ibid., pp. 41–3.

[3] *Report of the Committee of the Representative Church Council on the Report of the Archbishops' Committee on Church and State*, London, 1918, p. 11.

[4] Kenneth A. Thompson, *Bureaucracy and Church Reform. The Organizational Response of the Church of England to Social Change, 1800–1965* (Oxford, 1970), p. 143.

[5] Charles Gore, *The Religion of the Church. A Manual of Membership* (London, 1917), p. 6.

[6] Thompson, *Bureaucracy and Church Reform*, p. 175. The Nature of Church membership, and the baptismal test, were next dealt with by the Church in the 1971 Report by the Bishop of Ely (Dr. Edward Roberts); see *Christian Initiation* (London, 1971), G.S. 30.

[7] Henson, *Retrospect*, i. 305.   [8] Ibid., p. 306.

formists from interfering in Church government, and a careful compromise between the spiritual independence of the Church and ultimate parliamentary responsibility. Henson's dislike of a sectarian Church was shared by erastians in Parliament—he had, once again, hit chords of sympathy with common English attitudes to religion. Davidson had to explain to Haldane that in sponsoring the Enabling Act he was 'taking no line of a revolutionary sort or trying to impose ecclesiastical thraldom on the King's lieges'.[1] Dibdin also explained the necessity 'of finding some remedy for the present paralysis of Church legislation'.[2]

The existence of the 'Life and Liberty' movement explains a lot of the suspicions surrounding the issue of Church legislative autonomy. This pressure-group for reform, originally set on foot in 1917 by Dick Sheppard,[3] Vicar of St. Martin-in-the-Fields, was dominated by Temple—who in fact resigned the living of St. James in Piccadilly in order to give all his energies to it. In July 1917, at a meeting in the Queen's Hall, 'Life and Liberty' began its agitation by calling on Parliament to grant legislative autonomy to the Church.[4] Henson alone voted against the resolution. The real suspicion of the movement, however, lay as much in its association with social radicalism as with its intention of seeing the Selborne Report implemented. Although 'Life and Liberty' was supposed to represent all sections of Church opinion its leaders were all well known for their promotion of social radicalism. Tawney was on the Council; so were Albert Mansbridge of the W.E.A., Fred Hughes of the National Union of Clerks, and Miss E. Wilson of the Independent Union of Boot and Shoe Women Workers.[5] The movement also published a pamphlet on *The Social Message of the Church*, which embodied policies rather to the left of the C.S.U. The movement got quite a wide measure of support within the Church, however, and survived splitting up over the franchise question through Temple's leadership: it was he who led them to adopt the baptismal test.[6] 'Life and Liberty' was extremely eclectic, and tended to be a gathering of well-to-do radicals, with a few token working men on the Committee. In his withering, well-known, and completely accurate description of the Queen's Hall meeting, Henson categorized them as 'the academic, the feminist, the socialist, the clericalist'; the 'upper middle-class people who form the congregation of West-End churches'. The Headmasters of Eton, Harrow, and Rugby were all on the platform. They

[1] Davidson Papers, 1919, 'Church and State', Davidson to Haldane, 11 May 1919.
[2] Ibid., Dibdin to Haldane, 8 June 1919.
[3] Ellis Roberts, *H. R. L. Sheppard*, p. 118.
[4] Iremonger, *William Temple*, p. 230, Lloyd, *The Church of England*, p. 234; Bell, *Randall Davidson*, ii. 962.
[5] Thompson, *Bureaucracy and Church Reform*, p. 148.
[6] Iremonger, *William Temple*, p. 260.

were, in short, 'Gore's crowd'.[1] The importance of 'Life and Liberty' as
a preparation for Temple's C.O.P.E.C. movement, early in the 1920s,
cannot be overstated. The type of person attracted to both agitations was
the same. It was not all high-minded agreement, however, and when the
Council of 'Life and Liberty' met at Cuddesdon in October 1917, the
Principal (J. B. Seaton) refused to allow the secretary, who was a woman,
to sleep in the College. They had to spend the first day of the Council
discussing the higher principles involved.[2] This slight incident illustrates
a dimension of the movement which some found rather ridiculous.

In 1906 the Liberal administration appointed a Royal Commission on
the Churches in Wales, with the clear intention of bringing in a disestablishment measure. The Welsh Church issue never became a major
question, compared with the other issues of the time (or compared with
the Irish Church question in the later 1860s); though it did manage to fire
what Henson called 'a period of acute controversy'[3] in the relations of
Church and State. The Church of England once more stood by its traditional teaching, and defended the Church in Wales not just on the principle
that the Establishment of religion was in itself necessary, but because the
Welsh dioceses were inseparable from the rest of the Church. In 1910 the
Royal Commission reported. As everyone had expected, it offered statistical
evidence—whose accuracy both churchmen and Nonconformists at once
contested[4]—to show the huge numerical inferiority of the Church. The
Report did not regard the actual issue of disestablishment as within its
terms of reference, and made no recommendation; but in 1909 a Disestablishment Bill had been introduced to Parliament, and had only
foundered because of the general absorption in political controversy over
the Finance Bill. In 1912 the Government introduced new legislation to
disestablish the Church in Wales. There was also to be a substantial
disendowment, with the secularization of appropriated ecclesiastical
revenues: £87,000 was to be retained by the Church, and £173,000 was to
be secularized. The Bill was opposed by the Conservatives; passed by the
Commons; twice rejected in the Lords by large majorities; and in 1914
finally became law (only under the new procedures of the Parliament Act):
its operation was then suspended until the end of the war. The fate of the
Welsh Church was decided. In 1917, when Lord Robert Cecil and Bishop
Owen tried to secure further postponement of disestablishment, the
Church Times realistically remarked that there was no hope of this.[5] After
the war, in 1919, a Temporalities Act was passed which considerably

---

[1] Henson, *Retrospect*, i. 207. For the original account, written for Davidson, see Henson's
Journals, vol. 21 (18 Mar. 1917–12 Oct. 1917), p. 108.

[2] Iremonger, *William Temple*, p. 236.

[3] *The Chronicle of Convocation* (1912), p. 448 (3 July 1912).

[4] Morgan, *Wales in British Politics*, p. 261.

[5] *Church Times*, 7 Sept. 1917: 'Reconstruction in Wales'.

softened the disendowment provisions: £3,400,000 was paid back to the Church.[1] This in some measure represented the long-term success of Sir Henry Lunn's attempts in 1911 and 1912 to get a compromise on the disendowment terms.[2] The possibility of a concurrent endowment solution had again come up, but there was little support for it. In 1913 an amendment to the Bill had been proved which would have provided for the Welsh ecclesiastical revenues to be employed for the general advancement of Christianity in Wales. It was defeated in the Commons by 278 to 167.[3]

The Church of England's leaders were almost unanimous over the Welsh question and it was opposed with tremendous conviction. Disestablishment, as Davidson said in his *Charge* of 1912, was 'a sweeping change',[4] the end of a national recognition of God. 'The deliberate ending of these things by a parliamentary vote would in the popular mind mean a great deal more than can be expressed in statistical tables and balance sheets,' he argued; 'we should have lost, and lost in the most harmful way, something which compels the State in its corporate capacity to recognize the power and influence of religion; something which compels the Church to be in touch with thoughts and interests which are wider and deeper than it always sees'.[5] In Convocation Davidson called the Church to resistance: 'We are striving to draw the attention of the whole people of the country to the dangers impending over them if the present proposals become law.'[6] During the later Convocation and parliamentary debates it became clear that three prelates dissented—Gore of Oxford, Percival of Hereford, and Hicks of Lincoln. Percival argued a sort of inverted Coleridgian case, similar to the Whig and radical critique of Church property used in the 1830s. The endowments of the Church, he said,

were a trust for the whole community, and for a long period they were used for the whole community; and now that the circumstances have so changed that the Church is no longer in a position to fulfil that trust in its largest sense, these endowments have become, as a matter of indisputable fact, the monopoly of a small minority of the people of the principality of Wales.[7]

Gore was unable to imagine how churchmen could oppose disestablishment, which he saw as a great act of justice: 'I cannot conceive, on principles which would be accepted in modern society of any kind, of possible justification for a religious Establishment after it has ceased to commend

[1] P. M. H. Bell, *Disestablishment in Ireland and Wales*, p. 310. For the Texts of the Acts of 1914 and 1919, see Flindall, *The Church of England, 1815–1948*, pp. 308 and 346.
[2] Morgan, *Wales in British Politics*, p. 262; P. Bell, *Disestablishment in Ireland and Wales*, p. 245.
[3] P. Bell, *Disestablishment*, p. 287.
[4] *The Character and Call of the Church of England*, p. 89.
[5] Ibid., p. 102.
[6] *The Chronicle of Convocation* (1912), p. 65 (16 Feb. 1912).
[7] Hansard, *Fifth Series*, xiii. 1113 (12 Feb. 1913).

itself to the great majority of the inhabitants.'[1] But Gore, of course, was an advocate of English disestablishment too—and not on numerical grounds, but because of the need, as he saw it, to preserve the spiritual independence of the Church. Davidson asked if the principles thought applicable in Wales were to be used for England.[2] It fell to Lang to offer a remarkable defence of the Church in Wales, and of all Established religion. He was concerned with the consequences for the State, and for public life, of a secular constitution. The question, he said, is

whether in the public corporate life of the nation there is to be any assertion at all of its religious basis, of its acknowledgment of Almighty God, of its concern with the religious life of the people. The old Liberationist policy was clear, logical, and intelligible. It followed from the conception of the State as a sort of police committee protecting the competitive interests of the individuals who composed the State. But surely there has come to us a deeper and wider conception of the State. To some of us it is something which we do not as individuals compose but which as individuals we enter, and which from the very first, by virtue of its own intrinsic character, moulds and frames our life and being. It has an organic unity and spirit of its own, and that character and spirit are built up by tradition and associations running far back into the past. Its life is expressed not only by the policies and pursuits of the present, but also by a sort of subconscious continuity which endures and profoundly affects the character of each generation of citizens who enter within it. The question before us, as some of us consider it, is whether just there, in that inward region of the national life where anything that can be called its unity and character is expressed, there is or is not to be this witness to some ultimate sanction to which the nation looks, some ultimate ideal which it professes. It is in our judgment a very serious thing for a state to take out of that corporate heart of its life any acknowledgement at all of its concern with religion.[3]

Parliamentary politics were empirical, little influenced by organic concepts of the State. But Lang's speech in 1913 remains one of the clearest twentieth-century statements of the case for the Establishment of religion.

[1] Hansard, *Fifth Series*, xiii. 1195, (12 Feb. 1913).
[2] Ibid. 1142.   [3] Ibid. 1205.

7
Christian Politics, Economics and Citizenship 1919–1924

It was at discussions in Temple's 'Collegium' in 1919 that the idea of a general Christian Conference on social questions first seems to have taken serious form. In that year, at the Interdenominational Conference of Social Service Unions the movement was actually started. The result, in April 1924, was the assembly in Birmingham of the Conference on Christian Politics, Economics and Citizenship—'C.O.P.E.C.' (or 'Copec'). The Archbishop of Uppsala, attending the Conference on a visit from Sweden, remarked that 'Copec had given a new word to the English language'.[1] Its importance is not only in the history of the social attitudes of the Church. It was also a pioneering interdenominational venture, 'the biggest manifestation of such unity hitherto', as Temple said at the time.[2] 'As the expression of a common mind amongst social Christians in all the Churches of this country it was unique, and it will probably be epoch-making', wrote Samuel Keeble, the Methodist minister who wrote one of the official accounts of the Conference.[3]

The Church of England, and especially Temple, was the real force behind the movement, however, and it marks 1924 as a watershed in the development of social teaching in the Church. On the one side it brought to a more systematic and coherent statement the social radicalism of the preceding decade, and stamped the mind of the Church with a definite bias towards a social interpretation of Christianity; on the other, it prepared the ground for the mood of criticism and social writing known as 'Christian Sociology', which, in the years between the wars, did so much to condition the future attitudes of the Church. For these reasons it is worth especially close attention. Many writers have recognized the seminal importance of C.O.P.E.C. Temple himself traced its origins to the S.C.M. Matlock

---

[1] *The Proceedings of C.O.P.E.C. Being a Report of the Meetings of the Conference on Christian Politics, Economics and Citizenship held in Birmingham, April 5–12, 1924* (London, 1924), p. 261 (hereinafter cited as *Proceedings*).

[2] Ibid., p. 18.

[3] S. E. Keeble, *'C.O.P.E.C.' An Account of the Christian Conference on Politics, Economics and Citizenship*, issued by the C.O.P.E.C. Continuation Committee (London, n.d.) [1925], p. 3. For another account published by the Committee, see *C.O.P.E.C.: The Purpose, Scope and Character of the Conference* (London, 1924).

Conference in 1909, over which he presided,[1] and in his *Christianity and Social Order* (1942), he referred to the Conference as having been the 'fullest expression' of the movement for the rediscovery of a Christian social creed.[2] Canon Charles Raven, one of the two secretaries of the C.O.P.E.C. Executive Committee, looking back after forty years, regarded its real achievement as 'having aroused the social conscience at a time when it was still hardly vocal'.[3] That, of course, is a generous exaggeration: the preceding decades had seen the growth of a hugely vocal social conscience in the Church. But one of the most important characteristics of C.O.P.E.C. was the belief of those who took part in it that the movement heralded the first real advance. Later commentators have tended to follow their valuation. 'Never had so serious an effort been made by Christians to understand the world in which they lived', wrote one;[4] for two others it represented further progress 'by forward looking Christians of all denominations to consider the application of Christian Social ethics to the contemporary problems of human relationships.'[5] Leslie Paul has referred to 'that tremendous work which William Temple undertook through C.O.P.E.C.'.[6] David Edwards, in his account of the Church Leaders' Conference held in 1972, also in Birmingham, argued that 'a lot of hard thinking would have to be done before Christian social thought could return to the level reached at the Conference on Christian Politics, Economics and Citizenship held under William Temple's leadership'.[7] Clearly C.O.P.E.C. has left an influential impression in the minds of many who have sought to discuss the progress of social thinking in the Church. C.O.P.E.C. was among the first occasions on which the public became aware of the extent to which social radicalism had penetrated the leadership of the Churches—and that is one of its most important features.

Above all, C.O.P.E.C. marked the rise of William Temple to ascendancy over the social teaching of the Church of England. 'Copec itself made it clear where that leadership would be for the next two decades,' wrote Maurice Reckitt. 'To say that its presiding genius was William Temple is not in this case to employ a cliché but to give an exact description of the

[1] Iremonger, *William Temple*, p. 333.

[2] Temple, *Christianity and Social Order*, p. 9.

[3] Charles E. Raven, 'C.O.P.E.C. Then and Now—I', in *Crucible, The Quarterly Review of the Church Assembly Board for Social Responsibility* (Oct. 1962), p. 108.

[4] James Parker, 'The Churches and the Social Order', in *Religion in Britain since 1910*, ed. Spinks, p. 99.

[5] M. Penelope Hall and Ismene V. Howes, *The Church in Social Work. A Study of Moral Welfare Work undertaken by the Church of England* (London, 1965), p. 36.

[6] A tribute which would be all the more authoritative had Dr. Paul not disclosed an ignorance of what C.O.P.E.C. actually was. He identified it as the 'Christian Organisations' Political and Economic Conference'. *A Church by Daylight. A reappraisement of the Church of England and its future* (London, 1973), p. 78 (fn).

[7] David L. Edwards, *The British Churches Turn to the Future* (London, 1973), p. 66.

facts.'[1] F. A. Iremonger, Temple's biographer—an early colleague in 'Life and Liberty' and later Dean of Lichfield—also testified that C.O.P.E.C. was 'not only remarkable in itself; it also centred to so striking a degree on Temple, both in its inception and achievements'.[2] By 1928 it was possible for Iremonger to refer to Temple as 'the leader of the largest "Christian social" movement which has yet risen in the Churches'.[3] In 1924, at Birmingham, this reputation was established: Sidney Dark, an editor of the *Church Times*, traced the resulting rise of Temple's influence—'with clearly expressed sympathy for the demand for radical changes in the nation's social and economic life he has become the chief figure in the Anglican communion'.[4] Temple's leadership in some large measure derived from his social opinions. It is for them that he has been remembered in the Church. Of the 'prophets of social righteousness whom God has raised up', wrote W. G. Peck (Director of Clergy Schools in the Industrial Christian Fellowship), none made a more signal impact upon the mind and conscience of the nation; none was more gladly heard by the common people; none gave himself more fully to the support of social justice'.[5] Temple, in fact, made a whole generation of younger clergy see things the way he saw them; his achievement was finally to push the orthodoxy of social radicalism further down the ecclesiastical hierarchy, until it reached the parish pulpit with the frequency with which, previously, it had reached the episcopal palace. Very many middle-aged priests in the modern Church of England would elect to attribute their social conscience to Temple's influence. One theologian has even supposed that Isaiah's prophetic gifts were such as 'to make him the William Temple of his day'.[6]

Temple's social thinking was in fact rather unoriginal. It derived from the general deposit of ideas current in the more daring wing of the Christian Social Union around the turn of the century. He never went beyond the sort of radicalism expressed in the Archbishops' Fifth Report of 1918. He was not even a 'socialist'—a name which 'uninformed people, even some eminent ones, continued to apply to him to the end of his life'.[7] In 1921 he resigned from the Labour Party, after only three years, apparently regarding membership of a political party as incompatible with

---

[1] Reckitt, *Maurice to Temple*, p. 172.

[2] Iremonger, *William Temple*, p. 328.

[3] F. A. Iremonger, *Men and Movements in the Church. A Series of Interviews* (London, 1928), p. 24.

[4] Sidney Dark, *The People's Archbishop. The Man and his Message* (London, n.d.) [1942], p. 7.

[5] W. G. Peck. 'William Temple as Social Thinker', in *William Temple: An Estimate and Appreciation*, ed. W. R. Matthews (London, 1946), p. 59.

[6] S. B. Frost, *Old Testament Apocalyptic* (London, 1952), p. 112. I am grateful to the Revd. Dr. Ernest Nicholson, Dean of Pembroke College, Cambridge, for drawing my attention to this astonishing comparison by Professor Frost.

[7] Peck, 'William Temple', p. 64.

the office of a bishop—he had just been raised to the see of Manchester.[1] This was to adhere to the conventional attitude that party politics were no concern of the Church corporately. It was a view from which he never departed. Temple belonged pretty centrally to the Westcott tradition of social criticism; he shared the same sort of guilty moralism, and he often failed, also, to translate his social observations into realities. Charles Raven, one of Temple's closest associates in the C.O.P.E.C. movement, later noticed this quality rather clearly: 'some of my friends, not least the Bishop of Manchester', he said in 1926, 'are very fond of talking about industrial problems as if all you had to do was to speak of them as vocation, and the whole spirit in which they were undertaken was changed'.[2] Attempts have been made to show that his social ideas came from his philosophical studies,[3] and especially that his book, *Mens Creatrix*, published in 1917, and inspired by his appreciation of Plato and Aristotle, provided the basis for his 'ethico-social idealism'.[4] But this was not so. Temple's social ideas came from the C.S.U. tradition; what he did academically was to satisfy himself that the thought of the Greek Idealists was not incompatible. Most others who were interested in social issues were quite able to arrive independently at precisely the same conclusions without any reference to the Sophists. Temple's philosophical ideas had, additionally, the disadvantage of belonging to a school—to Oxford neo-metaphysics—which was intellectually discredited in his own lifetime;[5] 'questions which Temple regarded as central have ceased to be the chief subjects of debate', as Dean Matthews wrote.[6] Temple saw social questions in a vision which, after offering the usual pieties to Maurice and Westcott, he seems to have believed original. There was a lot of very ordinary *naïveté* in Temple. At the age of seven, while on holiday with his parents in the Lake District, he wept when told that the servants at their hotel were not allowed to eat the chicken he was himself consuming, an incident which was later rightly seen as a formative one in the development of his sense of social guilt.[7] As a man he was always far too impressed by

[1] Robert Craig, *Social Concern in the Thought of William Temple* (London, 1963), p. 20.

[2] C. E. Raven, 'Calling and Duty', a paper read at the Anglo-Catholic Summer School of Sociology; see the report, *The Social Teaching of the Sacraments*, ed. Maurice Reckitt (London, 1927), p. 81. On Raven's part in the preparations for C.O.P.E.C., see F. W. Dillistone, *Charles Raven, Naturalist, Historian, Theologian* (London, 1975), p. 120.

[3] See A. M. Ramsey, *From Gore to Temple. The Development of Anglican Theology between Lux Mundi and the Second World War, 1889–1939* (London, 1960), p. 154.

[4] Peck, 'William Temple', pp. 60–4.

[5] Craig, *Social Concern*, p. 151; Owen C. Thomas, *William Temple's Philosophy of Religion* (London, 1961), p. 3.

[6] W. R. Matthews, 'William Temple as Thinker', in *William Temple: An Estimate and Appreciation*, p. 22.

[7] Iremonger, *William Temple*, p. 328.

ideas; he tended not to ask perceptive questions, or any questions at all, about the emotional impulsions which lead to the adoption of ideas. He accepted the reasons given by the others at their own valuation and was in consequence a poor judge of people,[1] lacking elementary human shrewdness.[2] Those who heard his philosophy lectures at Oxford thought him a man of 'emotional poverty'.[3] This ceased to be true, as a passion for social justice flooded in to fill the gap—but it was all ideas, resting upon an innocent unawareness of the real nature and expectations of working-class life in England. He was, as Iremonger remarked 'a Conservative with a bad conscience';[4] he managed to hold in suspension a conviction, on the one hand, that the broad structure of existing society was satisfactory, with, on the other, a number of political and economic schemes to give to those less privileged than himself the advantages he enjoyed. His vision can in the end be stripped down to an educational one: everyone was to be given the opportunity of attaining the standards, material and cultural, then usual within the intelligentsia, to which he looked for his own values. Because he was so easily impressed by ideas, he became extremely eclectic, 'believing that Christian theology might produce a social philosophy having points of contact with many secular theories, but completely governed by none of them'.[5]

In thus seeking to describe the mechanics of Temple's social outlook, there is a danger that the real stature of the man will be obscured. This would be an error. Even Hensley Henson, no friend of Temple's, on hearing Provost Barnard of Trinity College, Dublin, discuss Temple, noted that this estimate 'was not high enough'.[6] Temple's spirituality, his immense personal generosity of affection, and clear thought, were qualities which placed him above his contemporaries. However second-hand his social thought, and however inept—as some of it was—his other qualities and his theological writing guaranteed his social outlook an ascendancy in the Church of his day. His social opinions prevailed until his death in 1944. Despite his distance, as an academic theoretician, from the ordinary assumptions of most people, he did manage to inspire popular affection. At an S.C.M. Summer Conference at Swanwick, when he was Archbishop of York, the students stood in formation and saluted him with the chant 'Heil Ebor!'.[7] It was not, in view of contemporary political practice else-

---

[1] A. E. Baker, 'William Temple—the Man', in *William Temple: An Estimate and Appreciation*, p. 97, Canon Baker writes, 'But he was not such a fool as some people think'.
[2] Edwards, *Leaders of the Church of England*, p. 288.
[3] Iremonger, *William Temple*, p. 104.
[4] Quoted in Craig, *Social Concern*, p. 12.
[5] Peck, 'William Temple', p. 66.
[6] Henson Papers, Durham Chapter Library, Journals, vol. 37 (21 Apr.—6 Sept. 1924), p. 56 (1 June 1924).
[7] A. E. Baker, 'William Temple—the Man', p. 95.

where, a particularly appropriate gesture, but it indicated the loyalty Temple elicited from those who knew him. C.O.P.E.C. in 1924 was the first occasion on which Temple really stood before the public as a social reformer.

The declared purposes of C.O.P.E.C. were a reliable indication of the movement's continuity with preceding decades of social radicalism. In language and enthusiasm unchanged since the 1860s, the leaders denounced the evils of *laissez-faire* and declared the need for 'co-operation' in industrial relationships. The message was repeated time and time again—that the Church had ignored the social implications of the Gospel. There must indeed have been something rather second-rate about the minds of those given to such repetitive exercises. The objects of C.O.P.E.C. were easily ascertained, for after 1921 they were printed within a sort of rectangular enclosure at the top of Temple's notepaper.

The Basis of this Conference is the conviction that the Christian faith, rightly interpreted and consistently followed, gives the vision and the power essential for solving the problems of to-day, that the social ethics of Christianity have been greatly neglected by the Church with disastrous consequences to the individual and to society, and that it is of the first importance that these should be given a clearer and more persistent emphasis. In the teaching and work of Jesus Christ there are certain fundamental principles—such as the Universal Fatherhood of God, with its corollary that mankind is God's family, and the law 'that whoso loseth his life, findeth it'—which, if accepted, not only condemn much in the present organisation of society but show the way of regeneration. Christianity has proved itself to possess also a motive power for the regeneration of the individual without which no change of policy or method can succeed. In the light of its principles the constitution of society, the conduct of industry, the upbringing of children, national and international politics, the personal relations of men and women, in fact all human relationships must be tested. It is hoped that through this Conference the Church may win a fuller understanding of its Gospel and hearing a clear call to action may find courage to obey.[1]

The saving clause about the need for a prior conversion of the individual was important, in view of the scepticism of those like Henson for whom most Christian social programmes were vitiated by the fact of individual sin. Some efforts were made to preserve a balance. Thus the C.O.P.E.C. Report on *Industry and Property* declared 'That this Kingdom of God is a spiritual kingdom, ruling the inner life of men—their thoughts and desires, their trust and their will—rather than a mere alteration of circumstance, so far from being an objection, as not infrequently urged, is the very heart and core of the position here taken'.[2] The tension between prior individual

---

[1] There are many copies of this notepaper in the Temple and Davidson Papers. The superscription bears all the marks of Temple's own authorship.

[2] *Industry and Property*, C.O.P.E.C. Report IX (London, 1924), p. 4.

conversion (because redeemed men were those capable of a Christian social reconstruction) and the prior reformation of social structures (that they should mould good men) was not resolved in the literature and discussions of C.O.P.E.C. It is, anyway, a permanent problem of the involvement of Christianity with the world. But the problem was at least clearly seen in C.O.P.E.C.

'C.O.P.E.C. is but the advance guard of a mighty moving spiritual host,' according to Samuel Keeble, 'which has declared war upon the present social order.'[1] The movement, in fact, echoed the social message which Church leaders had declaimed for years; but C.O.P.E.C. both summarized them and, to some extent, popularized them with the Churches. On the first day of the Conference, on 5 April 1924, the Bishop of Winchester, Dr. Frank Woods, offered the familiar version of their purpose, 'The Church is waking up to the social implications of her message,' he told the delegates; 'the Christianizing of conditions at home.'[2] He followed Temple's Opening Address, with its (again familiar) call to apply religion 'to those phases of life from which any direct reference to God has usually of late been excluded'.[3] On the next day Temple referred to C.O.P.E.C. as a continuation of the universal growth of social consciousness in the Church—evidenced by the Encyclicals of Leo XIII, by the Archbishops' Fifth Report, and by the Report of the American Interdenominational Committee on 'Christianity and Industrial Reconstruction'.[4] Miss Lucy Gardner, one of the two secretaries, said that they wanted 'to establish a norm of Christian thought and action for the further working out of a Christian order'.[5] In the *Guardian*'s 'C.O.P.E.C. Supplement', published the day before the Conference opened, the Hon. and Revd. 'Jimmy' Adderley remarked that their hope was 'to commit the whole body of the Church more definitely and more irrevocably to the principle that former Conferences have been occupied in elucidating and recommending to small bodies of earnest men'.[6]

This sense of continuity with preceding movements for social criticism was well illustrated in another aspect of C.O.P.E.C.: the familiar insistence on the Church's guilt for neglecting a social message in the past. This was a faithful echo of the Anglican social apologists of the C.S.U., and Samuel Keeble's ideas showed its spread to the Methodists. Writing in 1922 on the 'guilt of the Church,' he reproduced the false version of the nineteenth-century world of Christian social endeavour which C.S.U. propaganda had established as orthodoxy: 'A generation ago the Christain Church in England, Evangelical and Catholic, stoutly maintained that

[1] Keeble, 'C.O.P.E.C.', p. 17.
[2] *Proceedings*, p. 4.　　　　　　　　[3] Ibid., p. 1.
[4] Ibid., p. 20.　　　　　　　　[5] Ibid., p. 7.
[6] *Guardian*, 4 Apr. 1924, 'C.O.P.E.C. Supplement', p. ii, 'A look Forward'.

it had nothing to do with things social.'[1] Those who believed this version of the past did not bother to explain away the massive Church concern with schools for the poor, with industrial conditions, and so forth, in the nineteenth century—they did not even regard it all as attributable to subtle 'social control' as their successors have done: they simply ignored it, and were perhaps ignorant of its existence. Miss Lucy Gardner, at the Birmingham Conference, spoke of Christians as 'complacent, stereotyped, self-satisfied'.[2] Bishop Kempthorne of Lichfield, Chairman of the C.O.P.E.C. Commission on *The Social Function of the Church*, and himself for years a self-confessed guilty party to the Church's social intransigence, had by the time of the Conference got a bit fed up with it all. 'We have heard much of "the failure of the Church",' he told the delegates; 'I confess I am not enamoured of the phrase.' Christ does not fail, he declared, though Christian people do: 'But I fear that very many who use the phrase "failure of the Church" mean the failure of everybody but themselves.'[3] The inability of churchmen at this time to appreciate the scale of social criticism within the Church's leadership in the last decades of the nineteenth century itself bears witness to the vicarious and armchair quality of a lot of that thought. So little had the social critics actually translated into reality, that not much trace apparently remained even of their intentions.

It was the hope of Temple that C.O.P.E.C. would keep free of party politics, but this was never quite possible for one simple reason: the social analysis used in the movement, the solutions recommended, and the very vocabulary employed, were all characteristic of the Labour movement. Furthermore, the Birmingham Conference actually took place three months after the formation of Ramsay MacDonald's Labour administration, and the consequent euphoria had not entirely evaporated by the time the delegates assembled. No one bothered to disguise the fact that C.O.P.E.C. exhibited, as Henson put it, 'Christian Socialism in its latest phase'.[4] Temple seems to have imagined that his own resignation from the Labour Party had purified the entire enterprise from any suspicion of political partiality; and it is certainly true that the old C.S.U. *penchant* for failing to associate 'Christian Socialism' with party politics was well represented at Birmingham. C.O.P.E.C., Temple wrote, was 'not the sudden fancy of a few enthusiasts'; it was 'the form taken for the moment by that great movement in the Church which is associated, in the Anglican Communion, with the names of Kingsley, Maurice, Westcott, Scott Holland and

---

[1] S. E. Keeble, *Christian Responsibility for the Social Order* (London, 1922), p. 115. Keeble was also the author of *Industrial Day-dreams*.

[2] *Proceedings*, p. 7.

[3] Ibid., p. 231.

[4] H. Hensley Henson, *Quo Tendimus? The Primary Charge Delivered at his Visitation to the Clergy of his Diocese in November, 1924* (London, 1924), p. 78.

Gore'.[1] To that extent at any rate, Temple agreed with Henson. All the contributors to the *Guardian* supplement on C.O.P.E.C. saw the movement as a continuation of Christian Socialism. 'Our ideas have triumphed,' Percy Dearmer wrote there. 'The whole Christian Church has grappled with the social problem in earnest.' He went on to pay tribute to the memory of Westcott.[2] In a sympathetic appraisal of C.O.P.E.C. which Bishop Woods offered to the Convocation of Canterbury in May 1924, it was affirmed that the movement marked the real emergence of a Christian social position which hitherto 'had been confined to the efforts of small groups, including indeed such men as Maurice, Kingsley, Westcott'.[3] The political affinities of C.O.P.E.C. were shown in the adhesion of members of the League of the Kingdom of God. This was the new association of Christian Socialists which had emerged from the Church Socialist League in 1923.[4] It was led by Fr. Widdrington, and supported by Sir Henry Slesser—Solicitor-General in Ramsay MacDonald's Government and a prominent Anglo-Catholic layman. League members got themselves put onto several of the C.O.P.E.C. preparatory commissions. Charles Raven, one of the central planners of C.O.P.E.C., certainly envisaged radical political consequences of the movement rather in advance of Temple's intentions. In an interview with Archbishop Davidson early in June 1921, Raven was emphatic that 'the starting point' of C.O.P.E.C. 'was going to be quite different and much further back' than preceding social criticism; 'not assuming that the existing order of things is to be taken for granted and Christianity brought into it, but rather that a new order of things should be created'.[5] It is not surprising that Davidson was alarmed, nor that C.O.P.E.C. should have been so widely associated with left-wing political attitudes.

In March 1923 in fact, Davidson contemplated retirement—'he wondered', according to Bishop George Bell, his biographer, 'how far he was in sympathy with the modern social interpretation of Christianity'.[6] Bell was, as Davidson's domestic Chaplain at the time, in a good position to assess his mind. The Archbishop preserved a public silence over the preparations for C.O.P.E.C.[7] An examination of the correspondence

---

[1] *Guardian*, 4 Apr. 1924, 'C.O.P.E.C. Supplement', p. i, 'C.O.P.E.C. by the Bishop of Manchester' (the *Guardian* was a Church newspaper).

[2] Ibid., 'A look Back', p. ii. See also the feature articles on Scott Holland and Temple, p. iii.

[3] *The Chronicle of Convocation, 1924* (London, 1924), p. 228 (7 May).

[4] Reckitt, *P. E. T. Widdrington*, p. 94.

[5] Davidson Papers, Lambeth Palace Library, 1921/3 (Packet of Papers marked 'Christian Politics', in fact covering the years 1919–24), Davidson to Temple, 10 June 1921.

[6] Bell, *Randall Davidson*, ii. 1154.

[7] It is interesting that Bell's *Life* of Davidson, written when Temple was Archbishop of York, makes no difference to C.P.O.E.C.; perhaps a tactful omission in deference to Temple.

between himself and Temple, however, reveals a hidden hostility. Early in June 1921 the two secretaries of C.O.P.E.C.—Miss Lucy Gardner and Charles Raven—called upon Davidson at Lambeth, at his own request, to inform him exactly what the proposed Conference was for. 'My fear is,' Davidson wrote to Temple after the interview, 'that the purport of this Conference is so wide that it cannot help becoming vague or a mere repetition of what we are always saying as to the need of bringing Christianity into our common life, industrial, educational, political, etc.' He was against still more committees on these questions.[1] Davidson, meanwhile, through Bell, was collecting opinions. Lang, who was much more sympathetic to C.O.P.E.C. as it matured, was not much help at this preparatory stage. He forgot, when asked by Bell to sound Temple on the real intentions of the Conference, and so had 'really nothing to report' except a personal conviction that the Church of England Men's Society and the Industrial Christian Fellowship were the appropriate bodies to investigate social questions.[2] Hubert Burge, the Bishop of Oxford, who eventually joined the C.O.P.E.C. Council, was another asked to advise the Archbishop.[3] Burge also found it 'very difficult to see how a Conference on the lines proposed is going to avoid being a mere repetition of what has been put out over and over again during the last two or three years'. He favoured an expression of 'Church people *generally*' (his own italics) on this sort of question, rather than the views of a section, but doubted 'whether the time has come for that expression to be at all general'.[4] Temple himself urged Davidson to support his enterprise, admitting the difficulties:

All along I have felt the danger that we may only succeed in saying the old platitudes again, and the danger that if we escape this it will be by claiming as necessary parts of the Gospel what are really most fallible inferences from it. Yet I have felt sure the attempt ought to be made to focus Christian thought on the structural principles of social life in the hope of two things:
(1) The recovery of the constant Christian tradition in these matters in the ages when the thought of the Church was steadily directed to them.
(2) The assertion (or re-assertion) of some principles by a really representative body, which would be more explicit than the great platitudes and less particular than a political programme.[5]

Early in July 1921 Miss Gardner was pressing the Archbishop to give his decision 'with regard to giving his name to the Conference'.[6] Armed with the impression that Lang and Burge shared his own reservations, Davidson

[1] Davidson Papers, 1921/3, Davidson to Temple, 10 June 1921.
[2] Ibid., Lang to Bell, 8 June 1921.
[3] Ibid., Bell to H. M. Burge, 16 June 1921.
[4] Ibid., Burge to Davidson, 24 June 1921.
[5] Ibid., Temple to Davidson, 15 June 1921.
[6] Ibid., Lucy Gardner to Bell, 9 July 1921.

instructed Bell to reply that 'at any rate at this stage' he could not comply. This did not represent any lack of sympathy, Bell was instructed to suggest; but that 'apart altogether from the reports of recent committees on industrial problems, the Archbishop is obliged to recognise the fact that at the present moment there is a rather large number of proposals for Conferences or Councils dealing with social, political and international matters', awaiting the attention of the Church.[1]

There, for a time, matters rested. Preparations for the Conference went on. In May of 1922, Temple appealed to Davidson for 'co-operation in making this Conference known to the Church people, both clergy and laity, of your diocese'.[2] Davidson appears to have handed this over to J. V. Macmillan, the Archdeacon of Maidstone (later Bishop of Guildford), who was an enthusiastic supporter of C.O.P.E.C. and a member of one of its Commissions.[3] Early in the following year Temple asked Bell to sound the Archbishop about the possibility of the two Convocations sending official elegates to the Conference. Davidson was against this.[4] In March Temple was inquiring about 'the possibility of a provisional agreement' whereby Davidson should address the opening meeting of the Conference which was, Temple forecast, 'going to be a genuinely important event'.[5] Davidson would not commit himself and in May it was Miss Gardner's turn to try to convince him; this time to address a great London preparatory meeting in the autumn of 1923: 'as the Conference grows in weight and importance, the necessity for this becomes more and more clear'.[6] Davidson was blunt; 'I find some difficulty myself in sharing the full expectations which I find entertained,' he replied, and declined on account of the pressing obligations which would keep him at Lambeth.[7] In his place Lang presided at the Albert Hall meeting. In October Temple, ever persistent, asked Davidson if he would attend the Conference itself— now fixed for 5 April of the following year—and if he would speak.[8] Davidson declined, again stressing the importance of his daily attention to routine business at Lambeth. (Davidson actually went off on holiday to Italy during the week of the Conference.) In his letter of refusal he was bland: 'This is a real disappointment, but it is the kind of disappointment which I suppose one must face as years multiply.'[9] The last chapter of the episode came a month before the Birmingham gathering, when Temple

---

[1] Ibid., Bell to Miss Gardner, 18 July 1921.
[2] Ibid., Temple to Davidson, 31 May 1922.
[3] Ibid., Macmillan to Bell, 11 July 1922.
[4] Ibid., Temple to Bell, 22 Jan. 1923 (Bell has written 'No' against the paragraph which makes the request).
[5] Ibid., Temple to Davidson, 21 Mar. 1923.
[6] Ibid., Miss Gardner to Davidson, 3 May 1923.
[7] Ibid., Davidson to Miss Gardner, 5 May 1923.
[8] Ibid., Temple to Davidson, 22 Oct. 1923.
[9] Ibid., Davidson to Temple, 3 Nov. 1923.

sought a letter of support from the Archbishop, which could be read out.[1] This was duly given. 'In regard to this gathering,' Davidson then wrote, 'the aim has been so steady, the arrangements so deliberate and the choice of leaders so careful, and, above all, the prayers so real and expectant, that I am not afraid.' Davidson's eventual, if distant, recognition of C.O.P.E.C. —and his thoughts of retirement as the preparations advanced—are a clear indication of the strength of social radicalism within the Church. He contented himself now with a reminder to the Conference that most social questions could 'be regarded Christianly from quite different standpoints'.[2]

The preparations for the Conference really had been very extensive. Twelve Commissions were appointed in 1921 by the Executive Committee to inquire into specialized areas of social concern. Each consisted of experts and clergy, carefully balanced denominationally. It was intended, as Temple said, that their propaganda work, and the reports they composed, should 'be more important than the Conference itself'.[3] Temple was himself President of the C.O.P.E.C. Council of 300, on which there were fourteen Anglican bishops. Numerous bodies were affiliated to the Council—including the I.C.F., the S.C.M., and the Social Service Unions. Dr. Hugh Martin was Chairman of the Executive. Charles Raven, one of the two Secretaries, on whom most of the daily organization fell over the three years of preparation, was Rector of Bletchingly. He had been Dean of Emmanuel College, and after 1925 was Lady Margaret Professor of Divinity at Cambridge. In 1920 he had published a sympathetic account of the origins of Christian Socialism.[4] Miss Lucy Gardner, the other secretary, was a Quaker. She had acted as secretary to Temple's 'Collegium', and was inspired to social radicalism by her work in the Charity Organisation Society. 'I do not believe any man could have shown such ruthless and untiring efficiency', Raven wrote of her—an observation which Davidson would no doubt have confirmed. Her enthusiasm indeed attained ecstasy: on the first night of the Birmingham Conference she 'fell out of bed in a sort of delirium' and was only restored through the ministrations of Raven's wife, who, according to Raven, 'had an almost miraculous control over neurotics'.[5] The twelve preparatory Commissions, whose reports were before the Conference, were on 'The Nature of God and His Purpose for the World' (I); 'Education' (II); 'The Home' (III); 'The Relation of the Sexes' (IV); 'Leisure' (V); 'The Treatment of Crime' (VI); 'International Relations' (VII); 'Christianity and War (VIII); 'Industry and Property' (IX); 'Politics and Citizenship' (X); 'The Social Function of the Church' (XI); and 'Historical Illustrations of the

---

[1] Davidson Papers, Temple to Davidson, 10 Mar. 1924.
[2] *Proceedings of C.O.P.E.C.*, p. 15.
[3] Davidson Papers, 1921/3, Temple to Davidson, 15 June 1921.
[4] Charles E. Raven, *Christian Socialism, 1848–1854* (London, 1920).
[5] Raven, 'C.O.P.E.C. Then and Now—I', p. 110.

Social Effects of Christianity' (XII). The Commissions sent out 200,000 questionnaires, whose findings were collated at seventy-five centres.[1] Copies of study material and preliminary reports were sent to parishes, and to public schools.[2] The bishops of each diocese in the Church of England were asked in 1923 to write commendatory letters to their clergy, urging the study of C.O.P.E.C. literature among the congregations: this was intended as part of 'a very large educational campaign throughout the country'.[3] Advertisements were placed in Church newspapers, which called for an effort 'to understand exactly what the social ethics of Christianity are', and also 'to apply them without fear to all human relationships'.[4] A number of large meetings were held to stimulate interest still further.[5] Finance was always something of a problem, but local help was all voluntary, and only the staff of the London Office were salaried. Printing costs were the chief item of expenditure. In 1923 the campaign cost £4,611, and in 1924, £2,958.[6] One other problem was the resignation of the two Roman Catholic priests—Fathers O'Hea and Walker (both Jesuits)—from the Executive Committee, before the Conference met. This made the enterprise a little less ecumenical than intended. Tired of all the Anglicans' talk about the guilt and failure of the Church, the Roman Catholics withdrew on the grounds that their Church had not failed in its social teaching. Bishop Gore said he was 'amazed' at this 'almost unbelievable' claim.[7]

The actual Conference at Birmingham, between 5 and 12 April 1924, was much less important than the research it had initiated into Christian social attitudes. The official account was compiled by the Revd. Will Reason.[8] Of the 1,500 delegates, 700 were drawn as representatives from various Christian societies of the different denominations, and there were eighty visitors from overseas Churches; the other 800 were delegates allocated to the Churches, with the Church of England providing 340. The Anglicans constituted the real solidity of the Conference; it was from Anglican literature—such as the Archbishops' Reports of 1918—that most of the ideas expressed in C.O.P.E.C. literature took their origin. And Temple, the founder of C.O.P.E.C., despite his interdenominational courtesies, was a very Anglican figure. His opening Address, on Sunday 5 April,[9]

---

[1] Davidson Papers, 1921/3, contains copies of all the questionnaires sent out.

[2] The Revd. Meredith Dewey, former Dean of Pembroke College, Cambridge, who was a boy at Rugby when the C.O.P.E.C. papers were being studied as part of school religious instruction, recalls his own, and his contemporaries', extreme boredom.

[3] Davidson Papers, 1921/3, Miss Gardener to Davidson, 16 Mar. 1923.

[4] See the *Church Times*, 13 Oct. 1922: 'C.O.P.E.C.'

[5] e.g. the Queen's Hall Meeting on 26 Oct. 1922; and the Albert Hall Meeting on 4 Dec. 1922.

[6] Davidson Papers, 1921/3, C.O.P.E.C. circular 'Concerning Finance' (n.d.).

[7] *Proceedings*, p. 212.   [8] The author of *Poverty* (London, 1909).

[9] *Proceedings*, p. 1; the manuscript copy of the speech is in the Temple Papers, Lambeth

launched a week of very uneven discussion. As if in self-parody, a 'Junior C.O.P.E.C.' assembled in Eastbourne, composed of children, and dedicated to imparting to the young a sense of social concern. The adult version received formal letters of goodwill from King George V—'such discussion must surely be welcomed by the citizens of a Christian Country'[1] —from the Prime Minister, Ramsay MacDonald,[2] from Baldwin and Asquith,[3] and of course, the painfully extracted letter from Archbishop Davidson.[4] The *Guardian* 'C.O.P.E.C. Supplement' was also full of testimonial letters, including a warning from Lang about 'a danger lest enthusiasm should evaporate in mere generalities', an assurance from Bishop Burge 'that many will gain a new point of view',[5] and the usual doxology—this time from Adderley—about the overthrow 'of the blinding influence of the doctrine of laissez-faire'.[6] The Church press in general gave warm support to C.O.P.E.C.[7] and the Conference was well covered by the national press. The prevailing atmosphere at Birmingham, indeed, 'nearly took away the breath of the press', according to Keeble's account of the Conference.[8] At the end of a week spent debating the Reports and passing resolutions based on them, the delegates approved a 'Message of the Conference'. This was a predictable one: 'We have realised with a fresh intensity the scandal to our civilization and religion involved in the fact that thousands of our fellow-countrymen are without decent homes, are without work, are without education that would develop their faculties to the full.'[9] It seemed, in all, a very satisfactory week.

The C.O.P.E.C. Reports made a serious contribution to the Church's social teaching. Most of the developed ideas were rather contentious, but somehow managed to strike chords of sympathy with a large number of influential bishops and clergy in the Church of England. Some parts of the Reports were inventive—the results of the three years of research by the Commissions; these parts tended to go beyond the limits Temple set himself. The style and language used reflected the contemporary interests of the 'progressive' intelligentsia. The Reports, like the discussions, revealed very little difference of opinion over social analysis, and the critique of industrial society, or the effects of capitalism; but some really huge divergences of opinion emerged over questions of personal morality— over divorce and contraception—and over the issues of pacifism and tem-

---

Palace Library, in a Folder marked 'C.O.P.E.C. 1924'; for the text see also Flindall *The Church of England*, p. 388.

[1] *Proceedings*, p. 14; manuscript copy in Temple Papers (dated 3 Apr. 1924).
[2] *Proceedings*, p. 16.
[3] Ibid., pp. 16–17.   [4] Ibid., p. 51.
[5] *Guardian*, 4 Apr. 1924, 'C.O.P.E.C. Supplement', p. i.
[6] Ibid., p. ii.
[7] Oliver, *The Church and Social Order*, p. 66.   [8] Keeble, '*C.O.P.E.C.*', p. 9.
[9] *Proceedings*, p. 273; manuscript copy in the Temple Papers.

perance. Temple, whose main interest was in economic and social matters, was able to record his impression that 'very few' of the resolutions 'aroused any signs of serious opposition';[1] whereas Adderley, whose interests were a little more general, observed that 'many of the reports disclose serious differences which must delay for some time anything like final judgements'.[2] In fact the reports were no more radical than the Archbishops' Reports of 1918—and in some particulars a little less radical—and were in general far from being 'proposals for root and branch remedies for the ills of society'.[3] Hence, of course, their importance in the progressive development of the social teachings of the Church, and the need to examine the circumstances and contents of the C.O.P.E.C. movement rather closely. It was precisely because, although expressions of a familiar enough social radicalism, they were still recognizably moderate and authoritative, that the C.O.P.E.C. Reports exerted such influence in finally committing the Church to what increasingly became popularized as 'the Temple view' of social questions. Bishop Woods told Convocation that 'for many years to come the Reports would be regarded as text-books on the subjects with which they dealt and would be standard literature which should be on the shelves of every clergyman'.[4] Davidson privately recorded Lord Salisbury's shocked dislike of the Reports, which he believed involved 'a materializing of some parts of Our Lord's teaching'; yet the Archbishop himself supposed that 'no one can fail to find the Reports interesting'[5]—which was indeed a tribute.

The first report on *The Nature of God and His Purpose for the World* elicited, as Will Reason remarked in his account, 'no discussion'. Raven said the object of the Report was 'to bring the whole sum of human life into full co-operation with God', the 'goal of Christian citizenship'.[6] The Conference did, however, hear a short paper written by Evelyn Underhill —whose *Mystics of the Church* was published in the same year. She had taken a prominent part in the organization of C.O.P.E.C. and had spoken at a number of the preparatory public meetings. Although she was unable to attend the Conference itself because of the death of her mother,[7] her paper was read by Walter Moberley (later first Chairman of the University Grants Committee). It was a fairly conventional statement of the need for social change and for improvement in the conditions of the working classes: 'We continue our devotional basking in the sun, our religious cultivation,

---

[1] William Temple, *Essays in Christian Politics and Kindred Subjects* (London, 1927), p. 32.
[2] *Guardian*, 'C.O.P.E.C. Supplement', p. ii.
[3] Dark, *The People's Archbishop*, p. 27.
[4] *The Chronicle of Convocation, 1924*, p. 228 (7 May).
[5] Davidson Papers, 1921/3, Davidson to Archdeacon Macmillan, 17 May 1924.
[6] *Proceedings*, p. 24.
[7] Margaret Cropper, *Evelyn Underhill* (London, 1958), p. 121.

and let the maiming influence of environment play on these myriads of other souls, pushing them back to animal levels—we just don't give them a chance.'[1] On the eve of the Conference she had written that 'its deliberations and findings will exhibit to the world the immense amount of theoretical agreement which exists among all types of Christians as to the civil, moral, and political obligations of our faith, and the width of the gulf which now separates Christian ideals and public action'.[2] The Report itself, like these preliminary sentiments, was very much a restatement of the truism that God calls men to social concern.

The second report, on *Education*, upheld the essential requirement that religion should be associated with the education of children. 'At the very outset', said Salter Davies (a member of the preparatory Commission), 'it protests against the common tendency to regard education as primarily an intellectual process, concerning itself only incidentally with moral issues and with personal relationships.'[3] But it was quite clear that the Report envisaged '*undenominational* education in the Schools'[4]—the solution naturally favoured by the Nonconformists at the Conference, and by Temple, who was himself out of step with most of his colleagues in the Church of England on the education question. The Conference adopted the formula of 'religious instruction based on the Bible and leading to a progressive understanding of the right relations of man to God and man to man'.[5] The Report also urged the need to regard adult education as essential; to build better schools; and there was considerable emphasis on the need, also brought out in the discussion, to remove social-class distinctions from the educational system[6]—though this does not seem to have suggested to anyone the need to consider the position of independent schools. A special resolution, passed at the end of the Conference, called for the raising of the school-leaving age to sixteen and a reduction in the size of classes.[7] It was, altogether, an interesting summary of the opinions of educational reformers in the 1920s.

'In our Report', wrote the Commissioners on *The Home*, the third Report, 'we discuss the application of Christian principles to the vital relations of husband and wife, of parent and child, and of the family as a whole to the community of which it is a part.' As such, therefore, the Report concerned 'personal, political and social morality'.[8] The most suggestive sections were on the housing question. There was an idealistic

---

[1] *Proceedings*, p. 34.

[2] *Guardian*, 'C.O.P.E.C. Supplement', 4 Apr. 1924, p. i.

[3] *Proceedings*, p. 54.

[4] *Education* (C.O.P.E.C. Report II) (London, 1924), p. 29.

[5] *Proceedings*, p. 277, Resolution 2.

[6] Ibid., p. 57.   [7] Ibid., p. 274.

[8] *The Home* (C.O.P.E.C. Report III) (London, 1924), p. 3. For public comment, see the *Birmingham Post*, 9 Apr. 1924: 'The Voice of the Church'.

quality about a lot of the Report, whose Chairman, Captain R. L. Reiss, was also Chairman of the Executive of the Garden Cities Association, a director both of Welwyn Garden City Ltd., and of the Hampstead Garden City Trust Ltd. He called for 2,000,000 workers' houses to be built,[1] without any explicit hint as to how this might be financed. There was a clue:

We may differ [he said] as to whether the results we want should be achieved by an entire change in our economic system such as is involved by what is commonly called 'socialism', or whether it is possible under a private and capitalist system to secure the results, but those who believe it can be secured under the existing system are bound to recognise that it has not so far been achieved, and that drastic alterations are needed in our administration and legislation and in the conduct of business if the present system is to be justified.[2]

The Report itself laid emphasis on the moral consequences of bad housing,[3] in a way almost unchanged since the episcopal charges of the 1820s. The Conference resolved, accordingly, that 'the building up of Christian homes lies at the root of the social problem'.[4]

A social dimension was also imparted to *The Relation of the Sexes*, the fourth Report. This was characterized by a high-minded detachment from inhibitions. 'Only in an assembly of Christians earnestly seeking the truth could there safely be such frankness', Keeble remarked with pride.[5] There was enough praise of sex as 'a joyous and complete self-surrender'[6]—in, of course, carefully controlled moral conditions—to please any clinical therapist. The Chairman of the Commission, Professor W. F. Lofthouse, an Old Testament Scholar, and a Methodist, spoke of sex as 'too holy a thing for vulgar jesting'. The other members of the Commission, headed by Mrs. Alcock, agreed.[7] They also agreed that it was immoral to exploit others for sexual pleasure,[8] and that the great evil of female prostitution could be overcome by men 'showing self-control and chivalry'.[9] Sex education for children was also recommended.[10] This found a sponsor during the discussion in the person of the Revd. G. H. Martin, of the Surbiton Study Groups, who pleaded for sex education with the words 'If only someone had told me'.[11] The Conference eventually resolved 'to uphold before society the Christian standard of purity and the Christian ideal of love',[12] but only after it had become clear that there was no real agreement as to what they were. The differences corresponded to those between church-men and Nonconformists over the issues of divorce[13] and contraception[14]—

[1] *Proceedings*, p. 98.   [2] Ibid., p. 99.   [3] *Report*, pp. 67 ff.
[4] *Proceedings*, p. 279.   [5] Keeble, 'C.O.P.E.C.', p. 12.
[6] *The Relation of the Sexes* (C.O.P.E.C. Report IV) (London, 1924), p. 36.
[7] *Proceedings*, p. 107.   [8] Ibid., p. 109.   [9] Ibid., p. 110.
[10] *Report*, pp. 73 ff.   [11] *Proceedings*, p. 116.   [12] *Proceedings*, p. 280.
[13] *Report*, pp. 168-74.   [14] Ibid., p. 154.

two questions about which many Nonconformists had no clear moral theology, yet were insistent on the Christian value of both. Churchmen could not agree. 'The matter of contraceptives was a damnable scandal and was playing the very devil with the nation', as Studdert Kennedy, in his own style, expressed the Lambeth teachings of the Church of England.[1] Mrs. Wise, however, representing the alternative view, and claiming that the Conference 'ought to face facts', called for birth-control clinics to be set up in order to provide expert advice.[2] Temple led the Conference in a moment of prayer. But Mrs. Wise's amendment, in discreetly veiled language, was passed.[3] The major differences of opinion were left unresolved both in the Report and the discussion.

Similarly the fifth Report on *Leisure*, elicited another set of divergences of view—this time over the questions of Sunday Observance—or rather the extent to which Sunday Observance should be taken[4]—and temperance. On the 'Drink Problem' the Report favoured the universal adoption of the principle of local option in the granting of liquor licences[5]—a solution in accordance with legislation suggested by the Bishop of Oxford. This was also resolved by the Conference,[6] but a lot of the political problems associated with the liquor question, and the general touchiness of the Liberal Nonconformists on the matter, cast a subdued light upon the discussions.[7] On the next day, whilst considering the question of crime, Bishop James Cannon of the American Episcopal Church rather added to the moral tone by speaking strongly in favour of the Prohibition experiment in his country.[8] Gambling was condemned by everyone.[9] About other uses of leisure there was a euphoric consensus. The Revd. T. W. Pym, Head of Cambridge House in Camberwell, who was Chairman of the Commission, said that it was 'foolish for Christians to plead for a better general standard of life for the people in wages, housing, working conditions if we are not at the same time striving to secure better opportunities for the happiest use of the material advantages they may one day gain'.[10] The new utopia described in the games and pastimes recommended to the working classes by the members of the Conference were redolent of the romanticized passion for 'folk' culture characteristic of the progressively minded within the intelligentsia of the period. The working classes, who not unreasonably wanted leisure in order to play football or to drink in the pub, were seen by Miss Dashwood as given instead to the performance

---

[1] *Proceedings*, p. 115.   [2] Ibid., p. 119.
[3] Ibid., Resolution 8, p. 281.
[4] *Leisure* (C.O.P.E.C. Report V) (London, 1924), p. 14; *Proceedings*, p. 125.
[5] *Report*, pp. 105-6.
[6] *Proceedings*, p. 282 (Special Resolution).
[7] Ibid., p. 135.   [8] *Proceedings*, p 144.
[9] *Report*, p. 65; *Proceedings*, p. 282, Resolution 3.
[10] *Proceedings*, p. 125.

of medieval Mystery plays;[1] by Miss Shepherd, as introduced to 'community music';[2] by the Revd. A. B. Bateman, as attaining to 'the joy of creation, the sphere of art and handicrafts';[3] by Lord Aberdeen, as well as by almost everybody else, as enjoying folk-dancing;[4] by Miss Cropper, as devotees of drama.[5] When it came to the cinema, the new and popular entertainment, there was a call for censorship.[6] The Report itself had only referred to a boycott of 'the frivolous and the vicious' in films, as in the theatre; such things were to be defined by 'people of lofty ideals'.[7] The recommendations of the Report on games for children would seem to reflect the practice of the sort of schools to which most of those in the C.O.P.E.C. movement had gone. 'All individualism should be sunk in team work,' the Report urged; 'young boys and girls should engage in team games whether they like it or not.'[8] It has been argued that the C.O.P.E.C. Report on Leisure was a venture into a largely new area for the Christian conscience,[9] but in fact the Church Congresses regularly discussed it during the last three decades of the nineteenth century, and, apart from all the stuff about folk-dancing for the poor, the C.O.P.E.C. Report added nothing new.

The sixth Report, on *The Treatment of Crime*, pointed to the social causes of crime, to the poor housing conditions and inadequate educational facilities which created the circumstances in which criminality thrived. 'Crime must be considered not as an isolated phenomenon, but as intimately related to the home, to education and to the social and industrial order and to religion', according to Lleufer Thomas, a Welsh Stipendiary Magistrate who was a member of the Commission.[10] 'We no longer believe', he added, 'that crime is due to the innate depravity of the individual—the causes have to be sought outside the individual himself—in conditions that are intimately associated with sociological and industrial problems.'[11] The environmental element in crime had been stressed by the Church of England as far back as the start of the nineteenth century, as part of the vision of the Church Extension movement and its concern over 'Spiritual Destitution'; but C.O.P.E.C. appeared ignorant of these early beginnings—it did, however, add some useful ideas about child offenders,[12] the treatment of unconvicted prisoners,[13] and the reform of the Prison System.[14] On the question of capital punishment the Commission was divided, and called

---

[1] *Proceedings*, p. 129.   [2] Ibid., p. 130.
[3] Ibid., p. 131.   [4] Ibid., p. 132.
[5] Ibid., p. 132. See also *Report*, p. 51.
[6] Ibid., p. 132, from the Revd. Martyn Roberts, of the Hull Christian Social Council.
[7] *Report*, p. 53.   [8] Ibid., p. 35.
[9] Oliver, *The Church and Social Order*, p. 69.
[10] *Proceedings*, p. 139.   [11] Ibid., p. 140.
[12] *The Treatment of Crime* (C.O.P.E.C. Report VI) (London, 1924), pp. 68, 70.
[13] Ibid., p. 72.   [14] Ibid., p. 81.

merely for further study,[1] but a motion in support of abolition, introduced at the Conference by a Quaker delegate (C. R. Simpson) was carried by a large majority.[2]

Neither the seventh Report on *International Relations*, nor the eighth, on *Christianity and War*, contained material of direct relevance to social policy. Both were extremely idealistic—G. P. Gooch, for example, in the Conference discussion, seeking to model international relations on the medieval concept of Christendom,[3] 'The Christian faith is fundamentally opposed to the spirit of imperialism as expressed in desire of conquest, the maintenance of prestige, or the pursuit, in other forms, of the selfish interests of one nation at the expense of another', the Conference resolved.[4] Inevitably, they all clamoured to support the League of Nations as the embodiment of the Christian ideal of world order.[5] The Report on War was rightly described by Henson as 'a very pacifist production',[6] though in fact it represented a compromise attained only after the most difficult struggles both on the Commission and in the Conference discussion. At least, as the Revd. Dr. A. E. Garvie, Chairman of the Commission, was able to report, 'both pacifist and non-pacifist members found themselves at one in their condemnation of war as opposed to the distinctively Christian ethic'.[7] Quaker members led the attempt to commit C.O.P.E.C. to pacifism, and, after another of those short interludes of silent prayer to which Temple resorted when the Conference got out of hand, an ambiguous formula was adopted.[8] It became Resolution 1: 'That all war is contrary to the spirit and teaching of Jesus Christ'.[9] Another Resolution sought to oblige Christians to condemn any war started, for whatever purpose, without prior attempts at arbitration.[10] These discussions 'aroused great resentment'[11] among the public. It was hardly surprising, within a few years of the sacrifice endured in the Great War.

It was the Report on *Industry and Property*, the ninth Report, that reflected most fully the sort of social consciousness which the preceding decades had seen growing in the Churches. Yet the Report, and the Conference discussion (on 9 April) were essentially unoriginal—almost nothing emerged that had not formed part of the general deposit of Christian social radicalism for many years. This was not for want of talent. The Commission, chaired by Miss Constance Smith (of Temple's Collegium), contained, among others, Sir Max Muspratt (Vice-President of the Federation

---

[1] *The Treatment of Crime*, pp. 78 ff.
[2] *Proceedings*, p. 148. See the report in the *Birmingham Post*, 10 Apr. 1924.
[3] *Proceedings*, p. 153.   [4] Ibid., p. 285, Resolution 1.
[5] Ibid., p. 287, Resolution 9.
[6] Henson Journals, vol. 37, p. 147 (13 Aug. 1924).
[7] *Proceedings*, p. 165.
[8] Ibid., p. 178.   [9] Ibid., p. 287.
[10] Ibid., p. 288, Resolution 3.   [11] Keeble, 'C.O.P.E.C.', p. 13.

of British Industry), Sir Henry Slesser (the Solicitor-General), J. W. Ogden and Ben Turner (of the T.U.C.), H. A. Mess (Social Secretary of S.C.M.), Sir George Paish (a Governor of the L.S.E.) and R. H. Tawney (at the time a lecturer at the L.S.E.). With the exception of Sir Max Muspratt's dissent over property and over some of the economic arguments used, the Commission was of one mind. Tawney's influence was especially evident.

It is not only repugnant to the principles of the Christian, but revolting to the taste of an educated person, that one class in a country, a small class of which the individuals are not necessarily distinguished above their fellow-citizens for virtue or ability, should command more money than they can possibly spend in any rational or profitable fashion.[1]

The evidence of the distribution of wealth was drawn from Sir Josiah Stamp's conclusion that in 1914, 45 per cent of the national income went to $5\frac{1}{2}$ per cent of the income-receivers—an estimate which appeared to verify Sir Leo Chiozza Money's findings for 1905. The Commission accepted the estimates uncritically.[2] Their Report unfolded all the arguments deployed in the Archbishops' Fifth Report in 1918: on the evils of economic individualism, of the moral difficulties of capitalism, of the need for co-operation in industry, worker participation, a 'living wage', the conditions according to which property could be held without moral hazard, the evils of inherited wealth.[3] The repetitions were enormous. In presenting their findings to the Conference, Miss Smith referred—as if speaking of a wholly new revelation—to 'the fatal results of banishing God from the world's business and making the teaching of Christ of none effect by the maxims of trade'.[4] Once again, *laissez-faire* was attacked, and so was the Church, for its 'silent and apparently indifferent' acquiescence in that economic doctrine, 'buttressed by the eloquence of great statesmen', throughout the preceding century.[5] And her solution, which was that of the Commission, was still the old C.S.U. one: 'the transformation of industry by the spirit of service and of brotherhood'.[6]

Sir Henry Slesser, in agreeing, did not disguise from the Conference 'that in demanding a substitution of the motive of service for that of gain we make a vast demand upon human nature'. But he cited numerous examples 'in the case of the professions' where men had already attained altruism.[7] As for co-operation, Slesser fell back on the medieval guild 'as one pattern at any rate of the achievement of a social industrial combination'.[8] At the Anglo-Catholic Congress in 1923, Slesser had argued the

---

[1] *Industry and Property* (C.O.P.E.C. Report IX) (London, 1924), p. 25.
[2] Ibid., p. 95.
[3] For a summary, see the *Birmingham Post*, 11 Apr. 1924.
[4] *Proceedings*, p. 182.
[5] Ibid., p. 183.   [6] Ibid., p. 185.
[7] Ibid., p. 186.   [8] Ibid., p. 188.

same case: medieval Europe organized its whole life, 'their politics, their economics, their social structure according to the mind of Our Lord'.[1] Sir George Paish followed the Solicitor-General by agreeing that the world contained superabundant natural wealth for everybody: 'fundamentally there is no economic justification for poverty in any part of the world'; poverty was 'the result of lack of co-operation and of good-will'.[2] This case came to look rather dated by the 1960s after the recognition of the rate of population growth, and the finite nature of natural resources. In 1924 the earth seemed limitless. Paish was followed by a Scottish clergyman who attacked the profits of Standard Oil.[3] Before the discussion ran away into details, it was recalled to first principles by Conrad Noel—present at the Conference despite the diabetes which first seriously began to afflict him in 1924.[4] 'We must labour not for mere modification of evils, but for a fundamental transformation,' he said.[5] The Report itself had put the case for gradualism: 'This great transformation for which we look, from conflict to peace, from chaos to order, from morally repugnant to just conditions, may not be wrought by sudden and violent change, but by a gradual process.'[6] No doubt Noel's version of fundamental change would have differed considerably from that of the C.O.P.E.C. membership in general. This was all glossed over at Birmingham.

The only discordant notes to disturb the chorus, in fact came from Sir Max Muspratt, whose industrialist's realism was quite at variance with the academic tone of the other leading speakers in the debate on the Report. 'I think the ideal has been allowed to obscure the practical,' he said. He pointed to what he argued was a 'grave fallacy in economics' in the section on the distribution of wealth, and whilst agreeing that poverty was certainly repugnant to the Christian conscience, he maintained that wealth was justifiable.[7] 'It is the successful and wealthy industrialist who normally sets the example to the less wealthy in wages and conditions and wide philanthropy, and it is the nations with the largest number of wealthy people which have in practice the highest standard of living all round.[8] Muspratt also observed of the Report, that 'it states the problems rather than suggests the solutions', because of 'the complexity of the subject'.[9] He might have added that it was also due to a wish to keep the Report clear of party political identification. Even Slesser had pointed out that the Commission were anxious 'not to actualise this combination of social co-operation into any specific dogmatic form as between the State Collec-

---

[1] *Report of the Anglo-Catholic Congress, 1923* (London, 1923), p. 99.
[2] *Proceedings*, p. 192.   [3] Ibid., p. 195.
[4] Reg. Groves, *Conrad Noel and the Thaxted Movement. An Adventure in Christian Socialism* (London, 1967), p. 298.
[5] *Proceedings*, p. 196.   [6] *Report*, p. 196.
[7] *Proceedings*, p. 200.   [8] Ibid., p. 201.
[9] Ibid., p. 200.

tivists, the Guildsmen, or any other theorists'. They could, he said, 'afford to remain neutral'.[1] The Report had itself—on the question of unemployment—established the principle that it was improper 'to give judgment upon questions which divide technical experts'.[2] But to almost everybody outside C.O.P.E.C. such claims must have looked specious. The presuppositions of the Report were patently those of the moderate political Left. Will Reason's attacks on existing property rights for not being 'based on any principle, whether of desert or ability', and for symptomizing the extent to which 'economic forces have been allowed to slip out of moral control'[3]—or Bishop Gore's attack on 'personal philanthropy'[4]—can hardly have belonged to any other political tradition. Nor could the Resolutions which were adopted. The first concerned the need 'to procure the predominance of the motive of service over the motive of gain'.[5] This was uncontroversial as it stood. The second, in support of the co-operative principle in industry, although it was not to be taken to 'involve one particular type of organisation', was clearly an outward formula pointing to an inner doctrine which had become highly political. So was the third Resolution: for worker participation, 'an increasingly effective voice' in the management of industry. The fourth called for a 'living wage', defined as 'sufficient to maintain the worker and his family in health and dignity'. The fifth condemned unemployment, as morally intolerable. The Conference also passed a special Resolution calling on the Government 'either to hold, or to invite and assist the Churches to hold, a searching enquiry into the causes of unemployment', in preparation for any changes which might be required 'in our financial, economic and industrial system'.[6] The sixth ordinary Resolution condemned 'extremes of wealth and poverty', and deposed that 'a Christian order involves a juster distribution'. In the seventh the title to property was made dependent on its contribution to 'the development of personality and the good of the whole community'. There were echoes here, as there had been in the discussion,[7] of the volume on *Property* edited by Gore in 1913.[8] The eighth Resolution attacked inherited wealth. Very little of this was without pretty obvious political association, although the Conference leaders were careful to avoid overt party identification.

The tenth Report, on *Politics and Citizenship*, went some way to soften the political implications of the other Reports, by coming out very decisively against any direct party-political role for the Churches. Even Henson admitted it was 'distinctly saner than the other reports'.[9] 'I want no

---

[1] Ibid., p. 188.   [2] *Report*, p. 85.
[3] *Proceedings*, p. 208.   [4] Ibid., p. 211.
[5] Ibid., p. 289. The other Resolutions are printed on pp. 289 and 290.
[6] Ibid., p. 270.   [7] Ibid.; see p. 207.
[8] See Chap. 7, p. 228.
[9] Henson Papers, Journals, vol. 37, p. 145 (11 Aug. 1924).

Christian party', Temple had declared on the eve of the Conference; 'I want Christians to leaven and control all parties.'[1] The Report, indeed, contained traces of that superior detachment from the bickering squalor of mere politicians which moralists sometimes find it necessary to adopt: 'Parties too often deliberately try to create disagreement where none exist,' wrote the Commissioners; 'in social reform questions, especially, each party tries to outbid the other, and this bidding often comes very near pure money bribery.'[2] The Commission contained Maurice Reckitt and Sir Henry Slesser; it was chaired by Brigadier-General Sir Wyndham Deedes (described, in the list of members, as 'a worker' at Oxford House, Bethnal Green). The fundamental contention of the Report was that the Church could well decide on the need for action in specific fields, but that 'she can hardly claim to be a judge of method'.[3] Further: 'Economic laws do exist', but 'the Church is not the best interpreter of them'.[4] This was too much for some of the enthusiasts. Miss Kenyon, herself a member of the Commission, reminded the Conference that 'The Church is so penetrated by the idea that it must be non-party that it fears to say anything that might coincide with something said by some party'.[5] Professor H. G. Wood of the Birmingham C.O.P.E.C. Committee (as is the way with intellectuals who venture into realities), was impatient with the Conference for not sponsoring the Labour Party, which he called 'a positive engine for good'.[6]

In its attitude to the Divine nature of civil authority the Report claimed nothing that was not insisted upon by the Church of England as traditional teaching throughout the nineteenth century. But it offended the Nonconformists, and criticisms of the Report made at the Conference, on the ground that its view of the State was unsound, evoked loud applause—Temple later observed that he was unable to understand 'either the criticism or the applause'.[7] Members of the Conference imbued with the Dissenters' traditional suspicion of the State, with all their loathing of confessional claims, and allied with left-wing politics, moved to substitute a Resolution describing the State as 'an organization which may be reactionary and may lag behind public opinion'.[8] Temple would not allow it to be put.[9] What the Report had in fact suggested was based upon Scripture: that the State was not just a coercive power to keep order, but that 'the action of the State is to be directed to an end determined by the moral and spiritual character of human nature'.[10] Lord Eustace Percy, the member of the Commission who introduced the Report to the Conference, said 'We believe that the State is not merely the creation of some social contract,

---

[1] *Guardian*, 'C.O.P.E.C. Supplement', 4 Apr. 1924, p. i.
[2] *Politics and Citizenship* (C.O.P.E.C. Report X) (London, 1924), p. 38.
[3] Ibid., p. 45. [4] Ibid., p.46.
[5] *Proceedings*, p. 223. [6] Ibid., p. 228.
[7] Temple, *Essays in Christian Politics*, p. 32. [8] *Proceedings*, p. 218.
[9] Ibid., p. 219. [10] *Report*, p. 4.

but is ordained by God for certain purposes and derives its authority from Him'. In consequence, 'right political action is the duty of every citizen'. But the Nonconformists were really insulted by his further criticism of 'the whole tendency of the last hundred years', which had been 'to decry that God's will has anything to do with the regulation of political societies'.[1] The issue was absolutely basic. For it had, of course, been the policy of the Liberation Society, and of the whole weight of nineteenth-century Dissent, to make just such a denial, in the interests of pulling down the fabric of the confessional State in England. Their view of the State, as a result, was in direct theoretical opposition to the central C.O.P.E.C. ideal: that Christianity should *not* exclude itself from concern with the State and the use of state power for social improvement. The *laissez-faire* view of the State was not as dead as Temple supposed, and the row about the Divine purpose of civil authority brought it all out. Thus H. J. Morland, the Treasurer of C.O.P.E.C., attacked the Report for seeking to establish 'sacred obligations' on 'a rotten foundation'; and he defined the State as 'closely connected with brute force', as concerned with 'mostly matters of secondary importance, things called crimes, and other matters of social convenience'.[2] There was clearly some way still to go before the voice of British Nonconformity would adjust to the ethical idealism required to assemble a state doctrine adequate to construct the fabric of collectivist welfare legislation.

One other aspect of the Report merits comment: its observations on class.

Class divisions are no accidental feature of a modern society: they are an essential element of its present structure [the Report noticed]. We have to face this fact; and when we examine it more closely we must find ourselves unable, either to approve the basis on which those divisions are founded, or to doubt that so long as this basis remains, a proper relationship between the different elements that go to compose society is impossible.[3]

The Conference resolved that the Church 'must use its influence against any recognition of class distinctions which might offer an obstacle to true communion'.[4] There was nothing new here; the Report reflected, again, the preceding tradition of class-consciousness within Church social radicalism. But there was no apparent recognition by the Commission, or the members of the Conference itself, that class differences required much more than mutual esteem to overcome. Class was not linked to economic circumstances very clearly. It is also pertinent to notice the influence of Guild Socialism in the Report—no doubt the work of Reckitt. It emerged in the form of vocationalism, faintly suggestive of the corporatist-state

---

[1] *Proceedings*, p. 215.   [2] Ibid., p. 218.
[3] *Report*, p. 57.   [4] *Proceedings*, p. 290.

doctrines already beginning to enjoy a vogue in Europe. 'Functional associations', the Report declared, 'have a quasi-personality which is not merely a legal fiction, but a vital fact, not created by the State, not merely recognized by it.'[1] These were built into a view of political association.

Political democracy will never fulfil its promises until it is united to a social order in which opportunity is based in no way upon economic power, but is the heritage of all [the Report argued]. In such an order 'Functional' organizations would doubtless supply fresh nuclei to replace the 'class-conscious' solidarities of to-day; social differentiation could become, as it were, vertical rather than horizontal.[2]

The *Industry* Report had also referred to a 'natural grouping according to occupations'[3] as preferable to class society. These ideas were eliminated from most Christian social thought in England—though not in Ireland—when their practical possibilities were demonstrated in Europe.

The same attitude to party politics taken in the tenth Report was pursued in the eleventh, on *The Social Function of the Church*. The Chairman of this Commission, Bishop Kempthorne, said that 'in pleading for the real application of Christian faith and truth to social problems' they only did 'what the Church in its best periods has been doing through the centuries'.[4] The Report explicitly followed the recommendations of the Archbishops' Fifth Report of 1918.[5] 'We cannot agree with those who urge the Church incontinently to throw itself into the arms of some political party,' the Commissioners remarked; 'on the other hand, we again repeat our repudiation of the theory that Christianity has no message except for the individual.'[6] They did also notice 'that it is as possible to "take sides" by inaction or by silence as by speaking or working for the promotion of some policy which (owing to our present system) has become identified with some party'.[7] The eleventh Report, that is to say, was beginning to acquaint C.O.P.E.C. with some of the real complexities of the political questions. The Report also touched, though lightly, on another central issue: whether, in a society of divided or no clear religious affiliation, such as England was becoming, it was proper to use the force of law to compel Christian ideals. C.O.P.E.C., like Temple—who was a 'Church and State' man to the end of his life, and always supposed that England had a Christian Constitution —in general imagined that a Christian society was the only conceivable basis for the sort of social morality it envisaged. 'Certainly the Church has no business to dictate to the State, and if on the question of marriage or any other subject we try to impose "the morality of the Church as such"

---

[1] *Report*, p. 12. [2] Ibid., p. 60.
[3] *Industry and Property*, p. 113. [4] *Proceedings*, p. 232.
[5] *The Social Function of the Church* (C.O.P.E.C. Report XI) (London, 1924), p. 3.
[6] Ibid., p. 44. [7] Ibid., p. 51.

on the whole body politic, we are guilty of the gravest folly', the Report stated. But the Church could use its moral influence collectively, as individual Christians would in their own individual capacities. 'Nor would we wish', the Report continued, 'to force upon the nation a measure which does not appeal so strongly to the conscience of that country that it is able to range the force of enlightened public opinion generally on its side.'[1] In his criticism of C.O.P.E.C. Henson wrote that its programme was proposed 'for acceptance as the policy of a nation, the majority of whose citizens are in no effective sense Christian, that is, lack the essential condition of applying Christian ethics in the life of Society'.[2] The issue was in fact left unclear. Despite the disclaimer made in this Report, Henson's criticism generally hits the mark, for most of the C.O.P.E.C. writing or discussion certainly assumed that the State had a duty to base itself on Christian morality, despite the differences of opinion about the Divine nature of civil authority, and despite the existence in the State of those who dissented from Christian belief. Henson's first impression of the eleventh Report was of its 'immature and doctrinaire' character; explicable, to him, as 'Quaker precedents and Roman methods'.[3]

The eleventh Report also prepared the way for the continuation of C.O.P.E.C. The Revd. Malcolm Spencer, one of the founders of the movement, called for organization by the Churches to spread the C.O.P.E.C. message, to attend to local social needs, to educate the public in social principles, to lead public opinion, to form local committees to carry out the C.O.P.E.C. programme. There was also a need, he maintained, for a research department.[4] Reckitt added his support for a programme of social research,[5] so did Professor Vernon Bartlett—'the special need today is for correlation and co-operation of Christian religion and Social Science'.[6] C.O.P.E.C. became the stimulus for much of the so-called 'Christian Sociology' in the years between the wars.

The twelfth Report, *Historical Illustrations of the Social Effects of Christianity*, appears to have been written largely under the influence of Tawney, who was himself a member of the preparatory Commission. It attempted 'to show how Christian social principles have actually been applied' during the whole period of the Church's history.[7] The findings were predictable. The medieval world most fully enjoined a social message and an economic order conducted according to Christian morality. The Reformation broke it all up; the new commerce of the Protestant nations

---

[1] Ibid., p. 47.   [2] Henson, *Quo Tendimus?*, p. 87.
[3] Henson Papers, Journals, vol. 37, p. 139 (5 Aug. 1924).
[4] *Proceedings*, p. 241.   [5] Ibid., p. 245.
[6] Ibid., p. 249. Bartlett, Professor of Church History, Mansfield College, Oxford, was Chairman of the twelfth Commission.
[7] *Historical Illustrations of the Social Effects of Christianity* (C.O.P.E.C. Report XII) (London, 1924), p. 2.

threw aside moral sanctions. Even though 'the Reformation gave an impetus to the growth of the modern dualism between religion and business', it was conceded, however, 'it did so without design and against the intention of most of the reformers'.[1] The growth of economic individualism in the nineteenth century was explained,[2] and so was 'the reaction from Individualism' after 1870.[3] There was a conclusion: 'the fact that Christian thought as a whole is now once more recovering the great trail from which in some important matters it has been wandering more or less for centuries, makes the possibilities of progress in the immediate future immensely greater than we readily imagine'.[4] C.O.P.E.C. was seen as the great initiator of further advance. It is not surprising, in view of this version of historical preparation for it, that the delegates took the events at Birmingham seriously.

The Reports together constituted a body of ideas and attitudes which, while not especially original or systematic, provided a whole generation with statements of social teaching. In varying degrees of acceptance, they imparted a progressive bias to a lot of Church social opinion. The Birmingham Conference itself was less impressive, and in considering its place in the development of religious opinion it is as well to record the eclectic and often eccentric atmosphere which hovered around it. The Labour movement of the early 1920s was anyway 'a rag-bag of attitudes, purposes, programmes and intentions which were held together by a common language'.[5] C.O.P.E.C. tended to reflect it. The period flavour was very strong—as was the form in which the ideas were expressed. Despite their own belief that their ideals were drawn from the Gospels, the members of C.O.P.E.C. in fact got them, of course, from the attitudes fashionable within the intelligentsia and the professional class of which they were a part. In political character, the members of C.O.P.E.C. tended to reflect the bourgeois or the liberal social-service idealism shared by so many in the moralistic world of public school and University. Yet there was also a strong flavouring of eccentricity, though some went out of their way to deny it. 'At present', Adderley wrote, 'almost anything said by a prophet on social questions is looked upon as freakish.' C.O.P.E.C., he judged, 'would make it difficult' to sustain such a view any more.[6] 'No longer can Christian social reformers be set down as cranks, or as men who dream dreams but refuse to face realities', wrote Keeble.[7] Bishop Woods told Convocation that social theorists 'had been regarded in many quarters if not as faddists, at any rate as idealists and visionaries'—but that was all over now.[8] Lord Eustace Percy had criticized 'the rather feverish explana-

[1] *Historical Illustrations of the Social Effects of Christianity*, p. 103.
[2] Ibid., pp. 133 ff.   [3] Ibid., pp. 144 ff.   [4] Ibid., p. 166.
[5] Maurice Cowling, *The Impact of Labour, 1920–1924* (Cambridge, 1971), p. 28.
[6] *Guardian*, C.O.P.E.C. Supplement, 4 Apr. 1924, p. ii.
[7] Keeble, 'C.O.P.E.C.', p. 16.
[8] *The Chronicle of Convocation, 1924*, p. 228 (7 May).

tion of social problems in which earnest Christians feel compelled to engross themselves to-day'—at the Conference itself.[1] But some of the contributions make it difficult to acquit C.O.P.E.C. There were too many single women with obsessions; there was too much sponsorship of every high-minded panacea, from eugenics (the Eugenics Education Society was well represented)[2] to Esperanto (upheld 'not as a crank but as an incorrigible idealist' by the Revd. W. J. Downer, a Tonbridge Congregationalist Minister).[3] What is to be made of Miss Gollock's plea for them all to regard their servants as 'not merely servants but friends'?[4] Or the attempt to get weekend cottages banned, so that they could be occupied by farm labourers—a scheme put up by the Revd. H. Monks of the Church of England Men's Society?[5] And what of the proposed 'Christian trademarks' to be affixed to goods produced under approved moral conditions;[6] or the advocacy of Major Douglas's Social Credit programme?[7] These things were not suggested simply because they were thought to be interesting ideas, but because their advocates actually claimed they corresponded with the teachings of the Gospels. In such circumstances it was not surprising that the *Christian Science Monitor* should be claimed as the paper nearest to the ideals of C.O.P.E.C.,[8] or that some public-school boys were so excited by the whole enterprise that they sent a donation of £1 from their tuck-shop—a fact reported to the Conference by Miss Gardner, who went on to balance their virtue by disclosing a comparable contribution from a girls' school whose pupils, 'thrilled about it all', had gone out to work to earn something to send to C.O.P.E.C. funds.[9] There was something familiar enough about the speeches advocating sectional interests, on Christian grounds, made at the Conference by such as Miss Zoe Fairfield (S.C.M.); Miss Hodson (Eugenics Education Society); Miss Amy Pennethorne (Parents National Education Union); and Miss Gertrude Eaton (Howard League for Penal Reform). Even Bishop Woods, in his eulogy of C.O.P.E.C. before Convocation, referred to 'indiscretions' and exaggerations made at Birmingham; 'purple passages had been seized upon by certain sections of the Press', he complained.[10] But why not? For although the Reports were in general respectable and, in their way, authoritative documents, the Conference discussions really were characterized by a good deal of sectional eccentricity. This was to have been expected in view of the class moralism of the delegates. Keeble may have asserted that at Birmingham 'there was an entire obliteration of class, racial, and other distinctions',[11] but in reality, of course, the delegates' radicalism and social conscience represented class characteristics. The delegates were certainly

[1] *Proceedings*, p. 217.   [2] Ibid., p. 68.   [3] Ibid., p. 66.
[4] Ibid., p. 93.   [5] Ibid., p. 102.   [6] Ibid., p. 204.
[7] Ibid., p. 210.   [8] Ibid., p. 235.   [9] Ibid., p. 9.
[10] *The Chronicle of Convocation, 1924*, p. 229 (7 May).
[11] Keeble, 'C.O.P.E.C.', p. 7.

not classless, as indeed was clearly revealed when the Revd. T. W. Roff of Manchester bluntly asked 'How many of the Conference have been unemployed?',[1] in response to all the solemn analysis of the unemployment question given off by the delegates. And Lord Tavistock, representing the Y.M.C.A., after giving his attention to the speeches, said that 'many of the clergy did not recognize the limited vocabulary of the masses'.[2] Yet the delegates were all supposed to be, in Raven's unhappy phrase, 'God's storm-troops'.[3]

The members of the C.O.P.E.C. movement believed themselves to be espousing unpopular ideas—though not, of course, because of their own occasional eccentricities, which they often seem not to have noticed. They derived a grim pleasure from contemplating the opposition their championship of truth would meet. 'The scoffers will fail,' wrote Adderley, 'because the whole trend of knowledge and the lessons of experience are on the side of those who, with C.O.P.E.C., are returning to the principles of Christ.'[4] Keeble, in his account of the Conference, affirmed that it had 'stirred up that unsleeping opposition to Christian Social Reform which exists within as well as outside the borders of the Churches themselves'.[5] Gore, at Birmingham, 'solemnly asked the assembly whether it was ready for the consequences—scorn, misunderstanding and hostility'. C.O.P.E.C., he declared, had learned 'to live dangerously'.[6] Bishop Hamilton Baynes, of the Birmingham Committee, reminded the Conference that their ideas 'were far ahead of the bulk of the people', and that they 'would have to go back to puzzled folk who would, many of them, think them dreadful'.[7]

In reality, of course, the C.O.P.E.C. movement was well received within the Churches, and in the Church of England the only appreciable reservations came from those like Davidson, who doubted if there was much point in repeating again social principles already well approved within the Church. No doubt some were additionally suspicious of Temple's ascendancy in the movement. Bishop Frank Weston, the Anglo-Catholic leader, 'expected nothing but talk' from C.O.P.E.C.[8] Will Spens, later Master of Corpus Christi College in Cambridge, and a leading Anglo-Catholic layman, was privately 'resentful of Copec'.[9] Most Anglo-Catholics stood in a tradition of social concern and were warmly in favour, however. The Church press generally gave support,[10] and there was journalistic appraisal

[1] *Proceedings*, p. 205.   [2] Ibid., p. 247.
[3] Quoted in Henson's *Quo Tendimus?*, p. 112.
[4] *Guardian*, 'C.O.P.E.C. Supplement', 4 Apr. 1924, p. ii.
[5] Keeble, 'C.O.P.E.C.', p. 9.
[6] Quoted ibid., p. 14.   [7] *Proceedings*, p. 199.
[8] Maynard Smith, *Frank, Bishop of Zanzibar*, p. 312.
[9] Henson Papers, Journals, vol. 37, p. 27 (4 May 1924). Henson added, 'but I cannot lightly believe in the candour of an Anglo-Catholic!'
[10] See *British Weekly*, 17 Apr. 1924: 'C.O.P.E.C.—Some Reflections', by the Revd. F. C. Spurr.

from even the most secular sources.[1] The movement clearly achieved one of its objectives: many who had never really absorbed the social radicalism characteristic of Church leadership (and therefore mostly clerical), now opened themselves to it. For such persons it often came as quite new. R. G. Longman, the publisher of the C.O.P.E.C. Reports, attended the Conference himself and afterwards wrote to Temple to say 'I have a feeling that for a long time the Church has started at the wrong end of the stick by telling people to be converted and then to start out to do good . . . for some years I have been profoundly uncomfortable about Industry, and only gradually has the thought penetrated that Christ's way is the only way'.[2] This view can be taken as typical of the new enthusiasm of those laymen who first came to the Social Gospel ideals in 1924. But it was also amongst the laity that the greatest resistance was encountered; among those still loyal to economic individualism, and resentful of the intellectuals' simple moralism. English dislike of clerical 'interference' in secular matters was not to be overcome so easily as C.O.P.E.C. seemed to assume. Another of Temple's admirers, a year later, wrote to him about the resistance he was meeting, as a member of the Barnet Parish Council, in trying to get the C.O.P.E.C. programme adopted. The Council, apparently, reflected 'the prevalent charge against the C.O.P.E.C. outlook that it is a dislocation of the appeal for individual conversion and dedication'.[3] The penetration of the new idealism was imperfect.

The most distinguished opponent of 'the C.O.P.E.C. outlook' was Hensley Henson. He had refused an invitation to attend the Conference because he regarded it as 'the worst conceivable method of arriving at the truth'.[4] He had also refused to allow the diocese of Durham to send official delegates. At the time of the Conference, in April 1924, Henson was immersed in the preparation of his Rede Lecture on Byron.[5] It was not until August that he got round to reading the C.O.P.E.C. Reports, with the intention of devoting the second part of his Primary *Charge* to a criticism of them. 'I want to challenge the main assumption of "C.O.P.E.C",' he wrote in his journal, as he read through the Reports, 'that the Christian Revelation includes adequate direction on political and economic matters.' Then he intended to examine the 'actual policies' proposed, to reveal a 'paradox'—'they require the surplus wealth gained by "industrialism" for their social schemes while they labour to destroy "industrialism" by

---

[1] See *Freethinker*, 18 May 1924.

[2] Temple Papers, Folder marked 'C.O.P.E.C. 1924', Longman to Temple, 17 Apr. 1924.

[3] Ibid., Cyril L. M. Roxby to Temple, 'Tuesday before Easter' 1925.

[4] Henson Papers, Letter Books (July 1923–Dec. 1924), Henson to Miss Lucy Gardner, 6 Dec. 1923.

[5] Henson Papers, Journals, vol. 36 (1 Oct. 1923–20 Apr. 1924), pp. 213 ff. The Lecture was delivered in Cambridge on 3 May.

disallowing its motives and methods'. He also supposed that the ideal Christian man, envisaged by C.O.P.E.C., would be one deprived of personal liberty and personal responsibility.[1] Another theme suggested itself as he read the Reports:

The parallel between 'Christianity' as represented by 'C.O.P.E.C.', and 'Labour' as represented by its extremists is suggestively close in at least one important particular. Both insist on a distinctive and isolated handling of history and politics. They will not accept the general stream of human tradition, and take their place within it; but must vindicate a separate point of view, a recognizable distinct influence and objective. The result is bad enough in the case of 'Labour', for the particularist temper known as 'class-consciousness' obliterates the frontiers of right and wrong; and leads (as in the conspicuous case of Russia) to the most shocking violations of the moral law. Can the result be wholesome in the case of Christianity? Will not this passionate insistence on a definitely 'Christian' version of every human concern carry those who make it into the difficult business of life with minds closed to truth, and obsessed with politics which are not in any genuine sense Christian at all?[2]

Further reflection confirmed another impression, that the recent past had witnessed a substantial slide in Christian attitudes:

The demand is made, and pressed ever more insistently that the direction and emphasis of Christian teaching should be transferred from the personal to the social implications of Christ's Religion; that the redemption of Society should be dwelt upon rather than the salvation of the individual: that the 'Kingdom of God' should be set up visibly and by direct action in the economic and political spheres.[3]

Antipathy to these positions never departed from Henson. His *Charge*, delivered in November 1924, developed the criticism of C.O.P.E.C. and 'the grandiose scale and audacious character of its proposed programme'.[4] He correctly pointed to the lack of originality in the social creed of the movement. 'Whatever novelty "C.O.P.E.C." possessed was not so much in the substance of its message, as in the method of its messengers and the magnitude of its claim.'[5] This claim, in fact, amounted to saying that 'The Kingdom of Christ on Earth would be established according to plan'; every detail of the Christian life was to be laid down, as exclusively the right and moral course.[6] But the main C.O.P.E.C. assumption, that 'the Gospel provides the Christian with the solution of all the problems involved in our earthly life',[7] was a false one, Henson asserted, and the true position reversed. For it 'is fundamental in Christ's religion that the redemption of the world must be effected through the redemption of indi-

---

[1] Henson Papers, Journals, vol. 37 (21 Apr.–6 Sept. 1924), p. 141 (8 Aug. 1924).
[2] Ibid., p. 142 (9 Aug. 1924).   [3] Ibid., p. 145 (11 Aug. 1924).
[4] Henson, *Quo Tendimus?*.   [5] Ibid., p. 78.
[6] Ibid., p. 80.   [7] Ibid., p. 84.

viduals'.[1] C.O.P.E.C., on the contrary, 'enters the arena of current politics, formulates for Christian citizens an elaborate programme of civic action covering the whole field of national life'.[2] This was not only foolish, it was also irresponsible—the members of the Conference had felt themselves 'free to indulge the luxury of programme-framing without reference to those obstinate facts which a responsible statesman, tied to the necessity of carrying his policies into practice, must needs consider'.[3] They had not considered the cost of their social reforms: had they done so they would not 'have been content to leave this crucial matter of "ways and means" in such obscurity'.[4] He then described the 'paradox' of those who sought to appropriate the wealth of an industrial system and yet who sought to destroy its wealth-producing qualities. 'The critics of "Industrialism" are so obsessed by its darker features that they do not perceive its substantial merits.'[5] Christ had laid down no specific plan of social order. Henson's *Charge* was of uneven quality, but a lot of his arrows found the target. He did, it is true, rather undervalue the contributions made by the Reports, tending to suppose that the eccentricities and enthusiasms of the Conference were typical of the whole undertaking. Thus W. M. Pryke, Rector of Risby and a delegate at Birmingham, who was invited by the editor of the *Modern Churchman* to compose a critique of Henson's critique—a task which he performed rather indifferently—could write that 'one who had learned about C.O.P.E.C. for the first time by a perusal of the Bishop's Charge would be left with the impression that the personnel of the Conference consisted of a heterogeneous collection of unbalanced enthusiasts, persons altogether ignorant of the real nature of the problems which they presumed to discuss'.[6] That was only half the truth.

The value and importance of C.O.P.E.C. lay in its propagandist influence. 'I am sure', said Temple in 1928, about the results of the movement 'that there are many Christian folk seriously thinking about these things who had never dreamed of doing so before.'[7] C.O.P.E.C. popularized the old C.S.U. ideals, and they reached further into the Church—though it is difficult to say exactly how far, in view of the rank-and-file resistance founded upon reservations similar to Henson's. C.O.P.E.C.'s practical success, on the other hand, was negligible; it remained, as the old C.S.U. had been, too academic, and too conscious of its own supposed novelty. Gore had warned the Conference that the movement 'would be judged by its practical work'—for which he 'trembled', he added.[8] It had always been intended that the Conference would be followed up by a quasi-permanent

[1] Ibid., p. 86.   [2] Ibid., p. 87.   [3] Ibid., p. 95.
[4] Ibid., p. 96.   [5] Ibid., p. 98.
[6] W. M. Pryke, 'Dr. Henson and C.O.P.E.C.', in the *Modern Churchman*, xiv, No. 10 (Jan. 1925), 557.
[7] Iremonger, *Men and Movements in the Church*, p. 28.
[8] *Proceedings*, p. 212.

organization,[1] and as early as June 1921 Temple had informed Davidson of the possibility of a 'Continuation Committee' to be set up in 1924.[2] This duly came to pass. At the closing of the Conference Miss Gardner outlined a scheme for regional Conferences to follow up the work—the first was to be at Ipswich on 12 May, and twelve others were already arranged for later in the year.[3] These were to be interdenominational ventures; the separate Churches were also to be encouraged to develop C.O.P.E.C. ideals independently.[4] There were a few practical results. In Birmingham the movement set up a 'House Improvement Society' to purchase and renovate slum properties and to let them to the needy.[5] In one London borough a group of C.O.P.E.C. sympathizers approached the Council with a demand that their rates should be increased in order to pay for housing improvements for the poor.[6] The Continuation Committee arranged a number of Conferences on specific issues, too. There were also publications inspired by C.O.P.E.C. Committees—the most famous of these was Henry Mess's *Industrial Tyneside*, published in 1928 after an impressive and extensive survey of the conditions of life and work in the north-east. Even Henson praised it.[7] An additional C.O.P.E.C. Report on *Rural Life*, added to the other twelve in 1927, was less impressive and very doctrinaire. There had been those at Birmingham who had recognized the neglect of rural society,[8] and the 1927 Report sought to put this right. Written under the inspiration of the Chairman of the preparatory Commission, Noel Buxton (who had joined the Labour Party in 1920), it put the case for nationalization of agricultural land. 'Under public ownership of the land,' the Report claimed, 'the landlord's duties will be taken over by the State and the result of this transference will be seen in the provision of up-to-date equipment, improved buildings, and a well-drained soil.'[9] C.O.P.E.C. also published some *Present Day Papers*, including one on 'Democracy' by Temple, in 1926, which defended democratic government against the growth of Fascism in Italy and Communism in Russia.[10] But the C.O.P.E.C.

[1] See *C.O.P.E.C. and the Immediate Future*, a pamphlet put out by the Committee in 1924.

[2] Davidson Papers, 1921/3, Temple to Davidson, 15 June 1921.

[3] *Proceedings*, p. 266. There is a mention of the West Ham Conference in David Sheppard, *Built as a City. God and the Urban World Today*, p. 109.

[4] For the Nonconformists' hopes, see *Manchester Guardian*, 23 Apr. 1924: 'The Free Churches—C.O.P.E.C. and After'. For the first attempts in the Church of England, see Bishop Kempthorne's address on C.O.P.E.C. to the Canterbury Diocesan Conference reported in *The Times*, 27 June 1924. And Bishop W. W. Hough (of Woolwich) on 'Problems of Today' at the 1924 Church Congress; *The Official Report of the Church Congress, Oxford 1924*, especially pp. 41 and 45. The Congress met at the end of September.

[5] Oliver, *The Church and Social Order*, p. 72; Lloyd, *The Church of England*, p. 325.

[6] Temple, *Christianity and Social Order*, p. 19.

[7] Lloyd, *The Church of England*, p. 361.   [8] *Proceedings*, p. 205.

[9] *Rural Life, A Report prepared by a Commission appointed by the C.O.P.E.C. Continuation Committee* (London, 1927), p. 13.

[10] 'Democracy', repr. in Temple, *Essays in Christian Politics*, p. 68.

Committees were rapidly running out of steam, and it is only because he was considering the stature of Temple himself, and his reputation as a social thinker, that Bishop Bell was able to write of the 'far-reaching results' of the C.O.P.E.C. organization.[1]

The permanent result of C.O.P.E.C. was in fact Temple's leadership of the Church of England. That is why it is so important in the development of the social teachings of the Church. As an institutionalized movement for Christian social action it failed—in 1929 it was formally wound up, and its work passed to the 'Christian Social Council'. 'The weakness of "C.O.P.E.C." has been that it is "C.O.P.E.C." and not the Church,' wrote H. W. Fox in 1925; 'it speaks as the scribes and not with authority; its voice is that of experts, experts in Christianity, experts in some department of economics, politics or citizenship, but they do not possess official credentials.'[2] Raven believed that the movement declined because its members relied too greatly on Biblical texts and not on 'the new cosmology, anthropology, psychology and sociology of the twentieth century'.[3] That was a superfluous, as well as a foolish explanation. The decline was to some extent to be attributed to Temple himself. Between 1919 and 1924 he had sustained the entire movement with a gigantic energy. After the Conference he seems to have become wary of the political ambiguities into which he was running, and to have pulled back. He became more critical and by the time of his elevation of the archiepiscopal see of York, in 1929, there were some who thought they discerned a decline in his social interests, 'This was never for a moment true,' Peck later wrote of these suppositions; 'but he certainly found himself in perplexity as he strove to apply his ethico-social Idealism to the intractible problems rising on every side'[4]—which is a way of saying that he began to realize that social questions did not have easy solutions.

[1] 'Memoir' of William Temple, by George Bell, in *William Temple and His Message*, ed. A. E. Baker (London, 1946), p. 21.

[2] H. W. Fox, *Christianity in Politics* (London, 1925), p. 91.

[3] Raven, 'C.O.P.E.C. Then and Now—II', in *Crucible*, Jan. 1963, p. 12.

[4] W. G. Peck, 'William Temple as Social Thinker', in *William Temple: An Estimate and Appreciation*, ed. Matthews, p. 64.

8

Between the Wars: Social and Political Ideas

The acceptance of radical attitudes towards social questions within the Church's leadership, extended and given an interdenominationalism by C.O.P.E.C., continued its ascendancy through the 1920s and 1930s. The 'Christian Socialist' tradition also developed during these years according to a series of studies and conferences which became known, collectively, as 'Christian Sociology'. And to the left of those whom Dean Inge, in his crticism of Tawney, rather accurately called 'armchair Socialists',[1] were the surviving groups of socialist militants in the League of the Kingdom of God, and in Conrad Noel's Thaxted movement. But events themselves tempered the heady enthusiasm: the General Strike and the Depression revealed not only the true complexity of most of the economic questions which Church leaders had tended to simplify, but also showed the gulf which had been opened between the ordinary assumptions of the lay world and the Church's leadership. There was, in consequence, a slight recession, and much more reserve, in the advocacy of social radicalism by the clergy during the 1930s. This was not a decisive change: it was a matter of adjustment, of tone and emphasis. A lot of the optimism had gone. 'Christian teachers are apt to observe that if everyone would accept Christianity our economic difficulties would solve themselves,' wrote F. R. Barry in 1931; 'but unless the Churches show themselves capable of constructive and realistic thinking to vindicate these enormous generalizations they are bound to appear futile and almost meaningless.'[2] P. T. R. Kirk, the General Director of the Industrial Christian Fellowship, and a prominent Christian Socialist, was also touched by the new realism. 'We trust to conferences and are disappointed', he wrote in a compendium of essays on the economic Depression, edited by Percy Dearmer in 1933; 'schemes fondly believed likely to save society at last are heralded with the ringing of bells, but they are shelved almost as soon as formulated.'[3] In 1932 Bishop George Bell of Chichester, one of the Presidents of the ecumenical and international 'Life

---

[1] W. R. Inge, *Lay Thoughts of a Dean*, popular edn. (London, 1933), p. 208.

[2] F. R. Barry, *The Relevance of Christianity. An Approach to Christian Ethics*, revd. edn. (London, 1936), p. 284. Barry, who was a Canon of Westminster, was one of the most popular Church writers of the period; later he became Bishop of Southwell.

[3] P. T. R. Kirk, 'The Social and Economic Confusion', in *Christianity and the Crisis*, ed. Percy Dearmer (London, 1933), p. 99.

and Work' Council, actually refused to sign the report on *The Churches and the World Economic Crisis* on the ground that its arguments were purely economic, and not distinctively Christian.[1] In the preceding year Cyril Garbett, Bishop of Southwark, and the Church's main spokesman on housing problems, had emphasized that the Church did 'not exist to promote some particular political or economic principles, but to proclaim the Gospel of Christ and through the power of God to change, uplift and transform men and women'.[2] It was not that men like these had abandoned their social criticism: it was simply that they now recognized more of the difficulties. They also saw, to some extent, that they were in mixed company; that the temper of the political and social world from which they drew their terms of reference was not so easily accommodated as they had once thought. C.O.P.E.C. had enshrined the belief that social and economic experts would provide the basis for the new Christian view of society. But in 1935 V. A. Demant, Director of Research of the Christian Social Council, declared bluntly 'Scratch an expert today and you will find a moralist, though not a Christian one, and not generally one who knows that he is a moralist'.[3] One of the most popular attitudes of the previous decades of Christian social radicalism involved the belief that the Church had been too 'other-worldly', too pietistic to become concerned with the nasty realities of social evils. In this assumption, too, there was for many an adjustment. 'The only Church that could abolish Exploitation, War, Slums and Unemployment would be one that was in this world but not of it,' wrote Dick Sheppard in 1935; 'if it had maintained its other-worldly character it could long ago have torn these things out by the roots.'[4] Events in Europe—the collapse of democratic governments—appeared to reinforce the growing sense of caution amongst Church leaders. 'We have suffered so many disillusionments', Lang said, when he was Archbishop of Canterbury in 1935, in a review of the Italian invasion of Abyssinia.[5] In 1937 Maurice Reckitt summarized the new situation.

The call made by the Christian reformer to his fellows a generation back to identify themselves with the social movements of their age was, on the whole, a justifiable one, even independently of the validity of the particular programme for which those movements stood. For it emphasised an aspect of human life which religion and society had alike tended to leave on one side, to the grave disadvantage of both. But today it is precisely the social movements of the age which exhibit that age's most destructive characteristics. No longer are the

---

[1] Ronald C. D. Jasper, *George Bell, Bishop of Chichester* (London, 1967), p. 99.
[2] Cyril F. Garbett, *In the Heart of South London* (London, 1931), p. 132.
[3] *Faith that Illuminates*, ed. V. A. Demant (London, 1935), p. 14.
[4] H. R. L. Sheppard, *If I were Dictator* (London, 1935), p. 20.
[5] *Christianity in the Modern State*, ed. Maxwell S. Leigh (A Report of the Proceedings of the Church Congress, Bournemouth, Oct. 1935) (London, 1936), p. 74.

organized efforts after social change permeated by Christian aspirations and manned by those nurtured in the atmosphere, if not of Christian doctrine, at least of Christian ethics.[1]

The change of atmosphere was not universal, however; nor was it complete. In the years between the wars the leadership of the Church continued to retain a general adhesion to quite radical social criticism. 'The cause which I plead,' said Gore in 1927, 'is a cause which has been vocal in the religious world since the days, at least, of Frederick Maurice.'[2] The old impetus was still there; Christian Socialism, in some guise or other, still held an allurement. In 1923 Ramsay MacDonald and the Labour Party, when they became, for the first time, the official parliamentary Opposition, were sent the formal congratulations of 510 Anglican priests. Ten of those who signed later became bishops.[3] Baldwin remarked on the popularity of that aspect of Christianity 'which takes into view all kinds of activities for the social betterment of the people'—and added, with great truth, that there were among politicians and 'especially among the Labour Party, many men who fifty years ago would inevitably have gone into the Christian ministry'.[4] All the ideas which had excited Church opinion in the preceding decades were reproduced again in the years following C.O.P.E.C. The Bishop of Plymouth, J. M. B. Masterman, even went so far as to predict, in 1926, that the Church's 'long-standing alliance with the Conservative Party is gradually coming to an end'[5]—and that was after almost fifty years in which it had been difficult to find any sort of coherent political Conservatism in the leadership of the Church at all. But the assumption that a reaction was needed against established political and social values was still necessary for many Christians, who were apparently able to ignore the fact that the views for which they contended had held the field within the leadership of the Church since the 1880s. Masterman, indeed, also showed his dependence on existing custom when he maintained that 'the programme of the Labour Party constitutes a challenge to the present economic system, and to the whole structure of society'.[6] This opinion was offered at a time when most lay politicians of the Left were in fact extremely disillusioned with Labour, following the first Labour Government of 1924 and the apparent revelation that it did not constitute a challenge to the present economic system.

The publication of Tawney's *Religion and the Rise of Capitalism* in 1926

---

[1] Maurice B. Reckitt, *Religion in Social Action* (London, 1937), p. 154.

[2] Charles Gore, *Christ and Society* (London, 1928), p. 163 (the Halley Stewart Lectures, 1927).

[3] Oliver, *The Church and Social Order*, pp. 968, 118.

[4] Stanley Baldwin, *On England, And other Addresses* (London, 1926), p. 196.

[5] J. M. B. Masterman, 'The Church and Political and Economic Problems', in *The Future of the Church of England*, ed. Sir James Marchant (London, 1926,) p. 156.

[6] Ibid., p. 151.

was important. It was the most systematic, and most well-known statement of one doctrine essential to the structure of Church social radicalism since the mid-nineteenth century. It was a historical explanation of the transition from the medieval practice of Christian economic teachings to modern competitive individualism. Economics and religion had then become separated with the unhappy result reported by every Christian Socialist—and many others not of that school: 'its essence is a dualism which regards the secular and religious aspects of life, not as successive stages within a large unity, but as parallel and independent provinces, governed by different laws, judged by different standards, and amenable to different authorities'.[1] Tawney's analysis had been composed in 1922 and delivered as the Scott Holland Memorial Lectures. He dedicated the book to Gore. It was when he was up at Balliol that Tawney had come under Gore's influence in Oxford. Three years at Toynbee Hall, membership of the Labour Party, a lectureship (and later a chair) at the L.S.E., and friendship with Temple,[2] gave Tawney the essential qualifications, quite apart from his extraordinary intellectual and personal qualities, for being the Anglican layman who most influenced academic opinion within the Church in the years between the wars. His other books, notably his *Acquisitive Society* (1921), and *Equality* (1931), were absorbed within the canon of works which those interested in social criticism took as essential reference. The 'Protestant ethic' explanation of modern economic individualism was not, of course, original to Tawney. It was expounded by Max Weber and by Ernst Troeltsch,[3] and in some form or other had been lying around in nineteenth-century popular thought—William Cobbett, for example, argued a similar case against the social effects of Protestantism.[4] But Tawney's book gave a final and authoritative *imprimatur*. Within the Church few criticized it—although historians have never quite assimilated it. Ernest Barker told the Bournemouth Church Congress in 1935 that he doubted whether, 'as some have contended, Puritanism was the nursing mother of Capitalism'. He also remarked that Protestantism, in that stage of its development, 'was hardly a religion of social sympathy'.[5] Roman Catholics anxious to propagate the ideals of state corporatism, were especially fortunate beneficiaries of the Tawney thesis. 'It was but natural that the social institutions which had grown out of the ideals of Christianity would find but little sympathy in

---

[1] R. H. Tawney, *Religion and the Rise of Capitalism. A Historical Study*, revd. edn. (London, 1944), p. 279.

[2] See Temple's praise of *Religion at the Rise of Capitalism* in his *Christianity and the State* (London, 1928), p. 1; and the use he made of Tawney's historical evidence in *Christianity and Social Order*, p. 8.

[3] See Gore's introductory note to the English edition of Ernst Troeltsch's *The Social Teaching of the Christian Churches* (London, 1931), vol. 1.

[4] See Cobbett, *A History of the Protestant 'Reformation' in England and Ireland* (1826).

[5] Ernest Barker 'Christianity and Economics', in *Christianity in the Modern State*, p. 172.

an atmosphere of individualism,' wrote one noted Irish Catholic. 'Under the guise of liberty, the unbridled licence of the individual developed into heartless oppression of the weak.'[1] He meant the Reformation.

This was the sort of thing that Gore used to say in the early years of the century but with a socialist, not a corporatist purpose. He said them still. In 1927 his own Halley Stewart Lectures, called *Christ and Society*, unfolded the message he had proclaimed unaltered throughout his life. How he looked for radical social change to come 'from the influence in society of groups of men, inspired probably by prophetic leaders, who have attained to a true vision of the source of our evils'.[2] His actual proposals were those made in the C.O.P.E.C. movement.[3] All the old familiar themes can be found in the writings of the period, in fact.[4] W. G. Peck was still urging the overthrow of 'other-worldly' pietism—for the material world had, for him, a 'sacramental significance'[5] so great that the Holy Eucharist was itself a 'protest against Capitalist industrialism'.[6] Conrad Noel did actually suggest that the influence of pietism had diminished a little, 'but many utterances of bishops and clergy might be quoted in this year of grace 1939, to show that the pulpit rings with the same kind of teaching'.[7] For the Nonconformists, Alfred Garvie's massive study of *The Christian Ideal for Human Society*, published in 1930, carried on the tradition of social criticism. Garvie, who was Dean of the Faculty of Theology in London University, had been a member of the Executive Committee of C.O.P.E.C. His book asked the usual questions. 'The Christian Church has been too content with, too acquiescent in, the existing order of society,' he wrote. 'The more advanced and sensitive Christian conscience is compelled to cast down the challenge: can a competitive industrial system, an acquisitive society, realise the Christian ideal of equal love to self and neighbour?'[8] The familiar question had a familiar answer: Nonconformity was rapidly assimilating the social attitudes which had dominated the leadership of the Church of England since the end of the nineteenth century.

The leading socialist movement in the Church of England was now the

---

[1] A. M. Crofts, O.P., *Catholic Social Action. Principles, Purpose and Practice* (London, 1936), p. 75.

[2] Gore, *Christ and Society*, p. 16.

[3] Ibid., p. 169.

[4] As noticed by Malcolm Muggeridge: "Denunciations of slums from the pulpit have been more common than denunciations of sin'—*The Thirties, 1930–1940, in Great Britain*, [1940], (London, 1972), p. 35.

[5] W. G. Peck, 'Fellowship and Sacrifice', in *The Social Teaching of the Sacraments, being the Report of the Second Anglo-Catholic Summer School of Sociology, held at Keble College, Oxford, July, 1926*. ed. Maurice Reckitt (London, 1927), p. 122.

[6] Ibid., p. 125.

[7] Conrad Noel, *Jesus the Heretic* (London, 1939), p. 10.

[8] Alfred E. Garvie, *The Christian Ideal for Human Society* (London, 1930), p. 397.

'Christendom Group'—constituted from members of the Church Socialist League, just before the League was itself transformed into the League of the Kingdom of God. It was Fr. Widdrington who first seems to have suggested the idea of a comprehensive study of the ideals of medieval Christian society, and it was he who called together the group of Anglo-Catholics to discussions at Coggeshall in Essex during 1920. They published their findings in 1922, under the title which gave the group its lasting identity: *The Return of Christendom*. They were, as Gore remarked in his introduction to the essays, 'all socialists in a general sense'. But when he went on to define just what he meant by that, it became clear that their socialism was the usual Anglican eclectic mixture. 'That is to say,' Gore wrote, 'they are all at one in believing that no stable or healthy industrial or social fabric can be built upon the principle of Individualism, or is consistent with the assertion of an almost unrestricted Right of Private Property.'[1] But the writers also 'repudiate the ideal of Communism and the older ideal of State Socialism, as both of them tending to bureaucracy and tyranny'.[2] The result, of course, was the familiar 'Christian Socialist' one: they were full of ideas and social criticism but had no adequate concept of state sovereignty or of the power and civil coercion required to introduce any of their panaceas. The Christendom writers were Maurice Reckitt, Henry Slesser, L. S. Thornton, P. E. T. Widdrington, A. J. Carlyle, A. J. Penty, Niles Carpenter, and Paul Bull. G. K. Chesterton wrote an 'Epilogue'. None of them really said anything in their essays which they had not said before, but they were not without realization of the difficulties germane to attempting a resuscitation of medieval social ideas. 'The subjection of the community to capitalist industrialism and the distortion of property by plutocracy', Reckitt wrote, 'have made the very conception of Christendom not only unrealizable, but for the majority of men today even incomprehensible.'[3] Things were, in fact, felt to be so bad that Fr. Paul Bull of the Community of the Resurrection employed characteristically exaggerated language to declare that 'the doom of a Godless civilization is sealed'.[4] Reckitt, in his autobiography, acknowledged the weaknesses of the book: 'it came too soon . . . our new sociology was quite undeveloped'.[5] But this was hardly the case. It was not original enough for that to be said with any accuracy. It really restated, once more, social beliefs which have been heard within the Church for a couple of decades. The book was widely read, however, and helped still further to spread the ideals of Church social radicalism. It also confirmed the Group as the leaders of the Christian

---

[1] *The Return of Christendom by a Group of Churchmen* (London, 1922): Introduction, p. 9.
[2] Ibid., p. 10.
[3] Ibid., 'The Idea of Christendom in Relation to Modern Society', by Maurice B. Reckitt, p. 20.
[4] Ibid., 'The Kingdom of God and the Church Today', by Paul Bull, p. 241.
[5] Reckitt, *As It Happened*, p. 261.

Socialist movement. In 1931 a quarterly was started—*Christendom. A Journal of Christian Sociology*; and from the following year, annual summer conferences were held at St. Leonards-on-Sea.[1] Like most radicals within the Church, the Group tended to see themselves as battling heroically against entrenched opposition. In reality, of course, their ideas were generally greeted with respect and clothed in respectability.

For the movement of 'Christian Sociology', which they did so much to foster, and which in Maurice Reckitt had an effective popularizer, was sympathetically accommodated by Church leadership. C.O.P.E.C. had called for more Christian research into social questions, and the writers of Christian Sociology in the 1920s and 1930s to some extent complied—so that even by 1928 Temple could say that 'one of the most prominent features of recent religious history has been the steadily increasing effort to recover something like a real Christian sociology'.[2] What in fact he meant by this was the whole movement of opinion since the mid-nineteenth century, but his use of the new term indicates the extent to which contemporaries were conscious of a new attempt to direct Church social thinking. Christian 'Sociology' was not really sociology. It was not, that is to say, a quantitative and comparative study of society and opinion. It was normative, propagandist, not descriptive: but it was a serious attempt to define distinctly *Christian* principles of society, derived from Christian doctrine, and not just an attempt to conflate Christianity with secular social ideas. It rarely reached anything like that sort of goal, however, and most of the writings of the period which claimed the label of 'Christian Sociology' turned out to be the sort of moralistic social criticism which had been produced in the Church for decades.

From 1925 the annual 'Anglo-Catholic Summer Schools of Sociology' set themselves, in Charles Raven's words, 'to attempt to do what we tried to do when we first projected C.O.P.E.C., to start with certain eternal verities involving the very nature and operation of God, and to see how far we can formulate the consequences of those principles in terms of the social problems with which we are confronted'.[3] In 1926 an interdenominational dimension was given to 'Christian Sociology' by the establishment of the annual Social Service Lectures. The trustees were appointed by the Wesleyan Methodist Conference, but the lecturers were drawn from the various Protestant bodies. They made a distinguished contribution.

'There is still a colossal task before the Church in arousing the Christian community to the existence of and the possibility of redeeming the more flagrant social evils,' wrote Demant in 1934. 'In this respect one of the tasks of Christian Sociology is to discover as widely as possible how far

---

[1] Reckitt, *P. E. T. Widdrington*, p. 113.
[2] Temple, *Christianity and the State*, p. 1.
[3] C. E. Raven, 'Calling and Duty', in *The Social Teaching of the Sacraments*, p. 73.

evil social conditions can be traced to the motives and methods of people actually concerned with those conditions in positions of control or administration.'[1] This last aspiration was one suggesting genuine sociological inquiry—though it remained unfulfilled. The real intention was normative: to convert the Church to radical social principles. The object of Christian Sociology, according to Demant, was 'to decide which particular political structure best directs the community to order its life', and, as a consequence, the Church had 'a prophetic duty' and was 'justified in intervening in political affairs'.[2] Demant was, in addition to being Director of Research in the Christian Social Council, also a member of the Editorial Board of *Christendom*. He was a long way removed from the rather inept thinking of a lot of Christian Socialists. Demant had a clarity of mind, and a knowledge of political philosophy, which enabled him to get to the heart of many of the theoretical problems of political association. He attacked the C.O.P.E.C. view of the State, for example, for its impractical insistence that the duty of the State was to uphold 'some moral order'. This was not possible within the present terms of reference, which were also the ones agreeable to C.O.P.E.C. 'The State, in the theory at least of modern democracy, is the executor of the prevalent public will,' Demant wrote. 'If that public will is divided about what constitutes "the good life", to define the purpose of the State as "some moral order" is not a very practical guide for political conduct.'[3] It was a situation he lamented, but which he had the clarity of mind to recognize—most of those with whom he co-operated did not.

The question of state authority introduced a curious conclusion to the thought of most Christian Socialist writers. It was that once the problem of identifying the true Christian social order had been solved, the State would simply adopt it. They tended to assume the continuing obligation of the State to profess Christianity. Reckitt, who derived a lot of his ideas from Demant, like him, saw the problem. 'If the development of a Christian sociology is to be a genuine achievement of the twentieth century,' he observed in 1932, 'its emergence will necessitate clear thinking upon the degree to which such a body of teaching is held to be applicable to Christian people only, or to society as a whole.'[4] Yet he had little doubt about the proper course.

We are bound to claim, not merely that the Christian citizen shall continue to act as a Christian while he is functioning as a citizen, but that the Christian Community shall combine to make the whole community of which it is—or at least

---

[1] V. A. Demant, *God, Man and Society. An Introduction to Christian Sociology* (Milwaukee, 1934), p. 12.
[2] Ibid., p. 177.
[3] Ibid., p. 92.
[4] Maurice B. Reckitt, *Faith and Society* (London, 1932), p. 249.

aspires to become—the conscience, face up to and embrace the consequences of such moral and economic truth as it is capable of recognizing.[1]

Fr. Widdrington had been equally addicted to a confessional view of the State in his own contribution to *The Return of Christendom*. 'The revival of the influence of the Church on national and international affairs will follow when once the Kingdom of God becomes the regulative idea of our theology and propaganda: to demonstrate, in a word [sic], that upon the effective republication of the Gospel depends the force of civilization.'[2] 'The Church', as Fr. Bull wrote in the same place, 'by withdrawing from the political and economic spheres has lost its power to consecrate them.'[3] Demant, fully conscious of the problems of a secularized modern state, still looked to a Christian order. 'The Christian ethic embodies obligations to all men, not only to members of the Christian Brotherhood, and it is necessary to find a definition of the object of political action which will reflect that obligation.'[4] Thus the general tendency of most of the influential writers of Christian social radicalism in these years was towards the maintenance of the confessional State. State power, and state coercion— though this aspect was left implied rather than explicit—were to be employed to reintroduce a Christian social order. It was a scheme that Reckitt came to question: 'We had not entirely rid ourselves of our inherited beliefs,' he later wrote in explanation.[5]

The eclectic and still rather naïve quality of so much social criticism was shown by the headlong rush to support Major Douglas and his Social Credit programme. Very few Christian Socialists were not attracted to this ideal at one time or another, despite Sir Josiah Stamp's verdict that it was 'a dangerous delusion'.[6] For many well-meaning churchmen it must simply have appeared as a good moral ideal, worthy of their support, but without requiring a realistic grasp of its economic teaching. 'I have never been able to understand the Social Credit System,' declared the Bishop of London, Winnington-Ingram;[7] but he none the less felt that 'the present system showed such intolerable folly that it was well worth looking into the matter to see if a better system could not be devised'.[8] Social Credit also had a degree of influence on the Christendom Group.[9] Reckitt, who recognized a number of practical obstacles to the achievement of Social Credit, never-

---

[1] Maurice B. Beckitt, *Faith and Society*, p. 250.
[2] 'The Return of the Kingdom of God', by P. E. T. Widdrington, in *The Return of Christendom*, p. 92.
[3] 'The Kingdom of God and the Church Today', p. 227.
[4] Demant, *God, Man and Society*, p. 91.
[5] Reckitt, *P. E. T. Widdrington*, p. 122.
[6] Josiah Stamp, *Motive and Method in a Christian Order* (London, 1936), p.182.
[7] Winnington-Ingram, *Fifty Years' Work in London*, p. 212.
[8] Ibid., p. 216.
[9] J. L. Finlay, *Social Credit. The English Origins*, (Montreal, 1972), pp. 222–225.

theless wished to make 'no secret of his personal conviction of the general validity of the Social Credit analysis and synthesis'.[1] For Hewlett Johnson it never quite lost its appeal—even after he had been converted to Communism. He knew Douglas well, and spoke at Social Credit meetings throughout the country in 1933 and 1934. Douglas in fact sent him off to Alberta to see Premier William Aberhart's experiment in Social Credit government for himself;[2] an experiment which led to the growth of a political party out of the combination of economic radicalism and Evangelical Christianity.[3] For a time he was content with the doctrines.[4] 'If later I have moved on to other solutions, it has been on moral and practical rather than technical grounds,' he wrote in 1939; 'social reformers will always owe a debt to Douglas.'[5] The attraction and pervasiveness of Social Credit to Church radical thinkers is an unhappy testimony to their economic gullibility, and their ability to fall for almost any social panacea dressed up in moralistic language.

Although many bishops, during these years, assumed the general social outlook of the old Christian Social Union tradition, there was now no particular society or ginger-group to give that tradition a particular expression or coherence. To some extent the ideas of 'Christian Sociology' filled the gap. But it was the ascendancy of William Temple in the years after C.O.P.E.C. that gave the only effective cohesion that Church Social radicalism had. Temple was translated from Manchester to the Archbishopric of York in 1929—according to advice given to Baldwin by Lang himself, on his own removal to Canterbury. Temple, in fact, continued to sober up; he was no longer the young enthusiast, capable of elliptical espousal of almost any high-minded idealism. After 1929 he became of markedly better judgement, his social thought was touched with a degree of realism it had not demonstrated before. There were a number of lapses—especially his insistence, in 1943, in propagating some absurd notions about the banking and monetary systems.[6] But he also made some impressive contributions to 'Christian Sociology'. It was Temple who gathered the small committee that conducted a survey into unemployment. Bishop Bell helped him in this, and the resulting work, under the auspices of the Pilgrim Trust, was published in 1938 as *Men Without Work*. Temple also became much more cautious in the application of political solutions to social problems; he gave increasing emphasis to the priority of Christian conversion, before the solution of the world's evils should be attempted. At the

---

[1] Reckitt, *Faith and Society*, p. 386.
[2] Hewlett, Johnson, *Searching for Light, an Autobiography* (London, 1968), p. 136.
[3] See Norman, *The Conscience of the State in North America*, p. 15.
[4] See his exposition of Social Credit principles in 'The Social and Economic Order: The Basis of Exchange', in *Christianity and the Crisis*, ed. Dearmer, p. 358.
[5] Hewlett Johnson, *The Socialist Sixth of the World* (London, 1939), p. 40.
[6] Iremonger, *William Temple*, p. 580.

Southport Church Congress in October 1926, in the difficult months following the General Strike, he said,

There has never been a political movement which has used brotherhood and fellowship and comradeship as watchwords in anything like the degree the Labour movement of our time had used them. Yet we are also familiar with occasions on which the cause of brotherhood and fellowship has been advocated in the spirit and with the accents of pugnacity, and when that happens one knows at once something has gone wrong . . . And we know this Labour Movement, as a movement, is not religious. It is a movement after one of the fruits of the spirit without any conscious or deliberate reference to the spirit Himself. That will never succeed. Here our chief hope seems to lie in those members of such a movement who are Christians.[1]

The C.O.P.E.C. movement, he said on the same occasion, had succeeded because it was distinctively Christian; composed of 'people of the most diverse antecedents and points of view welded together in real fellowship because they were seeking to apply the principles of Christ'.[2] Temple also gave an increasing prominence to the Church's real and legitimate function as the source of general principles, rather than as an institution suited to be concerned with applications, in economic and political questions. It was a view he had always maintained—a traditional view—but in the mid-twenties he began to give more and more weight to it. This idea formed the centre of his Scott Holland Lectures in 1928, published as *Christianity and the State.*

First may I stress with all possible emphasis that there is no such thing as a Christian Social ideal, if by that is meant a particular constitution deducible from the Christian Gospel, to which we ought to conform the actual arrangements of our various states? [he said]. If Christianity committed itself to such an ideal, it would be hard indeed to believe that it is the absolute and universal religion.[3]

Temple also developed the view of the State for which he had contended at the C.O.P.E.C. Conference. The State was a Divine institution: God was 'immanent' in the world's sense of order.

We shall not seek the divine operation chiefly in any kind of interventions, or in the delegation of authority as from above, but rather in that irresistible logic which appears in the development and history of States, attaching success to some methods and failure to others, stability and prosperity to some aspirations and calamity to others.[4]

Similarly, in his judgement of actual political devices, it was possible to discern a slight hardening in these years. Temple rejected the view that

---

[1] *The Spirit in Life and Thought. Papers Read and Addresses Delivered at the Southport Church Congress, October, 1926* (Liverpool, 1927), pp. 174-5.
[2] Ibid., p. 177.
[3] Temple, *Christianity and the State*, p. 3.   [4] Ibid., p. 41.

the majority are right, and that it is necessary to have a voice in the enactment of law in order to be morally obliged to obey it.[1] He defined Democracy as 'respect for individual personality', which 'closely touches Christianity, which teaches the infinite worth of every individual'.[2] But he saw
dangers arising from the working class. 'Unless they respond to that respect' for individualism, he wrote, democracy 'will itself crush out their
individuality'.[3] Hence the real reason, as he now saw it, for the development of working-class education—'to make the working classes zealous of
individuality'.[4] This appeal was itself determined by another priority:
'reliance upon spiritual power'.[5] Temple had no conception of how the
false consciousness of the working classes needed to be overcome before
real choices could be made by them; his view of education did not allow
it. Faced with the realities of the economic Depression early in the 1930s,
Temple was again convinced of the duty of the Church to concern itself,
corporately, only with the definition of general moral principles, rather
than with the detailed applications suggested by various parties—'between
such theories the Christian is no more competent to judge than anybody
else', he wrote in 1933. 'The Gospel contains no illumination concerning
the rights and wrongs of bi-metallism, or social credit, or "technocracy".'
The true concern of Christianity was 'human welfare', and it 'has a great
deal to say about it'.[6] In one other notable field of interest Temple's thought
in these years arrived at a hardened position. After the rejection of the
Revised Prayer Book by Parliament in 1927 and 1928, Temple declared
firmly in favour of the continued Establishment of religion; so firmly, indeed, that it reduced Henson, who came out on the opposite side, as usual,
to scorn.[7] But Temple had always supported the idea of Establishment,
and his judgement was reinforced by the view of the State defined, through
his insistence, at the C.O.P.E.C. Conference in 1924. 'The question of
Establishment is very difficult in modern conditions,' he wrote in 1928;
'I believe it is good for the State to be (so to speak) affiliated to the Divine
Society; and so far as Establishment means this, it is altogether wholesome.' He went on to reject Establishment if it meant 'a special degree of
control over the Church' by the State—he himself, after all, in the 'Life
and Liberty' Movement at the end of the Great War, campaigned for
autonomy within Establishment. But he believed that, despite the parliamentary conflict over the Prayer Book, that was not, in the longest perspective, the case in England.[8] To that extent his view of the Divine nature of

---

[1] Temple, *Essays in Christian Politics*, p. 71.
[2] Ibid., p. 73.   [3] Ibid., p. 75.
[4] Ibid., p. 76.   [5] Ibid., p. 77.
[6] William Temple, 'The Conclusion of the Matter', in *Christianity and the Crisis*, ed.
Dearmer, p. 599.   [7] Henson, *Retrospect*, ii. 243.
[8] *Christianity and the State*, Appendix II, 'On the Relations Between Church and
State', p. 196.

secular authority derived from his 'theory of the social order'.[1] It is interesting to notice, however, that confronted with the intervention of the
Fascist States in the organization of the European Churches, in 1935,
Temple was prepared to make a practical reduction in the area covered
by the normal relations of Church and State. 'To such intervention', he
said, 'the Church must offer uncompromising resistance; but, if it is left
free to preach and minister, it has no concern with the State, except so
far as the Word of God itself directs obedience to established authority.'[2]
But European experience was regarded as exceptional, and, it was hoped,
transient.

These adjustments of Temple's position are not to be exaggerated, however, for Temple remained the symbol of the general adhesion of the
Church leadership to a respectable version of social radicalism. But this
pervasiveness had not extended to every part of the leadership: the Church
did contain men whose conservatism, though usually lacking echoes in
Convocation and at the Church Assembly, was often more in sympathy
with the ordinary assumptions of the lay world. The most distinguished
of these was Herbert Hensley Henson, Bishop of Durham. Henson was,
and felt he was, an isolated figure in the Church. 'I am too far out of sympathy with the methods and ideals of the clergy to be able to influence
them,' he reflected in 1924.[3] In 1931 Inge recorded Henson's unhappiness
at his 'isolated position in the Church'.[4] His criticism of the main assumptions of social radicalism separated him from most of the bishops and
clerical academics; his broad-Church theology was not conducive to the
Evangelicals—though he attacked a lot of Biblical scholarship for the
aridity of its language, and for its insensitivity to the faith of simple be-
lievers. His sharp attacks on the 'Catholicks' in the Church made enemies
of them, too. Henson's conversion to disestablishment in 1929, as he reflected gloomily at Carcassonne whilst on holiday in France that year,
'startled and alienated most of those who might fairly have been described
as my supporters'.[5] He really was a man outside the conventional ecclesiastical parties.

Because he was sceptical of social radicalism, there has been a tendency
by social radicals to do Henson the injustice of supposing him given to the
most caricatured version of conservatism possible—a misrepresentation of
opinion not uncommon in the Church of England. Henson was in effect
an old-fashioned Gladstonian Liberal. He believed in economic individualism, the competitive system, tempered by some restraints in the interests

---

[1] Ramsey, *From Gore to Temple*, p. 155.
[2] *Christianity in the Modern State*: Congress Sermon at Bournemouth Church Congress,
p. 16.
[3] Henson Papers, Journals, vol. 37, p. 155 (21 Aug. 1924).
[4] W. R. Inge, *Diary of a Dean* (London, 1949), p. 159.
[5] Henson, *Retrospect*, ii. 250.

of social justice, but as few of those as possible. He imagined social in-equality to be ineradicable. He really had few positive political or social beliefs—a lot of his sharp opinions came in the form of personal reactions to the fashionable social idealism of the other bishops. There was a touch of ordinary snobbery: 'You cannot make a silk purse out of a sow's ear,' he wrote, in criticism of the educational aspirations of social reformers.[1] This sort of thing reflected Henson's middle-class sense of gentility; he never could quite understand the patrician liberalism of the upper-class men who ran the Church. He refused to associate himself with any political party. His views on this matter were not unlike those expressed by Temple in the 1930s. 'There is nothing distinctively Christian about forms of policy, economic systems, and social programmes,' Henson wrote. 'These must commend themselves to the acceptance of intelligent and considering citizens by practical considerations, the force of which will be variously estimated.'[2] Time and time again he returned to the evil consequences of clerical politicking. 'Why is it that sincere and devout men, undismayed by the melancholy records of clerical politics in the past, are ever prepared to dogmatise "in the name of the Lord" about practical problems of which neither morality nor religion can provide the solution?', he asked, in refer-ence to the part taken by some clergy in the industrial troubles of 1926.[3] In the same year he complained that the clergy 'who might have been regarded as the obvious champions of individual rights and responsibilities, are as servile as the rest'. His condemnation was impartial; it fell on all who gave themselves to politics, conservative or radical: 'they are either the creatures of the mine-managers, or the tools and toadies of "Labour" '.[4] He was also impressed by the relativity, in a larger perspective, of clerical political sympathy.

If, therefore, in a democratic age, the clergy also shall become democratic in faith and feeling, they will exhibit a familiar feature. Democracy will be entering on its heritage, when it garners the benediction of the Hierarchy. The Empire, Feudalism, the Landed class, the Middle class, in the past, the organized powers of 'Big Money' and 'Labour' today: perhaps (who knows?), the 'Proletariat' tomorrow. Whatever the centre of political dominance may be, it will command the parasitic homage of the clergy.[5]

Henson's opposition to socialism was moral. He was, as he called himself, 'in temper and fundamental belief, an Individualist'.[6] It should be noticed,

---

[1] Ibid., p. 220.
[2] Henson, *Bishoprick Papers*, 'The Role of the Clergy in Modern Society', p. 177.
[3] *The Times*, 12 Aug. 1926.
[4] Henson, *Retrospect*, ii. 120; Journals, vol. 40, p. 279 (6 May 1926).
[5] Henson, *The Church of England*, p. 160.
[6] Henson, *Retrospect*, ii. 115.

however, that he condemned American religion for 'excesses of individual-ism'.[1] He disliked social-class categorization for political purposes, because it obscured the true individuality of men. This was another aspect of his 'Gladstonianism'. He hated talk of the interests of 'Capital' and 'Labour'. 'Nothing indeed can be more inconsistent with the spirit of Christianity than this submerging of individuals in such impersonal categories,' he wrote; 'morality has no use for such rhetorical figments. It is inexorably personal.'[2] The General Strike of 1926 seemed to confirm his worst fears about 'the effect of the constant preaching of the new "class-ethic" '. The result was that it 'has completely replaced the morality of Christianity even in the minds of regular church-goers'.[3] It also made ordinary working men easily manipulable by militant leaders.[4] 'Christian Socialism' seemed to be just a contradiction in terms. To Henson it was 'sentimental'; with 'its Nicaea at C.O.P.E.C.' and Temple as 'its pope'.[5] Above all, Christian Socialism was an assault upon the individual value of men—'it is suggested that men are so largely the creatures of their circumstances that the quickest way of making them Christians would be to Christianize their circum-stances'. This, for Henson, involved the immoral postulate that the end would justify the means and 'a coercive element' would be required 'for bridging the chasm between a Christian Society and its non-Christian members'.[6] Henson had spotted one of the central weaknesses in the Christendom Group's advocacy of state coercion for the creation of a Christian society. He developed his opposition to this aspect of Church socialism in his Gifford Lectures at Oxford in 1935:

In this secularist modern epoch, the absorption of Christians in the social application of their religion predisposes them to welcome in the State the advent of a power plainly superior to the Church in effectiveness. In the vulgar phrase, the State 'can deliver the goods'. A new Erastianism is emerging in a Christendom born, not of individual timidity and ambition, nor yet of the low-toned policies of hierarchical self-interest, but of a short-sighted and impatient, but not essentially ungenerous desire to Christianize society as quickly as possible.[7]

Henson differed, of course, from the prevalent view within the Church's leadership on economic issues. In his own words, Christianity had 'no essential association with any specific type of economic organization, though it cannot but affect for good whatever type is associated with it';[8]

---

[1] In his Introduction to Ray Strachey, *Group Movements of the Past, and Experiments in Guidance*, revd. edn. (London, 1934), p. 7.

[2] Henson, *Bishoprick Papers*, p. 170.

[3] Henson, Journals, vol. 40, p. 276 (5 May 1926); see *Retrospect*, ii. 119.

[4] Henson, Journals, vol. 36, p. 192 (14 Mar. 1924).

[5] *Retrospect*, ii. 223.

[6] H. Hensley Henson, *The Kingdom of God, Sermons* (London, 1929), p. 17.

[7] H. Hensley Henson, *Christian Morality. Natural, Developing, Final* (Oxford, 1936), p. 251.   [8] Ibid., p. 271.

and he differed from others, also in the extent that he denied the propriety of defining specific solutions. 'Christians as such have no private and plenary illuminations as to the solution of the obscure and puzzling problems which confront the statesman and the economist.'[1] That was why he had been so opposed to the whole idea of the C.O.P.E.C. movement. But he did not accept the prevailing practice of individualistic ethics uncritically. In 1935 he wrote:

Now it is certainly true that there is much in the industrial order, as it now exists, inspired by the principle of competition, which offends the conscience, and insults the reason of considering citizens, and among them especially of Christian citizens. Christianity has never accepted the current economic and social system of society as congruous with its own principles.

But if a particular social solution had too many unpredictable consequences, then the *status quo* might be preferable. Henson's respect for the present order did not mean total approval of it. It was, he wrote, 'possible to combine a clear vision of social evils with an acquiescence in them since their removal would create new evils and perhaps even greater'.[2] It was this aspect of his thought that his critics overlooked: they took him to stand for existing capitalist society just as it was. Henson denied that industrial society was Christian—'what Christianity is responsible for is the troubled conscience with which the evils of industrialism are regarded in Christendom, and the strenuous efforts to mitigate them which are being made'.[3] He censured commercial interests for their conduct towards the people of Africa.[4] At home, he was appreciative of 'the unsatisfactory conditions of the miners' lives', especially the bad housing—which he saw around him in the Durham diocese—and wrote saying so to Lord Londonderry, the spokesman of the coal-owners. He blamed the owners for 'shortsightedness and lack of imagination'.[5] This should be set against his criticisms of the miners for their readiness to take industrial action to settle wage claims. He was also sensitive about unemployment. In 1931 he circularized the clergy of the diocese in preparation for his Visitation, requiring them to declare both their knowledge of the unemployed and what steps they had taken to help them.[6] In the same year he rebuked one of his clergy for becoming Master of the Beagles in a local hunt, on the grounds that, at 'a time of unemployment', it was insensitive to be associated 'with mere amusement'.[7] He advocated housing reform, and explained the evils of bad

[1] Ibid., p. 290.
[2] *Bishoprick Papers*, 'Christ and Communism', p. 317.
[3] H. Hensley Henson, *Theology and Life* (London, n.d.) [1957], p. 43.
[4] Ibid., p. 127.
[5] E. F. Brayley (ed.), *More Letters of Herbert Hensley Henson. A Second Volume* (London, 1954), p. 28 (Mar. 1924).
[6] *Retrospect*, ii. 399.
[7] E. F. Brayley (ed.), *Letters of Herbert Hensley Henson* (London, 1950), p. 61 (Jan. 1931).

housing with extensive reference to Mess's report on *Industrial Tyneside*.[1] Henson also believed, as did most of the exponents of radical Church policies, that the whole of life, 'the entire life of mankind', was 'directed by a Divine purpose'.[2] There was no area—least of all economic ethics— from which Christianity was excluded. One of the worst evils of the new age, as he saw it, was the tendency to place Christianity 'in the category of private opinion which a man may cherish but by which he must not seriously guide his civil behaviour'.[3] The Church must be concerned with social issues—but in the right perspective. 'The advent of modern demo-cracy, with its keener appetite for material concerns, and its secularization of life, can best be met by a Church which, by its system and traditions, is interested in the general course of society.'[4] Henson's association of 'demo-cracy' and 'materialism' was important in his thought. He was sceptical of the rule of ignorance, rule by majorities—just as Temple was. Unlike Temple, he had no hope that education would create a responsible public opinion—that was an error 'which deceived the nineteenth century'.[5] In fact he seems to have identified 'democracy' with government according to the behests of organized labour. This he deplored because labour was obsessed, as he thought, with class-consciousness. Henson seems to have regarded those men most fitted for political judgement who were indepen-dent—rather in the sense that nineteenth-century liberal reformers of Parliament attempted to isolate and enfranchise those who, not being part of the 'residuum' of hopeless dependence, were in a position freely to exercise a vote. This was another aspect of his individualism, his 'Glad-stonianism'. Christian men had civic duties, and they were alone respon-sible, individually, for their exercise. The Christian 'cannot divest himself of his Christian character when he enters the polling booth, for, though the methods of government must in some respects differ from those of private duty, yet the principles of morality are immutable, and the grand objective of all rightful human action is the same'.[6] Henson had an English-man's distaste for authoritarian government, and when some European nations turned to Fascism in the 'thirties, Henson was their sharpest critic.

The same cannot be said for A. C. Headlam, Bishop of Gloucester, the other member of the episcopal bench noted for his political conservatism. Headlam supported Nazi Germany right up to the start of war in 1939. In his views on domestic politics he was a more straightforward exponent of a free competitive economy than Henson. He singled out the Industrial Christian Fellowship for special attack: it seemed to summarize all the

[1] H. Hensley Henson, *Fourth Quadrennial Charge, 1936*, printed in *Ad Clerum* (London, 1958), p. 15.
[2] *Bishoprick Papers*, 'Christianity and Nationality', p. 36.
[3] *Retrospect*, ii. 213 (Aug. 1928).
[4] H. Hensley Henson, *Church and Parson in England* (London, 1927), p. 44.
[5] *Retrospect*, ii. 220.   [6] *Christian Morality*, p. 174.

wrong assumptions of the Christian Socialist tradition.[1] Especially, he criticized the I.C.F. for its part in the industrial disputes of 1926—'underlying their actions lie certain theories of the relations of Christianity to the science of economics which, if carried out in practice, might bring disaster both to the industry of the country and the authority of the Christian religion'.[2] 'There seems to be an idea that if you approach economic questions as a Christian you can alter or modify economic laws,' he wrote. 'That you cannot do.'[3] His arguments were of the simplest: 'Unless a business can be carried on at a profit it must come to an end, and if wages are so high as to prevent it from being so carried on they will have to be reduced.'[4] This was indeed to maintain the integrity of capitalism. 'Wages are paid out of wealth; if they are increased there is less wealth for someone else,' he wrote. 'Any injury, therefore, to Capital is an injury to the working man, and the best way to benefit him is to increase the amount of capital available for improving the industry of the country.'[5] He used the same argument in opposing Garbett's motion on unemployment in the Upper House of the Convocation of Canterbury in January 1933: 'the only way in which one could improve the situation was by increasing the amount of productive employment, and at the same time doing away with all the restrictions upon trade which prevented people being employed'.[6] Garbett had called for 'centres' for the unemployed, to provide occupation for the workless.[7] Headlam had in 1927 compared the success of capitalism in America—which seemed to prove his contentions—with Russia, where 'the creed of the German-Jew has been quite successful', but where 'the misery of the wealthy has not been compensated for by any increased prosperity of the working classes'.[8] These observations were a little shaken by the Depression early in the 'thirties; but what Headlam said about the hard realities of capitalism corresponded to the opinions of very large numbers of middle-class and lower-middle-class people, as well as of industrialists. So did his attack on strike action, as an instrument of organized labour which hurt the innocent public.[9] Yet Headlam did believe that Christianity required social action; in this he went some way towards the views current within Church leadership.

There have been periods and circles of society when the Christian Church has kept itself aloof from political, economical and social questions. It has seemed at any rate to act as if the duty of a Christian was to save his own soul, and he was not concerned with the conditions of human life at all. Such an attitude is one clearly inconsistent with the duty of Christians to help their fellow men. Now the

[1] Arthur C. Headlam, *What it Means to be a Christian* (London, 1933), p. 149.
[2] Arthur C. Headlam, *Economics and Christianity* (London, 1927), p. 2.
[3] Ibid., p. 22.   [4] Ibid., p. 3.   [5] Ibid., p. 11.
[6] *The Chronicle of Convocation*, 1933, p. 130 (19 Jan. 1933).   [7] Ibid., p. 122.
[8] Headlam, *Economics and Christianity*, p. 9.   [9] Ibid., p. 23.

danger is of an opposite character. Many good Christians are not only eager to take part in political life that they may help others, and build up a Kingdom of God upon earth, but are inclined to identify the particular action which they support with the teaching of Christianity.[1]

He referred to this danger frequently, as the other bishops did. 'If we look back in history we shall find that again and again the course of religion has been invoked on the side which subsequent history has shown was not beneficial for the human race.'[2] Political opinions, he affirmed, were in the end less important than the moral character of those who governed.[3] He also argued strenuously for the maintenance of a Christian constitution in England—for the Establishment of religion. Those who held that the State ought to be neutral in religion were, to Headlam, simply unrealistic: 'neutrality very often speedily becomes opposition'.[4] And anyway, all religious bodies in England had some degree of connection with the State, for Acts of Parliament protected their property, titles, and trusts.[5] This point, ultimately derived from Archbishop Frederick Temple, was also made by William Temple as part of his defence of Establishment.[6] Headlam advocated not neutrality but a levelling up, a broadening of the basis of the Establishment, in the sense once suggested by Arnold. He believed the wisest course was 'not to diminish the prestige of the National Church but gradually to raise the status of the other bodies',[7] so that eventually all would have some place in the national Christianity.

Headlam's realism about the hard facts of capitalist economics were to some extent shared, though in a much more informed way, by Sir Josiah Stamp, a Methodist layman (originally a Baptist) whose works were extremely influential amongst Christians in the 'thirties. Stamp was an accomplished economic thinker, whereas Headlam of course, was very much an amateur. 'Exaggeration of the power of the moral element to overcome social evils is not a mere careless exercise, which does no good but leaves no harm,' Stamp said in *The Christian Ethic as an Economic Factor* (the Social Service Lecture for 1926): 'It is positively vicious.' Far too much was heard from the pulpit about the social implications of Christianity.[8] 'It is in the fast-developing field of collective action that the Christian ethic has scope for bridging the gulf between the individual whom *it has converted*, and who is already acting on the highest standards, and his group, which is only slowly getting the power to act as an entity beyond

---

[1] Headlam, *What it Means to be a Christian*, pp. 148–9.

[2] Arthur C. Headlam, *The Building of the Church of Christ. University and other Sermons* (London, 1928), p. 185.

[3] Ibid., p. 186.   [4] Ibid., p. 190.

[5] Arthur C. Headlam, *The Church of England* (London, 1924), p. 195.

[6] Temple, *Christianity and the State*, p. 197.

[7] Headlam, *The Building of the Church of Christ*, p. 191.

[8] Josiah Stamp, *The Christian Ethic as an Economic Factor* (London, 1926), p. 20.

the dictates of bare business.'[1] But society was so complicated and differences of interest and opinion so great, that the Church was not in a position
to offer single solutions: 'Everyone can introduce Christian ethics into his
personal relations with others, but it is another thing to prescribe a system
by which others must live and shall "work" society.'[2] Stamp, too, was
worried about the coercive element in prescribing solutions which required
legislative enactment. 'No economic problems can be solved by Christian
principles alone', though, equally, few could be solved 'without those principles as a powerful element in the solution'.[3] Stamp believed in the virtues
of individual exertion. There was nothing wrong with wealth as such: 'Rich
people are not intrinsically wicked by the possession of more than others,
but by their attitude of mind towards their possessions,' he wrote in 1936.[4]
He criticized churchmen for loose talk about unemployment and a 'living
wage'. These things were more technical, and depended on many more
contingent circumstances, than they ever realized. Economic developments
in the 'thirties confirmed his scepticism: 'I am also old-fashioned enough
to believe that, however well the world evolves, there will always be new
problems created by human relationships for which Christianity at any
given moment will have no clear programme.'[5] Similar views to these,
though expressed with rather less expertise, came from Sir Charles Marston, an industrialist himself, and author of *The Christian Faith and
Industry* (1927)—a work fairly representative of the thought of Christian
businessmen of the period, but which one recent writer has dismissed to
'the oblivion where it belongs'.[6] Marston argued for the competitive principle in industrial enterprise. This sort of view, rather than the social
radicalism of the bishops, was representative of Christian lay thought.

Dean Inge was as isolated a figure in the Church as Henson or Headlam,
but he, also, enjoyed a large public following; he was a popular figure with
the laity. He wrote a great deal—and in 1921 he began a series of articles
in the London *Evening Standard* which lasted through most of the period
between the wars. Inge was the only other conservative in the Church's
leadership whose opinions were well known. He was educated at Eton and
King's, and subsequently held fellowships at both Oxford and Cambridge;
he became Lady Margaret Professor at Cambridge and then Dean of St.
Paul's, an appointment he held until retirement. He had also been a schoolmaster (at Eton) and once held a living. Like most of the young Christians
of his class, he was attracted to the radical atmosphere of the Christian
Social Union when an undergraduate.[7] He was also influenced, in a contrary direction, by Henson, and became his lifelong friend. By 1918 Inge

[1] Ibid., p. 29.
[2] Ibid., p. 56.   [3] Ibid., p. 70.
[4] Stamp, *Motive and Method in a Christian Order*, p. 129.
[5] Ibid., p. 48.   [6] Oliver, *The Church and Social Order*, p. 115.
[7] Adam Fox, *Dean Inge* (London, 1960), p. 83.

was assailing 'wild-cat socialistic' resolutions in Convocation, in opposition
to Temple and Garbett.[1] Like Henson, he was as strongly opposed to
authoritarian government as he was to socialist collectivism and to the
vague 'socialism' of the episcopal bench. He also ridiculed Liberalism,
as 'a fair-weather creed' which was 'useless in a house divided against
itself'.[2] Events in Europe appeared to confirm this judgement. His mind
was as eclectic as Temple's. During his life, Inge pronounced on just about
everything. Central to his beliefs, however, was scepticism about the possibility of a Christian social programme. This was because, as he explained
most fully in his Social Service Lectures for 1930, Christ taught the prior
need for inward cleansing and conversion, before there was any hope of
social righteousness. Marxists, he said, proposed the opposite course; that
by reforming institutions it was possible to make men good. It was a view
to which he had given an early, and characteristic, expression: 'Put
shortly,' he wrote in 1912, 'Socialism always assumes that the sty makes
the pig, while Christianity declares that the pig makes the sty.'[3] Inge, too,
was full of scepticism about the propriety of state coercion for moral ends
in a society in which men differed about the true nature of human life.
'If Lenin and his disciples had turned Russia into an earthly paradise, we
might have some qualms about the wisdom of the Christian method', he
concluded in 1930.[4] 'There is no Christian economics, but only a Christian
and an unchristian way' of approaching such questions as wealth, property,
terms of employment, and so forth.[5] He criticized the old C.S.U. for
having been too worldly, with all its emphasis on social conditions and
its vilification of pietism.[6] 'The Gospel is a message of moral and spiritual
regeneration, not of social reform.'[7] Inge denounced all attempts, from all
quarters, to turn the Gospel into a vehicle for sectional interests or beliefs.
Thus he attacked nineteenth-century scientists for a specious 'Naturalism',
when in reality they were 'living on Christian capital' anyway.[8] On another
occasion he went for the scientists of his own generation. 'In the last century we tried to turn religion into economics,' he wrote in 1937; 'we are
now trying to turn it into psychology.'[9] And also of course, 'Churchmen
are likely to differ in politics', and it was as well to recognize that there
was nothing wrong with that. A religion of universal truth would strike the
diverse natures of men in different ways.[10] Individualism of response, for
Inge, was the most human result. He believed in the rule of the intelligent

[1] Adam Fox, *Dean Inge*, p. 127.
[2] Iremonger, *Man and Movements in the Church*, p. 3.
[3] Inge, *The Church and the Age*, p. 72.
[4] W. R. Inge, *The Social Teaching of the Church* (London, 1930), p. 29.
[5] Ibid., p. 32. [6] Ibid., p. 70. [7] Ibid., p. 91.
[8] *The Listener*, IV, No. 100, 10 Dec. 1930: 'Science and Religion', by W. R. Inge.
[9] *Evening Standard*, 14 Apr. 1937: 'The Religion of All Sensible men', by W. R. Inge.
[10] W. R. Inge, *Christian Ethics and Modern Problems* (London, 1930), p. 244.

and saw no harm in translating it into a clear political creed: 'Conservatives wish the country to be governed by intelligence, and therefore they cannot really be in favour of democracy.'[1] But in practice he *was* in favour of democracy, for the same sort of reason that Henson was: it was better than the alternatives, especially in view of the alternatives becoming available in Europe. He disliked the Labour Party—'once a pioneer and model for other countries'—because it had 'lost all inspiration and independence, and has become a mere organization for the progressive pillage of minorities'.[2] A lot of this independence had been lost to 'the tyranny of trade unions', who, he believed, were willing to hold the country to ransom by collective bargaining. This was 'an unexpected development of *laissez-faire*, though perhaps a legitimate development'.[3] This last realism reflected his own opposition to state interference with the economy. Like Stamp, he regarded the possession of wealth as morally indifferent; moral quality attached only to its use.[4]

Inge's advocacy of eugenics formed a consistent thread in his thinking on social questions. It was not only among liberal moralists of the sort who turned up in C.O.P.E.C. that eugenic theories had Christian exponents. Inge was involved in the Eugenics Society from 1912,[5] although for a time he came to disagree with them about the policy of sterilization of those thought unsuitable for parenthood.[6] 'Sir Francis Galton used to say that eugenics ought to be a religion,' Inge remarked in 1930. 'It is a religion, and its name is Christianity.'[7] The argument had to do with the quality of human life—'the qualitative problem'[8]—and led to an endorsement of birth-control. 'The main facts to bear in mind are, that restriction of numbers is inevitable; that our business is to find the least objectionable method of effecting it; that the world is filling up, and that the law of diminishing returns is asserting itself.'[9] He took the longest view; and poured scorn on those who spoke of birth-control as leading to 'race suicide' in Europe, categorizing them as 'old-fashioned theologians, militarists, and "record" fanatics'.[10] He had accused the Marxists of seeking to inhibit the spread of birth-control, because they 'are violently antagonistic to any course of action which would diminish human misery and thus make men less discontented and ready for a revolution'.[11] He also opposed the extension of the franchise to women, on the ground that 'emancipated women' were poor at fulfilling the obligations of family life

---

[1] W. R. Inge, *Assessments and Anticipations* (London, 1929), p. 135.
[2] Ibid., p. 144. [3] Ibid., p. 129.
[4] W. R. Inge, *England* (London, 1926), p. 193.
[5] Fox, *Dean Inge*, p. 126.
[6] Iremonger, *Men and Movements in the Church*, p. 3.
[7] Inge, *Christian Ethics and Modern Problems*, p. 271.
[8] Ibid., p. 269. [9] Ibid., p. 266.
[10] W. R. Inge, *Our Present Discontents* (London, 1938), p. 198.
[11] Inge, *England*, p. 208.

—of bringing up their children as quality human beings.[1] He thought 'the servant problem' so serious that it was 'a matter of national importance' in 1938, since 'our young middle-class couples are not those who ought to be deliberately childless'. But this was the class that was most effectively resorting to birth-control, because without servants, the quality of their lives was too greatly depressed if there were children.[2] It was all rather far from the usual teaching of the Church, even accounting for the slight adjustments made at Lambeth in 1930. Inge even argued for 'some kind of compulsion' of birth-control by the State; and finally returned to the idea of sterilization of the unfit, and a withdrawal of free education by the State for more than three children in a single family.[3] These ideas, it should be noticed, were not derived from Inge's Conservatism. Similar notions were commonplace in the eugenics movement, and were more characteristic of progressive intellectuals than right-wing thinkers. Inge's influence, which was very considerable with the ordinary public, lay in his 'common-sense' English approach to social and economic issues of the day; his interest in eugenics, though well known, was not especially appealing.

Before leaving this review of conservative attitudes in the Church, it is worth giving brief consideration to the influence of the Oxford Group movement in the 'thirties. The movement itself, inspired by Frank Buchman, an American Lutheran pastor, eschewed politics and concentrated on group experience, 'Guidance', 'sharing', inner conversion, and the moral strength of the individual.[4] But its method of seeking to influence leaders in industry, politics, and the Church, did seem to some to suggest a right-wing tendency, and Conrad Noel was not alone in condemning the entire enterprise on the ground that prominent German Nazis had expressed approval of Oxford Group principles.[5] It is true that Buchman, in 1936, praised Hitler as a defender of the world against Communism.[6] But the movement in England, although it attracted the support of some members of the 'Cliveden Set' of German sympathizers, really was relatively free of politics. The Groups taught self-reformation to set right the evils of the world, rather than the 'endeavour to eradicate these by legislation or some other method of compulsion'.[7] Ultimately, of course, this sort of attitude *could* lead to the Fascist ideal of abolishing party solutions to

---

[1] Inge, *Christian Ethics and Modern Problems*, p. 286.

[2] Inge, *Our Present Discontents*, p. 225.

[3] Inge, *Christian Ethics and Modern Problems*, p. 272.

[4] See Peter Howard, *Frank Buchman's Secret* (London, 1961), Chap. 3, p. 28, 'Not Left, Not Right, but Straight'.

[5] Conrad Noel, *Jesus the Heretic*, p. 14

[6] Walter Houston Clark, *The Oxford Group. Its History and Significance* (New York, 1951), pp. 77–8.

[7] Philip Leon, *The Philosophy of Courage or The Oxford Group Way* (London, 1939), p. 174.

national problems in order to attain the national will—there was certainly
a sense in which this was true in Ireland in the 1930s, as it was in Italy
or Spain or Germany. But the ideal of prior individual reformation, according to Henson, and to Temple, and to many except the more doctrinaire
Christian Socialists like Fr. Bull, was pretty central to the usual understanding of Christianity. In 1934 a volume of essays on 'The Influence of
the Groups' was published in Oxford, with an Introduction by Richard
Crossman, which showed the extent to which caution and faint approval
of the ideals of the movement were held in balance by many informed
observers. J. W. C. Wand, future Bishop of London, and in 1934 a Fellow
of Oriel, admitted 'some hesitancy and suspicion' by the Churches, but
felt there was no real need for this.[1] The Groups, indeed, 'lay a new and
fresh emphasis upon certain basic truths of the Christian religion, which
had become dim through long familiarity'.[2] Fr. D'Arcy, the Jesuit Master
of Campion Hall, made some criticisms, but approved of the Christian core
of the movement and imagined that they were, anyway, 'threatened by too
many dangers to neglect anything which can be of real help'.[3] The bishops
of the Church of England, meeting at Lambeth in October 1933, discussed
the Groups for two days and did not arrive at a common mind.[4] Some
bishops were clearly in favour; some, led by Henson, were very emphatically against. Henson saw the movement as yet another student diversion.
'Schoolmasters and College tutors ever impress me as excessively deferential to the opinion of boys and undergraduates', Henson wrote to the
Bishop of Oxford (Dr. Strong) about the influence of the Groups.[5] He
nevertheless took them seriously enough to devote half of his *Quadrennial
Charge*, in 1933, to a denunciation of the movement—which he identified
with the 'sect type' of religious enthusiasms categorized by Troeltsch.[6] He
disapproved of the movement's 'attitude to absolute authority'.[7] Dick
Sheppard also attacked the Groups for their sectarian quality: he found
them 'the old-fashioned Moody and Sankey business in a modern dress'.[8]
Suspicions of the Oxford Group Movement, therefore, were aroused both
by its sectarian religious associations and by the supposition that its political implications were potentially sinister. Quite a lot of junior clergy were
attracted to it—though it is not possible to say exactly how many—as well
as a number of their seniors. But its influence in the formulation of social
and political teachings or attitudes in the Church is scarcely discernible.

The almost euphoric adhesion of most of the leadership of the Church

---

[1] *Oxford and the Groups*, ed. by the Revd. Dr. W. B. Selbie (Oxford, 1934), p. 155.
[2] Ibid., p. 169.   [3] Ibid., p. 187.
[4] Henson, *Retrospect*, ii. 290.   [5] Ibid. 282 (13 Mar. 1932).
[6] H. Hensley Henson, *The Group Movement. Being the First Part of the Charge Delivered
at the Third Quadrennial Visitation of his Diocese* (Oxford, 1933), p. 20.
[7] Ibid., p. 33.
[8] Ellis Roberts, *H. R. L. Sheppard*, p. 231.

to principles of social radicalism received its first real check in 1926. The General Strike and the associated industrial unrest offered the bishops the opportunity for which their social views had prepared them. They implemented their principles and intervened—sometimes in the most hesitant manner, but clearly. The public rejected both their claim to speak and what they actually said. Randall Davidson, as Archbishop of Canterbury, was the centre of the controversy. Henson and Temple were both removed from the scene at the crucial moment: Temple was abroad undergoing a cure for his gout;[1] Henson was admitted to a Newcastle hospital in the middle of the strike in order to have his appendix removed.[2] Davidson began rather reluctantly—he had little taste for this sort of thing now— on 5 May 1926, by disapproving of the Strike, for its 'unwisdom and mischievousness', in a speech in the House of Lords.[3] But he also, on 11 May, complained to Baldwin about the militant language used about the strikers by some of the Cabinet—who in his judgement, seemed to want to defeat the trade unions rather than to reach a settlement.[4] By then, his relations with public men had been greatly strained by the publication of an *Appeal from the Churches* dated 7 May 1926. Davidson had consulted with other leading churchmen, and with the heads of some other denominations, and his *Appeal* was the result. It called for the cancellation of the Strike by the T.U.C.; renewal, for a short period, of government subsidy to the mining industry (thus reversing the course set out in the Samuel Commission Report); the withdrawal of the reduced wage scales declared by the coal-owners; and the resumption of negotiations between the Government and the strikers in a spirit of fellowship and co-operation.[5] Taken together with a letter published in *The Times* on the eve of the Strike by Bishops Garbett and Woods (before the negotiations had broken down) which sympathized with the miners and made them appear the injured party,[6] this looked like an episcopal attempt to assist in the direction of events. It came at a time when the supercharged political atmosphere responded to the lightest currents. The negotiations between the Government and the T.U.C. had ended amidst tactical balancing; each side seeking to avoid the responsibility for a breakdown. Public emotion was divided by class antipathy to an extent unknown before. Many expected a revolution. Into this delicate balance came Davidson's *Appeal*. Although most churchmen in the C.S.U. tradition welcomed it, for it seemed exactly what was expected of them, public men, and the public in general, deeply resented the 'interference' of the bishops. John Reith initially refused to have it broadcast over the B.B.C. wireless. 'Although', as he explained to David-

---

[1] Iremonger, *William Temple*, p. 337.   [2] Henson, *Retrospect*, ii. 122.
[3] Bell, *Randall Davidson*, ii. 1306.   [4] Ibid. 1313.
[5] For the text, see ibid. 1308.
[6] Henson, *Retrospect*, ii. 117. *The Times* letter was on 3 May 1926.

son, 'it might appear that we were neglecting to do right in this respect',[1] they were in fact trying to avoid the greater evil of putting the B.B.C. under government pressure. The press was full of denunciation of Davidson and the bishops: the whole governing class, as Tawney later remarked of the crisis, roared 'in every accent of grief and indignation'.[2] 'Few can remember', Temple said in 1928, 'any statement made on behalf of the Churches which aroused such divisive judgments in the country.'[3] Sir Henry Slesser told the Anglo-Catholic Summer School of Sociology at Oxford, in July, that during the Strike 'many Churchmen took it upon themselves to speak of the Archbishop of Canterbury in a manner which made one fear lest the martyrdom of St. Thomas was going to be repeated'.[4] Henson was able to lead this, just after his release from hospital. He wrote to the Archbishop disapproving his action and speaking of 'the practical mischiefs' which were following: 'a great impetus has been given to the tendency, already dangerously active, of many parochial clergymen—and they are often the least equipped with knowledge or character—to substitute for religious teaching, a declamatory, sentimental socialism as far removed from sound economics as from Christian morality'.[5] Henson, of course, regarded the Strike itself as 'criminal', and imagined a civil war possible.[6] All good Christians, he believed, should support the Government.[7] Temple, who came to see the Strike as having raised 'great issues in the field of political philosophy',[8] did not really think it was justified. 'But this is not because there can be admitted no directing authority within the State except the Government; it is not because there was some treasonous usurpation in the action of the General Council of the Trade Union Congress; it was simply because that course of action was bound to do more harm than good.'[9]

The attempt by the Industrial Christian Fellowship—a centre of Christian Socialism—to mediate in the coal dispute which continued after the General Strike had been called off, continued to draw the wrath of both public and politicians. A 'Standing Committee' was set up, with Temple, Gore, Woods, and six other bishops, and eleven Nonconformists, to attempt to settle the dispute. It was convened by P. T. R. Kirk, General Director of the I.C.F.[10] There was a very great amount of hostile press reaction.[10] Davidson secretly dissociated himself from the enterprise. He

---

[1] Davidson Papers, 1926, Reith to Davidson, 8 May 1926.
[2] R. H. Tawney, *Equality* (London, 1931), p. 33.
[3] Iremonger, *Men and Movements in the Church*, p. 27.
[4] *The Social Teaching of the Sacraments*, ed. Reckitt, p. 44.
[5] Bell, *Randall Davidson*, ii. 1316 (9 June 1926).
[6] Henson, *Retrospect*, ii. 119; Journals, vol. 40, p. 279.
[7] Journals, vol. 40, p. 286 (8 May 1926); see *Retrospect*, ii. 121.
[8] Temple, *Essays in Christian Politics*, 'Industry and Community', p. 48.
[9] Ibid., p. 56.   [10] Iremonger *William Temple*, p. 337.
[11] Oliver, *The Church and Social Order*, p. 90.

had no wish to intervene 'in any way' in the economic controversy, he wrote at the end of May, but he would hold himself 'alert to watch for any opportunity of throwing such weight as we possess into the arguments in favour of conference and negotiation'.[1] At the same time he declined to lend any appearance of moral assistance even to the dependants of striking miners.

I am anxious that the Church should not be backward in giving counsel and aid when it can rightly and advantageously be tendered; but I confess that I see considerable difficulty in arranging on a large scale and in a formal way an appeal for funds to help the families of those who are determined not even to negotiate about the conditions of the industry except under a virtual pledge that the outcome of the negotiating shall meet certain conditions which they lay down.[2]

The I.C.F. 'Standing Committee' had no such reservations; but then it was openly supporting the miners' claims. This was the situation in which Baldwin likened the Committee's attempt to secure a settlement in the miners' dispute to an attempt by the Federation of British Industry to bring about a revision of the Athanasian Creed.[3] 'The Prime Minister's little joke', Temple pithily remarked, 'ignores all claim on the part of the Church to be the Minister of reconciliation.'[4] That was, more or less, the claim which the public reaction to the episcopal attitude to the industrial troubles of 1926 had indeed rejected. Temple was largely unmoved; but many churchmen less well versed, and less committed to, social criticism, had learned a lesson. Church social radicalism had developed in isolation from realities—in episcopal palaces, at Conferences and study-groups, in Theological Colleges and University common rooms. In 1926 the door had been opened and a very cold blast had withered the hot-house growths. The Church's passion for social criticism survived the experience, but its growth was stunted. The views of Henson were much more nearly attuned to the common assumptions of most Englishmen. The Church had failed to realize that.

Thus bloodied, churchmen went into the economic Depression of the early 'thirties with considerable caution. Very little was either proposed or done by the Church in the face of recession—a great contrast to the United States, where the 'Social Gospel' underwent a revival of popularity and prestige in these years.[5] Many Church radicals experienced another instalment of disillusionment with the Labour Party—who saved the pound in

---

[1] Davidson Papers, 1926, Davidson to Chisholm, 26 May 1926.

[2] Ibid., 'Women's Committee for the Relief of Miners' Wives and Children', 26 May 1926.

[3] Cited in Temple, *Christianity and Social Order*, p. 7.

[4] Iremonger, *Men and Movements in the Church*, p. 28.

[5] Robert T. Handy, *The American Religious Depression, 1925–1935* (Philadelphia, 1968), p. 16.

the financial crisis, by capitalist devices: there were also 2¾ million unemployed in 1931.[1] The Depression did elicit *Christianity and the Crisis*,
a volume edited by Percy Dearmer for Victor Gollancz. Yet this collection
of essays, by Lang, Temple, Hewlett Johnson, Bell, Reckitt, Kirk, Masterman, Berdiaeff [Berdyaev], Raven, Garvie, Keeble, and others, appears to
have fallen into a void.[2] Its contributors offered predictable pieces; but
there was a sort of weariness and reserve about the book, characteristic of
Christian thought in the years following the General Strike. 'The financial
structure of Western civilization is shaking because it is not founded on a
moral basis,' declared Kirk.[3] It was all very familiar. Temple struck the
authentic note of the new caution, by refusing to diagnose the true cause
of the crisis, or to sift the 'Christian' explanation from among the many
which were available. 'Between such theories the Church is no more competent to judge than anybody else,' he wrote in Dearmer's volume.[4] It was
a telling admission. C.O.P.E.C. had not hesitated to make such judgements
ten years before.

The crisis in the relations of Church and State implicit in the rejection
of the Revised Prayer Book by Parliament in 1927, and again in 1928, was
another contributory cause of the Church of England's increasing reserve.
It came unexpectedly: the Church had got so used to the practical exercise
of a fairly wide degree of autonomy in the Assembly set up by the Enabling
Act of 1919, that few had imagined that Parliament would wish to override
its decisions—in such matters as liturgy and public worship, at any rate.
The events of 1927 came as a shock. 'In a single hectic night the House of
Commons had apparently destroyed the work of more than twenty years,'
Bell wrote.[5] Lang attributed the rejection of the Revised Prayer Book to
those who could not 'forget the Bishops who dabbled in the Coal Strike'.[6]
There was, perhaps, some substance to this. There was rather less to Garbett's belief that 'it was the Labour vote that defeated the measure'.[7] The
vote was humiliating; it was an unpleasant reminder of the legal realities
of the Establishment. 'It revealed in unmistakable fashion the subordination of the Church to a Parliament which might consist largely of non-
Christians, and does consist largely of persons who are not members of the
Church of England.' This was the verdict of the Archbishops' Commission
set up to look into the consequences of the catastrophe.[8] A majority of
M.P.s from English constituencies had voted for the measure in 1928: it

---

[1] Gilbert, *British Social Policy 1914–1939*, pp. 166–74.
[2] Oliver, *The Church and Social Order*, p. 184.
[3] *Christianity and the Crisis*, ed. Dearmer, p. 118.
[4] Ibid., p. 599.   [5] Bell, *Randall Davidson*, ii. 1347.
[6] Lockhart, *Cosmo Gordon Lang*, p. 303.
[7] Charles Smyth, *Cyril Foster Garbett, Archbishop of York* (London, 1959), p. 178.
[8] *Church and State: Report of the Archbishop's Commission on the Relations between
Church and State, 1935* (London, 1935), i. 41.

was not a *Labour* vote, as such, that had defeated it, but a vote of the *non-English*, and of the Nonconformists, who distrusted the 'Ritualism' of the proposed Book, of the Welsh and Scottish members, among whom, of course, many were Labour. Davidson faced the defeat of the Church in his usual statesmanlike fashion: no principles were allowed to cause an unnecessary confrontation; he moved in 'to smooth it all out'—as Temple said[1]—and prevent anyone rocking the boat. His resignation from the Primacy, some weeks later, however, was not due to the rejection of the Prayer Book, but was required by his conviction that a younger man should make the preparations for the Lambeth Conference coming up in 1930.[2] With four dissentients, the Upper Houses of both Convocations voted to allow the clergy to use the rejected services at their discretion: a tacit violation of the law,[3] which itself contributed to a feeling, quite widespread in England, that the bishops had behaved rather feebly. Public esteem, never too high in regard to bishops, was lowered further.[4] The Archbishops' Commission on Church and State—which contained Temple—reported in 1935 and took general stock of the legal position of the Church. A number of adjustments in the relationship to the State were recommended: a draft bill was suggested, setting out a scheme to allow the Church Assembly to pass its own 'spiritual measures';[5] a proposal by a Church Assembly Commission in 1929, on the appointment of bishops, which made few alterations to existing practice but abolished the *congé d'élire*, was endorsed. Disestablishment was rejected, although the Commission did admit that the case for it had some strength. The reasons for rejecting it were a testimony to the ideal of national religion:

The history of Church and nation is, in England, so closely intertwined that the separation could not be effected without injury to both of a kind impossible to forecast [the Commissioners reported]. Nor must it be forgotten that to many the Establishment is the symbol of the official acceptance of Christianity as the national religion, and that if England, by Disestablishment, should seem to become neutral in the fight between faith and unfaith in Christianity, that would be a calamity for our own people and, indeed, for the whole world.

It was proper that there should be 'a power of consecration' in the nation's life.[6] The Establishment principle was still very much alive. Convocation accepted the Report.[7]

One interesting consequence of the Prayer Book crisis was the conversion of Hensley Henson to disestablishment. He was unable to accept

---

[1] Iremonger, *William Temple*, p. 355.   [2] Bell, *Randall Davidson*, ii. 1361.

[3] *The Chronicle of Convocation*, 1929, p. 15 (10 July 1929: motion of Lang's).

[4] Horton Davies, *Worship and Theology in England. The Ecumenical Century, 1900–1965* (Princeton, 1965), p. 305.

[5] *Church and State*, p. 62.   [6] Ibid., p. 49.

[7] *The Chronicle of Convocation 1937*, p. 218 (22 Jan. 1937, Motion of Bishop Bell).

Davidson's bland refusal to discuss principles; he was shocked by what had happened to the logic of the idea that had grown in his mind since his opposition to the 'Life and Liberty' agitation of the war years. 'Indeed I have always held that in principle the Church was disestablished by the Enabling Act,' Henson wrote to J. E. Watts-Ditchfield, Bishop of Chelmsford, in 1923; 'we cannot go on as we are without forfeiting all legitimate title to the name and character of a living Church'.[1] Henson was, at that time, very sceptical of Prayer Book revision because he saw it as an 'attempt to re-open and revise the Reformation settlement'.[2] He also recognized that the Church Assembly was in effect 'the organ of an autonomous sect', incompatible with the idea of a National Establishment. 'There is much to be said for organizing Christians on a contractual basis into autonomous sects', he wrote in 1925, 'and much to be said for organizing them into a national system, but the two things can't permanently be combined: and the Enabling Act attempted the combination.'[3] Henson later came to terms with Prayer Book revision. The rejection of the 1927 scheme appeared to him to indicate a new political dimension to the Establishment question. 'The rise to power of "Labour" has introduced a new and most menacing factor to the whole question of Establishment, for "Labour" does not respect the conventions, or accept the principles which are implicit in the existing relations of Church and State,' he observed in December 1927. By 'Labour' he did not mean the Labour Party as such, but all who formed an organized opposition to individual ethics, social and political. This body of opinion 'is secularist, and it requires of the Christian Church the hallowing (if that word may be employed) of its secular policy'. It replaces the ethic of the individual with 'the ethic of class'.[4] In 1929 his famous *Second Quadrennial Charge*, on *Disestablishment*, and the long *Introduction* he added to it, reviewed the entire position of the Church in its relations with the State, and reluctantly concluded that the anomalies were stacked up too thickly to allow arrangements to continue. He traced the pattern of his thinking since the Enabling Act.[5] In retrospect it seemed to him that the final discussions among the bishops at Lambeth, when the scheme for the Prayer Book revision was put into shape, had not been (although he approved of the scheme itself) like the way a National Church ought to be doing things.[6] He considered what he took to be the three main grounds for having an Established Church—'as providing a spiritual organ for the nation, as securing an effective provision of Church teaching and

---

[1] Henson Papers, Letter Books (May 1920–July 1923), Henson to Watts-Ditchfield 10 May 1923.   [2] Ibid.
[3] Ibid. (Dec. 1924–Nov. 1925), Henson to Bishop Frodsham, 28 Feb. 1925.
[4] Henson, *Retrospect*, ii. 168 (18 Dec. 1927).
[5] H. Hensley Henson, *Disestablishment, The Charge Delivered at the Second Quadrennial Visitation of his Diocese* (London, 1929), pp. 8–9.
[6] Ibid., p. 41.

pastorate throughout the country, and as preserving the clergy from cleri-
calism'—and believed the existing Establishment failed to secure all three.[1]
Regretfully, he decided that the withdrawal of a formal link between the
State and religious belief must be made: 'Parliamentary action will always
be just as Christian as the Christianity of its members makes possible.'[2]
And, as he pointed out, 'it was not thought inconsistent with the Christian
character of the British Monarchy that the King's representative in India
should be a Jew'.[3] He felt there was some moral advantage to the Church
in a real Disestablishment, not just in a series of radical adjustments, giving
the Church more and more practical autonomy, and which would in the
end become indistinguishable from disestablishment anyway.[4] Parliament's
rejection of the Revised Prayer Book had introduced a note of clarity. 'It
is indeed apparent that only on the Erastian view of the States' religious
omnipotence, could the action of the House of Commons be justified, and
only on the Erastian assumption of the Church's complete subordination
to the State, could that action be acquiesced in.'[5] And finally, 'when the
mass of the people lie outside the membership of the Christian Society in
any of its organized sections, and no religious conditions whatever attach
to civic rights, Establishment is incapable of defence'.[6] Henson was increasingly impressed by the defection of the people from church attendance, and by the State from its confessional duties. 'The strong but
waning tradition of Christian feeling', he wrote in 1939, 'still obscures the
general abandonment of Christian principle, but nothing can finally avert
the effect of de-Christianized National habit.'[7] The relations of Church
and State, he told a meeting of the Church Union at the Albert Hall in
1930, represented 'a survival from a state of society which has wholly
passed away; that the assumption on which they were shaped and by which
alone they can be defended, have failed'.[8] These were the sort of principles
which Davidson refused to have discussed after the Prayer Book rejection.

Lang, as Archbishop of Canterbury in succession to Davidson (from
1928), continued this practical adhesion to the Establishment—which he
saw as a fact of political life. Lang, indeed, with his greater historical sense,
and his belief that his own national role should be carefully preserved, disguised the sort of weaknesses in the Church's position to which Henson
had drawn attention. In the abdication crisis, at the end of 1936, Lang was
involved in a very public demonstration of the surviving influence of Establishment. The crisis concerned, among other considerations, the maintenance of the Church's teaching on divorce.[9] To some it seemed that the

---

[1] Henson, *Disestablishment*, p. 43.
[2] Ibid., p. 56.   [3] Ibid., p. 59.
[4] Ibid., p. 73.   [5] Ibid., p. 97.
[6] Ibid., p. 105.   [7] Henson, *The Church of England*, p. 49.
[8] Henson, *Bishoprick Papers*, 'Church and State in England', p. 94.
[9] Lockhart, *Cosmo Gordon Lang*, p. 398.

Archbishop was interfering where he ought not to; but most of the public 'torrent of abuse' which arose from Lang's broadcast about the abdication, in December 1936, came from those offended by his rather tactless references to the King's conduct.[1] Occasionally Lang's political involvements in the House of Lords went rather beyond the sort Davidson had established as the proper sphere for the bishops. In 1934, when he received a letter from Lang eliciting his vote in support of the Government on the India resolution, Henson remarked: 'It can hardly be maintained that the bishops take no part in politics, if the Primate acts as a Government whip'.[2] Temple, as Archbishop of York, concerned himself with ordinary national issues, too.

Despite the events of 1927 and 1928, most churchmen continued to defend the practice of Establishment—few followed Henson's defection. 'It is the National Church not because it has more or fewer adherents, but because it is the ancient and official expression of our nation's Christianity', Canon Anthony Deane told the Bournemouth Church Congress meeting in 1935.[3] For the future, he went on, 'let us look for the continuance of a national Church, influencing and co-operating with a Christian State under a Christian and consecrated King'.[4] Dick Sheppard believed the Prime Minister ought to be asked 'to consider how the existing establishment could be enlarged and adjusted so that every approved Christian Church, if willing, could share with the Church of England the task of confirming and encouraging the nation in the Christian Faith'. This was in 1935. There was to be concurrent endowment, too. Sheppard was ready 'to pool the Church's endowments in the interests of other denominations'.[5] Headlam had also suggested this, so extending one nineteenth-century idea for helping the principle of Established religion to survive. There was, at the same time, a practical recognition by defenders of the Establishment that the law of the State must sometimes depart from the law of the Church—where there was a considerable body of opinion which rejected Christian morality. Marriage law was the centre of this realism. The Archbishops' Report on Church and State in 1935 had found no reason why a divergence between ecclesiastical and State law should either effect the spiritual freedom of the Church or have wide implications for the principle of Establishment.[6] In 1938 both Convocations agreed that the legal enactment of the Christian view of marriage 'may not always be possible in a State which comprises all sorts and kinds of people, including many who do not accept the Christian way of life'.[7] Rather than vote

[1] Ibid., p. 404. [2] Henson, *Retrospect*, ii. 358 (12 Dec. 1934).
[3] *Christianity in the Modern State*, ed. Leigh, p. 227.
[4] Ibid., p. 229. [5] H. R. L. Sheppard, *If I were Dictator*, p. 67.
[6] *Church and State*, p. 92.
[7] *Acts of the Convocations of Canterbury and York, passed since the reform of the Convocations in 1921* (London, 1961), p. 92 (June 1938: 'The Church and Civil Legislation').

against such a practical divergence from Church law, Lang chose to abstain from voting on A. P. Herbert's Bill of 1937 which extended the grounds of divorce.[1] By the 'thirties the existence of anomalies like these was well established, after all. 'No legislation which passes too far beyond public opinion is wise', Headlam remarked of the marriage law.[2] Henson maintained that the great force for Christian personal morality 'has not been legal coercion but personal example'. When employed, 'law has been surprisingly helpless'.[3] Temple contended that 'a compulsory virtue is no virtue', in his address to the Southport Congress in 1926. 'There may be a place for discipline, and even a place for coercive discipline, but they are merely, so to speak, to clear the way in order that the free action of the human spirit guided by the divine may press forward along the path which God has marked out for it.'[4] In the same year, as it happened, Sir Henry Slesser told the Anglo-Catholic Summer School of Sociology that Parliament was a 'pagan' institution. 'There is no morality assumed in Parliament that would not have been equally acceptable to the Emperor Marcus Aurelius.'[5] But churchmen were prepared to co-exist with such anomalies at the centre of the legal basis of the Establishment. They had very little choice, except for Henson's logical alternative.

In 1936 one of the last public obligations to support the National Church was ended with legislation which provided for the phased extinction of commuted tithe and rent-charge. The Act followed a Royal Commission of Inquiry—itself appointed after the withdrawal of an attempted Bill in 1934. The question was at the time the cause of some agitation. In 1933 anti-tithe militancy in rural Suffolk had actually attracted the support of the Fascist Blackshirts, some of whom went down from London to join in the disturbances.[6] In 1935 an effigy of Archbishop Lang was burned by a crowd at Ashford in Kent.[7] Lang was not opposed to the extinction of tithe, but he did believe the proposed compensation inadequate. This line was followed by Convocation, which, in 1936, welcomed the government legislation but regretted 'the proposal to inflict further heavy losses upon the tithe owners'.[8] The Act of 1936 brought more than a century of tithe difficulties to an end. The legislation was itself one of the last in a long sequence of measures, most of them initiated in the nineteenth century, to free the public from the obligation of maintaining the National Church. But a lot of commuted tithe payment was anyway in lay and secular hands.

---

[1] Lockhart, *Cosmo Gordon Lang*, p. 378.
[2] Headlam, *What it Means to be a Christian*, p. 147.
[3] Henson, *Christian Morality*, p. 202.
[4] William Temple, *The Spirit in Life and Thought* (Liverpool, 1927), p. 171.
[5] *The Social Teaching of the Sacraments*, p. 43.
[6] Robert Benewick, *The Fascist Movement in Britain*, revd. edn. (London, 1972), p. 90.
[7] Lockhart, *Cosmo Gordon Lang*, p. 379.
[8] *The Chronicle of Convocation* (1936), p. 105 (27 May 1936).

However willingly the Church surrendered these sorts of privileges, by the 1920s and 1930s, and however much there was an agreement that the state law on marriage may not necessarily have to correspond to the law of the National Church, there were many areas in which churchmen still looked emphatically to the State to safeguard Christian morality. Artificial birth-control was one of these: here the Lambeth Conference of 1930 modified the Church's total prohibition. But at the same time the bishops pressed 'for legislation forbidding the exposure for sale and the unrestricted advertisement of contraceptives, and placing definite restriction upon their purchase'. This was required 'in view of the widespread and increasing use of contraceptives among the unmarried'.[1] The end of the total ban of artificial birth-control reflected the thinking of the overseas bishops, who now greatly outnumbered those from England, and whose views on such matters were 'advanced'. The Lambeth Resolutions declared that 'complete abstinence from intercourse' was still the preferred method of contraception; 'nevertheless in those cases where there is such a clearly felt moral obligation to limit or avoid parenthood, and where there is a morally sound reason for avoiding complete abstinence, the Conference agrees that other methods may be used, provided that this is done in the light of the same Christian principles'.[2] The Conference was forced by sharp differences of opinion into taking a vote: the Resolution was carried by 193 to 67. The Committee which recommended this modification to the Church's teaching was presided over by Dr. Frank Woods, Bishop of Winchester. This was the bishop who had supported the miners in the strike of 1926, and whose Christian Socialism was well known. But there was no clear correlation on this issue between social radicalism and preparedness to see liberal reform of the Church's moral teaching, as Henson, for example, supposed.[3] Gore was a great opponent of artificial contraception.[4] There was some dissension in the Committee itself and a lot of negotiation was needed in order to arrive at a compromise. 'Circumstances of income, housing and education'—very wide grounds—were all reported by the Committee as justifying the practice of birth-control, as well as ordinary medical grounds. Yet they were 'unable to accept conception control as the right solution of unsatisfactory social and economic conditions which ought to be changed by the influence of Christian public opinion'.[5] They made one theological innovation: in addition to the primary purpose of marriage—procreation—they added a 'secondary end within the natural sacrament of marriage'. This 'secondary end' might still need to be fulfilled when for some good

[1] *The Lambeth Conference 1930. Encyclical Letter from the Bishops, with Resolutions and Reports* (London, 1930), Resolution 18, p. 44.
[2] Ibid., Resolution 15, p. 43.
[3] Henson, *Retrospect*, ii. 260.
[4] Gore, *Christ and Society*, pp. 160, 166.
[5] *The Lambeth Conference, 1930*, Reports of Committees, p. 91.

reason procreation was impossible. The 'secondary end' was not defined.[1]
Lang did not attempt to influence the outcome of the controversy. He
appeared, in fact, 'to have been curiously uninterested in the points at
issue'.[2] Others were victims of the hot afternoon on which the main debate
took place. Many of the bishops fell asleep.[3] So the Church of England
departed from its traditional teaching. 'Widespread criticism' followed,[4]
particularly from the laity, who were often shocked by the liberal attitudes
of the bishops.

Churchmen were prepared to call upon the State to do something about
the problem of gambling, too. There was a wide variation of view among
Christians about what actually constituted gambling, and what were the
degrees of culpability. Many thought that gambling was increasing among
the poor especially. Garbett, in his survey of social conditions in south
London, in 1931, wrote, 'It has become a mania. In every street there is
a bookmakers' tout who thrusts slips into the hands of passers-by and calls
at every house'.[5] In the same year, the Convocation of York condemned
gambling on social grounds—as a 'source of social evil'.[6] In 1933 the Lower
House of the Convocation of Canterbury was asked by P. T. R. Kirk, of
the I.C.F., to set up a Committee to inquire into 'practical steps' which
might be taken to combat gambling. He was, he said, 'attempting to try
to get rid of the gambling industry, which had now become an organized
trade and business'.[7] Temple had in 1927 defined gambling as 'the distribution of money by chance', and censured it as 'a socially wrong principle'.[8] The most widely read book on the subject was by Canon Peter
Green of Manchester, published in 1925. He had two main reasons for
objecting to gambling: it was bad stewardship,[9] and it was 'injurious to
character'.[10] Inevitably, of course, the Christian Socialist wing of the Church
classified financial speculation as gambling, and in 1920 Fr. Francis Belton,
the Anglo-Catholic incumbent of Highgate, Birmingham, had indeed
written to that effect: 'There is something wrong with the moral sense
of a community which receives with open arms the gambler on the Stock
Exchange . . . at the same time ostracizing the bookmaker on the race-
course.'[11] Green argued that business speculation was not gambling; 'the
object of the business man is to earn money by rendering some useful

[1] *The Lambeth Comference, 1930*, p. 92.
[2] Lockhart, *Cosmo Gordon Lang*, p. 350.
[3] Henson, *Retrospect*, ii. 260.
[4] Lockhart, *Cosmo Gordon Lang*, p. 349.
[5] Garbett, *In the Heart of South London* (London, 1931), p. 65.
[6] *Acts of the Convocations*, p. 108 (22 Jan. 1931; Upper House).
[7] *The Chronicle of Convocation, 1933*, p. 323 (31 May 1933).
[8] Temple, *Essays in Christian Politics*, 'Gambling and Ethics', p. 127.
[9] Peter Green, *Betting and Gambling* (London, 1925), p. 51.
[10] Ibid., p. 54.
[11] Francis G. Belton, *Present Day Problems in Christian Morals* (London, 1920), p. 90.

service to the Community, and the object of the gambler is to obtain something for which he makes no useful return'.[1] In 1933 R. C. Mortimer, Student of Christ Church (and later Bishop of Exeter), offered some early reflections in the field in which he was to become expert—moral theology— with a work on gambling. He differed from Green in that he did not regard all gambling as in its nature immoral. It was 'a legitimate indulgence, and as such neither Church nor State has the right to issue a general prohibition of it'.[2] But the facts appeared to show that it led some to excess, and this was both individually and socially pernicious. The State, therefore, 'should restrict the opportunities for its indulgence, so as to minimize the possibilities of excess'.[3] Here too then, was an issue where even the most qualified opinion looked to the State to safeguard morality.

In the continuing advocacy of social reforms, the Church between the wars looked to the State to initiate the required changes: the acceptance of collectivist principles was now very general in its leadership. Housing was the centre of concern, and it was in this area that churchmen were most influential both as propagandists and as practical reformers. When in 1933, as part of the celebrations to mark the centenary of the start of the Oxford movement, the Archbishops issued an appeal calling for the abolition of the slums and for 'decent housing of the people',[4] it was to Garbett that they turned. He wrote, in response, *The Challenge of the Slums*, in which the appalling conditions were again described and the need for action re-emphasized.[5] Garbett had by then moved from Southwark to Winchester. He had become the Church's spokesman on housing. In February 1930 the Convocation of Canterbury unanimously passed his motion condemning 'the overcrowded and insanitary conditions under which so many are now compelled to live as a menace to the moral and physical welfare of the nation', and calling on churchmen 'to do their utmost to remedy those evils in their own parishes and elsewhere', and urging the Government 'to introduce as soon as possible legislation which will facilitate the abolition of the slums'.[6] Lang, in supporting the motion, referred to the impressive achievements already made—which had transformed the Leeds he had known as a young priest.[7] In fact the Housing Act of 1930 went some way in the direction Garbett had indicated, and in 1933 he urged churchmen to use it to clear away the poor housing in their localities.[8] Garbett was himself responsible for inspiring much work in south London.

[1] Green, *Betting and Gambling*, p. 65.
[2] R. C. Mortimer, *Gambling* (London, 1933), p. 28.
[3] Ibid., p. 29.
[4] *Acts of the Convocations*, p. 108 (1 June 1933).
[5] Smyth, *Cyril Foster Garbett*, p. 219.
[6] *The Chronicle of Convocation, 1930*, p. 70 (13 Feb. 1930; Upper House).
[7] Ibid., p. 84.
[8] *The Chronicle of Convocation, 1933*, p. 343 (1 June 1933; Upper House).

More would have been known of this work had the Church not had 'a nervous horror of advertisement and sensationalism', with the result that 'very little is said about the work of its clergy and laity in the poorest parishes'.[1] Garbett's purpose was quite emphatic: 'The foulness of every slum denies that God is love.'[2] Elsewhere equally impressive practical steps were being taken, as they had been in the preceding decades, by individual clergymen. Birmingham had the C.O.P.E.C. housing scheme, still in operation in the 'thirties; in Bristol there was a Church Tenant Association; in Leeds Charles Jenkinson, a local parson and a Labour City Councillor used the Act of 1930 for extensive work in slum clearance;[3] in Somers Town Basil Jellicoe and the St. Pancras House Improvement Society hammered away at the slums from 1925.[4] It was an impressive record, but the main work in the field, of course, was done by local-government authorities.

The 1930s presented the Church with political ideas which, for the first time, really did oblige a measure of fundamental reassessment. A lot of time had been exhausted during the preceding hundred years with the conflict between individualism and collectivism, between acceptance of existing social and economic practice and radical criticism of it. The European confrontation of Communism and Fascism in the 'thirties, with its ripples extending even across English political waters, rather placed the Church's social analysis on the periphery. There were suddenly rather dangerous political alternatives. The Church discovered that politics really was about power.

Churchmen had tended to look upon Communism either as some exotic accident, like the Russian catastrophe of 1917, or as the perverse obsession of such as Conrad Noel or Hewlett Johnson. Social radicalism was safe and acceptable, so was flirtation with English Labour politics; but anyone who actually attempted a logical application of the principles of which these things were vulgarizations was at once labelled as eccentric. Some of those who were logical in this way actually were eccentric, and this, in a number of cases, gave some substance to the dismissal. But few Church leaders had studied Marxism or had any adequate appreciation of what it was. Its advocacy, in the 'thirties, by bourgeois intellectuals, did little to commend Marxism, although intellectual ballast was a quality the bishops were liable to find sympathetic. Roger Lloyd, indeed, found Communism preferable to Fascism precisely because 'in every country there is a solid block of intellectual opinion which places itself behind the banner of the hammer and sickle'. Communism, therefore, for Lloyd, attracted a 'higher type of

---

[1] Garbett, *In the Heart of South London*, p. 132.
[2] Ibid., p. 133.
[3] Lloyd, *The Church of England*, p. 327.
[4] Ibid., p. 313.

disciple'.[1] Gore was less impressed by the nice class of persons who became Communists, though he did apply an intellectual test of sorts. Walt
Whitman, he believed, was 'far more reasonable and enlightening than
Trotsky'.[2] Frank Salter, a Cambridge historian, who had taken part in
C.O.P.E.C., said that Marx 'would have liked to be a don'.[3] But there
were informed Christian assessments of Communism. In 1935 Gollancz
published a volume of essays intended to explore the meeting-points of
Christianity and Communism. In his introduction, Charles Raven, then
the Regius Professor of Divinity at Cambridge, remarked that the Soviet
revolution had 'falsified the predictions of its critics, and has shown a remarkable power not only to establish a new type of social order, but to
inspire its people with a zest for life'.[4] He believed that Marxism was beginning to become 'elastic and transformable'—'we are no longer confronted with a dogma that leaves no room for a spiritual interpretation of
life'.[5] For their part, the Churches had 'a similar task of re-examination
and restatement'. This imposed an obligation on them to seek a *modus
vivendi*: 'it is surely worth considering whether the traditional system can
afford to oppose a blind resistance to an experiment in which many are
discovering a new hope and a profound satisfaction'.[6] In the same volume
Conrad Noel wrote of Jesus as a revolutionary. He criticized many modern
socialist revolutionaries for lacking Christ's priority of love: 'in this measure
modern Communism falls short of the standard of Jesus the Communist'.[7]
Joseph Needham, Fellow (and later Master) of Caius College, Cambridge,
compared the Christian values of the early Church and the medieval world
with those of the modern; an exercise familiar from the writings of the
Guild Socialists to whom he owed some of his ideals. To this sort of
analysis, Needham brought the additional perspective of his distinguished
work in oriental scholarship. 'We reach the paradox', he wrote, 'that Marx
and Engels would have been more acceptable to the martyrs and Fathers
than the comfortable theologians contemporary with them, seeking to ex-
cuse and support the phenomena of class oppression.'[8] Needham was an
influential lay reader of the Church of England, associated with the Thaxted
movement. 'The phoenix of the Kingdom', he wrote—meaning Marxism—
'is rising from the ashes of the Church's failure.'[9] Some of the most
severe criticism of Marxism came from Christian socialist intellectuals.
V. A. Demant rejected Marxism because Marxism rejected 'transcendental

[1] Roger Lloyd, *Revolutionary Religion: Christianity, Fascism, and Communism* (London,
1938), p. 12.
[2] Gore, *Christ and Society*, p. 155.
[3] Quoted in Inge, *Assessments and Anticipations*, p. 139.
[4] *Christianity and the Social Revolution*, ed. John Lewis, Karl Polanyi, and Donald K.
Kitchen (London, 1935), Introduction, p. 22.
[5] Ibid., p. 25.   [6] Ibid., p. 26.   [7] Ibid., p. 73.
[8] Ibid., p. 427.   [9] Ibid., p. 441.

spiritual reality': 'it is in this matter, and not in its materialism, that Marxism is in deepest conflict with Christian dogma'.[1] He saw both Hegelianism, and Marxism as doctrines of mere 'becoming'; his ultimate rejection of both was for philosophical reasons. Most rejections of Communism, however, reflected practical objections to the supposed fruits of the system. Garvie, like so many others, disliked it because it appeared to rest on force. 'A socialistic system, aiming at economic equality, could be maintained only by such a subordination of the individual to society as would amount to tyranny, in the absence of an inner motive which would make social service personal freedom.'[2] Kirk contended that 'the first moral objection to Communism, apart from all question of its workability, is its dependence upon force, not only in its inception, but for its maintenance'.[3] Reckitt argued that Communism was 'the last ditch of a secularized economics', and an 'opportunity for the individual to link his aspirations and his energies to a reality and a purpose greater than himself'. It was thus a rival, as well as a false, system of salvation: 'this is the core of its challenge to Christianity'.[4] Inge had a similar view of the emotional threat of Communism. 'Though Marx was a poor economist, a poor philosopher, and a very poor prophet', he wrote, 'he brought into the political arena something more effective than argument. He is the apostle of class-hatred, the founder of a satanic anti-religion.'[5] Donald Soper, the Methodist preacher (and eventual Labour life peer), had still simpler objections: 'As a general principle I would agree with Marx that man has been governed by his circumstances,' he said from his box on Tower Hill, in 1935, 'but that is exactly what's wrong with us all.'[6]

The most important Anglican exponent of Marxism was Hewlett Johnson. This was in some measure because as 'Red' Dean of Canterbury, especially in the 1940s and 1950s, he travelled extensively in the Communist world and was regarded there as the spokesman for a school of thought in the Church of England. He was, in fact, confused with the Archbishop of Canterbury. Hewlett Johnson was a serious Marxist; his understanding of the philosophy, and the nature of its application, though open to charges of over-simplification, was very much more intelligent than much of the advocacy of social radicalism by reformist clergymen, and also usually a good deal more informed than his critics. He made the transition which reformist liberals found went too far beyond the conventional area of vicarious moralizing: he applied his social principles systematically, and was regarded by the Church, in the 1930s and subsequently,

[1] V. A. Demant, *The Religious Prospect* (London, 1939), p. 84.
[2] Garvie, *The Christian Ideal for Human Society*, p. 100.
[3] *Christianity and the Crisis*, ed. Dearmer, p. 111.
[4] *Christianity in the Modern State*, ed. Leigh, p. 191.
[5] Inge, *Assessments and Anticipations*, p. 142.
[6] Donald Soper, *Question Time on Tower Hill* (London, 1935), p. 60.

as a crank.[1] It was only in his enduring sponsorship of Social Credit ideas that any substantial grounds exist for doubting his analytical capabilities: but in this, as has been noticed, he erred in distinguished company in the 'thirties. He came from an entrepreneurial background: the Johnson Wire Works in Manchester—a background similar to Reckitt's. His education was conventional and stable. At Oxford he became the captain of the Wadham College Boat Club; at Manchester University he qualified as an engineer, and later became an Associate of the Institute of Civil Engineers. In 1908 he went as Vicar to St. Margaret's, Altrincham; in 1924 he became Dean of Manchester (while Temple was the Bishop); and in 1931 was moved (by Ramsay MacDonald) to succeed Dick Sheppard in the Deanery of Canterbury. He first seems to have learned of socialism from two young apprentices who worked in his own family factory.[2] He was subsequently influenced by Tawney's writings,[3] and also studied Blatchford and Ramsay MacDonald—finally arriving at Marx. These socialist ideas were all 'profoundly Christian'.[4] By 1933 he had already decided that 'if a system inevitably brings disastrous results, it is surely up to us to frame another'.[5] By 1938 he was organizing the East Kent W.E.A. with the help of George Wigg of the Army Pay Corps (and Paymaster-General in the Labour Government of 1964-70).[6] Like many in his generation, he was deeply influenced by the Spanish Civil War, and went to see conditions for himself on two occasions, in 1937 and 1938. 'The rise of fascism and my experience in Spain', he wrote, 'predisposed me to turn my attention more earnestly towards the Soviet Union.'[7] In 1939 he published *Act Now*, at the behest of Victor Gollancz. It argued for an alliance with Russia against Fascism in Germany.[8] He had visited the Soviet Union for the first time in 1937; and the fruit of the visit was *The Socialist Sixth of the World*, published on the eve of the war in 1939. It was an unfortunate moment. The book appeared just as the Russians invaded Finland, and when English feelings towards the Soviet system were most critical. The Canons of Canterbury Cathedral published a letter protesting at their Dean's defence of Russia.[9]

The book is an explanation and a practical description of socialist principles in the Soviet Union; it was an attempt to show why applied Marxism

---

[1] e.g. Miss Valerie Pitt, a radical member of the General Synod of the Church of England, said that Hewlett Johnson was 'as nutty as a fruitcake' in a B.B.C. Radio 4 discussion: 'Analysis', 8 Dec. 1972.

[2] Hewlett Johnson, *Searching for Light*, p. 32. [3] Ibid., p. 76.

[4] Ibid., p. 151. Hewlett Johnson's early views on social and economic questions are to be found in a magazine published in Altrincham—the *Interpreter*—to which he was principal contributor for many years.

[5] Hewlett Johnson, 'The Social and Economic Order: The Basis of Exchange', in *Christianity and the Crisis*, ed. Dearmer, p. 351.

[6] *Searching for Light*, p. 150. [7] Ibid., p. 149.

[8] Ibid., p. 151. [9] Ibid., p. 159.

could be regarded as Christianity. *The Socialist Sixth of the World* was also influential, written with great simplicity—it went into twenty-two editions and was translated into twenty-four languages. Johnson drew, at the start, upon the conventional criticism that Christianity was not applied in economic relationships; he wrote of 'the gap between Sunday, with its sermons on brotherhood, co-operation, seeking of others' good, and Monday, with its competitive rivalries, its veiled warfares, its concentration upon acquisition'.[1] There was an alternative: the Soviet Union, 'where co-operation replaces competitive chaos and a Plan succeeds the riot of disorder', and where 'the elimination of the profit-seeking motive makes room for the higher motive of service'.[2]

We call our Western economic and social order Christendom. It is hard to justify the term. Looked at through the eyes of artisan, engineer, employer of labour, or Christian minister, and I have been all four, I see it rather as an order flagrantly unChristian and palpably unscientific—an order which, if it possessed any substantial understanding of what Christian ethics really involved, or suspected its practical and immediate application, would dismiss it as a dream, or, like Hitler and Rosenberg, suppress it as a menace.[3]

He called for a revolution in attitudes. Justice, not charity, was the end of social righteousness—charity had become 'a dangerous clearing of conscience'.[4] Jesus 'had identified himself with the depressed classes; he had challenged the possessing classes'. Modern Biblical scholarship had at last 'rescued' Jesus from the advocates of 'other-worldliness'.[5] Hewlett Johnson's Marxism was orthodox, uncomplicated; capitalism had divorced the workers from the ownership of their labour.[6] Individual 'freedoms' in liberal philosophy were 'formal freedoms' only; '*bourgeios* society acknowledges with its lips the social ideals of liberty and believes them to be "rooted in eternal law"—but they are just instruments of class oppression'.[7] Working-class children, if they somehow escaped from their class, were capable of astonishing self-development. He cited Charlie Chaplin, the film comedian, as the best example of this.[8] Johnson's praise of Stalinism has dated some of the analysis. He was quite conscious of the need 'to guard against a too rosy and optimistic view of life in the Soviet Union',[9] and did not expect 'a Utopia' anywhere on earth.[10] But he also believed that 'when historians have settled down quietly to weigh the facts, there is small doubt that Stalin will stand out as a giant among pigmies, the man who, unlike those smaller men who clutch at power for themselves, trained and guarded that great family of peoples that we call the Soviet

---

[1] Hewlett Johnson, *The Socialist Sixth of the World*, p. 15.
[2] Ibid., p. 16.   [3] Ibid., p. 21.   [4] Ibid., p. 37.
[5] Ibid., pp. 64, 66.   [6] Ibid., p. 47.   [7] Ibid., p. 76.
[8] Ibid., p. 44.   [9] Ibid., p. 18.   [10] Ibid., p. 29.

Union towards the right exercise of power'.[1] He also believed that the free expression of religion was permitted in Russia.[2]

Hewlett Johnson was not worried about the atheism of the Soviet system, since he believed it originated in a misunderstanding. 'Marx, Lenin, and Stalin were anti-religious just because they believed that religion had consistently aligned itself with organized injustice.'[3] That was the sort of reason that fitted most sympathetically with the prevailing atmosphere of guilty self-criticism in which Church liberal thinkers of the C.S.U. tradition had immersed themselves. Johnson was not ignorant of the philosophical reasons that had led to rejection of Christianity by the Marxists— but these, too, were not insurmountable. He was, in fact, at his most perceptive in his attempts to separate dialectical materialism from 'the largely discredited doctrine of "materialism" which had gripped scientists a quarter of a century ago'. He found in dialectical materialism a human participation which seemed, to his judgement, to release the springs of spirituality at the basis of the material explanation of human phenomena. 'Lenin's belief in personality as something alive, creative, originating, and dignified, is wholly opposed to a devitalizing and degrading materialism.'[4] What he was really doing, however, was demolishing one of the false tenets of 'vulgar Marxism'. The philosophical problems of the relation of the superstructural to the structural in human motivation, and the inexorable nature of the movement of the dialectic, which were at the centre of Marxist objection to the reality of religious experience, were not resolved by his argument. He had, it should be recorded, noticed some aspects of the case which others had not; and his contribution to removing false misunderstandings between Marxism and Christianity was considerable.

The advocacy of Communism was rare in the Church, isolated to individual thinkers. The advocacy of Fascism was rare, too. Since a lot of European Fascism had racist associations there was, at the foundation, very little common ground with official Christian thinking in England.[5] Opposition to racism was well developed in the Church by the 'thirties. There was a major work on the question, *Christianity and the Race Problem*, published in 1924, which was widely respected and which provided Christians of all denominations with a scholarly and definitive (for its day) study of the whole question. Its author was J. H. Oldham, originally the Studies Secretary of S.C.M., and then secretary of the International Missionary Council. He wrote with a sense of urgency. 'The doctrine of racialism', he pointed out, 'is sowing in men's minds seeds which like the dragon's teeth

---

[1] Ibid., p. 356.   [2] Ibid., p. 358.
[3] Ibid., p. 357.   [4] Ibid., p. 361.
[5] See Sir Charles Grant Robertson, *Religion and the Totalitarian State* (London, 1937) (The Social Service Lecture, 1937), Appendix III, p. 64.

will reappear as armed hosts.'[1] He examined the circumstances which produced race consciousness: economic and political conditions, the differences of custom, and physical differences between the races. 'Racial antipathy is not instinctive or inborn', he concluded.[2] Belief in race superiority was not peculiar to any one race, but historical accidents had placed white men in a position where their surrender to the habit could cause the greatest harm —'the white man's claim to superiority is sometimes blatantly proclaimed, and more often quietly taken for granted'.[3] But as all men were brothers in the great creative purpose of God, he pointed out, so their stewardship of the people of the world must be according to the divine purpose—'the establishment on earth of God's kingdom of truth and righteousness'.[4] The chief battle would be against ignorance: 'Christian guidance in racial questions can be effective only if it is based on knowledge.'[5] The case presented by Oldham received almost universal acceptance among the clergy of the English Church. The Lambeth Conference of 1930 insisted that 'the issue is vital for the future of the world', and, like Oldham, pointed to the consequences of an inadequate appreciation of it: 'to fail here would be to leave the door open to racial and national animosities, the outcome of which it is awful to contemplate'.[6] The bishops also warned, in their *Encyclical*, against 'the peculiar form of pride known as race superiority', for 'Anglo-Saxons, perhaps, are especially liable to this infection'.[7] The Conference laid down the terms on which the administration of colonial peoples ought to be conducted. 'The ruling of one race by another can only be justified from the Christian standpoint when the highest welfare of the subject race is the constant aim of government, and when admission to an increasing share in the government of the country is an objective steadfastly pursued.'[8] The Oxford Conference called by the 'Life and Work' movement in 1937— an important stage in the history of Christian unity—also condemned the sin of 'racial pride' and 'the exploitation of other races'.[9] There was, in fact, during the 'thirties, a single view on the race issue inside the Christian ministry, if not among the laity, in England. Inge never allowed his interest in eugenics to slide into racism; he regarded all forms of race-consciousness as wrong, and anti-Semitism as shameful.[10] Henson's conservatism did not contain a trace of race feeling. He praised Oldham's book,[11] and in refer-

---

[1] J. H. Oldham, *Christianity and the Race Problem*, 4th edn. (London, 1925), p. 12.

[2] Ibid., p. 36.   [3] Ibid., p. 41.

[4] Ibid., p. 225.   [5] Ibid., p. 238.

[6] *The Lambeth Conference of 1930. Encyclical Letter from the Bishops, with Resolutions and Reports* (London, 1930), p. 24.

[7] Ibid., p. 23.

[8] Ibid., Resolution 21, p. 45.

[9] *The Churches Survey Their Task. The Report of the Conference at Oxford, July 1937, on Church, Community and State*, ed. J. H. Oldham (London, 1937), p. 72.

[10] Inge, *Lay Thoughts of a Dean*, pp. 177–81

[11] Henson, *Christian Morality*, p. 229.

ence to colonialism he wrote: 'No blacker chapters can be found in the record of humanity than those which tell the story of greed, cruelty, and lust which the white race has contributed to the experience of mankind'.[1] There were, no doubt, many lay Christians who gave themselves to race prejudice, but they did so in opposition to the clearly declared, and clearly maintained, teaching of the Church.

The racist ideas found in European Fascism raised an immediate barrier to the compatibility of Fascism and Christianity, at least as far as *English* understanding of Christianity was concerned. The European Fascists were themselves Christians, and in the Italian and Spanish versions of Fascism, which were very much less full of race analysis than German National Socialism, there were some who believed they had found an authentic Christianity. The English Churches contained no clergy who developed Fascist views of the State—except for some Catholics who imported versions of the corporatist State from contemporary Irish thinking. The Church of England produced only a handful of articulate priests who were known for their extreme right-wing politics in the years between the wars. There was the Revd. K. L. Kempthorne, the local officer of the British Fascists at Falmouth after 1923;[2] and there was Prebendary Alfred Gough—but he was not a member of any Fascist organization; he belonged to right-wing groups like the National Citizens' Union.[3] In 1939 the 'Militant Christian Patriots' distributed anti-Zionist pamphlets, and supported the Nazis in Germany for a short period. But this body, which was anyway small and insignificant, and does not appear to have had clerical support, disappeared after disillusionment over Hitler's pact with Stalin.[4] But in Ireland the Roman Catholic Church contained very many who were attracted to southern-European Fascism. The matter is worth a brief examination, since the corporatist leanings of the Irish Church in the 1930s and 1940s form an unusual departure from the general experience of religion in the British Isles.

Italy provided the source of the corporatist view of the State for Irish Catholics: the Italy of Mussolini, and especially the Italy of Pius XI's *Encyclical* of 1931, *Quadragesimo Anno*, with its scheme of vocationalist groups held together by the Nation-State.[5] The tradition of Irish nationalism found a niche here, as well: its emphasis on the subordination of class and party interests to the national ideal, on military glory, on the

[1] Ibid., p. 243.

[2] Benewick, *The Fascist Movement in Britain*, p. 33.

[3] Gough was a prebend of St. Paul's and a prominent Freemason; the author of *God's Strong People* (1915) and *Repentance and Strength* (1916). He advocated universal military service.

[4] Benewick, *The Fascist Movement in Britain*, p. 276.

[5] See Michael Oakeshott, *The Social and Political Doctrines of Contemporary Europe* (New York edn., 1950), pp. 57–60.

purity of the Irish race and culture, and in the national destiny,[1] all found echoes in Fascist views of the State. Irish exponents of the corporatist State in fact developed an analysis of the sickness of capitalist society not dissimilar to that of the English Guild Socialists. Professor Michael Tierney, one of the publicists of the Irish Fascist Blueshirt Movement—active between 1932 and 1934, and for almost a year in alliance with the main opposition party in the Irish Parliament—described the proposed vocationalist State as 'the medieval guild system brought up to date'.[2] He attacked the competitive ethic of 'individualist capitalism' for having produced appalling social conditions.[3] The most influential clerical writer who supported the ideal of the corporatist State was Fr. Edward Cahill, a Jesuit priest who was Professor of Church History and Social Science at Milltown Park, Dublin. In his *Framework of a Christian State*, published in 1932, Cahill outlined a systematic plan for the creation of such a State. He blamed Protestantism for having destroyed the true relationship which ought to exist between Christianity and economic and social life;[4] this was the Irish version of the Weber–Tawney thesis. The pluralistic nature of the State was described in language not unlike that used by Fr. Neville Figgis, the Anglican Christian Socialist, in his *Churches in the Modern State*. The State, as rightly conceived, Cahill argued, was organic. It could be 'compared in some respects to the composition of bodies', for 'in the properly constituted state there are several organic units intervening between the individual person and the completely organized body, such as families, municipalities, and social or professional classes'. Such groups were all 'natural institutions like the State itself'.[5] Furthermore,

these smaller units are constituted in various ways according to natural needs and historical developments, some founded upon a territorial basis like communes and municipalities, some being professional unions, such as lawyers' Guilds, Labour Unions, and vocational Corporations; each having its own privileges, rights and duties; some being contained within larger units . . . but all chartered, protected and co-ordinated by the central authority in accordance with the common good of the whole.[6]

The corporatist ideal was also unfolded in a work by the Passionist, Fr. A. M. Crofts, published in 1936 by the Catholic Book Club. He, too, lamented the break-up of the medieval guild system, and saw 'individualist capitalism and material socialism' as 'the twin children of the so-called

---

[1] Norman, *History of Modern Ireland*, 1973, p. 237.

[2] Quoted in Maurice Manning, *The Blueshirts* (Dublin, 1970), p. 222.

[3] Ibid., p. 220.

[4] E. Cahill, *The Framework of a Christian State. An Introduction to Social Science* (Dublin, 1932), p. 82.   [5] Ibid., p. 471.

[6] Ibid., p. 473. These sorts of ideals should be compared with Mussolini's Italy, and the Catholic view of the State there. See Adolf Keller, *Church and State on the European Continent* (London, 1936), 'The Ideology of the Fascist State', pp. 97–100.

Protestant Reform'.[1] In the reconstruction of a Christian constitution 'under the guidance of the hierarchy and above all party politics',[2] the workers were to be organized into associations, each one centralized in the State itself.[3] The book is full of quotations from *Quadragesimo Anno*. Another clerical exponent of corporatist doctrine was Fr. Denis Fahey, of the Holy Ghost Fathers. In 1931 he published *The Kingship of Christ*— with an appreciative introduction by Dr. John Charles McQuaid, Superior of Blackrock College and later Catholic Archbishop of Dublin.[4] Fahey's book contained the usual endorsement of medieval social organization and pressed for an authoritarian state structure to remodel society according to Christian morality. His work was less influential than Cahill's or Crofts's— which may have been just as well, since he developed some of the anti-Semitism to be found in an earlier work of Cahill's entitled *Freemasonry and the Anti-Christian Movement* (1929). An international conspiracy of Jews and Freemasons was there seen to be at work, undermining the fabric of the Christian political order of western civilization. 'Suffice it to say', Cahill had written, 'that the real inner Masonic religion upon which the whole system hinges is founded upon some type of Cabalistic or Jewish Pantheism, and implies, or is, a deification and worship of unregenerate humanity.'[5] The conspiracy extended, he believed, to 'the secularist Press, which is mostly controlled by the great Jewish financiers'.[6] It was, however, not necessary to 'condemn the Jewish people as a whole'.[7] These opinions went largely unnoticed in England, and anyway would have found no sympathizers among Church leaders. Hensley Henson was a Freemason, and so were some other members of the episcopal bench in England. In Ireland the influence of corporatist ideals (though less developed than in the writings of these priests), was very important. They were reflected in the support of the Irish hierarchy for Franco in the Spanish War, in the Éire Constitution of 1937,[8] and they cast a long shadow across the social thought of public men in Ireland in the 1940s.

For the clergy of the Church of England, Fascism had almost no appeal. The prevailing social radicalism of the Church leadership had by the 'thirties acquired the authority of several decades of prestigious existence. The clergy were not attracted to Fascism for the same reason that Englishmen in general were not. Its methods did not seem to recommend it to the familiar political culture. Dick Sheppard, for example, was a friend of the Mosley family and had actually assisted at Sir Oswald Mosley's wedding. But in June 1934 he attended Mosley's Olympia rally and was shocked

---

[1] Crofts, *Catholic Social Action*, p. 76.
[2] Ibid., p. 81.   [3] Ibid., pp. 213, 227, 234.
[4] J. H. Whyte, *Church and State in Modern Ireland, 1923–1970* (Dublin, 1970), p. 73.
[5] E. Cahill, *Freemasonry and the Anti-Christian Movement* (Dublin, 1929), p. 57.
[6] Ibid., p. 75.   [7] Ibid., p. 72.
[8] Whyte, *Church and State in Modern Ireland*, p. 51.

at the violence of the Blackshirt stewards towards the hecklers; he published a denunciation of the movement in the press as a result.[1] It was a characteristic revulsion, exaggerated, perhaps, in one who was about to emerge as a prominent pacifist. Sheppard was otherwise the type who might, in another context, have been attracted: he had a Labour political background, like Mosley, and he had the sort of mind which readily accepted large ideas, comprehensive explanations of things. He also believed in national virtues. But the English clergy were never likely to stomach immoderate political conduct. Everything had to be according to rules they could recognize—the ideas might change, they could be radical or 'socialist': but a wall of resistance went up against anything which went beyond the conventions of their class. And British Fascism lacked leadership by a section of the bourgeois intelligentsia—such as socialism had. That is why the clergy thought it alien. There was little risk that they would find Fascism conducive, with its shirted columns, its torchlight parades, its propaganda of violence, and its racist undertones. The close proximity of much of Henson's social and political thinking to the ordinary assumptions of the lay world also emerged in his attitude to Fascism. He opposed extreme nationalism and saw that it fed on hatred and 'monstrous popular fears'.[2] The Nazi version he found particularly despicable: 'how baseless are the racial doctrines which inspire the barbarous anti-Semitism of Germany, and give a fallacious appearance of scientific justification to the fanatical nationalism which now disturbs the civilized world'.[3] In 1934 he saw the German revolution as 'true to type', and particularly condemned the personal vices of the Nazi leadership; 'pederasty and suicide are the familiar marks of paganism'.[4] He was shocked by the murder of Dollfuss;[5] he wrote a pamphlet against the Italian invasion of Abyssinia; he spoke vigorously against the 'appeasement' policy in the House of Lords in 1938. It was his last speech in Parliament before he retired from the see of Durham.[6] With the start of the war, he had little difficulty in finding his diagnoses from the preceding years substantiated—'an appalling recrudescence of violence and racial hatred and social oppression'.[7]

Henson was especially incensed by the persecution of the German Jews. This brought him into opposition to Headlam, who, 'to the surprise and regret of his friends', in Henson's own words, 'came forward as the pertinacious apologist of the Nazi Government in its treatment of the German Churches'.[8] A lot of Headlam's support of Germany appears to have arisen from a perverse disgust at the moral outrage which his colleagues paraded

---

[1] Ellis Roberts, *H. R. L. Sheppard*, p. 266.
[2] Henson, *Bishoprick Papers*, p. 46.
[3] Henson, *Christian Morality*, p. 222. [4] Henson, *Retrospect*, ii. 334.
[5] Ibid. 337. [6] Ibid. 409.
[7] H. Hensley Henson, *Last Words in Westminster Abbey* (London, 1941), p. 132.
[8] *Retrospect*, ii. 413.

over the European situation. He was not really an apologist of National Socialism as such; but he did have a preference for an authoritarian regime of the Right, rather than of the Left, in Germany. He also had an extraordinary admiration for German scholarship and culture.[1] He believed that a united National Church was a blessing for any country, and some of his praise of the German Church for supporting the Government of Hitler reflected this.[2] In 1933 he sent the Dean of Chichester off to Berlin to report on conditions at first hand. After meeting Hitler, the Dean (A. S. Duncan-Jones) came back with a favourable account.[3] In October 1933 Headlam wrote to *The Times* regretting the hostile attitude to Germany then prevalent,[4] and his views became, thereafter, public. When, in January 1938, the Convocation of Canterbury resolved against the persecution of the Churches by the Government in Germany, Headlam alone spoke against the motion, deploring what he called 'the habit of expressing judgments on political matters' which Convocation was increasingly doing.[5] Lang rebuked him: the resolution, he said, 'deals with matters which transcend politics and concern the welfare of Christianity throughout the world'.[6] Headlam maintained his position until the outbreak of the war, when events overtook his optimism about the true intentions of the German Government.[7] He did not appear to have any particular sympathy for British Fascism.

The Church's opposition to the whole idea of totalitarianism in the 'thirties derived from the conviction that it embodied an immoral view of the nature of the State. 'We must remember', Lang told the Bristol Church Congress in 1938, 'that power politics are an essential contradiction of Christianity.'[8] 'As the totalitarian theory militates against the Christian doctrines of God and man,' Temple said on the same occasion, 'so it is only by renewed apprehension of those doctrines that human liberty can be preserved or made worthy to be preserved.[9] 'The real menace to Christianity', Oldham wrote in 1935, 'is the attempt to use the supreme authority of the State and all the agencies at its command to impose on the whole Community a philosophy of life and a pattern of living which

---

[1] Headlam, *The Church of England*, p. 196.

[2] Jasper, *Arthur Cayley Headlam*, p. 290.　　　　[3] Ibid., p. 291.

[4] Ibid., p. 293 (letter published 24 Oct. 1933).

[5] *The Chronicle of Convocation, 1938*, pp. 110–11 (20 Jan. 1938; Upper House).

[6] Ibid., p. 111. The Church Assembly call of Nov. 1938 for £50,000 to help the German refugees was subscribed in two months. Lang was especially enthusiastic in propagating this 'ministry of succour'; *Chronicle*, 1939, p. 3 (18 Jan. 1939; Upper House).

[7] Jasper, *Arthur Cayley Headlam*, p. 301. I am indebted to Professor Desmond Williams, of University College, Dublin, for the information, drawn from his research in the German Foreign Office archives, that the Berlin Government looked upon Headlam as a dependable ally in Britain. They also, mistakenly, supposed that Henson was a possibility.

[8] *The Gospel of this Generation*, ed. M. H. Fitzgerald, Report of the Bristol Church Congress, 1938 (London, 1938), p. 48 (the Archbishop's opening speech, 4 Oct. 1938).

[9] Ibid., p. 16, 'The Gospel in the Modern World' (opening Sermon).

are wholly, or in important respects, contrary to the Christian understanding of the meaning and ends of human existence.'[1] Bishop Bell, whose links with the European Churches were close (a consequence of his work for Christian Unity), was something of an expert in the evils of totalitarianism —both of the Right and of the Left. He led the Church in periodic denunciations of the systems of government obtaining in Russia, Germany, Turkey, and Italy. 'They one and all spring out of the breakdown of the existing capitalist system', Bell said in 1935, though, he hastened to add, there was nothing wrong with 'the use of private wealth for economic production'. What he censured was 'economic individualism'.[2] It was the C.S.U. ideal applied to the European powers. To support this loyalty to domestic social radicalism, he added, 'I would venture to declare that Christianity in its own way is as much opposed to the *status quo* in the existing international system, especially in the international economic situation, as is National Socialism'.[3] Yet Bell did see that an English version of totalitarianism would offer a familiar face if it ever came to pass.

We in England may not be in special danger of seeing the Fascist or Communist State established on our shores. But the dominion of the state is all the while encroaching on our life in a much more subtle way, through a parternal democratic régime with its apparatus of social services. The type of totalitarian State which might prevail with us would be more akin to Anglo-Saxon than to Prussian traditions.[4]

The virtue of survival was not among the strongest of the qualities of democracy. Englishmen were becoming aware of this. 'Democracy is neither white magic nor black, neither a formula of easy salvation nor a sanctimonious fraud,' Tawney had said in 1929. 'It is a tool which, like any other tool, is to be judged by its results.'[5] Reckitt argued for a better Christian defence of democracy; 'The presumed congruity of Christianity and formal democracy has been much too lightly accepted by Christian people.'[6] It could not be assumed: it needed to be fought for in a hostile world. The nation did not realize, he considered, how secularized its political experience had in fact become; the realities were 'still masked in England by the increasing anachronism of an established Church'. But they were nearer to 'a completely secularized state, claiming to dictate its own social values' than they realized. This, he said, in the language of Huxley, was the 'Brave new world' just round the corner.[7] The threat seemed to increase as events in Europe moved political authoritarianism

---

[1] J. H. Oldham, *Church, Community and State: A World Issue* (London, 1935), p. 14.
[2] Bell, *Christianity in the Modern State*, p. 147.
[3] Ibid., p. 149.   [4] Ibid., p. 151.
[5] Tawney, *Equality*, p. 288.
[6] Maurice Reckitt, 'Religion and Politics', in *Faith that Illuminates*, ed. Demant, p. 150.
[7] Ibid., p. 125.

nearer. 'The Church is clearly facing to-day one of the major crises in its history,' Oldham observed in 1933. 'It is confronted once again with a problem analogous to that which met it in its early days as it faced the Roman world.'[1] The threat was to the integrity of the Church. 'The Christian', said Sir Charles Grant Robertson, the Vice-Chancellor of Birmingham University, in his Social Service Lectures for 1937, 'cannot admit that any organization of a political community, called a state, can be co-extensive with the social organization of those who are its members.'[2] Demant, who had the wisdom to recognize that all 'liberal doctrine is based upon a dogma'[3]—and was not at all the prejudice-free, open system of values its adherents deluded themselves into actually believing—thought that he recognized the real threat to Christian society in its effects.

The decline of freedom is therefore not due primarily to totalitarian politics: it is inherent in the dogma of historic Liberalism which makes man a function of the temporal process [he wrote in 1939]. Where free discussion is still acknowledged as a good, it is, we might almost say, where there can be no real discussion at all, for everything is an open question and there is only a fortuitous wrangle to secure by mass-suggestion the support of man for political propaganda or commercial activity or cult and counter-cult.[4]

This sort of perspective found no common ground with the intellectual assumptions of Demant's contemporaries, however. Instead, they awaited the outcome of events in Europe; events which were seen to be 'essential for everyone interested in Christianity'.[5] W. G. Peck, the Christian Socialist publicist (and Rector of St. John's in Manchester), managed to break loose from most of the orthodox opinions about the collapse of democratic principles—opinions which churchmen picked up from the press more obviously than they derived them, as they supposed, from their theological learning. The modern breakdown, Peck wrote in 1935, 'began with theological and philosophical confusion, born of man's turning away from God as the ground and end of human existence'.[6] The 1930s had not seen the demise of radical social criticism in the Church—far from it—but these years had seen the accumulation of a realization that the advocacy of social values really did involve coercive political action. They had all lost a lot of their innocence.

---

[1] *The Churches Survey their Task*, Introduction by Oldham, p. 9.
[2] Robertson, *Religion and the Totalitarian State* (London, 1937), p. 25.
[3] Demant, *The Religious Prospect*, p. 56.
[4] Ibid., p. 73.
[5] William Teeling, *Crisis for Christianity* (London, 1939), p. 16. This book, though not especially perceptive, is a good illustration of the conventional English Christian's attitude to European political experience in these years.
[6] W. G. Peck, 'Religion and Economics', in *Faith that Illuminates*, p. 110.

9

Political Realism 1940–1960

The noticeable growth of a more realistic attitude to social criticism and political analysis, which had characterized many churchmen in the 1930s, continued in the following decade. Events in Europe, finally issuing in general warfare, had blighted the optimism assumed within the old Christian Social Union tradition, and impressed Church thinkers with the truth that politics was about real power and actual coercion, and not merely the adoption of ideas; the economic dislocation of the 'thirties had made them see that economic and social questions were too technical and too contingent upon political action, to be of easy Christian solution. In the 1940s, and into the 1950s, the toughened realism of churchmen elicited some of the most distinguished social and political analysis in the whole history of the modern English Church. 'The disillusionment is all the greater', wrote Inge of the general evaporation of optimism and progressive idealism, 'after the secularized apocalyptism which was the lay religion of that period.'[1] His view was an extended one; Inge believed that the disillusion of the 1940s followed two centuries of optimism. He was, anyway, a man who was always looking out for the opportunity to be disillusioned. But on this occasion he reflected a general view. The writers who most influenced Church thought in those years were critical of the easy assumptions of Christian social analysis prevalent in the first third of the twentieth century. *The End of Economic Man* published in 1939 by Peter Drucker, an expert on international banking, offered a view of social development which had little in common with the analysis offered by Church social radicalism. Nicholas Berdyaev's works suggested a disillusionment with human nature as represented in liberal thinking, and with all the barrenness of Humanism. His works, and especially, perhaps, *Slavery and Freedom*, published in 1939, breathe the spirituality and fatalism of Russian Orthodoxy. They appealed greatly to English churchmen wearied by the deflated hopes of the 1930s. Christopher Dawson's belief that the end of liberal democracy was in sight, that totalitarian tendencies were about to converge upon the remnants of Christian civilization, was, of all the pessimistic writing of the period, the most influential. In 1935 he had published *Religion and the Modern State*. In

[1] W. R. Inge, *The End of an Age* (London, 1948), p. 52; on 'The Sickness of Christendom'.

1939 came *Beyond Politics*, and in 1943 *The Judgment of the Nations*. Dawson was a Catholic; but his appeal to his generation was nowhere greater than in the Church of England.[1] Church thinkers were also attracted to the works of Maritain and Niebuhr. These writers offered an explanation of the ills of Christian society on a wide scale; they isolated long-term developments and postulated general results. No doubt the accuracy of their conclusions was uneven, but as social analysts they were clearly removed for the rather second-rate minds which had unfolded the 'Christian Sociology' of the years between the wars. Charles Raven, who was among that company, remarked in 1943 that 'since the outbreak of war such theology as has been produced has been plainly pathological'—the work of men who had, in the 'thirties, declared solemnly against the sin of warfare only to find themselves 'constrained within a couple of years to do evil or at least to advocate the doing of evil that good might come'.[2] Raven, who was a pacifist, found this pathological. But to others it could appear a growth of realism.

Social radicalism in the Church was, therefore, in eclipse. And it is important to notice that the reason was not a change of generation, but a feeling of disillusionment amongst the writers who had previously created 'Christian Sociology'. Reckitt, Temple, Peck, Demant: in the 'forties these men combined their earlier social concern with a toughened sense of how humanity actually behaves, and provided the Church with some really impressive writing. It was probably the Malvern Conference in 1941 that finally revealed the malaise of social radicalism. Its advocates, and particularly Temple, had misread the times. They sought to reproduce C.O.P.E.C.—to use the war years in preparing a Christian programme for social reform. 'If, as seems certain, the end of the war is bound to usher in a vast social transformation,' wrote Temple in 1941, 'the Church must be ready with its system of principles, and the Christian citizens must be ready to press for attention to these in the action taken by the State.'[3] Reckitt believed that the evacuation of civil populations from the cities was revealing the social problems of the poor to the comfortable classes,[4] just as the experience of the trenches had fostered a measure of social awareness in the Great War. It was Prebendary P. T. R. Kirk, General Director of the Industrial Christian Fellowship, who first seems to have conceived the idea of a Conference of churchmen to consider post-war reconstruction.[5] Reckitt's 'Christendom Group' appears to

---

[1] See 'The Importance of Christopher Dawson', in V. A. Demant, *Theology of Society. More Essays in Christian Polity* (London, 1947), pp. 185 ff.

[2] Charles E. Raven, *Science, Religion, and the Future. A Course of Eight Lectures* (Cambridge, 1943), p. 78.

[3] Temple, *Citizen and Churchman*, p. 83.

[4] Maurice B. Reckitt and J. V. Langmead Casserley, *The Vocation of England* (London, 1941), p. 85.　　　　　　　　[5] Iremonger, *William Temple*, p. 428.

have done the actual planning,[1] though the conditions of the war did not allow the extensive preparation which had preceded C.O.P.E.C. in 1924, and when the Conference finally assembled at Malvern College, a boys' public school, in 1941, it bore clear signs of too hasty preparation. It lasted three days, and, unlike C.O.P.E.C., with which it was frequently compared by those who took part, it was purely Anglican in composition.[2] Temple presided. There were fifteen bishops, and, among the other notables present were V. A. Demant, Kenneth Ingram, W. G. Peck, D. M. Mackinnon, and T. S. Eliot. Reckitt was prevented by illness from actual attendance, but his paper was read out. Their object, as Temple declared in his invitation, was 'to consider from the Anglican point of view what are the fundamental facts which are directly relevant to the ordering of the new society that is quite evidently emerging, and how Christian thought can be shaped to play a leading part in the reconstruction after the War is over'.[3] The papers read at Malvern, however, were quite unlike the C.O.P.E.C. attempts to describe social policies: they were 'predominantly theological', as Temple said; they were intended more 'to lay down sound principles than to draw up anything resembling a political programme'.[4] The arguments at the Conference, as Bernard Causton wrote, 'rarely declined to a debating society level of Left *versus* Right',[5] but this was, perhaps, because the Right was not present anyway. Temple had written to Kirk: 'we must be very careful that we do not give the impression that the Church is an agency for supporting Left-wing politics which are often based on presuppositions entirely un-Christian'.[6] These precautions did not, as it turned out, do much to alter the image of the enterprise. Cyril Garbett, Bishop of Winchester (and in 1942 Temple's successor as the Archbishop of York), described Malvern as 'a gathering of the Left Wing intelligentsia', who intended 'to commit the Church to an economic programme'.[7] Garbett's political sympathies were actually with Labour; but it was not surprising that Hensley Henson, from his retirement at Hintlesham in Suffolk, should have attributed the Conference to those whose 'feelings and passions are strong in proportion to the narrowness of their experience,

---

[1] Lloyd, *The Church of England*, p. 310.

[2] The official account of proceedings was very heavily edited: *Malvern 1941. The Life of the Church and the Order of Society, Being the Proceedings of the Archbishop of York's Conference* (London, 1941). There were, according to Lloyd (p. 310), 240 members; and according to Iremonger (p. 430) there were 400. In his extracts from some of the Malvern resolutions, Flindall incorrectly attributes the gathering to 1942: Flindall, *The Church of England, 1815–1948*, p. 429.

[3] Iremonger, *William Temple*, p. 429.

[4] *Malvern 1941*, Introduction, by Temple, p. vii.

[5] Ibid., p. 3.

[6] Iremonger, *William Temple*, p. 433.

[7] Smyth, *Cyril Forster Garbett*, p. 292.

the smallness of their knowledge, and the strength of their prejudices'.[1] The Conference tried to cram too much into a small space; the speakers overran their time; there was a pervasive donnishness about the whole gathering. The only real disagreements came over the question of private property and followed W. G. Peck's declaration, in his address, that he saw 'in the denial of all private ownership only an alternative embarrassment of the whole idea of status, since it must remove from men the material instrument of freedom'.[2] Some, and especially Kenneth Ingram, the author of several works sympathetic to Russian Communism, sought a total end to all private property. Temple thought this question 'the most vital' at the Conference, and regretted the controversy.[3] Ingram, in his own paper, had argued for the end of 'dual control' in economic life: an attack on the concept of a mixed economy, of capitalism and state enterprise existing in friendly rivalry. Only central planning, he believed, could bring a just society after the war. 'I do not, in fact, see how a planned order can preserve social freedom and avoid becoming a slave-state, without achieving common ownership and a socialist system.'[4] As at C.O.P.E.C. in 1924, there was also a strong pacifist wing at Malvern. Its leading spokesman was Professor D. M. Mackinnon. Heavily influenced by what he called 'the hideous crime of Franco's revolt' (the Spanish War), Mackinnon's distinguished contribution described the 'paradox' of a 'war to make the world safe for Christianity'.[5] Malvern in fact was hugely different from C.O.P.E.C. The debates were more learned, less practical, more systematic in the presentation of theory. But it made little impact on the Church, there were no discernible results, except in the minds of the individuals who took part; and Temple's claim that it had 'put the Church on the map again', as an organization for engineering social change, was clearly unwarranted.[6]

Temple's last great contribution to the social Christianity he had done so much to foster was not the Malvern Conference—it was the publication of his Penguin Special in 1942, just before his translation to Canterbury on Lang's resignation. This was *Christianity and Social Order*. The importance of this little book lay not in its originality—for Temple offered nothing he had not been saying for years—but in its reservations and cautiousness, and in its national appeal. Over 140,000 copies were sold, and the main assumptions of 'Christian Sociology' were handed down to levels of the Church and of educated society they had not reached before. The intellectual content of the book was familiar. It raked again over the 'claim of the Christian Church to make its voice heard in matters of politics and

[1] *Letters of Herbert Hensley Henson*, ed. Braley, p. 132.
[2] *Malvern 1941*, p. 34.
[3] Ibid., p. 219. [4] Ibid., p. 167.
[5] Ibid., p. 98. [6] Ibid., p. 224.

economics'—a claim, he admitted, 'very widely resented, even by those who are Christian in personal belief and devotional practice'.[1] There were short historical surveys of the separation of religious teaching from business practice,[2] of the consequences of the rise of Puritanism,[3] and all other requisites of the Tawney view of the consequences of economic individualism. Tawney and Keynes, in fact, read the book before publication, and advised Temple on the correct presentation of their opinions.[4] The book traced the 'recovery' of the Church's obligation to espouse economic and social teaching in the, by now, conventional way, starting with Ludlow, Maurice, and Kingsley, and proceeding via Westcott, Gore, and Scott Holland to 'its fullest expression' in C.O.P.E.C. This led to the contention that 'the claim of the Church today to be heard in relation to political and economic problems is no new usurpation, but a re-assertion of a right once universally admitted'.[5] The book argued the right of the Church to be the foundation of the State, to guide its principles. Temple did not envisage the notion of a secular State. Such a concept he would have found quite outside his references. Temple was at his best in pointing to the educative influence of social arrangements and environment, and their importance in the assistance or hindrance of Christian character in the individual.[6] Yet his distinctions between the individual action of Christians in politics, which was legitimate, and the corporate action of the Church, which should *never* go beyond the definition of general principles, looked conservative in the thoroughness with which Temple applied it. 'A policy always depends on technical decisions concerning actual relations of cause and effect in the political and economic world; about these a Christian as such has no more reliable judgment than an atheist.'[7] And certainly with issues like trade disputes 'the Church, acting officially, should stand aside'; for 'it is very seldom that Christianity offers a solution of practical problems; what it can do is to lift the parties to a level of thought and feeling at which the problem disappears'.[8] There was 'no such thing as a Christian social ideal', only Christian principles: 'Now the most fundamental requirement of any political and economic system is not that it shall express love, though that is desirable, nor that it should express justice, though that is the first ethical demand to be made upon it, but that it shall supply some reasonable measure of security against murder, robbery and starvation.'[9] This was indeed to return to first principles in political theory. The contrast with the 'Christian Sociology' of the years between

---

[1] Temple, *Christianity and Social Order* (London, 1942), p. 7.

[2] Ibid., p. 8.   [3] Ibid., p. 33.

[4] Iremonger, *William Temple*, p. 439.

[5] *Christianity and Social Order*, p. 9.

[6] Ibid., p. 14. This dimension had been explained quite fully in Temple's *The Hope of a New World* (London, 1940); see especially pp. 49 ff.

[7] Ibid., p. 18.   [8] Ibid., p. 21.   [9] Ibid., p. 38.

the wars was fairly sharp. The thinkers of that school, including Temple himself, had contended that political systems were fundamentally concerned with justice. In *Citizen and Churchman*, published in 1941, Temple had been more radical; envisaging a wider definition of 'order' than he now gave.

But the State does not, and cannot, stop short at the maintenance of order. Indeed the very conception of 'order' expands as it becomes relatively secure. At first the maintenance of order may mean little more than the prevention of riots or of physical violence. But when personal immunity from attack is secured, the question arises whether cut-throat competition is not in the same category of disorder as the cutting of throats.[1]

In *Christianity and Social Order*, Temple emphasized Original Sin,[2] and the effect its action has upon even the highest intentions of men's political actions. All Christian thinking about society should begin not with men and their needs, but with God.[3] The inherent sin of mankind required redemption; and so there was 'no hope of establishing a more Christian social order except through the labour and sacrifice of those in whom the Spirit of Christ is active'.[4] This view was a traditional statement of Christian teaching. Temple's arguments in this book in fact, were ones he had used often enough before; but there were subtle new emphases; certain points were underlined, others were heavily qualified. The general impression was of a growing moderation. Very few conservatives should in theory have found anything disagreeable in the book.

There was also a good deal of internal consistency. In a section entitled 'The Task before us' Temple offered some suggestions for post-war social reconstruction, and these were elaborated in an Appendix as 'A Suggested Programme'. There was to be state promotion of better housing, and more provision for leisure;[5] workers were to be given the opportunity to participate in the management of industry;[6] there was to be educational reform, smaller classes, and a later school-leaving age;[7] measures were to be devised to reduce the problems of unemployment.[8] Yet he made it quite clear that these policies were advanced in his capacity as 'a Christian citizen' and that, as Archbishop of York, he would actually oppose their adoption as the official policy of the Church: 'The Church is committed to the everlasting Gospel and to the Creeds which formulate it; it must never commit itself to an ephemeral programme of detailed action.'[9] This corresponded to the arguments for Christian 'social witness' used by Temple in his Beckley Social Service Lectures in 1943. 'We cannot obtain a hearing for our primary message if with regard to the evils of

---

[1] Temple, *Citizen and Churchman*, p. 30.
[2] Temple, *Christianity and Social Order*, p. 38. [3] Ibid., p. 39.
[4] Ibid., p. 74. [5] Ibid., p. 63. [6] Ibid., p. 64.
[7] Ibid., p. 65. [8] Ibid., p. 72. [9] Ibid., p. 19.

which men are chiefly conscious we have to say that for these it contains no remedy.'[1] Yet there, again, he emphasized the impossibility of a corporate adhesion to a single policy, and pointed out that 'a Christian approach to the questions of social justice will lead us back to a renewed belief in the need for individual conversion and dedication'.[2]

The distinction between his public and his private duties as a Christian was not very realistic for one so excited by political issues, however, and Temple's last years were disturbed by his insistence on giving public voice to his extraordinary views on banking. He got them from Sir Reginald Rowe's *The Root of All Evil*, published by the Economic Reform Club.[3] Temple argued that note issue by the banks should be restricted to the size of their deposits, and that all new credit should be issued by the State. His first public declaration for this policy came at a meeting in the Albert Hall on 26 September 1942, on a platform shared with Sir Stafford Cripps. 'When something which is universally necessary becomes a monopoly, that monopoly should be taken under public control', he said.[4] Despite the widespread disapproval, both of his ideas on banking, and of his articulating them at all as an Archbishop, Temple later addressed the Bank Officers' Guild, on 'The Christian View of the right relationship between Finance, Production and Consumption', in February 1943.[5] In 1944 he published some of the most important sermons and speeches he had made as Archbishop of Canterbury, and this book, *The Church looks Forward*, was full of advice and advocacy of causes, apparently at variance with the canons laid down in his *Christianity and Social Order*. In this later work he condemned the 'crime' of speculation in foreign currencies,[6] and put all his views on banking into permanent form. Temple did often declare that these were his private opinions; but the public did not take them so, and it is questionable whether a Primate can have published private opinions on public matters. His biographer believed that 'there can be little doubt that he went astray'.[7]

Temple had succeeded Lang at Canterbury in 1942. In October 1944 he died unexpectedly at a hotel in Westgate-on-Sea. The dominance of social radicalism in the leadership of the Church of England passed with him. Temple's life, in this sense, 'marked the final end of Victorian Christianity'.[8] He had shown some signs of the tougher qualities which characterized the Church thinking of the last years of his life, but essentially he belonged to the old tradition of the Christian Social Union. He died

---

[1] William Temple, *Social Witness and Evangelism* (London, 1943), p. 7.
[2] Ibid., p. 9.
[3] See his debt to this work in *The Hope of a New World*, p. 63.
[4] Text in William Temple, *The Church Looks Forward* (London, 1944), p. 112.
[5] Ibid., pp. 140 ff.   [6] Ibid., p. 148.
[7] Iremonger, *William Temple*, p. 579.
[8] Lloyd, *The Church of England*, p. 462.

just as some of his ideas were about to be recognized as obsolete. 'I could not but reflect on the Archbishop's good fortune', wrote Henson of Temple's death, 'on being called away precisely at the juncture when popular hopes were fresh and full, before the chill of reaction had chastened enthusiasm, and the exasperation of disillusionment had replaced the exultation of success.'[1] The influence of Temple's detailed policies came very rapidly to an end. What survived was a proper veneration for the memory of a very great theologian and churchman, and an enduring respectability for reformist ideas in Church social attitudes. But Temple's own ideas did not endure, his philosophy was outmoded before he died, his Christian social radicalism, too, went into decline. Reckitt, speaking in 1954 about the very little real influence Temple seemed to have left behind him in social and political questions, remarked that he died before 'the era of atomic power' and before the 'Cold War'. But above all, Temple had believed that society was redeemable, and he had always assumed that the National Church would be the obvious basis of a reformed social morality in England.[2] He 'did not engage himself closely enough with the problem of how to bring a Christian impact to bear upon a post-Christian society', Reckitt concluded.[3] From this distance it is now possible to see that Temple's true greatness lay in his spirituality and the sheer energy of his Churchmanship, in the personal inspiration of service he generated in others. As a social and political thinker he reflected the views of the moderate left-wing intellectuals, but he never attained anything like a really professional knowledge of academic Political Science.

The whole orthodoxy of social radicalism, which had so permeated Church leadership in the first half of the twentieth century, was moving to the periphery; and there it stayed until the revival of the 1960s. In 1956 Dr. Michael Ramsey, Bishop of Durham, and later Archbishop of Canterbury, sought reasons for the decline of 'Christian Sociology', then so clearly 'under the weather'. He wrote: 'The tradition of thought about the bearing of the Christian Faith upon the problems of society has not in recent years been conspicuous within the Church of England'.[4] It was an opinion that required some modification. There was quite a lot of such thought going on; but it was not liberal thought. Nor was there much attempt to derive radical political ideas from theological construction. There had never been much of that anyway: churchmen had always tended to derive their social and political notions from the surrounding

[1] Henson, *Retrospect*, iii. 276.

[2] Maurice B. Reckitt, *Militant Here in Earth. Considerations on the prophetic function of the Church in the twentieth century* (London, 1957), p. 107 (Lectures in Chelmsford Cathedral, 1954).

[3] Ibid., p. 154.

[4] Michael Ramsey, *Durham Essays and Addresses* (London, 1956), 'Faith and Society' p. 41.

culture of the intelligentsia, and then clothe these ideas with theological reinterpretations compatible with them. Ramsey, who believed, on the contrary, that 'it is in theology that sociology has its creative springs', was naturally unable to find a source for it in the 'fifties.[1] He did, however, praise the Gifford Lectures of Charles Raven,[2] evidently seeing in them an example of the sort of enterprise which might regenerate 'Christian Sociology'. Raven was a veteran of C.O.P.E.C., and had increasingly given himself to the controversy about the relation of science and religion—at a time when many had opted for premises which had made them appear mutually exclusive. Whatever the merits of Raven's scientific outlook, his social thought preserved the old pre-war moulds.[3] Ramsey also believed the decline of 'Christian Sociology' had been associated with a growth of 'other-worldly' pietism in the Church. The post-war Welfare State had removed so many of the 'gross injustices' in society, he argued, that the ground had been cut away from beneath the social radicals in the Church.[4] The realities of nuclear weaponry, and the nuclear deterrent—which Ramsey called 'the Churchill thesis', and for which he said he could find no theological basis—had induced men to look to an 'other-worldly' version of their faith, to 'escape' from the challenges of this world.[5] He also argued that 'Fundamentalist Evangelicalism', which appealed to 'less than the whole man', by omitting the rational will of men, left them unable to see the need to contend for a view of society and social needs.[6]

These points were all doubless arguable, but they were symptoms, not causes. 'Christian Sociology' declined because Christian social critics had themselves seen the need for a more realistic approach to the hard realities of the world of the mid-century. They were overtaken by events. By the 'thirties the Church found itself with a new context for social and political analysis—a world context; a context full of totalitarianism and threats even to the survival of Christian values at all. In this wider and more dangerous context the refinements of social justice in industrial and social benefits, though still important, appeared much less significant than the need to preserve the general future of a recognizably Christian social order and civilization. The events of the 'thirties, and especially the economic Depression, had made churchmen conscious of the real complexities of the questions to which 'Christian sociology' had, until then, brought too simple, and too doctrinaire, a solution. Geoffrey Fisher, Temple's successor as Archbishop of Canterbury, symbolized the new realism.

[1] Michael Ramsey, *Durham Essays and Addresses*, p. 43.

[2] *Science and Religion*, and *Experience and Interpretation* (Cambridge, 1955).

[3] For an evaluation of Raven's Gifford Lectures, see F. W. Dillistone, *Charles Raven, Naturalist, Historian, Theologian* (London, 1975), p. 247.

[4] Ramsey, *Durham Essays*, p. 41.

[5] Ibid., p. 42.

[6] Ibid., p. 43.

Fisher was not an original, or even a skilled, thinker in political or in theological questions. He was, indeed, a schoolmaster; Headmaster of Repton until 1932 (where he had brought organization after the relative laxity of Temple's headship), and then Bishop successively of Chester and of London. He came from the 'Victorian clerical upper middle class'.[1] His instincts were inherently conservative, and he had a marked respect for the concept of authority. But in politics he pursued an independent course, characterized by a sense of the growing world context of events. Fisher's independence sometimes involved him in political controversy— as in 1956, when he attacked the Conservative administration over the Suez invasion; and as in 1958, when he invited Archbishop Makarios, who at the time was the leader of Cypriot nationalism, supporting armed insurrection against the authority of the Crown, to attend the Lambeth Conference.[2] In domestic questions, Fisher was conciliatory but in general unmoved by the sort of passions which had occupied his predecessor. He was an ardent anti-Communist, in the years of the Cold War, and an upholder of the nuclear-deterrence thesis. His 'common-sense' approach to political and social questions coincided much more readily with the conventional attitudes of most Englishmen than had Temple's idealism; but Fisher was not popular. His pedagogic style apparently irritated the press.[3]

At the Malvern Conference Professor Mackinnon had pointed to one of the contemporary weaknesses of 'Christian Sociology'—that its advocates had not 'faced up to the problems raised by modern propaganda techniques'.[4] It was an aspect of their general failure to cope with the impact of European totalitarianism on the general political outlook. The difficulties were recognized in *Prospect for Christendom*, edited by Maurice Reckitt in 1940. This volume was an attempt by writers of the 'Christendom Group' of Christian Socialists 'to suggest the shape of a Christian society' for the future.[5] But it was the threat offered to liberal institutions by totalitarianism that preoccupied the contributors to the volume. Reckitt, in his own essay, accepted Drucker's thesis that Europe had reached the end of 'Economic Man', and also saw that there could be no real return to the Christian economic and social relationships of the medieval world. The urgent task, however, was to avoid the 'Servile Man' who seemed to loom in the immediate future—the advance of England 'to a society in which the individual exists only to function as an agent of the power-

---

[1] William Purcell, *Fisher of Lambeth. A Portrait from Life* (London, 1969), p. 21.
[2] Ibid., pp. 259–64.
[3] See Edward Carpenter, *Cantuar. The Archbishops in their Office* (London, 1971), p. 510.
[4] *Malvern, 1941*, p. 101.
[5] *Prospect for Christendom. Essays in Catholic Social Reconstruction*, ed. Maurice B. Reckitt (London, 1940), p. 7.

striving of an idolatrous collectivity'.[1] William Peck, of the Industrial
Christian Fellowship, denounced the falseness of the 'attempt to identify
political man with the whole man' made in contemporary society. 'The
modern world has seen the exaggeration of the State', he wrote in his
essay, 'and the assertion of its claims in fields where it has no natural
right, until the modern mind is in danger of losing all power to discriminate
the realm in which politics is valid.'[2] These opinions were in some contrast
with the belief of Christian social radicalism in the first decades of the
century that the sphere of politics ought, indeed, to be enlarged: to
include such matters as economic and social relationships between men.
Temple, in 1941, had felt the need to emphasize more emphatically than
ever before that the State existed for individuals, not individuals for the
State: 'human personality has a status, worth, and dignity quite independent of the State, and superior to that of the State itself'.[3] V. A. Demant,
the most systematic thinker of the 'Christian Sociology' School—and by
any standards a moral and political philosopher of great distinction—said
in his 1949 Scott Holland Lectures that 'the collectivist reaction has not
therefore been a response to the call of man's total nature, but only an
outbreak from frustrations', the consequence of disillusionment with
liberalism; and 'unless renewal takes the form of a response to the ground
of all human purposes which constitute man's personality, there is bound
to be a surrender to some natural or economic absolutism where he loses
his individuality without recovering his personality'.[4] Garbett also
realized the dangers in the collectivism he had encouraged when part of
the social-radical school in the 1920s. He now saw the duty of the Church
to preach liberty against 'the ever-increasing encroachments of a Totalitarian State'.[5] There should be no total allegiance required by any
government.[6] 'While the Church calls the nation to God,' he wrote in
1953, 'it must also call upon the nation to recognize and to respect the
rights and responsibilities of the individual.'[7] Most Christian writers at
this time referred frequently to these themes; most condemned what Inge
called 'the philosophy of the Wolf State', the aggrandizement of collectivism
over the individual.[8] 'Society exists to serve the needs of its members, not
to enslave and possess them wholly,' declared the bishops at the Lambeth
Conference of 1948, in their *Encyclical Letter*; 'and when a society treats
its members merely as means towards securing its ends, it becomes a

[1] Maurice B. Reckitt (London 1940), 'Catholic Sociology and the English Situation',
in *Prospect for Christendom*, p. 88.
[2] Ibid., 'The validity of Politics', p. 164.   [3] Temple, *Citizen and Churchman*, p. 27.
[4] V. A. Demant, *Religion and the Decline of Capitalism* (London, 1952), p. 195. Vigo
Demant was a Canon of St. Paul's, and later a Canon of Christ Church, Oxford.
[5] Garbett, *The Claims of the Church of England*, p. 220.
[6] Cyril Garbett, *In an Age of Revolution* (London, 1952), p. 155.
[7] Cyril Garbett, *The Church of England Today* (London, 1953), p. 113, 'Mass Man'
[8] Inge, *The End of an Age*, p. 196.

destroyer of men's souls'.[1] The point had been emphasized in the Conference Report on *The Christian Doctrine of Man*, in its insistence that 'belief in man's eternal destiny must profoundly and radically influence Christian political and social thought'. For the value of a man was not exhausted in his political worth: 'man is more than a function of his society, more than a producer or a citizen'. Human society was dependent on God. The claims of men to fulfil their purposes were established 'not on any concession by an earthly state, but upon a divine endowment and prerogative which no human agency gave, or can take away'.[2] The Chairman of the Committee which produced this Report was Dr. J. W. C. Ward, Bishop of London (formerly Archbishop of Brisbane). Wand had, in the previous year, published a book which sought to analyse the attack on Christian values implied in the ideologies of contemporary totalitarianism.[3] In 1949 the Methodist Conference also warned that the extension of the powers of the State 'threatens to become a totalitarian colossus to which the individual person is completely subordinate'.[4]

The Church retained a balance, however, in its attitude to the accumulation by the State of powers over social regulation. It welcomed the postwar Welfare State—at a time, too, when a lot of popular conservative opinion was deeply distrustful of any increased state activity. Temple had in 1941 written that 'all the conditions of modern life, so favourable to central administration, favour the extension of State activity',[5] and had gone on to link welfare with the State's concern for the spiritual nature of its citizens: 'it has at least an indirect spiritual function'.[6] The Welfare State was usually welcomed because it was seen to be identifiably Christian. Bishop Wand wrote in 1947 that it was 'an expression at the national level of the humanitarian work of the Church'.[7] Canon Roger Lloyd, the historian of the Church in the twentieth century, wrote a small work in 1952 called *The Church and the Artisan Today* in which he justified the Welfare State in explicitly Christian terms. 'In the Bible, and therefore in Christian theology, there is every warrant for believing that a reasonable degree of material security is part of God's desire for every one of His human creatures.'[8] In the same year Garbett declared that the Welfare State was 'the embodiment of the principle "Bear ye one another's burdens,

---

[1] *The Lambeth Conference, 1948. The Encyclical Letter from the Bishops; together with Resolutions and Reports* (London, 1948), p. 19.
[2] Ibid., 'The Christian Doctrine of Man', First Report, p. 10.
[3] See J. W. C. Wand, *God and Goodness* (London, 1947), pp. 45 ff.
[4] *Declarations of Conference on Social Questions*. The Methodist Church; ed. Edward Rogers (London, 1959), p. 17, 'Christian Social and Political Responsibility' (1949). For a Methodist view of collectivism, with a recognition of some of the dangers, see Maldwyn Edwards, *Church and Society* (London, 1954), p. 80.
[5] Temple, *Citizen and Churchman*, p. 32.
[6] Ibid., p. 36.   [7] Wand, *God and Goodness*, p. 56.
[8] Roger Lloyd, *The Church and the Artisan Today* (London, 1952), p. 32.

and so fulfil the law of Christ" '.[1] Garbett, however, also pointed to some dangers—dangers which might arise for the spiritual destiny of mankind if the State concerned itself only with the material needs of men, and the danger that state provision might 'weaken the sense of personal responsibility'.[2] And in 1953 Garbett lamented this weakening, 'hastened by central planning', and even observed that 'the nationalisation of the mines, the railways, and other industries, however justifiable, has resulted in the undermining of local responsibilities'.[3]

These reservations were expressed by many Church writers. Demant had spoken of them at Malvern in 1941, anticipating things to come. One of the results of the war, he then predicted, 'will undoubtedly be a large measure of totalitarianism, that is, a restriction of personal and group initiative, and a merging of all social functions in one overwhelming mass policy'. The Church ought not to resist this, he believed, because it was 'the only way in which modern society, having lost its Christian bearings, can try to cope with its problems'; but the Church should 'rather seek to transcend and work through this coming phase, so as to build up anew centres of liberty and social life with a robustness that has been missing in the late liberal epoch'.[4] Bell had in 1940 made a similar point: 'The citizen of a democratic State may be deprived of his freedom, by the subtle influence of the universal provision of social services, from ante-natal clinics to euthanasia couches, just as effectively as the German subject is robbed of his liberty by the system of spies and concentration camps.'[5] Reckitt, in 1941, had blamed 'advanced' and 'progressive' thinkers for the possibility of a future loss of personal freedom in England. 'Their dream is only of bigger and better social services, larger and more influential committees, a people less and less responsible for the day to day conduct of its own way of life.'[6] Reckitt, seeing the plans for state activity at the end of the war, even suggested that it had all gone too far; that 'the extension of State activities has very considerably outrun the development of public consciousness.[7] The advocates of Christian Socialism were not alone in awakening to these possibilities. In 1948 the Lambeth Conference declared that 'the Church should welcome the growing concern of the State for human welfare', but the bishops added the rider that 'there must be constant endeavour to resist encroachments by the State which endanger human personality'.[8] Resolution 19 of the Conference adhered the Church to the Welfare State:

[1] Garbett, *In an Age of Revolution*, p. 151.   [2] Ibid., p. 152.
[3] Garbett, *The Church of England Today*, p. 114.
[4] *Malvern, 1941*, p. 121.
[5] G. K. A. Bell, *Christianity and World Order* (Penguin Special, London, 1940), p. 69.
[6] Reckitt and Langmead Casserley, *The Vocation of England*, p. 73.
[7] Reckitt, *The Christian in Politics*, p. 43.
[8] *The Lambeth Conference, 1948, Encyclical Letter*, p. 20.

We believe that the State is under the moral law of God, and is intended by Him to be an instrument for human welfare. We therefore welcome the growing concern and care of the modern State for its citizens, and call upon Church members to accept their own political responsibility and to co-operate with the State and its officers in their work.[1]

The Lambeth Committee which drew up the second part of the Report on *The Christian Doctrine of Man*, presided over by G. Ashton Oldham, Bishop of Albany (U.S.A.), had reminded the Church of its special role, in the modern Welfare State, as the guardian of personal freedom, as the counter-weight to 'the natural bias of the State towards totalitarianism'.[2] The Church must also preserve the spirit of voluntary social service.[3] Commentaries on the Lambeth Conference emphasized this aspect of its message on the modern State.[4] Archbishop Fisher welcomed the Welfare State, and joined others in pointing to the dangers of too great a measure of state control, and the danger that the State would regard man merely as a material being, 'a mouth, a body, an end in himself'. Yet Fisher believed that 'the Welfare State calls for a far higher level of citizenship'.[5] Perhaps the most balanced appraisal of the Welfare State in these years came from Alec Vidler, Dean of King's College, Cambridge, writing in *Theology* in 1952. No one, he argued, should claim the Welfare State as a 'final norm or standard of what a State should be according to the law of God', for no particular type of State has been ordained by God. 'In our historic circumstances, the "Welfare State" is the best means by which the human needs of all citizens can be met—by which as a national community we can be assisted to love our neighbours as ourselves.'[6] Most Church leaders would probably have agreed to the Welfare State on these terms, however reluctant some sections of the laity, dependent still on older liberal doctrines of self-help and private social initiative, may have been. Nor should the Church's acceptance of the Welfare State be taken too much for granted. In Southern Ireland attempts to introduce health and social welfare measures were heavily and successfully resisted in the years after the war. The Catholic hierarchy refused to countenance the interference of the State with the rights of families.[7]

The fears which churchmen entertained about the extension of state powers in England were reinforced by their realization of the growing attraction of secular humanism among sections of the intelligentsia. 'It is very hard to resist the Totalitarian claim on any humanist basis,' wrote Temple in 1941; 'if a man has no status or worth except his status as a

---

[1] Ibid., *Resolutions*, p. 32.   [2] Ibid., No. II Report, p. 17.   [3] Ibid., p. 18.
[4] See Dudley Symon, *Lambeth Questions* (London, 1948), p. 30.
[5] *The Archbishop Speaks*, 'The Welfare State' (Address at Brisbane, Nov. 1950), p. 124.
[6] Alec R. Vidler, *Essays in Liberality* (London, 1957), p. 119, 'The Welfare State: A Christian View'.
[7] See Whyte, *Church and State in Modern Ireland*, pp. 120 ff. and 196 ff.

citizen and his worth to an earthly community, he can have no rights against the State which acts for that community.'[1] And Fisher, speaking to the Labour Party's annual Conference at Margate in 1947, declared that 'man's struggle to-day at its deepest level is not so much to secure his rights or his freedom as to recover belief in his own significance, his own spiritual value'.[2] Humanism, in its atheist and secular form, was recognized as the leading influence in England for a view of man and of human nature which eliminated the Divine foundation of human personality. Churchmen were aware of the dangers. 'Each age', as Bell wisely wrote, 'is marked by the doctrine of man which it upholds.'[3] The Church was anxious that the years after the war should not fall under the dominion of what *Towards the Conversion of England*—the Report edited by Christopher Chavasse, Bishop of Rochester—called 'Humanism the Age-long lie'.[4] The dangers existed at more than one level of society. The espousal of humanism was not only a characteristic of some of the intellectuals: there was a widely diffused, popular version, which equated Christianity with a vague but beneficent moralism. This was still Christian, at least in the minds of those who adopted it; but many Church leaders feared that its inadequate grounding in solid Christian knowledge could easily give way to atheism. After the war it seemed to many Christians as if 'an Age without Standards'[5] was opening up. Humanism in practical guise appeared to advocate an assault upon the Christian understanding of morality. The phrase 'the New Morality' came into use—though the morals complained of looked rather traditional compared with those which prevailed in the 1960s, when the label was again applied. In criticizing the values of humanism, Wand said in 1947 that 'the basic mistake lies in the fact that the followers of this new morality have ceased to look for any standard outside humanity, or to believe that any absolute standard exists'.[6] In the face of the cosmic relativism of secular humanism, nearly all the leaders of the Church responded, in these years, with a clear and uncompromising contrast: 'The humanist believes that man is all sufficient and can work out his own destiny; the Christian believes that man is a sinner, unable to do anything by himself', as Garbett put it in 1952.[7] 'Between the dogma that man is a child of God, and the dogma that he is a chance assemblage of physical forces without freedom or responsibility, there can be no accommodation at all and no progress can be made until that is clear', said Spencer Leeson (later the Bishop of

---

[1] Temple, *Citizen and Churchman*, p. 74.   [2] *The Archbishop Speaks*, p. 102.
[3] Bell, *Christianity and World Order*, p. 17.
[4] *Towards the Conversion of England, Being the Report of a Commission on Evangelism Appointed by the Archbishops of Canterbury and York Pursuant to a Resolution of the Church Assembly Passed at the Summer Session, 1943* (London, 1945), p. 6.
[5] Ibid., p. 5.   [6] Wand, *God and Goodness*, p. 107.
[7] Garbett, *In an Age of Revolution*, p. 81.

Peterborough), in his great Bampton Lectures for 1944.[1] In the upheaval of values which took place in the 1960s—after this post-war interlude in which reapplications of traditional Christian teachings usually predominated—some churchmen found reasons for violating Spencer Leeson's rule, and for seeking just such an accommodation. In 1956 Archbishop Ramsey criticized the Lambeth Report on *The Doctrine of Man* (1948) precisely because, in anticipation of the thinking of the 1960s, he was offended by its sharp distinction between humanism and Christianity; because 'here the distinction between the natural and the supernatural slips out of sight'. He found Raven's Gifford lectures more 'noble' than the Lambeth Report of 1948.[2]

It was the first part of the Lambeth Report on *The Doctrine of Man* that considered the challenge of secular humanism. This was the section compiled by Bishop Wand. It was a clear and uncompromising statement of Christian teaching. 'The drama of contemporary history is a conflict between the Gospel and secularism for the possession of the human soul,' the Report declared. 'Now, if ever, the Church must be ready and equipped to accept its historical mission as the spiritual guardian and trustee of a civilization painfully built up under Christian auspices.'[3] Some Christian content in contemporary humanism was acknowledged, but these surviving qualities—'derivatives from Christianity'—disclosed no 'eternal dimension for the human spirit'; they were 'avowedly man-centred', regarding man as 'his own sovereign'. Humanism offered no valid sanctions: 'We have all had vivid experience of the power of evil wrecking the hopes of men, and against this the secular form of humanism can offer no ultimate defences.' Humanism 'treats man, in theory and in practice, as no more than a product of natural forces, whether biological or economic, within which his experience is confined and by which his motives are determined'. Between such a doctrine of human nature, and Christianity, 'there can be no compromise; and it seems to be increasingly probable that it is between these two that the world must choose'.[4] The Lambeth Report recognized not only the clear differences in these two views of human nature, but saw also that in the new world-context of totalitarian political ideologies, secular humanism was the version of a materialistic doctrine of man most likely to take root in England. The political implications were enormous, since the collectivist modern State, with all its educational apparatus, was increasingly in a position to influence its citizens according to whatever view of human nature it favoured. 'The youth of a democratic State may be moulded on a pattern, and given a particular philosophy, by a so-called

---

[1] Spencer Leeson, *Christian Education* (London, 1947), p. 115.
[2] Ramsey, *Durham Essays and Addresses*, p. 47.
[3] *The Lambeth Conference, 1948*, Report No. I, 'The Christian Doctrine of Man', p. 2.
[4] Ibid., p. 4.

democratic education, just as truly as the Hitler Youth is moulded on the Hitler pattern,' Bell had warned in 1940.[1]

In opposition to secular humanism, churchmen returned to the doctrine of Original Sin, to the inherent tendency to corruption and self-regard which describe the ambiguity of human motivation. Again, there were political implications. And the application of Original Sin in opposition to the world political ideologies of the 1940s makes the period an exceptional one in the history of the English Church. It was a rare example of the Church really applying theological concepts to political behaviour— rather than, as was more usual, employing theological reinterpretation to justify political values derived from the surrounding class and intellectual culture. Most English opinion in the 1940s was opposed both to totalitarianism and to humanism: to that extent the Church reflected conventional beliefs. But general opinion did not find in Original Sin an explanation for the limits of human capacity to contrive desired social objectives. Churchmen really were being forced by the alien political ideas they saw at work in the world to return to first principles of the traditional theological view of man—or what they thought of as such a view. The emphasis on the theological basis of political scepticism was really the result of the increased secularization of the culture: Victorian Christianity had had less need to spell out the subtle consequences of Original Sin, or had not even to be conscious of them, because the world of values in which it operated, despite the much-publicized criticisms of Biblical theology, had not in general departed from a Christian view of things. This was not true of the mid-twentieth century. The most systematic statement of the real implications of Original Sin, furthermore, did not come from a conservative churchman, but from Canon Demant, the Christian Socialist. Of all the writing on political and social questions by churchmen in the last century and a half, Demant's essays in Christian polity, published as *Theology and Society*, in 1947, stand out for their intellectual coherence. Demant was then a Canon of St. Paul's. The essays were drawn from several years of writing—some were pre-war. The clearest applications of the doctrine of Original Sin to political behaviour were offered in essays entitled 'The Mischief of Ideals', which first appeared in the American edition of *Christendom*, and in 'The Formation of Consciences', which was first published in *The Rebel Church* in 1943. Demant pointed to the absurdity of those Christians who spoke of politics as essentially concerned with the adjustment of 'a discrepancy between ideals and practice'.[2] This, of course, was exactly what 'Christian Sociology' had done in the years between the wars, in its contrast between the economic order of medieval Christendom, and modern competitive

[1] Bell, *Christianity and World Order*, p. 69.
[2] Demant, 'The Mischief of Ideals', in *Theology of Society*, p. 149.

society. Demant now argued that 'the whole conception of a conflict between practice and ideals is misleading and even mischievous'. For Christianity is about man as he really is, man whose highest aspirations are alloyed with the ambiguities and corruptions germane to his fallen condition. Christianity takes account of man realistically: it is concerned with 'the forces which cause him to violate his essential nature'.[1] The spiritual tradition which is Christianity has grown inside internal references which require grace and redemption for an adequate comprehension of human life. Men are mixed up in the world—in it but not of it; their efforts to seek goodness are only intelligible in the vocabulary of spirituality; and this is not immediately compatible with political or social theories derived from a view of man which does not recognize the screen of Original Sin.

The dilemma is made more intolerable by the Pelagian habit of Anglo-Saxon religion which encourages the notion that the will can act as the agent of the absolute good in any social situation. Men are thus continually mistaking their relatively better decisions for decisions that embody the absolute good. That is the whole ethos of modern politics and economics. To take a moral outlook which for generations has been confined to making judgments upon the motives and acts of men, and attempt to apply it in a concrete social structure which has grown up in entire independence of a religious philosophy, is to deepen and not to relieve the tragedy of man and to foster disillusionment instead of encouragement.[2]

Demant's own disillusionment with earlier 'Christian Sociology' became evident. 'Most of the slogans of the liberal "social gospel" have become unreal,' he wrote; 'and such catchwords as fellowship, service, sacrifice, have the effect of making one stifle a shriek of spiritual pain when they reach the ear of Christian realism.'[3] Unless the true and fallen natures of men are the centre of the Christian view of the world there can be no adequate Christian attitude to social life. 'The most pernicious and debilitating results have followed from the identification of the morality of social living as such with the supernatural values of the life in grace,' Demant pointed out. 'It has led to a utopian idealism in social ethics which leaves all real problems outside it.'[4]

The believer who has won some insight into the meaning of original sin and the need of grace knows also that the extent of what is wrong in organized society is out of all proportion to the deliberately anti-social or defective behaviour of persons and groups in it at any one time. He knows the corrupting effects of the collective miasma of sinfulness upon the best intentions, the good motives and the altruistic actions of personal and corporate wills . . . The first question which

[1] Ibid., p. 150.
[3] Ibid., 'The Formation of Consciences', p. 164.
[2] Ibid., p. 156.
[4] Ibid., p. 167.

the Christian mind will ask of a social order is whether its organization recognizes the moral frailty of man.[1]

It was precisely this view of social and political questions, based upon the doctrine of Original Sin, that some Church thinkers in the 1960s in practice abandoned—though most were apparently unaware either of what they were abandoning or of the extent of their defection. Original Sin, as Demant and 'traditional' Christianity saw it, was not an accidental attribute of human nature, attached to Christianity in the centuries before men had come through 'modern knowledge' to understand cultural conditioning and psychological necessity, which, once explained, was to be reinterpreted in some picture language. Original Sin was not a myth or a parable, to describe men's evil actions—and particularly men's sexual actions. It was a basic account of essential human nature, known in the religious and spiritual tradition of the world; sustained in those who through the centuries transmitted the wisdom of religious experience. It was not an explanation of evil acts which unenlightened or wrongly principled men might do; it was an explanation of the force of evil itself in the world, in and through the natures of men. The later optimism, and the taste for social engineering, which characterized the liberal approach of radical churchmen to political questions in the 1960s, was founded upon a practical refusal to believe the doctrine of Original Sin as traditionally understood, and to accept, instead, contemporary views of human nature at the valuation set upon them by the secular humanists within the intelligentsia who increasingly formed opinions on such questions.

Demant was far from being alone in his attempt to counter the false optimism of liberal attitudes to social improvement. A continuous stream of commentary came from Church leaders during the 1940s. In his *Christianity and Social Order*, Temple had acknowledged that the 'assertion of Original Sin should make the Church intensely realistic, and conspicuously free from Utopianism',[2] an opinion he was rather better at offering than observing. Vidler pointed to the wrong assumption of humanism that men are naturally reasonable. 'The Christian insight is far more realistic,' he wrote in 1940; 'it is expressed in the traditional dogma of original sin.'[3] Reckitt, under the influence of Demant (who belonged to the 'Christendom' party), also showed signs of appreciating the consequences of the doctrine in the political sphere. In 1946 he wrote—in a book which he declared was 'a practical study of the relationship of the Christian to politics in Britain to-day'—[4]

---

[1] Demant, 'The Formation of Consciences' in *Theology of Society*, p. 168.
[2] Temple, *Christianity and Social Order*, p. 38.
[3] Vidler, *God's Judgement on Europe* (London, 1940), p. 27.
[4] Reckitt, *The Christian in Politics*, p. 9.

Repudiation of the doctine of Original Sin, or even the failure to recognize its existence as a fact, not only makes for an unrealistic diagnosis of political possibilities. It tends to lead to ruthlessness in political conflict and prepares the way for totalitarianism. For since moral fallibility is no longer assumed to be in some measure universal, so that its influence will affect all policies and all parties, but is regarded rather as an exceptional and even monstrous sort of malice, the 'liberal', his optimism thus so unfairly falsified, hates the 'sin' of his opponents.[1]

Reckitt and Demant both lived to see the world of the later 1960s and 1970s, when leading churchmen, and the World Council of Churches, spoke unambiguously of the 'evil' of certain classes and parties, and of the value of humanist social morality, in just the manner they lamented. Charles Smyth, Fellow of Corpus Christi, Cambridge, and later Rector of St. Margaret's, Westminster, spoke in 1942, at Winchester Cathedral, of a 'widespread and very serious delusion that certain sins are confined to certain classes of the community, or that they are likely to be dangerous only when society is organized in a specific manner'.[2] The Lambeth Report on *The Doctrine of Man* in 1948, also underlined the essential fact of man's sin, and the fact, also, of man's Redemption. Only the grace of God could fit men for free institutions in society; in their own strength every political structure, of whatever apparent morality or social justice, would become destructive. 'The hope that free institutions can be safeguarded on a secular basis must prove self-defeating.' Already, indeed, 'many in their despair are surrendering to a historical determinism which paralyzes all moral enterprise and murders all spiritual hope'.[3]

Against the determinism of humanism, and against the relativity of secular sanctions, the Church reiterated its adhesion to Natural Law, and to the human rights derived from it. 'The Christian Church', declared the bishops at Lambeth in 1948, 'demands essential human rights for all, irrespective of race or colour'; though they warned, too, of the duties which men also have in society.[4] Resolution 7 of the Conference defined that 'among such rights are security of life and person; the right to work, to bring up a family, and to possess personal property; the right to freedom of speech, of discussion and association, and to accurate information; and to full freedom of religious life and practice, and that these rights belong to all men'.[5] The Atlantic Charter—a similar Natural Law statement— was approved by the Conference.[6] Temple had founded his attitude to human freedom on Natural Law,[7] and it was usual for churchmen to oppose the claims of totalitarianism with appeals to a law outside the

[1] Ibid., p. 15.   [2] Charles Smyth, *Religion and Politics* (London, 1943), p. 21.
[3] *The Lambeth Conference, 1948*, No. 1 Report, 'The Christian Doctrine of Man', p. 8
[4] Ibid., *Encyclical Letter*, p. 20.   [5] Ibid., p. 30.
[6] Ibid., 'The Doctrine of Man', No. II Report, p. 12.
[7] Temple, *Christianity and Social Order*, p. 57.

control of men.'There is a law higher than the law of the State, and that is the law of God', wrote Bell, in classic Thomism, an adhesion to the Divine Laws as well as to the Natural Laws: 'The reason why morality is encouraged, why faithfulness, honesty, justice are promoted in the State is not because they help the efficiency of the State but because they are the Will of God.'[1] Demant, too, preserved the priority of Natural Law as the culture in which the spiritual discernment of men was embedded. The family, especially, could only be protected from violation because of its place in the natural order.[2] Garbett frequently referred to the Natural Laws; they were 'promulgated by God in making human nature'.[3] In this, then, as in the doctrine of Original Sin, the realism of churchmen in the mid-century was expressed in traditional teachings of the Church. Fisher linked the two practically. 'No man is ever better merely for having got his rights,' he said at Sydney, in Australia, in 1950. 'No man is ever made better in any significant sense, more noble, more true-hearted, less selfish and egoistic, except in proportion as he gives himself to his duty—that is, of course, the significance of the one supreme spiritual law which Christ declared.'[4] It was the point Temple had made in *Christianity and Social Order*, and which was at the centre of the Christian view of human society: individual redemption must precede social improvement.

Humanism may have appeared—and truly appeared—the immediate threat to faith and morals in England, but, after the defeat of Fascism and National Socialism, the rapid spread of Communism, in the world context, became equally alarming. It was as a form of philosophical determinism, as well as because of its atheism, that it attracted the hostility of the Church in England—quite apart from conventional class opposition to Communism which the clergy shared with the social levels from which they were drawn and whose prejudices they reflected. 'Mankind has only recently escaped conquest by totalitarian States which deified their own power,' observed the bishops at the Lambeth Conference in 1948. 'It now finds itself threatened by the new menace of Marxian Communism which exalts atheism, puts supreme confidence in material progress, and proclaims its gospel with a militant enthusiasm which expects to conquer the world.' The bishops were anxious to link Marxist teaching with the tactical devices and the violence used to attain its ends. 'Christians must repudiate this form of Communism, and must condemn the cruelties, injustice, and lying propaganda which are inherent in it.' They were also, on the other hand, not insensitive to those who found in Communism 'a protest against social injustice', who believed that Communism had

[1] G. K. A. Bell, *The Church and Humanity* (*1939–1946*) (London, 1946), 'A War of Ideals', p. 213.

[2] V. A. Demant, 'The Ideas of a Natural Order', in *Prospect For Christendom*, ed. Reckitt, p. 38.

[3] Garbett, *In an Age of Revolution*, p. 58.   [4] *The Archbishop Speaks*, p. 96.

'inherited a concern for the depressed and downtrodden which is—wherever it is true to its vocation—a glory of the Church'. Communism was not, therefore, 'the only influence in our political and economic world against which the Christian conscience must take its stand'. In the western world, there were 'forms of economic domination' which were also to be condemned for not exhibiting 'any clearer recognition of moral law'.[1] The bishops had not lost sight of the criticism and suspicions of competitive economic principles which had characterized their outlook on English society in the pre-war years. The Report on *The Doctrine of Man* regarded Marxism as 'a "heresy" of Christianity'—'a secularized form of the Christian hope, drawing some of its springs from the Bible and presenting something like a caricature of the Christian hope, of the Christian doctrine and culture, and above all of the Christian eschatology'.[2] The last point was especially apposite: Communism was seen as a version of the secular redemption so central to modern political thinking—in this case to be procured through the purifying, cataclysmic events of the revolution. The Report was also, however, careful to distinguish atheistic Communism from the ideas of those 'who call themselves Christian Communists and believe in the removal of class distinctions through Communal ownership, but who combine such views with belief in God'.[3] Thus the 'Christianity of the Left' movement, associated particularly with Professor John Macmurray and Kenneth Ingram, and which was at its greatest point of influence—though that was not very great—during the war years, escaped condemnation. The Lambeth teaching on Communism was endorsed at the World Anglican Congress, held in Minneapolis, Minnesota, in 1954. The State was there encouraged 'to protect good order and peace from all subversive movements', and the Church, at the same time, was called upon to 'be a fearless witness against political, social and economic injustice'.[4]

Garbett later dissented from the Lambeth view that Communism was a 'Christian heresy'. This was because the 'fundamental differences' between Marxism and Christianity were 'so deep' that it was impossible for him to consider Marxist materialism, the Marxist view of human nature, the Marxist conception of morality, and the absence of any hope for a future life in Marxism, as being in any way the teachings of a system related to Christianity.[5] He also identified Communism with what seemed to be its methods—with terror, propaganda, revolution[6]—and

---

[1] *The Lambeth Conference, 1948, Encyclical Letter*, p. 19. For the formal condemnation of Communism, see Resolution 25 (p. 33).

[2] Ibid., 'The Christian Doctrine of Man', No. I Report, p. 4.

[3] Ibid., No. II Report, p. 20.

[4] *Report of the Anglican Congress, 1954*, ed. P. M. Dawley (Seabury Press, Conn., 1954), p. 202.

[5] Garbett, *In an Age of Revolution*, pp. 203-4.   [6] Ibid., p. 185.

believed that by its fruits it was known. In 1950 Bishop Bell, with the approval of Fisher, initiated a series of discussions on the Anglican attitude to Communism. The conclusions were published in 1953. Bell, in his introduction, regarded Communism in itself as a religion, and its appeal to men to be explained appropriately. The Church was, he wrote, open 'to the necessity of the use of force on an adequate scale to meet a Communist aggressor'.[1] The discussions had taken place under the shadow of the Berlin blockade; the 'Cold War' was at its height. Donald Mackinnon, Professor of Moral Philosophy at Aberdeen, was the editor of the published essays. In Marxism, he pointed out, there was 'no natural law, other than the fact of the class struggle', and ' no place for the exercise of such human virtues as pity and compassion this side of the ending of that struggle'. He recognized that a lot of liberals would be caught in the net, however. 'The Marxist may, of course, for the purposes of propaganda, try to "sell" to the liberal the actual reforms carried out in the so-called "People's Democracies" as truly humanitarian in the traditional sense,' Mackinnon observed; 'but this is little more than sales-talk.'[2] In answer to Communism, the Church must discover how to present 'the mystery of Christ's resurrection in a scientific age'.[3] The contrast was, for Mackinnon, a sharp one: between two faiths, between the mysterious truths of the Christian dispensation and the materialistic and ruthless view of man offered in Communism. One of the contributors to these discussions, however, was less willing to see these distinctions with such clarity. Dr. J. A. T. Robinson, Dean of Clare College, Cambridge, sought to reinterpret Christianity to show that its 'other-worldly' dimension was not really part of its essential nature. 'What the Communist programme offered was quite simply to restore to earth the hope—and therefore the justice—of which it had been robbed by heaven.'[4] This Feuerbachianism was balanced by a recognition that 'anything that can rescue human nature from the consequences of itself must come from outside'.[5]

It may be said that the English Church had, therefore, come out very emphatically against Communism. In later years the spread of humanist values, the further decline of a system of values which related man to his eternal expectations, and the accumulation of left-wing political idealism in western society, made the post-war blanket opposition of the Church to Communism appear unfortunate to some. The realities of the 'Cold War' had by then slipped from vision. Yet Europe really had appeared to be under actual military threat; the Stalinist Marxism of the post-war years

---

[1] *Christian Faith and Communist Faith. A Series of Studies by Members of the Anglican Communion*, ed. D. M. MacKinnon (London, 1953), p. x.

[2] Ibid., 'Christian and Marxist Dialectic', p. 231.

[3] Ibid., 'Prayer, Worship and Life', p. 249.

[4] Ibid., 'The Christian Hope', p. 212.   [5] Ibid., p. 218.

had not presented itself as compatible in any practical degree with institutional Christianity.

There were, of course, a few within the Church who believed otherwise at the time. Kenneth Ingram managed to suppose that the Soviet State, once viewed separately from the anti-Russian propaganda of the press, was really an instrument 'to give the individual the fullest opportunities for his own development, spiritual, mental, physical', for Communism 'exists to provide the fulfilment of individual expression'.[1] Ingram even identified the Christian conception of 'love' with Marx's 'theory that everything develops by means of a struggle of opposites'. Real 'love' was concerned with an actual struggle to secure justice against the currents of resistance in human society.[2] This view came into vogue again in the 1960s, when 'liberation' movements of minorities in western society, or of race groups in the under-developed world, were identified by some Christian bodies and writers as the embodiments of true Christian 'love'. The 'Christianity of the Left' of the 1940s attacked 'other-worldliness' and 'dualism' indiscriminately, for leaving this world in all its injustices, as they imagined, and directing the attention of men to spiritual, and not material, service. 'As "Left-Wing Christianity" uses the term "Dualist" it can be applied to any view which supposes any contrast of quality or worth between one element of the world and another'—so, in 1940, wrote Dr. Edwyn Bevan, a classical scholar and writer on Christianity; a man expertly acquainted with Greek concepts of philosophical dualism.[3] ' "Left-Wing Christianity" has a word by which it thinks apparently it can make short work of any opposing view.'[4] Charles Raven devoted a lot of his energies, over many years, to assaulting 'Dualism' in Christianity: one of the qualities which commended him to Archbishop Ramsey.[5] Of Communism itself Raven had a simple view, derived, not from a resignation to the fallen condition of men, which makes all human endeavour ambiguous, but from totting up the pros and cons. There was good and bad on both sides of the Iron Curtain, he concluded. There was also, he believed, 'a landslide back to the Church' in Russia.[6] Such is the peril of prophetic judgement.

The most well-known Christian advocate of Communism in these years was still Hewlett Johnson, Dean of Canterbury until his retirement in 1963. But despite the seriousness of the contribution he made to the political thinking of the Church in the years between the wars, Hewlett

---

[1] Kenneth Ingram, *Christianity—Right or Left?* (London, 1937), p. 157.

[2] Kenneth Ingram, *The Christian Challenge to Christians* (London, 1938), p. 86.

[3] Edwyn Bevan, *Christians in a World at War* (London, 1940), p. 132.

[4] Ibid., p. 131.

[5] Ramsey, *Durham Essays and Addresses*, p. 47.

[6] Charles E. Raven, *Christ and the Modern Opportunity* (London, 1956), 'Christ and Social Problems', p. 50.

Johnson's judgement, in the 1940s and 1950s, was open to question. He travelled extensively in socialist countries, yet the more he experienced of Communism the less he seems to have applied even the most elementary critical faculties. He welcomed the 'new China' and was received by Mao Tse-Tung in 1952. He was in China again in 1956, in 1959, and in 1964. He denounced the involvement of Chinese Christianity with 'imperialism'.[1] He also travelled in Russia and in Eastern Europe often, and in 1964 he went to Cuba. In 1951 he was awarded the Stalin Peace Prize. In 1956 he supported the Russian suppression of the Hungarian 'counter-revolution'.[2] At home, he gave himself to the Campaign for Nuclear Disarmament in the early 'sixties, and went on the Aldermaston marches several times. His writings included books about the achievements of Russian and of Chinese Communism; but the only really theoretical work of these years was the publication in 1956 of *Christians and Communism*—sermons preached in Canterbury Cathedral. The book appeared at an unfortunate moment: at the time of the Hungarian uprising. It argued that between Communism and Christianity it was possible 'to discover many points of contact' which would 'pave the road to unity'.[3] As in the *Socialist Sixth of the World* (1939), he sought to interpret dialectical materialism as a Christian truth. Marx did not use the term, he wrote, in a way that 'denies spiritual values'.[4] But the subtleties of Johnson's earlier work were absent here. A crude attack on 'other-worldliness' became the basis of his materialism: 'Idealism, in its extremes, despairs of this world altogether and taking its ideas aloft leaves this world to the ruthless, the exploiter, the profiteer, the profligate.'[5] He was, indeed, attracted to socialism by the sexual purity which struck him in the countries he visited—so different from the commercialized sex of western capitalism.[6] Like Conrad Noel, he saw Christ as a political revolutionary. 'Jesus' dialectical insight,' he wrote, 'His insight into a nature of the intrusion of ideas and acts which cracked the crusted surface of the static order, of the process by which it operates and of the course it takes—made Him perceive the inwardness of revolutionary change.'[7] He also saw the Virgin as a sort of urban guerrilla: 'Within the home circle at Nazareth Mary seems to have trained several as pioneers of new revolutionary thought and action.'[8] Jesus was a prophet of female emancipation.[9] The identification of contemporary Communism with the Gospel was extremely close. The Soviet offer of atomic aid to China was described as 'a further outburst of that same Christian movement which Jesus launched so dramatically on the world by His declaration that it was God's purpose to

---

[1] Hewlett Johnson, *Searching for Light*, p. 319.   [2] Ibid., p. 370.
[3] Hewlett Johnson, *Christians and Communism* (London, 1956), p. 13.
[4] Ibid., p. 24.   [5] Ibid., p. 27.   [6] Ibid., p. 65.
[7] Ibid., p. 43.   [8] Ibid., p. 49.   [9] Ibid., p. 50.

create a world-wide family'.[1] But extraordinary as this sort of thing looks from a later vantage-point, it is as well to remember that the complete identification between the Gospel and the 'liberation movements' of the later 1960s was no less extravagant in its claims upon the intelligence. Archbishop Fisher felt obliged to repudiate Hewlett Johnson's opinions publicly on several occasions.[2]

Alongside the censures of totalitarianism, humanism, and Communism, the Church continued to preach against the ills of industrial society at home. This was a straight continuation of the tradition of social criticism institutionalized within the leadership of the Church in the earlier decades of the century. But it was more cautious; less easily given to facile judgements on complicated and technical matters of economic doctrine and practice. A lot of time was taken up in the Convocations with canon-law revision between 1948 and 1960, and to some extent this deprived churchmen of the occasion for lengthy collective discussion of social issues. There were, of course, plenty of examples of churchmen attacking the profit motive and capitalism as 'damaging to the human spirit',[3] and as 'industrial slavery'.[4] Churchmen still found it necessary to rake guiltily over what—in the orthodoxy of the C.S.U. tradition—was now unreflectingly accepted as the failure of the nineteenth-century Church to concern itself with social questions.[5] Reckitt was still prepared, in 1941, to contend for the benefits of Social Credit,[6] although by that date its other advocates in England had mostly surrendered. But the keen edge had gone from social criticism. The Welfare State held out great promise, and 'the world of *laissez-faire* is dead, in so far as it ever existed at all'.[7] The remnants of Christian Socialism were in general happy to settle for what they had got. D. L. Munby, of King's College, Aberdeen, and later a Fellow of Nuffield College, Oxford, was among those who argued for the Christianity of a mixed economy. 'It is to be preferred,' he wrote, 'because it allows for the variety and experiment necessary to human life, and because it sets no rigid and dogmatic bounds to action by the State or private initiative.' It also avoided the totalitarian perils of complete collectivism. The Labour Party, in Munby's judgement, was better suited to the operation of a mixed economy than the Conservatives.[8] Garbett found the controlled capitalism of post-war England acceptable, and quite unlike the old

[1] Ibid., p. 62.
[2] Carpenter, *Cantaur, The Archbishops in their Office*, p. 495; Purcell, *Fisher of Lambeth*, p. 142.
[3] Eric Gill, *Christianity and the Machine Age* (London, 1940), p. 35.
[4] *Towards the Conversion of England*, p. 14.
[5] For an authoritative statement of this view, see *The Lambeth Conference, 1948*, 'The Christian Doctrine of Man', No. II Report, p. 21.
[6] Reckitt and Casserley, *The Vocation of England*, pp. 92-3.
[7] D. L. Munby, *Christianity and Economic Problems* (London, 1956), p. 233.
[8] Ibid., p. 235.

system he had attacked so frequently in the 1920s.[1] Yet enough of his former suspicions survived to make him an outspoken opponent of the introduction of Independent Television in 1954. He had, he told the Church Assembly, 'serious scruples' about commercial broadcasting.[2] His real fears were not so much that capitalistic exploitation might result, however, as that the need for advertising revenue would lead to cultural debasement by lowering the standard of programmes.[3] The Church continued to condemn most forms of gambling because of its moral consequences, and because of the social effects on the standard of living in a family whose head was tempted to hazard his income in this way. The Lambeth Conference of 1948 attacked the 'grave moral and social evils' of gambling.[4] The Conference of 1958 added, to its censure of gambling, a warning about the use of drugs for pleasure.[5] Fisher opposed the Conservative Government when it introduced its Premium Savings Bond Scheme in 1956. He saw it as a form of national lottery. It was 'private gain divorced from responsibility'. The Government should see 'that money gained shall be truly earned and that money earned shall be used reasonably, thoughtfully, and for the general good'.[6] In 1958 the Lambeth Conference Report on *The Family in Contemporary Society* laid down some essential conditions for employment, to prevent 'industrial pressures' from vitiating home and family life. Human needs were to come before production; working shifts were to be arranged so as to cause a minimum interference with normal home life; migrant and contract labour must be controlled; and more care was to be taken in the training of youth for industry.[7] It was a sensible and moderate programme, concerned with the realities of labour. The call for co-operation in industry, made so often in the early years of the century, was set out in Sir George Schuster's *Social Service Lecture* for 1951. He was opposed to nationalization, and argued that the social ills of industry could be cured by 'a form of Community Co-operation'.[8] He also hoped for an end to the 'two sides' of industry language, with its suggestion of inherent conflict; and like the radical bishops of the old C.S.U., he contended that all men, both employers and employed, were, after all, 'workers'.[9] Archbishop Fisher spoke on many occasions about 'co-operation and partnership' in industry.[10] In 1956 he

---

[1] Garbett, *In an Age of Revolution*, p. 117.

[2] *Church Assembly, Spring Sermon, 1954. Report of Proceedings*, Vol. XXXIV, No. 1, p. 110 (18 Feb. 1954).

[3] Ibid., p. 111.   [4] *The Lambeth Conference, 1948*, Resolution 44, p. 36.

[5] *The Lambeth Conference, 1958*, Resolution 126, p. 1, 60.

[6] *The Archbishop Speaks*, p. 177.

[7] *The Lambeth Conference 1958. The Encyclical Letter from the Bishops together with the Resolutions and Reports*, p. 2, 161.

[8] George Schuster, *Christianity and Human Relations in Industry* (London, 1951), p. 64.

[9] Ibid., p. 17.

[10] *The Archbishop Speaks*, 'Christianity and Industry' (1953), p. 110.

addressed the T.U.C. at Brighton on the need for a change 'from force to reason' in industrial relations: the militancy once required by unions to secure their demands was inappropriate in modern conditions, he said.[1] Churchmen, in general—no doubt in reaction against the difficulties and disillusionments of the 'thirties—were optimistic about the prospects for industrial harmony and justice in the years after the war. But the Church never managed to arrive at a satisfactory doctrine of work—although the need for one had long been recognized. In *Prospect for Christendom*, Reckitt's 1940 book of essays on the hopes of 'Christian Sociology', T. M. Heron, the Managing Director of Cresta Silks Ltd. (a prominent layman of the Church, and an expert on the problems of unemployment), had lamented not only the absence of a doctrine of work but the absence also of a sense that one was needed.[2] Temple, writing about unemployment in his Penguin Special, in 1942, had suggested this need too.[3] The Lambeth Conference of 1948 called upon the Church 'to think out afresh the Christian Gospel of Work in terms relevant to modern working conditions'.[4] Despite some good attempts to put this right,[5] no clear doctrine of work received recognition in the Church.

It can be seen from all this that the Church in the 1940s and 1950s had some clear things to say about the threats to Christian social order, including a need to preserve industrial justice at home. Its view of the State as such, and of the relationship between the Church and politics, was not significantly different from its pre-war position. First in priority, the Church retained the belief that it ought not to be 'identified with any particular political or social system'—as the bishops declared at the Lambeth Conference of 1958.[6] And however much there may have been a need for the Church to concern itself with political *principle*, there was an almost universal adhesion to the traditional practice of keeping out of party politics. This was the burden of Temple's *Christianity and Social Order* in 1942, and Charles Smyth's *Religion and Politics*,[7] of the same year—these men representing the most balanced and intelligent thought of the moderate Left and the moderate Right in the Church. Henson's mission of informing the Church of the laity's disapproval of 'political' clergymen seems to have fallen to Garbett. He knew that 'unless the Church permeates with its influence the political parties, they may become increasingly indifferent to the claims of Christianity';[8] but he also knew the

---

[1] Ibid., 'Partnership in Industry', p. 119.

[2] *Prospect for Christendom*, 'Men at Work', p. 114.

[3] Temple, *Christianity and Social Order*, p. 12.

[4] *The Lambeth Conference, 1948*, Resolution 22, p. 32.

[5] See Demant, *Theology of Society*, 'Vocation in Work', pp. 175 ff., and Garbett, *In an Age of Revolution*, 'The Church and Work', pp. 370 ff.

[6] *The Lambeth Conference 1958*, Encyclical Letter, Part 1, p. 20.

[7] Smyth, *Religion and Politics*, p. 8.

[8] Garbett, *The Claims of the Church of England*, p. 220.

English 'suspicion of the parson who preaches political sermons and appears on party platforms'.[1] He argued that much of the bitterness attaching to the Roman Catholic Church in some European countries was explicable not in terms of its Christian faith, but of its political activity.[2] Vidler wisely advised in 1955 that 'Political resolutions by ecclesiastical assemblies or political pronouncements by clerics frequently encourage irresponsibility'.[3] Reckitt blamed left-wing Christians for 'always appealing to the Church to "throw in its lot with the revolution" or "identify itself with the principle of common ownership" '. They 'want religion for the sake of something they have come to value already', he pointed out; 'they do not want that something for the sake of religion'.[4] In this observation, from the most influential lay 'Christian Sociologist' in the Church, the realism of these years is fully illustrated.

Although its teachings prohibited the Church from adhering itself to a particular form of political society, the Church was clear that, in the historical circumstances of the time, and faced with the threats that it was, democratic government appeared the most suited to England's needs. Temple, with his usual reference to classical and to medieval political thought, realized that democracy was not the ideal form of government. '*Vox populi vox dei*: What nonsense!', he said in 1944; 'the defence of government by a majority is not that the majority is always right; on the contrary, the only thing you know for certain about a majority with regard to any new issue is that it's sure to be a little wrong.' But, he added, 'you have no earthly means of finding out which of the minorities, if any, is right, and it is very unlikely that the majority will be as wrong as some of the minorities are likely to be'. Therefore, he concluded, 'it is a great deal safer to let the majority rule than a minority'.[5] Garbett was just as pragmatic and just as certain.

There is nothing specifically Christian in the demand for representative government or the broadeast possible franchise [he wrote in 1952]. The Church is attracted to democracy as a method of government which gives the individual citizen an opportunity of responsibility which would not be found under an oligarchy or despotism: but provided that the State is encouraging the good life among its citizens, the Church need neither accept nor reject on Christian grounds any particular form of government.[6]

The Lambeth Report of 1948 believed that the dependence was on the side of the State: 'Democracy cannot work without the Christian qualities

---

[1] Cyril Garbett, *Church and State in England* (London, 1950), p. 296.

[2] Ibid., p. 297.

[3] Alec R. Vidler, *Christian Belief and This World* (London, 1956), p. 117 (Firth Lectures, Nottingham, 1955).

[4] Reckitt, *The Christian in Politics*, p. 31.

[5] Temple, *The Church Looks Forward*, p. 142.

[6] Garbett, *In an Age of Revolution*, p. 137.

of self-restraint and discipline, and the training provided by Christian fellowship.'[1] There was also some lingering case to be made for the old Guild Socialist notion of the State, 'the Community of Communities', as Temple, in the language of Figgis, put it in his Penguin Special of 1942.[2] Liberty resided in 'the various cultural and commercial and local associations men form', he went on; and then, as if willing to demonstrate the closeness of Guild Socialism to state corporatism, he cited Pius XI's *Quadragesimo Anno* with approval.[3] Reckitt, in 1946, still looked for an 'associative quality' in society; the development of 'a complex of social groupings with an inherent life of their own', and the growing responsibility of these 'corporate bodies' for those who belong to them, the State itself being the coping stone of the whole structure.[4] Very little was heard of such ideas after the mid-'forties anywhere except in Southern Ireland.

The Church's attitude to the relationship of Church and State remained unchanged during these years. The experience of the war, between 1939 and 1945, appeared to reinforce the old notion of the interdependence of religion and civil order in England. Broadcasts and speeches by public men included Christian references and often tended to identify national political and social arrangements with divine will.[5] 'Early in the war some of our leaders declared with truth that we were fighting to defend Christian civilization', Spencer Leeson wrote in 1944.[6] For many, it was seen as a simple conflict to preserve a *Christian* country.[7] Church leaders echoed these sentiments. At the Stoll Theatre meetings, in 1941, Fisher associated the war aims with religion: 'if there is to be any strength and stability in any better order of civilization, it must be based upon the Christian faith and built on the lines of Christian tradition, and principle'.[8] Temple, also, provided a similar view of the war. 'It has often been said that we are fighting for a Christian civilization,' he wrote in 1940; 'my whole contention is that it is our duty to prove that to be a true claim.'[9] It was a war 'for the principle of national morality'.[10] Bell applied these pieties rather strictly, and earned considerable odium—and some thought lost him the Primacy, too—by criticizing the policy of obliteration bombing as unworthy of a Christian country.[11]

---

[1] *The Lambeth Conference 1948*, 'The Christian Doctrine of Man', No. II Report, p. 17.
[2] Temple, *Christianity and Social Order*, p. 47.
[3] Ibid., p. 48.   [4] Reckitt, *The Christian in Politics*, pp. 44–5.
[5] See W. E. Sangster, *Ten Statesmen and Jesus Christ. A Christian Commentary on our War Aims* (London, 1941).
[6] Spencer Leeson, *Christian Education*, p. 194.
[7] Lord Elton, *St. George or the Dragon. Towards a Christian Democracy* (London, 1942), p. 170.
[8] G. K. A. Bell, *The Church and Humanity*, p. 228.
[9] Temple, *The Hope of a New World*, p. 64.
[10] William Temple, *Thoughts in War-Time* (London, 1940), p. 20.
[11] Bell, *The Church and Humanity*, pp. 129 ff; see also Jasper, *George Bell*, p. 262.

These national aspirations for Christianity had to be set against the realities of formal religious practice within the population. In 1945 the Evangelistic Committee, set up by Temple two years previously, reported. Temple was by then dead. There had been a measure of disagreement among the members of the Committee,[1] but their Report was emphatic in one particular: the decline of any real sense in which Christianity was a matter of daily reference for most Englishmen.

Seen from a distance, Britain is the country which seems most nearly to approach the ideal of a Christian community. The ceremony of the Coronation, the regular openings of the sittings of Parliament with prayer, the Mayor's chaplain, the provision for religion in the services and in all State institutions, the religious articles in popular periodicals, the Religious department of the British Broadcasting Corporation, and many similar phenomena, go to show that the ethos of the State remains Christian . . . the Established Church is 'still entwined by countless subtle threads around the life of the realm and nation.' The English are still more deeply influenced by Christianity than they themselves know . . . But behind the facade the situation presents a more ominous appearance.[2]

The mobility of the population during the war years, the Report argued, had revealed 'a wholesale drift from organized religion'.[3] And with it had come a collapse of personal morality—there was a spread of gambling, and an increase in divorce; advertisements, plays, novels, and films had become 'continuous propaganda for sex-indulgence'.[4] Compared with the public display of sexual advertisement which became commonplace twenty years later, these observations seem unduly alarmist; but to many Christians in the 1940s it seemed to be already 'an Age without standards'.[5] Demant said it could at 'best be described as post-Christian'.[6] Reckitt also felt justified in speaking of a 'post-Christian age', to describe a society in transition, still sustaining a Christian view on some things, but riddled with inconsistencies.[7] Yet he did record that, compared with fifty years before, when he was a young man, and when it seemed to be assumed in intellectual circles that religion was 'on the way out', there was in post-war England a growing intellectual respect for Christianity.[8] There were many churchmen for whom Christianity seemed now to be 'a minority opinion in a predominantly pagan world'.[9] But there were also many who supposed that the popular religiosity which faintly glowed in the war years promised better things. Few, it is true, went as far as Lord Elton in speaking of an existing revival of Christianity.[10] But the C. of E. Youth Council, remarking in

[1] Lloyd, *The Church of England*, p. 473.
[2] *Towards the Conversion of England*, p. 2.
[3] Ibid., p. 3.   [4] Ibid., p. 4.   [5] Ibid., p. 5.
[6] Demant, *Theology of Society*, 'Christianity and Civilization', p. 45.
[7] Reckitt, *Militant Here in Earth*, p. 7.
[8] Ibid., p. 12.   [9] Symon, *Lambeth Questions*, p. 27.
[10] Elton, *St. George or the Dragon*, p. 174.

1955 on the half-a-million young persons in its affiliated groups, believed this sufficient evidence to claim that 'England still has a Christian tradition'.[1] Canon Roger Lloyd, a practised observer of religious trends, noted the return of intellectual respectability to Christianity which Reckitt pointed out. It was a hopeful sign; though the increase in adult confirmations, in student religion, in the size of congregations, and in Sunday Schools, which was discernible early in the 1950s, was a middle- and lower-middle-class movement of opinion. The urban working class were apparently unmoved.[2] Lloyd had noticed a rather temporary ripple on the surface. The religious stability of the 1940s and 1950s, which allowed such optimism, did not survive into the next decade. And the success of Billy Graham's London Crusade in 1954—and the public interest in the vast meetings held nightly for three months at the Harringay Arena—were no indication of the malaise ahead. Among those who heard Graham were more than 250 M.P.s.[3] Archbishop Fisher himself wrote that the Crusade came at a time when 'a fairly widespread beginning of a return to the Christian religion had already set in'.[4]

There was, in fact, a conflict of opinion about whether Britain was becoming more Christian or not. One lay writer, who based his findings on nearly two years of interviewing officer cadets—young men of eighteen to twenty-two years—found that over half believed Christianity to be true, and thought the figure would have been higher had religious education been better conducted in the schools.[5] This sample came only from the well educated. Class inhibitions continued to be offered as the leading reason why working men did not go to church—just as they had been throughout the preceding century. A lot of the old problems of 'the class barrier between the clergy and the artisan', Lloyd suggested, were no longer in existence, but the differences were still deep—'a difference of cultural standards'.[6] A Report by the British Council of Churches, published in 1945, which looked at the problems of the Church in rural areas, concluded that the Anglican parson, like the local schoolmaster, 'is frequently regarded as belonging to another social order and a different educational stratum from most of his parishioners'.[7] Nothing new here, either; this was the familiar difficulty, well known to Victorian Christianity.

---

[1] *The Church and Young People. The Story, setting and development of the Youth Work of the Church of England* (London, 1955), p. 15 (published by the Church of England Youth Council).

[2] Lloyd, *The Church and the Artisan Today*, p. 1.

[3] Charles T. Cook, *London Hears Billy Graham. The Greater London Crusade* (London, 1954), p. 107.

[4] Ibid., 'A Remarkable Campaign', by the Archbishop of Canterbury, p. vii.

[5] B. G. Sandhurst, *How Heathen is Britain?* (London, 1946), Part I, p. 27.

[6] Lloyd, *The Church and the Artisan Today*, p. 89.

[7] *The Land, the People and the Churches*, published for the British Council of Churches (London, 1945), p. 40.

At the Minneapolis Anglican Congress in 1954 Bishop Leslie Hunter of Sheffield asked why the workers did not go to church, and also concluded, in classic style, that it was class that kept them away. The Church ought, in consequence, to identify with men 'from the base of the pyramid of industrial society and the majority nowadays in every society'.[1]

Yet many observers? noticed the wide diffusion of a vague Christianity in English society. This was the sense in which Reckitt believed it was possible to speak of England as a Christian country only if Christianity was not closely defined.[2] 'We can at least claim with some confidence that the vast majority of our people are in some real, if shadowy sense theistic in conviction, and at least show no desire to replace the Christianity for which their "National Church" stands by any other faith.' Atheism had no popular appeal, and was still found only among the intelligentsia.[3] Demant believed this vague Christianity positively harmful. 'It equates Christianity with good ideals,' he wrote. 'It attaches no real, vital meaning to sin, grace, redemption, or to the Church as a divine society . . . instead this religion is one of moral exhortation.'[4] The result was 'widespread pronouncements from pamphlets, platforms and pulpits which are merely religiously tinged versions of what the writer or speaker believes to be the most progressive effort of the world to improve itself'.[5] This recorded a constant feature of Christian thought in England, but did some injustice to the widespread spirituality of the working population—it was more a description of what intellectuals in the Church tended to do. Similarly, Bishop Wand was rather too hasty in dismissing popular conceptions of Christianity, which, he believed, regarded Christianity 'merely as a sentiment'. Yet he noticed, correctly, that the absence of people from Church did not mean that they were prepared to be thought unchristian.[6] Temple, too, was clear that the people were far from being irreligious. 'There is a very widespread Theism—a belief in a righteous God who in a general sense rules the world, though He is not regarded as demanding of the individual any more exacting requirement than what may enable him to say, "I have not done any harm to anyone" .' Temple also noticed that 'there is a deeper stratum of real though latent faith which is tapped by great national occasions or by some personal or family events'.[7] Men who, as E. L. Mascall wrote, were perplexed by 'what appear to them to be entirely capricious world-forces', in their daily lives, in the management,

---

[1] *Report of the Anglican Congress, 1954*, p. 163.
[2] Reckitt and Casserley, *The Vocation of England* (1941), p. 135.
[3] Ibid., p. 141.
[4] Demant, *Theology of Society*, 'The menace of National "Christianity" ', p. 240.
[5] Ibid., p. 243.
[6] *Has the Church Failed?*, ed. Sir James Marchant (London, 1947), Introduction, by J. W. C. Wand, p. xi.
[7] Temple, *Social Witness and Evangelism*, pp. 3–4.

by others, of their labour, still found in Christianity an uncomprehended but sure instinct for goodness.[1] The Church still saw in this widely diffused spiritual instinct the basis for a national religious profession.

When he was enthroned at Canterbury in 1945, Archbishop Fisher remarked that Church and State had for many years been drawing apart, and that there was a possibility that this might continue. But there was also the possibility—which he saw it as their duty to explore—that 'they should come together again in a Christian faith which is not ashamed to be definite, explicit and binding, wherein Church and nation, each in its own sphere and function, may glorify God'.[2] The principle of Established religion was still very much taken for granted. During the 1940s and 1950s very few within the Church of England questioned it; and the few Nonconformists or secularists who spoke of disestablishment were responding to historical instincts which were not live politics.[3] The *Church Times*, reviewing Garbett's *Church and State in England*, in 1950, noted that the question of the Establishment was so little discussed that there was 'not enough wind at the moment' even to fly the kite of internal Church reform put up by Garbett.[4] Temple had always assumed the permanent existence of the National Church, and so did Fisher. Nearly every leading churchman in these years felt the same. Garbett was perhaps the most persistent exponent of maintaining close relations between Church and State. 'There is little doubt that if the Church of England were disestablished at the present time,' he wrote in 1950, 'the world would interpret this as the national repudiation of Christianity.'[5] His reasons for the preservation of the Establishment were the traditional ones. The Church 'has the responsibility of arousing and educating the conscience of the State and the nation on matters of public policy and administration'.[6] In his *Claims of the Church of England*, in 1947, Garbett had also argued for the territorial advantages of an Established Church— that provision was made for the spiritual welfare of the smallest communities, of people who could not otherwise pay for the upkeep of religion themselves.[7] There, too, he had written of the Church as the representative of 'the religious aspect of the nation', symbolized in the hallowing of the sovereign in the Coronation ceremonial, which revealed 'the meaning of a

---

[1] E. L. Mascall, 'The Person and the Family', in *Prospect for Christendom*, ed. Reckitt, p. 44. Mascall, Sub-Warden of Lincoln Theological College, was one of the most influential theological writers in the years after the war.

[2] Text of the Enthronement Sermon, in Charles Smyth, *The Church and the Nation* (London, 1962), p. 15.

[3] For one interesting contemporary recognition of the problems raised for the place of religion in a possible secular State, however, see E. G. Rupp, *Is this a Christian Country?* (London, 1941), pp. 2–3. Professor Rupp is a Methodist.

[4] *Church Times*, 10 Mar. 1950.

[5] Garbett, *Church and State in England*, p. 146.   [6] Ibid., p. 131.

[7] Garbett, *The Claims of the Church of England*, p. 188.

Christian State'.[1] Dr. Norman Sykes, Dixie Professor of Ecclesiastical
History at Cambridge, and later Dean of Winchester, spoke of 'the
important and symbolic part' which the Coronation played in the Establishment of religion in England. He was addressing the Church Assembly
after the death of George VI.[2] Charles Smyth was another academic
advocate of the Church as 'the keeper of the public conscience',[3] and
criticized Sir Stafford Cripps in 1942 for suggesting that if the Church
wanted to dissociate itself from 'privilege' it should seek disestablishment.

The real trouble with Left-Wing intellectuals in every generation is self-
righteousness and the claim to a monopoly of principle: which explains not only
the moral recklessness with which they inflict criticism and the moral indignation
with which they suffer it, but also their curious trick of demanding that other
people shall make sacrifices in order to demonstrate their sincerity.[4]

Smyth had written an essay in *Prospect for Christendom* (1940) which
showed how Church and Nation in England were historically interrelated
to such an extent that separation would do injury to both.[5] Reckitt, who
explicitly endorsed Smyth's detailed case for the Establishment,[6] believed
that disestablishment would involve the Church 'in grave prejudice of its
trusteeship of the Christian faith in this age and among the people'.[7] For
F. R. Barry, the Bishop of Southwell, and one of the most popular religious
writers of the period, the Establishment was 'the recognition by the State
that the ultimate ends and sanctions of politics lie in a realm which is
beyond politics'—and was, as a result, a guarantee of freedom against
autocracy.[8] Arthur Headlam (who had retired as Bishop of Gloucester in
1945 and was by 1947 finally convinced that German National Socialism
was built upon the 'repudiation of Christianity'[9]) saw that the close
relationship of Church and State in England 'bids King and Parliament
alike to be guided by Christian principles'.[10] The extent of the commentary
to this effect, from many writers, was very great, and the terms of reference
were sometimes very wide. T. S. Eliot, speaking at the Malvern gathering
in 1941, declared that 'the task of the Church is to Christianize the State
and society'.[11] Eliot was associated with the 'Christendom Group'. His was

---

[1] Garbett, *The claims of the Church of England*, p. 189.
[2] *Church Assembly. Spring and Summer Sessions, 1952. Report of Proceedings*, vol.
XXXII, No. 1, p. 95 (18 June 1952).
[3] Smyth, *Religion and Politics*, p. 13.
[4] Ibid., p. 15.
[5] Charles Smyth, 'The Meaning of a Nation', in *Prospect for Christendom*, ed. Reckitt,
p. 184.
[6] Reckitt, *The Christian in Politics*, p. 84.
[7] Ibid., p. 96.
[8] F. R. Barry, *Church and Leadership* (London, 1945), p. 46.
[9] 'The Duty of the Christian Church', in *Has the Church Failed?*, p. 16.
[10] Ibid., p. 20.
[11] *Malvern, 1941*, p. 212.

a conventional opinion—a sign that, for the time being, the nineteenth-century questionings of the position of religion in national life appeared to be in abeyance. Even Henson, the one surviving influential exponent of disestablishment within the episcopacy, though now in retirement, saw in 1940 that it was the influence of Christianity 'within the national life' that preserved 'the stability of our civilization'.[1]

The Establishment needed reform. There was also a general agreement about that within the Church. Indeed, unlike the Church reform movements of the past, the opinion for reform this time was almost entirely located within the Church—and especially within the clergy. This in itself was an indication of how, in practice, the relations of Church and State had become a minor feature of national life. Church leaders hoped to apply the logic of the Enabling Act of 1919: they hoped to reverse the set-back of 1928 when the Revised Prayer Book had been defeated in Parliament. They hoped, in short, to secure control over the worship of the Church, and to do this without prejudice to the general relations of Church and State in England. Feelings among the clergy were strong on the matter. Temple had said in 1941 that the absence of absolute freedom to order its own worship was, for the Church, 'in the proper sense intolerable'.[2] Bell, who was particularly interested in Church reform, got the bishops to look again at the 1935 *Report of the Church and State Commission*, in July 1943.[3] But still the recommendations of the Report lay unimplemented. After the war Bell gave himself increasingly to his ecumenical work. Garbett then became the leading exponent of reforms in the relationship of Church and State,[4] and Fisher began the work of revising the canons—which he described as 'the most absorbing and all-embracing topic of my whole archiepiscopate'.[5] Garbett's programme for 'some readjustment in the existing relationship between Church and State',[6] included the preservation of Crown appointment of the bishops, but with the right of chapters to submit names, and with the abolition of the formal penalties of *praemunire*;[7] a revised Prayer Book, with complete control of worship vested for the future in the Church and not in Parliament; and reforms of ecclesiastical courts and the Canon Law.[8] These were all objects very much in the tradition of the 1935 Report. In 1949 the Church Assembly had appointed a Commission under Sir Walter Moberly, on the resolution 'That the Assembly, while valuing the "Establishment" of the Church of England as an expression of the nation's recognition of religion, nevertheless is of

---

[1] Henson, *Last Words in Westminster Abbey*, 'Christianity and Liberty' (Sermon in Cambridge, 1940), p. 65.

[2] Temple, *Citizen and Churchman*, p. 67.

[3] Jasper, *George Bell, Bishop of Chichester*, p. 190.

[4] Garbett, *The Claims of the Church of England*, pp. 196 ff.

[5] Purcell, *Fisher of Lambeth*, p. 206.   [6] Garbett, *Church and State in England*, p. 5.

[7] Ibid., pp. 201–2.   [8] Ibid., p. 204.

opinion that the present form of it impedes the fulfilment of the responsibilities of the Church as a spiritual society'. This Commission
reported back unanimously in 1952;[1] their recommendations were accepted
without dissent. They agreed that the Establishment was right in principle,
and that, as Garbett said in the debate, 'disestablishment might lead to the
loss of various opportunities which they now had as a national Church in
giving their message to the nation'.[2] The Report detailed the Church's
case for control of worship and, in effect, reaffirmed the recommendations
of the 1935 Commission. So little, in fact, did the Report discuss the
general principles of the relationship of Church and State that the Dean
of Winchester felt able to point out the need for some study of the serious
issues raised by the continued departure of the State from the law of the
Church in questions of marriage and divorce.[3] The Moberly Report, like
its predecessor, was not implemented. There was, however, an adjustment
in these years which placed one aspect of the relationship of Church and
State upon a surer footing. In 1948 Queen Anne's Bounty was amalgamated with the Ecclesiastical Commission to form the Church Commissioners for England.[4]

The presence of the bishops in the House of Lords was not among
issues raised for reform in the Church. Throughout these years, 'when
some question of national importance is debated', in Garbett's words,
'nearly always one of the archbishops or bishops is present to express the
view not only of the Church but of all Christians on the religious and
moral issues involved'.[5] Diocesan duties kept attendance low, however—
and the old self-imposed rule that the bishops normally spoke only on
moral, religious, or welfare questions, was in general observed, although
the sort of legislation required by the machinery of the post-war Welfare
State sometimes made it extremely difficult for a clear separation to be
made between the traditional issues on which the Church had had a
parliamentary view—housing, for example—and new welfare questions
which had become matters of party political contention. The bishops
tended to avoid anything which divided the House on party lines. Both
Temple and Fisher, however, frequently ventured opinions on national
issues which fell outside the conventional definitions. Temple had never
been an effective parliamentary speaker, but Fisher spoke often and
revealed a great knowledge of public affairs.[6] Garbett, too, was often in
Parliament.[7]

---

[1] *Church Assembly, Spring and Summer Sessions, 1952. Report of Proceedings,* vol.
XXXII, No. 1 (18 June 1952), p. 77.

[2] Ibid., p. 93.   [3] Ibid., p. 77.

[4] Best, *Temporal Pillars,* p. 512.

[5] Garbett, *The Claims of the Church of England,* p. 191.

[6] Purcell, *Fisher of Lambeth,* p. 266.

[7] Smyth, *Cyril Forster Garbett,* p. 433.

As the State extended its collectivist machinery of welfare, so did the Church. These years saw the centralization and departmentalization of most of the Church's own welfare work. In 1942 the Church of England Youth Council was created by the Church Assembly, and in 1947 the Council for Education.[1] The old Board for Moral Welfare, originally constituted in 1917 and re-formed in 1932 and 1934 as the Moral Welfare Council, was in 1958 absorbed into the Board for Social Responsibility. The real growth of an ecclesiastical civil service belonged to the next decade, and the reuqirements of synodical government early in the 1970s expanded it still further.

Part of the stability in the relations of Church and State in these years may be attributed to the absence of a conflict over education. This was due to the acceptance by the Church and the Nonconformists—though not by the Roman Catholics—of the Education Act of 1944. The Act was designed by R. A. Butler, President of the Board of Education in the wartime National Government. It was the most comprehensive educational measure ever passed by parliament. A Ministry of Education replaced the old Board; it was to work in co-operation with Local Education Authorities. The 'dual system' of Church and state schools was modified but perpetuated. Church schools were divided into two categories: 'Voluntary aided schools' were to continue denominational teaching according to their trust deeds, provided that they (or the dioceses) could themselves put up half the costs required to bring their buildings in line with the Ministry's required standards. The Local Authorities would furnish all other expenses. 'Controlled schools'—those unable to raise half their building costs—were to open two-thirds of their management bodies to representatives appointed by the Local Authority; they were to be fully maintained, and were allowed to teach religion only according to the 'agreed syllabus' prescribed by the Local Authority for its own schools. The Church had clearly given some ground here, but rising costs had made it evident that the Church could no longer finance the improvements needed in all its schools.[2] But the Act did establish religious teaching in the state schools, and this, from the Church's point of view, was its greatest advantage. Until 1944 there was no legal provision for religious instruction in state schools at all: the law simply required that those Local Authorities who did provide it should ensure that it was non-denominational—in practice nearly all Authorities did make a provision. The 1944 Act required two things: that there should be religious instruction, and that each day 'should begin with collective worship on the part of all pupils'—with the usual conscience clauses for those parents who wished to withdraw their children. Neither the religious instruction nor the act of worship

[1] The Church and Young People, p. 32.
[2] Murphy, Church, State and Schools in Britain, p. 114.

was to be denominational. Local Education Authorities were empowered to set up advisory bodies to draw up an 'agreed syllabus' for each area. Many such syllabuses were already in use in fact, and these were simply readopted under the terms of the Act; many L.E.A.s accepted successful syllabuses operated by their counterparts in other districts.[1]

The Church had given early approval to the principle of the Act—when the Government's White Paper was published in July 1943. Temple realized that the Church could never hope to regain the initiative in education, and that these were the best terms they were likely to get to preserve the 'dual system'.[2] He was anyway interested in educational reform, and was enthusiastic about the general improvements and the 'parity of esteem' which the Act held out. 'The most serious inequality today is found in the matter of educational opportunity', he had written in 1940.[3] In *Christianity and Social Order* (1942) he had suggested 'regular corporate worship' in the state schools.[4] This was now guaranteed. He hoped that under the Act two other necessary reforms would eventually follow—a reduction in the size of classes, and the raising of the school-leaving age.[5] Garbett later came to believe that Temple had in fact entrusted too much of the Church's share in education to the State; that no safeguards existed to preserve religion in the schools should the State later move to less clear Christian intentions.[6] These fears were certainly justifiable; but in 1944 it did not look that way.

For the first time the consideration of national education was unsullied by a row between the Church and the Nonconformists; and there was a swell of public feeling, doubtless influenced by the war aims, in favour of religious education in the state schools. As Spencer Leeson wrote, 'a wide and deep desire was expressed, outside the Churches as well as within them, that Christianity should be restored to its true and traditional place in English education'.[7] Leeson's Bampton Lectures, on *Christian Education*, were actually delivered as the Education Bill was being discussed in Parliament, in 1944. They are the finest statements of the Church of England's view of education written this century. His vision was a large one, extending back to Plato, and tracing the educational vocation of the Church through the centuries. For the guidance of Church schools, he summarized two principles: the first was the duty 'to initiate the children into membership of this society of the Church, not simply to teach about

---

[1] *Religious Education in Schools. The Report of an Inquiry made by the Research Committee of the Institute of Christian Education into the Working of the 1944 Education Act* (London, 1954), p. 26.

[2] Iremonger, *William Temple*, p. 571.   [3] Temple, *The Hope of a New World*, p. 47.

[4] Temple, *Christianity and Social Order*, p. 69.

[5] Hansard, *Fifth Series*, cxxxii. 34 (6 June 1944).

[6] Smyth, *Cyril Forster Garbett*, p. 287.

[7] Spencer Leeson, *Christian Education* (London, 1947), Foreword, p. v.

it'.[1] The second, to conduct the life of the schools around the truth 'that all human beings are of equal value in the sight of God'.[2] As training in worship was essential to the Christian profession, Leeson welcomed the Education Bill for 'requiring a continuation of worship and instruction' in the state schools.[3] And that would make for good citizenship, since 'a good Christian must necessarily be a good citizen, for with him it is an axiom that no man lives to himself . . .'.[4] The State, however, was not itself a fit teacher of religion—it must 'show itself scrupulously fair to religious convictions of all varieties, provided always that they have attained a recognized place in the unity of the nation's life'. But the State must 'do all in its power to encourage good religious teaching'.[5] The 1944 Bill showed that 'the State apparently recognizes that it is, in idea and intention at any rate, Christian, and so far as the State can contribute effectively to that end, the children of the nation shall be brought up in the faith'.[6] Further: 'Parliament has declared by and through this requirement the will of the nation that it shall be a Christian nation'.[7]

The Church Assembly welcomed the Bill, as it was going through Parliament, on a motion of the Bishop of London (Fisher).[8] Opposition was led by A. H. Rees, a minor Canon of St. Paul's, who claimed to speak for 'the great majority of the rank and file of Church people'.[9] The claim was possibly well founded. As with educational compromises in the past, there was quite a difference in attitude between Church leaders, who were generally willing, as a result of their parliamentary and administrative experience, to give and take a lot, and the lower clergy and laity, who, less well accomplished in the liberal arts of compromise, were suspicious. Rees objected to the 'greater obstacles which were placed in the way of giving denominational instruction' in Church schools.[10] 'The progressive decay of religion had made it clear that religious instruction did not reach its proper goal unless it attracted the child to a worshipping community.' The 'agreed syllabuses' were hardly likely, in his estimation, to foster Christian conviction.[11] But the Bill was approved in the Church Assembly by a large majority.[12] In the House of Lords Temple acknowledged that 'it writes religion into national education in a way which has never been done before'.[13] It offered 'a reform of the dual system such as has won a very large measure of assent', which, in view of past bitterness, was a 'very great achievement'.[14] Although the Bill did not contain all the Church might, in other circumstances, have preferred, its future was 'promising'

---

[1] Ibid., p. 120.   [2] Ibid., p. 123.   [3] Ibid., p. 129.   [4] Ibid., p. 137.
[5] Ibid., p. 190.   [6] Ibid., p. 193.   [7] Ibid., p. 194.
[8] *Church Assembly, Spring Session, 1944. Report of Proceedings*, vol. XXIV, No. 1, p. 59 (16 Feb. 1944).
[9] Ibid., p. 100.   [10] Ibid., p. 67.   [11] Ibid., p. 68.   [12] Ibid., p. 102.
[13] Hansard, *Fifth Series*, cxxxii. 37 (6 June 1944), Debate on the Second Reading of the Education Bill.   [14] Ibid., 39.

—Temple's fulsome response rather evaporated as the amendments proceeded.[1] Lang, from his retirement, sent a letter approving the Bill.[2] Henson, in his retirement, regretted that the dual system had been preserved at all. He favoured 'undenominational' religious teaching, because, in his view, English Christianity, though genuine enough, *was* 'undenominational'.[3] Bell, in the Lords' debate, took 'a less cheerful view' than Temple.[4] He regretted that religious instruction was to be made compulsory in the state schools, for as no religious tests were allowed in the appointment of teachers there was no guarantee as to the religious character of their teaching, and the result might, in practice, be far from Christian.[5] This consideration became much more significant in later years. The 1944 Act, however, passed with the approval of most Church leaders. Headlam appears to have regretted it on the ground that it added too much to collectivism, that it was 'a great advance towards totalitarianism', by increasing the powers of the State to mould the thoughts of children.[6] But this was not a view held by many in the leadership of the Church. The Act was welcomed by the press and in public discussion generally. The Roman Catholic Church did not join the Establishment in co-operating with it: the Catholic schools declined 'controlled' status.[7] In 1948 the Lambeth Conference commended the Act for providing for worship and instruction in the state schools,[8] and it noticed the need for the Church and the State to continue to co-operate in the furtherance of Christian education.[9]

During the next two decades, more satisfaction was expressed in the Church over the provision of worship in the state schools than over the quality of the religious instruction. The recognition in the Act of the importance of corporate worship had, in the first ten years, 'encouraged schools to pay more attention to form and content', according to the Research Committee of the Institute of Christian Education, an interdenominational body linked with the British Council of Churches. There was 'no tendency to foster a "school religion", impoverished in itself, and mischievous in so far as it might offer a substitute for worship in the Churches'.[10] But the Church remained unhappy about the religious instruction. For some, of course, the real disquiet derived from dislike of 'undenominational' education in any form, although, according to

[1] Hansard, *Fifth Series*, cxxxii. 972 (18 July 1944).
[2] Ibid. 42 (read out by Temple in the debate).
[3] *Letters of Herbert Hensley Henson*, ed. Braley, p. 147 (2 Nov. 1943).
[4] Hansard, cxxvii. 45.　　　　　　　　　　[5] Ibid. 46.
[6] Arthur C. Headlam, 'The Duty of the Christian Church', in *Has the Church Failed?*, ed. Marchant, p. 24.
[7] Murphy, *Church, State and Schools*, p. 118.
[8] *The Lambeth Conference, 1948*, p. 34; Resolution 31.
[9] Ibid., 'The Christian Doctrine of Man', No. II Report, p. 22.
[10] *Religious Education in Schools* (1954), p. 109.

Professor Jeffreys of the Durham Department of Education, the 'prevailing view' in the Churches after the passing of the 1944 Act was that the Churches 'could best serve the cause of Christian education by co-operating with the lay authorities in making the "undenominational" religious instruction in the provided schools as good as possible'.[1] But dissatisfaction at the quality of the instruction grew.[2] Archbishop Fisher, addressing the students at Hockerill Training College in 1952, pointed out that at a time when 'no system of basic truth is presented to pupils by the social environment in which they live', a very clear statement of Christianity was required to be imparted at school.[3] The year after the passage of the Act, in fact, the Commission on Evangelism had observed that the religious instruction in the schools 'has not allowed Christian teaching to take its proper place as the unifying factor in education, co-ordinating all learning'.[4] Many churchmen still looked to their own schools to act as the spearhead of advance in proper Christian education—and not only to the primary and secondary schools related to the national system, but also to the public schools. The Fleming Report[5] of 1944 had sought to broaden their social basis by encouraging Local Education Authorities to send pupils to selected places in public schools on special scholarships. 'The overwhelming majority of these schools were born of, and remain strongly attached to, one or other religious denomination,' wrote Spencer Leeson, in 1957, the year of his death; 'it is largely in order to preserve that character that they will contend for their independence.'[6] Leeson also noticed that there was 'an even stronger disposition in 1955 than there was in 1944 to serve and strengthen Christian education in the schools'.[7] It is interesting, however, that already he found it necessary to argue against the notion—which by the later 1960s had almost become an orthodoxy among liberal educationalists absorbed in 'child-centred' concepts—that teachers ought not to 'impose' their religious and moral views upon the children, that children should find out such things for themselves. 'A negative attitude towards these high spiritual and moral issues turns out on examination to be affirmative; for by suppressing all reference to them, the teacher will create the impression that they are irrelevant and insignificant.'[8] The Church held on to its own schools in order to provide at least one area in which, as they supposed, truth could be protected from such fashions of thought. In the Education Act of 1959 the state grants to

---

[1] M. V. C. Jeffreys, *Education—Christian or Pagan* (London, 1946), p. 64.

[2] See B. G. Sandhurst, *How Heathen Is Britain? A Revised and Enlarged Edition* (London, 1948), p. 17.

[3] *The Archbishop Speaks*, 'Change and Crisis in Education', p. 169.

[4] *Towards the Conversion of England*, p. 11.

[5] *The Public Schools and the General Educational System* (London, 1944).

[6] Spencer Leeson, *Christian Education Reviewed* (London, 1957), p. 81.

[7] Ibid., p. 28.   [8] Ibid., p. 4.

maintained Church Schools were increased from 50 to 75 per cent. Parliament was still anxious to preserve the religious tranquillity which had settled upon the education issue after 1944.

There were a number of further issues involving questions of social morality about which the Church declared a public voice in those years. Of these the use of nuclear energy was perhaps closest to the political sphere, particularly during the later 1950s when the Campaign for Nuclear Disarmanent attained a considerable standing among liberal and left-wing intellectuals. In 1946 the British Council of Churches, disturbed by the implications of the use of nuclear weapons in Japan at the end of the war, had produced a Report called *The Era of Atomic Power*. This rather diffuse statement was not satisfactory to the Church Assembly, who appointed its own Archbishops' Commission under the Dean of Winchester (Gordon Selwyn). It reported in 1948: *The Church and the Atom*. There was a division of opinion in the Commission itself, which came out in their Report—which pronounced the use of nuclear weapons immoral, yet also, in line with the deterrent argument, declared the *retention* of nuclear armaments to be morally acceptable.[1] In the same year the Lambeth Conference recommended that all nuclear energy should be brought under international inspection and control, 'to prevent its use as a weapon of war'.[2] At Minneapolis in 1954 the Anglican Congress, similarly, called upon the nations to use nuclear energy 'only for God's peaceful and creative purpose'.[3] And at Lambeth again, in 1958, the division of opinion surfaced. In their *Encyclical Letter* the bishops declared that 'the use of nuclear weapons is repugnant to the Christian conscience'; but they added, 'some of us would go further and regard such use in any circumstances as morally indefensible, while others of us, with equal conviction, would hold that so long as such weapons exist there are circumstances in which to use them might be preferable to political enslavement'.[4] They called for an international ban of nuclear weapons, and, in the words of Resolution 106, 'To this end governments should accept such limitations to their own sovereignty as effective control demands'.[5] The extent of the division of opinion which lay behind the careful wording of the Lambeth teaching was underlined when the Church Information Board put out a statement by Archbishop Fisher explaining why the vote on Resolution 106 had not been published, and why it had been decided to refer to the differences of view in the Encyclical instead.[6] It was clearly a matter of the utmost

---

[1] Lloyd, *The Church of England*, p. 477.

[2] *The Lambeth Conference, 1948*, Resolution 11, p. 30.

[3] *Report of the Anglican Congress, 1954*, p. 202.

[4] *The Lambeth Conference, 1958*, Encyclical Letter, p. 1.21.

[5] Ibid., p. 1.54, 'Modern Warfare and Christian Responsibility'.

[6] The Church Information Board, 'Voting at Lambeth Conferences'; Circular of 2 Oct. 1958.

delicacy. The two Archbishops were less careful of the consciences of the nuclear disarmers in their public utterance. Fisher, in speaking of the hydrogen bomb, once observed realistically that the survival of mankind could not automatically be assumed to be God's will;[1] and Garbett always argued for the retention of the bomb as a condition of world peace.[2] Both opinions were by some regarded as controversial. Another issue, not dissimilar in its way, which was already beginning to attract the notice of a few churchmen, was the stewardship of the earth. Ecology and conservation did not really get added to the list of social issues worrying the intelligentsia until early in the 1970s, but it is interesting to notice that Demant spoke of the dangers to survival, from misuse of the earth's resources, at the Malvern Conference in 1941.[3] And in 1954 Reckitt demanded that the Church 'take a firm and informed stand on the literally vital question of the preservation of the earth and the whole of our natural heritage from the dangers of reckless use and ruthless exploitation, and not least by appliances and practices which claim the authority of science for their employment'.[4]

The Church was greatly exercised over the growing problem of race relations—a problem, in the 1940s and 1950s, still largely isolated overseas, in the African colonies especially. The heavy immigration of the later 1950s and 1960s had not yet created a problem in England. Africa and its tensions dominated the social conscience of the Church of England during the 1950s. There were few men who were so short-sighted as Bishop Barnes showed himself to be when, in 1949, he denied that the race question was 'either the most dangerous, or even a permanently dangerous, element in the present turmoil of mankind'.[5] The Lambeth Conferences of 1948 and 1958 both repeated the Church's condemnation of the practice of racial discrimination as unchristian.[6] It was again condemned at Minneapolis in 1954.[7] The Methodist Conference condemned racial policies in Southern Africa in 1950.[8] It was, indeed, in South Africa that the Church of England came into direct collison with the State over the question of apartheid—of separate development of the coloured and white races. The implementation of this policy had been hastened by the replacement of Smuts by Malan in the South African general election of 1948. Under the new Nationalist administration apartheid was promoted as a systematic solution to the problem of a mixed-race society. The Church

---

[1] Purcell, *Fisher of Lambeth*, p. 23.

[2] Smyth, *Cyril Forster Garbett*, p. 373.

[3] *Malvern 1941*, p. 145.

[4] Reckitt, *Militant Here in Earth*, p. 48.

[5] Ernest William Barnes, *Religion and Turmoil* (Cambridge, 1949), p. 7.

[6] *The Lambeth Conference 1948*, Resolution 43, p. 36; *The Lambeth Conference, 1958*, Resolution 110, p. 1.55.

[7] *Report of the Anglican Congress, 1954*, p. 201.

[8] *Declaration of Conference on Social Questions*, ed. Rogers, p. 115.

of England, whose strength in the Province naturally lay mostly with citizens of English descent, instead taught the concept of a multi-racial parity. At the centre of the gathering storm was Geoffrey Clayton, Bishop of Johannesburg from 1934, and Archbishop of Cape Town from 1949. He was an Englishman; Dean of Peterhouse, Cambridge, and later Vicar of Chesterfield, before his call to Africa. Clayton conducted the Church exactly according to Anglican practice. He and the bishops of the Province spoke out against legislative enactments of the doctrine of apartheid— against the Bantu Education Act and the Criminal Law Amendment Act in 1953, and during the clearance of the Sophiatown quarter of Johannes-burg by the Government in 1955—a further attempt to resettle the native population in segregated areas. But the corporate Church confined itself to the declaration of the general principle, and was careful not to condemn the Government as such, or to incite anyone to disobey the law. This was not an easy position to maintain; many of the more radical clergy were anxious for greater militancy. The most distinguished of these was Fr. Trevor Huddleston, Provincial of the Community of the Resurrection. In 1956, after his recall to England, he published *Naught for Your Comfort*, an impassioned indictment of racial discrimination, and a book which filled the Church in England with righteous indignation about the events in South Africa. Huddleston compared the racialism of Southern Africa with Germany under Hitler.[1] He saw that the situation had raised 'funda-mental' issues about 'the function of the Christian Church in Society',[2] and contemplated the propriety of the use of force to remove the evils of apartheid, much to the disquiet of the Archbishop of Canterbury.[3] Clayton was also a man to shrink from that. As long ago as his 1934 *Charge*, as Bishop of Johannesburg, he had criticized 'the methods of some of my fellow-churchmen' as being too political.[4] During the excitements of the 'fifties he wrote, 'I have done my best to make clear to fellow Anglicans in England and elsewhere how complex the situation in this country is, and to discourage pronouncements on points of detail and condemnation of particular persons'.[5] Clayton disapproved of the political involvements of Ambrose Reeves, his successor as Bishop of Johannesburg, and of the Revd. Michael Scott, whom he dismissed after failing to receive assurances that parochial duties should come before political agitation.[6] His relations with Huddleston were strained, and he refused to continue as Visitor to the Community of the Resurrection while Huddleston was Provincial.[7] In 1955 he told Selby Taylor, Bishop of Pretoria, that he

---

[1] Trevor Huddleston, *Naught for Your Comfort* (London, 1956), p. 232. Huddleston later became Bishop of Stepney.   [2] Ibid., p. 235.   [3] Ibid., p. 234.

[4] Alan Paton, *Apartheid and the Archbishop. The Life and Times of Geoffrey Clayton, Archbishop of Cape Town* (London, 1974), p. 52.

[5] Quoted in Lloyd, *The Church of England, 1900-1965*, p. 506.

[6] Paton, *Apartheid and the Archbishop*, p. 152.   [7] Ibid., p. 247.

found men like these unbalanced in judgement and given to exhibitionism. He believed, in the words of his biographer, 'that Reeves, Huddleston, and Scott grew too emotional over South Africa'.[1] He disapproved of attempts to organize boycotts of South Africa or its produce (then common among intellectuals in England);[2] though he did support the 'Black Sash' movement. The Church of England has tended to accept the views of militants like Huddleston and Reeves and Gonville ffrench Beytagh, with a sort of uncritical eagerness. Archbishop Clayton offered another view of the tragedy of apartheid; a more balanced opposition. In 1957 the South African Government introduced a Native Laws Amendment Bill, with provisions for the State to exclude black Africans from attending churches in areas designated for European residents only. This was an interference by the State in the worship of the Church, and therefore an infraction of religious freedom, and Clayton recognized that his duty now lay in a formal rejection of the law. After consultations with the bishops he drafted a letter to the Prime Minister, Verwoerd, which announced 'that obedience to secular authority, even in matters about which we differ in opinion, is a command laid upon us by God'. But they were also, he pointed out, obliged to render to God the things which are God's: 'it is because we believe this that we feel bound to state that if the Bill were to become law in its present form we should ourselves be unable to obey it or to counsel our clergy and people to do so'.[3] Clayton died of a heart attack immediately after he had signed the letter. The Bill was passed but its offensive clauses were never enforced. The Church had confronted the State, and proved its traditional teaching not only on the conduct of the relations of the Church to Government, but on racial equality. 'Not that the question of race relations is confined to the continent of Africa,' Ambrose Reeves had written in a charge of 1955, when Bishop of Johannesburg; 'racial issues are becoming almost a universal problem.'[4] In the next decade they were to become an issue inside England itself.

The Church continued to uphold its traditional teaching about the family, and the permanence of the marriage contract, as well. Temple, in his *Christianity and Social Order*, had insisted that the family was, as an institution, essential to man's social being; and on the duty of the State to preserve it.[5] Professor James, of the Department of the History and Philosophy of Religion in the University of London, in a popular comparative anthropological study published in 1940, had sustained the traditional Christian belief that it was the family that had 'enabled mankind to go forward as a social organism rather than merely as a biological species, till at length the goal was reached in the ideal relationships of a

[1] Ibid., p. 253.   [2] Ibid., p. 241.   [3] Ibid., p. 280.
[4] David M. Paton, *Church and Race in South Africa* (London, 1958), p. 24.
[5] Temple, *Christianity and Social Order*, p. 41.

C S E—O

supernatural fellowship'.[1] The Anglican tradition, which also tended to give a concrete expression to a general concept, took the opportunity of the Lambeth Conference in 1948 to link the preservation of the family with the need for better housing. Every family, the bishops resolved, should have a home of its own.[2] This was repeated at the 1958 Conference: 'There is a sacramental relationship between good housing and good homes which does not allow Churchmen to be indifferent to the basic need for more and better housing.'[3] The bishops, in their *Encyclical*, in noticing the increased pressures placed upon the integrity of the family by modern life, affirmed their belief 'that the Christian faith has something unique which must be said both on the idea of the human family as rooted in the God-head, and on its creative possibilities under God'.[4] The family was founded upon the authority of Natural Law.

The institution of marriage also needed protection against the conditions of modern society. 'Public opinion is shocked by the growing number of divorces', according to the Bishop of Norwich (Dr. Percy Herbert) in 1948.[5] The 'New Morality' of which churchmen complained in the post-war years seemed to be centred in 'the decay of the sense of sin'—the words are those of Dr. W. R. Matthews, Inge's successor as Dean of St. Paul's—'the Gospel is a message of redemption and forgiveness and speaks in an unknown tongue to those who feel that they have done nothing to require forgiveness and no need of redemption'.[6] Dr. Wand, the Bishop of London, observed in the same year, 1947, that 'the new theory appears to be that love is an impulse that seizes upon the individual and must be obeyed at all costs'. This notion was to be rejected by Christians, because it was 'nothing less than a denial of the rights of the major part of the human personality'.[7] But as Garbett reflected a few years later: 'now the Christian ideals of sex are not only disregarded in practice, but criticised and rejected as mischievous and dangerous'.[8] He was, however, glad to record the diminution of a lot of the 'unhealthy secrecy' which had previously encompassed sexual questions; and also regarded the emancipation of women as a moral gain.[9] The position of women in society was one which the Church had sought to improve, at any rate in its formal declarations, at least since the start of the century.

---

[1] E. O. James, *The Social Function of Religion. A Comparative Study*, 2nd edn. (London, 1948), p. 192.

[2] *The Lambeth Conference, 1948*, Resolution 45, p. 36.

[3] *The Lambeth Conference, 1958*, Report 5, 'The Family in Contemporary Society', p. 2.158.

[4] Ibid., *Encyclical Letter*, p. 1.21.

[5] *The Lambeth Conference, 1948*, Report No. V, 'The Church's Discipline in Marriage', p. 97.

[6] W. R. Matthews, 'The Crisis for Religion', in *Has the Church Failed?*, p. 139.

[7] Wand, *God and Goodness*, p. 104.

[8] Garbett, *In an Age of Revolution* (1952), p. 74.   [9] Ibid., p. 73.

In 1948 the bishops resolved at Lambeth for better opportunities for women in professional and business life.[1] In 1958 polygamy was condemned—it restricted the lives of women overseas.[2] Both the Lambeth Conferences of 1948 and 1958 and the Anglican Congress in 1954, in the face of the threats to marriage discipline, declared firmly for the Church's traditional insistence on the indissolubility of marriage, and continued to discountenance the remarriage of the divorced by the Church.[3] Fisher was always insistent on the Church's marriage teaching,[4] and in 1955, in fact, got a very bad press for appearing to influence Princess Margaret against marriage to Group-Captain Peter Townsend, who had been the innocent party in the dissolution of his marriage. The Princess, in a press statement, issued after a visit to Lambeth Palace, said she was 'mindful of the Church's teaching that marriage is indissoluble'.[5]

Another matter of sexual morality which came into prominence in these years was homosexual misconduct. Publicity surrounding a number of prosecutions under existing law early in the 1950s prompted the Church of England Moral Welfare Council to approve the setting up of a small committee of doctors, lawyers, and clergy, to look into the law and practice of homosexuality in England.[6] Their Report in 1954 ('The Problem of Homosexuality') favoured the removal of legal penalties from misconduct between consenting adults. The Government's committee under Sir John Wolfenden, appointed to look into this question in 1954, reported along these lines in 1957; though legislation waited for public opinion to catch up—in the next decade. The Wolfenden proposals were approved by the Church's Moral Welfare Council.[7] Fisher wrote that the Report drew 'attention forcefully to the distinction between a crime and a sin'. Homosexual misconduct was certainly sinful, he maintained, in his *Canterbury Diocesan Notes* (October 1957), but in a civilized society 'most sins are not and ought not to be treated as crimes'.[8] But Fisher also acknowledged, in a considerable qualification, that 'it is always hard to draw a line between what is private sin only and what is an offence against public order and general good'. For the standards of a society *were* ultimately set by what citizens did 'in the privacy of their own hearts and habits'. So Fisher saw the difficulty of libertarian legislation after all: 'If in any matter of morality there are enough weak, misguided or evil-minded citizens to form, by

---

[1] *The Lambeth Conference, 1948*, Resolution 48, p. 37.

[2] *The Lambeth Conference, 1958*, Resolution 120, p. 1.58.

[3] *The Lambeth Conference, 1948*, Resolution 92, p. 49; Resolution 94, p. 49; *1958*, Resolution 114, p. 1.57; Resolution 119, p. 1.58; *Report of the Anglican Congress 1954*, p. 200.

[4] See Fisher's statement on the remarriage of the divorced in the Convocation of Canterbury: *Chronicle of Convocation*, 1957 (London, 1957), p. 208 (1 Oct. 1957).

[5] Purcell, *Fisher of Lambeth*, p. 244.

[6] Hall and Howes, *The Church in Social Work*, p. 66.   [7] Ibid., p. 68.

[8] Reprinted in *The Archbishop Speaks*, p. 127.

their mere existence in the life of the nation, a centre of active poison of a serious kind, then the law could rightly invade their private lives to restrain them.'[1] And that, of course, could define anything or any group. The relationship between law and morality was far too difficult, and involved far too many larger considerations, for Fisher's simple distinction between crime and sin to be especially helpful. But it got publicity at the time, and appears to have persuaded a number of people.

In the question of birth-control the Church shifted its ground. It happened fairly suddenly—at the Lambeth Conference of 1958, a Conference at which only seventy-three of the 310 Anglican bishops were actually from dioceses within the British Isles. The overseas bishops were more liberal in their attitude to contraception, and one of them, Stephen Bayne Jr., the Bishop of Olympia (U.S.A.), was chairman of the Committee on 'The Family in Contemporary Society'. Bayne was educated at Trinity School, New York City, Amherst, and at the General Theological Seminary. He had then been a tutor at the Seminary and chaplain at Columbia University, as well as holding two parishes and serving as a Naval chaplain during the War. He had, that is to say, spent half his ministry in academic appointments until, in 1947, he was elected Bishop of Olympia. He almost at once established a reputation as an ecclesiastical diplomatist, using his considerable personal charm to smooth over differences of view within the American Church. He was the American equivalent of an English public-school and Oxbridge prelate, and the English bishops clearly recognized the similar characteristics, too. Fisher said they all owed 'an immense amount to Steve Bayne'.[2] That immense amount included the abandonment of the Church's teaching on contraception. As Chairman of the Committee it was Bayne who used his diplomatic skills in favour of change. The 'Theology of Sexuality' approved by the Committee was, they argued, derived from the Book of Genesis—an odd resort to Scripture, since most of the members of the Committee were noted for liberal attitudes to Biblical scholarship; and the literal acceptance of the moral behaviour described in that Book was scarcely characteristic of their general outlook. There two purposes were suggested for marriage: the procreation of children, and 'the need of men and women for each other, to complement and fulfil each other'.[3] To these it was possible to add a third—'the establishment of a stable environment within which the deepest truths about human relationships can be expressed and communicated'. From this they deduced that it was 'clearly not true that all other duties and relationships in marriage must be subordinate to the procreative one'.[4] Having crossed the rubicon the

---

[1] *The Archbishop Speaks*, pp. 128–9.

[2] Purcell, *Fisher of Lambeth*, p. 198.

[3] *The Lambeth Conference, 1958*, Report 5, 'The Family in Contemporary Society', Part 2, p. 143.   [4] Ibid., p. 144.

Committee advanced quickly into a lush eulogy of 'family planning'. 'Responsible parenthood' was 'a far richer one than merely the reproduction of the species.' Retaining a balance between the various purposes of sex was 'an art man has had a long fight to learn'.[1] There were, of course, dangers. Couples who delayed having children for career reasons, or in order to conserve prosperity, might be selfish; but 'similarly those who carelessly and improvidently bring children into the world trusting in an unknown future or a generous society to care for them, need to make a vigorous examination of their lack of concern for their children and for the society of which they are a part'.[2] And, anyway, sexual intercourse, as the 'language of earthly love', had a positive virtue quite independently of any desire for children. Tensions between the world and the Spirit were not regarded as proper considerations. Indeed 'Dualism' was brushed aside as an attitude they 'can no longer accept.' The 'theology of St. Augustine', too, was no longer, apparently, acceptable—though in stating this, the Report observed that 'the Church holds as strongly as ever that continence, chastity, and self-control are a positive and creative element in Christian living'.[3] It was quite a volte-face. All the qualifications which had accompanied the 1930 Lambeth ruling that contraception could be permitted only in cases of exceptional social or medical need were abandoned. Contraception was now to be freely allowed because of the human values implicit in sexual union. This was a revolution in the Church's attitude to sexual morality. In the *Encyclical Letter* issued by the Conference, the bishops accepted these teachings, and referred to the 'sacramental' nature of sexual intercourse. 'We believe that family planning', they declared, 'in such ways as are mutually acceptable to husband and wife in Christian conscience, and secure from the corruptions of sensuality and selfishness, is a right and important factor in Christian family life.'[4] Abortion and infanticide were ruled out as acceptable methods of population control.[5] In this alteration of the teaching on contraception, the Church of England had gone further than the Methodist Conference which had, in 1939, agreed to suspend judgement between conflicting views on the issue, and leave it all up to 'the individual conscience'.[6] The new teaching caused a measure of disquiet in the Church; some thought that the abandonment of principle had been too precipitate,[7] and remained unconvinced by the appeal to human values. But many others

[1] Ibid., p. 145.   [2] Ibid., p. 146.   [3] Ibid., p. 147.

[4] Ibid., Part I, p. 122. 'Acceptable' methods declared themselves at once. For a few years after the publication of the Lambeth decrees, a well-known brand of contraceptives for men included a short extract from Resolution 115 on birth-control (suitably printed in gothic letters), in each packet of their product: a bizarre testimony to the strength religious sanction was thought by market researchers to hold upon the minds of society.

[5] Ibid., Part I, p. 23.

[6] *Declarations of Conference on Social Questions*, ed. Rogers, p. 104.

[7] Purcell, *Fisher of Lambeth*, p. 198.

were clearly delighted to discover that, after all, 'family planning is not against the Will of God'.[1] Bayne's success was recognized. In 1959 he became the first Executive Secretary of the Anglican Communion.

For those who would see in the Church's abandonment of its teaching on contraception a change of principle, there were other straws in the wind. The stability and the general caution which characterized the Church between 1940 and 1960 perhaps threw exceptions into greater relief than they really warranted. The changed values which the Church was to reflect in the 1960s were already throwing out the occasional early warning. In 1949 there was considerable excitement over the publication of Bishop Barnes's book *The Rise of Christianity*—an indifferent and often wrong study which was almost universally condemned.[2] Barnes owed his preferment to the see of Birmingham to Ramsay MacDonald. He was a mathematician, largely ignorant of theology; a publicist who wrote articles for the *Sunday Pictorial* explaining his liberal beliefs. Fisher thought he had disqualified himself from episcopal office, and said so publicly.[3] Barnes's opinions were certainly unusual ones—at least for the period in which they were offered. In his Rede Lecture in 1949 he argued that the opinions of traditional Christians would have to be discarded: 'their teaching, of course, makes no appeal to men and women of modern education'.[4] He was absorbed by world problems, and appeared to bring no distinctively Christian ideas to bear upon the solutions he favoured. He would have thrived in the atmosphere of the later 1960s, but in his own generation he was still very much an exception. Nearest to him in outlook and interests was Charles Raven, and, although Raven retained a stronger hold upon orthodoxy, he too became occupied with 'the tremendously exciting concrete problems which are clamouring for solution in the world at this present time'.[5] He also was impressed by the notion that science offered its own solutions to things. Bishop Stephen Neill was another Church leader who anticipated later attitudes. Viewing Christianity from the non-European standpoint of an expert on missionary enterprise throughout the world, he lamented the conservative tendencies of Christians in 1952. Too many, he wrote, found in Christianity a 'nostalgia' for the form of society they were most comfortable in; 'even if the Church does not lend itself directly to the forces of reaction, as at certain times it has been prone to do, there is yet a danger that it may find itself the home of those out of touch with the movement of the times'.[6] He regretted that 'Christian bodies have come to believe in the virtue of property and

[1] Dewi Morgan, *Lambeth Speaks* (London, 1958), p. 49.
[2] See Smyth, *Cyril Forster Garbett*, p. 472.
[3] Purcell, *Fisher of Lambeth*, p. 167.
[4] Barnes, *Religion and Turmoil*, p. 36.
[5] Raven, *Christ and the Modern Opportunity*, p. 45.
[6] Stephen Neill, *The Christian Society* (London, 1952), p. 288.

security'—virtues, of course, which Temple, in line with accepted Christian teaching, had supported for reasons suggested by his view of human nature. For Neill 'the Christian Society is called to recognize how many of its contemporary difficulties arise from its too close identification with the principles and practices of bourgeois society'.[1] It was a point of view that had considerable truth. In Neill's liberal attitudes to social and political questions the discerning will recognize that explicit readiness to accept the analysis of contemporary world problems at the valuation placed upon them by the currents of secular thought, which came to dominate the attitudes of Church leaders in the years after 1960. To some a collapse of values: to others an affirmation of the value of the secular. A new world of Christian divisions was about to open up.

[1] Ibid., p. 289.

IO

After 1960

The first impression of the social and political thinking of churchmen after 1960 seems to be one of increasing confusion. After the relative stability of the preceding two decades, pent-up desires to review the most basic teachings and attitudes of the Church were quite suddenly released, in an earnest and even frantic wish to relate the truths of the Christian dispensation to the knowledge and values of contemporary society; to reinterpret and remould; to learn from the secular culture. It was, as the bishops at the Lambeth Conference of 1968 declared, 'a world in which inherited institutions and ways of thought are increasingly questioned'. It was a world, too, in which 'the familiar teaching through which ordinary Christians learn their faith is being re-examined and in part rejected by some theologians'.[1] To some, the 'sixties appeared to disclose that Bishop John Robinson, one of the more radical theologians of the period, described as 'a climacteric in the transition from the paternalistic to the permissive society'; a sequence to be recognized in 'the cracking of the containers within which power, influence and leadership in the community has hitherto been exercised'.[2] Yet despite all the sound and fury of those years, and the collapse of social and moral values which was reflected in the Church, it is important to realize that the changes within Christian attitudes in England were not as extensive or as complete as conservatives complained. In the broadest perspective it is possible, in fact, to discern a familiar terrain beneath the landslips. Once again Church leaders—particularly theologians and some of the more academic bishops—were in effect accommodating the general cultural assumptions and social and political values of the intelligentsia around them; they joined in the transition to a more radical criticism of existing arrangements. Many Church radicals believed that they derived their new radicalism from their theological studies, but, as usual, the influence flowed the other way—Biblical scholarship was made to correspond almost exactly to the moral canons of contemporary humanism and to the idealism of the 'youth culture' of the period. This also illustrated how 'in touch' with contemporary society and its values the leading thinkers of the Church actually were,

[1] *The Lambeth Conference 1968. Resolutions and Reports* (London and New York, 1968), 'A Message from the Bishops', p. 23.
[2] John A. T. Robinson, *Christian Freedom in a Permissive Society* (London, 1970), p. 242.

how closely, still, they were integrated within the intelligentsia. But after 1960, as it happened, current intellectual values increasingly promoted a discontent with society and its institutions. Advocates spoke of a refusal to accept single solutions, of their rejection of orthodoxies, of 'pluralism' and 'openness'. But in reality the assumptions constituted a new liberal orthodoxy—uncritical in its essential acceptance of the main canons of secular humanism. To its values and its norms some of the leading churchmen of the period have found a compelling attraction. Yet despite all the publicity given to ecclesiastical radicals by the press and broadcasting, and the internal respect which protects them within the Church, they are a minority. It is a fact of which some of the leading radicals are very conscious. By the early years of the 1970s a failure of radical attitudes seemed to some to be revealing itself in a new conservatism.[1] Bishop John Robinson wrote that he felt 'increasingly alienated from the mind (or mindlessness) of the Establishment'—by which he meant the social and political establishment—because of the tenacity of its conservatism.[2] A journal for chaplains in higher education, circulated by the Church of England's Board of Education, referred gloomily, in the autumn of 1973, to the 'in-built dynamism' of capitalism.[3] The revolution seemed to have run out of steam.

The separation of the radical minority from the ordinary assumptions of most churchmen has in fact led to a situation in which it is possible to speak of 'two Christianities'. The expression was used by Canon David Edwards about the Church Leaders' Conference held at Birmingham in September 1973. 'Conservatives and radicals seemed to have utterly different conceptions of the Church,' he noticed. 'The theological split revealed was almost one between two Christianities'.[4] Edwards also defined two religious psychologies—'a psychology of openness, supporting a theology of adventure', and a 'psychology of reverence and humble study, supporting a doctrinal system'.[5] Bishop Robinson has made the same distinction (though in language drawn from Donald Schon's Reith Lectures for 1970), and called it 'the crucial divide in the Church today'.[6] Lord Fisher of Lambeth, from his retirement, pointed to the same sort of differences in 1967. The Church, he wrote, was 'torn between those who questioned the old norms too little and those who questioned them too much'; there was a 'noise of new ideas on everything', and 'those who spoke out loudest on morals appeared to be joining their voices to those of the humanists rather than expounding Christian verities'. Meanwhile, he

---

[1] John A. T. Robinson, *The Difference in Being a Christian Today* (London, 1972), p. 17.
[2] Ibid., p. 59.
[3] *Sensation. A Bulletin for Chaplains in Higher Education* (London, Autumn 1973), p. 3 (Report of the Aarhus Conference of Chaplains).
[4] Edwards, *The British Churches Turn to the Future* (London, 1973), p. 1.
[5] Ibid., p. 31.   [6] Robinson, *The Difference in Being a Christian Today*, p. 13.

believed, 'the quiet part of the nation still respected the basic principles of Christian morality in which they, and their parents, had been brought up'.[1] In 1968 the Lambeth Conference committee on 'Renewal in Faith' declared 'that recent theological discussion, while it has been liberating to some, has been thought by others to be destructive of faith'.[2] The divisions were becoming very noticeable.

'For better or worse, theological beliefs do affect social development and at the same time social structures and social dynamics influence the formation of theology.' So observed the Church Report on Education, compiled under the chairmanship of Ian Ramsey, Bishop of Durham. 'Theology will therefore wisely take note of the kinds of questions which sociologists are asking and benefit from many sociological conclusions'.[3] This view pervaded the theological upheaval of the 1960s: with the implication that modern knowledge, however apparently antipathetic to received religious thought, should be accommodated on its own terms. Theologians were seized with respect for the secular culture around them, and many believed that traditional notions of God and His operations in the world would have to be altered to correspond to the information and resource available to 'mankind come of age'. The resulting propositions have seemed, to some, 'iconoclastic'; they 'present a new image of Christianity, involving a radical recasting of the theology, the piety, and the moral attitudes of the Church'.[4] It was the publication in 1963 of Dr. Robinson's *Honest to God*—he was at the time Bishop of Woolwich—that stamped the decade with theological questioning, and first brought out the 'two Christianities'. The enormous sales of the book, and the press publicity, meant that 'in 1944 the image of the theologian was for most people Archbishop William Temple; for most in 1964 it was Bishop John Robinson'.[5] It is for this reason that Robinson's thought may not unfairly be taken to represent the central tendencies of radical theology in the 'sixties and early 'seventies'. In America a comparable movement of opinion was taking place—there associated with Dr. Paul van Buren and Bishop James Pike. By 1965 it was possible for Professor E. L. Mascall, a critic of the new theology, to remark that it had 'obtained a foothold in many academic circles', and he added that 'until the publication of *Honest to God* it was little known to the general public and to the majority of the parochial clergy'.[6] In the next few years radical theology became very prestigious, and within the rather enclosed atmosphere of theological

---

[1] Lord Fisher of Lambeth, *Standards of Morality, Christian and Humanist* (London, 1967), p. 4.   [2] *The Lambeth Conference*, 1968, p. 63.

[3] *The fourth R. The Report of the Commission on Religious Education* (London, 1970), p. 47.

[4] Horton, Davies, *Worship and Theology in England*, p. 201.   [5] Ibid., p. 20.

[6] E. L. Mascall, *The Secularization of Christianity. An Analysis and a Critique* (London, 1965), p. viii.

faculties at universities, and theological colleges, it thrived with very little internal criticism of its general conceptual assumptions and methods. It was often justified on the grounds not only of academic pedigree, but because it had assisted people of integrity who harboured honest doubts. 'My own little contribution', as Bishop Robinson himself described *Honest to God*, 'evidently articulated a good deal of hidden questioning.'[1] The questioning of received ideas went very far, and caused a good deal of dismay among many of the parochial clergy and laity. Church leaders, however, increasingly imagined the new theology to be a proper intellectual attempt to restate Christianity in the style of contemporary knowledge and were not, in consequence, prepared to arrest its advance. It is true that Archbishop Michael Ramsey—who succeeded Fisher in 1961—criticized Robinson in Convocation for some of his views,[2] but by the end of the decade it could be noticed that Ramsey was 'increasingly hospitable to the positive challenge of the ferment'.[3] The Lambeth Conference in 1968 also welcomed the new questioning—'out of this present travail new understandings of the Christian faith' would emerge. 'If, when the world changes, the Church does not reorientate itself, it fails for want of fresh insights.' The Conference did also warn against 'disproportionate reaction against customary and valued spiritual practices'.[4]

By 1970 radical attitudes in theological learning clearly predominated among academic clergy, and were receiving a sympathetic hearing from Church leaders, some of whom—and notably Ian Ramsey, Bishop of Durham—were anyway promotions from among the ranks of the academics.[5] Although the new theology was well received at the top end of the Church, it was not highly regarded by non-Christian academics in contiguous fields of study, who criticized *Honest to God*, and subsequent works, for lack of intellectual coherence. Bishop Robinson himself seems to have attributed much of the opposition he encountered in the lay world to press sensationalism, to 'slogan-thinking',[6] and to the 'psychological need' of traditional Christians to see a perfect Christ.[7] But when he was described

---

[1] Robinson, *Christian Freedom in a Permissive Society*, p. 243.

[2] David L. Edwards, ed., *The Honest to God Debate. Some reactions to the book 'Honest to God'* (London, 1963), p. 7.

[3] Kenneth Slack, *The British Churches Today*, 2nd edn. (London, 1970), Introduction to 2nd edn., p. xv. In 1973, however, Ramsey admitted that in the preceding decade theology had rather slipped from its moorings, but that things were now more stable—B.B.C. Radio 4, 13 Dec. 1973 (interviewed by Ian MacIntyre).

[4] *The Lambeth Conference*, 1968, Report No. 1, 'Renewal of Faith', p. 69.

[5] See 'Pathways to Theological Atheism?'—Ian Ramsey's attempt to defend himself against charges of having gone too far; in *Models for Divine Activity* (London, 1973), pp. 56 ff.   [6] Robinson, *Christian Freedom in a Permissive Society*, p. 19.

[7] John A. T. Robinson, *The Human Face of God* (London, 1973), p. 74. ('A progressive wishing to discredit a particular person or viewpoint does not use the straightforward language of moral disapproval but employs the language of pathology'—David Martin, *A Sociology of English Religion* (London, 1967), p. 65.)

as 'an Anglican Bishop who does not believe in God'—a phrase which stuck in the public mind—it was by T. E. Utley, a political philosopher.[1] 'First and foremost', wrote Alasdair MacIntyre, 'he is an atheist.'[2] MacIntyre is himself a distinguished atheist philosopher. Renford Bambrough, the Cambridge philosopher, and an agnostic, spoke of Robinson and his followers as 'a Cambridge Agnostic Church, a haven for fundamentalist "free thought" '.[3] So although there were no doubt some who dismissed the new theology out of hand, and with insufficient grasp of its subtleties and modifications, it can hardly be said that the secular academic world was impressed. As the new learning filtered down to the laity it confused Christian apologetics still further. Bambrough refers to a woman contributor to the B.B.C.'s 'Any Questions?' programme, who explained her own attempt to give an equivocal interpretation to the language of the marriage vows by saying she had heard about 'a bishop or parson who said there was no God'.[4] The new theology, which may have liberated the consciences of ecclesiastical intellectuals, sometimes had predictable but disagreeable consequences for ordinary people. Furthermore, the rapid expansion of religious publishing in the 1960s—the market perhaps stimulated by the requirements of compulsory religious instruction in the state schools, as well as by the paperback revolution—dispersed the new ideas quite extensively.

The attitudes of the radical theologians are important within the present terms of reference for two reasons. The theologians themselves, in the first place, believed that their new insights into the value of secular thought provided a basis for far-reaching adjustments to the ethical teachings of the Church. In the second place, the theological ferment began to precipitate at a time, in the later 1960s, when a renaissance of left-wing idealism in the universities and elsewhere made a political dimension to the 'open' theology inevitable. Assessment of the second point is more difficult than of the first, because the world of political values in which theologians became immersed was less frequently defined in Church discussions; whereas ethical questions were on the agenda all the time, forced forward by public discussion of issues like divorce, abortion, and homosexuality. What clearly emerges from the confusions, however, is the abandonment of the Church's hostility to secular humanism. It is the hallmark of most radical theologians: a belief that the Church had been mistaken in its

---

[1] Edwards, *The Honest to God Debate*, p. 95. Edwards actually described Utley (p. 11) as a 'journalist'—which he is also; but Utley's published work in political philosophy is better known to political scientists. [2] Ibid., p. 215.

[3] 'Praising with Faint Damns', in *Religion and Humanism* by Ronald Hepburn and others (London, 1964), p. 64. Bambrough's hostile criticism of *Honest to God*, in the *Cambridge Review*, was strangely omitted from Edwards's compendium of reviews (*The Honest to God Debate*).

[4] 'Pickwickian Christianity', in *Religion and Humanism*, p. 54.

previous insistence on a distinct and unique spiritual interpretation of human life. It now seemed that to man 'come of age' the secular values of humanism might well provide a key to the reality of God's 'immanence' in the world.[1] Although humanism has 'neither the height nor the depth of the Christian doctrine of man' as Archbishop Ramsey said in his Scott Holland lectures in 1964, Christian criticism 'must be accompanied by the most reverent understanding' of it.[2] Ramsey's desire to learn from contemporary culture was, however, tempered by his disbelief both in the notion of human moral progress,[3] and in the idea that making men more cultured would make them morally better.[4] These were traditional views, related to the doctrine of Original Sin. The Church, he argued, must 'never commend itself to the world by providing what the world would most like to approve'.[5] Radical theologians would have agreed with this last sentiment for they usually thought of 'the world' as meaning 'establishment' values and self-interests. Their conservative critics saw radicalism itself as merely a part of the fashionable orthodoxy of the world of the intelligentsia, and believed that radical thinkers in the Church were liable to commend the world's priorities for that reason. Radicals themselves seemed unaware of how orthodox their assumptions had become within the academic élite: they preferred to see themselves as locked in an uphill battle against the 'establishment' and its ways of thinking. Lord Fisher of Lambeth certainly thought this was the case.[6] The radical theologians themselves did state their adhesion to humanist positions with reservations—thus although Robinson declared that 'because I am a Christian, I am a radical humanist',[7] he also criticized 'a closed humanism' since 'man is not the measure of all things'.[8] But the reservations in his position were either not noticed or carried little conviction. David Boulton, reviewing *Honest to God* in *Tribune*, remarked on 'the spectacle of a humanist holding a bishop's office in the Church of England'.[9] The whole range of radical theology tended to accept the value placed on human rationality, responsibility, and maturity, by secular humanism. Everywhere there was the influence of Tillich and Bonhoeffer; the rejection of 'triumphalism'; the desire to probe the insights of secular morality with friendly instru-

[1] David L. Edwards, *Religion and Change* (London, 1969), pp. 19, 25.

[2] Arthur Michael Ramsay, *Sacred and Secular. A Study in the other-worldly and this-worldly aspects of Christianity* (London, 1965), p. 66.

[3] The Archbishop of Canterbury, *The Crisis of Human Freedom* (Waley Cohen Memorial Lecture, 1961) (London, 1962), p. 13.

[4] Michael Ramsey, *Freedom, Faith and the Future* (London, 1970), p. 43.

[5] Arthur Michael Ramsey and Leon-Joseph Suenens, *The Future of the Christian Church* (London, 1971), p. 24.

[6] Fisher, *Standards of Morality*, p. 30.

[7] Robinson, *Christian Freedom in a Permissive Society*, p. 5.

[8] Robinson, *The Difference in Being a Christian Today*, p. 18.

[9] Edwards, *The Honest to God Debate*, p. 106.

ments of analysis. Christians have discovered, as Canon Hugh Montefiore said at Lincoln Theological College in 1964, that 'in a post-Christian
society, Christian charity is not confined within the Christian Church'.[1]
The acceptance of humanist values became essential as the basis of
'situation ethics', and for the sponsorship of 'liberation' movements
amongst minority groups in society. And the doctrine of Original Sin,
which above all else had restrained Christians in the past from espousing
ideas essential to humanistic confidence about the ability of mankind
to control his choices and actions, has been either ignored, or not really
known about, or denied. Some contemporary churchmen, in fact, have
apparently regarded it as essentially explicable in terms of former Christian
inhibitions about sexual conduct.[2] Radical Christians who have realized
the extent to which belief in Original Sin has suggested scepticism about
the beneficial consequence of political action have modified the doctrine
rather than abandon their political preferences. 'While the doctrine of
original sin is not denied,' declared the Church of England's Board of
Education, in their annual report for 1972, 'some of its traditional implications are challenged.' The Board's own challenge was to the idea that
Christians should hold back from using schools for the 'process of liberation' in the political as well as in the personal sphere.[3]

Churchmen of the extreme Left in the earlier years of the century—like
Conrad Noel or Hewlett Johnson—had devoted much energy to an assault
upon the 'other-worldly' pietism implicit in Christianity. Their objections
were still those of Feuerbach. Christians of the Westcott, liberal 'socialist'
school, and the 'Christian Sociology' movement of the years between the
wars, had also attacked 'other-worldly' attitudes for seeming to deny the
value of commitment in this world to the passions and struggles of
humanity. The attitudes attacked were usually caricatured. During the
1960s traditional spirituality was subjected to tremendous criticism by
radical theology, and by 1970 it was becoming difficult to find any influential churchmen who did not assume that Christians in the past had left
the miseries of the world to get more miserable, while men were directed
to think of heavenly rewards. In some measure this resulted from a
simple ignorance of the past—of all the work and all the social thought of
preceding Christianity. Thus Bishop John How, the Secretary of the
Anglican Consultative Council, was able to say, in an interview given to
the B.B.C. after the Dublin meeting in 1973, that the Council's concern
with social justice was their most important achievement, because it was an

---

[1] Hugh Montefiore, *Awkward Questions on Christian Love* (London, 1964), p. 115.
Montefiore was Vicar of Great St. Mary's, Cambridge (the University Church). He later
became Bishop of Kingston-upon-Thames.

[2] See Don Cupitt, *Crisis of Moral Authority. The Dethronement of Christianity* (London,
1972), p. 65, for such an interpretation of Original Sin.

[3] *Annual Report of the Board of Education (1972–3)*, G. S. 152 (London, 1973), p. 25.

area in which the Church had scarcely concerned itself in the past.[1] The Council itself had declared that it was 'aware of lopsided emphases within the Church in the work of spiritual formation, resulting often in faith being used as a buffer against life's problems'.[2] The Lambeth Conference of 1968 had indicated a similar attitude though rather less bluntly: 'In this age above all, Christians should not regard the contemporary world as an alien order'.[3] It seemed as if the balance between concern for the worldly condition of men, and for their eternal expectations—a balance which the Church has always taught—was liable to become weighted at the worldly end, so great was the reaction. The Archbishop of Canterbury, in his Scott Holland lectures, had contended for the maintenance of the balance. It is Christianity that brings the supernatural to the world: 'Christian supernaturalism will carry with it, as a very part of itself, the will to "muck in" (if the vulgarism is allowed) with the secular while living the life that is "hid with Christ in God".'[4] But a lot of contemporary theological speculation has germinated upon the ruins of 'other-worldly' spirituality, and in its more popular expressions the assault has been very drastic. Fr. Trevor Beeson, an Anglican churchman who has become something of an expert in communications, and is himself a frequent broadcaster, actually compared the evangelistic techniques of the Church with those 'of Goebbels and other notorious propagandists'.[5] He wrote: 'all attempts to present the Christian faith as if its primary concern was with what happens to a man after his death, a common feature of much manipulative evangelism, are nothing more than a total distortion and denial of the Christianity of the New Testament'.[6] The consequence of this sort of opinion, translated into social and political morality, will be considered in due course. The assault upon the 'other-worldly' dimension of Christianity, like the emphasis upon the humanist view of man's responsibility, has tended to concentrate the attention of contemporary Christian radicalism upon social and political change. It has become, for some, the essence of Christianity, the paradoxical adoption of materialist premises.

This partial acceptance of contemporary humanism at its own valuation has been accompanied by a great volume of discussion about 'secular' and 'pluralistic' societies, and their implications for Christianity. The greatest influence here was, perhaps, the publication in 1965 of a work by an American theologian: *The Secular City* by Harvey Cox. This book, with its sharp criticisms of past Christianity, its gratitude for the absorption of

---

[1] B.B.C. Radio 4, 28 July 1973. (interviewed by Douglas Brown).

[2] *Partners in Mission. Anglican Consultative Council. Second Meeting, Dublin, July, 1973* (London, 1973), p. 15.

[3] *The Lambeth Conference* (1968), p. 73.

[4] Ramsey, *Sacred and Secular*, p. 65.

[5] Trevor Beeson, *An Eye for an Ear* (London, 1972), p. 11.

[6] Ibid., p. 27.

Christianity by humanism, and its exultation of 'technocracy', has enjoyed a considerable success with religious thinking in England. It is hardly appropriate, in the present study, to offer an analysis of the concepts of 'secularism' and 'pluralism', but rather to point to their practical result in the priorities of contemporary Christian social attitudes. There has, in fact, been a tendency to exaggerate the extent to which English society really is secularized. 'Dr. Robinson writes as if the secularization of the modern world were an accomplished and recognized fact', observed Alasdair MacIntyre in his criticism of *Honest to God*.[1] That part of English society which contains the highest and most articulate element of atheism and agnosticism—the intelligentsia—is also the least in contact with the religious convictions of ordinary people, and, in consequence, exaggerates the degree of irreligion in society—just as upper-class leaders in the nineteenth century failed to comprehend the latent religiosity of the working classes, writing them off as pagan. Academic churchmen, with their reverence for intellectual values, have tended to accept the secularist analysis uncritically, and have joined in the general proclamation of the secular society. Yet English society has for a very long time been 'secularized'—at least in the sense that ordinary Englishmen were reluctant either to go to church or to regard themselves as 'religious' in the conventional sense. But the mass of the people in England do still regard themselves as Christian, and a considerable injustice is done to their sensibilities when churchmen discount their rather imprecise religious instincts as too diluted to be of value. Acceptance of society as 'secular' is realistic to the extent that public reference to religious sanction or morality is becoming unusual; but this may not be an adequate test. It may also be suggested that the English people are the subjects of secularization, rather than its advocates—a point made by E. R. Wickham, Bishop of Middleton, whose study of industrial society has earned respect in the Church. 'The nation may be deeply secularized,' he wrote in 1966, 'but is the victim of the secular forces, surely, rather than open-eyed, conscious and determined agent of those forces.'[2] Public opinion surveys indicate that a very large majority of the population claims allegiance to a religious denomination—'almost the whole adult population' in the mid-1960s.[3] During those years 66 per cent of the population still received Anglican baptism, and if the initiation rites of other Christian Churches are added, a figure above 80 per cent becomes apparent.[4] All available surveys show the 'continued hold of the

---

[1] Edwards, *The Honest to God Debate*, p. 223.

[2] See E. R. Wickham, 'What should be the New Look', in *The English Church. A New Look*, ed. Leslie Hunter (London, 1966), p. 148.

[3] *Television and Religion. Prepared by Social Surveys (Gallup Poll) Ltd. on behalf of A.B.C. Television Ltd.* (London, 1964), p. 9.

[4] *Church and State. Report of the Archbishops' Commission* (London, 1970), p. 4; Martin, *A Sociology of English Religion*, p. 37.

Church over the nation, at least in idea, if not in activity such as church-going'.[1] Most of those who do not go to church attribute this to lost habit, or uninteresting services, or absence of free time; very few admit to dis-belief.[2] Bishop Wand wrote of the average Englishman: 'If you ask him whether he was a religious man he would probably say No, but he would regard it as the greatest insult if you told him he was no Christian'.[3] And in 1965 the Church's Industrial Committee confirmed that Christianity 'however attenuated, remains the acknowledged norm' for most people in England.[4] Parish priests usually know from pastoral experience not to dismiss this vague Christian attachment as a meaningless cultural deposit—many 'have memories of how something which appeared nominal went very much deeper or how the merely superficial became entirely sincere when confronted with one of life's turning points'.[5] Many people in fact find their spiritual sense satisfied in popular television religious programmes: by early in the 1970s one of these was achieving audiences of 12,000,000 to 15,000,000—figures equal to the most popular entertainment programmes, and which, according to I.B.A. research, comprise a fair cross-section of society measured by age, class, and sex.[6] So although there has been a slow decline in religious observance—a decline which has shown signs of accel-eration since the mid-'sixties—there is no straightforward correlation between formal observance and ultimate conviction. The Report of the Archbishops' Commission on Church and State, under the chairmanship of Professor W. O. Chadwick (1970), pointed out that the Church was 'not the only organization to discover a gulf between active and passive members'. Attendance at political meetings, youth clubs, evening classes, theatres, and cinemas, had all experienced the same decline.[7] A majority of the members of the Commission which produced this Report, in fact, saw 'a general, diffused, inarticulate assent to Christianity, in the body of the nation, by people participating in Christian services at birth, or mar-riage or death, seeking at times to relate their lives to a frame broader than the frame by which they normally live'.[8] There also seemed to be support for this frame to have national recognition. 'The people of England still want to feel that religion has a place in the land to which they can turn on the all too rare occasions when they think they need it; and they are not

---

[1] The Deployment and Payment of the Clergy. A Report by Leslie Paul, p. 27.

[2] Ibid., p. 14.

[3] J. W. C. Wand, Anglicanism in History and Today (London, 1961), p. 179.

[4] Industrial Mission. A Paper Issued by the Church of England Industrial Committee (London, 1965), p. 7.

[5] Dewi Morgan, The Church in Transition. Reform in the Church of England (London, 1970), p. 71. The author is Rector of St. Bride's, Fleet Street.

[6] Broadcasting, Society and the Church. Report of the Broadcasting Commission of the General Synod of the Church of England (London, 1973), p. 50.

[7] Church and State. Report of the Archbishops' Commission (London, 1970), p. 5.

[8] Ibid., p. 6.

likely to be pleased by legislation which might suggest that the English people as a whole were going un-Christian.'[1]

These considerations, then, suggest a continuing popular desire to retain a Christian identity; they are not evidences, however, that a secular society does not also exist. Many Christian thinkers today welcome the notion of a secular society, on grounds of abstract justice, in a 'pluralistic' condition where there appears to be no agreement about the moral basis of society or the State. The Church's 'system of values is held to be only one option among many, even by some of her members, and the alternatives are assumed to be equally valid for our society'.[2] But does a 'secular society' exist in England in the form so many Church leaders appear to assume? Up to a point it is a matter of definition. Many Christian thinkers have followed the outlines suggested in 1962 by D. L. Munby's lectures on *The Idea of a Secular Society*—which were commended by Archbishop Ramsey himself.[3] This analysis, which was not without an element of political polemicism (especially its moralistic rejection of 'the cynical claim of vulgar Conservative leaders such as Baldwin and Macmillan in decline that they give the people what they want')[4] welcomed the advent of secularism. Munby, an economist of Nuffield College, Oxford, noticed that the Church was adjusting well to the secular society, 'as it has acclimatized itself to most previous forms of society'.[5] His definition has generally been accepted: 'A secular society is one which explicitly refuses to commit itself as a whole to any particular view of the nature of the universe and the place of men in it.'[6] Further, 'A secular society is in practice a pluralist society, in so far as it is truly secular', and as a result, 'Societies which enforce, whether by State coercion, or by social pressures, a uniform attitude of behaviour in important matters of human behaviour and values, whether or not these are regarded as religious, are in effect sacral societies of the traditional form, and not secular societies'.[7] Yet England does not in fact fit Munby's definition. It is true that in the last decade the divided will of the intelligentsia, with its element of humanist morality, has persuaded Parliament to remove legal restrictions in a number of areas of 'private' moral behaviour, such as the grounds of divorce or homosexuality. But this has been more than compensated by the protection of other moral beliefs and practices by the rule of law—the race-relations legislation, for example, or the whole apparatus of social-welfare benefits, or the attempt to contrive social equality through the state educational system. Some of these issues have a majority support; some, like the race laws, probably do not. Some may also be defended on the ground that they are really an attempt

[1] *Church and State. Report of the Archbishops' Commission*, p. 65.

[2] *Broadcasting, Society and the Church*, p. 5.   [3] Ramsey, *Sacred and Secular*, p. 64.

[4] D. L. Munby, *The Idea of a Secular Society, And its significance for Christians* (London, 1963), p. 51.

[5] Ibid., p. 11.   [6] Ibid., p. 14.   [7] Ibid., p. 17.

to keep the peace, rather than to enforce moral beliefs as such by law—the race-legislation code, again, has been defended in this way. But all law in the end involves a prior morality for legitimate enforcement, and the social morality incorporated in the legislation of the last decade certainly removes this country very far from being a 'secular society' in Munby's sense. Parliament has, in fact, avoided defining the moral basis of its legislation in recent years; politicians speak of 'consensus' for or against action; popularized versions of humanist ethics are frequently offered as explanations for social morality in television discussions of law reform; but no one of real influence outside the circles of the intelligentsia has propagated genuinely secular principles of law. In view of the latent Christian sense in society, they would get a cool hearing if they did. Radical churchmen, however, continue to argue that the Church as an institution should adjust its teaching as if there was a general and agreed doctrine of secularity operating throughout society. It is a view which requires modification. But however inadequately based, the assumption that modern society is inherently secular has been of the greatest importance in the recent formation of Church attitudes to social and moral questions. It is also evident that talk about the values of a 'pluralistic' society ignores a lot of hidden class reference. Most of the components of the plurality, when examined, turn out to exist only within the professional class and the intelligentsia—there is a much greater agreement about the moral bases of society within the working classes. 'Pluralistic societies', anyway, are not stable: they are societies caught in transition from one set of orthodoxies to another—they are found where a failure of nerve by ascendant opinion in a society leads to a progressive disintegration of values. During the interlude it may be possible to speak of a pluralism, but it does not last, and eventually society will slide, or be coerced, into the acceptance of a new set of moral values. When the liberal advocates of moral diversity have more or less destroyed the fibre of a society's values, and weakened its institutions, minorities with clear and hard opinions can easily take over and impose their own norms, usually through the appeal to a universal ideology. 'Pluralism' is really just a luxury device used by western bourgeois intellectuals to explain the paralysing effects of their own class dissatisfaction with existing social practices. The social diversities they describe are usually all to be located within their own class, and to them they bring a set of social doctrines no more characteristically tolerant than any others.

One of the most important fruits of these attitudes, and one which has penetrated the Church's thinking on morality in several areas, is the notion of 'situation ethics', or 'self-authenticating morality'. All the radical theologians of recent years have been affected by this in some degree; the 'New Morality' has been closely linked with the 'New Theology'.[1] It is

[1] *The fourth R.*, p. 20.

interesting to notice that most of the advocates of 'situation ethics' have attacked the Church for dwelling too much on sexual morality in the past, and for encouraging 'a widespread Christian deviation which all but equates sex and sin'.[1] And yet they, too, have applied their 'situation ethics' almost exclusively to sexual behaviour. A great deal has been written about the need to abandon 'legalistic' approaches to morality, to treat people as 'responsible' and 'adult': yet none of these thinkers has suggested, for example, that 'man come of age' should be allowed to exercise his own responsibility in such moral questions as racial discrimination or capital punishment. 'Situation ethics' has not really been applied to social morality at all; though it has been applied pretty thoroughly to sexual morality, to the 'private' sphere, where men are thought to be sufficiently responsible to exercise stewardship over the bodies of others without the need of legal inhibitions. 'Obsession with sex is likely to strike future historians as one of the outstanding characteristics of the age';[2] and the radical churchmen of the last decade have certainly been men of their age in this sense. There has been a tremendous effort to change the sexual repression which, it has been assumed, has hung around traditional Christianity. By 1965, however, it was possible for Howard Root, Dean of Emmanuel College, Cambridge, to declare that those offended by discussion of sex 'are in fact members of a minority which is steadily dwindling, and which they know to be steadily dwindling'.[3] By 1973 the transformation seemed to some observers to be complete. Peregrine Worsthorne, remarking on the speeches of the bishops in the House of Lords, in support of the Government's decision to allow contraceptives to be prescribed on the National Health Service, wrote of their 'most indelicate enthusiasm, exchanging expertise' with 'proud mastery of detail'. He added, 'One doubts, perhaps, whether the Bishops would be quite so outspoken with their expertise in the privacy of their own palaces with their own children around, but at least on show, speaking officially to the nation as a whole, it would be a bold prelate who would dare to confess to unseemly reticence'.[4] During the 1960s this change in attitudes by churchmen reflected the changed attitudes of the intelligentsia and the media as a whole. 'Situation ethics' were not original to theologians after all; they were the adoption by theologians of existing humanist standards of morality. 'This new crisis in ethics had been building up because Christians had noticed—some more acutely than others—that new decisions had been demanded by new situations created by scientific

---

[1] Howard Root, 'Ethical Problems of Sex', in *God, Sex and War*, ed. D. M. Mackinnon (London, 1963), p. 37.

[2] R. H. Fuller and B. K. Rice, *Christianity and the Affluent Society* (London, 1966), p. 115.

[3] Howard Root, 'Love, Law and Liberty', in *We must Love One Another or Die*, ed. Hugh Montefiore (London, 1966), p. 49.

[4] *Sunday Telegraph*, 1 Apr. 1973; 'Non-birth of a Nation' by Peregrine Worsthorne.

progress,' as David Edwards put it; 'the availability of contraceptives produced another debate about whether sexual intercourse could now be treated as hand-shakes had been in the old Western Society.'[1] Hugh Montefiore, in the vanguard of the 'New Morality', and critical of social arrangements too, wrote that 'in a capitalist form of society' the 'popularity of hire-purchase' is such as to influence the 'attitude towards matters of sex'.[2] This critical element involved radical churchmen with the much-publicized 'crisis of authority' in the later 1960s. 'The challenge to authority in ethics', as Professor John Macquarrie wrote in 1970, 'is only part of a much wider phenomenon, seen also in the challenge to the universities, the family, political institutions, and so on.'[3] But radical views on sexual ethics had a much wider appeal in the Church than social or political radicalism, and attracted the support or the lip-service of rather a larger group than the progressive theologians and their supporters within the leadership of the Church. In 1970 even the Archbishop of Canterbury's press officer was contributing articles advocating 'situation ethics' in sexual questions to advanced secular journals.[4] Nor were the Non-conformist Churches hesitant. The publication of *Towards a Quaker View of Sex* in 1963 was one of the milestones on the road to sexual liberation. 'The impression created', as the Bishop of Durham's Report on Education observed in 1970, 'was that not only Christian doctrines but also Christian ethics were in the melting pot.'[5] As early as 1963 Archbishop Ramsey had pronounced that 'sexual morality is in a mess'.[6]

As Bishop Robinson has rightly noticed, the phrase 'the New Morality' covers widely differing views.[7] The 'New Morality' had also begun before the 1960s—the first significant shift in the Church's attitude to sexual morality had come in the theological reinterpretations used to justify the abandonment of the teaching on contraception in 1958. Perhaps the next step—a symbolic and a very public step, at any rate—came in October 1960. This was Bishop Robinson's evidence, on behalf of Penguin Books, in the proceedings under the Obscene Publications Act over *Lady Chatterley's Lover*. Of the adultery, which forms the story-line of the book, Robinson said in court that 'Lawrence tried to portray this relation as in a real sense an act of holy communion'.[8] This shocked a lot of opinion—not accustomed, as it was later to become, to the new attitudes among church-men. In 1962 Harry Williams, the Dean of Trinity College, Cambridge,

[1] Edwards, *Religion and Change*, p. 313.
[2] Montefiore, 'Personal Relations before Marriage', in *God, Sex and War*, p. 81.
[3] Macquarrie, *3 Issues in Ethics* (London, 1970), p. 26.
[4] Michael De-La-Noy, *A Day in the Life of God* (Derby, 1971), Appendix One, p. 94.
[5] *The fourth R.*, p. 20.
[6] Michael Ramsey, *Canterbury Essays and Addresses* (London, 1964), p. 88; 'Sex and Civilization' (from the *Sunday Times*, 17 Feb. 1963).
[7] Robinson, *Christian Freedom in a Permissive Society*, p. 10.
[8] Quoted in Peter Howard, *Britain and the Beast* (London, 1963), p. 8.

wrote an essay in *Soundings*, a volume of critical writing on theological issues, which justified sexual relations outside marriage 'whatever the Church may say about fornication'.[1] The following year, 1963, brought not only *Honest to God* into the world, but also Dr. Frank Lake's 'Clinical Theology' centre at Nottingham. This application of psychiatry to religious experience necessarily had a tendency to reinterpret the sexual teachings of the Church. Many bishops approved.[2] Robinson's *Honest to God* itself had a chapter on 'The New Morality'—though public outrage at the apparent tendency of the book to deny the existence of a personal God screened this section of the book from attack for some months. Its author attributed the delay to the public's shocked absorption with the Profumo scandal.[3] In this chapter Robinson argued for 'situation ethics', pointing out that the revolution 'required in morals' had 'long since broken out'.[4] He argued that the legalistic approach to morality, which Christianity had practised, did not have the authority of Jesus and His teaching about absolute love. 'Love alone,' he wrote, 'because, as it were, it has a built-in moral compass, enabling it to "home" intuitively upon the deepest need of the other, can allow itself to be directed completely by the situation.'[5] The whole fabric of 'situation ethics' was created from this position. Canon Edward Carpenter, a prominent member of the Modern Churchmen's Union, wrote in 1961 that Christianity 'seeks to lift men out of the area in which law operates and a coercive jurisdiction is necessary into the territory where creative love becomes the controlling loyalty'.[6] There were 'situations', he believed, in which 'the normative may have to give way to more personal needs'.[7] In 1964 Archbishop Ramsey wrote that 'narrow moralism must be cleared away', for 'the Christian ethic is not primarily a set of rules and prohibitions'.[8] In the same year Canon Douglas Rhymes wrote an influential little book attacking legalism—'this long-standing traditional morality, based upon authoritarian law and suspicion of the flesh, is to-day being rejected on all sides, and especially among the younger generation'.[9] Jesus, he said, taught that 'the needs of men come before the law'.[10] Rhymes also declared his aim as 'not a lower code of morality, but a high attitude towards the person, a personal relationship

---

[1] Harry Williams, 'Theology and Self-Awareness', in *Soundings. Essays Concerning Christian Understanding*, ed. A. R. Vidler (Cambridge, 1962), p. 82.

[2] Paul Ferris, *The Church of England*, revd. edn. (London, 1964), p. 256. See also Dewar, *An Outline of Anglican Moral Theology*, pp. 18–19.

[3] Robinson, *Christian Freedom in a Permissive Society*, p. 8.

[4] John A. T. Robinson, *Honest to God* (London, 1963), p. 105.

[5] Ibid., p. 115.

[6] Edward Carpenter, *Common Sense About Christian Ethics* (London, 1961), p. 152.

[7] Ibid., p. 147.   [8] Ramsey, *Canterbury Essays*, p. 88.

[9] Douglas Rhymes, *No New Morality, Christian personal values and sexual morality* (London, 1964), p. 19.

[10] Ibid., p. 22.

of responsibility and love which will pervade all human relationships; a relationship which will be based not upon the observance of laws but upon concern for the person in the situation of the person'.[1] This contention reveals the affinity of the 'New Morality' with secular humanism: the respect of human rational choice and moral autonomy—the 'higher law' of private judgement. The Christian advocacy of this view of ethics reached its most systematic statement in two works by an American academic theologian, Joseph Fletcher—*Situation Ethics* (1966), and *Moral Responsibility* (1967). In its final form, 'situation ethics' was summarized by Professor William Barclay, in a series of television lectures in 1971. 'According to this theory of ethics, there is no such thing as a predefinition of goodness or badness,' he said in a fairly critical assessment; 'what we have to take to any situation is not a prefabricated decision, but an act of judgment.'[2]

For the most influential English advocate of 'situation ethics' it is necessary to turn again to Bishop Robinson, but in doing so it is always as well to realize that he is not an isolated theoretician. Within the world of academic theology, and within the leadership of the Church, his position attracts considerable respect, and a general inclination, even in those who do not share his convictions, to accept some of his essential criteria for ethical questions. Many feel he goes a little too far; but it is in a general direction which they have come to regard as legitimate. Robinson's first premise is that 'the Christian ethic is not an unchanging body of fixed teaching'.[3] 'Situation ethics' have of necessity to rest upon radical reinterpretation of Scriptural texts, since to most readers of the Bible, and to the Church for nearly two thousand years, Christ has seemed to have prescribed some clear and fixed moral laws. Robinson applied his New Testament scholarship to show how, in his judgement, either the words of Jesus do not imply what they seem to, or that they were so conditioned by the culture of his day that they can be regarded as inapplicable to the modern world. Robinson wrote of the modern Christian: 'Christ does not supply him with an ethical code, any more than he supplies him with a legal system, or a polity, or an economy'.[4] Radicalism (which the Bishop correctly realizes is 'an attitude or temper of mind'), when applied to Christian ethical teaching, can have only one result: 'the radical believes with the revolutionary in "the ethic of the situation", with nothing prescribed— *except love*'.[5] This love is to be taken in all senses, and Robinson's severest critics have been those most offended by his observations on the sexuality of Christ himself.[6] In numerous places Robinson has suggested the removal

[1] Ibid., p. 29.

[2] William Barclay, *Ethics in a Permissive Society* (London, 1971), p. 69 (Baird Lectures, B.B.C. Television).

[3] Robinson, *Christian Freedom in a Permissive Society*, p. 15.   [4] Ibid., p. 12.

[5] Ibid., p. 5.   [6] Robinson, *The Human Face of God*, p. 64.

of legal and other restraints upon sexual conduct as a positive part of the Christian Gospel. He has also argued the same case in the interests of civil liberty and social justice: in a 'pluralistic' society it is improper for moral norms to be enforced in matters which relate solely to 'private' behaviour; 'As long as we allow for this relativistic factor in all ethical judgments and are not afraid to face it as Christians, then we shall not be unduly disturbed by our divergent moralities.'[1] God himself 'is characteristically to be found on the shifting frontiers of social change, in the relativities of events rather than in a timeless absolute'.[2] Hence the Christian contribution to contemporary society: 'The aim should be to *move towards* a mature society where the moral choice in issues of this sort (including sex relationships, divorce, euthanasia, gambling, drugs, reading-matter and the rest) is taken by the individuals concerned and safeguarded by society against exploitation or abuse.' The law should not interfere. There should be 'a free, responsible, secular society—all to the end that life can be more deeply and truly human'.[3] Don Cupitt, the Dean of Emmanuel College, Cambridge—a theologian friendly to the Robinson view of morality—has noticed the corollary of Christian advocacy of such aims. 'Christians have themselves increasingly been persuaded by the free-thinkers' picture of Church history, and are themselves also critical of the form of the Church as they have received it,' he has written. 'The main reason for this is that vast changes in Christian ethics have almost destroyed the moral authority of the Christian past.'[4] It is interesting to notice that two moral spheres are constantly being mixed in the theological debate about 'situation ethics'. Those ethics are, first, identified with the teachings of the Gospel: they are, in the religious sphere, promoted as Christian. And then, they are thought applicable to society in general, in the public sphere, through the sponsorship of the State—which will have to agree with this moral attitude in order to repeal the various laws which contravene freedom of moral choice. Robinson and others quite freely move from one sphere to the next, often evidently unaware that their prior argument means that it is for a Christian State that they are now seeking an existence; for law to recognize a moral scheme which they are commending to the Church because it corresponds to the Gospel. And because the Gospel itself also happens to correspond with scientific humanism and with the facts of social pluralism, no apparent inconsistencies get in the way.

Extensive use has been made by radical moralists within the Church—as outside it—of the 'youth culture' of the contemporary western world. Church leaders have been much attracted to the 'idealism' of the young,

[1] Robinson, *Christian Freedom in a Permissive Society*, p. 13.
[2] Robinson, *The Human Face of God*, p. 25.
[3] Robinson, *The Difference in Being a Christian Today*, p. 27.
[4] Cupitt, *Crisis of Moral Authority*, p. 89.

and their taste for social protest. 'The questionings of young people today are often an indication not of irresponsibility but of the beginning of depth', according to Canon Rhymes, writing in 1964.[1] It has become a conventional view. In 1968 the bishops at the Lambeth Conference declared that it was 'the impatient protests of young men and women' that convinced them that they must depict a 'servant Church' as the one appropriate to the age.[2] In 1973 the Anglican Consultative Council exemplified 'the role of the servant' as 'the place of youth in the Church'. The youth dimension must make the Church 'willing to confront its own ecclesiastical structures with their oppressive role'.[3] Churchmen, in fact, have identified youth with radicalism. Harold Loukes, an Oxford Education-alist who has studied the moral beliefs of young people, has concluded that 'they are, to put it crudely, "Robinson-men" '. They are, that is to say, ignorant of the traditional language of Christian values, and 'demand that the whole matter should be dealt with in thought-forms they can al-ready handle'.[4] And Leslie Paul, reviewing the Church and its place in society in 1973, ten years after the publication of his Report on the deploy-ment of the clergy, declared that 'the youth culture is hostile to establish-ment institutions'.[5] These sorts of judgements have become common-place in Church thought. It is as well to notice that they are open to question. It may be true that 'the youth culture' is hostile to religious, as to other institutions; but it is not clear that 'the youth culture' originates with 'youth', or is even believed by them in any significant sense. It may be true of middle-class youth or of working-class youth stimulated to respond sympathetically by middle-class research-workers. It can be argued that 'the youth culture' is as much the contrivance of the middle-aged of the middle classes—whose latter-day radicalism has been fed to the young, through the media, through advertising, and through the schools—as the genuine invention of the young themselves. Youth radicalism is also a minority movement. Most young people remain fairly conservative in a wide range of their instincts and beliefs, reflecting the tenacity of family custom against the dissolvent incitements of educationalists. A lot of the recent evidence for 'youth culture' as a radical force has been drawn from the student unrest since 1968: it is evidence of the behaviour of a middle-class élite.

However prestigious radical attitudes may have become among academic theologians and with those parts of the leadership of the Church most in touch with the assumptions and intellectual fashions of the intelligentsia, radical ideas have not enjoyed widespread approval in the Church in

[1] Rhymes, *No new morality*, p. 58.
[2] *The Lambeth Conference 1968*, 'A Message from the Bishops', p. 24.
[3] *Partners in Mission* (London, 1973), p. 22.
[4] Harold Loukes, *Teenage Morality* (London, 1973), p. 115.
[5] Paul, *A Church by Daylight*, p. 161.

recent years. From his retirement in Dorset, Archbishop Lord Fisher noted in 1967 that despite the loud voices of the 'humanists' within the Church, 'the quiet part of the nation still respected the basic principles of Christian morality'.[1] In 1971 he added, 'In this country the disturbing thing is that too many groups and interests are at one and the same time seeking publicity for their own grievances and demanding under threats some reform which will give more power to the less responsible and less respect to the more responsible'.[2] This belief in the conservatism of the 'silent majority'—to use a phrase still current—was widespread in the Church. The 'broad assent' given to diluted Christianity in English society was an assent to traditionally conceived Christian theology and morality, not to 'situation ethics' and 'religionless Christianity'. 'It is as a basis for morality or "civilization" that Christianity is so widely applauded, and especially as a means for inculcating distinctions between right and wrong amongst children', according to a sociologist who has studied the Church in England.[3] The 'nominal' Christian public were amazed by the ideas put out by radical churchmen, most of which reached them through broadcasting. And religious broadcasting, as the Archdeacon of Hastings remarked in 1965, appeared 'primarily concerned to publicise the utterances of ecclesiastical radio stars with *avant-garde* views'.[4] The Report on Broadcasting presented to the General Synod of the Church of England in 1973 gave some indication that things had not changed too much: 'judging from some of the evidence the Commission has received, it seems that some members of the Church are too easily persuaded that the fashionable sociological view is the right attitude for them to adopt'.[5] The minority, however, had the initiative, the weight of academic respectability, influential representation among the episcopacy, and a disproportionate representation in the Church press. The *Church Times* gave sympathetic airing to a lot of the theological radicals' opinions, and only the distinctly Evangelical religious press has been really hostile. Of the national prints there was no marked opposition, perhaps through lack of interest, and the *Spectator*, alone, carried a series of rather polemical criticisms of radical opinions early in the 1970s.

A growing number of radical clergy have recently become impatient of parish work, and have sought appointment either in educational institutions or in central societies and agencies of the Church. They have carried their own sense of a 'crisis of identity', and their general radical outlook, into the expanding 'specialized ministries' of the Church. This too has

[1] Fisher, *Standards of Morality, Christian and Humanist*, p. 5.

[2] Archbishop Lord Fisher, *Touching on Christian Truth* (London, 1971), p. 177.

[3] David Martin, *A Sociology of English Religion*, p. 55.

[4] Guy Mayfield, *Like Nothing on Earth* (London, 1965), p. 149.

[5] *Broadcasting, Society and the Church* (1973), p. 6.

given radical opinion a public voice its numerical following would not warrant. But despite the domination of so much religious discussion by radical ideas in the 1960s and early in the 1970s, there have been signs that the enthusiasm has slightly cooled recently. In a few areas resistance to change has exerted itself with some results. Thus although liturgical reforms got through, because they were more broadly based in lay and parochial support, changes in the marriage discipline were resisted. Radical theology is essentially a talking shop, it develops in isolation from the real world of parish experience; it is intellectual, not practical. The slightest breeze can blow it onto some new tack—as conservatives within the Church began to discover early in the 1970s. But conservative churchmen lacked leadership, and, because of their very nature, the will to organize and proselytize for their view of Christianity within the Church. The situation was like that between the wars, when radical opinion led the Church although the men in the pews and their ministers were far from following. Perhaps the last Church debate on Christian morality which did not become the vehicle for liberals to sound their trumpets was in October 1961, when Convocation approved a motion deploring standards of morality in contemporary society. But even then, it was necessary for Dr. W. M. Askwith, the Bishop of Gloucester, to regret 'the use of the word "anti-social" instead of the word "wrong" in relation to conduct'.[1]

There has been some criticism of the moral beliefs of the radicals from within academic theology. Canon V. A. Demant, the Christian Socialist writer whose distinguished contribution to Anglican thinking in the 1940s has already been discussed,[2] in 1963 published a work which defended Christian marriage as a permanent covenant.[3] And in 1965, speaking at the University Church in Cambridge, he defended chastity—the Christian teaching of temperance in sexual behaviour: 'It rules out adultery which is fornication when one or both parties are married, it rules out pre-marital venereal union, it rules out free love, homosexual practices and other counterfeits of the normal acts of intercourse between a man and a woman.'[4] Demant pointed to the universal need for rules to govern sexual conduct. It was spiritual wisdom implanted in generations of men, and not ignorance of the true nature of sexuality, as the radicals supposed, that lay behind the providential provision of religious laws about sexual conduct. 'Because of this complex nature of the sex life, human nature has always made rules about it,' he said. 'People talk about human life as though it could be regulated entirely by spontaneous good-will and charity, and they call for a Christianity without rules.' And above all, he argued, the 'New

[1] *The Chronicle of Convocation*, 1961 (London, 1961), p. 492 (Upper House, 3 Oct. 1961; Debate on 'Standard of Morality'). [2] See Chap. 9, pp. 380–83.

[3] V. A. Demant, *An Exposition of Christian Sex Ethics* (London, 1963).

[4] V. A. Demant, 'Chastity and Charity', in *We must Love one another or Die*, ed. Montefiore, p. 75.

Morality' ignored 'the imperfection of human nature', and the 'demonic element in sex'.[1] The Christian rules 'are not arbitrary, nor do they belong to a patriarchal state of society; they really represent the truly human interest';[2] they recognize human life as it actually is. R. M. Fuller and B. K. Rice, writing in 1966, also pointed to the traditional wisdom and utility embodied in Christian rules. 'The "new freedom" for the young sounds all right in theory,' they wrote: 'the trouble is that in so many families it must be paid for with unhappiness and ruined lives.'[3] In 1967 Fisher, in similar vein, wrote that ethical radicalism involved 'the all-too prevalent fashion of hedging on fundamental moral questions', and always meant 'exalting the rights of private judgment or prejudice to a point where it was destructive of community co-operation and cohesion'.[4]

Professor Mascall condemned both the new theology and the 'New Morality' outright. In 1965 he attacked *Honest to God* for the secularization of Christianity. 'The outlook of what Robinson calls the "lay" world has become radically unchristian,' Mascall wrote of the prevailing humanism of the intellectuals; 'he himself has been dangerously influenced by it.'[5] The unique claims of Christianity seemed to have been surrendered or denied, all in the interests of accommodating humanism. 'It is quite illegitimate to redefine Christianity in order to include all men of good will', Mascall contended, though 'this is what Robinson's programme in fact amounts to.'[6] Canon Waddams has argued against the tendency to abandon law and substitute love—*Agape*—as anyway based upon mis-understandings of Scripture: 'it is not the subjective *Agape* of the indi-vidual, but the *Agape* of God which alone sets the standard for all men'.[7] Professor John Macquarrie's criticism of the new moral attitudes pointed to their inadequacy, both practically and theoretically. 'Anyone looking to Christian thinkers for guidance on the problems of the day will find him-self bewildered,' he wrote in 1970; 'we have heard a great deal about the virtues of "situation ethics", but much of this discussion has been pitiably irrelevant to the major ethical problems of our time.'[8] He agreed that legalism certainly 'distorts' Christianity—for which Christ had criticized the Judaism of the Pharisees—but he believed the present revolt against 'supposedly legalistic forms' was sometimes conducted 'extravagantly'.[9] The facts of personality were ignored. 'A situational ethic breaks up the moral life into separate acts in such a way as to deny the reality of a unitary personal self that grows and deepens through its successive experiences.'

---

[1] V. A. Demant, 'Chastity and Charity', in *We must Love one another or Die*, p. 77.
[2] Ibid., p. 78.   [3] Fuller and Rice, *Christianity and the Affluent Society*, p. 126.
[4] Fisher, *Standards of Morality*, p. 30.
[5] Mascall, *The Secularization of Christianity*, p. 108.   [6] Ibid., p. 110.
[7] Quoted, with approving commentary and explanation, in Dewar, *An Outline of Angli-can Moral Theology*, p. 10.
[8] Macquarrie, *3 Issues in Ethics*, p. 13.   [9] Ibid., p. 28.

The mechanistic approach, adequate for humanism, is inadequate for Christianity; 'For the situationist, man is simply "functional" man: he is what he does, in one situation after another.'[1] This point was similar to the difficulties in too close a conflation of Christianity and humanism suggested by Fr. D'Arcy, the Catholic scholar. The exclusive nature of Christian truth was dissipated if men entrusted it to 'human society without any qualification'.[2] William Barclay, Professor of Divinity at Glasgow, and a Presbyterian theologian, though himself sympathetic to new approaches in Biblical study, has popularized some of the objections to 'situation ethics'. They present men with 'a terrifying degree of freedom'.[3] He declined to agree with Robinson that man had 'come of age'—an idea popularized by the Bonhoeffer cult—and so rendered the moral attitudes constructed upon that assumption questionable.[4] Like Demant, Barclay sustained the value of law in ethical guidance as 'the distillation of experience', and not a crude imposition by those ignorant of modern knowledge. 'Law seeks to ensure that those courses of action which experience has shown to be beneficial are followed, and to eliminate those courses of action which experience has shown to be harmful or injurious to society and its members.' A lot of suffering could be eliminated as a result; 'to discard law is to discard experience'.[5] The distinction between public and private morals breaks down in practice, and so there is always cause for law to control 'private' conduct.[6] And finally, Barclay could not see any Scriptural basis for 'situation ethics'. Christ condemned fornication at least eighteen times. 'There is no way of making Jesus a supporter of the permissive society,' he concluded. 'If we support sexual intercourse before marriage or outside marriage, then I do not see how we can continue to call ourselves Christian, for a man cannot be a Christian and flatly contradict the teaching of Jesus Christ.'[7] Exponents of 'situation ethics' within the Church have, in fact, been far from advocating 'permissiveness' in moral conduct. Very much the reverse: not only have their actual moral recommendations, when all the agonized calculations are done, turned out to be extremely prescriptive in most instances, but the radicals are also very insistent moralists. Their claims are to exclusive truth; there is no compromise with traditionalist morality at all. And those who find it so difficult to approve the application of fixed principles in questions of sexual morality are also those noted for a highly authoritarian and normative attitude to social and political morality. They do not allow that 'situationist' considerations may introduce flexibility into such questions as race relations or social equality or educational policy.

[1] Ibid., p. 33.
[2] Martin C. D'Arcy, *Humanism and Christianity* (London, 1969), p. 185.
[3] Barclay, *Ethics in a Permissive Society*, p. 80.   [4] Ibid., p. 81.
[5] Ibid., p. 84.   [6] Ibid., p. 90.   [7] Ibid., p. 208.

Academic criticism of the humanist lobby within the Church has never attracted much publicity. In actual discussions of moral issues by the Church of England in the years after 1960 the influence of 'situation ethics' has increasingly been felt, but it has encountered the conservatism of the parishes—often represented in the Church Assembly and its successor, the General Synod—and never got very far. A more liberal line in moral teaching certainly declared itself in some of the Church documents of the period—produced by committees on which academic theologians were well represented, offering apparently authoritative advice: but really radical ideas are not automatically accepted. Thus although the Church's Report, *Ought Suicide to be a Crime?*, published in 1959, was followed in 1960 by legislation to remove criminal liability, as the Report had suggested, and although the general attitudes in the *Abortion* Report, 1965, were those the legislation of 1967 in effect adopted, the influence of the Church was not decisive. It was convenient. It enabled the secular humanist liberalism of those who sought reform for reasons which had nothing to do with the interpretation of Christianity to get their way without too much embarrassing religious opposition—except from Roman Catholics. The Church of England's formal teaching remained unchanged however; the force of conservative opinion was in general sufficiently strong to prevent a collective declaration for humanist morality, whatever the theologians might hope one day to see. It is not surprising that Leslie Paul should have noticed the fears 'of some Churchmen that the Church had not (and perhaps never would) come to terms with enlightened secular teaching on sex'.[1] There was a still large, and still largely silent, majority which hoped to see the Church adhere to the traditional teaching. It is possible that as synodical government develops it will foster a greater sectarian self-identification which may well benefit radical ideas. But ultimately it will depend on what happens in the general world of the intelligentsia: if radical moral and social ideas continue to thrive there, they will be reflected in the Church. On that, and not on Biblical scholarship, radical theology depends. Teachers of religious education in secondary schools are also sometimes a vehicle for the diffusion of radical ideas, and in the fullness of time this too could favour more extensive adjustments to the Church's teachings.

The discussions of the Church of England's attitude to marriage and divorce have furnished the most frequent occasions for the 'situationists' to get their views aired within Church government. After a decade of talking, the issues remain unsettled (1974). But the advance of liberal attitudes can be measured in the arguments used as the debate developed over the years. Like most churchmen since the mid-nineteenth century, contemporary leaders of the Church have recognized the practical diver-

---

[1] *The Deployment and Payment of the Clergy*, p. 13.

gence of Church and State law. Churchmen of all shades of opinion saw
that in a question like marriage discipline it was doubtful if 'it was right to
seek to impose in any way Christian standards on an agnostic or indifferent
population'—as Dr. Edward Henderson, the Bishop of Bath and Wells said
in 1961—'a moral code should be the product (not in the sense of originated by, but with the consent) of public opinion and not its tyrant'.[1]
Archbishop Ramsey expressed similar opinions in 1962, during the parliamentary discussion of the Matrimonial Causes Bill. This unsuccessful
measure, promoted by Leo Abse and Lord Silkin (neither of whom was
Christian), would have allowed divorce by consent after a seven years'
separation. Ramsey's opposition to the principle of divorce by consent was
absolute: 'it alters by reflex implication the meaning of the marriage
covenant'.[2] The Church, on the other hand, did not wish to force its
teachings 'upon the law of the country', Ramsey affirmed. 'While the
churches have their beliefs and standards which they urge their members
to follow and teach, that they can follow by the help of God's grace, they
accept the fact that a great many citizens do not share their beliefs and that
this is reflected in the divorce laws of the country.'[3] Yet the Church was
concerned with the general welfare of the country, and would, as a result,
seek to assist in divorce-law reform despite the Church's own teachings
against divorce. The Church was seeing if 'it were possible to find a
principle and a law of breakdown of marriage which was free from any
trace of the idea of consent, which conserved the point that offences and
not only wishes are the basis of the breakdown, and which was protected
by a far more thorough insistence on reconciliation procedures first'.[4]
This view reflected a general feeling within the leadership of the Church
at the time. Bishop Robinson, of course, did not agree with Ramsey's
objections to divorce by consent—in 1963 he attacked the 'supernaturalist
ethic' of marriage upheld by 'traditional' Christianity,[5] and came to believe
the Church would 'live to regret' its opposition to Leo Abse's bill.[6] That
opposition had, in the event, been general—the statement rejecting the
principle of the Bill, in April 1963, was issued in the name of the Church
of England, the Roman Catholic Church, and the Free Church Federal
Council.

The inquiry to which Ramsey had referred led to the appointment, early
in 1964, of the 'Archbishop's Group'—a working party set up under the
chairmanship of Dr. Robert Mortimer, Bishop of Exeter, to examine the
whole question of divorce law.[7] Mortimer's opinions were perhaps
flexible, but not radical; he had established a substantial reputation as an

---

[1] *The Chronicle of Convocation 1961*, p. 493 (3 Oct. 1961).
[2] Ramsey, *Canterbury Essays*, p. 93.   [3] Ibid., p. 92.
[4] Ibid., p. 95.   [5] Robinson, *Honest to God*, p. 109.
[6] Robinson, *Christian Freedom in a Permissive Society*, p. 15.
[7] A. R. Winnett, *The Church and Divorce* (London, 1968), p. 87.

expert on moral theology. The report of the Group was published in 1966 with the title *Putting Asunder*. They were careful to declare that their suggestions were intended to assist the realities of 'a secular society', and that the law of the Church against divorce remained.

It is right and proper for the Church to co-operate with the State, and for Christians to co-operate with secular humanists and others who are not Christians, in trying to make the divorce law as equitable and as little harmful to society as it can be made [the Report declared]. Any advice that the Church tenders the State must rest, not upon doctrines that only Christians accept, but upon premises that enjoy wide acknowledgement in the nation as a whole.[1]

The involvement of the Church was also justified on the ground of its national position: it had special responsibilities as an Establishment.[2] Professor Norman Anderson, an academic lawyer and a member of the Archbishop's Group, later explained this involvement to the Church Assembly. 'Our own attitude to divorce is quite plain,' he said in February 1967. 'But the State allows divorce, and our proposals are designed to suggest a better civil law of divorce, better for the people and the nation.'[3] Archbishop Ramsey took the same opportunity to underline the point. 'I am sure that it is right for the Church to be concerned about and interested in the State's law of divorce,' he told the Church Assembly. 'This is part of the Church's service to the community, whatever the community may like.'[4] *Putting Asunder* argued for liberal reform. The concept of matrimonial offence was to be removed from the law and 'irretrievable breakdown' substituted. Courts were to proceed by inquiry into the past history of a marriage, not with the intention of determining whether there were innocent or guilty parties, but seeking evidence that the intended relationship had failed.[5] 'Irretrievable breakdown' must be the sole grounds of divorce, and not merely an addition to existing grounds of matrimonial delinquency. The Church Assembly endorsed the Report.[6]

The problem with liberal reforms is that they tend to replace laws which, though formally offensive, have often found their own level and work tolerably in practice, with a heavy machinery for the enforcement of the enlightened opinions enshrined in the reforming legislation. The recommendations of *Putting Asunder* were like this. The inquisitorial powers to be handed to the courts were to be very extensive; the private lives of petitioners were to be opened up without effective limitation. The Law Commission, to which the Report was referred by the Lord Chancellor (Lord Gardiner), criticized it on just those grounds. It would cause distress

---

[1] *Putting Asunder: A Divorce Law for Contemporary Society* (London, 1966), p. 12.
[2] Ibid., p. 13.
[3] *Church Assembly. Report of Proceedings*, vol. XLVII, No. 1 (1967), p. 239.
[4] Ibid., p. 250.   [5] *Putting Asunder*, p. 37.
[6] *Report of Proceedings*, vol. XLVII, No. 1, p. 230 (16 Feb. 1967).

and humiliation—'public opinon would be unlikely to regard it as an improvement if in every case the whole matrimonial history were ventilated in public'[1] Dr. Edith Summerskill, the Labour M.P., attacked the Report for its refusal to consider the special security needed for women in the break-up of marriage; it in effect replaced a lifelong contract by 'trial marriage'.[2] *Putting Asunder*, in fact, was a typical piece of academic liberalism. On the one hand it correctly caught the spirit of contemporary legal thinking on the need for adjustments in existing arrangements; on the other hand it proposed a blueprint for a machinery of enforcement more offensive to the public than the equivocal procedures of the old law. This unpopularity was proved in practice. The reconciliation officers provided by the Divorce Reform Act of 1969 have had very few cases referred to them.[3] The Divorce Act itself followed the thinking of *Putting Asunder* at least to the extent of providing for 'irretrievable breakdown'; but the inquisitorial procedures were dropped, and the use of the reconciliation service was entirely optional. It can hardly be said that this reform was the result of Christian thought in any immediate sense, however. The truth is that the authors of *Putting Asunder* were themselves under the influence of opinions pretty general among liberal law reformers—opinions which were already acceptable to the Law Commission. The Church Report reflected the 'enlightened' thought around them; it was not distinctively Christian. Archbishop Ramsey, who had supported the scheme suggested in *Putting Asunder*, was critical of the 1969 Act, fearing its effect on the stability of marriage. He believed the provisions for divorce where 'irretrievable breakdown' could be established by a two-year separation, and where innocent parties could be divorced against their will after five years, encouraged the idea of temporary marriage.[4] He retained his total opposition to divorce by consent. It would 'make such a big contrast between a civil marriage and a Church marriage that it would raise the question of whether the Church could continue to recognise civil marriages as a contract for a lifelong union'.[5] English law, even under the new legislation of 1969, continues to require civil registrars to declare that the marriage contract is permanent. It is an important survival of Christian teaching within the law. The large numbers of clergy who act as marriage-guidance counsellors also indicates the surviving closeness of Church and State on marriage questions, despite the different attitudes of Church and State to divorce.

Procedure by inquisition into the circumstances of moral conduct did not lose its appeal for liberal churchmen, and in 1971 the idea cropped up

[1] Quoted in Winnett, *The Church and Divorce*, p. 93.   [2] Ibid., p. 95.
[3] *Marriage and the Family in Britain Today. A Survey presented by the Board for Social Responsibility*, G.S. 169 (London, 1973), p. 17.
[4] Winnett, *The Church and Divorce*, p. 99.
[5] *Church Assembly. Report of Proceedings*, vol. XLVII, No. 1, p. 250 (16 Feb. 1967).

again in the Report of a Commission set up by the Archbishop of Canterbury according to a Resolution of Convocation, to formulate 'a statement
of the Christian doctrine of marriage'. Its immediate purpose was to see if
grounds existed for changing the rule against the remarriage of the divorced in Church. The Commission reported to the new General Synod.
Its Chairman was Professor Howard Root (an exponent of 'situation ethics'
who had once expressed the opinion that not all sex outside marriage was
'irredeemably wrong').[1] Hugh Montefiore, now Bishop of Kingston-on-
Thames, was another radical member. The Commission also contained
Professor G. R. Dunstan, a distinguished theologian, widely respected for
his balanced attitude towards the adjustment of Christian teachings to
contemporary conditions. The Commission sought to discover if a 'moral
consensus' for change existed in the Church. Some rather prejudicial
means of inquiry were used. 'Which is more important, the institution of
marriage or the welfare of the two people concerned?' they asked.[2] It was
not exactly, in this formulation, an unweighted question. The Commission,
not surprisingly, came down unanimously in favour of the view that remarriage of the divorced should be allowed in Church.[3] But 'a competent
church authority' was to make 'discreet but adequate inquiry' into the
moral circumstances which had led to the failure of the previous marriage, and into the characters of the two persons now seeking marriage, to
get 'an assurance that they are both the kind of people who are capable of
the stable and permanent relationship of marriage'.[4] The exact form of this
inquiry never came to be laid down. In February 1972 the General Synod
debated the Commission's recommendations and a lot of dissatisfaction
was voiced. A new Committee was appointed under the Bishop of Leicester,
Dr. Ronald Williams, who, although he was also the Chairman of the Board
for Social Responsibility—a body noted for the radicalism of its publications—is in general a fairly conservative churchman. In a first report to the
Synod in 1973, the new Committee attacked the ambiguity of the 'consensus' sought by the previous inquiry, and decided that two-thirds of the
Church could be considered an adequate sanction for change in the
Church's marriage discipline.[5] They were able to report, also, that of the
twenty-six bishops who had replied to their inquiry, seventeen favoured
some change, eight were against, and one 'deferred comment'.[6] They
contented themselves with reiterating the cases for and against a change;

[1] See Howard Root, 'Ethical Problems of Sex', in *God, Sex and War*, ed. Mackinnon,
p. 44.
[2] *Marriage, Divorce and the Church. The Report of a Commission appointed by The
Archbishop of Canterbury to prepare a Statement on the Christian Doctrine of Marriage*
(London, 1971), p. 28.
[3] Ibid., p. 72.   [4] Ibid., p. 73.
[5] *Report of the Working Group on Marriage, Divorce and the Church*, G.S. 156, p. 6.
[6] Ibid., p. 7.

'a clearing of the air'.[1] In November 1973 the Synod voted against change, amidst some procedural confusions, and at the Spring Session of 1974 the Archbishop of Canterbury announced that the question was now put off for another year.[2]

The marriage and divorce questions absorbed a great deal of Church attention in the years after 1960. But there has also been a considerable ferment in other areas of sexual morality; areas in which some churchmen have brought a radical critique either to the attitudes or to the formal teaching of the Church. The question of homosexual misconduct has been one of the most prominent of these, an issue given much publicity by interested parties and by liberals anxious to release minorities from 'discrimination'. St. Paul declared that homosexuals could not inherit the Kingdom of Heaven (1 Cor. 6:9), and the Church of England has always taught that homosexual misconduct is a sin. At the time of the Wolfenden Report in 1957, Archbishop Fisher had made it clear that whereas he was prepared to consider that homosexual practices should no longer constitute a crime when performed between consenting adults, they remained a sin in the eyes of the Church.[3] In 1967 Parliament did in fact follow the Wolfenden recommendations and legislation in that year removed legal restraints upon practices between consenting adult men. Church leaders generally supported the change in the law. In their enthusiasm for 'situation ethics' and for minority rights, however, some radical opinion in the Church now asks whether homosexual misconduct should be deleted from the list of sins. In 1967 Montefiore suggested the possibility that Christ Himself was homosexual. At the Conference of Modern Churchmen meeting in Oxford he said, 'If Jesus were homosexual in nature (and if this is a true explanation of his celibate state) then this would be further evidence of God's self-identification with those who are unacceptable to the upholders of "the Establishment" and social conventions'.[4] Robinson has also considered the possibility.[5] Robinson also pointed to the conviction within Christian liberal opinion—which he called 'responsible opinion'—that modern knowledge about the facts of human sexuality required the abandonment of traditional teachings on homosexuality.[6] This style of thinking had grown during the 1960s, as liberal opinion generally came to adopt the main assumptions of humanist ethics and what were taken to be the scientific proofs of sexual relativism.[7] In 1963 the Quaker Report on Sex had

---

[1] Ibid., p. 14.   [2] Synod Report, Spring 1974, vol. 4, No. 1, p. 4.
[3] See Chap. 10, p. 411.
[4] Christ for Us Today. Papers read at the Conference of Modern Churchmen, Somerville College, Oxford, July, 1967, ed. Norman Pittinger (London, 1968), p. 110.
[5] Robinson, The Human Face of God, p. 68.
[6] Robinson, Christian Freedom in a Permissive Society, p. 37.
[7] See Rhymes, No New Morality, Appendix, 'The Predicament of the Homosexual', p. 91.

recommended that 'one should no more deplore homosexuality than left-handedness'.[1] Early in the 1970s several groups emerged within the Churches, seeking to propagate sympathetic opinion on homosexuality and to encourage a separate ministry to homosexuals. One of these—which calls itself 'Reach' and is 'a Christian homophile group'[2]—began to extend its activities in universities, following a 'Gay Rights' programme adopted by the National Union of Students in 1973. The most systematic case for an alteration of the Church's teaching on homosexuality, based on radical theology, came with the publication in 1970 of Dr. Norman Pittinger's book *Time for Consent*—an elaboration of his 1967 pamphlet on the question. Pittinger, who is an Anglican theologian, argues that homosexual acts are not sinful,[3] and that homosexuals ought not to be patronized, but regarded as capable of full human love.[4] He proposes 'an Ethic for Homosexuals', within which relationships can be considered as blessed by God.[5] The Church has not, so far (1974), given formal consideration to the possibility of altering its teaching on the question. Propagandists for a change have claimed that their publications are met with 'a conspiracy of silence.'[6]

The family-planning issue has remained unaltered since the Lambeth Conference in 1958; the bishops at Lambeth in 1968 merely adding a dissentient resolution on the Encyclical *Humanae Vitae*, in which Pope Paul VI repeated the opposition of the Catholic Church to artificial birth-control.[7] In many parishes enthusiasm has been such, indeed, that local family-planning counselling has been added to parochial moral concerns alongside the Mothers' Union and the Boy Scouts. Many clergy have begun to teach the positive obligation of limiting families artificially, as a contribution to the solution of the world's population and ecological problems. Bishop Robinson, in making just this point, suggested in 1970 that married couples who wanted more than two children should regard it as a matter of conscience to adopt a 'coloured' child instead of having another of their own.[8] In 1973 the Church of England's Board for Social Responsibility supported the decision of the National Health Service to provide contraceptives for the unmarried—'to help people', as the Board declared, 'to avoid the consequences, in terms of unplanned pregnancies, which may otherwise flow from sexual intercourse'.[9] The Boards' action attracted

---

[1] *Towards a Quaker View of Sex*, p. 21.

[2] See a circular letter of 27 Oct. 1973, sent by 'Reach' to all University Chaplains.

[3] Norman Pittinger, *Time for Consent* (London, 1970), pp. 29 and 100.

[4] Ibid., p. 69.   [5] Ibid., p. 122.

[6] Ibid., p. 9; the phrase was also used by the Revd. Denis Nadin, organizer of 'Reach', in a letter to the *Spectator*, 1 June 1974.

[7] *The Lambeth Conference 1968*, Resolution 22, 'Responsible Parenthood', p. 36.

[8] *Church Assembly. Spring Session 1970. Report of Proceedings*, vol. L, No. 1, p. 191 (5 Feb. 1970).

[9] *Marriage and the Family in Britain Today. A survey presented by the Board for Social Responsibility*, p. 14.

criticism in the General Synod.[1] The question of abortion has not disturbed the Church of England to the extent that it has the Roman Catholic Church, and the Act of 1967, which liberalized the law on the termination of pregnancies, attracted a lot of episcopal support in the House of Lords, as well as some opposition.[2] The Board for Social Responsibility, noting the division of opinion within the Church, stated in 1973 that it was 'particularly misleading to convey the impression that Christians are by the nature of their faith opposed to abortion as such'.[3] Whereas the Lambeth Conference Report of 1958 on *The Family in Contemporary Society* had condemned abortion 'in the strongest terms',[4] the Lambeth Conference of 1968 had been silent on the matter, and clearly by then it had become an acceptable means of birth-control for some Anglicans. In his textbook on Anglican Moral Theology, written in 1968, Canon Lindsay Dewar wrote that there appeared, from pronouncements of Lambeth Conferences, to be a rejection of abortion, and that this was 'also the teaching of the Anglican Church, so far as it is ascertainable'.[5] The matter has been very obscure. 'Real love can only desire people to be as truly free as they possibly can be,' Bishop Robinson told the Abortion Law Reform Association in 1966; people should 'not have what should be their moral decision taken for them by others'.[6] In 1974 the General Synod resolved that the Act of 1967 ought to be tightened up a little, to prevent abuses, but that the essential provisions should remain. Dr. Donald Coggan, the Archbishop of York—who later in the same year succeeded Ramsey at Canterbury—declared in the debate that the Act 'was like one of those old-fashioned street cars running downhill, the brakes of which had failed'.[7] The Church of England lacks a clear view of the question, tending to reflect the divisions of opinion prevailing in society generally.

The divisiveness of the 'two Christianities' has been apparent in the Church's attitude to obscenity and censorship. Bishop Robinson's behaviour in the *Lady Chatterley* case in 1960 had already established a radical position: Robinson there formulated distinctions between the 'erotic', the 'obscene', and the 'pornographic' which, ten years later, the Board for Social Responsibility found commendable.[8] The Board had by 1970 become conscious of the depth of the division, in society and in the Church, between those who sought to retain effective and extensive regulation of

[1] *Synod Report*, Spring 1974, vol. 4, No. 1, p. 14.

[2] Lord Longford, 'The Permissive Society', in *Christianity and Change*, ed. Norman Autton (London, 1971), p. 21.

[3] *Marriage and the Family in Britain Today*, p. 24.

[4] *The Lambeth Conference 1958* (London, 1958), Part 2, p. 148.

[5] Dewar, *An Outline of Anglican Moral Theology*, p. 85.

[6] Robinson, *Christian Freedom in a Permissive Society*, p. 63.

[7] *Synod Report*, Spring 1974, vol. 4, No. 1, p. 9.

[8] *Obscene Publications, Law and Practice*, Issued by the Board for Social Responsibility of the General Synod (London, 1970), p. 10.

what the public should read or see, and those who favoured the abolition of censorship. 'The Church's role is not that of censor', the Board reported; yet it had 'some responsibility for the education of the people's spiritual discernment and judgment'. The Board came down in favour of existing legal controls. In effect, the Board argued the duty of the Church to be concerned in the legal control of obscenity on grounds very similar to those employed to justify the role of the Church in divorce legislation. 'It must be understood that when questions concerning the law of the land are under discussion the criteria to be used, must be the criteria which "all reasonable men" or "the general run of the population" are ready and able to accept.' Churchmen would take some part in the formulation of this opinion; but there was 'a quite different set of considerations by which Christian people will wish to formulate their own attitudes, and seek to influence those who are ready to accept their guidance'.[1] Thus in the matter of public decency, as in divorce, the legislative expression of non-Christian moral attitudes has tended to increase the sectarian self-identification of the Church. By 1970, however, some radical opinion within the Church had acclaimed as Christian the moral attitudes which such legislation embodied; and some had come to oppose censorship altogether as 'a hangover from the paternalistic society'.[2] The opposition to censorship has been fairly selective however. It has come principally from those who believe that violence is obscene, but that sexual licence is not. Bishop Robinson declared that *Playboy* magazine had 'done a liberating job in releasing all kinds of inhibitions about sex' and had helped to make 'the erotic acceptable in a pseudo-puritanical culture'.[3] Such a view of things was still exceptional among the episcopacy, with, perhaps, only another two or three bishops in England happy to share it. But among the radical forces at work in the universities, among Christian students, and in the Student Christian Movement especially, it was common enough by 1970. The opposition to censorship has not cared to define its political limits, but there can be little doubt, in view of the prevailing political atmosphere of the contemporary Church, that the radicals, for all their theoretical opposition to censorship, would clamour for the use of legal restriction to prevent, for example, the dissemination of racialist ideas in society. The progressive lobby, which advocates freedom of thought among school children, and the removal of normative moral teaching in the schools, always assumes that the ideas the liberated children will opt to espouse are liberal ones. In reality, of course, the liberated children are to be encouraged to think liberal thoughts, to adopt a normative set of values under a specious appearance of freedom of choice. So is the debate about censorship. It has so far been defined by relatively safe issues like sex. How sys-

---

[1] *Obscene Publications, Law and Practice*, p. 14.
[2] Robinson, *Christian Freedom in a Permissive Society*, p. 69.   [3] Ibid., p. 75.

tematic radical opinion will become when important issues impress themselves into the area of discussion it is not within the province of this study to ask. Certainly the Broadcasting Commission of the Church of England, in its Report of 1973, declined to accept the fashionable radical claim that moral neutrality is possible. 'Broadcasting does not simply reflect the attitudes of society but helps to form them,' the Commission noted. 'It follows that producers cannot be neutral or disclaim responsibility for the attitudes they help to propagate.'[1] Archbishop Coggan, a fairly consistent advocate of censorship in the area of public morals, quoted the words of President Nixon with approval—'pornography is to freedom of expression what anarchy is to liberty'—in an appeal, written in 1971, for Christian determination to end the evils of materialism.[2] In the attitudes adopted on the question of censorship, the divisions of view between liberal and conservative churchmen are likely to continue. These, too, represent a Christian expression of a general divergence of view in society.

Liberal Christian attitudes have been especially active in the question of education. Here the Church has continued to find, in the terms of the 1944 Education Act, a beneficial relationship with the State, and a substantial stake in social service. 'A partnership, in terms undreamed of only twenty-five years ago,' Archdeacon Guy Mayfield wrote in 1963, 'has been set up between Church and State; it penetrates the whole field of education.'[3] The day-to-day operation of the aided and controlled Church schools has required continuous contact between diocesan officials and Local Education Authorities throughout the country, and this has given a reality to the recognition of Christianity within the state system which those not directly concerned with education are unable to appreciate. Furthermore, the teaching of Christianity within the state schools, as provided in the 1944 Act, continues to be extremely popular with the public—as opinion polls have indicated.[4] The State, for its part, has remained convinced of the need to maintain religious education: the Newsom Report, in 1963, for example, was in favour of it.[5] The Church's role in the training of teachers has also continued to receive the support of the State—it has, in fact, increasingly been recognized as one of the most important educational services of the Church, and Teacher Training Colleges, conducted by the Church of England, are 'ready to make a distinctive contribution' to the future development of professional training.[6]

---

[1] *Broadcasting, Society and the Church* (1973), p. 77.

[2] Donald Coggan, *Word and World* (London, 1971), p. 122.

[3] Guy Mayfield, *The Church of England. Its Members and Its Business*, 2nd edn. (London, 1963), p. 172.

[4] Martin, *A Sociology of English Religion*, p. 53.   [5] *The fourth R.*, p. 23.

[6] *A Submission by the Board of Education to the Secretary of State for Education and Science on 'Teacher Education and Training'—the James Report*, G.S. Misc. 16 (May 1972), p. 7. See also *The Future of the Church Colleges of Education*, G.S. 194 (1973).

In 1970 the Commission constituted jointly by the Church's Board of
Education and the National Society (in 1967) to look into the entire basis of
religious education, reported in favour of the maintenance of the 'dual
system' of Church and State schools. This Report was influenced to some
extent by the radicalism of the chairman, Dr. Ian Ramsey, Bishop of
Durham. As Canon Wedderspoon, Secretary of the Commission, remarked
of Ramsey's attitude, he made it 'clear that it was not the Commission's duty
to manufacture reasons for the preservation of the *status quo*'.[1] Ramsey was
not especially knowledgeable about schools, in fact. It was only a few
days before his death, in October 1972, that he had his 'first and only
experience of teaching in a classroom'.[2] But with characteristic attention to
detail and unsparing hard work, he had applied himself to the education
Commission. Its more radical recommendations concerned the content of
the proposed studies. Religious education, as such, was supported because
of its 'educational significance'; it was 'an act of exploration', on an 'open
basis'; to be fashioned 'by exploring the distinctive vocabularies of faith
and those of many modern disciplines which relate to man and his environment'. The Report projected a sort of situational education. 'It seeks
neither to impose nor to indoctrinate,' the Commissioners wrote of
Christianity as it was in future to be in the schools. 'Indeed, in the exploration of beliefs, it must endeavour to provide for the possibility of a built-in
self criticism so as to anticipate from the start the possibility of reasoned
choice.'[3] Moral education, in the wider sense, too 'must enshrine possibilities for built-in criticism,' the Report urged, 'otherwise moral education
would be no more than training in social conventions'; and it might even,
they added, 'be authoritarian in the worse sense, and the teaching of
morals could be mere conditioning'.[4] Moral teaching, therefore, was to
be 'open', 'encouraging people to think for themselves', to stimulate
them 'to consider arguments against one's own position'.[5] In any new
educational legislation the term 'religious instruction', which had been
used in the 1944 Act, ought to be replaced by 'religious education'.[6] The
Church schools, though they were to continue, were not to be used by the
Church for 'denominational instruction', and the number of voluntary-
aided schools was to be reduced for financial reasons.[7] The Report did
recognize the value of worship in the schools, however,[8] though it offered
little advice about how the children were to worship a Deity who was to be
understood upon an 'open basis'. The main ideas of the Durham Report
for an 'open' teaching of religion have found a lot of favour with educationalists—whose growing criticism of Christian teaching in schools the
Report itself in fact reflected. Conservative opinion, worried by what has

---

[1] David L. Edwards, *Ian Ramsey, Bishop of Durham, A Memoir* (London, 1973), p. 93.
[2] Ibid., p. 96.   [3] *The fourth R.*, p. 58.   [4] Ibid., p. 63.
[5] Ibid., p. 80.   [6] Ibid., p. 277.   [7] Ibid., p. 281.   [8] Ibid., p. 60.

seemed to be the rapid advance of doctrinaire liberalism in educational theory, has not been happy with proposals like those made in the Report. In May 1972, when the Schools Council—a teachers' body which advises the Government—recommended that all religions should be taught equally in the state schools, the *Sunday Telegraph* led the public criticism. 'Faith cannot be taught through scepticism', declared a leader writer: 'Nobody would think of suggesting that the young should be taught all political doctrines equally, with the schools neutrally suggesting that Communism, fascism, oligarchy, autocracy, are all as worthy as democracy. We still take our politics seriously.'[1] The radical parts of the Durham Report have not, so far, been adopted by Church opinion in general. In 1974 the Church's Board of Education noted that huge financial inflation since the Report was published had greatly increased the problems, to which it had addressed itself, of maintaining the aided schools. But the Board urged the Church to make every effort to do so.[2]

Some contemporary churchmen have also been critical of the public schools, and of the Church's involvement with independent education generally. This has been for reasons of social justice, because of the social divisiveness of 'privilege' in education. The Durham Report remarked, 'It is certain that the Church of England has never properly come to terms with the facts of exclusiveness and privilege implied by the existence of independent schools'. The schools themselves, as the Report correctly noticed, 'are all too conscious these days of the contradiction between their professed Christian ideals and their actual social make-up'. There is perhaps some difference here between the major and the minor public schools, to which the Commissioners were not altogether insensitive. The more prestigious schools have generally reflected the liberal questionings of the intelligentsia: radical theology, voluntary religious worship, liberal political and social ideas spread quite rapidly to them during the later 1960s. It is the minor schools who have shown themselves less open to the waves of new thought, and who have, in consequence, adhered with more tenacity to traditional Christian teaching. This situation is hinted at in the Report. 'They should all', prescribed the Commission, 'as many are doing, encourage experiment and critical inquiry, welcome dissent.'[3] It has recently become quite usual for bishops to argue that the independent schools should be compelled to integrate with the state system of education.[4] And the sort of criticism of the state schools made by Hewlett Johnson for Marxist reasons—which in 1963 he called 'our class-ridden educational

---

[1] *Sunday Telegraph*, 28 May 1972: 'Honest to God' (as the leader was entitled, itself an interesting testimony to the legacy of radical theology).

[2] *Crisis in Church Schools. Progress Report I*, G.S. Misc. 28 (Jan. 1974), p. 11.

[3] *The fourth R.*, p. 168.

[4] See e.g. David Sheppard, *Built as a City*, p. 151.

system'[1]—has now spread so effectively that many Church leaders accommodate quite easily, and for *social* reasons, to the Comprehensive schools which, after the mid-sixties, have replaced the old grammar and secondary modern schools in most local-government areas. Everywhere the Church secondary schools have adjusted to the new arrangements.

'The key concept for the progressively-minded is freedom, and this achieves peculiar concentration in their concern for the right kind of education.'[2] Dr. Martin's observation is well illustrated in contemporary Christian radicalism. The criticism by churchmen themselves of traditional Christianity in the content of religious education first became influential early in the 1960s with the writings of Sir Richard Acland[3] and R. J. Goldman.[4] Acland had in 1955 resigned from the Labour Party and from Parliament, over the question of nuclear defence, and had become a teacher in a Comprehensive school. In his book he called for a revolution in the approach to Christianity in the schools; modern knowledge about man required it. 'The Church has enjoyed its long propaganda experience and won its wide propaganda success only within the childhood of the human race,' Acland contended.[5] An adult version of religion, suited to the modern intellect, was now needed. Coinciding as it did with the change to Comprehensive education, the radical approach to morals and theology which so preoccupied the more academic section of the Church during the last ten years, has achieved a significant foothold in the classroom. In 1969, for example, the Student Christian Movement began to publish a series of booklets under the collective title of *Probe*—'designed to provide school groups and teachers with information about important topics, as a basis for discussion'.[6] Although there is some indication, in each number, that various conflicting opinions on each selected topic are given space, the general presentation of the material clearly favours the assimilation of radical opinion. Thus the first booklet, on *Population and Family Planning*, does give a brief account of the opinions of those who object to contraception for moral or religious reasons,[7] but most of the space is taken up with information about the world's population explosion, and there is no doubt that family planning by artificial means is presented as the only effective answer. The children are even informed about the 'small loop or coil, known as an "intra-uterine device" ', widely used in 'developing countries' because 'it is more suitable for use among uneducated

---

[1] Hewlett Johnson, 'Education for Today', in the *Cambridge Review*, vol. 84, No. 2048, 9 Mar. 1963.

[2] Martin, *A Sociology of English Religion*, p. 66.

[3] See Richard Acland, *We Teach Them Wrong* (London, 1963).

[4] See R. J. Goldman, *Religious Teaching from Childhood to Adolescence* (London, 1964).

[5] Acland, *We Teach Them Wrong*, p. 27.

[6] This description is printed at the front of each booklet. The books are anonymous.

[7] *Population and Family Planning*, *Probe* 1. (London, 1969), p. 20.

and unsophisticated people' than 'the pill'.[1] In 1970 *Probe* No. 5 was on *Protest*. 'The students' demand for changes in structure to meet the requirements of a new day reminds us that from Abraham to Jesus and from Jesus to the present, the man of God has been a pilgrim and often a revolutionary.' These words, offered to the children 'for discussion' could perhaps be interpreted equivocally; but they are printed opposite a photograph of German students destroying copies of right-wing newspapers during a riot in West Berlin.[2] The message the children are intended to get is quite clear. A *Probe Special* in 1972 was actually on *Revolution*, and it gives what purports to be a balanced discussion of the various attitudes to violent and non-violent change; introducing the children, in the course of it, to the opinions of Stokely Carmichael.[3] *Probe* 17, on *Women and Men*, in 1973, teaches the relativity of sexual roles, and the way in which sexual identification is part of social conditioning. 'There is a very large variety of sexual behaviour and it is difficult to draw sharp distinctions between what is "normal" and what is not', the booklet declares, as part of a plea for relativism of judgement in sexual morality.[4] This is among the least 'objective' of the *Probe* series, at least to the extent that its hidden advocacy of radical beliefs is less hidden than in some others in the series. It is difficult to say, as yet, how extensively propaganda like this is used in the schools; but the series appears to be extremely popular with teachers if the sales are any indication. Several modern hymn books, which have been adopted for use in a lot of schools, are also thought, by some, to insinuate radical political ideas. One such contains the verse:

> Polaris subs, atomic bombs,
> Germ research in progress
> That's the way the money goes,
> What price the homeless?[5]

Many others are about 'freedom' and the need for 'liberation'. Those who authorize the use of hymns like these justify them on the grounds that they merely declare an agreed morality. Early in 1972 a complaint about the 'left-wing' bias in some contemporary hymns was crushingly dismissed by the governors of a London Comprehensive school.[6] But there can surely be little doubt that the allocation of national resources for defence, the subject of the hymn cited, is an issue of current political controversy.

[1] Ibid., p. 19.
[2] *Protest. Probe* 5 (London, 1970), p. 19.
[3] *Revolution, Probe Special* (London, 1972), p. 35.
[4] *Women and Men, Probe* 17 (London, 1973), p. 11.
[5] *New Life. Songs and Hymns for Assemblies, Clubs and Churches*, ed. John Bailey (1971), p. 40. Mr. Bailey is London Secretary of the Christian Education Movement, a body which has the support of the Church of England's Board of Education.
[6] *Spectator*, 23 Dec. 1972: 'Christianity in the Schools', by Edward Norman.

Most children, anyway, have to have the words of hymns like these explained to them by the teachers—so far removed are they from the normal interests of children—and it is perhaps then that the real filters of political bias begin to operate in the schools. Yet it is not to be supposed that massive radical inroads have been made in the schools. The situation is both confused and patchy. The strength of conservative opinion in the Church is echoed, though in places rather faintly, in the local schools themselves. The Church has, however, given a generous hearing to radical views on education at the highest levels. 'If education is polarised, as Paulo Freire says it must be, into either domestication or liberation,' commented the Church's Board of Education in 1973, 'much of the educational activity of the Church would seem to be in the area of domestication, of giving instruction, whereas increasingly education is seen to be a process of liberation.'[1] Freire'a ideas have acquired a fashionable following among Church leaders in recent years. Freire is a Chilean intellectual; he became a professor at Harvard and then a consultant to the Office of Education at the World Council of Churches.[2] His educational attitudes suggest the influence of left-wing political idealism: they were reflected in the thought of the Anglican Consultative Council at its meeting in Dublin in 1973. The Council declared:

Education is no end in itself and therefore is never a neutral process. Education basically is used either to *domesticate* or to *liberate* man. It is always carried out within the context of the struggle of a community or a nation to achieve its own goals. To be authentic, these goals should be formulated and reformulated through processes of political participation in which everyone is able to share. Involvement in such decision-making processes is a primary prerequisite for a relevant education. Education is relevant in as far as it enables people to 'become aware of their own problems' . . . The Church has often failed to recognize the intrinsic link between education, political self-determination, and social responsibility. We have often been, and often still are, on the side of those who determine value-systems and educational goals *for* others instead of *with* others. In many situations our churches are allied with the minority élite in power, determining what the majority of the people should be educated for. However, if we are to serve people educationally rather than impose, and to liberate them instead of domesticating them, we must establish a partnership with those seeking knowledge in a process to determine the goals and methods of education. This implies a critical view of our relationship to the power-élite in our societies.[3]

It is a tribute to the astonishing adaptability of the Church of England that these opinions—expressed in language which itself clearly indicates doc-

[1] *Annual Report of the Board of Education* (*1972–3*), G.S. 152 (London, 1973), p. 25.
[2] See Paulo Freire, *Cultural Action for Freedom* (London, 1970), and *Pedagogy of the Oppressed* (London, 1972).
[3] 'Education: A process of Liberation for Social Justice', in *Partners in Mission. Anglican Consultative Council. Second Meeting, Dublin, July, 1973* (London, 1973), p. 20.

trinaire political preference— have apparently been found agreeable to its Board of Education. In a homely fashion, the Board seems to have identified this Marxist polemic with Dr. Ian Ramsey's plea for an end to 'prescriptive theology' in the schools' religious curricula.[1] The Church of England will increasingly encounter committed political thinking in the various Christian international bodies; perhaps, too, it will continue to assimilate these ideas without any clear awareness that the revolution for which they appeal is intended to be a real one. In its more gentle English form, the radical approach to education is perhaps well expressed in the liberal belief of David Sheppard (then Bishop of Woolwich) that education should encourage 'creative discontent with society'.[2]

The successful operation of the 1944 Act has removed education as one of the potential causes of friction at the centre of the relations of Church and State. The Establishment of the Church has also continued to the present time with very little movement of public opinion about it. The Free Churches have not agitated for disestablishment, 'whatever residual resentments there may be about her privileges'.[3] The Nonconformists, in fact, have, as Archbishop Fisher put it, 'discovered that the Establishment has positive advantages both for them and for the country as serving well the whole place of the Christian religion in the life of the nation'.[4] Nonconformist and Roman Catholic chaplains have continued to be paid by the State, alongside the provision of chaplains from the Establishment, to serve in the armed services of the Crown, in hospitals, prisons, and other national and local institutions. Each day's sitting of Parliament begins with prayers said in the Lower House by one of the chaplains, and in the Upper House by one of the bishops.[5] The whole concept of national religion has been well supported by churchmen in recent times, despite all the talk about secularism. 'The fact that the Church of England still has the framework of a national church, as distinguished from that of a gathered church, or sect, or a religious denomination, is a constant reminder to its members and to the nation that it is inescapably involved with the whole of the society in which it is set'—Dr. Vidler wrote in *Soundings* in 1962, as part of a considerable defence of the Establishment of religion on practical grounds.[6] Fears of increasing sectarianism within the Church have led many to hold on to Establishment. 'The purer the Church attempts to make itself by regulation,' as Guy Mayfield remarked, 'the more sectarian and less churchlike it will become.'[7] It is a view held by many. The early experiences with synodical government have so far done little to allay such

---

[1] *Annual Report* (1972–3), p. 25.   [2] Sheppard, *Built as a City*, p. 133.
[3] Slack, *The British Churches Today*, p. 17.
[4] Fisher, *Touching on Christian Truth*, p. 140.
[5] For the text of the Parliamentary Prayer, see *The English Church. A New Look*, ed. Hunter, p. 7.
[6] *Soundings*, ed. Vidler, p. 257.   [7] Mayfield, *The Church of England*, p. 12.

fears either, although most of the scepticism with the new forms of ecclesiastical polity has derived from weariness at the cumbersome discussions
at national, diocesan, and deanery levels, rather than suspicion that sectarian instincts are being fostered. In the larger perspective, however, there
can be little doubt that the Synodical Government Measure of 1969 has,
in the sense meant by Hensley Henson in opposing the Enabling Act in
1919, accelerated the practical separation of Church and State. It may, on
the other hand, be pointed out that measures passed by the General Synod
—which in 1970 took over from the Church Assembly—still need formal
parliamentary approval: 'Parliament has not surrendered its ultimate control over the Church, but simply transferred to it the detailed legislative
work for which it was no longer fitted and had no time.'[1] In his enthronement sermon at Canterbury in 1961, Archbishop Ramsey had asked for
Church freedom in the ordering of her forms of worship; and he had
actually said that if the links of Church and State were broken in the process it would be the fault of those 'who denied that freedom to us'.[2]
Autonomy in this area was granted without serious opposition. The will
to preserve the Establishment was greater than Ramsey evidently supposed. Disestablishment, wrote Bishop Wickham, himself a liberal in
social questions, 'would constitute an overt act radically un-churching the
nation and the bulk of its people—who have, on their part, no deliberate,
expressed will to be de-Christianized'.[3] Bishop Stephen Bayne, Executive
Officer of the Anglican Communion from 1960 to 1964—a leader of liberal
opinion in moral questions—supported the Establishment of the Church
England because it 'gives to the nation a solid rooting in the Christian
tradition', and to the Church, 'a responsibility to the nation which it cannot escape'.[4] Like some other liberal or radical churchmen, Bayne believed
that the appointment of bishops by the Crown enabled liberals or radicals
to rise to Church leadership: a state of affairs less likely to occur if bishops
were elected by relatively conservative representative bodies of the Church,
who tended to promote 'safe' men.[5]

The practical opportunities for contacts between the Church and local
institutions of government, have continued to assist the social work of the
Church in recent years. As the welfare services of the State have expanded,
those of the Church have tended to integrate with the state system. The
Church, in these conditions, has come to fulfil 'one of the classic roles of
the voluntary organization, that of drawing attention to a hitherto un-
recognized need, filling a gap in existing services as long as this exists,
but of being ready to withdraw as soon as adequate statutory provision

[1] Paul, *A Church by Daylight*, p. 109.

[2] Quoted in Morgan, *The Church in Transition*, p. 72.

[3] *The Church of England. A New Look*, ed. Hunter, p. 148.

[4] Stephen Fielding Bayne, *An Anglican Turning Point. Documents and Interpretations*
(Austin, Texas, 1964), p. 182.   [5] Ibid., p. 179.

is made'.[1] The effect of the Welfare State's expansion in diminishing the social-welfare work of the Church can be exaggerated, however, and reference to the *Directory of Church of England Social Services*, published by the Church in 1974, will show the very extensive national and local undertakings, and the tremendous effort and resources still invested in social work. Opinion surveys have found a very general belief that the Churches should express their views 'on day-to-day social questions and not merely confine themselves to the spiritual life of the individual'.[2] This attitude, indeed, resounds deeply in the vague spiritual sense of Englishmen: they see Christianity as essentially concerned with good neighbourliness, with social good works. It is the English belief again: pelagianism. There is also a widespread impression that the Church's ability to influence social questions is declining, and this is deplored.[3]

Opposition to the concept of Established religion has in recent years come from small groups within the educated classes—like the National Secular Society—whose influence is not great, and from a section of radical opinion within the Church, whose influence is greater than its numbers might indicate. It is also clear that some Anglicans in overseas Churches regard 'the English form of Establishment as a grave embarrassment to the whole Anglican Communion'.[4] A minority of the members of the Archbishops' Commission on Church and State found themselves, because of their opposition to the principle of Establishment, unable to sign the Report in 1970. To these members of the Commission 'the Church must take account of the general questioning of authority and so learn to make its way in the modern world'. They would like the Church 'to be seen to be a minority, that no man may charge them with professing their faith for the sake of custom, or advantage, or social pressure, or convention'.[5] They saw the Church as a 'gathered community'. Miss Valerie Pitt, in her memorandum of dissent from the Report, remarked: 'To be a Christian a man must himself answer—*Jesus is Lord*. Writing "C of E" on a form is not quite enough'.[6] The evidences of 'inarticulate Christianity' residually present in the nation, were dismissed as 'nostalgia', as childhood memories. To Miss Pitt, risen up, as she declared, from 'the great conurbations',[7] the whole idea of national religion was simply unrealistic: society had become secular and the Church ought to come to terms with it and seek disestablishment.[8]

---

[1] Hall and Howes, *The Church in Social Work*, p. 262.

[2] *Television and Religion. Prepared by Social Surveys (Gallup Poll) Ltd. on behalf of A.B.C. Television Ltd.* (London, 1964), p. 62.

[3] Martin, *A Sociology of English Religion*, p. 57.

[4] Peter Whiteley, *Frontier Mission. An Account of the Toronto Congress, 1963* (Toronto, New York, and London, 1963), p. 61.

[5] *Church and State. Report of the Archbishops' Commission* (London, 1970), p. 7.

[6] Ibid., p. 74.   [7] Ibid., p. 73.   [8] Ibid., p. 78.

The Commission, under the chairmanship of Professor Owen Chadwick, the Master of Selwyn College, Cambridge, was appointed by the Church Assembly in 1967 'to make recommendations as to the modifications in the constitutional relationships between Church and State which are desirable and practicable and in so doing to take account of current and future steps to promote greater unity between the Churches'.[1] The terms of reference, therefore, did not themselves envisage disestablishment, but 'qualification'; and they also had an ecumenical dimension. The Commission, once down to work, found it had to look into 'Church and Society' as well as 'Church and State'.[2] Their Report was, at least as far as the majority were concerned, conservative in tone. All the members were able to agree that *some* adjustments were required: greater freedom to determine doctrine and order worship, and some reform of the manner of appointing bishops. On this last point, unanimity did not extend beyond the need for reform: the majority recommended a scheme based essentially on the proposals of the 1964 Howick Commission, which would have retained the Prime Minister's powers but provided for formal consultations with the Church;[3] the more radical members wanted to abolish the Prime Minister's functions altogether and have bishops elected by Church bodies.[4] (In July 1974 the General Synod, meeting in York, voted by 270 to 70 to implement this part of the Report's recommendations—they voted to seek a decisive voice for the Church in the appointment of bishops.)[5] The Commission did recommend the continued presence of the bishops in the House of Lords, and, in a practical recognition of religious diversity, favoured the Government adding leaders of other Churches to the Lords, from time to time, as Life Peers.[6] A general revision of laws touching ecclesiastical matters was suggested.[7] The majority Report was within the tradition of the 1935 and 1952 inquiries; it was moderately reformist, intending to preserve the advantages of the national position of the Church in the life of the country. 'We have not recommended a total severing of the historic links', the majority declared, 'first, because we think such a programme to be impracticable in the present state of opinion; and second, because even if such a programme was practicable, most of us would not like it, though we should not shrink from it, if the State decided it to be either wise or politically necessary.'[8] The State has itself shown no inclination at all to contemplate disestablishment. The matter has not been raised within political life, and apart from a ritual adhesion to disestablishment in the fine print of the Liberal Party's programmes—a survival from the Gladstonian

---

[1] *Church and State. Report of the Archbishops' Commission* (London, 1970), p. ix.
[2] Ibid., p. 4.
[3] Ibid., p. 32, 'Proposal A'.   [4] Ibid., p. 37, 'Proposal B'.
[5] See also *Crown Appointments. A Report by the Standing Committee*, G.S. 210 (1974).
[6] *Church and State*, p. 47.
[7] Ibid., p. 56.   [8] Ibid., p. 65.

inheritance, now reinforced by the allure of minority-rights arguments—the political parties have shown no interest in the question. The Establishment is tenacious in national life. The people of the country still see themselves as retaining their Christian identity, and regret the decline of religion.[1] Christian morality sustains its place as the cohesive force in the popular idea of the national conscience. There is, as Archbishop Fisher has said, still 'no viable alternative'.[2]

Churchmen have continued to teach that the State is a divine institution. Even the divided Chadwick Commission were all agreed about that.[3] 'The apostolic injunctions about the divine role of the State were given at the time of a Nero and a Domitian, and are no less relevant for the State under a Stalin or a Kruschev', as Archbishop Ramsey has said.[4] In this conviction, the Church has always been consistent. The Dean of York, in a recent survey of the early development of Christian attitudes to the State, declared this in classic style: 'The truth is that all societies need government and its laws because of the defect of human nature, just as a lame man needs crutches.'[5] The contemporary Church has also, in general, attempted to practise the traditional formula about political involvement: that the Church has the duty to define the general principles within which human society may be ordered, but that individual applications are best left to the expertise of political and other leaders. The Church should never be involved in party politics. 'Of course the Church is to be found in the political arena', wrote Archbishop Joost de Blank in 1964, for the Church has an obligation to be concerned with human welfare; but 'the Church as the custodian of the Eternal Gospel can never commit herself to any particular political party, or herself become a political party'.[6] The Christian, according to Walter James, is to be involved in politics to the extent of pursuing 'a single course'—like Shaftesbury in the nineteenth century; he should not become concerned with the ordinary conduct of political debate, though he can and should co-operate with non-Christians in the promotion of desired social ends.[7] Sir Frederick Catherwood, writing with all the experience of Industrial Adviser to the Ministry of Economic Affairs, in 1964, offered the same view: 'The Church cannot subscribe to broad political platforms which include many issues on which it is not qualified to comment, but it must be in a position to advise its own members on matters of conduct when they find themselves in uncharted seas.'[8]

---

[1] Martin, *A Sociology of English Religion*, p. 57.
[2] Fisher, *Standards of Morality*, p. 32.
[3] *Church and State* (1970), p. 8.   [4] Ramsey, *Sacred and Secular*, p. 61.
[5] Alan Richardson, *The Political Christ* (London, 1973), p. 101.
[6] Joost de Blank, *Out of Africa* (London, 1964), p. 25. The former Archbishop of Cape Town; then Canon of Westminster.
[7] Walter James, *The Christian in Politics* (London, 1962), pp. 16, 127.
[8] H. F. R. Catherwood, *The Christian in Industrial Society* (London, 1964), p. 28.

Archbishop Ramsey's opinions on this question have corresponded exactly with those of Temple. Whilst enjoining the clergy to concern themselves with 'the tremendous issues of the world we live in: poverty, affluence, pollution, race, war, violence, revolution', he also warned the clergy not to hold out assured solutions.[1] Although he disapproved of the priest whose concern was only with the eternal deserts of humanity, he equally condemned the priest 'whose time is spent in the organizing of protests and campaigns, in leading the people in demonstrations for the causes which fire him'.[2] And in a direct allusion to Temple, he wrote 'It is one thing to state main Christian principles, or to denounce a particular down-right evil', but it was quite wrong 'to commend a particular programme, on which the technical skills and wisdom of competent Christians may differ'.[3] Ramsey, unlike Temple, did apply these rules to himself. In his Presidential Address to the General Synod in February 1974, in which he spoke of the national economic crisis, the Archbishop remarked that as he was 'not versed in economics' he was 'unable to suggest particular economic policies'.[4] Similarly, Archbishop Coggan, in his Presidential Address to the General Synod in July 1974, declared that the Christian 'cannot, just be-cause he is a Christian, lay claim to any special insight into the mysteries of economic problems'.[5] Even the Church's Board for Social Responsi-bility, in its 1971 document on *Civil Strife*—a paper otherwise redolent of political radicalism—declared that it would 'rightly be regarded as in-tolerable if Church Assemblies and Synods sought to direct Church mem-bers into one or other of the political parties'.[6]

It can therefore be said that the great weight of authoritative opinion in the Church's leadership has adhered to the traditional ban on party-political allegiance by the corporate Church—leaving political judgement to individual Christians. Yet the press and the public have received a dis-tinct impression, in recent years, that the Church has become sympathetic to the politics of the Left. This general impression is not entirely un-founded, but it is an exaggeration based upon the behaviour and utterances of a few radical churchmen which have acquired undue publicity. These churchmen have on the whole been those nearest to the political interests of the intelligentsia—those most impressed by the liberal-left politics of the quality Sunday press, of the universities, of the B.B.C. Occasionally they have fallen off the tightrope between principles and applications. Dr. Ian Ramsey, Bishop of Durham from 1966 until his early death in 1972, frequently appeared to lapse into partisan political positions. It could be

---

[1] Michael Ramsey, *The Christian Priest Today* (London, 1972) (Ordination Charges), p. 24.

[2] Ibid., p. 35.   [3] Ibid., p. 38.

[4] *Synod Report, Spring 1974*, vol. 4, No. 1, p. 3.

[5] *Synod Report, Summer 1974*, vol. 4, No. 2, p. 3.

[6] *Civil Strife*, published for the Board for Social Responsibility (London, 1971), p. 18.

said, even by friendly observers, that the political ideas he encouraged in
his diocese were 'based on the day's newspaper rather than on the New
Testament'.[1] Ramsey had in fact given as his reason for accepting his
bishopric the need of the Church to have a spokesman on moral issues in
the House of Lords—and he became, in fact, a frequent parliamentary
speaker,[2] noted for his radical polemicism. He was a socialist, though he
preferred the title of 'radical', as many left-wing intellectuals have recently
done. In 1970 he led a deputation to the new Conservative Prime Minister,
Edward Heath, to protest against the rumoured sale of arms to South
Africa.[3] In 1971 he criticized the Conservatives for their proposed Rhodesian settlement. He also attacked the Prices and Incomes Policy for not
having a statutory foundation[4] (a position most other socialists abandoned
after Ramsey's death). And in what his biographer calls 'the bravest speech
of his career', he assailed the Conservatives' Industrial Relations Bill in
1971.[5] These were all issues in which Ramsey himself believed his opinions
were moral, rather than political. But it did not seem so to the press and
the public—for these were issues of directly partisan character, supercharged with political passion. Ramsey's dislike of political Conservatism
was not disguised.[6] Observers outside the Church do not make the delicate
distinctions which sometimes appeal within. Thus Paul Ferris, a journalist,
has been able to write with justice that the clergy involved in full-time
social work 'are usually Socialists'[7], who have not hidden their party feelings. Bishop Robinson objected to the Conservatives' hopes for a Rhodesian
settlement, believing that it was 'as discreditable as anything in the Tory
record'.[8] In the context of political debate this sort of judgement could
only appear politically partisan. Robinson wrote in 1972 that it was impossible to 'love your neighbour' without 'getting involved in politics'—
the idea that it was possible to avoid doing so was 'so absurd that I don't
propose to waste time on it'.[9] For Robinson, as for some other radical
Christians, the Church's most effective and least compromising political
activity would lie in local 'community politics'. Robinson, indeed, has a
vision of the Church developing as a sort of cohesive element within
'clusters' of minority groups concerned with 'the variety of law reform and
liberation movements'.[10] Bishop Sheppard's plea for political involvement
by the Church was also given a local-community basis: 'it does not necessarily mean party politics, but it may mean the politics of pressure groups
concerning themselves with particular issues' in 'a pluralist society'.[11]

---

[1] Edwards, *Ian Ramsey, Bishop of Durham*, p. 76.   [2] Ibid., p. 80.
[3] Ibid., p. 14.   [4] Ibid., p. 84.   [5] Ibid., p. 85.   [6] Ibid., p. 13.
[7] Ferris, *The Church of England*, p. 174.
[8] Robinson, *Christian Freedom in a Permissive Society*, p. 85.
[9] Robinson, *The Difference in Being a Christian Today*, p. 27.
[10] Ibid., p. 69.
[11] Sheppard, *Built as a City*, p. 335.

Christians, as a result, 'may find themselves pushed into being the spokes-men for unpopular, minority groups'.[1] But 'community politics', though they have no necessary connection with socialism or political radicalism, are as a matter of fact associated with left and liberal thinking. Bishops like Robinson and Sheppard and Montefiore or Stockwood (Bishop of Southwark)—who have become well known as advocates of radical politics—are careful in trying to avoid partisan utterances within the moral refer-ences they have set themselves. They are not always successful. There are very few bishops who are thought to be sympathetic to the Conservative Party, and none who makes any public profession of Conservative political principles. Most bishops are still caught up in the legacy of the old Christian Social Union spirit, and probably entertain liberal political ideals. But it is not easy to calculate these inclinations because most have been notably scrupulous in avoiding partisan declarations. Similarly, in the House of Lords most bishops have tried to avoid party issues, and this has again involved some difficulty, since morality and politics are not separable, and party divisions have occurred on a number of issues which churchmen have believed to be primarily moral ones.

The problems of race relations have been among these. The principles of the Race Relations Acts of 1965 and 1968 have been, in parliamentary terms at least, fairly bi-partisan. Opposition came only from those who objected to the legislation because it interfered with freedom of speech and action—opposition which radical supporters of the legislation were quick to stigmatize as disguised racism. Church leaders vigorously sup-ported the Acts.[2] In 1968 the Lambeth Conference repeated former con-demnations of racial discrimination and gave formal approval to the anti-racist declarations made at the Uppsala meeting of the World Council of Churches.[3] When, in the same year, the Labour Government felt the need to control the entry of 'coloured' immigrants to Britain, and passed the Immigration Act, protests were made by many Church leaders, including the Archbishop of Canterbury. Bishop Robinson resigned from the Labour Party and joined the Liberals. Bishop Ian Ramsey had told the Church Assembly, in the previous year, that Britain must become 'a multi-racial and multi-religious community'.[4] He, too, was among objectors to the Act. The immigration controls, which appeared to discriminate against coloured rather more than white prospective entrants to the country, appeared to some Church leaders to be immoral. It was a view promoted by liberal intellectuals. Opinion among the laity divided according to social and poli-tical prejudice. The race question has seemed to some critics to be exactly

---

[1] Sheppard, *Built as a City*, p. 199.

[2] David Edington, *Christians and Colour in Britain* (London, 1970), p. 84.

[3] *The Lambeth Conference, 1968*, Resolution 16, p. 33.

[4] *Church Assembly. Report of Proceedings*, vol. XLVII, No. 1 (1967), p. 680 (7 Nov. 1967), Debate on Race Relations.

the sort of issue in which the Church, whatever its moral intentions, necessarily steps over the line into partisan politics. Perhaps both the situation and the consequences are unavoidable. The declaration of the Church's Board for Social Responsibility on the Rhodesian question—itself judged largely in terms of race ethics rather than of political theory—has been a recent example of how thinly the line is drawn. The Board has argued that 'forceful intervention from outside is needed to defeat the illegal regime',[1] and in 1972 the British Council of Churches welcomed the rejection, by the African majority, of the Salisbury proposals for a settlement.[2] Such opinions, perfectly tenable according to given moral propositions, are inevitably partisan when set within the context of actual political debate.

Because this sort of demarcation raises insoluble difficulties, it is all the more surprising that leading churchmen have on the whole been very successful in keeping the Church out of party politics. 'A Christian political document which runs against the grain of contemporary political assumptions is not likely to gain much of a hearing, but one that accepts them is apt to water down its Christianity with the prevailing humanitarian fashions':[3] Walter James's observation well applies to the contemporary Church. Yet few Church leaders actually wish to go against the grain; most accept the political values and references current among the intelligentsia. They are, in fact, internally divided, but with a clear preference towards liberal attitudes. Churchmen who do seek to define general principles of political morality are accused by their opponents of actually offering party-political advice—and sometimes they actually are. Churchmen who really are advocates of deliberate party politics usually believe that their ideals are the concrete versions of moral truths. But in general, the political reserve of modern English Church leaders has been marked. The odd lapses, the few 'political' bishops and clergy, get a lot of publicity, some of which they seem to seek themselves. But they are very untypical, and the natural prejudice of Englishmen, and the tradition of the Church, would wish to keep it that way. Below the level of the formal leadership of the Church, the impression of increased political interest takes on rather more substance. Quite a number of parochial clergy, middle-aged as well as more junior men, make frequent reference to political issues of the moment in their sermons and counselling—in order to illustrate moral points or to express the Gospel in social concern. Their interests are characteristic of their class and education: they reflect the contemporary obsession of the intelligentsia for 'current affairs', and the moralistic attitude which requires that everyone should be involved with the great issues of the day. It would

[1] *Force in the Modern World. A document prepared by the Board for Social Responsibility*, G.S. 168 (London, 1973), p. 66.

[2] *Britain and Rhodesia now. A Statement on the Rhodesian situation following the publication of the Pearce Report*, British Council of Churches (London, 1972), p. 2.

[3] James, *The Christian in Politics*, p. 128.

have been surprising if the clergy had not taken part in this aspect of present culture.

There has been one particular field, that of industrial relations and the distribution of wealth—the centre of the 'Christian Sociology' critique of the years between the wars—in which the contemporary Church has noticeably failed to translate its ideas into political language. The reasons are unclear. The continuing Church interest in these sorts of questions has been largely confined to the liberal centre of the Church: they have had less appeal to the radicals, who have tended to follow fashionable progressive thought in espousing other issues—minority rights, the 'Third World', ecology, educational experiment, sexual freedom, and so forth. It is certainly a feature of present ecclesiastical radicalism that it has been little concerned with the redistribution of wealth, industrial relations, or wages policies—issues which have formed the substance of working-class politics. Radicals all agree that something needs to be done in these areas, and they support reforms intended to allow greater rewards for labour in the working classes; but those questions are not the things which most occupy them. Liberal churchmen in the C.O.P.E.C. tradition continue to promote social and industrial reform: but they have also become increasingly impressed with the complexity of these questions, and have become hesitant to prescribe distinctively Christian policies on particular issues. The Board for Social Responsibility has itself recognized that social reform by legislation is a 'hazardous business', because technical expertise is required to determine the consequences of change, and there is anyway a large area where results cannot be adequately predicted.[1] Recent annual reports of the Board have shown the continued spread of social concern—especially the reports on Housing, Gambling, Social Aid, and the reports of the Industrial Committee. The Industrial Christian Fellowship has also continued its work in the field; and it has retained too, its mild socialist atmosphere. Yet in this sort of work there has been a considerable growth of realism. Many would now agree with Archbishop Coggan's reminder, of 1969, that 'social concern is not the Gospel, though it is part of the Gospel'.[2] Coggan censured those who propagated the false idea that social concern as such equalled Christianity—'it seeps, like some chilly fog, into the pulpits of the land'.[3]

There have been some notable contributions to the old 'Christian Sociology' tradition in recent years, even though these have not been years in which the tradition has especially flourished. Mervyn Stockwood, Bishop of Southwark, has, in the press and in the House of Lords, given contem-

---

[1] *Annual Report of the Board for Social Responsibility* (1972), G.S. 91 (London, 1972), p. 32.

[2] Donald Coggan, *Sinews of Faith. A Primary Visitation Charge to the Diocese of York, April 1969* (London, 1969), p. 17.   [3] Ibid., p. 18.

porary form to the old Christian Socialist ideal, and has remained largely untouched by the new-left radicalism of the later 1960s. To the same tradition belongs Bishop Wickham of Middleton. His *Church and People in an Industrial City*, originally published in 1957, but reissued in six successive reprints in the following ten years, has familiarized a whole generation of younger clergy and laymen with the style and interests of the Christian Social Union critique of society. The book breathes the spirit of Temple. In 1961 a Congregationalist Minister, Daniel Jenkins, made a distinguished contribution in the same genre. His *Equality and Excellence* contained an influential assemblage of arguments in favour of participation in industrial management by workers and by the public interest,[1] of a national wages policy,[2] and of educational reform.[3] These were all items ultimately derived from the 'Christian Sociology' school, and presented in familiar conceptual forms—brought up to date. Jenkins's appeal for a new radicalism was fulfilled—but not quite as he had hoped: 'the best radicalism is not that which thinks that you must always try to find a visible enemy in society, who can be denounced as the source of all evil and overthrown in a heroic outburst of revolutionary fervour; it is that which recognizes that all our earthly societies are imperfect'.[4] The radicalism of the World Council of Churches in the later 1960s was very far from this model. It more or less exactly represented the partisan approaches which Jenkins had deplored. A balance of judgement like that found in Jenkins's book was also found in Sir Frederick Catherwood's *The Christian in Industrial Society*, published in 1964. It too brought the old 'Christian Socialist' idealism up to date, around some practical proposals for social reform. Catherwood stressed that there was no 'social gospel': the Gospel 'is addressed to the individual', for 'society collectively cannot be redeemed'. Yet society could be reconstructed, and it was the duty of the Christian to work for righteousness in those 'spheres' of society in which he was involved. 'To leave them to secularism or humanism would be a complete abdication of our responsibility as Christian citizens.'[5] His study concerned practical issues: the Christian attitudes which he believed appropriate to the balance between market capitalism and state control;[6] fair trading;[7] the morality of the Stock Exchange;[8] the duty of Christians as employers of labour;[9] trades unions and their responsibilities;[10] the social duties of big business,[11] and so forth. A similar catalogue might also describe the contents of Bishop Sheppard's *Built as a City*, published in 1974. This work, too, stands in the old 'Christian Sociology' tradition, and

---

[1] Daniel Jenkins, *Equality and Excellence. A Christian Comment on Britain's Life* (London, 1961), p. 74.

[2] Ibid., p. 81.   [3] Ibid., p. 125.   [4] Ibid., p. 162.

[5] Catherwood, *The Christian in Industrial Society*, p. xi.

[6] Ibid., p. 17.   [7] Ibid., p. 72.   [8] Ibid., p. 83.

[9] Ibid., p. 93.   [10] Ibid., p. 39.   [11] Ibid., p. 28.

although there are occasional touches in the book which suggest an acquaintance with the new-left radicalism of the last few years, the main substance of the book clearly belongs to the Temple school. The Bishop advocates a 'social audit' to make private enterprise more accountable to society;[1] a statutory national wages policy;[2] educational reform intended to promote social equality;[3] greater control of housing by local authorities;[4] and worker participation in the management of industry.[5] This is, again, a list comparable to those found in the C.O.P.E.C. tradition. Perhaps the most interesting contemporary manifestation of the old spirit of industrial criticism has been the issue of South African investments. A series of studies undertaken for the Board for Social Responsibility by Canon Gonville ffrench-Beytagh (formerly Dean of Johannesburg), argued the case for moral disapproval of apartheid to be registered through indirect action —by exploiting the opening given by existing Church financial investments to try to force changes in the practice of companies operating in South Africa, and to encourage African Trade Unionism.[6] Such a solution— working within existing arrangements—is very much within the 'Christian Sociology' tradition: indeed, Gore had proposed the use of investments as a form of moral coercion before the Great War. This is all quite different in tone and method from the newer radicalism of the World Council of Churches, which has advised the Churches to dispose of all South African investments in order to remain completely untainted by them, and in order to offer some sort of economic sanction against the South African Government.

In the second half of the 1960s the spread of a new left-wing idealism, influenced by Trotskyite Marxism, by Maoism, and by philosophical anarchism, began to exercise a considerable influence in the 'Third World', and among some of the students in western universities. Politically conscious sections of the intelligentsia in Britain were quickly responsive. The new ethos spoke the language of 'liberation', sometimes appealing to violent revolution. Its influence was very much less evident in England than in some other western countries, but it achieved a handsome measure of notoriety, due to extensive press coverage of student political demonstrations, and, predictably, was taken extremely seriously by university teachers and journalists. From these sources, and as a result of increasing contact with the ideas of Church leaders from the 'Third World', small groups of English Christians absorbed some of the fervour of the later 'sixties. The influence of the World Council of Churches must also be taken into the calculation. At the fourth General Assembly of the World

---

[1] Sheppard, *Built as a City*, p. 212.   [2] Ibid., p. 214.   [3] Ibid., p. 133.
[4] Ibid., p. 161.   [5] Ibid., p. 183.
[6] *Investment in South Africa: Challenge for the Church. A memorandum by the Board for Social Responsibility*, G.S. Misc. 23 (London, 1973), p. 4. See also *Investment in South Africa. A Second Memorandum*, G.S. Misc. 23A (London, 1973).

Council at Uppsala, in 1968, a rift emerged between radicals and conservatives—so great was the insistence of the former on the duty of the Churches
to support rebellions and revolutions 'against all establishments, civil and
religious'.[1] By that date the World Council's own staff were quite frankly
left-wing.[2] The Churches in Britain have declined to follow the leadership
of the World Council in some of its more extreme statements of political
radicalism, but individual churchmen have certainly been influenced. One
of the effects of the entry of Britain to the E.E.C. has been an increase in
the exchange of ideas between the European Churches, an addition to the
accelerating ecumenism of the last thirty years. These contacts, too, have
tended to introduce some British Christians to the left-wing politics now
quite widespread among many younger European Christians. Thus the
chaplains of British universities who attended the Aarhus conference of
'European Student Pastors' in 1973 found a prevailing Marxist analysis,
and an assumption among their European counterparts that Marxism was
the only moral political critique.[3] The British representatives were less
politicized, yet attracted to radical attitudes. The Revd. John Allen, Chaplain at Bristol University, in his account of the Aarhus gathering, lamented
the tenacity of political conservatism, which, to some extent, he blamed on
the 'élitism' of theology as an academic study—'If, in the last resort, we
can say that the failure of the revolution, the failure of democratisation,
the failure of the liberation movement, are basically *theological* failures,
need we look beyond ourselves to discover the character of the conservative
set-back?'[4]

This sense of failure was inevitable in those Christians who had, after
1967, been attracted to the revolutionary politics of the student Left. For
a few years the ferment had appeared to hold out the possibility of really
radical changes. It was an appearance only: the student movement, in
England at any rate, was full of romanticism; it was all intellectual analysis,
excited demonstrations, and petty acts of indiscipline, with a good deal of
paraded sexual liberation. Undergraduates invited 'workers' at their universities to join them in the overthrow of bourgeois 'power-structures'.
But the 'workers' were unwilling to become a *jacquerie*, and went home
to their families instead. The mood changed: by 1973 or so, it was clear
that the 'militant' students now formed only a small if permanent group in
each university—in many places excited to action by radical dons—but it
was clear also that the revolution was off for the time being. In the few
heady years after 1968, when a lot of 'responsible' opinion took the student
protest seriously, a number of Church leaders, as well as many chaplains

---

[1] Barry Till, *The Churches' Search for Unity* (London, 1972), p. 263.
[2] Ibid., pp. 272–511.
[3] *Sensation. A Bulletin for Chaplains in Higher Education* (London, Autumn 1973), p. 9.
[4] Ibid., p. 18.

in the universities, were induced to see politics the way the militants did. First among them was Bishop Robinson, who went to Cambridge as Dean of Trinity in 1969. He was far from being a revolutionary, but was attracted to the idealism and radicalism of the militants. In 1968, the *annus mirabilus* of the student ferment, Robinson told the Cambridge students

If society is to be changed it must be through those with the education and intelligence to see how the masses—all of us—are being subverted and pulped by the mass media. The majority now signifies nothing. Consensus politics is the bogus consensus induced by those who control the instruments of communication. The real situation is not going to be changed by the ballot box . . . The only hope is a revolutionary élite, prepared to stand out, or sit in, until something gives.[1]

Since Robinson really is not a Marxist, or a revolutionary, it is likely that this classic appeal to the Marxist doctrine of false consciousness was offered in innocent unawareness of its implications for democratic government. But it illustrates the preparedness of a few liberal churchmen to go to some lengths to accommodate the political radicalism of the period. The Student Christian Movement has been particularly influential in disseminating the atmosphere of revolutionary politics. In January 1973 the S.C.M. held a conference at Sheffield, on 'The Seeds of Liberation'. Three hundred and fifty attended. 'For most Christians, the last decade has been dominated by questions of politics,' the Conference organizers declared. 'It's pretty safe to say that the debate in principle is over and for a great number of Christians, a new spiritual home has been found in the (extra-parliamentary) political community.' Theology was pronounced to be bankrupt; 'but we have found that we cannot live by Marx alone and that there are spiritual dimensions'.[2] The Conference attempted to identify the 'Beast' in the thirteenth chapter of the Book of Revelation, and settled for Vorster and Nixon—but failed to agree on a 'credible' British conservative figure to join 'an unholy trinity'.[3]

The appeal to revolutionary political action has carried with it an approval of violence for political ends. In the student politics of Britain this has not been a serious matter. The talk of violence has been romantic, vicarious. In the developing world, however, the use of force for social change has begun to receive a lot of well-publicized support. And British Churches have on the whole been prepared to sympathize with radical political changes in those parts of the world where 'oppression' has been established. The list of countries concerned is rather selective and contains almost no socialist ones. In 1968 the Lambeth Conference recommended

---

[1] Sermon at the University Church, Oct. 1968, printed in *Christian Freedom in a Permissive Society*, p. 93.

[2] From the S.C.M. leaflet announcing the Conference.

[3] *Sensation* (Jan. 1973), p. 5 (an account of the Conference).

the setting up of 'study groups' in the constituent churches of the Anglican Communion to examine 'all aspects of violent and non-violent social and political change'.[1] The first subcommittee report to the Conference, in seeking to encourage a radical attitude to the political development of the world, remarked that 'in political and economic matters excessive deference has been paid to conventional wisdom and outdated institutions'.[2] And 'in the struggle for justice and freedom, the Church must be deeply involved in the search on the part of some for nationhood; in indigenous movements for the transformation of society; in dialogue with Marxists and humanists as well as with those who control power structures, political, economic, and industrial'.[3] At Lambeth the influence of the overseas bishops, especially those from developing countries, was irresistible; the earnest goodwill of the English bishops inclined them to accept this sort of statement—whose vocabulary, as well as the tone and intention, was suggestive of international left-wing thinking. At the 1973 Anglican Consultative Council in Dublin, the appeal to the Church to side with the 'liberation' of the 'oppressed' was in flood-tide. The Council duly called for a recognition of the need for 'violence'—'It is necessary to understand that the injustice that exists in pluralist societies is violent by nature', the Council declared. Examples of this 'violence' were such things as denial of political rights, and pollution of the environment: 'violent injustice also exists where the imposition upon people of political, social, economic, cultural or religious structures de-humanizes both groups, the oppressed and the oppressors'.[4] The Church, the Council said, must support the oppressed. The appeal was in classic revolutionary language: 'With initiative from élitist groups who control power the State may itself bring about the transference of resources.' 'Sometimes their transference may be accompanied by violence.' On other occasions, apparently, this might not be necessary.[5] To determine the appropriate method, the Council recommended 'A Theology of Liberation in the Contemporary Situation'.[6] The Church must be committed 'to following Jesus in the work of liberation for personal and social renewal, justice, development, and wholeness of life in our respective societies'.[7]

The Anglican Consultative Council was not alone in recommending the use of violence for political ends in some circumstances of desired social change. The Board for Social Responsibility, in applying the traditional Christian teachings about the concept of a 'Just War' to a possible 'Just Revolution', in 1973 endorsed the principle of violence for political ends— but only if non-violent action, which was to be preferred, really was in-

---

[1] *The Lambeth Conference 1968*, Resolution 18, p. 34.			[2] Ibid., p. 72.
[3] Ibid., p. 74.
[4] *Partners in Mission. Anglican Consultative Council, Second Meeting, Dublin, July, 1973* (London, 1973), p. 14.		[5] Ibid., p. 16.		[6] Ibid., p. 17.		[7] Ibid., p. 19.

appropriate.[1] 'A Christian can never acquiesce in the *status quo*', the Board declared. Whereas 'conservative Christianity seeks to change society by changing individuals' and 'Marxist Communism concentrates on changing the power structure of society while leaving power centralized'—a fashionable Trotskyite critique of Soviet Marxism, though it is not clear the Board was actually conscious of this—'Revolutionary Christianity seeks a change in both individuals and society.'[2] This was the sort of Christianity the Board recommended. The Modern Churchmen's Union also discussed the question of political violence at its Conference in 1971, and there was some support for it in circumstances in which non-violent means were ineffective. The Revd. Sebastian Charles, in urging this, defined also the terms on which the Church ought to side with the oppressed—'In Britain there are many such groups: the poor, the homeless, the black, the young, and the opposite sex (women)'.[3] In 1971 a Church working party under Professor Norman Anderson, Chairman of the House of Laity of the General Synod, considered the attitude the Church of England should adopt towards the World Council of Churches' policy (1970) of giving financial aid to guerrilla fighters in Southern Africa. It was a policy that had attracted some surprise and a great deal of unfavourable publicity in the British press, and had proved offensive to the consciences of many moderate churchmen. The World Council's action had also raised the question of violence for political ends in a very practical manner: men were actually being killed for political reasons with Christian assistance— even though the Council tried to see that the grants it made were directed to the provision of medicine rather than weapons for the 'freedom fighters'. A majority of the working party supported the Council's policy, however, including, paradoxically, the pacifist members: it was 'a practical way of declaring our moral solidarity with the oppressed'.[4] A minority professed non-violent demonstrations of solidarity.[5] The majority did believe that 'every effort should be made by the Church to promote dialogue between the unjust government and the prospective rebels . . . only when this effort has been consistently made and has manifestly failed should violent revolution even be contemplated by Christians'.[6] Whatever the merits of the arguments for or against the use of force by Christians to overthrow established governments, the real difficulty has, of course, been a difference of view among Christians as to how to define 'oppression' and 'tyranny'. The 'freedom fighters', some of whom are inspired by atheist Communism, and

---

[1] *Force in the Modern World. A document prepared by the Board for Social Responsibility,* G.S. 168, p. 45.

[2] Ibid., p. 47.

[3] *Freedom and Responsibility. Papers Read at a Conference Organized by the Modern Churchmen's Union,* in the *Modern Churchman* (Oct. 1971), N.S., vol. XV, No. 1, p. 46.

[4] *Civil Strife,* published for the Board for Social Responsibility, p. 18.

[5] Ibid., p. 20.   [6] Ibid., p. 17.

some of whom are no doubt Christians, are usually at work against governments actually conducted by Christians. At the centre of the debate is an
awkward deficiency: the English Church does not seem to have any accomplished experts in political science to assist the definition of what may be
thought oppressive government. Churchmen fall into the use of highly
suggestive political vocabulary with apparent innocence of the technical
use to which it is conventionally applied. 'The so-called "theology of
revolution" lacks the hard thinking needed to make it convincing,' as
Alan Richardson, the Dean of York, has rightly observed. 'Relying on a
picture of Jesus the revolutionary which historical study does not authenti-
cate, it frequently seeks justification for violence by its assertion that the
State itself is the prime perpetrator of violence against the people and that
it must therefore be met by violence.' In this, such 'theology' does not
adequately distinguish between violence and force.[1] A more traditional
view of human nature would not allow this to happen. 'Original Sin is not
an abstract dogma invented by theologians,' Richardson has written, 'but
a verifiable empirical judgment concerning the human condition.'[2] The
astonishing innocence of the political vocabulary they use indicates the
extent to which churchmen are susceptible to manipulation by propagandist
ideas. They are amateurs in a very professional business.

It is important to set the radical instincts of contemporary Christianity
in England into perspective. Most English Christians—both nominal and
worshipping—have probably remained unconvinced both by 'situation
ethics' and by attempts to identify the Church with radical politics. They
have often been confused by the shifts of opinion within Church leadership; many have looked for a more coherent direction from the bishops
than they have received in the last ten years. On their side of the 'two
Christianities' division, moderate and conservative Christians have also
identified their faith with the morality and the political values of the social
classes from which they are drawn—with a heavy balance in favour of a
lower-middle-class sense of order and 'decency', and of deference to traditionally conceived authorities. But if this is a class ethic, so too, of course,
is that of radical opinion. Because they have adopted 'progressive' moral
positions, and 'Left' politics, Christians of this temperament have failed
to realize how characteristically bourgeois their attitudes actually are. They
are often hurt to find that for all their sympathy for the Left in politics
they have moved no nearer to the working classes. All they have done, in
fact, is to reflect the movement of a section of the intelligentsia in the
transition from acquiescence in existing social beliefs to radical criticism
of them. Their new ideas are no less class ones. The bourgeoisie is internally divided over political preferences—as in the past—but the various

---

[1] Richardson, *The Political Christ*, p. 111. This point was also made by Archbishop
Fisher in *Touching on Christian Truth* (1971), p. 175.   [2] *The Political Christ*, p. 93.

sections have retained their essential class presuppositions, and to observers from the working class, their class identity.

The leadership of the Church of England has remained in the hands of men from public-school and Oxford and Cambridge backgrounds. In 1960 only six of the bishops were not educated in public-schools. There remains 'a strong bias towards public school candidates in Church selection procedures'[1]—as Leslie Paul remarked in 1964; and the succeeding ten years has not changed this. In these years the public schools and the universities have encouraged liberal attitudes, and this has led some to suppose that the class nature of the younger clergy (who are now less obviously marked off by wealth, and assumptions of 'natural' leadership, than they once were) has somehow diminished. But it has not. The phenomenon is a constant one in modern Church history. Educated in isolation from the realities of working-class and lower-middle-class life, the clergy have still acquired their social knowledge and attitudes from books and the communications media. In tastes, in accent, in pastimes, in social relationships, and finally through the clerical profession as a profession, they are still marked off by class reference. Yet they rarely seem conscious of it: assuming, somehow, that working people will see in their liberal social attitudes a sign that differences have been removed. 'The ministry does constitute a social stratum, its centre of gravity is middle to upper class: the centre of gravity is higher upper middle to upper class for dignitaries',[2] Leslie Paul wrote. 'Christ was the greatest public schoolboy who ever lived', an English bishop has remarked, apparently without intended irony.[3] The leading radical bishops of recent years have all been public-school men—Robinson, Montefiore, Sheppard, Huddleston. Ramsey of Durham was an exception. Indeed, he cultivated a working-class image—arriving at Buckingham Palace in 1966, to pay homage to the Crown on his appointment, wearing a cloth cap.[4] This sort of thing disguised his real social identity, for, after a lifetime spent as a don at both Oxford and Cambridge, he had adopted a set of left-wing political beliefs whose content derived almost entirely from the bourgeois radicalism and the moralistic attitudes of the progressive intellectuals around him. Ramsey's own origins, in Lancashire, in fact contributed very little to this. His socialism was a characteristic of his 'embourgeoisement'. It is a common paradox. With all the goodwill of the English upper-middle class, the clergy have believed they are, in their generation, almost the first to fall upon radical attitudes. Knowledge of the past radicalism of Church leaders hardly exists. In their judgement, the Victorian Church was simply given over to unthinking conservatism. As Carmichael and Goodwin wrote in their criticism of

---

[1] *The Deployment and Payment of the Clergy*, p. 112.
[2] Ibid., p. 114.   [3] Quoted in Mayfield, *Like Nothing on Earth*, p. 145.
[4] Edwards, *Ian Ramsey*, p. 59.

Temple's influence in the Church, 'Left-wing Anglican dignitaries have all been inclined to think of themselves as pioneers, but the pioneering task was ended by the time William Temple appeared as the new Christian socialist leader'.[1] Radical opinion has been a minority opinion in the Church, yet it has been the most publicized in recent years; a group whose intellectual prestige, at least within the Church, has allowed them a disproportionate influence. Their vision of radicalism has remained, despite the almost romantic language used about social realities, extremely academic—Canon Edwards remarked that 'many people were puzzled by the donnish style of the radical lecturers' at the Birmingham Church Leaders' Conference in 1972.[2] At the same gathering, Professor Torrance, in regretting that radical churchmen seemed 'to jump on every passing bandwagon', spoke of the tendency to reduce Christianity to the 'pathological moralism' of the 'guilty intellectual'.[3] It was an acute remark. The radicalism of contemporary churchmen has reproduced all the vicarious qualities which have characterized progressive attitudes in the Church throughout the preceding hundred years. It is a talking shop, where consciences are displayed, but very little actually happens. There is an obsessive emphasis on ideas, on analysis of social problems: qualities which themselves make the radicals incomprehensible to working-class people. Paul has noticed that the Church is 'unwilling to be radical about those parts of the church structures which relate to the norms of society',[4] and Cupitt has accused the Church of behaving 'rather like Henry James' Lord Warburton in holding progressive opinions without thought of applying them to himself'.[5] Harry Williams has written: 'There is still a general background of feeling that Christianity is not concerned to make an impact upon the structures of society—whatever bishops and other Christian leaders say or do'.[6] Radical churchmen have blamed all this on the intransigence of the conservative majority within the Church. But it is only half the truth. They are themselves also responsible: the academic and vicarious quality of their radicalism has limits of which they scarcely seem conscious.

Radical opinion in the Church also likes to suppose that its attitudes are derived from theological study. But this too does not bear examination. There is certainly a correlation between the espousal of radical theological ideas and radical social idealism: but the link is not causal—it is personal. Both are indications of a taste for academic analysis. Biblical reinterpretation has been necessary to remove the clear opposition of many Scriptural passages to modern humanistic morality or social doctrines—about sexual equality, or the worth of human rationality, for example.

[1] J. D. Carmichael and H. S. Goodwin, *William Temple's Political Legacy. A Critical Assessment* (London, 1963), p. vi.

[2] Edwards, *The British Churches Turn to the Future*, p. 11.   [3] Ibid., p. 43.

[4] Paul, *A Church by Daylight*, p. 160.   [5] Cupitt, *Crisis of Moral Authority*, p. 57.

[6] H. A. Williams, *True Resurrection* (London, 1972), p. 123.

'Situation ethics' are borrowed from the morality of the prevailing humanism of the intelligentsia, and radical politics come from the bourgeois
socialism current in academic circles, and found pretty evenly spread across
sections of the professional class. Theological reinterpretation merely ad-
justs Christian ideas to render them compatible with the latest developments in the class morality and political preferences of the class from which
the clergy are drawn. Radical laymen either accept the area of inquiry as
defined by the critical theologians, or are themselves in direct correspondence with the sources of social radicalism. Most of the laymen who take
part in government of the Church anyway come from the same social class
as the clergy. Altogether, contemporary Christian radicalism in England
illustrates the permanent tendency of the Church to assimilate the prevailing social and political beliefs of the intelligentsia. And its class presuppositions are more or less completely out of touch with working-class and
lower-middle-class society. Church radical politics are all about moralistic
issues, such as race, 'Third World' development, minority rights, sexual
liberation, censorship, and so forth, which have very little in common with
working-class labour politics, and nothing at all, of course, with the conventionally conservative social attitudes of the lower-middle classes.
Working-class socialism is about status, wages, and the distribution of
wealth. In fact, the more concerned Church leaders have become with
radical politics, Professor Torrance has said, 'the less had Church leaders
been in touch with the common people and their spiritual needs'.[1] Church
interests in issues like ecology are similar. The Lambeth Conference
of 1968 urged the importance of the question,[2] and the Church Assembly emphasized the need for the Church to become involved.[3] This
question is, no doubt, an important one: but it is characteristically an issue
which attracts little working-class interest. Similar to this in practical
appeal is the matter of women's rights. In its milder form it has become
involved in the arguments now current about the propriety of ordaining
women to the priesthood of the Church[4]—another idea characteristic of
bourgeois reformism, with no sort of sympathetic rapport with working-
class custom. The differences between the radicalism of Christian and
popular thought is even more clearly revealed in the controversies over
personal morality. 'Situation ethics' are class ethics: they are, perhaps,
arguably only for those who are *already* moral, and appropriate for those
whose traditional moral sense has been blunted by acquaintance with
rationalistic thinking. The application of such ethical attitudes requires

---

[1] Edwards, *The British Churches Turn to the Future*, p. 43.

[2] *The Lambeth Conference 1968*, Resolution 6, p. 30.

[3] *Church Assembly, Spring Session 1970. Report of Proceedings*, vol. L, No. 1, p. 177
(5 Feb. 1970).

[4] *The Ordination of Women to the Priesthood. A consultative document presented by the
Advisory Council for the Church's Ministry* (London, 1972), p. 54.

calculation and balance of judgement of a range found in academic life, or among the professional classes. They are an ethic for the bourgeoisie. It is not reasonable to expect a sheet-metal worker, at the end of his day's labour, to begin the sort of agonized self-criticism which the calculations involved in 'situation ethics' require. They are the ethics of leisure; appropriate, perhaps, for those with a taste for moral inquisition, for the moralistic, or for those who live life at second-hand. Professor Macquarrie has criticized Bishop Robinson's ethical scheme as 'a remarkable example of the situationist's utopian belief in his own and other people's sensitivity to complex situations'.[1] When, in 1972, Robinson advocated lowering the age of consent for sexual intercourse to fourteen years of age—in a speech to the Methodist Conference—he was sharply rebuked by Father Joe Williamson. This priest, well known for his rescue work among young prostitutes in London's East End, knew about the social realities which Robinson's ethical analysis did not take into account. 'The lecherous would have a clear field for raping children of 14', he wrote.[2] This exchange illustrates the gap between the intellectual and the actual, between the bourgeois world of personal rights and liberation and the ordinary assumption of ordinary people. Although some of the radical ideals of 'situation ethics' may have begun to filter down the social scale—and there has been enough publicity to help the process—signs of 'common sense' attitudes to morality among the working classes, which radicals occasionally take to be evidence of their influence, usually turn out to be the Englishman's traditional dislike of 'religious' moralizing; as true in the early nineteenth century as today. The influence of 'situation ethics' within the intelligentsia can be exaggerated as well. It is to be expected that many will seem to give a favourable hearing to the new ideas yet remain unconvinced by them. This is because modern churchmen are terrified of not seeming open-minded about almost every aspect of faith and morals (though not of social morality)—an attitude also encouraged by the experience of synodical government. T. E. Utley, at the time of the publication of *Honest to God*, remarked on 'a new obsession, which appears to afflict the entire Episcopal Bench, with the importance of not appearing to be old-fashioned'.[3]

Identifying the class basis of religious opinion in moral, social, and political questions is not, of course, to denigrate the possible validity of particular attitudes, or to deny that changes in modes of thought on such matters inevitably originate within an élite of some sort or other. But it is lack of awareness by Church thinkers themselves of just how crucial class reference is in the adoption of ideas which makes the Church's approach to social problems sometimes appear so unreal. Churchmen often seem to

---

[1] Macquarrie, *3 Issues in Ethics*, p. 37.

[2] Joseph Williamson, *A Reply to the Lecture 'The Place of Law in the Field of Sex,'* (London, 1972), p. 7.   [3] Edwards, *The Honest to God Debate*, p. 96.

imagine that sociological inquiry only reveals the class basis of conservative opinion: they never seem to find it necessary to wonder how radical
attitudes arise within the intelligentsia—always assuming that it reflects
rational choice. Working-class values are probably as little regarded, and
perhaps as little known about, by the contemporary Church as they were
in the nineteenth century. For all the shifts in class orientation, in the
relative distribution of wealth, and for all the social mobility, things
have changed very little in the mechanics of social consciousness. It is
certain that in twenty years from now, or in a hundred, Church leadership will continue to reflect whatever social and political attitudes are then
fashionable with the intelligentsia—it is certain that a few, in their enthusiasm, will completely identify Christianity with ideals which today would
seem intolerable. 'Ecclesiastical policies in secular concerns are hardly ever
original', Hensley Henson wrote in 1924; for on the one hand Christians
'wish to placate their consciences by reconciling their actual practice with
their professed belief: on the other hand, they seek to conciliate secular
society in order to Christianize it'. But these characteristics, he noticed,
were largely 'unperceived' by men of the time.[1]

In this generation, as in others, some churchmen have made their identification between the ideals of the secular intelligence and the spiritual
culture of the Church an almost complete one. Rather more, however, have
no doubt been content to suffer the confusions which usually surround
the attempt to detach the Living Christ from the cultural preferences of
each age. They proclaim, still, the Lord whose followers were called to
be in the world, but not of it; the God whose providential purpose is believed to hedge the ambiguities of present realities with intimations of the
eternal; removed, infinite, yet evident to the discernment of men, through
all the chaos of successive human expectations. Each generation of Christians offers up what in each age they judge most to convey the presence
of Christ. A lot of what is transient gets caught up in the process. It is
unavoidable, even necessary. The Incarnate truth presents itself in the
realities of human experience—in the mechanics of social class, or communal tradition, or inherited wisdom, or economic fact. In such things
humanity discovers and practises its values, and so Providence discloses
the Creator. Christ is borne in human hands. 'In the middle of all this
eddy and flux the faith still stands,' as Spencer Leeson said in 1944. 'Its
stability and strength does not, we may be thankful to remember, depend
upon us who try to serve it.'[2]

---

[1] Henson, *Quo Tendimus?*, Part II, p. 150.   [2] Leeson, *Christian Education*, p. 114.

Bibliography

OF WORKS REFERRED TO IN THE TEXT

I. MANUSCRIPT SOURCES

A substantial part of the material in this study is drawn from primary printed sources—from episcopal *Charges*, from pamphlet literature and books by contemporaries, and from public speeches. These are here classified as 'Principal Texts', below. In some places, however, and more frequently in the twentieth century, where there is very little secondary literature of interpretation, considerable use has been made of manuscript material in order to illuminate particular points. The following are the Collections consulted:

Samuel Horsley: Fulham Papers, Lambeth Palace Library.
Charles James Blomfield: Fulham Papers, Lambeth.
Lord George Beresford: Library of the Representative Church Body, Dublin.
Edward White Benson: Trinity College, Cambridge.
Randall Davidson: Lambeth Palace Library.
Herbert Hensley Henson: Chapter Library, Durham.
William Temple: Lambeth Palace Library.

II. REPORTS, NEWSPAPERS, JOURNALS, ETC.

The Chronicle of Convocation (London).
Reports and Resolutions of Lambeth Conferences (London).
Official Reports of the Church Congresses (usually where held).
Church Assembly, Reports of Proceedings (London).
Reports of the General Synod of the Church of England (London).
Annual Reports of the Board for Social Responsibility of the General Synod (London).
Annual Reports of the Board of Education of the General Synod (London).
Hansard's Parliamentary Debates (London).
Reports of the Anglo-Catholic Congresses (London).
Evangelical Magazine (London).
Guardian of Education (London).
Anti-Jacobin Review (London).
Churchman (London).
Modern Churchman (London).
British Critic (Oxford and London).
Crucible (London).
Oxford House Papers (London).
Christian Spectator (London).
Guardian (London).
Church Times (London).
Interpreter (Altrincham).
Sensation. A Bulletin for Chaplains in Higher Education (London).
British Weekly (London).
Hibbert Journal (London).

Freethinker (London).
Edinburgh Review (Edinburgh).
The Times (London).
Daily News (London).
Birmingham Post (Birmingham).
Evening Standard (London).
Listener (London).
Sunday Telegraph (London).
Spectator (London).
Cambridge Review (Cambridge).
Journal of Ecclesiastical History (Edinburgh and London).
Transactions of the Royal Historical Society (London).
Historical Journal (Cambridge).
Economic History Review (London).
Victorian Studies (London).

III. PRINCIPAL TEXTS

ACLAND, RICHARD, *We Teach Them Wrong*, London, 1963.
ACTS OF THE CONVOCATIONS of Canterbury and York, passed since the reform of the Convocations in 1921, London, 1961.
ALLEN, JOSEPH, *A Charge Delivered to the Clergy of the Diocese of Bristol*, London, 1835.
ARCHBISHOPS' COMMITTEE on Church and State. Report, London, 1918.
ARNOLD, MATTHEW, *Culture and Anarchy*, 1869, ed. J. Dover Wilson, Cambridge, 1960.
ARNOLD, THOMAS, *Principles of Church Reform*, London, 3rd edn., 1833.
AUTTON, NORMAN, ed., *Christianity and Change*, London, 1971.
BAGOT, RICHARD, *A Charge Addressed to the Clergy of the Diocese*, Oxford, 1834.
——, *A Charge Addressed to the Clergy of the Diocese of Oxford*, Oxford, 1838.
BAILEY, JOHN, ed., *New Life, Songs and Hymns for Assemblies, Clubs and Churches*, Great Yarmouth, 1971.
BALDWIN, STANLEY, *On England, And other Addresses*, London, 1926.
BARCLAY, WILLIAM, *Ethics in a Permissive Society*, London, 1971.
BARNES, E. W., *Religion and Turmoil*, Cambridge, 1949.
BARRY, F. R., *The Relevance of Christianity. An Approach to Christian Ethics*, London, revd. edn., 1936.
——, *Church and Leadership*, London, 1945.
BAYLY, W. D., *The State of the Poor and Working Classes Considered*, London, 1820.
BEESON, TREVOR, *An Eye for an Ear*, London, 1972.
BELL, G. K. A., *Christianity and World Order*, London, 1940.
——, *The Church and Humanity (1939–1946)*, London, 1946.
BELTON, F. G., *Present Day Problems in Christian Morals*, London, 1920.
BENSON, EDWARD WHITE, *The Church in Wales: Shall We Forsake Her?*, London, 1891.
——, *Church Education. A Sermon Preached at the Dedication of the Chapel of St. Chad's College, Denstone*, 1887.
BENTHAM, JEREMY, *The Church of England Catechism Examined*, new edn., London, 1824.
BERDYAEV, NICHOLAS, *Slavery and Freedom*, London, 1939.
BEST, S., *Parochial Ministrations*, London, 1839.

BETHELL, CHRISTOPHER, *A Charge Delivered at the Triennial Visitation of the Diocese of Gloucester*, Gloucester, 1828.

BEVAN, EDWYN, *Christians in a World at War*, London, 1940.

BLANK, JOOST DE, *Out of Africa*, London, 1964.

BLOMFIELD, C. J., *The Christian's Duty Towards Criminals*, London, 1828.

——, *A Charge Delivered to the Clergy of the Diocese of London*, London, 1834.

——, *The Uses of a Standing Ministry and an Established Church*, London, 1834.

——, *Proposals for the Creation of a Fund to be applied to the Building and Endowment of Additional Churches in the Metropolis*, London, 1836.

——, *A Charge Delivered to the Clergy of the Diocese of London*, London, 1838.

——, *The Duty of Prayer and Intercession for our Rulers*, London, 1838.

——, *Speech of the Lord Bishop of London on National Education at the Public Meeting held in Willis's Rooms*, London, 1839.

——, *A Charge Delivered to the Clergy of the Diocese of London*, 2nd edn., London, 1846.

——, *A Pastoral Letter to the Clergy of the Diocese of London*, London, 1847.

——, *A Charge Delivered to the Clergy of the Diocese of London*, London, 1854.

BLUNT, J. J., *The Acquirements and Principal Obligations and Duties of The Parish Priest*, 5th edn., London, 1856.

BOOTH, GENERAL WILLIAM, *In Darkest England and The Way Out*, London, 1890.

BREWSTER, JOHN, *A Sketch of the History of Churches in England: Applied to the Purposes of the Society for Promoting the Enlargement and Building of Churches and Chapels*, London, 1818.

BROADCASTING, *Society and the Church. Report of the Broadcasting Commission of the General Synod of the Church of England*, London, 1973.

BROUGHAM, HENRY, *Opinions of Lord Brougham*, Paris, 1841.

BURGES, GEORGE, *Reflections on the Nature and Tendency of the Present Spirit of the Times*, Norwich, 1819.

BURGESS, THOMAS, *A Charge Delivered to the Clergy of the Diocese of Salisbury*, Salisbury, 1832.

BURKE, EDMUND, *Reflections on the Revolution in France*, London, 1790.

BUSSELL, F. W., *Christian Theology and Social Progress*, London, 1907.

——, *The National Church and the Social Crisis*, London, 1918.

BUTLER, SAMUEL, *A Charge Delivered to the Archdeaconry of Derby*, London, 1834.

CAHILL, E., *Freemasonry and the Anti-Christian Movement*, Dublin, 1929.

——, *The Framework of a Christian State. An Introduction to Social Science*, Dublin, 1932.

CALVERT, THOMAS, *The Rich and Poor shewn to be of God's Appointment*, Cambridge, 1820.

CARPENTER, EDWARD, *Common Sense About Christian Ethics*, London, 1961.

CASE FOR DISESTABLISHMENT: *A Handbook of Facts and Arguments in Support of the Claim for Religious Equality*, published by the Society for the Liberation of Religion from State Patronage and Control, revd. edn., London [1884], 1894.

CATHERWOOD, H. F. R., *The Christian in Industrial Society*, London, 1964.

CHALMERS, THOMAS, *Lectures on the Establishment and Extention of National Churches*, Glasgow, 1838.

CHRIST for us Today. *Papers read at the Conference of Modern Churchmen*, ed. N. Pittinger, London, 1968.

CHURCHMAN, A. LAY, [Anon.], *Church and Party: being some Remarks on the Duty of Churchmen in and out of Parliament with particular reference to the Coming General Election*, London, 1865.

CHURCH AND STATE, *Report of the Archbishops' Commission on the Relations between Church and State*, London, 1935.

CHURCH AND STATE, *Report of the Archbishops' Commission*, London, 1970.

CHURCH AND YOUNG PEOPLE. *The Story, setting and development of the Youth Work of the Church of England*, London, 1955.

CIVIL STRIFE, published by the Board for Social Responsibility, London, 1971.

CLAYTON, H. J., *Church Defence*, London, 1910.

CLIFFORD, JOHN, *Socialism and the Teaching of Christ* (Fabian Tract), London, 1897.

——, *Socialism and the Churches* (Fabian Tract), London, 1908.

COBBETT, WILLIAM, *A History of the Protestant 'Reformation' in England and Ireland*, Dublin, 1826.

COGGAN, DONALD, *Sinews of Faith, A Primary Visitation Charge to the Diocese of York*, London, 1969.

——, *Word and World*, London, 1971.

COLERIDGE, S. T., *On the Constitution of the Church and State According to the Idea of Each* [1830], London, 1972 edn.

COLES, V. S. S., *Pastoral Work in Country Districts*, London, 1906.

CONFERENCE on Christian Politics, Economics and Citizenship (C.O.P.E.C.), Reports (vols. I–XII), London, 1924.

COPLESTON, EDWARD, *A Letter to the Right Hon. Robert Peel, M.P. for the University of Oxford, on the Pernicious Effects of a Variable Standard of Value, especially as it regards the Condition of the Lower Orders and the Poor Laws*, Oxford, 1819.

——, *A Second Letter to the Right Hon. Robert Peel, M.P. for the University of Oxford, on the Causes of the Increase of Pauperism and on the Poor Laws*, 2nd edn., Oxford, 1819.

——, *A Charge Delivered to the Clergy of the Diocese of Llandaff*, London, 1833.

——, *A Charge Delivered to the Clergy of the Diocese of Llandaff*, London, 1836.

——, *A Charge Delivered to the Clergy of the Diocese of Llandaff*, London, 1839.

——, *A Charge Delivered to the Clergy of the Diocese of Llandaff*, London, 1848.

COXE, R. C., *A Charge Delivered to the Clergy of the Archdeaconry of Lindisfarne*, London, 1856.

CREIGHTON, MANDELL, *A Charge Delivered to the Clergy and Churchwardens of the Diocese*, Peterborough, 1894.

——, *The Church and the Nation. Charges and Addresses*, London, 1901.

CROFTS, A. M., *Catholic Social Action. Principles, Purposes and Practice*, London, 1936.

CUNNINGHAM, W., *Christianity and Socialism*, London, 1909.

——, *Christianity and Social Questions*, London, 1910.

——, *Christianity and Economic Science*, London, 1914.

——, *Christianity and Politics*, London, 1916.

——, *Personal Ideals and Social Principles*, London, 1919.

CUPITT, DON, *Crisis of Moral Authority. The Dethronement of Christianity*, London, 1972.

CURTEIS, G. M., *Dissent in its Relation to the Church of England*, 2nd edn., London, 1892.

DAVIDSON, RANDALL T., *A Charge Delivered to the Clergy of the Diocese of Rochester*, London, 1894.

——, ed., *The Church of the People*, London, 1894.

——, *The Character and Call of the Church of England. A Charge Delivered at his Second Visitation*, London, 1912.

——, *The Six Lambeth Conferences, 1867–1920*, London, 1929.

DAWLEY, P. M., ed., *Report of the Anglican Congress*, Seabury Press, 1954.

DAWSON, CHRISTOPHER, *Religion and the Modern State*, London, 1935.

——, *Beyond Politics*, London, 1939.

——, *The Judgment of the Nations*, London, 1943.

DEALTRY, W., *A Charge Delivered in the Autumn of 1834 at the Visitation in Hampshire*, London, 1835.

DEARMER, PERCY, ed., *Christianity and the Crisis*, London, 1933.

DEMANT, V. A., *God, Man, and Society. An Introduction to Christian Sociology*, Milwaukee, 1934.

——, ed., *Faith that Illuminates*, London, 1935.

——, *The Religious Prospect*, London, 1939.

——, *Theology of Society*, London, 1947.

——, *Religion and the Decline of Capitalism*, London, 1952.

——, *An Exposition of Christian Sex Ethics*, London, 1963.

DENISON, EDWARD, *A Charge Delivered to the Clergy of the Diocese of Salisbury*, London, 1842.

——, *A Charge Delivered to the Clergy of the Diocese of Salisbury*, London, 1845.

DISESTABLISHMENT, *Lectures On*, by the Bishops of London, Bangor, Stepney, and Others, London, 1895.

DOCTRINE IN THE CHURCH OF ENGLAND. The Report of the Commission on Christian Doctrine Appointed by the Archbishops of Canterbury and York in 1922, London, 1938.

DRUCKER, PETER, *The End of Economic Man*, London, 1939.

EDWARDS, DAVID L., *Religion and Change*, London, 1969.

EDWARDS, MALDWYN, *Church and Society*, London, 1954.

ELIOT, T. S., *The Idea of a Christian Society*, London, 1939.

ELTON, LORD, *St. George or the Dragon. Towards a Christian Democracy*, London, 1942.

FIGGIS, J. N., *Churches in the Modern State*, 2nd edn., London, 1914.

——, *Hopes for English Religion*, London, 1919.

FISHER, GEOFFREY, *Standards of Morality. Christian and Humanist*, London, 1967.

——, *Touching On Christian Truth*, London, 1971.

FITZGERALD, M. H., ed., *The Gospel of This Generation*, London, 1938.

FORCE IN THE MODERN WORLD. A Document Prepared by the Board for Social Responsibility (G.S. 168), London, 1973.

FOURTH R., The Report of the Commission on Religious Education in Schools appointed in 1967 under the chairmanship of the Bishop of Durham, London, 1970.

FOX, H. W., *Christianity in Politics*, London, 1925.

FRASER, JAMES, *Charge Delivered at his Second Visitation*, Manchester, 1876.

FREIRE, PAULO, *Cultural Action for Freedom*, London, 1970.

——, *Pedagogy of the Oppressed*, London, 1972.

FROUDE, R. HURRELL, *Remains*, London, 1838.

FULLER, R. H., and RICE, B. K., *Christianity and the Affluent Society*, London, 1966.

GARBETT, CYRIL F., *In the Heart of South London*, London, 1931.

——, *The Claims of the Church of England*, London, 1947.

——, *Church and State in England*, London, 1950.

GARBETT, CYRIL F., *In an Age of Revolution*, London, 1952.
——, *The Church of England Today*, London, 1953.
GARVIE, A. E., *The Christian Ideal for Human Society*, London, 1930.
GILL, ERIC, *Christianity and the Machine Age*, London, 1940.
GLADSTONE, W. E., *The State in its Relations with the Church*, 2nd edn., London, 1839.
——, *Church Principles Considered in their Results*, London, 1840.
——, *A Chapter of Autobiography*, London, 1868.
——, *The Vatican Decrees in their Bearing on Civil Allegiance: A Political Expostulation*, London, 1874.
GOLDMAN, R. J., *Religious Teaching from Childhood to Adolescence*, London, 1964.
GORE, CHARLES, ed., *Essays in Aid of the Reform of the Church*, London, 1898.
——, *The Mission of the Church*, London, 1899.
——, *Objections to the Education Bill, 1906, in Principle and in Detail*, London, 1906.
——, *Christianity and Socialism; Pan-Anglican Papers*, London, 1908.
——, *The Question of Divorce*, London, 1911.
——, ed., *Property. Its Duties and Rights*, London, 1913.
——, *The Religion of the Church. A Manual of Membership*, London, 1917.
——, *Dominant Ideas and Corrective Principles*, London, 1918.
——, *Christ and Society*, London, 1928.
GREEN, PETER, *Betting and Gambling*, London, 1925.
GREY, EARL, *Letter to John Bright respecting the Irish Church*, London, 1868.
HALE, W. HALE, *The Approaching Contest with Romanism Considered in a Charge Addressed to the Clergy of the Archdeaconry of London*, London, 1845.
HARE, JULIUS, *A Charge Delivered to the Clergy of the Archdeaconry of Lewes*, London, 1842.
HARVEY, JOHN, and others, *Competition. A Study in Human Motive*, London, 1917.
HEADLAM, A. C., *The Church of England*, London, 1924.
——, *Economics and Christianity*, London, 1927.
——, *The Building of the Church of Christ. University and Other Sermons*, London, 1928.
——, *What it Means to be a Christian*, London, 1933.
HEADLAM, STEWART D., *The Church Catechism and the Emancipation of Labour*, London, 1875.
——, *Christian Socialism*, London, 1892.
HENSON, H. HENSLEY, *Light and Leaven. Historical and Social Sermons*, London, 1897.
——, ed., *Church Problems. A View of Modern Anglicanism*, London, 1900.
——, *Christian Marriage*, London, 1907.
——, *Quo Tendimus? The Primary Charge Delivered at his Visitation*, London, 1924.
——, *Church and Parson in England*, London, 1927.
——, *Disestablishment. The Charge delivered at the Second Quadrennial Visitation*, London, 1929.
——, *The Kingdom of God. Sermons*, London, 1929.
——, *The Group Movement. Being the First Part of the Charge Delivered at the Third Quadrennial Visitation*, Oxford, 1933.
——, *Christian Morality, Natural, Developing, Final*, Oxford, 1936.
——, *The Church of England*, Cambridge, 1939.
——, *Last Words in Westminster Abbey*, London, 1941.
——, *Bishoprick Papers*, Oxford, 1946.

——, *Letters of*, ed. E. F. Brayley, London, 1950.

——, *More Letters of*, ed. E. F. Brayley, London, 1954.

——, *Theology and Life*, London [1957].

——, *Ad Clerum*, London, 1958.

HESSEY, J. A., *Sunday. Its Origin, History, and Present Obligation*, 3rd edn., London, 1866.

HOLMES, ROBERT, *A Sermon Preached before the Honourable House of Commons*, London, 1796.

HORNE, GEORGE, *Charge, Intended to have been Delivered to the Clergy of Norwich at the Primary Visitation*, Norwich, 1791.

HORSLEY, SAMUEL, *The Charge of the Bishop of St. David's, 1790*, Gloucester, 1791.

——, *The Abounding of Iniquity. A Sermon Preached in Quebec Chapel, Mary-le-Bone*, London, 1792.

——, *A Sermon Preached before the Lords Spiritual and Temporal*, London, 1793.

——, *The Charge of Samuel, Lord Bishop of Rochester to the Clergy of his Diocese, 1796*, London, 1796.

——, *The Speeches in Parliament of Samuel Horsley*, Dundee, 1813.

——, *The Charges of Samuel Horsley*, London, 1830.

HOWLEY, WILLIAM, *A Charge Delivered to the Clergy of the Diocese of London*, 2nd edn., London, 1818.

——, *A Charge Delivered to the Clergy of the Diocese of London*, London, 1822.

——, *A Charge Delivered at his Primary Visitation*, London, 1832.

——, *A Charge Delivered at his Ordinary Visitation*, London, 1844.

HUDDLESTON, TREVOR, *Naught For Your Comfort*, London, 1956.

HUGHES, H. PRICE, *Social Christianity*, 2nd edn., London, 1889.

INDUSTRIAL MISSION, *A Paper Issued by the Church of England Industrial Committee*, London, 1965.

INGE, W. R., *All Saints' Sermons*, London, 1907.

——, *The Church and the Age*, London, 1912.

——, *England*, London, 1926.

——, *Assessments and Anticipations*, London, 1929.

——, *The Social Teaching of the Church*, London, 1930.

——, *Christian Ethics and Modern Problems*, London, 1930.

——, *Lay Thoughts of a Dean*, popular edn., London, 1933.

——, *Our Present Discontents*, London, 1938.

——, *The End of an Age*, London, 1948.

——, *Diary of a Dean*, London, 1949.

INGRAM, KENNETH, *Christianity—Right or Left?*, London, 1937.

——, *The Christian Challenge to Christians*, London, 1938.

JAMES, E. O., *The Social Function of Religion. A Comparative Study*, 2nd edn., London, 1948.

JAMES, WALTER, *The Christian in Politics*, London, 1962.

JEFFREYS, M. V. C., *Education—Christian or Pagan*, London, 1946.

JENKINS, DANIEL, *Equality and Excellence. A Christian Comment on Britain's Life*, London, 1971.

JOHNSON, HEWLETT, *The Socialist Sixth of the World*, London, 1939.

——, *Christians and Communism*, London, 1956.

——, *Searching for Light, an Autobiography*, London, 1968.

JONES, WILLIAM, *A Small Whole-Length of Dr. Priestley, from his Printed Works*, London, 1792.

KAYE, JOHN, *A Charge Delivered at the Triennial Visitation*, London, 1834.

KEEBLE, S. E., *Christian Responsibility for the Social Order*, London, 1922.

KELLY, HERBERT, *England and the Church*, London, 1902.

KENNEDY, G. A. STUDDERT, *Lies!*, London, 1919.

KING, EDWARD, *Sermons and Addresses*, ed. B. W. Randolph, London, 1911.

KING, WALTER, *A Pastoral Letter to the Clergy and Other Inhabitants of his Diocese*, London, 1819.

LAND, the People and the Churches, The, published for the British Council of Churches, London, 1945.

LANG, COSMO G., *The Opportunity of the Church of England*, London, 1906.

LAW, G. H., *A Charge Delivered to the Clergy of the Diocese of Bath and Wells*, London, 1825.

——, *On Education. A Sermon Preached in the Cathedral Church of Wells*, London, 1827.

LEESON, SPENCER, *Christian Education*, London, 1947.

——, *Christian Education Reviewed*, London, 1957.

LEIGH, M. S., ed., *Christianity in the Modern State*, London, 1936.

LEON, PHILIP, *The Philosophy of Courage, or The Oxford Group Way*, London, 1939.

LEWIS, JOHN, and others, ed., *Christianity and the Social Revolution*, London, 1935.

LLOYD, Roger, *Revolutionary Religion: Christianity, Fascism and Communism*. London, 1938.

——, *The Church and the Artisan Today*, London, 1952.

LYALL, W. R., *Sentiments of the Clergy on the Question of Church Reform, Briefly Stated in a Charge Delivered to the Clergy*, London, 1833.

McCLURE, EDMUND, *Modern Substitutes for Traditional Christianity*, London, 1916.

MACKINNON, D. M., ed., *Christian Faith and Communist Faith. A Series of Studies by Members of the Anglican Communion*, London, 1953.

——, ed., *God, Sex and War*, London, 1963.

MACNUTT, F. B., ed., *The Church in the Furnace. Essays by Seventeen Temporary Church of England Chaplains on Active Service in France and Flanders*, London, 1917.

MACQUARRIE, JOHN, *3 Issues in Ethics*, London, 1970.

MALTBY, EDWARD, *A Charge Delivered to the Clergy of the Archdeaconry of Lewes*, London, 1834.

MALTHUS, T. R., *Principles of Political Economy, Considered with a View to their Practical Application*, [1820], Oxford edn., 1951.

MALVERN 1941. The Life of the Church and the Order of Society, Being the Proceedings of the Archbishop of York's Conference, London, 1941.

MANNING, H. E., *National Education. A Sermon Preached in the Cathedral Church of Chichester*, London, 1838.

MARCHANT, SIR JAMES, ed., *The Future of the Church of England*, London, 1926.

——ed., *Has the Church Failed?*, London, 1947.

MARRIAGE, Divorce and the Church. The Report of a Commission appointed by the Archbishop of Canterbury to prepare a Statement on the Christian Doctrine of Marriage, London, 1971.

MARRIAGE and the Family in Britain Today. A Survey presented by the Board for Social Responsibility (G.S. 169), London, 1973.

MARRIOTT, HARVEY, *Essay on the Madras System of Education*, London, 1819.

MARSH, HERBERT, *The National Religion the Foundation of National Education*, London, 1811.

MASCALL, E. L., *The Secularization of Christianity. An analysis and a Critique*, London, 1965.

MASTERMAN, C. F. G., *The Heart of the Empire. Discussions of Problems of Modern City Life in England*, London, 1901.

MAURICE, F. D., *On the Reformation of Society, and How all Classes may Contribute to it*, Southampton, 1851.

——, *The Conflict of Good and Evil in Our Day*, London, 1865.

——, *The Workmen and the Franchise*, London, 1866.

——, *Social Morality. Twenty-one Lectures Delivered to the University of Cambridge*, London, 1869.

——, *The Kingdom of Christ*, new edn., (A. R. Vidler, ed.), London, 1958.

MONK, JAMES HENRY, *A Charge Delivered to the Clergy of the Diocese of Gloucester*, London, 1835.

——, *A Sermon Preached before the University of Cambridge*, London, 1835.

MONTEFIORE, HUGH, *Awkward Questions on Christian Love*, London, 1964.

——, ed., *We Must Love one Another or Die*, London, 1966.

MORE, HANNAH, *Estimate of the Religion of the Fashionable World*, London, 1790.

——, *Village Politics. Addressed to all the Mechanics, Journeymen, and Day Labourers in Great Britain by Will Chip*, London, 3rd edn., 1793.

——, *Thoughts on the Importance of the Manners of the Great to General Society*, London, 1788.

MORTIMER, R. C., *Gambling*, London, 1933.

MUNBY, D. L., *Christianity and Economic Problems*, London, 1956.

——, *The Idea of a Secular Society, and its Significance for Christians*, London, 1963.

NEILL, STEPHEN, *The Christian Society*, London, 1952.

NEWMAN, J. H., *Discussions and Arguments*, London, 1872.

NICKOLLS, R. B., *The Duty of Supporting and Defending our Country and Constitution*, York, 1793.

NOEL, CONRAD, *Socialism in Church History*, London, 1910.

——, *Jesus the Heretic*, London, 1939.

OBSCENE PUBLICATIONS. Law and Practice, issued by the Board for Social Responsibility, London, 1970.

OLDHAM, J. H., *Christianity and the Race Problem*, 4th edn., London, 1925.

——, *Church, Community, and State: A World Issue*, London, 1935.

——, *The Churches Survey Their Task. The Report of the Conference at Oxford, July, 1937, on Church, Community and State*, London, 1937.

ORDINATION of Women to the Priesthood. A Consultative Document Presented by the Advisory Council for the Church's Ministry, London, 1972.

OTTER, WILLIAM, *A Charge Delivered to the Clergy of the Diocese of Chichester*, London, 1838.

OWEN, ROBERT, *A New View of Society, or Essays on the Formation of the Human Character* (1813), in *Robert Owen on Education*, Cambridge, 1969.

PAGET, FRANCIS, *This Church and Realm*, London, 1887.

PALEY, WILLIAM, *The Principles of Moral and Political Philosophy*, London, 1785,

——, *Works*, Edinburgh, 1822.

PALMER, ROUNDELL, EARL OF SELBORNE, *A Defence of the Church of England Against Disestablishment*, new edn., London, 1887.

PALMER, WILLIAM, *A Narrative of Events Connected with the Publication of the Tracts for the Times*, London, 1883 edn.

PARTNERS in Mission. Anglican Consultative Council. Second Meeting, Dublin, July, 1973, London, 1973.

PASHLEY, ROBERT, *Pauperism and Poor Laws,* London, 1852.

PAUL, LESLIE, *The Deployment and Payment of the Clergy. A Report by Leslie Paul,* London, 1964.

PEABODY, F. G., *Jesus Christ and the Social Question,* New York, 1902.

PEPYS, HENRY, *A Charge Delivered to the Clergy of the Diocese of Worcester,* London, 1845.

PERCIVAL, JOHN, *The Present State of the Church. A Charge Delivered to the Clergy and Churchwardens of the Diocese of Hereford,* London, 1898.

PHILLPOTTS, HENRY, *A Letter to the Right Honourable William Sturges Bourne, M.P.,* 2nd edn., London, 1819.

——, *A Letter to the Freeholders of the County of Durham,* Durham, 1819.

——, *Charge Delivered to the Clergy of the Diocese of Exeter,* London, 1833.

——, *Charge Delivered to the Clergy of the Diocese of Exeter,* London, 1836.

——, *Charge Delivered to the Clergy of the Diocese of Exeter,* London, 1839.

PITTINGER, NORMAN, *Time for Consent,* London, 1970.

PROBE, Booklets for use in schools published by S.C.M., London, 1969– .

PROCEEDINGS OF C.O.P.E.C. Being a Report of the Meetings of the Conference on Christian Politics, Economics and Citizenship, London, 1924.

PUBLIC SCHOOLS and the General Educational System, The, (Fleming Report), London, 1944.

PUTTING ASUNDER: A Divorce Law for Contemporary Society, London, 1966.

RAMSEY, A. M., *Durham Essays and Addresses,* London, 1956.

——, *The Crisis of Human Freedom,* London, 1962.

——, *Canterbury Essays and Addresses,* London, 1964.

——, *Sacred and Secular. A Study in the other-worldly and this-worldly aspects of Christianity,* London, 1965.

——, *Freedom, Faith and the Future,* London, 1970.

——, *The Christian Priest Today,* London, 1972.

——, and SUENENS, L.-J., *The Future of the Christian Church,* London, 1971.

RAMSEY, IAN, *Models for Divine Activity,* London, 1973.

RAUSCHENBUSCH, WALTER, *Christianity and the Social Crisis,* New York, 1907.

RAVEN, C. E., *Science, Religion and the Future,* Cambridge, 1943.

——, *Christ and the Modern Opportunity,* London, 1956.

RECKITT, MAURICE B., ed., *The Social Teaching of the Sacraments,* London, 1927.

——, *Religion in Social Action,* London, 1937.

——, *Faith and Society,* London, 1932.

——, ed., *Prospect for Christendom. Essays in Catholic Social Reconstruction,* London, 1940.

——, *The Christian in Politics,* London, 1946.

——, *Militant Here in Earth. Considerations on the prophetic function of the Church in the twentieth century,* London, 1957.

——, and BECHHOFER, C. E., *The Meaning of National Guilds,* London, 1918.

——, and CASSERLEY, J. V. LANGMEAD, *The Vocation of England,* London, 1941.

RELIGIOUS EDUCATION in schools. The Report of an Inquiry made by the Research Committee of the Institute of Christian Education into the Working of the 1944 Education Act, London, 1954.

REPORTS of the Archbishops' Committee of Inquiry (5 Reports), London, 1918.

REPORT of the Committee of the Representative Church Council on the Report of the Archbishop's Committee on Church and State, London, 1918.

RETURN of Christendom, The, by a Group of Churchmen, London, 1922.
RHYMES, DOUGLAS, *No New Morality. Christian Personal Values and Sexual Morality,* London, 1964.
RICHARDSON, ALAN, *The Political Christ,* London, 1973.
ROBERTSON, SIR C. G., *Religion and the Totalitarian State,* London, 1937.
ROBINSON, J. A. T., *Honest to God,* London, 1963.
——, *Christian Freedom in a Permissive Society,* London, 1970.
——, *The Difference in Being a Christian Today,* London, 1972.
——, *The Human Face of God,* London, 1973.
RUPP, E. G., *Is This a Christian Country?,* London, 1941.
RURAL LIFE. A Report prepared by a Commission appointed by the Copec Continuation Committee, London, 1927.
RYLE, J. C., *A Charge Delivered to the Clergy of the Diocese of Liverpool,* Liverpool, 1884.
SANDHURST, B. G., *How Heathen is Britain?,* London, 1946.
——, *How Heathen is Britain? A Revised and Enlarged Edition,* London, 1948.
SANGSTER, W. E., *Ten Statesmen and Jesus Christ. A Christian Commentary on our War Aims,* London, 1941.
SCHUSTER, GEORGE, *Christianity and Human Relations in Industry,* Lonon, 1951.
SHEPPARD, H. R. L., *If I Were Dictator,* London, 1935.
SMITH, SYDNEY, *Works,* 3rd edn., London, 1845.
SMYTH, CHARLES, *Religion and Politics,* London, 1943.
——, *The Church and the Nation,* London, 1962.
SOPER, DONALD, *Question Time on Tower Hill,* London, 1935.
SOUTHEY, ROBERT, *The Book of the Church,* London, 1824.
STAMP, JOSIAH, *The Christian Ethic as an Economic Factor,* London, 1926.
——, *Motive and Method in a Christian Order,* London, 1936.
STANLEY, A. P., *An Address on the Connection of Church and State,* London, 1868.
STANLEY, EDWARD, *A Charge Delivered to the Clergy of the Diocese of Norwich,* Norwich, 1838.
SUMNER, C. J., *A Charge Delivered to the Clergy of the Diocese of Llandaff,* London, 1827.
——, *A Charge Delivered to the Clergy of the Diocese of Winchester,* London, 1834.
SUMNER, J. BIRD, *An Essay Tending to Show that the Prophesies, now Accomplishing, are an Evidence of the Truth of the Christian Religion,* Cambridge, 1802.
——, *A Treatise on the Records of the Creation and on the Moral Attributes of the Creator,* London, 1816.
——, *The Evidence of Christianity, Derived from its Nature and Reception,* London, 1824.
——, *A Charge Delivered to the Clergy of the Diocese of Chester,* London, 1832.
——, *A Charge Addressed to the Clergy of the Diocese of Chester,* London, 1845.
TAIT, A. C., *Middle Class Education. A Speech Delivered at the Devon County School, West Buckland,* London, 1865.
——, *The Present Position of the Church of England,* 3rd edn., London, 1873.
——, *Some Thoughts on the Duties of the Established Church of England as a National Church,* London, 1876.
——, *The Church and the Law,* 4th edn., London, 1877.
——, *The Church of the Future. A Diocesan Charge,* London, 1880.
TAWNEY, R. H., *Equality,* London, 1931.
——, *Religion and the Rise of Capitalism. A Historical Study,* revd. edn., London, 1944.

TEELING, WILLIAM, *Crisis for Christianity*, London, 1939.

TELEVISION AND RELIGION. Prepared by Social Surveys (Gallup Poll) Ltd., on behalf of A.B.C. Television Ltd., London, 1964.

TEMPLE, FREDERICK, *A Speech by the Right Honourable and Right Reverend the Lord Bishop of London, at the Annual Meeting of the Church Defence Institution*, London, 1892.

TEMPLE, WILLIAM, *The Church and the Education Bill*, Oxford, 1906.

——, *The Kingdom of God*, London, 1912.

——, *Church and Nation*, London, 1916.

——, *Essays in Christian Politics and Kindred Subjects*, London, 1927.

——, *The Spirit in Life and Thought*, Liverpool, 1927.

——, *Christianity and the State*, London, 1928.

——, *Thoughts in War-Time*, London, 1940.

——, *The Hope of a New World*, London, 1940.

——, *Citizen and Churchman*, London, 1941.

——, *Christianity and Social Order*, London, 1942.

——, *Social Witness and Evangelism*, London, 1943.

——, *The Church Looks Forward*, London, 1944.

THIRLWALL, CONNOP, *A Charge Delivered to the Clergy of the Diocese of St. David's*. London, 1842.

THORNTON, HENRY, *An Enquiry into the Nature and Effects of the Paper Credit of Great Britain*, London, 1802.

THORP, THOMAS, *A Charge Delivered to the Archdeaconry of Bristol*, Bristol, 1843.

TOWARDS THE CONVERSION OF ENGLAND. Being the Report of a Commission on Evangelism Appointed by the Archbishops of Canterbury and York, London, 1945.

TOWARDS a Quaker View of Sex, London, 1963.

TUCKWELL, W., *Reminiscences of a Radical Parson*, London, 1895.

VIDLER, A. R., *God's Judgment on Europe*, London, 1940.

——, *Christian Belief and This World*, London, 1956.

——, *Essays in Liberality*, London, 1957.

——, ed., *Soundings, Essays Concerning Christian Understanding*. Cambridge, 1962.

WAND, J. C., *God and Goodness*, London, 1947.

WARD, W. G., *The Ideal of a Christian Church Considered in Comparison with Existing Practice*, London, 1844.

WATSON, RICHARD, *A Defence of Revealed Religion in Two Sermons Preached in the Cathedral Church of Llandaff, 1795*, 3rd edn., London, 1806.

——, *An Apology for the Bible in a Series of Letters Addressed to Thomas Paine*, 9th edn., London, 1806.

WATTS-DITCHFIELD, J. E., *The Church in Action*, London, 1913.

WEIR, A. and MACLAGAN, W., eds., *The Church and the Age*, London, 1872.

WESTCOTT, B. FOSS, *The Christian Social Union*, London, 1895.

——, *The Obligations of Empire*, London, 1900.

——, *Lessons from Work*, London, 1901.

——, *Christian Social Union Addresses*, London, 1903.

WHATELY, RICHARD, *Thoughts on Church Government*, London, 1844.

WHITEHEAD, W. B., *Prosecutions of Infidel Blasphemers briefly Vindicated in a Letter to David Ricardo, Esqr., M.A.*, Bristol, 1823.

WHITELEY, PETER, *Frontier Mission. An Account of the Toronto Congress, 1963*, Toronto, New York, and London, 1963.

WILBERFORCE, SAMUEL, *A Charge Delivered at the Ordinary Visitation of the Archdeaconry of Surrey*, London, 1842.

WILBERFORCE, WILLIAM, *A Practical View of the Prevailing Religious System of Professed Christians in the Higher and Middle Classes in the Country Contrasted with Real Christianity*, 2nd edn., London, 1797.

WILLIAMS, H. A., *True Resurrection*, London, 1972.

WILLIAMSON, JOSEPH, *A Reply to the Lecture 'The Place of Law in the Field of Sex'* (by J. A. T. Robinson), London, 1972.

WINNINGTON-INGRAM, A. F., *Victory and After*, London, 1919.

——, *Fifty Years' Work in London (1889–1939)*, London, 1940.

WINTER, ROBERT, *Brief Statement of the Case of Protestant Dissenters*, London, 1834.

WORDSWORTH, CHRISTOPHER, *The Ecclesiastical Commission and the Universities*, London, 1837.

——, *Heathen and Christian Philanthropy. Their Practical Results Compared*, London, 1838.

——, *Miscellanies*, London, 1879.

YATES, RICHARD, *The Church in Danger, A Statement of the Course, and of the Probable Means of Averting that Danger Attempted: in a Letter to the Right Honourable the Earl of Liverpool*, London, 1815.

——, *The Basis of National Welfare: Considered in Reference Chiefly to the Prosperity of Britain and the Safety of the Church of England . . . In a Second Letter to the Right Honourable the Earl of Liverpool*, London, 1817.

——, *The Gospel Kingdom . . . A Sermon Preached in the Parish Church of Halstead in Essex*, London, 1818.

——, *Patronage of the Church of England*, London, 1823.

IV. BIOGRAPHY AND OTHER WORKS

ADDISON, W. G., *Religious Equality in Modern England, 1714–1914*, London, 1944.

AKENSON, D. H., *The Irish Education Experiment*, London, 1970.

ALINGTON, C. A., *A Dean's Apology. A Semi-Religious Autobiography*, London, 1952.

ANTHOLOGY of Chartist Literature, ed. I. O. B. Kobaneba, Moscow, 1956.

ARMSTRONG, Anthony, *The Church of England, the Methodists and Society, 1700–1850*, London, 1973.

ARNSTEIN, W. L., *The Bradlaugh Case: a Study in late Victorian Opinion and Politics*, Oxford, 1965.

ASHWELL, A. R., *Life of the Right Reverend Samuel Wilberforce, D.D.*, London, 1880.

BACKSTROM, P. N., *Christian Socialism and Co-operation in Victorian England*, London, 1973.

BAKER, A. E., ed., *William Temple and his Message*, London, 1946.

BALDICK, ROBERT, ed., *The Memoirs of Chateaubriand*, London, 1961.

BALL, J. T., *The Reformed Church of Ireland*, London, 1886.

BATHURST, HENRY, *Memoirs of the late Dr. Henry Bathurst*, London, 1837.

BATTISCOMBE, GEORGINA, *John Keble. A Study in Limitations*, London, 1963.

BAYNE, S. F., *An Anglican Turning Point. Documents and Interpretations*, Austin, Texas, 1964.

BELL, G. K. A., *Randall Davidson*, Oxford, 1935.

BELL, P. M. H., *Disestablishment in Ireland and Wales*, London, 1969.

BENEWICK, ROBERT, *The Fascist Movement in Britain*, revd. edn., London, 1972.

BENSON, A. C., *The Life of Edward White Benson*, new edn., London, 1901.

488 BIBLIOGRAPHY

BEST, G. F. A., 'The Protestant Constitution and its Supporters, 1800–29', in *Transactions of the Royal Historical Society*, 5th series, 8 (1958), 105.

——, *Temporal Pillars. Queen Anne's Bounty, the Ecclesiastical Commissioners, and the Church of England*, Cambridge, 1964.

——, *Bishop Westcott and the Miners*, London, 1967.

BIBER, G. E., *Bishop Blomfield and his Times*, London, 1857.

BINFIELD, CLYDE, *George Williams and the Y.M.C.A. A Study in Victorian Social Attitudes*, London, 1973.

BLAKE, ROBERT, *Disraeli*, London, 1966.

BLAUG, MARK, 'The Poor Law Report Re-examined', in *Journal of Economic History*, 24 (1964).

BLOMFIELD, ALFRED, *A Memoir of Charles James Blomfield, D.D.*, London, 1863.

BOLITHO, HECTOR, ed., *A Victorian Dean. A Memoir of Arthur Stanley*, London, 1930.

BOWEN, DESMOND, *The Idea of the Victorian Church*, Montreal, 1968.

BRADLAUGH, CHARLES, *Champion of Liberty* (issued by the Centenary Committee), London, 1933.

BRIGGS, ASA, ed., *Chartist Studies*, London, 1959.

BROCK, W. R., *Lord Liverpool and Liberal Toryism*, 2nd edn., London, 1967.

BROSE, OLIVE J., 'The Irish Precedent for English Church Reform: the Church Temporalities Act of 1833', in *Journal of Ecclesiastical History*, 7, no. 2 (1956).

——, *Church and Parliament. The Reshaping of the Church of England, 1828–1860*, Oxford, 1959.

BROWN, C. K. FRANCIS, *The Church's Part in Education, 1833–1941*, London, 1942.

BROWN, FORD, K., *Father of the Victorians. The Age of Wilberforce*, Cambridge, 1961.

CARMICHAEL, J. D., and GOODWIN, H. S., *William Temple's Political Legacy. A Critical Assessment*, London, 1963.

CARPENTER, EDWARD, *Cantaur. The Archbishops in their Office*, London, 1971.

CARPENTER, S. C., *Winnington-Ingram*, London, 1949.

CHADWICK, OWEN, *Westcott and the University*, Cambridge, 1962.

——, *The Victorian Church*, London, Part I, 1966; Part II, 1970.

CHANCELLOR, V. E., *History for their Masters. Opinion in the English History Textbook: 1800–1914*, London, 1970.

CHRISTENSEN, TORBEN, *Origins and History of Christian Socialism, 1848–54*, Aarhus, 1962.

CHURCH, R. W., *The Oxford Movement*, London, 1892.

CLARK, W. H., *The Oxford Group. Its History and Significance*, New York, 1951.

CLAYTON, JOSEPH, *Bishops as Legislators*, London, 1906.

COBBAN, ALFRED, *Edmund Burke and the Revolt against the Eighteenth Century*, 2nd edn., London, 1960.

COLE, G. D. H., and POSTGATE, R., *The Common People, 1746–1946*, revd. edn., London, 1946.

COLERIDGE, J. T., *A Memoir of the Revd. John Keble*, 2nd edn., Oxford and London, 1869.

COLSON, PERCY, *Life of the Bishop of London* (Winnington-Ingram), London, 1935.

CONFERENCE on Christian Politics Economics and Citizenship (C.O.P.E.C.)— and the Immediate Future (issued by the Committee), London, 1924.

COOK, CHARLES T., *London Hears Billy Graham. The Greater London Crusade*, London, 1954.

C.O.P.E.C. The Purpose, Scope and Character of the Conference (issued by the Committee), London, 1924.

COPLESTON, W. J., *Memoir of Edward Copleston, D.D.*, London, 1851.

CORNISH, F. WARRE, *The English Church in the Nineteenth Century*, London, 1910.

COWLING, MAURICE, *The Impact of Labour, 1920–1924*, Cambridge, 1971.

CRAGG, G. R., *The Church and the Age of Reason*, London, 1960.

CRAIG, ROBERT, *Social Concern in the Thought of William Temple*, London, 1963.

CREIGHTON, MANDELL, *Life and Letters*, by his Wife, London, 1904.

CROPPER, MARGARET, *Evelyn Underhill*, London, 1958.

D'ARCY, M. C., *Humanism and Christianity*, London, 1969.

DARK, SIDNEY, *The People's Archbishop. The Man and his Message* (William Temple), London, 1942.

DAVIDSON, R. T., and BENHAM, W., *Life of Archibald Campbell Tait*, London, 1891.

DAVIES, E. T., *The Political Ideas of Richard Hooker*, London, 1946.

DAVIES, G. C. B., *Henry Phillpotts. Bishop of Exeter, 1778–1869*, London, 1954.

DAVIES, HORTON, *Worship and Theology in England. The Ecumenical Century, 1900–1965*, Princeton, 1965.

DAWSON, CONINGSBY, *The Glory of Trenches*, London, 1918.

DE-LA-NOY, MICHAEL, *A Day in the Life of God*, Derby, 1971.

DEWAR, LINDSAY, *An Outline of Anglican Moral Theology*, London, 1968.

DILLISTONE, F. W., *Charles Raven, Naturalist, Historian, Theologian*, London, 1975.

DRUMMOND, ANDREW L., and BULLOCH, JAMES, *The Church in Victorian Scotland, 1843–1874*, Edinburgh, 1975.

EDINGTON, DAVID, *Christians and Colour in Britain*, London, 1970.

EDSALL, N. C., *The Anti-Poor Law Movement, 1834–44*, Manchester, 1971.

EDWARDS, DAVID L., *The Honest to God Debate. Some reactions to the book 'Honest to God'*, London, 1963.

——, *Leaders of the Church of England, 1828–1944*, London, 1971

——, *The British Churches Turn to the Future*, London, 1973..

——, *Ian Ramsey: Bishop of Durham. A Memoir*, London, 1973.

ENGELS, FREDERICK, *The Condition of the Working Class in England* (1844), Blackwell ed., Oxford, 1958.

FACTS AND FIGURES about the Church of England, ed. R. F. Neuss, London, 1959, 1962, 1965.

FALLOWS, W. G., *Mandell Creighton and the English Church*, London, 1964.

FAULKNER, H. U., *Chartism and the Churches*, New York, 1916.

FERRIS, PAUL, *The Church of England*, revd. edn., London, 1964.

FINLAY, JOHN L., *Social Credit: the English Origins*, Montreal, 1972.

FISHER, GEOFFREY, *The Archbishop Speaks. Addresses and Speeches by the Archbishop of Canterbury*, selected by Edward Carpenter, London, 1958.

FITZPATRICK, W. J., *The Life, Times, and Correspondence of the Rt. Revd. Dr. Doyle*, Dublin, 1861.

FLETCHER, RONALD, *The Akenham Burial Case*, London, 1974.

FLINDALL, R. P., *The Church of England, 1815–1948. A Documentary History*, London, 1972.

FOX, ADAM, *Dean Inge*, London, 1960.

FREEMANTLE, ANNE, ed., *The Papal Encyclicals*, New York, 1956.

GASH, NORMAN, *Politics in the Age of Peel*, London, 1953.

——, *Mr. Secretary Peel. The Life of Sir Robert Peel to 1830*, London, 1961.

GAY, J. D., *The Geography of Religion in England*, London, 1971.

GERTH, H. H., and WRIGHT MILLS, C., *From Max Weber: Essays in Sociology*, London, 1948.

GILBERT, BENTLEY B., *British Social Policy, 1914–1939*, London, 1970.

GILL, J. C., *Parson Bull of Byerley*, London, 1963.

GROVES, REG., *Conrad Noel and the Thaxted Movement*, London, 1967.

HALL, M. P., and HOWES, I. V., *The Church in Social Work. A Study of the Mora Welfare Work Undertaken by the Church of England*, London, 1965.

HANDY, ROBERT T., *The American Religious Depression, 1925–1935*, Philadelphia, 1968.

HARCOURT, MELVILLE, *Tubby Clayton. A Personal Saga*, London, 1953.

HARFORD, J. B., and MACDONALD, F. C., *Handley Carr Glyn Moule, Bishop of Durham*, 3rd edn., London, 1922.

HARRIS, JOSÉ, *Unemployment and Politics. A Study in English Social Policy, 1886–1914*, Oxford, 1972.

HARRISON, BRIAN, *Drink and the Victorians. The Temperance Question in England, 1818–1872*, London, 1971.

HEASMAN, KATHLEEN, *Evangelicals in Action. An Appraisal of their Social Work in the Victorian Era*, London, 1962.

HEENEY, BRIAN, *Mission to the Middle Classes. The Woodard Schools, 1848–1891*, London, 1969.

HENSON, H. HENSLEY, *Retrospect of an Unimportant Life*, Oxford, vol. i, 1942; vol. ii, 1943; vol. iii, 1950.

HEPBURN, RONALD, and others, *Religion and Humanism*, London, 1964.

HERBERT, CHARLES, *Twenty-five Years as Archbishop of Canterbury* (Davidson), London, 1928.

HOBSBAWN, E. J., *Primitive Rebels. Studies in Archaic Forms of Social Movement in the 19th and 20th Centuries*, Manchester, 1959.

HODGSON, ROBERT, *The Life of the Right Reverend Beilby Porteus, D.D.*, London, 1811.

HOFSTADTER, RICHARD, *Social Darwinism in American Thought*, revd. edn., Boston, 1955.

HOW, F. D., *William Conyngham Plunket. A Memoir*, London, 1900.

HOWARD, PETER, *Frank Buchman's Secret*, London, 1961.

——, *Britain and the Beast*, London, 1963.

HOWSE, E. M., *Saints in Politics. The 'Clapham Sect' and the Growth of Freedom*, London, 1953.

HUGHES, E., 'The Bishops and Reform, 1831–2: Some Fresh Correspondence', in *English Historical Review*, 56 (1941).

HUGHES, HUGH PRICE, *Life*, by his Daughter, London, 1904.

HUNTER, LESLIE, ed., *The English Church. A New Look*, London, 1966.

HURT, JOHN, *Education in Evolution, Church, State, Society and Popular Education, 1800–1870*, London, 1972.

HYAMSON, A. M., *A History of the Jews in England*, 2nd edn., London, 1928.

HYNES, SAMUEL, *The Edwardian Turn of Mind*, Princeton, 1968.

ILLINGWORTH, J. R., *The Life and Work of John Richardson Illingworth*, ed. by his Wife, London, 1917.

INGLIS, K. S., *Churches and the Working Classes in Victorian England*, London, 1963.

IREMONGER, F. A., *Men and Movements in the Church. A Series of Interviews*, London, 1928.

——, *William Temple, His Life and Letters*, Oxford, 1948.

JASPER, RONALD, C. D., *Arthur Cayley Headlam, Life and Letters of a Bishop*, London, 1960.

——, *George Bell, Bishop of Chichester*, London, 1967.

JONES, ANDREW, *The Politics of Reform, 1884*, Cambridge, 1972.

JONES, P. d'A., *The Christian Socialist Revival, 1877–1914*, Princeton, 1968.

KEEBLE, S. E., '*C.O.P.E.C.*', *An Account of the Christian Conference on Politics, Economics and Citizenship*, London, 1925.

KELLER, ADOLF, *Church and State on the European Continent*, London, 1936.

KENT, J. H. S., 'The Role of Religion in the Cultural Structure of the Later Victorian City', in *Transactions of the Royal Historical Society*, 5th series, 23 (1973).

KINGSLEY, CHARLES, *His Letters and Memories of his Life*, ed. by his Wife, London, 1899.

KIRK, K. E., *The Story of the Woodard Schools*, London, 1937.

KITSON CLARK, G., *Churchmen and the Condition of England, 1832–1885*, London, 1973.

——, *An Expanding Society, Britain 1830–1900*, Cambridge, 1967.

LACEY, T. A., *Marriage in Church and State*, revd. edn., London, 1947.

LAMBERT, ROYSTON, *Sir John Simon, 1816–1904, and English Social Administration*, London, 1963.

LATHBURY, D. C., *Correspondence on Church and Religion of William Ewart Gladstone*, London, 1910.

LIDDON, H. P., *Life of Edward Bouverie Pusey*, 4th edn., London, 1894.

LLOYD, ROGER, *The Church of England, 1900–1965*, revd. edn., London, 1966.

LOCKHART, J. G., *Cosmo Gordon Lang*, London, 1949.

LOUKES, HAROLD, *Teenage Morality*, London, 1973.

McBRIAR, A. M., *Fabian Socialism and English Politics, 1884–1918*, Cambridge, 1962.

McCLAIN, F. M., *Maurice, Man and Moralist*, London, 1972.

McCLEOD, HUGH, *Class and Religion in the Late Victorian City*, London, 1974.

MACDONNELL, J. C., *The Life and Correspondence of William Magee*, London, 1896.

MACHIN, G. I. T., *The Catholic Question in English Politics, 1820 to 1830*, Oxford, 1964.

MACINTYRE, A., *The Liberator. Daniel O'Connell and the Irish Party, 1830–1847*, London, 1965.

MACKINTOSH, W. H., *Disestablishment and Liberation. The Movement for the Separation of the Anglican Church from State Control*, London, 1972.

MANNING, B. L., *The Protestant Dissenting Deputies*, Cambridge, 1952.

MANNING, MAURICE, *The Blueshirts*, Dublin, 1970.

MARRIN, ALBERT, *The Last Crusade. The Church of England in the First World War*, Duke University Press, 1974.

MARSH, P. T., *The Victorian Church in Decline. Archbishop Tait and the Church of England, 1868–1882*, London, 1969.

MARSHALL, J. D., *The Old Poor Law, 1795–1834*, London, 1968.

MARTIN, DAVID, *A Sociology of English Religion*, London, 1967.

MATTHEWS, W. R., ed., *William Temple: An Estimate and Appreciation*, London 1946.

MAYFIELD, GUY, *The Church of England. Its Members and Its Business*, 2nd edn., London, 1963.

——, *Like Nothing on Earth*, London, 1965.

MAYOR, STEPHEN, *The Churches and the Labour Movement*, London, 1967.

MEACHAM, S., 'The Church in the Victorian City', in *Victorian Studies*, xi (1968).

MILLER, DAVID W., *Church, State and Nation in Ireland, 1898–1921*, Dublin, 1973.

MOORE, D. C., 'Concession or Cure: The Sociological Premises of the First Reform Act', in *Historical Journal*, 9, 1 (1966).

MORGAN, DEWI, *Lambeth Speaks*, London, 1958.

——, *The Church in Transition. Reform in the Church of England*, London, 1970.

MORGAN, K. O., *Wales in British Politics, 1868–1922*, Cardiff, 1963.

MORLEY, JOHN, *The Life of William Ewart Gladstone*, London, 1905 edn.

MORTIMER, R. C., *The Elements of Moral Theology*, London, 1947.

MOZLEY, ANNE, ed., *Letters and Correspondence of John Henry Newman During his Life in the English Church*, new edn., London, 1898.

MURPHY, JAMES, *Church, State and Schools in Britain, 1800–1970*, London, 1971.

NEWSOME, DAVID, *Godliness and Good Learning. Four Studies on a Victorian Ideal*, London, 1961.

——, *The Parting of Friends. A Study of the Wilberforces and Henry Manning*, London, 1966.

NIEBUHR, H. RICHARD, *The Social Sources of Denominationalism* (1929), New York, 1959 edn.

NORMAN, E. R., *The Catholic Church and Ireland in the Age of Rebellion, 1859–1873*, London, 1965.

——, *Anti-Catholicism in Victorian England*, London, 1968.

——, *The Conscience of the State in North America*, Cambridge, 1968.

——, *A History of Modern Ireland*, Penguin edn., London, 1973.

OAKESHOTT, MICHAEL, *The Social and Political Doctrines of Contemporary Europe*, New York edn., 1950.

ODOM, W., *Fifty Years of Sheffield Church Life, 1866–1916*, London, 1917.

OLIVER, JOHN, *The Church and Social Order. Social Thought in the Church of England, 1918–1939*, London, 1968.

OVERTON, J. E., and WORDSWORTH, E., *Christopher Wordsworth, Bishop of Lincoln*, London, 1888.

PAGET, E. K., *Henry Luke Paget*, London, 1939.

PATON, ALAN, *Apartheid and the Archbishop. The Life and Times of Geoffrey Clayton, Archbishop of Cape Town*, London, 1974.

PATON, D. M., *Church and Race in South Africa*, London, 1958.

PAUL, LESLIE, *A Church by Daylight. A Reappraisement of the Church of England and its Future*, London, 1973.

PELLING, HENRY, 'The Working Class and the Origins of the Welfare State', in *Popular Politics and Society in Late Victorian Britain*, London, 1968.

PIKE, E. ROYSTON, *Human Documents of the Victorian Golden Age*, London, 1967.

PORT, M. H., *Six Hundred New Churches*, London, 1961.

PROTHERO, R. E., and BRADLEY, G. G., *The Life and Correspondence of Arthur Penrhyn Stanley*, London, 1893.

PRYKE, W. M., 'Dr. Henson and C.O.P.E.C.', in *The Modern Churchman*, 14, no. 10 (1925).

PURCELL, WILLIAM, *Woodbine Willie*, London, 1962.

——, *Fisher of Lambeth. A Portrait from Life*, London, 1969.

RAMSEY, A. M., *From Gore to Temple. The Development of Anglican Theology between LUX MUNDI and the Second World War, 1889–1939*, London, 1960.

RANDOLPH, B. W., and TOWNROE, J. W., *The Mind and Work of Bishop King*, London, 1918.

RAVEN, C. E., *Christian Socialism, 1848–1854*, London, 1920.

——, 'C.O.P.E.C. Then and Now', in *Crucible*, October 1962, and January 1963.

RAVITCH, NORMAN, *Sword and Mitre. Government and Episcopate in France and England in the Age of Aristocracy*, The Hague, 1966.

REARDON, B. M. G., *From Coleridge to Gore. A Century of Religious Thought in Britain*, London, 1971.

RECKITT, MAURICE, B., *As It Happened. An Autobiography*, London, 1941.

——, *Maurice to Temple. A Century of the Social Movement in the Church of England*, London, 1947.

——, *P. E. T. Widdrington. A Study in Vocation and Versatility*, London, 1961.

ROBERTS, R. ELLIS, *H. R. L. Sheppard, Life and Letters*, London, 1942.

ROGERS, EDWARD, ed., *Declarations of Conference on Social Questions*, London, 1959.

ROWELL, GEOFFREY, *Hell and the Victorians. A study of the nineteenth-century theological controversies concerning eternal punishment and the future life*, Oxford, 1974.

ROYLE, EDWARD, *Radical Politics, 1790–1900, Religion and Unbelief*, London, 1971.

RUSSELL, E. F., ed., *Alexander Heriot Mackonochie*, London, 1890.

RUSSELL, G. W. E., *Dr. Liddon*, London, 1905.

SALTER, F. R., 'Political Nonconformity in the 1830's', in *Transactions of the Royal Historical Society*, 5th series, 3 (1953).

SANDFORD, E. G., ed., *Memoirs of Archbishop [Frederick] Temple by Seven Friends*, London, 1906.

SAVILLE, J., 'Sleeping Partnerships and Limited Liability, 1850–56', in *Economic History Review*, April 1956.

SELBIE, W. B., ed., *Oxford and the Groups*, Oxford, 1934.

SHELFORD, L. E., *Twenty Years at St. Matthew's, Upper Clapton, 1866–1886*, London, 1886.

SHEPPARD, DAVID, *Built as a City. God and the Urban World Today*, London, 1974.

SHYLLON, F. O., *Black Slaves in Britain*, London, 1973.

SLACK, KENNETH, *The British Churches Today*, 2nd edn., London, 1970.

SMITH, ALAN, *The Established Church and Popular Religion, 1750–1850*, London, 1970.

SMITH, H., MAYNARD, *Frank, Bishop of Zanzibar*, London, 1926.

SMYTH, CHARLES, *Cyril Foster Garbett, Archbishop of York*, London, 1959.

SOLOWAY, R. A., *Prelates and People. Ecclesiastical Social Thought in England, 1783–1852*, London and Toronto, 1969.

SPINKS, G. STEPHENS, ed., *Religion in Britain since 1900*, London, 1952.

STANLEY, A. P., *The Life and Correspondence of Thomas Arnold, D.D.*, 15th edn., London, 1892.

STEPHENS, W. R. W., *The Life and Letters of Walter Farquhar Hook*, 3rd edn., London, 1879.

STRACHEY, RAY, *Group Movements of the Past, and Experiments in Guidance*, revd. edn., London, 1934.

STRANKS, C. J., *Dean Hook*, London, 1954.

SUMNER, MARY E., *Memoir of George Henry Sumner*, Winchester, 1910.

SUTHERLAND, GILLIAN, *Policy-Making in Elementary Education, 1870–1895*, Oxford, 1973.

SYKES, NORMAN, *Church and State in England in the XVIIIth Century*, Cambridge, 1934.

SYMON, DUDLEY, *Lambeth Questions*, London, 1948.

TATLOW, TISSINGTON, *The Story of the Student Christian Movement of Great Britain and Ireland*, London, 1933.

TEMPLE, WILLIAM, *Life of Bishop Percival*, London, 1921.

THOMAS, O. C., *William Temple's Philosophy of Religion*, London, 1961.

THOMPSON, D. M., *Nonconformity in the Nineteenth Century*, London, 1972.

THOMPSON, E. P., *The Making of the English Working Class*, Pelican edn., London, 1968.

THOMPSON, K. A., *Bureaucracy and Church Reform. The Organizational Response of the Church of England to Social Change, 1800–1965*, Oxford, 1970.

TILL, BARRY, *The Churches' Search for Unity*, London, 1972.

TOBIAS, J. J., *Nineteenth-Century Crime, Prevention and Punishment*, Newton Abbot, 1972.

TROELTSCH, ERNST, *The Social Teaching of the Christian Churches*, London, 1931.

TUCKER, H. W., *Memoir of the Life and Episcopate of George Augustus Selwyn*, London, 1879.

VIDLER, A. R., *The Orb and the Cross. A Normative Study in the Relations of Church and State with Reference to Gladstone's Early Writings*, London, 1945.

WAGNER, D. O., *The Church of England and Social Reform since 1854*, New York, 1930.

WAND, J. W. C., *Anglicanism in History and Today*, London, 1961.

WARD, W. R., *Religion and Society in England, 1790–1850*, London, 1972.

WARDLE, DAVID, *English Popular Education, 1780–1970*, Cambridge, 1970.

WEARMOUTH, R. F., *Methodism and the Working-class Movements of England, 1800–1850*, 2nd edn., London, 1946.

WEBSTER, A. B., *Joshua Watson*, London, 1954.

WELCH, P. J., 'Revival of the Convocation of Canterbury, 1852–8', in *Journal of Ecclesiastical History*, 10 (1959).

WESTCOTT, ARTHUR, *Life and Letters of Brooke Foss Westcott*, London, 1903.

WHYTE, J. H., *Church and State in Modern Ireland, 1923–1970*, Dublin, 1970.

WICKHAM, E. R., *Church and People in an Industrial City* (1957), London, 1969 edn.

WILBERFORCE, R. G., *Life of the Right Reverend Samuel Wilberforce, D.D.*, London, 1882.

WILBERFORCE, SAMUEL, *The Life of William Wilberforce*, revd. edn., London, 1872.

WINNETT, A. R., *The Church and Divorce*, London, 1968.

WOODROOFE, KATHLEEN, *From Charity to Social Work in England and the United States*, London, 1962.

YOUNG, KENNETH, *Chapel*, London, 1972.

Index